Theosophy across Boundaries

SUNY series in Western Esoteric Traditions

David Appelbaum, editor

Theosophy across Boundaries

Transcultural and Interdisciplinary Perspectives on a Modern Esoteric Movement

Edited by

Hans Martin Krämer *and* Julian Strube

Cover image courtesy of the Theosophical Society in Australia

Published by State University of New York Press, Albany

© 2020 State University of New York

All rights reserved

Printed in the United States of America

No part of this book may be used or reproduced in any manner whatsoever without written permission. No part of this book may be stored in a retrieval system or transmitted in any form or by any means including electronic, electrostatic, magnetic tape, mechanical, photocopying, recording, or otherwise without the prior permission in writing of the publisher.

For information, contact State University of New York Press, Albany, NY
www.sunypress.edu

Library of Congress Cataloging-in-Publication Data

Names: Krämer, Hans Martin, editor. | Strube, Julian, editor.
Title: Theosophy across boundaries : transcultural and interdisciplinary perspectives on a modern esoteric movement / edited by Hans Martin Krämer and Julian Strube.
Description: Albany : State University of New York Press, 2020. | Series: SUNY series in western esoteric traditions | Includes bibliographical references and index.
Identifiers: LCCN 2020018354 | ISBN 9781438480411 (hardcover : alk. paper) | ISBN 9781438480428 (pbk. : alk. paper) | ISBN 9781438480435 (ebook)
Subjects: LCSH: Theosophy—Influence.
Classification: LCC BP520 .T545 2020 | DDC 299/.934—dc23
LC record available at https://lccn.loc.gov/2020018354

10 9 8 7 6 5 4 3 2 1

Contents

List of Illustrations ix

Introduction: Theosophy across Boundaries 1
   Julian Strube and Hans Martin Krämer

Part I
New Perspectives on Theosophy

Chapter 1
Western Esotericism and the Orient in the First
Theosophical Society 29
   Wouter J. Hanegraaff

Chapter 2
Hinduism, Theosophy, and the *Bhagavad Gita* within a
Global Religious History of the Nineteenth Century 65
   Michael Bergunder

Chapter 3
Theosophying the Vietnamese Religious Landscape:
A Circulatory History of a Western Esoteric Movement in
Southern Vietnam 109
   Jérémy Jammes

Chapter 4
Theosophical Movements in Modern China: The Education
Provided by Theosophists at the Shanghai International Settlement 149
   Chuang *Chienhui*

Chapter 5
Absence Unveiled? The Early Theosophical Society and the
Entanglement of History and Historiography 179
   Ulrich Harlass

Chapter 6
Affinity and Estrangement: Transnational Theosophy in
Germany and India during the Colonial Era (1878–1933) 217
   Perry Myers

Chapter 7
"To Study Judaism in the Light of Theosophy and Theosophy in
the Light of Judaism": The Association of Hebrew Theosophists
and Its Missions to the Jews and Gentiles 253
   Boaz Huss

Part II
Theosophy in Literature, the Arts, and Politics

Chapter 8
International Religious Organizations in a Colonial World:
The Maha-Bodhi Society in Arakan 281
   Laurence Cox and Alicia Turner

Chapter 9
Euro-Asian Political Activist and Spiritual Seeker: Paul Richard
and Theosophy 317
   Hans Martin Krämer

Chapter 10
An Irish Theosophist's Pan-Asianism or Fant-asia? James Cousins
and Gurcharan Singh 345
   Hashimoto *Yorimitsu*

Chapter 11
Theosophy as a Transnational Network: The Commission of
the Golconde Dormitory in Puducherry (1935–ca. 1948) 373
   Helena Čapková

Chapter 12
From Healer to Shaman: Theosophy and the Making of
Esoteric Bali   401
Yan Suarsana

Chapter 13
Effects of Theosophy on Russian Cultural History   425
Björn Seidel-Dreffke

Contributors   455

Index   461

Illustrations

Figure 3.1   A Vietnamese Theosophist in the international networks of the Theosophical Society. *Source:* Nguyễn Văn Lượng, 1981.   126

Figure 10.1   James H. Cousins and Noguchi Yone. From Cousins, *New Japan*.   349

Figure 10.2   Koumé and his "Etherist" painting, Snow Covered Road at Dusk (1920). From *Asahi Shinbun*, May 1, 1920.   352

Figure 10.3   Cultural unity of Asia? "An Indo-Japo-Chinese Vase by Gurcharn [sic] Singh." From Cousins, *New Japan*.   353

Figure 10.4   Gurcharan Singh, Asakawa Takumi, and his brother Asakawa Noritaka's white vase. This is Gurcharan Singh's own picture; the caption says "Dear Singu [sic], August 31, 1920, Takumi." From Anuradha Ravindranath's archive concerning Gurcharan Singh, New Delhi, India.   358

Figure 10.5   Gurcharan Singh, *Three Symbol Vase* (1970s). From Ravindranath, *Pottery and the Legacy of Sardar Gurcharan Singh* (1998).   361

Figure 11.1   A long view of Golconde, 1948, Puducherry, photographer unknown, photographs copyright Sri Aurobindo Ashram Pondicherry, India.   374

Figure 11.2	Group photo, from the left: Stefan Łubienski, Antonín and Noémi Raymond, Philip St. Hilaire, Zina Łubienski, Keshoram Sabarwal, and two men, Tokyo, early 1920s, photographer unknown, photographs copyright private collection.	375
Figures 11.3 and 11.4	James H. Cousins's letter to the TS HQ in Adyar refers in detail to the foundation of the first TS lodge in Japan, the Tokyo International Lodge. Letter of February 15, 1920. Theosophical Society Archives, TS HQ Adyar, India.	378–379
Figure 11.5	Mme Metaxa and Stefan and Zina Łubienski at her Tokyo home, early 1920s, photographer unknown, photographs copyright private collection.	380
Figures 11.6 and 11.7	The foundational document of the Orpheus Lodge, Tokyo established on May 22, 1924. Theosophical Society Archives, TS HQ Adyar, India.	382–383
Figure 11.8	Group photo, from the left: Philip St. Hilaire, Gurcharan Singh, Stefan and Zina Łubienski, and Noémi Raymond, Tokyo, early 1920s, photographer unknown, photographs copyright Sri Aurobindo Ashram Pondicherry, India.	385
Figure 11.9	Zina and Stefan Łubienski performing at a children's Christmas party at Atami (?), early 1920s, photographer unknown, photographs copyright private collection.	387
Figure 11.10	Pavitra in Sri Aurobindo Ashram, Puducherry, undated, photographer unknown, photographs copyright Sri Aurobindo Ashram Pondicherry, India.	391
Figure 11.11	Golconde under construction, 1942, Puducherry, photographer unknown, photographs copyright Sri Aurobindo Ashram Pondicherry, India.	392

Figure 11.12 George Katsutoshi Nakashima (Sundarananda) at Sri Aurobindo Ashram Golconde Guest House, undated, photographer unknown, photographs copyright Sri Aurobindo Ashram Pondicherry, India. 393

Figure 11.13 One of the rooms in Golconde Puducherry, undated, photographer unknown, photographs copyright Sri Aurobindo Ashram Pondicherry, India. 395

Introduction

Theosophy: Across Boundaries

Julian Strube and Hans Martin Krämer

From its inception throughout the period of its highest influence toward the end of the nineteenth century and the beginning of the twentieth, the Theosophical Society has constantly transgressed boundaries. It has gone beyond geographical boundaries, from Europe to India and on to other Asian countries. It has blurred boundaries between religious traditions, mixing elements from various European and Asian traditions, appealing to individuals from a variety of religious backgrounds. And it has transgressed the boundaries between categories such as religion, philosophy, politics, and science.

Dealing with Theosophy may challenge our way of looking at things, such as the division of religion and science or the relationship between "East and West"—because they were challenged by Theosophy. A key to understanding the importance of Theosophy perhaps may lie in recognizing it as a crucial agent in historical debates about the very meaning of "religion" or "science." These debates took place within a truly entangled global context, in which transfers of knowledge were not monodirectional but polyphonic and often ambiguous. Indeed, the Theosophical Society is perhaps the most overlooked agent in these transfers. Until recently, it has barely received any attention in the most widely read studies of global history, although a more extensive analysis from a global perspective was provided by Peter van der Veer, who highlighted the impact of Theosophy on Indian religions.[1]

Despite such acknowledgements, the global dimension of Theosophy remains largely neglected. The reason for this neglect is twofold: it can be traced to a lack of attention to religions other than Christianity in studies of global history, and the fact that Theosophy so far has been studied mostly within the disciplinary framework of "Western Esotericism." When global history, which is often focused on economic exchanges and diplomacy, does take religion seriously, the focus is usually exclusively on the global spread of Christianity through newly invigorated missionary activities of the nineteenth century.[2] The other major movements that are acknowledged are the global spread of Islam, especially to Africa,[3] and that of the incursion of Asian "world religions" into Europe and North America, such as the interest in Hinduism or Buddhism as lived religions in the United States and Western Europe around the turn of the twentieth century.[4] The focus on Christianity persists, although more recent studies have done a lot to counter it. In his magisterial account of "The Birth of the Modern World" in the long nineteenth century, Christopher Bayly has devoted a whole chapter to "Empires of Religion" that takes pains to go beyond a Eurocentric and Christian-centric account. Still, Bayly's chapter is slanted toward his overarching thesis of nineteenth-century "uniformity," which he also applies to religions. Hence, his observation that change in this period "tended toward greater uniformity both within and between religions" privileges the large "world religions" as the source of this trend toward uniformity.[5]

Sebastian Conrad, who also devotes a long chapter to "Religion in the Global World" within his more recent overview of "A Cultural History of Global Transformation," implicitly rejects Bayly's basic assumption when he argues that, in the course of the nineteenth century, religion was understood less as an expression of universal values; rather, it was an emphasis on the connection between religion and the nation that was typical of the late nineteenth century. This strategic move allows Conrad to consider new religious movements, almost completely overlooked by Bayly, more seriously and also to locate the Theosophical Society as "the prototype of a transnationally active religion, a typical product of the cultural globalization at the end of the nineteenth century."[6]

Yet, while the impact of globalization on the Theosophical Society is duly noted, the importance of the Society for global history remains sketchy, as do its connections to other religious and nonreligious movements of the period under study. One can even go further and state that, with regard to global history, the neglect of Theosophy is not due merely to the fact that scholars such as Bayly, Conrad, and Jürgen Osterhammel seem to be largely unaware of the study of esotericism.[7] Even if they were aware of it, they would find that scholars of Western Esotericism have traditionally concluded that the Theosophical Society was first and foremost responsible for "globalizing" entirely "Western" ideas—if the global dimension of its history has been discussed at all.[8] In this vein, the recent *Handbook of the Theosophical Current* focuses exclusively on European and North American contexts and the Western Theosophists who have traditionally received scholarly attention.[9]

Yet some scholars of Western Esotericism have engaged in a fruitful discussion of the notion of "the West" that seeks to problematize the label of the field. Kennet Granholm has discussed the geographical limitations of the field and described the separation between "the West" and "the non-West" as largely imaginary.[10] Egil Asprem called for a "new comparativism" in the study of esotericism and described the delimitations of "Western Esotericism" as a product of boundary-work.[11] Wouter Hanegraaff has stressed the need for more research into the "globalization of Western Esotericism," but also suggested maintaining the category.[12] Michael Bergunder, on the other hand, has argued that the very emergence of "esotericism" per se can only be comprehended in the context of a global religious history.[13] This debate has considerably gained momentum in recent years. Julian Strube has argued that the study of esotericism would only benefit from an engagement with global and non-Eurocentric perspectives, for which Theosophy is an especially strong case in point. When seen in this light, the "Western" demarcation of the field of study that most extensively investigates Theosophy appears detrimental to an understanding of the subject, and the study of esotericism as a whole.[14] Regardless of one's position on these theoretical and methodological reflections, the fact remains that only a few attempts have been made so far to do practical research about the global dimension of esotericism.[15] The Theosophical Society is perhaps the most relevant and instructive example that can serve as a starting point for such an endeavor. This is reflected in a growing interest that most recently manifested itself in *Theosophical Appropriations*, a volume edited by Julie Chajes and Boaz Huss, which allows for significant insights into Theosophy's role for the transformation of traditions.[16]

There can be little doubt that the Theosophical Society was part of a truly global movement, thus providing an outstanding example of the complex entanglements of the global religious history of the nineteenth and early twentieth centuries.[17] Theosophy should not be regarded simply as a part of a "Western esotericism," that is, the product of a purely Orientalist imagination in which Western audiences defined their own identity with implicit or explicit reference to the "otherness" of the East.[18] Of course, its Western leaders were, certainly in the early phase of the Society, informed by Orientalist ideas of "the East." However, because they engaged in complex exchanges with Indians and other "non-Westerners," this relationship must not be seen one-dimensionally. An understanding of these exchanges requires an approach that leaves behind the classical notion of Edward Said's famous *Orientalism*, implying the passivity of the colonized, and instead highlights the mutual influences among all involved actors, despite differences in power and position. The ambiguities and contradictions of the agency of the colonized in the light of Orientalist knowledge have long been the subject of post-colonial debates.[19] Taking them into account is crucial for understanding the relationships between the many different members of the Theosophical Society.[20]

Despite the dominance of Western knowledge within the colonial framework, this knowledge was by no means adopted passively. Colonial relations were highly unstable and dynamic; knowledge was not reproduced identically by the colonized but inherently contained the potential for transformation and the articulation of opposition.[21] While it might be questioned whether esotericism could reasonably be regarded as "rejected knowledge," it certainly propagated an opposition to the hegemonic culture of what was perceived as the West.[22] In this light, the huge popularity of Theosophy and other esoteric currents underlines that "Western knowledge" was anything but monolithic: the colonized were not confronted by a homogenic Western understanding of religion or science, but they actively shaped the fragile meanings of these contested signifiers. The Theosophical Society offered them a unique platform for doing so. For people in Asia, esotericism could function as an entry point into Orientalist discourse and, at the same time, provide opportunities for a critical resignification of its contents, which in turn impacted Orientalist notions.

Much of this agency was derived from the Orientalist perception of Asia as the cradle of pristine wisdom, "spiritual" yet effeminate and otherworldly. It is thus important to be aware of the ambiguity of the Theosophical elevation of Asians, especially Indians. The glory of India was more often than not located in a distant past, and Theosophists such as Helena Petrovna Blavatsky tended to dismiss the real, living Indians as ignorants who had to be educated by the Western re-discoverers of their lost wisdom. This more or less implicit reproduction of colonial and Orientalist racial and hierarchical modes within the Theosophical Society demands further attention.[23] It should also complicate the perception of Theosophical attitudes as a kind of "positive Orientalism."[24] While it might very well be distinguished from more malicious attitudes—for instance, of the missionary variety that was denounced by Theosophists—it certainly is marked by an ambiguity that cannot simply be regarded as "positive."

A better understanding of these dynamics is of crucial importance for an analysis of the extraordinary role the Theosophical Society played in modern Asian history. It is well known that Theosophists and their collaborators were a driving force behind the emergence of the modern Buddhist identity in Sri Lanka.[25] Annie Besant (1847–1933), who became president of the Theosophical Society in 1907, was elected president of the Indian National Congress in 1917.[26] And Theosophical ideas significantly informed the man who would soon eclipse Besant as a political leader, Mohandas Karamchand Gandhi (1883–1944).[27] Farther to the East, the ideas of the Theosophical Society became a rallying point for Buddhist reformers in Japan. This movement culminated when Henry Steel Olcott (1832–1907) visited Japan in 1889 and was welcomed enthusiastically by Buddhists embracing inner-sectarian reform, although they soon became disillusioned about the potential of Theosophy for modern Buddhism.[28]

In the West, Theosophy was largely responsible for the wide-spread fascination with "Buddhism" or "Hinduism," resulting in the practice of yoga, meditation, and alternative lifestyles that would prepare the ground for New Age culture, remaining influential up to the present day.[29] As these examples demonstrate, the interaction of Theosophy with highly diverse cultural contexts resulted in mutual influences, the study of which enables us to better understand historical processes that far exceed Theosophy. The different perspectives offered in the contributions to his volume allow for instructive insights into how the meaning of "it," Theosophy, has been constructed in various cultural contexts, and how Theosophy could function as a nodal point for the emergence of new religious or political identities.

These discussions also allow for a better understanding of constructions of "the East" in contrast to "the West." The Theosophical shift toward India, within the first years after its formation, not only caused fierce polemics among esotericists, but also raised pressing questions that are crucial for future research. Clearly, the notion and location, be it imaginary or physical, of "the East" were subject to radical change, and the demarcations between "East" and "West" were obviously contingent. While "the East" was imagined as a pristine location since late antiquity, its exact position in the "esoteric landscape" was extremely fluid throughout the nineteenth and twentieth centuries.[30] The "Orient" could comprise Egypt, Chaldea, India, and China. This vast conflation reflected typical Orientalist notions and thus broader historical trends, but the "wandering" of the East from Egypt to India within esoteric discourses is especially remarkable. In the process, certain notions such as the "Oriental Kabbalah" were transformed into a part of "Western esotericism," and it is important to note that this was the outcome of polemical identity formations.[31] Whether one tends to subscribe to a demarcation between "Western" and "Eastern" esotericism in scholarship or not, there is little doubt that future approaches should be discussed against the background of global developments whose relevance extends well beyond the sphere of esotericism itself.

A Brief History of the Theosophical Society

Despite its outstanding historical significance, no recent attempt has been made to write a comprehensive history of the Theosophical Society.[32] Only some of the Society's leading figures have been studied in dedicated biographies—all of them Westerners.[33] Indeed, when it was formed in New York in 1875, the Theosophical Society was clearly situated against a Western Spiritualist and occultist background, although its name did not explicitly refer to the older notion of "theosophy."[34] Its founding leaders were the illustrious Blavatsky (1831–1891) and Henry Steel Olcott.[35] The Society was marked by polemical identity formations, initially against Spiritualism and other esoteric groups, before it went through several schisms toward the end of the century and fractured into numerous offshoots. A central issue in this respect was the increasingly "Eastern" orientation of the Society.[36] This orientation became obvious in May 1878, when it was renamed "The Theosophical Society of the Arya Samaj of India." This referred to the Indian reform movement Arya Samaj, which had recently been formed by Dayananda Saraswati (1824–1883).[37] Since 1878, the Theosophists were in direct contact with its leader, although the links between the two organizations did not last for long. Nevertheless, after Blavatsky and Olcott reached Mumbai (then Bombay) for the first time on February 16, 1879, the Theosophical Society would firmly establish itself in the Asian landscape of religious and political reform movements.

An important platform of communication was the journal *The Theosophist*, which commenced publication in 1879 and gave a public voice to educated Indians who otherwise were disregarded by the colonial communities. The Western Theosophists would become a recognizable, and soon a highly influential, force in the struggle for native identities, openly adhering to Hinduism and Buddhism—and eventually contributing to the formation of these terms. Olcott proved to be especially active in touring the subcontinent and protesting colonial and missionary policies. His efforts in Sri Lanka, which have been mentioned above, were commemorated with an "Olcott Day" on February 17. The Theosophists had early allies in the colonial community, such as Alfred Percy Sinnett (1840–1921), who edited the largest daily newspaper in India, *The Pioneer*. But they also developed close ties to learned Indians, such as Tallapragada Subba Row (1856–1890), whose activity as an advocate in Madras was one reason for the Society to move its headquarters to a nearby town, Adyar, in late 1882.

In the meantime, Theosophists such as Anna Kingsford (1846–1888) and Edward Maitland (1824–1897) began to voice their protest against the "Oriental" tendencies of the Society, which, among other internal and external quarrels, forced Blavatsky and Olcott to travel back to Europe in February 1884. One pressing issue revolved around the claim that Blavatsky received orders from unseen masters, the so-called Mahatmas, who were regarded as the guardians of supreme esoteric knowledge. The identity and influence of these masters became increasingly subject to scrutiny, which opened another front in India and forced Blavatsky and Olcott to return in October 1884 to face accusations of fraud. The affair took a devastating end when Richard Hodgson, a member of the Society for Psychical Research who was commissioned to write a report on the matter, concluded that the Mahatma letters, as well as the phenomena produced by Blavatsky, were forgeries. On March 31, 1885, Blavatsky left India forever, while Olcott remained as president of the Society.

In the following years, Annie Besant and Charles W. Leadbeater (1847–1934), who allegedly received training from the Mahatmas and Subba Row, would establish themselves as the "second generation" leaders of the Society. While they and Olcott remained highly active in Asia and increased their activities to promote Hinduism, Buddhism, education, and political emancipation, other Theosophists would emphasize the "Western" and/or "Christian" character of Theosophy. In 1894, this resulted in a major schism between the Theosophical Society of Adyar and the American branch under William Quan Judge (1851–1896), a founding member, and his successor, Katherine Tingley (1847–1929). Subsequently, a range of smaller schisms took place, notably the founding of the Anthroposophical Society by Rudolf Steiner (1861–1925) in 1912; again, at least partly due to Steiner's rejection of a more Asian inflection and his wish to pursue a path centered more on the European Christian heritage.[38] In 1907, Besant was elected president of the Theosophical Society (Adyar) and held that position until her death. Beginning in the late 1890s, she founded several boys' and girls' schools, focusing on education and social work, which finally resulted in her election as president of the Indian National Congress in 1917. During her office, the international membership of the Society grew from approximately 14,700 in 1907 to its peak in 1928 of 45,098 members.[39]

Since the 1930s, the majority of Theosophical groups have experienced a decline in membership and influence. In the case of Adyar, this was also due to the promotion by Besant and Leadbeater of a young boy, Jiddu Krishnamurti (1895–1986), as the "World Teacher"—a role that he eventually rejected, dissolving the Order of the Star in the East, which had been created for him and attracted around 30,000 members, in 1929. For these and other reasons, the multiple Theosophical Societies suffered heavy losses during the 1930s. The membership of Adyar reached a low of 18,216 in 1943 and has since ranged from about 20,000 to about 35,000.[40] Of course, Theosophical groups did not simply cease their activities after the 1930s, and Theosophical ideas would become enormously influential in new offshoots of the Societies and new religious movements well until the present day. While it is an important achievement of Hammer's *Handbook* to highlight this fact and give instructive insights into the more recent developments of Theosophy,[41] the present volume seeks to draw attention to the developments in non-Western contexts, focusing on the time around 1900 but allowing some glimpses into the second half of the twentieth century.

The volume does so by dividing its chapters into two parts, both following an innovative approach to Theosophy. The first part consists of seven perspectives on the activities of the Theosophical Society in very different regional contexts, ranging from India, Vietnam, China, and Japan to Victorian Britain and Israel/Palestine. Emphasis is thus placed on regional and historical contexts that have attracted little to no scholarly attention up to this day. This sheds new light on the entanglement of

"Western" and "Oriental" ideas around 1900, wherein the Theosophical Society played a crucial role.

In the second part, the point of view shifts from looking at Theosophy itself as the main object of inquiry to other contexts in which Theosophy played a formative role. The six chapters of the second part discuss specific cultural influences that Theosophy exerted in the spheres of literature, art, and politics. Again, the case studies selected cover a wide range not only of topics, but also of regional contexts, including Sri Lanka, Burma, India, Japan, Ireland, Germany, and Russia. The examples clearly show the international, global dimension of personal and institutional networks, highlighting the multifaceted and complex entanglement of cultural influences by and on the Theosophical Society and its affiliated actors.

This volume is the result of a conference held under the title *Theosophy Across Boundaries* from September 24 to 26, 2015. It was financed and facilitated by the Cluster of Excellence "Asia and Europe in a Global Context" at the University of Heidelberg, Germany. Among the many people who made this project possible, the editors would like to thank Russell Ó Ríagáin for his editorial work and Lena Paulsen for her translations of the contributions by Michael Bergunder und Björn Seidel-Dreffke, as well as Violetta Janzen, Sevgi Memov, and Alice Witt for help with several manuscripts included in this volume.

Summary of Part One: New Perspectives on Theosophy

The first part of this volume can be regarded as a pioneering attempt to map the global landscape of Theosophy's manifold and often ambiguous influences. By taking into account examples stretching from Europe to the Middle and Far East, it offers new perspectives on the development of a society whose doctrines have changed profoundly since the first years of its formation. This poses a number of challenges that are of consequence to many of the ongoing scholarly debates about the global role of Theosophy and by extension esotericism: how can we best historicize the fluid demarcations between "East" and "West"? And how can we approach the complex exchanges between actors from different parts of the world? How can we grasp the ever-changing, heterogeneous doctrines propagated by members of the Theosophical Society, and how were they transformed in a global context?

These issues are comprehensively addressed in the chapter by Wouter J. Hanegraaff, who discusses the changing notion of "the East" in the history of what he calls "the First Theosophical Society," between 1875 and 1878. Before leading Theosophists traveled to India and established their headquarters there in 1879, their interest in India was largely informed by the "Ancient Wisdom Narrative," which has thrived since the Renaissance and plays a crucial role for the concept of Western Esotericism. This so-called "positive orientalism" revolved around the notion of a "universal Kabbalah" with Oriental origins in Chaldea and Egypt. Although India did feature as a source of ancient wisdom from an early point on—a central example would be Blavatsky's article "A Few Questions to 'Hiraf'" from 1875—it was Egypt that stood at the center of Theosophical attention, while discussions of India relied on Western orientalist and popular literature. Hanegraaff makes an important point by highlighting the difference between the early Theosophical Society and its transformation after 1878, and it is crucial to keep this in mind when discussing later historical developments.

At the same time, our understanding of the global exchanges that underlie Theosophical identity formations is still limited, especially with regard to the role of "non-Western" actors. Michael Bergunder's chapter demonstrates that the traditional neglect of Indian agency has led to significant historiographical distortions. His discussion of the reception of the *Bhagavad Gita* radically questions the idea that the popularity of this text in India was due to earlier European and American appreciations. Not only does Bergunder show that these appreciations were much more marginal than they are usually perceived to be, but he can also establish that the *Bhagavad Gita*'s present-day popularity is largely due to the engagement of Indian intellectuals with the Theosophical Society. This deconstruction of a supposed "pizza effect" is in itself a significant achievement that is highly valuable for a historical understanding of one of the most popular and influential Hindu texts. In addition, Bergunder's argument emphasizes the urgent need to take into consideration the contributions of Indians, and other "non-Westerners," to the development of Theosophical ideas—and, by extension, to the conceptual formation of modern Hinduism under colonialism.

The pioneering contribution by Jérémy Jammes allows for instructive insights into the development of the Theosophical Society in Vietnam. As elsewhere, its foundation coincided with the colonial period. Jammes establishes a fascinating connection between present-day Vietnamese Theosophists and their historical predecessors, focusing on the period between

1920 and 1975, when the Society was banned by the socialist regime. The first lodge of the *Hội giáo Thông thần học*, literally "religious association of studies on communication with spirits," was founded in 1928 and was immersed in the atmosphere of contemporary reform Buddhism. Jammes discusses the Vietnamese Theosophists' concern, not only with "cultural synthesis," aestheticism, and religious comparativism, but first and foremost with social and political reform. This is especially instructive because it confirms the impression that Theosophy thrived especially in reformist contexts across Asia, and that local actors played a decisive role in its flourishing. Consequently, Jammes suggests a dynamic and trans-Asian reading of the "Vietnamese Orient" that interacts with philosophies and practices external to Vietnamese culture. The complex tangle of Western and Asian actors of different origin that becomes manifest in Jammes's discussion of Vietnamese Theosophy makes this article a treasure trove for those interested in one of the neglected Asian contexts of Theosophical history.

Modern understandings of "Kabbalah" were central to Theosophical identity formations across the globe, but the role of Jews in this context is often neglected. Boaz Huss's research on the Association of Hebrew Theosophists, founded in 1925, sheds light on the conflicted position in which Jewish Theosophists found themselves: on the one hand, they faced strong opposition from Jewish circles; on the other hand, they had to counter often blatantly anti-Semitic attitudes within the Theosophical Society. Given the outstanding role of Kabbalah in Theosophy, the latter circumstance seems to be bizarre at first. As indicated above, Blavatsky and other Theosophists had detached the Kabbalah from Judaism and established an antagonism between the (degenerated) Israelites and the Aryans. By contrast, Jewish Theosophists were arguing for the identity of modern Theosophy and ancient Jewish mysticism. This went hand in hand with a fierce critique of Jewish orthodoxy, which displayed typically "modern" reformist tendencies and often a strongly anti-rabbinic agenda. Yet at the same time, liberal Jewish trends were criticized as materialistic and lacking spirituality. Jewish Theosophists regarded Theosophy as a way of "spiritualizing unspiritual Judaism." They strived for the creation of a "modern, westernized, universalistic form of Judaism that embraced Kabbalah, and presented Jewish mysticism as the central component of the Jewish tradition." This tension between "modernity" and "tradition" is reminiscent of other local encounters with Theosophy, and it illustrates the great fluidity of central identity markers such as "Kabbalah," which calls for constant historical contextualization.

Theosophical identity formations are also the subject of Ulrich Harlass's chapter, which focuses on the role of A. P. Sinnett and the Mahatma letters within the historiography of the Theosophical Society. Harlass addresses two lacunae or "absences" in the historiography of Theosophy, namely an exclusive focus on Blavatsky that blots out the influence of other authors, and a more or less implicit exclusion of "the East." Harlass argues that much of the scholarship on Theosophy assumed that "the 'East' is referred to as a façade, set up by Blavatsky to refurbish the stage on which her *Western* esoteric Theosophical play was carried out." This is demonstrated by an analysis of the debates surrounding the Mahatma letters, Sinnett's writings, and the provenance of the concept of the septenary constitution. Harlass stresses that the Anglo-Indian milieu and Indian Theosophists are practically excluded from the scholarly accounts of these contexts, with Blavatsky appearing as *fons et origo* of the doctrines in dispute. This is at least partially misleading, because Indian Theosophists, most notably T. Subba Row, played a crucial role in these debates and significantly contributed to the development of Theosophical doctrines. Harlass argues that the distinction between East and West was strategic in these debates, in which the doctrines of "Eastern adepts" were juxtaposed with those of inferior "Western spiritualists." The genealogical approach suggested by Harlass helps to problematize the influence that such polemical narratives are still exerting, not only self-referential Theosophical historiography, but also on scholarship.

Chuang Chienhui's chapter on the Theosophical Society in China is another account of the deep entanglement of Theosophy, political reform, educational modernization, and the formation of religious identities. Focusing on the Theosophical educational movement of the 1920s and 1930s, Chuang shows that the establishment of Theosophical schools was intended not only for the propagation of Theosophy, but also for supporting China as it faced Western and Japanese imperialism. In that regard, contemporary Chinese authors made explicit references to Theosophical efforts in India, which shows an awareness of Theosophy's sociopolitical role across Asia. Chuang also offers fascinating insights into the merging of Theosophical ideas with local traditions. Her primary example is the diplomat Wu Tingfang, who functioned as an important propagandist for Theosophy in China after the 1910s and combined Theosophy with Taoism. The struggles to relate these systems to each other become tangible in the changing ways of translating "Theosophy," which was at times translated as *Tong shen* ("connected with God"), *Ming dao* ("to clarify the natural laws"), and *Ling hun xue shuo ming dao* ("to clarify the theories about the soul"). It becomes evident that Theosophy was widely regarded as a catalyst for the rethinking of religion and as mediator between Eastern and Western thought systems. In the turbulent years after the 1910s, Chinese intellectuals were striving to reconcile the "old" and the "new" to establish a national and "spiritual" identity. As elsewhere in Asia, Theosophy proved to be an attractive way of achieving this spiritual reconciliation and national renewal.

The chapter by Perry Myers takes another close look at the political ramifications of Theosophy in the Asian context—in his case, India—but at the same time juxtaposes it with developments in Germany. Despite a marked lack of direct interaction between German and Indian Theosophists, a comparison between German and Indian Theosophy during the late nineteenth and early twentieth centuries reveals strong transnational affinities yet at the same time certain estrangements through their local applications. The affinities between Germany and Indian Theosophy are best visible in what made Theosophy attractive to the respective societies. Myers cites three factors: first, a criticism of empirical science's predominant role as the exclusive source for determining human knowledge; second, a plea for the unification of modern science and spirituality; and, finally, the ideal of universality, that is, that all religions embody a core occult spiritual truth only accessible through Theosophy. These affinities were offset by estrangements most obviously visible in the field of socioeconomic ideals. German Theosophists, while criticizing materialism and capitalism, invoked a spirituality that would have preserved class status quo, viewing workers' movements as a threat to the nation-state. In India, however, Theosophists saw workers as an essential force in fomenting national sentiment in support of overthrowing British colonial power. Myers also exposes the recourse of German Theosophists to ancient India as the source of German culture in an attempt to circumvent the Greek-Mediterranean heritage, which might at first glance appear to provide a point of affinity, as actually a factor of estrangement. This is because Indian Theosophists envisioned a renewed Indian spirituality that emerged together with the Theosophical reawakening of ancient Hindu wisdom and practice, and that informed their (anticolonial) political agenda. German Theosophists, by contrast, denounced their own Christian traditions and pursued innovative esoteric avenues for reconstituting spirituality in direct opposition to Christianity.

Summary of Part Two:
Theosophy in Literature, the Arts, and Politics

The importance of Theosophy, especially in Asian contexts, for society and politics has already been emphasized in several chapters of the first part. The contributions to the second part demonstrate that Theosophy was a key player in politics as well as other areas of human endeavor, such as literature and the arts, even when outright representatives or members of the Theosophical Society were not directly involved. Rather, in the last decades of the nineteenth and the first decades of the twentieth centuries, Theosophy frequently had an indirect impact on these fields. This, however, has mostly been ignored by historical scholarship not concerned with esotericism, just as works on Theosophy have tended to neglect broader historical contexts. At the same time, recent years have witnessed a revived interest in the relationship between Theosophy and art in particular, although this interest is still centered on Western and especially North American actors.[42] For the most part, the following chapters follow less the concerns of Religious Studies or Western Esotericism, but seek to detect Theosophy as one among several factors within history, literature, or the arts beyond the West. It was not necessarily always those who remained within an organization who gave it significance, but also those who left it, or even those who were influenced by Theosophy without having ever been members.

A perfect example of this is presented by Laurence Cox and Alicia Turner in their chapter on the Burmese branches of the Maha-Bodhi Society. Founded in 1891 by Anagarika Dharmapala, the Maha-Bodhi Society was, like the Theosophical Society, an "international religious organization." In fact, the authors argue that the Maha-Bodhi Society was "theosophical with a small t," in that, like the Theosophical Society, it was a "borning organization," which enabled the formation of new religious organizations in ways that could diverge significantly from their official organizational structures. In the history of global Buddhism, both the Theosophical Society and the Maha-Bodhi Society were thus crucial catalysts, although their original purpose had been different. This was because in the global spread of international religious organizations, local actors followed their own agendas, over which the central organizations could often exert little control. As a result, the conventional perspective focusing on founders, texts, and organizational history misses local agendas such as those articulated in the Burmese region of Arakan, where anticolonial, pan-Theravada Buddhist networks soon declared their independence from larger international bodies such as the Maha-Bodhi Society.

Hans Martin Krämer introduces an individual who never was a member of the Theosophical Society—and indeed of no other international religious organization—but whose striking impact on Asia in the 1910s is difficult to conceive without the existence of Theosophy. The Frenchman Paul Richard had traveled the way from Protestant clergyman to adherent of esoteric practices in the early years of the twentieth century. He blended his religious or spiritual curiosity with a keen interest in progressive politics, leading him to India in 1910, where he met the revolutionary-turned-guru Aurobindo Ghose. Richard and his wife, Mirra, who was later to become the spiritual leader of the Aurobindo ashram, built extensive networks in India and Japan, where they lived for several years. Their activities were marked by the fusion of the politics of anticolonialism with a spiritual quest reaching out beyond Western materialism, bringing Richard into proximity with the budding pan-Asianist movement. While Theosophy played some part in the formation of Richard's thought and Theosophists were included in his personal networks, the greatest relevance of Theosophy for Richard lay in the opportunity structure it offered him. The fact that there was an eager audience for Richard's unique blend of religion and politics in Asia and Europe during the 1910s and 1920s was made possible in large part by Theosophy. Theosophists had done pioneering work in presenting a spiritual East as an alternative to the failed materialist civilizations of the West, at the same time embracing a political agenda of social reform and anticolonialism. Richard's existence as a public intellectual of his time—like that of his fellow traveler Rabindranath Tagore—was significantly enabled by Theosophy.

A similarly central figure connecting numerous strands of a sprawling network was the Irish poet James Cousins, who is the subject of the chapter by Hashimoto Yorimitsu. In fact, Cousins was close to Richard when their sojourns in Tokyo overlapped in 1919, but the networks highlighted by Hashimoto were primarily artistic, not political in nature. Cousins, himself a Theosophist, connected a surprising number of avant-garde painters, potters, composers, and writers from across Europe and Asia. While many of these had at most an indirect relationship to Theosophy, the direction their artistic work took was often influenced by their Theosophical acquaintances, an interest in Asian religions, a concern for Indian culture and politics, or other elements from Theosophical teachings or symbolism. In reconstructing Cousins's network, Hashimoto shows connections that have previously not been seen, connections that were largely made possible in some way or another by Theosophy. Most relevant for the history of Theosophy in Asia is his observation that pan-Asianism was not just a political movement with religious or spiritual overtones, but also an idea that was propelled by artistic circles, a connection that was facilitated by Theosophy.

The relationship between the arts and Theosophy is more deeply investigated in the chapter by Helena Čapková. Annie Besant had drawn this connection explicitly, especially for the visual arts, in arguing that good mental vibrations materialize in specific shapes created by spiritual devotion and create a spiritually advanced society. This argument came to inspire artists worldwide, and Čapková describes one wide-reaching network of artists inspired by Theosophy working in Europe, India, and Japan. Her prime example is the architectural project of the Golconde dormitory in Puducherry, India. Although this building belonged to the Aurobindo ashram, which generally was not on good terms with the Theosophical Society, a team of Theosophists was commissioned with designing it. Čapková argues that it was the architects' commitment to new spirituality generally that created an avenue for mutual understanding between the ashram members and spiritually attuned designers. More broadly, Theosophy appealed to a global audience sympathetic to the idea of a "universal brotherhood": Theosophical texts emphasized the importance of supernatural powers in Eastern belief systems, thus supplying Western artists with exciting new material creating an appetite for the "Orient" and the "exotic." Concretely, for the two couples at the center of Čapková's analysis, the Czech-French Raymonds and the Polish Łubienskis, living in Asia helped them gain a unique insight into Japanese art and prompted their interest in folk objects. These inspirations later became central to their artistic work, fusing Japanese, Asian, and European views on design. The Theosophical networks surrounding these European travelers to Asia provided an unexpected impulse or a spark for creating the Golconde dormitory, recognized as one of the best architectural creations in twentieth-century India.

The final two chapters of the volume trace the story of Theosophy between Asia and Europe up to the present time. Yan Suarsana sets out from contemporary images of Bali as a repository of esoteric wisdom and spiritual paradise, which was popularized by hippies and other spiritual tourists in the 1970s. Yet why was such an image plausible in the first place? Suarsana argues that this esoteric conception of Bali dates back to colonial times, when the island was forcefully opened to foreigners and the global discourses of religion and culture, including those initiated by Theosophists. Most saliently, Balinese religion came to be perceived as a part of global Hinduism. In India, Theosophists had been instrumental in establishing the "world religion" of Hinduism in the late nineteenth century. When the Dutch colonial administration started to (re)construct Balinese society as an essentially Indian culture, Balinese religion became a "legitimate part of the world religion of Hinduism." The enthusiasm of Balinese Hindu reformists for Theosophical ideas can be understood by the fact that these organizations were in intense contact with representatives of Indian Neo-Hinduism, who shared the idea of Balinese religion as part of worldwide Hinduism and were themselves often deeply entangled with Theosophy. Furthermore, not only did the Neo-Hindu conceptualization of Balinese religion as part of the world religion of Hinduism represent the leading guideline for the colonial administration, but it also continued to be an important element of religious politics of the Republic of Indonesia from 1945 onward. In this context, for which Theosophy had been crucial, the postwar popularization of "Esoteric Bali" became plausible.

In the existing literature on the cultural history of modern Russia, Theosophy is certainly not prominent among the many intellectual forces that are seen to be at work in the late nineteenth and early twentieth centuries. In his chapter, Björn Seidel-Dreffke shows that Theosophy was indeed a crucial factor in the cultural production of modern Russia in a number of realms. As he argues, many Russian intellectuals throughout the course of their lives gravitated toward the three poles of the materialist worldview, the idealistic worldview, and the mystical occult worldview, and Theosophy played an important role in the latter. The search for "true spirituality" became a constitutive element in the lives of many intellectuals around 1900, resulting in a cultural boom affecting literature, art, music, theater, and philosophy. Blavatsky's Theosophy was attractive at that time because it showed aspects of the search for the "new human," which was prominent in turn-of-the-century Russia. Theosophy appealed to those Russians who held an interest in spirituality, but had turned their backs on official religion, and it was also a way for Russian intellectuals to express their wish to distance themselves from the "decadent" West. A number of Theosophical lodges were thus successfully established in Russia toward the end of the nineteenth century. The movement took a downturn upon the split between Steiner and Besant in 1912, and shortly thereafter, all chapters of the Theosophical Society in Russia were shut down by the Bolsheviks in 1918. Since Perestroika, Theosophy has regained a footing in contemporary Russia, offering an alternative framework for interpreting the world in a society that hungers for innovations.

In sum, the chapters of this volume highlight not only the diversity and fluidity of Theosophy as a movement, but also the necessity to transgress geographical as well as disciplinary boundaries when investigating its rich history. When viewed from a global perspective, Theosophy offers far-reaching insights into the controversial negotiations of the meaning of science, religion, or art, and their complex relations to politics and social issues. Hopefully, this volume serves to stimulate scholarship in a similar vein and helps us understand the relevance of esotericism for some of the most significant historical developments of the nineteenth and twentieth centuries.

Notes

1. Peter van der Veer, *Imperial Encounters: Religion and Modernity in India and Britain* (Princeton: Princeton University Press, 2001), 55–82.

2. For instance, Judith Becker, ed. *European Missions in Contact Zones: Transformation through Interaction in a (Post-)Colonial World* (Göttingen: Vandenhoeck & Ruprecht, 2015) or the many recent titles dealing with "world Christianity."

3. See Christopher A. Bayly, *The Birth of the Modern World, 1780–1914: Global Connections and Comparisons* (Malden: Blackwell, 2004), 345–49.

4. See Thomas A. Tweed, *The American Encounter with Buddhism, 1844–1912: Victorian Culture and the Limits of Dissent* (Chapel Hill: University of North Carolina Press, 2000) or Volker Zotz, *Auf den glückseligen Inseln: Buddhismus in der deutschen Kultur* (Berlin: Theseus, 2000).

5. Bayly, *Birth*, 336.

6. Sebastian Conrad, "A Cultural History of Global Transformation," in *A History of the World*, vol. 4: *An Emerging Modern World, 1750–1870*, ed. idem and Jürgen Osterhammel (Cambridge, MA: Harvard University Press, 2018), 582.

7. Cf. the references in Jürgen Osterhammel, *The Transformation of the World: A Global History of the Nineteenth Century* (Princeton: Princeton University Press, 2014), 813.

8. Joscelyn Godwin, *The Theosophical Enlightenment* (Albany: State University of New York Press, 1994); James A. Santucci, "Theosophical Society," in *Dictionary of Gnosis and Western Esotericism*, ed. Wouter Hanegraaff et al. (Leiden: Brill, 2006); Nicholas Goodrick-Clarke, *The Western Esoteric Traditions:*

A Historical Introduction (Oxford: Oxford University Press, 2008); Jeffrey D. Lavoie, *The Theosophical Society: The History of a Spiritualist Movement* (Boca Raton: BrownWalker Press, 2012). See the statement in Nicholas Goodrick-Clarke, "Western Esoteric Traditions and Theosophy," in *Handbook of the Theosophical Current*, ed. Olav Hammer (Leiden: Brill, 2013), 303: "For all its Asian costume and fabulous intermediaries, modern Theosophy retains its Western Hermetic motive, logic, and end."

9. Olav Hammer, ed., *Handbook of the Theosophical Current*, Brill Handbooks on Contemporary Religion 7 (Leiden: Brill, 2013).

10. Kennet Granholm, "Locating the West: Problematizing the 'Western' in Western Esotericism and Occultism," in *Occultism in a Global Perspective*, ed. Henrik Bogdan and Gordan Djurdjevic (London: Acumen Publishing, 2014).

11. Egil Asprem, "Beyond the West: Towards a New Comparativism in the Study of Esotericism," *Correspondences* 2, no. 1 (2014).

12. Wouter Hanegraaff, "The Globalization of Esotericism," *Correspondences* 3, no. 1 (2015).

13. Michael Bergunder, "Experiments with Theosophical Truth: Gandhi, Esotericism, and Global Religious History," *Journal of the American Academy of Religion* 82 (2014); "'Religion' and 'Science' Within a Global Religious History," *Aries* 16, no. 1 (2016).

14. See the discussion in Julian Strube, "Towards the Study of Esotericism without the 'Western': Esotericism from the Perspective of a Global Religious History," in *New Approaches to the Study of Esotericism*, ed. Egil Asprem and Julian Strube (forthcoming).

15. Henrik Bogdan and Gordan Djurdjevic, eds., *Occultism in a Global Perspective* (Durham: Acumen, 2013); Nile Green, "The Global Occult: An Introduction," *History of Religions* 54, no. 4 (2015). For a first comprehensive attempt, see Julian Strube, *Tantra in the Context of a Global Religious History* (forthcoming).

16. Julie Chajes and Boaz Huss, eds., *Theosophical Appropriations: Esotericism, Kabbalah, and the Transformation of Traditions*, The Goldstein-Goren Library of Jewish Thought (Beer Sheva: Ben-Gurion University of the Negev Press, 2016), esp. part III about "Global Adaptations."

17. Cf. Olav Hammer and Mikael Rothstein, "Introduction," in *Handbook of the Theosophical Current*, ed. Olav Hammer (Leiden: Brill, 2013), 4: "it was perhaps the first global post-Christian organization . . ."

18. For a recent volume centering on such Orientalist imaginations, see Tim Rudbøg and Erik Reenberg Sand, eds., *Imagining the East: The Early Theosophical Society* (New York: Oxford University Press, 2020).

19. Milestones include Richard King, *Orientalism and Religion: Postcolonial Theory, India and "the Mystic East"* (London: Routledge, 1999); Dipesh Chakrabarty, *Provincializing Europe: Postcolonial Thought and Historical Difference* (Princeton: Princeton University Press, 2000); Talal Asad, *Formations of the Secular: Christianity, Islam, Modernity* (Stanford: Stanford University Press, 2003).

20. See Julian Strube, "Theosophy, Race, and the Study of Esotericism," *Journal of the American Academy of Religion* (forthcoming).
21. This was famously expressed by the notion of hybridity, for instance, in Homi K. Bhabha, *The Location of Culture* (London: Routledge, 1994), 22–26. See also the critical discussion of subaltern agency in Gayatri Chakravorty Spivak, "Can the Subaltern Speak?," in *Colonial Discourse and Post-Colonial Theory*, ed. Patrick Williams and Laura Chrisman (New York: Columbia University Press, 1994), esp. 71–73.
22. For a criticism of the conceptualization of esotericism as rejected knowledge, see Egil Asprem, "Rejected Knowledge Reconsidered: Some Methodological Notes on Esotericism and Marginality," in *New Approaches to the Study of Esotericism*, ed. Egil Asprem and Julian Strube (forthcoming). Blavatsky's oppositional strategy toward established forms of religion received recent scrutiny in by Gauri Viswanathan, "In Search of Madame Blavatsky: Reading the Exoteric, Retrieving the Esoteric," *Representations* 141, no. 1 (2018).
23. This was most clearly highlighted by Gauri Viswanathan, "The Ordinary Business of Occultism," *Critical Inquiry* 27, no. 1 (2000) and *Outside the Fold: Conversion, Modernity, and Belief* (Princeton: Princeton University Press, 1998), 177–207. Viswanathan's focus on Western actors and anglophone sources, however, tends to eclipse the very agency of non-Western actors that she otherwise seeks to highlight.
24. Granholm, "Locating," 24 and Christopher Partridge, "Lost Horizon: H.P. Blavatsky and Theosophical Orientalism," in *Handbook of the Theosophical Current*, ed. Olav Hammer and Mikael Rothstein (Leiden: Brill, 2013), 327. Although voicing important criticism of the notion of "positive orientalism," Partridge also maintains a binary of colonizer and colonized that demands complication.
25. David L. McMahan, *The Making of Buddhist Modernism* (Oxford: Oxford University Press, 2008), cf. Osterhammel, *Transformation*, 900.
26. Catherine L. Wessinger, *Annie Besant and Progressive Messianism*, Studies in Women and Religion (Lewiston: Mellen, 1988); Mark Bevir, "In Opposition to the Raj," *History of Political Thought* 19 (1998). Cf. Isaac Lubelsky, *Celestial India: Madame Blavatsky and the Birth of Indian Nationalism* (Sheffield: Equinox, 2012).
27. Bergunder, "Experiments."
28. Yoshinaga Shin'ichi, "After Olcott Left: Theosophy and 'New Buddhists' at the Turn of the Century," *The Eastern Buddhist* 43, nos. 1–2 (2012).
29. See, for instance, the key studies by Elizabeth de Michelis, *A History of Modern Yoga: Patanjali and Western Esotericism* (London: Continuum, 2004); Karl Baier, *Meditation und Moderne: Zur Genese eines Kernbereichs Moderner Spiritualität in der Wechselwirkung zwischen Westeuropa, Nordamerika und Asien* (Würzburg: Königshausen & Neumann, 2009); and Mark Singleton, *Yoga Body: The Origins of Modern Posture Practice* (Oxford: Oxford University Press, 2010). Also see Karl Baier, "Mesmeric Yoga and the Development of Meditation within

the Theosophical Society," *Theosophical History* 16, nos. 3–4 (2012) and "Theosophical Orientalism and the Structures of Intercultural Transfer: Annotations on the Appropriation of the Cakras in Early Theosophy," in *Theosophical Appropriations: Esotericism, Kabbalah, and the Transformation of Traditions*, The Goldstein-Goren Library of Jewish Thought, ed. Julie Chajes and Boaz Huss (Beer Sheva: Ben-Gurion University of the Negev Press, 2016).

30. Cf. the discussion in Geoffrey McVey, "Thebes, Luxor, and Loudsville, Georgia: The Hermetic Brotherhood of Luxor and the Landscapes of 19th-Century Occultisms," in *The Occult in Nineteenth-Century America*, ed. Cathy Gutierrez (Aurora: The Davies Group, 2005).

31. It should be added that the Kabbalah's place in "Western Esotericism" is still contested, although it is now firmly established as a subject within this field of study. For a seminal overview of relevant discussions, see Boaz Huss, Marco Pasi, and Kocku von Stuckrad, eds., *Kabbalah and Modernity: Interpretations, Transformations, Adaptations* (Leiden: Brill, 2010).

32. For classical studies, see Bruce F. Campbell, *Ancient Wisdom Revived: A History of the Theosophical Movement* (Berkeley: University of California Press, 1980); Michael Gomes, *The Dawning of the Theosophical Movement* (Wheaton: Theosophical Publishing House, 1987); Godwin, *Theosophical*. Cf. the overview in Santucci, "Theosophical Society," and the respective contributions to Hammer, *Handbook*.

33. For Helena P. Blavatsky, see S. L. Cranston, *HPB: The Extraordinary Life and Influence of Helena Blavatsky, Founder of the Modern Theosophical Movement* (New York: Putnam, 1993) and Ursula Keller and Natalja Sharandak, eds., *Madame Blavatsky: Eine Biographie* (Berlin: Insel-Verlag, 2013); for Besant, Arthur Hobart Nethercot, *The First Five Lives of Annie Besant* (Chicago: University of Chicago Press, 1960) and *The Last Four Lives of Annie Besant* (London: R. Hart-Davis, 1963); for Charles W. Leadbeater, see Gregory Tillett, *The Elder Brother: A Biography of Charles Webster Leadbeater* (London: Routledge & K. Paul, 1982). On Olcott, see Stephen R. Prothero, *The White Buddhist: The Asian Odyssey of Henry Steel Olcott* (Bloomington: Indiana University Press, 1996). While there are also several books on Jiddu Krishnamurti (1895–1986), none of them meets the standards of an academic monograph.

34. Until the end of the nineteenth century, "theosophy" usually referred to a Christian tradition including thinkers such as Louis Claude de Saint-Martin (1743–1803) and Jakob Böhme (1575–1624). For a comprehensive historical overview of this current, see Wouter Hanegraaff, *Esotericism and the Academy: Rejected Knowledge in Western Culture* (Cambridge: Cambridge University Press, 2012). Henry Steel Olcott explained that the name was chosen after looking at a dictionary.

35. For a recent study of Blavatsky, see Julie Chajes, *Recycled Lives: A History of Rebirth in Blavatsky's Theosophy* (New York: Oxford University Press, 2019).

36. Cf. Stephen R. Prothero, "From Spiritualism to Theosophy: 'Uplifting' a Democratic Tradition," *Religion and American Culture: A Journal of Interpretation* 3, no. 2 (1993); Marco Pasi, "Oriental Kabbalah and the Parting of East and West in the Early Theosophical Society," in *Kabbalah and Modernity: Interpretations, Transformations, Adaptations*, ed. Boaz Huss, Marco Pasi, and Kocku von Stuckrad (Leiden: Brill, 2010); Julian Strube, "Occultist Identity Formations Between Theosophy and Socialism in Fin-de-Siècle France," *Numen* 64, nos. 5–6 (2017).

37. The Arya Samaj is one of numerous subjects that would facilitate a dialogue between the study of esotericism, global history, and South Asian studies. See, for instance, the work of Harald Fischer-Tiné, most specifically "Marrying Global History with South Asian History: Potential and Limits of Global Microhistory in a Regional Inflection," *Comparativ* 28, no. 5 (2018).

38. Helmut Zander, *Anthroposophie in Deutschland: Theosophische Weltanschauung und gesellschaftliche Praxis 1884–1945*, 2 vols., vol. 1 (Göttingen: Vandenhoeck & Ruprecht, 2007), 151–70.

39. Catherine L. Wessinger, "The Second Generation Leaders of the Theosophical Society (Adyar)," in *Handbook of the Theosophical Current*, ed. Olav Hammer (Leiden: Brill, 2013), 46.

40. Ibid., 47.

41. See Olav Hammer and Mikael Rothstein, "Introduction," and the respective contributions.

42. See, for instance, Sarah V. Turner, Christopher M. Scheer, and James G. Mansell, eds., *Enchanted Modernities: Theosophy, the Arts and the American West* (Somerset: Fulgur Press, 2019); Marco Pasi, "Afterthought Forms: Theosophy in Modern and Contemporary Art," in *Hilma Af Klint Visionary*, ed. Kurt Almqvist and Louise Belfrage (Stockholm: Bokförlaget Stolpe, 2019); Christopher M. Scheer, "Enchanted Music, Enchanted Modernity: Theosophy, Maud Maccarthy, and John Foulds," *Journal of Musicological Research* 37, no. 1 (2018).

References

Asad, Talal. *Formations of the Secular: Christianity, Islam, Modernity*. Stanford: Stanford University Press, 2003.

Asprem, Egil. "Beyond the West: Towards a New Comparativism in the Study of Esotericism." *Correspondences* 2, no. 1 (2014): 3–33.

———. "Rejected Knowledge Reconsidered: Some Methodological Notes on Esotericism and Marginality," in *New Approaches to the Study of Esotericism*, edited by Egil Asprem and Julian Strube, forthcoming.

Baier, Karl. *Meditation Und Moderne: Zur Genese Eines Kernbereichs Moderner Spiritualität in Der Wechselwirkung Zwischen Westeuropa, Nordamerika Und Asien*. 2 vols. Würzburg: Königshausen & Neumann, 2009.

———. "Mesmeric Yoga and the Development of Meditation within the Theosophical Society." *Theosophical History* 16, nos. 3–4 (2012): 151–61.

———. "Theosophical Orientalism and the Structures of Intercultural Transfer: Annotations on the Appropriation of the Cakras in Early Theosophy." In *Theosophical Appropriations: Esotericism, Kabbalah, and the Transformation of Traditions*, edited by Julie Chajes and Boaz Huss, 309–54. Beer Sheva: Ben-Gurion University of the Negev Press, 2016.

Bayly, Christopher A. *The Birth of the Modern World, 1780–1914: Global Connections and Comparisons* [in Eng.]. Malden: Blackwell, 2004.

Becker, Judith, ed. *European Missions in Contact Zones: Transformation through Interaction in a (Post-)Colonial World*. Göttingen: Vandenhoeck & Ruprecht, 2015.

Bergunder, Michael. "Experiments with Theosophical Truth: Gandhi, Esotericism, and Global Religious History." *Journal of the American Academy of Religion* 82 (2014): 398–426.

———. "'Religion' and 'Science' Within a Global Religious History." *Aries* 16, no. 1 (2016): 86–141.

Bevir, Mark. "In Opposition to the Raj." *History of Political Thought* 19 (1998): 61–77.

Bhabha, Homi K. *The Location of Culture*. London: Routledge, 1994.

Bogdan, Henrik, and Gordan Djurdjevic, eds. *Occultism in a Global Perspective*. Durham: Acumen, 2013.

Campbell, Bruce F. *Ancient Wisdom Revived: A History of the Theosophical Movement*. Berkeley: University of California Press, 1980.

Chajes, Julie. *Recycled Lives: A History of Rebirth in Blavatsky's Theosophy*. New York: Oxford University Press, 2019.

Chajes, Julie, and Boaz Huss, eds. *Theosophical Appropriations: Esotericism, Kabbalah, and the Transformation of Traditions*. The Goldstein-Goren Library of Jewish Thought, vol. 21. Beer Sheva: Ben-Gurion University of the Negev Press, 2016.

Chakrabarty, Dipesh. *Provincializing Europe: Postcolonial Thought and Historical Difference*. Princeton: Princeton University Press, 2000.

Conrad, Sebastian. "A Cultural History of Global Transformation." In *A History of the World*, vol. 4: *An Emerging Modern World, 1750–1870*, edited by Sebastian Conrad and Jürgen Osterhammel, 413–659. Cambridge, MA: Harvard University Press, 2018.

Cranston, S. L. *HPB: The Extraordinary Life and Influence of Helena Blavatsky, Founder of the Modern Theosophical Movement*. New York: Putnam, 1993.

Godwin, Joscelyn. *The Theosophical Enlightenment*. Albany: State University of New York Press, 1994.

Fischer-Tiné, Harald. "Marrying Global History with South Asian History: Potential and Limits of Global Microhistory in a Regional Inflection." *Comparativ* 28, no. 5 (2018): 49–74.

Gomes, Michael. *The Dawning of the Theosophical Movement*. Wheaton: Theosophical Publishing House, 1987.

Goodrick-Clarke, Nicholas. "Western Esoteric Traditions and Theosophy." In *Handbook of the Theosophical Current*, edited by Olav Hammer, 261–307. Leiden: Brill, 2013.

———. *The Western Esoteric Traditions: A Historical Introduction*. Oxford: Oxford University Press, 2008.

Granholm, Kennet. "Locating the West: Problematizing the 'Western' in Western Esotericism and Occultism." In *Occultism in a Global Perspective*, edited by Henrik Bogdan and Gordan Djurdjevic, 17–36. London: Acumen Publishing, 2014.

Green, Nile. "The Global Occult: An Introduction." *History of Religions* 54, no. 4 (2015): 383–93.

Hammer, Olav, ed. *Handbook of the Theosophical Current*, Brill Handbooks on Contemporary Religion, vol. 7. Leiden: Brill, 2013.

Hammer, Olav, and Mikael Rothstein. "Introduction." In *Handbook of the Theosophical Current*, edited by Olav Hammer, 1–12. Leiden: Brill, 2013.

Hanegraaff, Wouter. *Esotericism and the Academy: Rejected Knowledge in Western Culture* [in Eng.]. Cambridge: Cambridge University Press, 2012.

———. "The Globalization of Esotericism." *Correspondences* 3, no. 1 (2015): 55–91.

Huss, Boaz, Marco Pasi, and Kocku von Stuckrad, eds. *Kabbalah and Modernity: Interpretations, Transformations, Adaptations*. Leiden: Brill, 2010.

Keller, Ursula, and Natalja Sharandak, eds. *Madame Blavatsky: Eine Biographie*. Berlin: Insel-Verlag, 2013.

King, Richard. *Orientalism and Religion: Postcolonial Theory, India and "the Mystic East."* London New York: Routledge, 1999.

Lavoie, Jeffrey D. *The Theosophical Society: The History of a Spiritualist Movement*. Boca Raton: BrownWalker Press, 2012.

Lubelsky, Isaac. *Celestial India: Madame Blavatsky and the Birth of Indian Nationalism* [in English translation of an unpublished manuscript in Hebrew.]. Sheffield: Equinox, 2012.

McMahan, David L. *The Making of Buddhist Modernism*. Oxford: Oxford University Press, 2008.

McVey, Geoffrey. "Thebes, Luxor, and Loudsville, Georgia: The Hermetic Brotherhood of Luxor and the Landscapes of 19th-Century Occultisms." In *The Occult in Nineteenth-Century America*, edited by Cathy Gutierrez, 153–81. Aurora: The Davies Group, 2005.

Michelis, Elizabeth De. *A History of Modern Yoga: Patañjali and Western Esotericism*. London: Continuum, 2004.

Nethercot, Arthur Hobart. *The First Five Lives of Annie Besant*. Chicago: University of Chicago Press, 1960.

———. *The Last Four Lives of Annie Besant*. London: R. Hart-Davis, 1963.
Osterhammel, Jürgen. *The Transformation of the World: A Global History of the Nineteenth Century*. Princeton: Princeton University Press, 2014.
Partridge, Christopher. "Lost Horizon: H.P. Blavatsky and Theosophical Orientalism," in *Handbook of the Theosophical Current*, edited by Olav Hammer and Mikael Rothstein, 309–33. Leiden: Brill, 2013.
Pasi, Marco. "Oriental Kabbalah and the Parting of East and West in the Early Theosophical Society." In *Kabbalah and Modernity: Interpretations, Transformations, Adaptations*, edited by Boaz Huss, Marco Pasi, and Kocku von Stuckrad, 151–66. Leiden: Brill, 2010.
———. "Afterthought Forms: Theosophy in Modern and Contemporary Art." In *Hilma Af Klint Visionary*, edited by Kurt Almqvist and Louise Belfrage, 92–109. Stockholm: Bokförlaget Stolpe, 2019.
Prothero, Stephen R. "From Spiritualism to Theosophy: 'Uplifting' a Democratic Tradition." *Religion and American Culture: A Journal of Interpretation* 3, no. 2 (1993): 197–216.
———. *The White Buddhist: The Asian Odyssey of Henry Steel Olcott*. Bloomington: Indiana University Press, 1996.
Rudbøg, Tim, and Erik Reenberg Sand, eds. *Imagining the East: The Early Theosophical Society*. New York: Oxford University Press, 2020.
Santucci, James A. "Theosophical Society." In *Dictionary of Gnosis and Western Estericism*, edited by Wouter Hanegraaff, Antoine Faivre, Roelof van den Broek, and Jean-Pierre Brach, 1114–23. Leiden: Brill, 2006.
Scheer, Christopher M. "Enchanted Music, Enchanted Modernity: Theosophy, Maud Maccarthy, and John Foulds." *Journal of Musicological Research* 37, no. 1 (2018): 5–29.
Singleton, Mark. *Yoga Body: The Origins of Modern Posture Practice*. Oxford: Oxford University Press, 2010.
Spivak, Gayatri Chakravorty. "Can the Subaltern Speak?" In *Colonial Discourse and Post-Colonial Theory*, edited by Patrick Williams and Laura Chrisman, 66–111. New York: Columbia University Press, 1994.
Strube, Julian. "Occultist Identity Formations Between Theosophy and Socialism in Fin-de-Siècle France." *Numen* 64, no. 5–6 (2017): 568–595.
———. *Tantra in the Context of a Global Religious History*. Forthcoming.
———. "Theosophy, Race, and the Study of Esotericism." *Journal of the American Academy of Religion* (forthcoming).
———. "Towards the Study of Esotericism without the 'Western': Esotericism from the Perspective of a Global Religious History," in *New Approaches to the Study of Esotericism*, edited by Egil Asprem and Julian Strube, forthcoming.
Tillett, Gregory. *The Elder Brother: A Biography of Charles Webster Leadbeater*. London: Routledge & K. Paul, 1982.

Turner, Sarah V., Christopher M. Scheer, and James G. Mansell, eds. *Enchanted Modernities: Theosophy, the Arts and the American West*. Somerset: Fulgur Press, 2019.

Tweed, Thomas A. *The American Encounter with Buddhism, 1844–1912: Victorian Culture and the Limits of Dissent*. Chapel Hill: University of North Carolina Press, 2000.

Veer, Peter van der. *Imperial Encounters: Religion and Modernity in India and Britain*. Princeton: Princeton University Press, 2001.

Viswanathan, Gauri. *Outside the Fold: Conversion, Modernity, and Belief*. Princeton: Princeton University Press, 1998.

———. "The Ordinary Business of Occultism." *Critical Inquiry* 27, no. 1 (2000): 1–20.

———. "In Search of Madame Blavatsky: Reading the Exoteric, Retrieving the Esoteric." *Representations* 141, no. 1 (2018): 67–94.

Wessinger, Catherine L. *Annie Besant and Progressive Messianism: Studies in Women and Religion*. Lewiston: Mellen, 1988.

———. "The Second Generation Leaders of the Theosophical Society (Adyar)." In *Handbook of the Theosophical Current*, edited by Olav Hammer, 33–50. Leiden: Brill, 2013.

Yoshinaga Shin'ichi. "After Olcott Left: Theosophy and 'New Buddhists' at the Turn of the Century." *The Eastern Buddhist* 43, nos. 1–2 (2012): 103–132.

Zander, Helmut. *Anthroposophie in Deutschland: Theosophische Weltanschauung und gesellschaftliche Praxis 1884–1945*. 2 vols. Göttingen: Vandenhoeck & Ruprecht, 2007.

Zotz, Volker. *Auf den glückseligen Inseln: Buddhismus in der deutschen Kultur*. Berlin: Theseus, 2000.

PART I

NEW PERSPECTIVES ON THEOSOPHY

Chapter 1

Western Esotericism and the Orient in the First Theosophical Society

Wouter J. Hanegraaff

Almost everybody knows that the Theosophical Society was founded in Helena P. Blavatsky's apartment in New York in 1875, but few people are aware of how little this original society resembled the international organization that began to operate from India in 1879.[1] My argument in this chapter is that Theosophy began as a specifically Western[2] esoteric current that became "entangled"[3] with Indian religions only *after* Blavatsky and Olcott arrived in Bombay on February 16, 1879. Prior to that event, Theosophical understandings of India and its religious traditions were dominated by the deeply ethnocentric Orientalist imagination typical of nineteenth-century European scholarship and popular literature.[4] This means that if we wish to "disentangle" the global history of Theosophy, we must first of all obtain a clear picture of what it looked like prior to 1879.

None of the above is meant to suggest that the arrival of Olcott and Blavatsky in Bombay caused them simply to move from a Western and merely "imaginary" vision of the Orient toward an "authentic" understanding of Indian religion.[5] Not only did they bring their Orientalist perspectives with them to India, but perspectives and assumptions quite similar to their own were already present among colonial elites and educated Indians well before their arrival. As far as their own ideas are concerned, there is no doubt that in their sincere efforts to give a voice to Buddhism, the founders ended up promoting what *they* believed Buddhism should be all about—whether Buddhists agreed or not. As formulated by Stephen Prothero,

When it came to constructing his understanding of Buddhism, [. . .] Olcott relied not on the living example of Asian Buddhists but on the scholarly works of academic Orientalists, most of whom were committed Christians. This key decision to attend to the bookish Buddhism of Orientalists rather than the lived Buddhism of Buddhists tilted Olcott's imaginative construction of Buddhism in a decidedly Protestant direction.[6]

It has been noted that Blavatsky's and Olcott's Theosophy reflected "a never-before-seen degree of admiration of non-Western culture and religion,"[7] and this is correct at least as far as Western Theosophists are concerned. However, what they found so admirable in India was largely what they had *already* been admiring before they ever arrived there. The "positive Orientalism" to which they adhered is a European invention with roots that reach far back in history;[8] and while this perspective highlighted certain dimensions of "the Orient" as emblematic of a "universal" ancient mystical wisdom,[9] such idealizations required the simultaneous suppression or marginalization of everything that did not fit the picture—notably the traditional bête noire of "idolatry."[10]

But Theosophy was more than just another example of colonialist "encompassment"[11] of Indian religion within a Western framework, for the lines of influence went in both directions. The Theosophical Society grew with stunning rapidity (as early as 1891, it had 258 branches on six continents[12]), and as more and more Indians joined its ranks, it was inevitable that they would begin to interpret Theosophy from *their* own perspectives. The result was a great variety of local variations and interpretations, all participating in a movement that may have been unified in theory, but was bound to become far more complex than anything Olcott or Blavatsky had in mind. Because of its great importance both from a historical and a theoretical perspective, I find it important to clarify my position on this point. In some of my earlier work, Theosophy is described as an "essentially Western movement" rooted in Western-esoteric rather than Eastern traditions;[13] and more recently I wrote about the larger context of esotericism as "an inherently Western domain of research."[14] These statements have received some criticism,[15] as the formulations could seem to suggest a residual East/West essentialism and a refusal to acknowledge esotericism as a global reality. Nothing could be further from my intentions, so I have tried to sharpen my formulations and clarify my position in a recent publication.[16] Interestingly, my critics seem to have overlooked a much more problematic statement that I made in 1996: "To my knowledge, there is no evidence to support the [. . .] idea that modern theosophy eventually came to interpret esotericism, occultism or western science from perspectives that are distinctly oriental and have no precedent in the west."[17] *That* statement was certainly mistaken! Today I realize that there is plenty of evidence indeed, but one will have to look for it in the writings and activities of Theosophists with *non*-European/American cultural, religious, or ethnic backgrounds.[18] It is in this regard that I expect the present volume will be able to break new ground and contribute to a truly global understanding of Theosophy.

Rather than framing the history of Theosophy in the simplistic terms of a confrontation between Western Orientalist "fantasies" and Indian "realities," then, we should focus on the extremely complicated historical processes of imaginal construction and reconstruction that took place in a variety of specific local contexts and on all levels of the Theosophical hierarchy. Such a project should start at the very beginning and at the very place of origin, *before* the moment of "first contact" on Indian soil. In other words, we need to travel back to New York City in 1875.

The First Theosophical Society

In studying early Theosophical history, it is crucial to resist the temptation of reading earlier developments in the light of later ones. If we try to imagine for a moment that Blavatsky and Olcott had died tragically in 1878 and never embarked for India: how—if at all—would we then remember the "Theosophical Society" today? From surviving sources, we might discover that on the evening of September 7, 1875, about seventeen people[19] gathered in the parlor at 46 Irving Place, the apartment of a recent immigrant from Russia, a certain Helena P. Blavatsky, where they established what some contemporary observers saw as "a school for sorcery" devoted to "the Practice of Witch-Craft."[20] Those who knew Blavatsky at the time were generally impressed by her mysterious and charismatic personality, but she was not yet famous as an occultist or writer. Since her arrival in the United States two years earlier, she had been sending letters to popular newspapers and Spiritualist magazines;[21] and her first real article on occultism, "A Few Questions to 'HIRAF,'" had appeared in one of those journals just a few months before.[22] With her powerful, passionate, and somehow authoritative style of writing, she had begun to be noted in Spiritualist milieus, and the popular press was fascinated with her. Still, nobody could have predicted in September 1875 that she would soon produce a spectacular best seller and become the world's most famous "occultist"—let alone that she would spearhead an international revival of Buddhism and Hinduism.

Blavatsky's understanding of occultism at this time is evident from an important letter she wrote on February 16, 1875 to Professor Hiram Corson,[23] who had contacted her about an article she had written in the Spiritualist paper *Banner of Light*.[24] Blavatsky was still presenting herself as a Spiritualist at this time: she wrote that "for the sake of Spiritualism" she had left her home and "become a wanderer upon the face of the earth," and when she sailed from France to the United States, she did so "with feelings not unlike those of a Mohammadan approaching the birth-place of his prophet."[25] But once having arrived in the Promised Land, she was sorely disappointed by what she found, and was soon lashing out at fraudulent practices and the "deplorable lack of accord between American spiritualists."[26] Clearly she had something different in mind: in her letter to Corson (the second one after an initial letter dated February 9, 1875), she explained that Spiritualism should be understood as part of a much larger tradition, unknown to most Spiritualists. The passage is of such importance to our concerns in this chapter that it must be quoted here in full:

> When I became a spiritualist, it was not through the agency of the ever-lying, cheating mediums, miserable instruments of the undeveloped Spirits of the lower Sphere, the ancient Hades. My belief is based on something older than the Rochester knockings, and springs out from the same source of information that was used by Raymond Lully, Picus della Mirandola, Cornelius Agrippa, Robert Fludd, Henry More, et cetera, etc., all of whom have ever been searching for a system that should disclose to them the "deepest depths" of the Divine nature, and show them the real tie which binds all things together. I found at last, and many years ago, the cravings of my mind satisfied by this theosophy taught by the Angels and communicated by them that the protoplast might know it for the aid of the human destiny. The practical, however small knowledge of the Principle, Ain-Soph, or the Endless and the Boundless with its ten Sephiroths or Emanations, goes more towards opening

your eyes than all the hypothetical teachings of the leaders of Spiritualism, let them be American or European. In my eyes, Allan Kardec and Flammarion, Andrew Jackson Davis and Judge Edmonds, are but schoolboys just trying to spell their A B C and sorely blundering sometimes. The relation between the two is in just proportion what were in the ancient ages the book called *Sohar*, based on the perfect knowledge of the Kabbala handed down by oral tradition from David and Solomon to Simon ben Jochai, the first man who dared write it down, and the *Massorah*, a book based on outside, not direct tradition, and which never vouchsafed the truth of what it taught.[27]

Note that Blavatsky already uses the term "theosophy" here, and clearly means it to refer to the classic traditions of *Western* esotericism or occult philosophy. Theosophy is supposed to have originated in the Kabbalah or, as formulated in her "HIRAF" article a few months later, "the primitive Oriental Cabala" that possessed all the "primitive secret powers of the ancient Chaldaeans."[28] In using the word "Oriental" here, she was hardly thinking of India or the Far East: her reference was to standard nineteenth-century concepts of a universal kabbalah with *non*-Jewish origins that, according to some of the most influential authors available to her (from a legitimate academic such as Adolphe Franck to the French occultist Éliphas Lévi), had ultimately emerged from the religion of Zoroaster.[29] Such perceptions of Kabbalah as Zoroastrian or Chaldaean may sound bizarre to us today but were perfectly normal in 1875. They ultimately reflected the Platonic Orientalist narrative of an "Ancient Wisdom Tradition" that had been promoted by countless European intellectuals since the fifteenth century, and remained remarkably widespread in nineteenth-century Orientalist scholarship.[30] Only in the early twentieth century did Gershom Scholem succeed in replacing these concepts of a universal kabbalah with Oriental origins by a proper understanding of kabbalah as a Jewish tradition.[31]

The Theosophical Microbe: George Henry Felt

That a journalist writing in 1875 could perceive the First Theosophical Society as "a school for sorcery" is not at all surprising, as will be seen. Discussions at Blavatsky's weekly gatherings tended to move all over the place, touching upon such diverse topics as

> [t]he phallic element in religions; the souls of flowers; recent wonders among the mediums; history; Italian character; the strangeness of travel; chemistry; poetry; Nature's duality; Romanism; Gravitation; the Carbonari; jugglery; Crook's new discoveries about the force of light; the literature of magic [. . .][32]

On the fateful evening of September 7, a military officer named George Henry Felt (1831–1906) gave a lecture about a book project of his. It was concerned with *The Kabbalah of the Egyptians*, which he interpreted as containing the lost "Canon of Proportion of the Greeks." It is important to get the title right: this is what Felt's book (which was frequently announced but would never appear in print[33]) was supposed to be titled; and when Olcott rendered it as "The Lost Canon of Proportion of the Egyptians," without mentioning kabbalah, he was clearly just collapsing title and subtitle into one. The report of this evening by the Rev. J. H. Wiggins was in fact titled "The Cabala," and it is perfectly clear from his description that the members of Felt's audience believed they were listening to a talk about *kabbalistic* mysteries. From the default perspective of a "universal kabbalah" referred to above, these mysteries were believed to hold the key for unlocking "the secrets of nature" already known to the ancient Egyptians (who, by the way, were claimed to have emigrated from Finland!), the ancient Greeks, the Hebrew scriptures, the "learned Rabbins," and the teachings of Jesus. No mention of Brahmans or India.

After Felt's lecture, Blavatsky's personal physician, Seth Pancoast (who seems to have owned a valuable library of occult books[34] and was particularly interested in medical applications of the kabbalistic "science of light"[35]), seems to have challenged Felt for discussing "the kabbalah" just a bit too safely from a theoretical perspective alone. He argued that "the ancient occultists" had not just been concerned with geometrical proportions, but had been practical alchemists who could "transmute the baser metals into gold" and "indefinitely prolong human life." Moreover, they knew how to summon "spirits from the vasty deep" as well as "ward off and neutralize the power of surrounding ill-boding demons."[36] From Wiggins's account, one gets the impression that Pancoast was deliberately and even aggressively trying to provoke Felt:

> Could Mr. Felt do this? Did he fully understand the meaning of the alphabet, numerals, and other Cabalistic signs? If so, nature was subject to his will, and he could not be confined

by bolts and bars. A crystal was then shown to the Cabalist, whose meaning he could not then and there explain. To the questions these were HIS STRAIGHTFORWARD REPLIES: He could, with his chemical circle, call into sight hundreds of shadowy forms resembling the human, but he had seen no signs of intelligence in these apparitions [etc.].[37]

It would seem that Felt took the bait. As regards the "bolts and bars," he boasted that he knew how to escape from prison if he wanted; but more importantly, he proposed to give a series of further lectures (for payment), during which he would "exhibit the nature-spirits to us all."[38] It was in response to these promises of invoking "elementals" that the idea was born "to form a Society for this kind of study."[39] Henry J. Newton was therefore correct in describing Felt (in a later hostile account) as "the theosophical microbe, the germ from which was constructed that 'crazy quilt' called Theosophy."[40]

Felt did indeed give several further lectures, on September 18, 1875, and June 21, 1876. The first of these must have been promising enough to inspire great expectations in Olcott, as one can see from his Inaugural Address of November 1875:

> Without claiming to be a theurgist, a mesmerist, or a Spiritualist, our Vice-President [= Felt] promises, by simple chemical appliances, to exhibit to us, as he has to others before, the races of beings which, invisible to our eyes, people the elements. Think for a moment of this astounding claim! Fancy the consequences of the practical demonstration of its truth, for which Mr. Felt is now preparing the requisite apparatus! [. . .] What will the Spiritualists say, when through the column of saturated vapor flit the dreadful shapes of beings whom, in their blindness, they have in a thousand cases revered and babbled to as the returning shades of their relatives and friends?[41]

These statements were an embarrassment to Olcott seventeen years later, when he admitted that these high expectations had been "a bit foolish." Presumably in reference to Felt's second lecture, on June 21, 1876, he now described the demonstration as "a complete and mortifying disappointment. Whatever he may have done by himself in that direction, he showed us nothing, not even the tip end of the tail of the tiniest

Nature-spirit. He left us to be mocked by the Spiritualist and every other class of sceptic."[42]

But was it really so simple? For his part, Felt claimed that he *had* been successful enough but had been forced to interrupt his demonstration because the "*illuminati* of the Society" (as he calls them) were spooked by the experience:

> Certain members of lower degree were impressed with a feeling of dread, as though something awful were about to happen; most of the probationers were rendered uncomfortable or uneasy; some became hypercritical and abusive; several of the novitiates left the room; and Mme. Blavatsky, who had seen unpleasant effects follow somewhat similar phenomena in the East, requested me to turn the drawing and change the subject.[43]

What was Felt's manner of operation? According to a hostile newspaper article from November 10, 1895, based on statements by Henry J. Newton, he claimed that "the methods used in Egypt and India in connection with their mysteries [. . .] produce[d] the phenomena of so-called materialization by a combustion of aromatic gum and herbs"[44] This detail is significant for two reasons. First, similar references in the work of Emma Hardinge Britten (see below) suggest that occultists during the later 1870s were trying to reintroduce a kind of Neoplatonic theurgy, including its use of herbal fumigations to create an atmosphere thick with smoke in which spectral visions would appear.[45] This fits perfectly with Olcott's reference to a "column of saturated vapor." If we compare this information with Emma Hardinge Britten's more detailed descriptions of occultist theurgy in *Ghost Land* (see below),[46] it seems clear that such rituals were perfectly capable of inspiring feelings of dread and gothic horror.

> [. . .] the sight itself can be rendered more subtle, the nerves more acute, the spirit more alive and outward, and the element itself—the air, the space—may be made, by certain secrets of the higher chemistry, more palpable and clear. [. . .] Now, in space there are millions of beings, not literally spiritual, for they have all [. . .] certain forms of matter, though matter so delicate, air-drawn, and subtle that it is, as it were, but a film, a gossamer, that clothes the spirit. Hence the Roscicrusian's [sic] lovely phantoms of sylph and gnomen [sic] [. . .] He who

would establish intercourse with these varying beings, resembles
the traveller who would penetrate into unknown lands. [. . .]
Because the very elixir that pours a more glorious life into
the frame, so sharpens the senses that those larvae of the air
become to thee audible and apparent.[47]

When Bulwer-Lytton's protagonist, Glyndon, inhales the "delicious odor" that comes from the "ecstatic liquid" kept in crystal vessels in the study of the master adept Mejnour, he does indeed begin to see the shapes of elemental beings—although soon enough, his experiment gives way to an experience of gothic horror, with the appearance of the terrifying "dweller on the threshold."[48] These pages from the most influential occult novel of the nineteenth century explain why the early Theosophists would be so excited about the idea of invoking elementals through procedures that they saw as "kabbalistic" alchemy. If Felt did indeed use fumigations in some kind of "theurgical" ritual, as seems very likely, then one easily understands the feelings of fear and dread that appear to have overwhelmed the participants when it dawned on them that he might actually succeed.

No wonder then that contemporaries could see the first Theosophical Society as a "school for sorcery," concerned as it was with theurgic invocations of elementals and other spiritual beings (as an alternative to the typical Spiritualist séance). Blavatsky and her friends saw themselves as heirs of the ancient "kabbalistic" tradition,[49] represented not just by Jewish practitioners, but also by Egyptian Hermetists, Neoplatonic theurgists, alchemists, and famous "adepts" or magicians such as Ramon Llull, Giovanni Pico della Mirandola, Cornelius Agrippa, John Dee, or Robert Fludd. Just two weeks after the founding of the Theosophical Society, Blavatsky described how she saw it at that time:

[i]t will be composed of learned occultists and cabbalists,
of *philosophes hermétiques* of the nineteenth century, and of
passionate antiquaries and Egyptologists generally. We want to
make an experimental comparison between Spiritualism and
the magic of the ancients by following literally the instructions
of the old Cabbalas, both Jewish and Egyptian.[50]

Once again, the primary reference is to Egypt and the kabbalah, not to India, Hinduism, or Buddhism. It should be clear then how little the First Theosophical Society resembled the movement that would become famous after 1878. Other leading Theosophists such as William Q. Judge likewise joined the Society not so much because of an interest in Buddhism or other Oriental religions, but "to investigate the same thing that Mr. Felt had investigated."[51] As the invocation of Elementals proved more problematic or frightening than first expected, they moved on to exploring other occult practices, notably astral travel.[52]

The Other Woman: Emma Hardinge Britten

We have seen that the early Theosophists believed in a "kabbalah" with non-Jewish Oriental origins in Chaldaea and Egypt. As such, they were faithful heirs of nineteenth-century Orientalism and the Platonic Orientalist tradition in Western esotericism. How then did they look at India and its traditions? To explore this question, I will focus on the case of Emma Hardinge Britten (1823–1899).

As the only woman apart from Blavatsky, Britten was among the most active founding members of the Theosophical Society. Significantly, its preamble and bylaws were adopted and its first officers elected not in Blavatsky's apartment, but in the reception rooms of Britten's husband and their residence on 38th Street, New York, on October 16 and 30.[53] At this time, Britten was busy preparing two books that would both appear in 1876 under the titles *Art Magic* and *Ghost Land*.[54] Blavatsky, for her part, was struggling mightily with a manuscript of her own that seems to have carried the provisory title *A Skeleton Key to Mysterious Gates*.[55] But, as she did not have Britten's long experience as an author and editor, she needed much help to produce a publishable version; and while it was certainly not in her character to show any signs of insecurity, she must have felt the pressure of the competition. It is important to realize that while Blavatsky had arrived in New York just two years earlier, Britten was already comfortably established as a celebrated speaker in the American Spiritualist milieu. A strong personality on top of her game, she had forceful opinions of her own and would hardly be inclined to play second fiddle to Blavatsky or anyone else. It is not hard to understand, then, that "the atmosphere was at times thick with tension"[56] between these two formidable women each working on her own mysterious manuscript about occultism. Because Britten would soon turn away from the Theosophical Society and become a vocal critic of Blavatsky and her "turn towards the East," there has been a tendency to see her not as a Theosophist, but as a Spiritualist and independent occultist. Understandable as this may be, such a view is anachronistic. In the early years of the Theosophical Society, from 1875 to 1876, Britten's perspective was perfectly typical of what "Theosophy" was supposed to be all about.

So who was Emma Hardinge Britten? We know that in 1823 she was born in England as Emma Floyd, but for many details about her life we have only her own testimony. This is unfortunate because, as noted by her biographer Mathiesen, she "consistently and deliberately obscured the record of her own early life."[57] For instance, she was a gifted musician and seems to have been a child prodigy—but should we believe that at the age of twelve she already had embarked on a public career as singer, concert pianist and organ player (not to mention her activities as a choral conductor and composer)?[58] Somewhat similar reservations are in order about the exact nature of her involvement in a mysterious "Orphic Circle," described by her as a secret society of magical practitioners that enlisted her as a child medium at about the same time (1836). Fourteen years later, in 1850, she claims to have renewed her acquaintance with one of its members, a mysterious "Chevalier Louis de B---," to whose significance we will return.

In 1854 Emma left England for Paris, where she worked as an actress. She now appeared on stage as "Mrs Hardinge," but it is doubtful whether she ever married the medical botanist and Mesmerist E. Hardinge or was even acquainted with him at all.[59] Be that as it may, in 1855 she (and her devoted mother) moved to New York, where Emma soon became involved in the Spiritualist movement. Having begun as a test medium, she found her true calling as an "inspired" lecturer who would address large audiences in a state of trance. Traveling widely at the invitation of Spiritualists all over the United States and England, she established a solid reputation as one of the most vocal and visible defenders of the Spiritualist cause.

From about 1858 on, her religious ideas began to change. She drifted away from Christianity to embrace a worldview grounded in the notion of an ancient and universal religion of Nature, an "astronomical religion" of Solar and phallic worship.[60] Emma's earliest statements to that effect were delivered in a state of trance and published in 1860 as *Six Lectures on Theology and Nature*.[61] Her career as a prolific writer began at about the same time, with numerous articles in Spiritualist journals and a long series of books.[62] Some of these were based on stenographed versions of her trance lectures; others were written under her own name: first that of Emma Hardinge and later (after her marriage to William G. P. Britten in 1870) that of Emma Hardinge Britten.

Britten was also active as a founder and editor of Spiritualist journals. Her first attempt, the short-lived *Western Star* of 1875, is most relevant to our present concerns. It carried a series of articles titled "'Ghost Land': or, Researches into the Mysteries of Spiritual Existence" by an author who concealed his identity behind the pseudonym "Austria," as well as a series entitled "Amongst the Spirits: or, Glimpses of Spiritual Men, Women, and Things" by another Anonymous who signed as "Asmodeus."[63] Whether for financial reasons or the Boston fire of 1875 (or both), the series was cut short; but it is here that we see the first beginnings of the two crucial books that Emma would publish four years later.

Mysteries of Authorship and the Orphic Circle

Art Magic was published in April 1876 as a limited edition of only 500 copies available only to subscribers.[64] Later that year, it was followed by *Ghost Land*, this time in a normal edition for the general public. Those readers who had read the original articles in *The Western Star* now learned that behind the pseudonyms "Austria" and "Asmodeus" were two members of the mysterious Orphic Circle. Britten insisted that *Art Magic* and *Ghost Land* were written not by herself, but by "Chevalier Louis de B---" (with some chapters based on materials written by his friend and fellow adept "John Cavendish Dudley"). She presented her own role as merely that of a modest editor and translator, but if we are to believe the Author's Preface, she was much more than that. She is presented there as a selfless hero who courageously volunteers to act as a buffer between an extremely timid Chevalier de B--- and the uncomprehending outside world. With characteristic pathos, the Chevalier writes how he had been "shrinking with unconquerable repugnance from any encounter with those butchers of human character, self-styled 'critics,' whose chief delight is to exercise their carving-knives upon the bodies of slain reputations, without regard to qualification for the act of dissection,"[65] and had been "equally averse to entrusting the dangerous and difficult processes of magical art to an age wherein even the most sacred elements of religion and Spiritualism are so often prostituted to the arts of imposture, or mean traffic."[66] In short, it was only because of Britten's insistence and her willingness to take the heat on his behalf that he finally consented:

> The reception which [the circular that announced *Art Magic*] met with, the unworthy jibes, sneers, and cruel insults which

have been leveled against the excellent lady who volunteered to stand between the author and his shrinking spirit, have caused him the deepest remorse for having placed her in such a position, and induced a frequent solicitation on his part that the publication of the book should be abandoned.[67]

But did this mysterious Chevalier de B--- and his friend Dudley really exist? Robert Mathiesen believed he could identify the former as Ernest de Bunsen (1819–1903), son of the more famous historian of religions Christian Carl Josias von Bunsen (1791–1860);[68] but Marc Demarest has contested this identification with strong arguments, and I am inclined to agree with him.[69] For John Cavendish Dudley, we might perhaps have a slightly more promising candidate in the person of Alexander Lindsay, the 25th Earl of Crawford (1812–1889),[70] but the evidence remains circumstantial and speculative.

Regarding the Orphic Circle, it does seem to have existed. However, we should imagine it not as a formal organization, but rather as a loose-knit social network of occult practitioners with different personal agendas, active between the 1820s and 1850s.[71] It seems to have emerged from a kind of mutual aid society for practicing astrologers that referred to itself as The Mercurii and took shape around John Varley senior (1778–1842), Robert Cross Smith (better known by his writer's pseudonym "Raphael," 1795–1832), Richard James Morrison (known as "Zadkiel," 1795–1874), and Thomas Oxley (1807–1837).[72] Eventually its participants began to experiment with clairvoyants and scrying, and as new figures joined the network (notably Frederick Hockley [1808–1880], Edward Bulwer Lytton [1803–1873], Philip Henry Stanhope [1871–1855], and Richard F. Burton [1821–1890][73]), they began to think of themselves as "Rosicrucians." Various anonymous members of the Orphic Circle mentioned in *Ghost Land* can be plausibly linked to these historical personalities: hence "Mr. B." would be Burton, "Sir James M---" would be Morrison, "Lord L---" would be Bulwer Lytton, and "Sir Peter S---" would be Stanhope.

The logic by which scholars have been operating is that *if* these identifications are indeed correct, then it should be possible to identify Chevalier Louis de B--- and John Cavendish Dudley as existing beyond the pages of the book as well.[74] However, this logic is questionable. It seems significant that, although *Ghost Land* contains much more precise and detailed information about these central protagonists than about any other member of the network, they still have resisted identification much more successfully than those shadowy companions of which we are told nothing but their initials. Based on the evidence presently at our disposal, it seems most likely that precisely Chevalier de B---, his Master Professor Felix von Marx, and his friend John Cavendish Dudley (with his daughter Blanche, see below) are fictional inventions by Emma Hardinge Britten, but that she placed them in a context of occultist networks and practices that has some basis in historical fact. I therefore agree with Marc Demarest that, in all likelihood, the true author of *Art Magic* is Emma Hardinge Britten herself,[75] and am inclined to believe that she wrote *Ghost Land* as well.[76] If this is so, it is of considerable importance for our concerns in this chapter. Whereas Chevalier Louis de B--- is claimed to have been born in Hindustan and to have spent a large part of his life there, we know for certain that Britten never visited India. If she is indeed the real author of *Art Magic* and *Ghost Land*, then these books are (exactly as one might expect) typical products of the mid-nineteenth century Orientalist imagination, illustrative of an imaginary Hindustan concocted from a limited number of Western literary sources.

The Contents of *Art Magic* and *Ghost Land*

It may be instructive to quote the title of the first volume in full:

> Art Magic; Mundane, Sub-Mundane and Super-Mundane Spiritism. A Treatise in Three Parts and Twenty-Three Sections: Descriptive of Art Magic, Spiritism, the Different Orders of Spirits in the Universe known to be related to, or in Communication with Man; together with Directions for Invoking, Controlling, and Discharging Spirits, and the Uses and Abuses, Dangers and Possibilities of Magical Art.[77]

This title shows that "Spiritism" and "Magic" are seen as inseparable from "occultism" or even synonymous with it.[78] *Art Magic* begins by outlining some basic metaphysical and *naturphilosophical* principles grounded in the primacy of Spirit over Matter. Historically, it is claimed, human consciousness has gone through a long process of evolutionary progress on earth; but on the individual level, each human spirit incarnates in our material world just one single time, after which it progresses further in a possibly infinite series of higher spiritual realities. Reincarnation therefore is rejected in favor of a traditional doctrine of "ascendant metempsychosis."[79]

India is described as the cradle of human civilization, and the oldest religious records are the Vedas. The original religion that first developed among the "Hindoos" was an "astronomical religion" grounded in veneration of the powers of nature, and more specifically of the Sun and the forces of sexual generation as the sources of all life. The same type of religion developed in China, and from Asia it spread toward Egypt and Chaldaea. The belief in intermediary beings is universal in all these forms of ancient religion, and the great hierarchy of such entities ranges from the "sub-mundane" realms of Elemental beings connected to the natural world, the "mundane" realms of discarnate human spirits, and the "super-mundane" realms of planetary angels and an enormous variety of even higher entities. It is only with Judaism and especially Christianity that the universal astronomical religion of solar and sexual worship began to be rejected by the priestly elites, who replaced it with a dogmatic and intolerant faith that demonized large parts of the celestial realms and persecuted spiritualists as pagans, heretics, or witches. Similar inquisitorial attitudes are typical of scientific materialism in our own time, which seeks to ridicule the belief in spirits and is still persecuting its adherents. But the future belongs to Spiritualism: as science will eventually be forced to accept the irrefutable evidence for spiritual manifestations, the ancient philosophy of Occultism will make its comeback as the most logical scientific framework for understanding the interrelation between spirit and matter.

Ghost Land has a shorter subtitle: *Researches into the Mysteries of Occultism. Illustrated in a Series of Autobiographical Sketches.* Significantly, it is presented as published "By the Editor." This detail is most plausibly an attempt at correcting a previous slip of attention: *Art Magic* had been presented as published "by the Author," which, according to Britten's official story, was not her but Chevalier Louis de B---. Be that as it may, in the Preface to *Ghost Land*, its author insists on the "strict veracity"[80] of his account and admits to a "special dislike to tales of fiction."[81] The book consists of two parts, one situated in Europe and the other in India.

In Part One we read how, at the age of twelve, Louis meets a professor of Oriental Languages at the University of Berlin, a certain Felix von Marx, who introduces him into a secret society of Mesmerist practitioners. Under von Marx's tutelage, Louis embarks on an extremely successful career as a clairvoyant medium adept at astral travel. Interestingly, the members of this "Berlin Brotherhood" are described as dogmatic scientific materialists who strictly reject the idea of immortality: Spiritualist manifestations therefore cannot be attributed to the souls of deceased human beings but are caused by non-human Elemental or Planetary beings. The confrontation between this quasi-materialist type of occultism and its Spiritualist alternative runs like a red thread through the narrative of *Ghost Land*.

As Louis develops into a virtuoso clairvoyant, the power of magnetic rapport eventually causes his own personality to be overwhelmed and almost obliterated by that of von Marx, who completes the process of "mental obsession" at the moment of his death, when he magically transfers his own life force to his pupil. Von Marx himself tries to present this as an ultimate sacrifice in which he gives up his life so that Louis may inherit his powers, but in fact it appears to be a perfectly selfish act: convinced as he is that there is no personal immortality, von Marx tries to prolong his own life by "taking over" the life of his pupil.[82] Notwithstanding, Louis is so shattered by his master's death that he withdraws deep into the forest, where he tries to starve himself to death. His spectacular dying visions of the invisible world and the splendor of the spiritual hierarchies are a literary highlight of the novel. Meanwhile, the spirit of von Marx appears in a séance of the Orphic Circle, telling its members to go find Louis and save his life. They manage to bring him back from the brink of death, but he no longer seems to be himself. In yet another spectacular magical séance, the spiritual forces of light succeed with great effort to cure Louis from what turns out to be his occult "obsession" by the spirit of von Marx (who after his death appears to have fallen victim to sinister sub-human Elementals).

The second part of *Ghost Land* is situated in Hindustan. Having returned to his normal state, Louis had moved to India, where for twenty years he enjoyed a successful political and military career. It is in this part of the novel that we encounter the Orientalist imagination in full swing. Louis joins a mysterious occult Brotherhood that meets at Ellora, "in the gloomy subterranean crypts of a vast range of ancient ruins, where the spirit of a grand, antique faith pervaded every stone and hallowed the scenes which were once consecrated to the loftiest and most exalted inspiration."[83] Wandering "beneath the shadows of the grim idols, the darksome caverns, the mighty banyan groves and memory-haunted forests,"[84] he meets an Indian initiate, Chundra ud Deen, who brings him to a large subterranean temple

> sculptured with the emblems of Egyptian and Chaldaic worship, interspersed with sentences emblazoned in gold, in Arabic, Sanskrit, and other Oriental languages. [. . .] The walls [. . .]

were thickly adorned with gigantic images of the Hindoo and Egyptian gods, surmounted by a border of gorgeous bas relievos, some of which represented ancient Chaldaic tablets; others were engraved with planispheres, astrological charts, and scenes in Babylonish, Assyrian, and Chaldaic history.[85]

Surrounded by masked initiates, he is granted an ecstatic vision of the spiritual universe. Like several similar visionary experiences, its phenomenology is so evidently psychedelic that one cannot help wondering about the numerous references to narcotics[86] that are sprinkled through both *Art Magic* and *Ghost Land*:

> These sparkling worlds swam, danced, sported, floated upwards and darted downwards, with all the erratic mobility of zigzag lightning. Could they be really living, sentient beings—glorious organisms not moved upon, but breathing, burning, rejoicing lives, acting in the unimitable procedures of fixed law? [. . .] Could they be all living organisms, and the immensity of the universe be filled, not with billions of manufactured automata, but with legions of living creatures, rushing through the orbits of illimitable space in the joy and glory of life everlasting? Could our own burning sun and its shining family of planetary orbs be all creatures of parts and passions, organs and susceptibilities, with a framework of rocky ribs and mountain bones and sinews; veins and arteries coursed by the fluid-life of oceans and rivers; heaving lungs aerated by the breath of winds and atmospheres; electric life evolved from the galvanic actions of metallic lodes threading their way like a gigantic nervous system through every globe [. . .] and one vast collective soul in the aggregated mass of soul atoms that maintain a parasitical life upon the surface of every planet?[87]

Part Two of *Ghost Land* moves toward its dramatic climax with the arrival in India of John Cavendish Dudley's angelic daughter Blanche and Louis's confrontation with a pair of black magicians, Helene Laval and her brother Paul Perrault. Helene is in love with Louis and her brother with Blanche. Both are using powerful magnetic techniques and dark Voodoo rituals to dominate and control the objects of their obsession, and it is only with great difficulty that Louis (assisted by his Indian brethren from the Ellora Brotherhood) succeeds in diverting their occult attacks. Louis ends up marrying Blanche, a typical example of the Victorian "angel in the house"; and as always in such narratives,[88] the price of love consists of the loss of his magical powers. But the story ends badly. After a period of marital bliss, the pure and innocent Blanche falls victim to yet another occult attack from Helene Laval and her brother. Louis fails to save her this time, and she dies in his arms. The only compensation is that he is now free to return to his study of the occult and continue exploring the mysteries of after-death survival.

This is where the novel ends. However, in 1892, Britten tried to continue it in separate installments published in her journal *The Unseen Universe*.[89] This series was never finished and is of no great interest to our present concerns, as it basically describes how Louis returns to the United States, where he becomes involved in Spiritualism.

India in the Early Theosophical Imagination

Early on in *Art Magic*, we are told about a child medium of twelve years old (later identified as Sonoma[90]), the niece of a "Noble Hindoo" from Malabar. Merely as a result of the medium falling asleep with her head on a tripod, sheets of paper lying on that tripod are filled by invisible hands with writing in ancient Sanskrit.[91] Four volumes of text have already been received in this manner, and they describe how "souls spring up like blossoms . . . in the Paradises of purity and love,"[92] which then descend into the world of matter to embark on a pilgrimage, first on "many earths" before the present one, until they become human beings on this earth. The doctrine of transmigration is based on an incorrect interpretation of this belief, for

> it is a sin against divine truth to believe that the exalted soul that has once reached the dignity and upright stature of manhood should, or could, retrograde into the bodies of creeping things, or crouching animals—Not so, not so![93]

So what we have here is a Hindu child medium transmitting texts in ancient Sanskrit to refute reincarnation and preach a doctrine of spiritual progress on broadly Swedenborgian foundations, quite compatible with the teachings of a Spiritualist theologian such as Andrew Jackson Davis or the French Swedenborgian Alphonse-Louis Cahagnet (a major influence on Britten). This very same passage was quoted by Blavatsky in *Isis Unveiled*[94] and may have its origin in a so far undiscovered story in the popular periodical literature.[95] That we have reason to doubt its credibility would be an obvious understatement.

Britten claimed that Louis de B---'s original manuscripts were full of footnotes that she did not care to reproduce in her published version. However, Marc Demarest has identified many of the tacit references in his annotated edition of *Art Magic* (2011). Most relevant here are the very lengthy descriptions of "Fakeer miracles" in Chapter XI and its supplement section devoted to India.[96] Its purpose is to demonstrate that Fakirs have such perfect control over the *ākāśa* (interpreted as the universal magnetic life force) that they can perform spectacular feats such as ripping open their abdomens with their own hands and curing the wound again. The reader is presented with lengthy and gruesome accounts, many of which are clearly (and even explicitly) based on well-known traveler's descriptions, notably the missionary's M. Régis Évariste Huc's *Souvenirs d'un voyage dans la Tartarie, le Thibet et la Chine* (1850, English translation 1851), and the Princess de Belgiojosa's travel memoirs, *Asie mineure et Syrie* (1858). Emma Hardinge Britten had lived in Paris and must have been able to read some French, but we need not assume that she had seen the originals: in fact, the relevant passages from these and similar sources were quoted at length in articles about Indian miracles in contemporary spiritual magazines, notably (in this case), a contribution to Jason Burn's magazine *Human Nature* (1873)[97] and an article by William Howitt in *The Spiritual Magazine* (July 1868)[98] that was based in turn on a piece by Z. J. Piérart published one month earlier in his French *Revue Spiritualiste*.

We find a similar pattern for the other descriptions of Oriental religion in *Art Magic*: typically, they can be traced without too much trouble to a limited number of contemporary publications. Among the more important ones are Thomas Maurice's three-volume *Indian Antiquities* (1806), Lydia Maria Child's three-volume *Progress of Religious Ideas* (1855), William Howitt's two-volume *History of the Supernatural* (1863), Joseph Ennemoser's *History of Magic* (1844; English translation by William Howitt 1854), Hargrave Jennings's *Indian Religions* (1858) and *The Rosicrucians* (1870), and Samuel Johnson's *Oriental Religions and Their Relation to Universal Religion* (1872). All of this provides further confirmation for Joscelyn Godwin's thesis that the new occultism of the 1870s was grounded in an anti-Christian Enlightenment mythography that focused on Solar and phallic worship and traced the origins of religion to India. The only point I would add is that an important part of this background goes back to *German* Romantic sources, to which Godwin was giving somewhat less attention. The relation between German Orientalism and Romantic Mesmerism, and the transmission of both to French and English contexts, requires more attention than it has so far received.

Whereas *Art Magic* is presented as a semi-scholarly overview full of quotations from unidentified (but partly identifiable) sources, the backgrounds to *Ghost Land* are much more difficult to determine. However, there is nothing in the book that suggests any firsthand acquaintance with Indian practices or traditions. The mysterious descriptions of the temples and caves of Ellora clearly reflect the Romantic "sublime" as pictured in a famous series of paintings by Thomas Daniell after James Wales, published in 1803,[99] and later publications such as John B. Seely's *The Wonders of Elora* (1824). And, of course, that these Indian temples are supposed to be full of "Egyptian," "Chaldaic," "Assyrian," "Babylonian," and "Arabic" script and symbolism (see the quotation above) really says it all. These temples never existed in India: their true location was in the occultist imagination.

Conclusion

We have seen that the Theosophical Society emerged as an organization devoted to occult practices that were generally seen as "kabbalistic." This occultist kabbalah was not considered to be a Jewish tradition but, rather, a universal religious philosophy that was believed to have existed since ancient times and had ultimately come from "the East." This historical vision was based on a standard "ancient wisdom narrative" that had been popular among Western intellectuals and the wider public since the fifteenth century and was adopted in its broadest outlines by nineteenth century Orientalist scholarship. Early Theosophists hardly cared to differentiate between Indian, Egyptian, Persian, Zoroastrian, and Chaldaean origins: what mattered to them was the universality and superiority of this ancient "oriental kabbalah." While India was beginning to be given a slightly privileged status in Emma Hardinge Britten's work, this was still the India of the popular Orientalist imagination, including its roots in a much older Platonic Orientalist tradition. This kabbalistic chapter in the history of Theosophy did not end when Blavatsky and Olcott boarded a steamship for India on December 17, 1878. However, their arrival in Bombay on

February 16, 1879, did open a new chapter in a different book: that of a mutual fertilization of Indian religions and Western esotericism that would finally transform both almost beyond recognition.

Notes

1. Michael Gomes, *The Dawning of the Theosophical Movement* (Madras: The Theosophical Publishing House, 1987); John Patrick Deveney, "Astral Projection or Liberation of the Double and the Work of the Early Theosophical Society," *Theosophical History Occasional Papers* 6 (1997); James Santucci, "Foreword," *Theosophical History Occasional Papers* 6 (1997): i–iii; Robert Mathiesen, "The Unseen Worlds of Emma Hardinge Britten: Some Chapters in the History of Western Occultism," *Theosophical History Occasional Papers* 9 (2001): 32–33; Marc Demarest, "A School for Sorcery: New Light on the First Theosophical Society," *Theosophical History* 15, no. 1 (2011); John Patrick Deveney, "The Two Theosophical Societies: Prolonged Life, Conditional Immortality and the Individualized Immortal Monad," in *Theosophical Appropriations: Esotericism, Kabbalah, and the Transformation of Traditions*, ed. Julie Chajes and Boaz Huss (Beer Sheva: Ben-Gurion University of the Negev Press, 2016). An important new volume appeared when the present chapter was already in press: *Imagining the East: The Early Theosophical Society*, ed. Tim Rudbøg and Erik Reenberg Sand (Oxford: Oxford University Press, 2020).

2. On the problematics of distinguishing between "Western" and "Eastern" in this context, see Wouter J. Hanegraaff, "The Globalization of Esotericism," *Correspondences* 3 (2015). I understand "Western" from a perspective of cultural history rather than in a strictly geographical sense, recognizing that important parts of this history have unfolded in areas that are nowadays seen as belonging to the Middle East and Northern Africa. As a manifestation of "Western esotericism" in this sense, modern Theosophy traveled to India after 1878, where its system of beliefs began to change under the influence of Hinduism and Buddhism. It is impossible to establish criteria for determining at what point this process caused Theosophy to be no longer "Western" but "Eastern" (not to mention "Universal") without reverting to essentialist notions of "East" and "West" or religionist notions of a generic supra-historical "esotericism." Opinions in favor or against the adjective "Western" are therefore just that: opinions, or preferences, based upon specific scholarly commitments or agendas. My own preference is to maintain the adjective "Western" as referring to the *cultural provenance* (rather than the geographical location) of specific worldviews or traditions.

3. On the fashionable notion of "entangled genealogies" (*verflochtene Genealogien*) in postcolonial discourse, see e.g. Shalini Randeria and Regina Römhild, "Das postkoloniale Europa: Verflochtene Genealogien der Gegenwart—

Einleitung zur erweiterten Neuauflage (2013)," in *Jenseits des Eurozentrismus*, ed. Sebastian Conrad, Shalini Randeria, and Regina Römhild (Frankfurt: Campus, 2013); Sebastian Conrad and Shalini Randeria, "Einleitung: Geteilte Geschichten—Europa in einer postkolonialen Welt," in *Jenseits des Eurozentrismus*, ed. Sebstian Conrad, Shalini Randeria, and Regina Römhild (Frankfurt: Campus, 2013). In my opinion, there is no such thing as *non*-entangled history, and hence the adjective is strictly superfluous; in other words, the recipe for overcoming Eurocentric perspectives does not consist of some new historical method but of radical and consistent historicization. Nevertheless, the language of entangling/disentangling remains useful for describing the intellectual historian's attempt at unraveling the complex tapestry of ideas by tracing its various threads backward in time. Needless to add, each thread is in turn the product of prior processes of entanglement, and so on ad infinitum.

4. For a useful historical overview of this shift, see Nicholas Goodrick-Clarke, "Theosophical Society, Orientalism, and the 'Mystic East': Western Esotericism and Eastern Religion in Theosophy," *Theosophical History* 13, no. 3 (2007).

5. On the problematics of "authenticity" in analyzing the relation between Theosophy and Indian religions, see e.g. Peter van der Veer, *Imperial Encounters: Religion and Modernity in India and Britain* (Princeton: Princeton University Press, 2001), 55–82, esp. 56–57.

6. Stephen Prothero, *The White Buddhist: The Asian Odyssey of Henry Steel Olcott* (Bloomington: Indiana University Press, 1996), 177–78. Cf. van der Veer, *Imperial Encounters*, 75.

7. Kennet Granholm, "Locating the West: Problematizing the Western in Western Esotericism and Occultism," in *Occultism in a Global Perspective*, ed. Henrik Bogdan and Gordan Djurdjevic (Durham: Acumen, 2013), 23.

8. For these deeper historical roots, see the discussion of "Platonic Orientalism" in Wouter J. Hanegraaff, *Esotericism and the Academy: Rejected Knowledge in Western Culture* (Cambridge: Cambridge University Press, 2012), esp. chapter 1; and cf. John Walbridge, *The Wisdom of the Mystic East: Suhrawardi and Platonic Orientalism* (Albany: State University of New York Press, 2001). Essentially, the notion of Platonic Orientalism stands for the extremely widespread idea, rooted in Hellenistic antiquity and promoted by many of the early Church fathers, that Platonism was a spiritual wisdom tradition ultimately derived from Oriental (Egyptian, Persian, Hebrew, even Indian) origins rather than just a rational philosophy founded by Plato in Greece. Edward Said's notion of Orientalism should be seen in this much larger historical perspective.

9. On this notion of the "mystical east" see e.g. Richard King, *Orientalism and Religion: Postcolonial Theory, India and 'The Mystic East'* (London: Routledge, 1999), esp. chapters 6 and 7.

10. See for instance Blavatsky's letter to Mme C. R. Corson a few months after the ill-fated "unification" of the Theosophical Society with the Arya Samaj:

"we go dead against *idolatry* in every shape and colour, whether in the heathen or Christian religions" (Eugene Rollin Corson, ed., *Some Unpublished Letters of Helena Petrovna Blavatsky, with an Introduction and Commentary* [London: Rider & Co, 1929], 197). In this regard, the Arya Samaj (founded by Dayananda Saraswati in 1875) simply continued the perspective of the older movement of the Brahmo Samaj, founded by Rammohun Roy in 1828 (on these movements and their relevance to Theosophy, see e.g. Joscelyn Godwin, *The Theosophical Enlightenment* [Albany: State University of New York Press, 1994], 307–31; van der Veer, *Imperial Encounters*, 55–82).

11. On the three "grammars" basic to the formation of identity/alterity ("orientalization," "segmentation," "encompassment"), see Gerd Baumann, "Grammars of Identity/Alterity: A Structural Approach," in *Grammars of Identity/Alterity: A Structural Approach*, ed. Gerd Baumann and Andre Gingrich (New York: Berghahn, 2004).

12. Prothero, *White Buddhist*, 131.

13. Wouter J. Hanegraaff, *New Age Religion and Western Culture: Esotericism in the Mirror of Secular Thought* (Leiden: Brill, 1996), 455.

14. Wouter J. Hanegraaff, *Western Esotericism: A Guide for the Perplexed* (London: Bloomsbury, 2013), 15.

15. E.g., Granholm, "Locating the West," 30; Michael Bergunder, "Experiments with Theosophical Truth: Gandhi, Esotericism, and Global Religious History," *Journal of the American Academy of Religion* 82, no. 2 (2014): 403.

16. Hanegraaff, "Globalization of Esotericism." I would still disagree with Bergunder's claim that the notion of Western esotericism "leaves no room for a global history understanding of esotericism" (Bergunder, "Experiments," 403, 420). On the contrary, I see Bergunder's own work as an excellent illustration of the approach I advocate: after all, he shows convincingly how Gandhi read "Hinduism" originally through the Western esoteric or occultist prism of Blavatsky's *Key to Theosophy*, which led him to construct a supposedly "authentic" Indian spirituality that would eventually be promoted worldwide. Of course, Blavatsky's *Key* was already the outcome of an earlier process of "entanglement" (see note 3, above) between the original Western occultist framework prior to 1878 and new influences derived from Blavatsky's Indian experience. In my opinion, we are dealing here with a typical case of "encompassment" (see note 11), where Indian materials are appropriated and incorporated in an already existing framework of assumptions that are themselves typical of nineteenth-century Western (European/American) culture.

17. Hanegraaff, *New Age Religion*, 455.

18. Important steps into that direction have been taken by Karl Baier: see especially Karl Baier, *Meditation und Moderne: Zur Genese eines Kernbereichs moderner Spiritualität in der Wechselwirkung zwischen Westeuropa, Nordamerika und Asien*, vol. 1 (Würzburg: Königshausen & Neumann, 2009), 315–76; and idem,

"Theosophical Orientalism and the Structures of Intercultural Transfer: Annotations on the Appropriation of the Cakras in Early Theosophy," in *Theosophical Appropriations: Esotericism, Kabbalah, and the Transformation of Traditions*, ed. Julie Chajes and Boaz Huss (Beer Sheva: Ben-Gurion University of the Negev Press, 2016).

19. Seventeen according to an early report: Anonymous, "A Theosophical Society," *The Spiritual Scientist* 3, no. 2 (September 16, 1875); but see also Anonymous [= Rev. J. H. Wiggin], "The Cabala," *The Liberal Christian* 30, no. 87 (September 25, 1875): 1 (I am grateful to John Patrick Deveney for his scan from this extremely rare journal); the article was reprinted in Michael Gomes, "Rev. Wiggin's Review of George Henry Felt's 1875 Lecture on the Cabala," *The Canadian Theosophist* 71, no. 3 (1990). Most participants are identified in Gomes, *Dawning*, 85; and for longer personal descriptions, see Josephine Ransom, *A Short History of the Theosophical Society, 1875–1937* (Adyar: Theosophical Publishing House, 1938), 110–15. If one attempts to establish the exact number, one runs into some problems, for instance with the need to add the wife of "Signor Bruzzesi" (see Henry Steel Olcott, *Old Diary Leaves: The True Story of the Theosophical Society, 1875–78* (Cambridge University Press, 2011 [1895]), 115).

20. Anonymous, "Latter-Day Magic," *The Daily Inter Ocean*, November 13, 1875. This article was discovered by Marc Demarest and reprinted in Demarest, "School for Sorcery," 15–19. The version in *The Daily Inter Ocean* seems to be a reprint of an earlier article published in the New York *Mercury* or its sister publication, the *Sunday Mercury*, but efforts to find that original have so far been unsuccessful (ibid., 19).

21. Gomes, *Dawning*, 36–61.

22. Helena P. Blavatsky, "A Few Questions to 'HIRAF,' Author of the Article 'Rosicrucianism,'" *Spiritual Scientist* 2, no. 19 (July 15, 1875) and no. 20 (July 22, 1875). Blavatsky was responding to an article written, apparently as a hoax, by her lawyer William M. Ivins and his friends F. W. Hinrichs, J. C. Robinson, C. F. Adams and W. E. S. Fales under the acronym "HIRAF": see HIRAF, "Rosicrucianism," *Spiritual Scientist* 2, no. 17 (July 1, 1875) and no. 18 (July 8, 1875). See also the editorial introduction anonymously written by Olcott: "Rosicrucianism," *Spiritual Scientist* 2, no. 17 (July 1, 1875). For background to this exchange and discussion, see Gomes, *Dawning*, 76–77; Boris de Zirkoff, "The 'Hiraf' Club and its Historical Background," in *Collected Writings* by Helena Petrovna Blavatsky (Adyar: The Theosophical Publishing House/The Theosophical Press, 1966); Marco Pasi, "Oriental Kabbalah and the Parting of East and West in the Early Theosophical Society," in *Kabbalah and Modernity: Interpretations, Transformations, Adaptations*, ed. Boaz Huss, Marco Pasi, and Kocku von Stuckrad (Leiden: Brill, 2010), 158–60.

23. Corson, *Some Unpublished Letters*, 127–29; see also Daniel H. Caldwell, *The Esoteric World of Madame Blavatsky: Insights into the Life of a Modern Sphinx* (Wheaton, IL: Quest Books, 2000), 63–66. Hiram Corson (1828–1911) was a professor at Cornell University and is still remembered as a significant scholar of

English literature today. He had become a convinced Spiritualist after the death of his daughter in 1874.

24. Helena P. Blavatsky, "The Philadelphia 'Fiasco,' or Who Is Who?," *Banner of Light* 36, no. 18 (January 30, 1875).

25. Letter by Blavatsky, as quoted in Anonymous, "Mme Blavatsky: Her Experience, Her Opinion of American Spiritualism and American Society," *Spiritual Scientist* 1, no. 13 (December 3, 1874): 149. See also Blavatsky, "Philadelphia 'Fiasco,'" 2 ("our belief," "our cause," "my rights [. . .] as a widely known Spiritualist" etc.).

26. Blavatsky, "Philadelphia 'Fiasco,'" 2.

27. H. P. Blavatsky, undated Letter to Hiram Corson (postmarked February 16, 1875), in Corson, *Some Unpublished Letters*, 128–29.

28. Blavatsky, "A Few Questions to 'HIRAF,'" 104, 107.

29. On Franck's and Lévi's understandings of "kabbalah," see Wouter J. Hanegraaff, "The Beginnings of Occultist Kabbalah: Adolphe Franck and Éliphas Lévi," in *Kabbalah and Modernity: Interpretations, Transformations, Adaptations*, ed. Boaz Huss, Marco Pasi, and Kocku von Stuckrad (Leiden: Brill, 2010). A deeper and more complex analysis of Lévi's "kabbalah" is now available in Julian Strube, *Sozialismus, Katholizismus und Okkultismus im Frankreich des 19. Jahrhunderts: Die Genealogie der Schriften von Eliphas Lévi* (Berlin: De Gruyter, 2016).

30. See, notably, Suzanne L. Marchand, *German Orientalism in the Age of Empire: Religion, Race, and Scholarship* (Cambridge University Press, 2009), xxiv, xxvii–xxix, 1–6. While Marchand still broadly relies on Frances Yates's grand narrative of "the Hermetic Tradition," her argument strongly confirms my more recent repositioning of Renaissance Hermeticism within the wider context of "Platonic Orientalism" (see note 8). Most relevant to our present concerns is not the "Hermetic" interpretation of Platonic Orientalism, but a common nineteenth-century conflation of the competing "Mosaic" interpretation (better known as "Christian kabbalah") and the "Zoroastrian" interpretation highlighted since Gemistos Plethon and Marsilio Ficino (see Michael Stausberg, *Faszination Zarathushtra: Zoroaster und die Europäische Religionsgeschichte der Frühen Neuzeit*, 2 vols. [Berlin: De Gruyter, 1998]).

31. It is significant that even as late as 1977, Scholem still found it necessary to juxtapose his perspective against common notions of a "universal kabbalah" in his large Eranos lecture about Alchemy and Kabbalah: Gershom Scholem, "Alchemie und Kabbala," in *Judaica* 4, ed. Rolf Tiedemann (Frankfurt a.M.: Suhrkamp, 1984 [1977]), 19–20 (see English translation and discussion in Hanegraaff, "Beginnings," 107–10).

32. Anonymous [= Rev. J. H. Wiggin], "Rosicrucianism in New York" [thanks again to John Patrick Deveney for his scan of this article from a journal that is impossible to find through regular channels]. The passage is quoted in Olcott, *Old Diary Leaves 1875–78*, 115.

33. For all known details about Felt and what happened to his book project, see the meticulous but still unpublished research by Marc Demarest and the "Felt Working Group," available online as a progress report (dated November 3, 2011) on www.ehbritten.org; Marc Demarest, "The Fate of George Henry Felt's The Kabbalah of the Egyptians" (unpublished paper presented at the biannual Conferences of the Association for the Study of Esotericism, 2012); John Patrick Deveney, *Paschal Beverly Randolph: A Nineteenth-Century Black American Spiritualist, Rosicrucian, and Sex Magician* (Albany: State University of New York Press 1997); idem, "Astral Projection," 58–60.

34. Ransom, *Short History*, 114.

35. Seth Pancoast, *The Kabbala: or the True Science of Light; an Introduction to the Philosophy and Theosophy of the Ancient Sages, Together with a Chapter on Light in the Vegetable Kingdom* (Philadelphia: J.M. Stoddard, 1877).

36. Anonymous [Wiggin], "The Cabala," 1.

37. Ibid., 1/4. Felt also suggested that, through his kabbalistic researches, he had been able to perfect the military signal rockets for which he had gained a patent (on Felt as an inventor, see James Santucci, "George Henry Felt: The Life Unknown," *Theosophical History* 6, no. 7 [1997]).

38. Olcott, *Old Diary Leaves 1875–78*, 117.

39. Ibid., 118 (cf. D. D. Home, *Lights and Shadows of Spiritualism*, 2nd ed. (London: Virtue & Co, 1878), 248: "The tree which Mr. Felt planted and African magicians are to water"). Olcott claimed that it was he who came up with the original idea for a Society, and was appointed as chairman to organize the initial meetings, but note the conflicting claim by Henry J. Newton twenty years later: "At the close of his [Felt's] lecture I moved a committee be appointed to organize and investigate the phenomena which he alleged he was able to accomplish. This committee was appointed. I was made chairman and called a meeting at my house where we continued to meet weekly until a society was formed and named 'The Theosophical Society of New York'" (Henry J. Newton, "Denied by Mr. Newton: He Characterizes Some of the Statements Made by George H. Felt as False," *The New York Herald*, December 15, 1895, 9).

40. Newton, "Denied," 9.

41. Hiram Corson, "The Theosophical Society and Its President's Inaugural Address," *Banner of Light* 38, no. 15 (January 8, 1876): 2; cf. Home, *Lights and Shadows*, 245–46. Blavatsky too seems to have been impressed: "And Mr. Felt *has done it* in the presence of nine persons in all" (handwritten comment to Corson, ibid.: see Deveney, *Paschal Beverly Randolph*, 294).

42. Olcott, *Old Diary Leaves 1875–78*, 138 (and cf. 126).

43. Felt, draft of a letter to the editor of *The Spiritualist* (London), signed June 19, 1878, as reprinted in Olcott, *Old Diary Leaves 1875–78*, 131. The description seems compatible with Olcott's account of Felt's September 18 lecture (ibid., 126); but if it refers to the lecture on June 21, 1876, the nature of its "success" might help explain why the Theosophical Society decided to turn toward

another and less practical direction (cf. Deveney, *Paschal Beverley Randolph*, 290, 293).

44. Anonymous, "Theosophy's Origin Exposed: The Herald Tells the Secrets of Its Birth in This City and the Jugglers Behind It [etc.]," *The New York Herald*, November 10, 1895. In his response, Felt states that Newton had omitted "one very important factor of the recipe—viz. rum, either Santa Cruz or New England" (Georg Henry Felt, "Mr. Felt's Disclaimer: He Takes Issue with Henry J. Newton's Statements About Theosophy," *The New York Herald*, December 1, 1895). While this may well have been an attempt at irony, as suggested by Deveney, it is noteworthy that an article in the Spiritualist *Banner of Light* of 1859 claimed that "In some yet unexplained manner we know that tobacco, rum, opium, hashish and other substances of like nature, produce an effect upon the spirit of man that opens the perceptions to the spirit world" (A. B. Child, "Hashish," *Banner of Light* 4, no. 17 [January 22, 1859]: 3). See also Newton, "Denied," 9.

45. Cf. Buddha, "Exotic Spirituality," *Spiritual Scientist* 4, no. 18 (July 6, 1876) (with long quotations from Jung Stilling and Eckartshausen). Buddha, of California, "What Is Occultism?" *Spiritual Scientist* 4, no. 10 (May 11, 1876). "Buddha" is a pseudonym of Dr. Augustus W. Baylis, an Englishman who had lived in Palermo and Ceylon (where he started the Kandy *Herald*) and finally settled in California. He began to contribute to the *Spiritual Scientist* in September 1875 and explicitly disavowed being a Rosicrucian, Brother of Luxor, or member of any other secret occult society, Eastern or Western (See Buddha, "Occult Philosophy," *Spiritual Scientist* 3, no. 1 [September 9, 1875]: 8). Under the additional pseudonym of "Don Fulano," he also contributed a long series to the *Spiritual Scientist* all through 1876 on various aspects of Buddhism, such as reincarnation (which he abhorred) and morality. Under his own name and as "Don Fulano" and "Medicus," he made regular contributions to the San Francisco Spiritualist journal *Common Sense* as well. Blavatsky called him "a marvellously gifted man" (Helena P. Blavatsky, "The Power to Heal," *The Theosophist* 4, no. 7 [April 1883]) (Deveney, personal communication, April 13, 2016).

46. Anonymous, *Ghost Land; or Researches into the Mysteries of Occultism. Illustrated in a Series of Autobiographical Sketches, in Two Parts* (Boston: Published for the Editor, 1876), 93–105, 247–61, 285–89.

47. Anonymous [= Edward Bulwer Lytton], *Zanoni*, vol. II (London: Saunders & Otley, 1842), 10–11. Such entheogenic occultism has clear and explicit precedents, especially in the writings of Alphonse-Louis Cahagnet (Wouter J. Hanegraaff, "The First Psychonaut? Louis-Alphonse Cahagnet's Experiments with Narcotics," *International Journal for the Study of New Religions* 7, no. 2 [2016]).

48. *Zanoni*, vol. II, 18–27.

49. On Blavatsky and kabbalah, cf. Julie Chajes, "Construction through Appropriation: Kabbalah in Blavatsky's Early Works," in *Theosophical Appropriations: Esotericism, Kabbalah, and the Transformation of Traditions*, ed. Julie Chajes and Boaz Huss (Beer Sheva: Ben-Gurion University of the Negev Press, 2016).

50. Vsevolod Sergyeevich Solovyoff, *Modern Priestess of Isis* (London: Longman, Green & Co, 1895), 256–57; cf. Joscelyn Godwin, "The Hidden Hand, Part III: The Parting of East and West," *Theosophical History* 3, no. 4 (1990): 108.

51. John Patrick Deveney, "An 1876 Lecture by W.Q. Judge on His Magical Progress in the Theosophical Society," *Theosophical History* 9, no. 3 (2003): 13, referring to William Q. Judge, "Giebt es eine Magie und Zauberer?," *Psychische Studien* 4, no. 4 (1877): 194 ("Ich verband mich mit der Gesellschaft zu dem Zwecke, dasselbe zu erforschen, was Mr. *Felt* erforscht hatte").

52. See the fundamental study by Deveney, "Astral Projection."

53. Mathiesen, "Unseen Worlds," 32; cf. Emma Hardinge Britten, "The Theosophical Society: Its Origin and Founders." *The Two Worlds* 4, no. 187 (1891): 359. See also Robert Mathiesen, "Britten, Emma (Floyd) Hardinge," in *Dictionary of Gnosis and Western Esotericism*, ed. Wouter J. Hanegraaff et al. (Leiden: Brill, 2005).

54. For their importance as foundational texts of the new occultist movement, see Godwin, *Theosophical Enlightenment*, 302–6. The two other key texts were Lady Caithness's *Old Truths in a New Light* (likewise 1876) and, of course, Blavatsky's *Isis Unveiled* (1877).

55. Solovyoff, *Modern Priestess of Isis*, 257.

56. Mathiesen, "Unseen World," 33.

57. Ibid., 1. However, see now Marc Demarest's invaluable blog *Chasing Down Emma* (ehbritten.blogspot.com), devoted to "resolving the Contradictions of, and filling in the Gaps in the Life, Work and World of Emma Hardinge Britten."

58. Source references for these claims in Mathiesen, "Unseen Worlds," 3 note 17.

59. Marc Demarest, "Revising Mathiesen: Updating Richard Mathiesen's Work on Emma Hardinge Britten" (revision 3, 2009, unpublished manuscript available at www.ehbritten.org) responding to Mathiesen, "Unseen Worlds," 4–10.

60. On the centrality of this worldview to the occultist movement, see the classic study by Godwin, *Theosophical Enlightenment*, esp. 200–3.

61. Emma Hardinge, *Six Lectures on Theology and Nature, together with the Outline of a Plan for a Humane Enterprise and an Autobiographical Introduction* (Chicago: for the author, 1860). Note that "the superb dynasties of India and Egypt" are always mentioned together here, and are described not as the origin but the inheritors of "the astronomical systems of the ancients" (ibid., 24–25, 105, 114, 123, 126–27).

62. For a chronological bibliography, see Appendix B in Mathiesen, "Unseen Worlds," 75–77.

63. Austria, "'Ghost Land;' or, Researches into the Mysteries of Spiritual Existence," *The Western Star* 1, nos. 1–5 (July–November 1872); Asmodeus,

"Amongst the Spirits; or, Glimpses of Spiritual Men, Women, and Things," *The Western Star* 1, nos. 2-6 (August-December 1872).

64. On the publishing history, see Marc Demarest, "Introduction to the Annotated Edition," in *Art Magic* by Emma Hardinge Britten, ed. and annot. Marc Demarest (Forest Grove, OR: Typhon Press, 2011), iii-lvi, esp. v-xv.

65. Anonymous, *Art Magic; Mundane, Sub-Mundane and Super-Mundane Spiritism. A Treatise in Three Parts and Twenty-Three Sections: Descriptive of Art Magic, Spiritism, the Different Orders of Spirits in the Universe Known to Be Related to, or in Communication with Man; Together with Directions for Invoking, Controlling, and Discharging Spirits, and the Uses and Abuses, Dangers and Possibilities of Magical Art* (New York: Published by the Author, 1876), 8 (Dem 5). All page references will be to both the first edition of 1876 and Marc Demarest's new annotated edition (who, because he considers the authorship question as settled, presents *Art Magic* as a book by Emma Hardinge Britten).

66. Ibid.

67. Ibid., 8-9 (Dem 5). On these hostilities, cf. Britten, "Theosophical Society," 346.

68. Mathiesen, "Unseen Worlds," 25-31.

69. Demarest, "Revising Mathiesen"; and idem, "Introduction," xl-xlii. Like Demarest, I am not impressed by the alleged similarity (Mathiesen, "Unseen Worlds," 28-29) between *Art Magic* and de Bunsen's published works.

70. Mathiesen, "Unseen Worlds," 31-32.

71. Marc Demarest, "Hypotheses on the Orphic Circle" (revision 5, June 2011, www.ehbritten.org); and see also Demarest's two fascinating "Orphic Circle Social Network Diagrams" at www.ehbritten.org. Cf. Godwin, *Theosophical Enlightenment*, 205-12; Mathiesen, "Unseen Worlds," 22-25.

72. On these personalities, see Godwin, *Theosophical Enlightenment*, 136-40 (Varley), 143-47 (Smith), 175-78 (Morrison); Ellic Howe, *Astrology: A Recent History Including the Untold Story of Its Role in World War II* (New York: Walker and Company, 1967), 28-32 (Smith), 33-47 *passim*, 49-50 (Oxley).

73. On Hockley, see John Hamill, *The Rosicrucian Seer: The Magical Writings of Frederick Hockley* (Wellingborough: The Aquarian Press, 1986); Godwin, *Theosophical Enlightenment*, 170-75; Samuel Scarborough, "Frederick Hockley: A Hidden Force behind the 19th Century English Occult Revival," *Journal of the Western Mystery Tradition* 14, no. 2 (2008). On Bulwer Lytton, see e.g. Godwin, *Theosophical Enlightenment*, 123-30, 192-96; on Stanhope, see Godwin, ibid., 162-67, 181-85; on Burton, see Godwin, "Burton, Sir Richard Francis," in *Dictionary of Gnosis and Western Esotericism*, ed. Wouter J. Hanegraaff et al. (Leiden: Brill, 2005).

74. Interestingly, I do not know of any attempts to identify Louis's master Professor Felix von Marx (on whom more below).

75. Demarest, "Introduction," xliii–xliv.

76. Demarest seems to leave this question open, while also questioning the purely fictional nature of *Ghost Land* ("Introduction," xlvii).

77. Anonymous, *Art Magic*, cover (Dem 1).

78. Note that while the noun "occultism" appears just twice in *Art Magic* (1876 edition, 287–88), it appears frequently throughout the text of *Ghost Land*, including in the book's very subtitle. The adjective "occult" appears regularly in both volumes.

79. On this crucial distinction, see Hanegraaff, *New Age Religion*, 474–75, 480–81.

80. Anonymous, *Ghost Land*, 5 (all references are to the first edition of 1876).

81. Ibid., 18.

82. On the central importance of such attempts (at preserving one's individuality after death) to the worldview of the First Theosophical Society prior to Blavatsky's and Olcott's acceptance of reincarnation, see Deveney, "Two Theosophical Societies."

83. Ibid., 333.

84. Ibid., 336–37.

85. Ibid., 347–48.

86. On this neglected dimension of occultism, and the probable sources from which Britten derived her interest in narcotics, see Hanegraaff, "First Psychonaut."

87. *Ghost Land*, 352–53.

88. Cf. e.g. Bulwer Lytton's *Zanoni*, where the adept Zanoni sacrifices his immortality and his magical powers to marry his beloved.

89. Anonymous, "Extracts from 'Ghostland,' vol. II. or, Researches into the Realm of Spiritual Existence. By the Author of 'Art Magic.' Translated and Collated by Emma H. Britten," *The Unseen Universe* 1, nos. 1–12 (1892–83). (1893).

90. Anonymous, *Art Magic*, 213 (Dem 222).

91. Ibid., 26–27 (Dem 25–26).

92. Ibid., 27 (Dem 26).

93. Ibid., 28 (Dem 29).

94. Helena P. Blavatsky, *Isis Unveiled: A Master-Key to the Mysteries of Ancient and Modern Science and Theology*, vol. 1: *Science* (New York: J.W. Bouton & London: Bernard Quaritch, 1877).

95. Cf. Britten, *Art Magic* (Demarest ed.), 25 note 134.

96. *Art Magic*, 174–218.

97. Ibid., 200 (Dem 208 with note 507).

98. W. H. [= William Howitt], "Modern Fire and Other Phenomena of the Eastern Nations," *The Spiritual Magazine* 3 (July 1868).

99. Thomas Daniell, *Hindoo Excavations in the Mountain of Ellora Near Aurungabad in the Decan* (London: Thomas and William Daniell, 1803).

References

Anonymous. "Mme Blavatsky: Her Experience, Her Opinion of American Spiritualism and American Society." *Spiritual Scientist* 1, no. 13 (December 3, 1874): 148–49.

———. "A Theosophical Society." *The Spiritual Scientist* 3, no. 2 (September 16, 1875): 21–22 (repr. in Britten, Emma Hardinge. *Nineteenth Century Miracles: Spirits and Their Work in Every Country of the Earth. A Complete Historical Compendium on the Great Movement Known as "Modern Spiritualism."* New York: William Britten, 1884, 296).

———. "Theosophy's Origin Exposed: The Herald Tells the Secrets of Its Birth in This City and the Jugglers Behind It [etc.]." *The New York Herald*, November 10, 1895: 2.

———. "Latter-Day Magic." *The Daily Inter Ocean*, November 13, 1875: 5, vols. 4–5.

———. *Art Magic; Mundane, Sub-Mundane and Super-Mundane Spiritism. A Treatise in Three Parts and Twenty-Three Sections: Descriptive of Art Magic, Spiritism, the Different Orders of Spirits in the Universe Known to Be Related to, or in Communication with Man; Together with Directions for Invoking, Controlling, and Discharging Spirits, and the Uses and Abuses, Dangers and Possibilities of Magical Art*. New York: Published by the Author, 1876.

———. *Ghost Land; or Researches into the Mysteries of Occultism. Illustrated in a Series of Autobiographical Sketches*. In Two Parts. Boston: Published for the Editor, 1876.

———. "Extracts from 'Ghostland,' vol. II. or, Researches into the Realm of Spiritual Existence. By the Author of 'Art Magic.' Translated and Collated by Emma H. Britten." *The Unseen Universe* 1, no. 1: 28–37; 1, no. 2: 66–75; 1, no. 3: 114–23; 1, no. 4: 168–76; 1, no. 5: 226–35; 1, no. 6: 284–91; 1, no. 7: 334–41; 1, no. 8: 390–96; 1, no. 9: 440–47 (1892); 1, no. 10: 507–13; 1, no. 11: 556–62; 1, no. 12: 613–19 (1893).

Anonymous [= Edward Bulwer Lytton]. *Zanoni*, 3 vols. London: Saunders & Otley, 1842.

Anonymous [= H. S. Olcott]. "Rosicrucianism." *Spiritual Scientist* 2, no. 17 (July 1, 1875): 199.

Anonymous [= Rev. J. H. Wiggin]. "Rosicrucianism in New York." *The Liberal Christian* 30, no. 84 (September 4, 1875): 4.

———. "The Cabala." *The Liberal Christian* 30, no. 87 (September 25, 1875): 1–4.

Asmodeus. "Amongst the Spirits; or, Glimpses of Spiritual Men, Women, and Things." *The Western Star* 1, no. 2 (August 1872): 131–42; 1, no. 3 (September 1872): 225–38; 1, no. 4 (October 1872): 299–313; 1, no. 6 (December 1872): 469–85.

Austria. "'Ghost Land'; or, Researches into the Mysteries of Spiritual Existence." *The Western Star* 1, no. 1 (July 1872): 53–66; 1, no. 2 (August 1872): 115–30; 1, no. 3 (September 1872): 207–24; 1, no. 4 (October 1872): 277–88; 1, no. 5 (November 1872): 373–86.

Baier, Karl. *Meditation und Moderne: Zur Genese eines Kernbereichs moderner Spiritualität in der Wechselwirkung zwischen Westeuropa, Nordamerika und Asien*. 2 vols. Würzburg: Königshausen & Neumann, 2009.

———. "Theosophical Orientalism and the Structures of Intercultural Transfer: Annotations on the Appropriation of the Cakras in Early Theosophy." In *Theosophical Appropriations: Esotericism, Kabbalah, and the Transformation of Traditions*, edited by Julie Chajes and Boaz Huss, 309–53. Beer Sheva: Ben-Gurion University of the Negev Press, 2016.

Baumann, Gerd. "Grammars of Identity/Alterity: A Structural Approach." In *Grammars of Identity/Alterity: A Structural Approach*, edited by Gerd Baumann and Andre Gingrich, 18–50. New York: Berghahn, 2004.

Belgiojoso, Cristina Trivulzio di. *Asie mineure et Syrie: Souvenirs de voyages*. Paris: Michel Lévy frères, 1858.

Bergunder, Michael. "Experiments with Theosophical Truth: Gandhi, Esotericism, and Global Religious History." *Journal of the American Academy of Religion* 82, no. 2 (2014): 398–426.

Blavatsky, Helena P. "The Philadelphia 'Fiasco,' or Who Is Who?" *Banner of Light* 36, no. 18 (January 30, 1875): 2–3.

———. "A Few Questions to 'HIRAF,' Author of the Article 'Rosicrucianism.'" *Spiritual Scientist* 2, no. 19 (July 15, 1875): 217–18 and no. 20 (July 22, 1875): 236–37.

———. *Isis Unveiled: A Master-Key to the Mysteries of Ancient and Modern Science and Theology*. Vol. 1: *Science*. New York: J.W. Bouton & London: Bernard Quaritch, 1877.

———. "The Power to Heal." *The Theosophist* 4, no. 7 (April 1883): 158–60.

Boyle, Robert. "Dialogue on the Converse with Angels Aided by the Philosophers' Stone." In *The Aspiring Adept: Robert Boyle and His Alchemical Quest. Including Boyle's "Lost" Dialogue on the Transmutation of Metals*, edited by Lawrence M. Principe, 310–17. Princeton: Princeton University Press, 1998.

Britten, Emma Hardinge. *Art Magic*. Edited and annotated by Marc Demarest. Forest Grove, OR: Typhon Press, 2011.

———. "The Theosophical Society: Its Origin and Founders." *The Two Worlds* 4, no. 186 (1891): 346–48; 4, no. 187 (1891): 359–60; 3, no. 188 (1891): 369–70.

Buddha. "Occult Philosophy." *Spiritual Scientist* 3, no. 1 (September 9, 1875): 8.

———. "What Is Occultism?" *Spiritual Scientist* 4, no. 10 (May 11, 1876): 109–10.

———. "Exotic Spirituality." *Spiritual Scientist* 4, no. 18 (July 6, 1876): 205–6.

Caldwell, Daniel H. *The Esoteric World of Madame Blavatsky: Insights into the Life of a Modern Sphinx*. Wheaton, IL: Quest Books, 2000.

Chajes, Julie. "Construction through Appropriation: Kabbalah in Blavatsky's Early Works." In *Theosophical Appropriations: Esotericism, Kabbalah, and the Transformation of Traditions*, edited by Julie Chajes and Boaz Huss, 33–72. Beer Sheva: Ben-Gurion University of the Negev Press, 2016.

Child, A. B. "Hashish." *Banner of Light* 4, no. 17 (January 22, 1859): 3.

Conrad, Sebastian, and Shalini Randeria. "Einleitung: Geteilte Geschichten—Europa in einer postkolonialen Welt." In *Jenseits des Eurozentrismus*, edited by Sebastian Conrad, Shalini Randeria, and Regina Römhild, 32–70. Frankfurt: Campus, 2013.

Conrad, Sebastian, Shalini Randeria, and Regina Römhild, eds. *Jenseits des Eurozentrismus: Postkoloniale Perspektiven in den Geschichts- und Kulturwissenschaften*. 2nd ed. Frankfurt: Campus, 2013.

Corson, Hiram. "The Theosophical Society and Its President's Inaugural Address." *Banner of Light* 38, no. 15 (January 8, 1876): 2.

Corson, Eugene Rollin, ed. *Some Unpublished Letters of Helena Petrovna Blavatsky, with an Introduction and Commentary*. London: Rider & Co, 1929.

Daniell, Thomas. *Hindoo Excavations in the Mountain of Ellora Near Aurungabad in the Decan*. London: Thomas and William Daniell, 1803.

Demarest, Marc. "A School for Sorcery: New Light on the First Theosophical Society." *Theosophical History* 15, no. 1 (2011): 15–32.

———. "The Fate of George Henry Felt's *The Kabbalah of the Egyptians*." Unpublished paper presented at the biannual Conferences of the Association for the Study of Esotericism, 2012.

———. "Revising Mathiesen: Updating Richard Mathiesen's Work on Emma Hardinge Britten." Revision 3, 2009. Unpublished manuscript available at www.ehbritten.org.

———. "Hypotheses on the Orphic Circle." Revision 5, June 2011. www.ehbritten.org.

———. "Introduction to the Annotated Edition." In *Art Magic* by Emma Hardinge Britten, edited and annotated by Marc Demarest, iii–lvi. Forest Grove, OR: Typhon Press, 2011.

Deveney, John Patrick. "Astral Projection or Liberation of the Double and the Work of the Early Theosophical Society." *Theosophical History Occasional Papers* 6 (1997): 1–84.

———. *Paschal Beverly Randolph: A Nineteenth-Century Black American Spiritualist, Rosicrucian, and Sex Magician*. Albany: State University of New York Press 1997.

———. "An 1876 Lecture by W.Q. Judge on his Magical Progress in the Theosophical Society." *Theosophical History* 9, no. 3 (2003): 12–20.

———. "The Two Theosophical Societies: Prolonged Life, Conditional Immortality and the Individualized Immortal Monad." In *Theosophical Appropriations: Esotericism, Kabbalah, and the Transformation of Traditions*, edited by Julie

Chajes and Boaz Huss, 93–114. Beer Sheva: Ben-Gurion University of the Negev Press, 2016.

Felt, Georg Henry. "Mr. Felt's Disclaimer: He Takes Issue with Henry J. Newton's Statements About Theosophy." *The New York Herald*, December 1, 1895: 8.

Godwin, Joscelyn. "The Hidden Hand, Part III: The Parting of East and West." *Theosophical History* 3, no. 4 (1990): 107–17.

———. *The Theosophical Enlightenment*. Albany: State University of New York Press, 1994.

———. "Burton, Sir Richard Francis." In *Dictionary of Gnosis and Western Esotericism*, edited by Wouter J. Hanegraaff et al., 217–18. Leiden, Boston: Brill, 2005.

Gomes, Michael. *The Dawning of the Theosophical Movement*. Madras: The Theosophical Publishing House, 1987.

———. "Rev. Wiggin's Review of George Henry Felt's 1875 Lecture on the Cabala." *The Canadian Theosophist* 71, no. 3 (1990): 64–68.

Goodrick-Clarke, Nicholas. "The Theosophical Society, Orientalism, and the 'Mystic East': Western Esotericism and Eastern Religion in Theosophy." *Theosophical History* 13, no. 3 (2007): 3–28.

Granholm, Kennet. "Locating the West: Problematizing the *Western* in Western Esotericism and Occultism." In *Occultism in a Global Perspective*, edited by Henrik Bogdan and Gordan Djurdjevic, 17–36. Durham: Acumen, 2013.

Hamill, John. *The Rosicrucian Seer: The Magical Writings of Frederick Hockley*. Wellingborough: The Aquarian Press, 1986.

Hanegraaff, Wouter J. *New Age Religion and Western Culture: Esotericism in the Mirror of Secular Thought*. Leiden: Brill, 1996.

———. "The Beginnings of Occultist Kabbalah: Adolphe Franck and Éliphas Lévi." In *Kabbalah and Modernity: Interpretations, Transformations, Adaptations*, edited by Boaz Huss, Marco Pasi, and Kocku von Stuckrad, 107–28. Leiden: Brill, 2010.

———. *Esotericism and the Academy: Rejected Knowledge in Western Culture*. Cambridge: Cambridge University Press, 2012.

———. *Western Esotericism: A Guide for the Perplexed*. London: Bloomsbury, 2013.

———. "The Globalization of Esotericism." *Correspondences* 3 (2015): 55–91.

———. "The First Psychonaut? Louis-Alphonse Cahagnet's Experiments with Narcotics." *International Journal for the Study of New Religions* 7, no. 2 (2016): 105–23.

Hardinge, Emma. *Six Lectures on Theology and Nature, Together with the Outline of a Plan for a Humane Enterprise and an Autobiographical Introduction*. Chicago: for the author, 1860.

HIRAF. "Rosicrucianism." *Spiritual Scientist* 2, no. 17 (July 1, 1875): 202 and no. 18 (July 8, 1875): 212–13.

Home, D. D. *Lights and Shadows of Spiritualism*. 2nd ed. London: Virtue & Co, 1878.

Howe, Ellic. *Astrology: A Recent History Including the Untold Story of Its Role in World War II*. New York: Walker and Company, 1967.

Howitt, William. "Modern Fire and Other Phenomena of the Eastern Nations." *The Spiritual Magazine* (2nd series), July 3, 1868: 289–96.

Huc, Régis Évariste. *Souvenirs d'un voyage dans la Tartarie, le Thibet et la Chine pendant les années 1844, 1845 et 1846*. Paris: Adrien le Clerc & Co., 1850.

Huss, Boaz, Marco Pasi, and Kocku von Stuckrad, eds. *Kabbalah and Modernity: Interpretations, Transformations, Adaptations*. Leiden: Brill, 2010.

Judge, William Q. "Giebt es eine Magie und Zauberer?" *Psychische Studien* 4, no. 4 (1877): 193–201.

King, Richard. *Orientalism and Religion: Postcolonial Theory, India and "The Mystic East."* London: Routledge, 1999.

Marchand, Suzanne L. *German Orientalism in the Age of Empire: Religion, Race, and Scholarship*. Cambridge University Press, 2009.

Mathiesen, Robert. "The Unseen Worlds of Emma Hardinge Britten: Some Chapters in the History of Western Occultism." *Theosophical History Occasional Papers* 9 (2001): 1–88.

———. "Britten, Emma (Floyd) Hardinge." In *Dictionary of Gnosis and Western Esotericism*, edited by Wouter J. Hanegraaff et al., 202–6. Leiden: Brill, 2005.

Newton, Henry J. "Denied by Mr. Newton: He Characterizes Some of the Statements Made by George H. Felt as False." *The New York Herald*, December 15, 1895: 9.

Olcott, Henry Steel. *Old Diary Leaves: The True Story of the Theosophical Society, 1875–78*. Cambridge University Press, 2011 [1895].

Pancoast, Seth. *The Kabbala: or The True Science of Light; an Introduction to the Philosophy and Theosophy of the Ancient Sages, Together with a Chapter on Light in the Vegetable Kingdom*. Philadelphia: J.M. Stoddard, 1877.

Pasi, Marco. "Oriental Kabbalah and the Parting of East and West in the Early Theosophical Society." In *Kabbalah and Modernity: Interpretations, Transformations, Adaptations*, edited by Boaz Huss, Marco Pasi, and Kocku von Stuckrad, 151–66. Leiden: Brill, 2010.

Piérart, Z. J. "Le merveilleux en Orient et en Europe: Faits divers fréquemment constatés." *Revue spiritualiste* 6, no. 6 (June 1863): 161–76.

Prothero, Stephen. *The White Buddhist: The Asian Odyssey of Henry Steel Olcott*. Bloomington: Indiana University Press, 1996.

Randeria, Shalini, and Regina Römhild. "Das postkoloniale Europa: Verflochtene Genealogien der Gegenwart—Einleitung zur erweiterten Neuauflage (2013)." In *Jenseits des Eurozentrismus*, edited by Sebstian Conrad, Shalini Randeria, and Regina Römhild, 9–31. Frankfurt: Campus, 2013.

Ransom, Josephine. *A Short History of the Theosophical Society, 1875–1937*. Adyar: Theosophical Publishing House, 1938.

Rudbøg, Tim, and Erik Reenberg Sand. *Imagining the East: The Early Theosophical Society*. Oxford: Oxford University Press, 2020.
Santucci, James. "Foreword." *Theosophical History Occasional Papers* 6 (1997): i–iii.
———. "George Henry Felt: The Life Unknown." *Theosophical History* 6, no. 7 (1997): 243–61.
Scarborough, Samuel. "Frederick Hockley: A Hidden Force behind the 19th Century English Occult Revival." *Journal of the Western Mystery Tradition* 14, no. 2 (2008). http://www.jwmt.org/v2n14/hockley_article.html.
Scholem, Gershom. "Alchemie und Kabbala." In *Judaica* 4, edited by Rolf Tiedemann, 19–128. Frankfurt a.M.: Suhrkamp, 1984 [1977].
Seely, John B. *The Wonders of Elora; or, the Narrative of a Journey to the Temples and Dwellings Excavated out of a Mountain of Granite, and Extending Upwards of a Mile and a Quarter at Elora, in the East Indies, by the Route of Poona, Ahmed-Nuggur, and Toka, Returning by Dowlutabad and Aurungabad; with Some General Observations on the People and Country*. 2nd ed. London: Geo. B. Whittaker, 1825.
Solovyoff, Vsevolod Sergyeevich. *A Modern Priestess of Isis*. London: Longman, Green & Co, 1895.
Stausberg, Michael. *Faszination Zarathushtra: Zoroaster und die Europäische Religionsgeschichte der Frühen Neuzeit*. 2 vols. Berlin: De Gruyter, 1998.
Strube, Julian. *Sozialismus, Katholizismus und Okkultismus im Frankreich des 19. Jahrhunderts: Die Genealogie der Schriften von Eliphas Lévi*. Berlin: De Gruyter, 2016.
Tilton, Hereward. "Of Ether and Colloidal Gold: The Making of a Philosophers' Stone." *Esoterica* 9 (2007): 49–128.
———. "*Alchymia Archetypica*: Theurgy, Inner Transformation and the Historiography of Alchemy." In *Transmutatio: La via ermetica alla felicità*, edited by Daniela Boccassini and Carlo Testa, 179–215. Alexandria: Edizioni dell'Orso, 2012.
Veer, Peter van der. *Imperial Encounters: Religion and Modernity in India and Britain*. Princeton: Princeton University Press, 2001.
Villars, Henri Montfaucon de. *Le Comte de Gabalis ou entretiens sur les sciences secrètes, avec l'adaptation du* Liber de Nymphis de Paracelse par Blaise de Vigenère *(1583)*, edited by Didier Kahn. Paris: Honoré Champion, 2010.
Walbridge, John. *The Wisdom of the Mystic East: Suhrawardi and Platonic Orientalism*. Albany: State University of New York Press, 2001.
W. H. [= William Howitt]. "Modern Fire and Other Phenomena of the Eastern Nations." *The Spiritual Magazine* 3 (July 1868): 289–96.
Zirkoff, Boris de. "The 'Hiraf' Club and Its Historical Background." In *Collected Writings* by Helena Petrovna Blavatsky, 95–100. Adyar: The Theosophical Publishing House/The Theosophical Press, 1966.

Chapter 2

Hinduism, Theosophy, and the *Bhagavad Gita* within a Global Religious History of the Nineteenth Century

Michael Bergunder

The *Bhagavad Gita* is widely considered the most important and most popular scripture of Hinduism, both within and without India. Nevertheless, there is a widespread consensus within current scholarship that its present popularity owes itself to developments of the nineteenth century.[1] According to this understanding, the *Bhagavad Gita* was remarkably well received in Europe and North America in the first half of the nineteenth century, and then, beginning in the 1880s, in India also. What remains unclear is the connection between its international and Indian reception.

The Austrian Indologist Agehananda Bharati (born Leopold Fischer) was among the first to suspect an interdependent relationship. He employs the metaphor of a "pizza effect":[2] similar to the pizza in Italy, the *Bhagavad Gita* became popular in India only after having won acclaim in Europe and America. Eric Sharpe's foundational study of the *Bhagavad Gita*'s reception shares this argument.[3] Such a narrative fits well into debates on Orientalism, which see today's Hinduism as a product of European imaginations during the time of colonialism. In this sense, the nineteenth-century reception of the *Bhagavad Gita* slots nicely into post-colonial debates,[4] and the theory of the "pizza effect" remains unchallenged. However, current scholarship has failed to demonstrate how the "Western" preoccupation with the *Bhagavad Gita* is meant to have precisely influenced Indian discourse since the 1880s. It is perplexing that recent examinations of the

Bhagavad Gita's reception in the nineteenth century have entirely refrained from tracing the historical connections between its reception in India and within European Orientalism.[5]

In the following, I argue that current scholarship has overestimated the "Western" interest in the *Bhagavad Gita* in the first half of the nineteenth century. The Indian reception of the *Bhagavad Gita*, which began in the 1880s, is no simple consequence of preceding European and American appreciation of the text; rather, it arose as a direct result of nationalist protest against a certain appropriation of Indian tradition by European Orientalism. It was Indian Theosophists who played a decisive role in this process. They were instrumental in the *Bhagavad Gita*'s eventual incorporation into Hindu reform movements, which subsequently caused its current popularity in India.

1. *Bhagavad Gita* in Precolonial India

Any appropriate evaluation of the developments of the nineteenth century necessitates a look at the preceding time period first. In precolonial India, the *Bhagavad Gita* was held in high esteem within the Brahmanical philosophy of Vedanta, where it belonged to the three classic commentaries (Skt. *prasthānatraya*), together with the Upanishads and the Brahma Sutras. Vedanta philosophy was the domain of the Brahmans. Advaita Vedanta, which can be traced back to Shankara (around 800), was fostered by Smarta Brahmans, in Brahmanical Shankara monasteries, and by followers of Dashanami asceticism.[6] Besides Advaita Vedanta, there was the widespread Vaishnavite Vedanta, whose most important tributary, the Vishishtadvaita Vedanta, was and is cultivated by Brahmanical Shrivaishnavas.[7] Additionally, there were smaller Vaishnavite schools, such as the Dvaita Vedanta, all of which were also Brahmanical in orientation.

Other than the highly elite Brahmanical Vedanta, the *Bhagavad Gita* seems to have had little or no significance until the nineteenth century.[8] Occasional references do not challenge this general picture. This is illustrated by the historical impact of a free-verse translation of the *Bhagavad Gita* with an extensive commentary into Marathi, undertaken in the thirteenth century by Nath-Yogi Jnandev.[9] It was the Marathi devotional poet Eknath who in the sixteenth century revitalized and popularized the tradition of Jnandev. He penned a sort of critical edition of Jnandev's *Bhagavad Gita* translation, which has since been received as the standard text.[10] However,

Eknath himself was not particularly interested in the *Bhagavad Gita*. His major work was a commentary in Marathi on the eleventh book of the *Bhagavata Purana*. Though Eknath was influenced by Jnandev's translation of the *Bhagavad Gita*,[11] he nonetheless chose a different text for his own major commentary. This is a clear indication that the *Bhagavad Gita* was of lesser standing within the literary circles in which Eknath was active.

On the other hand, the *Bhagavata Purana* was without a doubt an exceedingly popular text at the time. It also formed the basis for a Krishna bhakti, which began to make great inroads in India from sixteenth century onward.[12] Even to these ardent worshipers of Krishna, the *Bhagavad Gita* played a secondary role. The only notable exception was the Pushtimarg, founded by Vallabha at the end of fifteenth century. It displayed strong Brahmanical characteristics and, because of its Vedantic basis, counted the *Bhagavad Gita* among its central texts from the start.[13] Nevertheless, the *Bhagavata Purana* was the focus even within the Pushtimarg. Conversely, Gaudiya Vaishnavism, which also emerged in the sixteenth century and fostered a particularly intensive brand of Krishna bhakti, initially showed no interest in the *Bhagavad Gita*.[14] This remained the case until the eighteenth century, when Gaudiya Vaishnavism in Rajasthan underwent a massive Brahmanization,[15] over the course of which it came to align itself with the traditions of Vaishnavite Vedanta and refer to the *Bhagavad Gita* as one of the three classic Vedanta commentaries.

Accordingly, it were two scholars of Gaudiya Vaishnavism who first compiled their own commentaries on the *Bhagavad Gita*. The first step was made by Vishvanatha Cakravarti at the start of the eighteenth century.[16] With regard to the contents, however, he followed the *Bhagavata Purana*, in accordance with the interpretive conventions of Gaudiya Vaishnavism.[17] The second commentary to the *Bhagavad Gita* was drawn up by Baladeva Vidyabhushana in the mid-eighteenth century.[18] He sought to tie the *Bhagavad Gita* back to Dvaita Vedanta, and, in this way, tried to present Gaudiya Vaishnavism as part of the Vaishnavite Vedanta. Neither commentary, however, indicated that the majority of the followers of Gaudiya Vaishnavism had ever turned toward the *Bhagavad Gita* or to Vaishnavite Vedanta.

The central role played by the *Bhagavad Gita* in contemporary reform movements of Gaudiya Vaishnavism, such as the International Society for Krishna Consciousness (ISKON), is a recent development and presupposes the popularity of the text since the end of the nineteenth century. Even the first major publication in English by the ISKCON founder A.

C. Bhaktivedanta (1896–1977) was still a commentary on the *Bhagavata Purana*, the first volume of which first appeared in India in 1962. It was not until two years after his emigration to the United States, in 1968, that he published *The Bhagavad Gita, As It Is*.[19]

In short, according to current scholarship, the *Bhagavad Gita* was neither widely read nor particularly popular in precolonial India. At first glance, this would seem to confirm the thesis of Bharati and Sharpe that it was the Orientalist reception in Europe and America that allowed for the popularization of the *Bhagavad Gita* in India.

2. *Bhagavad Gita* and Europe

The 1785 English translation of the *Bhagavad Gita* by Charles Wilkins (1749–1836), who belonged to the circle of early Orientalists in Calcutta,[20] was the first Sanskrit text to be translated into a European language. There is ample reason to believe that the *Bhagavad Gita* was introduced to Wilkins as an expression of Vedanta philosophy by his Brahmanical informants in Banaras, and he himself mentions having partial access to a wide array of Sanskrit commentaries.[21] His statement that the *Bhagavad Gita* contains "all the grand mysteries of [the Brahman's] religion"[22] is reminiscent of Shankara's well-known foreword to his commentary on the *Bhagavad Gita*, in which he describes the *Bhagavad Gita* as the "core essence of the meaning of the Vedas."[23]

Moreover, according to Wilkins, the central message of the *Bhagavad Gita* was to "unite all the prevailing modes of worship in those days," to teach the "unity of the Godhead," and "to bring about the downfall of Polytheism."[24] This characterization not only indicates a Vedantic frame of interpretation, but also suggests that Wilkins wanted to divorce the *Bhagavad Gita* from contemporary European criticism of idol worship and sacrifice in India at the time, because "the most learned Brāhmăns of the present times" were in truth "Unitarians," and the *Bhagavad Gita* the "downfall of polytheism."[25] This stance was shared by the Orientalist Nathaniel Brassey Halhed (1751–1830), with whom Wilkins discussed his translation of the *Bhagavad Gita*.[26] Wilkins paved the way for a European interpretation of the *Bhagavad Gita* that, in the spirit of European deism, understood it as an alternative to traditional Christian doctrines.[27] This understanding was well received, and Wilkins's translation soon became well known in Europe. After only two years, it appeared in French translation, and it is worth noting that it has been reprinted numerous times in the near-century since.

The *Bhagavad Gita* experienced a major reception in the German Romantic philosophy, considerably advanced by its translation into Latin by August Wilhelm Schlegel in 1823.[28] This edition was reviewed extensively in 1826 by Wilhelm von Humboldt, who once spoke in a letter of his "thanks for the fortune [. . .] that allowed me to live to encounter this work."[29] Humboldt stands as an example of the "Romantic consensus," which saw a universal message of "oneness—with God and with nature" in the *Bhagavad Gita*.[30] In a way, this perspective was reinforced by Hegel in his highly critical response to Humboldt's essay. While Hegel's assessment of the *Bhagavad Gita* was the opposite of Humboldt's, it employs the same framework of interpretation. For Hegel, too, the *Bhagavad Gita* was a typical representation of an Indian philosophy of unity based on "yoga," that is to say, "meditation." However, he considered the Indian concept of unity deficient, abstract, and indeterminate ("religion of substance") because it failed to relate back concretely to the particulars of the world by developing the concept of the person and the autonomous subject.[31] This assessment is to be understood not only as a general critique by Hegel of "Eastern" religions, but above all as a critique aimed at Romantic philosophy. The *Bhagavad Gita*, as a supposedly typical example of a mysterious philosophy of unity, was thereby adapted to European debates. At the same time, its classification by Schlegel and Hegel confirmed its status as a Vedanta text.

Nevertheless, the effects of the Romantic enthusiasm for the *Bhagavad Gita* should not be exaggerated, lest one overlook that it did not make any significant headway into early Indology. In 1855, a new English translation by John Cockburn Thomson (1834–1860) appeared, together with an edition of the Sanskrit text and an extensive introduction to Indian philosophy, but no particular value was placed on the importance of the text.[32] Thompson did not adopt the Romantic interpretation. Instead of the "Romantic consensus," wherein the *Bhagavad Gita* teaches a monistic philosophy of unity, Thomson attributed the text to a theistic version of Samkhya and Yoga, neither of which possesses a monistic basis.[33] It is notable that his edition barely resonated in Indology, even though he advanced his own supplementary textual edition.[34]

Renowned Indologist Émile-Louis Burnouf (1821–1907), for his part, released a transliterated Sanskrit text with French translation in prose in 1861. Although in his introduction he writes that the *Bhagavad Gita* contains the "essence" of "Brahmanical philosophy" and offers certain access to the "knowledge of India,"[35] he never gets any more specific. His edition was thought of as an exercise book for students, and he did not assign particular value to the text.[36] In the *Akademische Vorlesungen über indische Literaturgeschichte* (1852,[2] 1876, French 1859, English 1878,[2] 1882,[3] 1892) by Albrecht Weber, the *Bhagavad Gita* was dealt with simply as a part of the *Mahabharata*, just as it would be fifty years later in Arthur Anthony Macdonell's *A History of Sanskrit Literature*.[37]

If the "Romantic consensus" can be said to have experienced any progression, then it might be most clearly visible in the case of Max Müller. While on the one hand his characterization of the *Bhagavad Gita* as not very old and "a rather popular and esoteric exposition of Vedantic doctrines"[38] indicates little particular interest on his part in the text, on the other hand he at least definitively classifies it as a Vedanta work. Furthermore, he allotted an entire volume to the *Bhagavad Gita* in *Sacred Books of the East*, although this volume seems to have been largely ignored by contemporary reviewers.[39] What is also noteworthy is that this was the only volume for which an Indian translator, Kashinath Trimbak Telang (1850–1893) of Bombay, was employed. It would seem that none of the established European Indologists at the time were interested in taking over this task themselves.

The reason that Telang, who was not only a Sanskritologist, but also an influential judge and social reformer, took a special interest in the *Bhagavad Gita* is explained in detail later, as it is of critical importance to the argument put forward in this chapter. For the moment, all that need concern us is that Telang, too, dealt with the *Bhagavad Gita* as a classic text in the style of an *Upanishad*, if one of a different age, and as a commentary on Vedantic philosophy.[40] The impression that emerges from these observations is that the Romantic enthusiasm for the *Bhagavad Gita* did not develop further in nineteenth-century European Indology. However, through Max Müller, the Romantic interpretation of the *Bhagavad Gita* as a Vedantic text was received and further established.

3. *Bhagavad Gita* and the United States

The Romantic interest in the *Bhagavad Gita* in Europe had a rough equivalent in the United States, where Transcendentalists referred to the text. Arthur Christy even judges that "no one Oriental volume [. . .] was more influential" there "than the *Bhagavadgita*."[41] This seems, however, to have been far too generous an assessment. With the benefit of hindsight, and given the present awareness of the significance of the text, one must caution against overstating the relevance of the Transcendentalist reception of the *Bhagavad Gita*. The *Bhagavad Gita* was simply one of many other "Eastern" primary and secondary sources of importance to Transcendentalism.[42]

It was probably Ralph Waldo Emerson (1803–1882) who introduced the *Bhagavad Gita* to Transcendentalism. Many years later, in a letter to Max Müller from 1873, he credited his discovery of it to the study of Victor Cousin's *Cours de Philosophie* (1828, Engl. 1832), which he had read in the early 1830s.[43] In this work, Cousin attempts, in an eclectic manner, to synthesize French Spiritism, in the vein of Maine de Biran, and German Idealism, especially as characterized by Schelling. He dedicated a separate segment to Asian philosophy, in which the *Bhagavad Gita* is mentioned. However, it was not until 1845 that Emerson had the opportunity to read and, shortly thereafter, acquire Wilkins's translation. Regarding this opportunity, he writes in a letter of "the much renowned book of Buddhism [as he saw it, M.B.], extracts of which I have often admired but never before held the book in my hands."[44] Emerson soon recommended and loaned the book to his friends (e.g., John Greenleaf Whittier, Moncure Conway).[45] Nonetheless, it would seem his enthusiasm was not without its bounds, because in response to a query from a publisher he advocated against an American reprint of the inaccessible work.[46] Furthermore, one would be hard pressed to make a case for a deeper textual engagement with the *Bhagavad Gita* by Emerson. Instead, he concentrated on single verses, which he interpreted according to his own understanding. Hence, he copied to his journal verses 4–5 of the *Bhagavad Gita*, in which—according to Wilkins's translation—"the speculative doctrines and practical are one."[47] Emerson, who admired great heroes and great thinkers alike, saw his belief, that the intellectual advance toward the "Over-Soul" and the active developing of individual perfection represent two equally valid methods of human aspiration, confirmed through these two verses.[48]

Another great Transcendentalist, Henry David Thoreau (1817–1862), is known to have also quoted the *Bhagavad Gita*.[49] During his time as a recluse at Lake Walden, he wrote: "In the morning I bathe my intellect in the stupendous and cosmological philosophy of the Bhagvat Geeta [sic]."[50] Yet he only dedicated a single longer passage to the *Bhagavad Gita* in his work *A Week on the Concord and Merrimac Rivers* (written

1840–1844, published 1849). Therein the scripture is simply a stand-in for an East/West dichotomy by which the Christian scriptures stand for "pure morality," and the Hindu for "pure intellectuality."[51] At that point, he considered the latter superior, an assessment that shifted considerably with his turn toward "civil disobedience." The *Bhagavad Gita* served above all as a background foil for the Transcendentalist discourse of self-realization. It was the "atmosphere, rather than the actual content"[52] that caught Thoreau's interest.

Bronson Alcott (1799–1888), a third great Transcendentalist, demonstrated an interest in Asian religions, especially because of Emerson's influence in the 1840s. During this time, he read the *Bhagavad Gita*, discussed it with Emerson, and presented on it at public lectures.[53] But in his published works, along with Asian texts in general, it is mentioned only tangentially. In 1846, Alcott advocated for the *Bhagavad Gita* to be included in a *Bible for Mankind*;[54] however, in his actual manuscript for a spiritual *Mankind Library* some years later there is no explicit mention of it, neither in the extant unpublished drafts[55] nor even in the publication project that Emerson later supported.[56] It follows that not even Alcott could be considered an exceptional admirer of the *Bhagavad Gita*.

Following the American Civil War, a second generation of Transcendentalists formed, tightly enmeshed with Unitarian and liberal religious circles, in which there was renewed interest in non-Christian religions. In the 1870s, this climate resulted in, among other things, three influential works of religious comparison (Clarke, Johnson, Conway).[57] These three works held a highly authoritative status at the time. In 1892, the evangelical missionary theologian Frank F. Ellinwood names them as the most important comparative religious works in North America.[58]

All three texts refer to the *Bhagavad Gita*, though in different ways. James Freeman Clarke (1810–1888) cites it in his explanation of the philosophy of Vedanta,[59] as does Samuel Johnson (1822–1882), who was, incidentally, the only scholar who, in addition to the translation of Wilkins, also drew on the translation by Thomson, and who dedicated an entire chapter to the *Bhagavad Gita*.[60] Both thereby advanced its reception as a religious-philosophical Hindu text without privileging it in any way. In doing so, they found themselves in accord with European Indology, which also acknowledged the *Bhagavad Gita* as being above all a work of Vedanta.

The third work set a slightly different tone. The *Sacred Anthology* by Moncure Conway (1832–1907) offered a thematically organized selection of texts from different religions. With it, Conway was in a way augmenting the aforementioned Transcendentalist project, the *Bible for Mankind*. He was not alone in this ambition: by that time, William Henry Channing (1810–1884) had also suggested something similar.[61] It was clear to Channing that the *Bhagavad Gita* absolutely ought to be included in the *Bible for Mankind*, not least because he counted it among his daily devotional texts, together with Confucius, Laozi, and the *Dhammapada* of the Pali Canon. Accordingly, the *Bhagavad Gita* was also given a place in Conway's work. We know from Conway that he learned of the *Bhagavad Gita* from Emerson, and that it "thenceforth became part of my canon."[62] Thus, in the context of the Transcendentalist conception of a *Bible for Mankind*, the *Bhagavad Gita* emerged as a central text of Hinduism. The cited passages, however, seem to have been chosen arbitrarily, and with regard to Hinduism, the *Bhagavad Gita* is neither the only nor the most cited text in the *Sacred Anthology*.[63] Thus, Conway cannot really be said to have prioritized the *Bhagavad Gita* either.

4. Theosophy and the *Bhagavad Gita*

From the evidence presented thus far, the following picture emerges. The reception of the *Bhagavad Gita* in Europe and the United States in the first half of the nineteenth century was indeed remarkable. However, it was nowhere near as far-reaching nor as clear-cut as has often been claimed. The enthusiasm of the European Romantic movement for the text stagnated. After all, in the latter half of the nineteenth century, European Indology mostly viewed the *Bhagavad Gita* as a commentary of Vedanta, if a subordinate one, as, for instance, Max Müller did. The second generation of Transcendentalists in the United States also reacted rather reservedly to the *Bhagavad Gita*. The project for a *Bible for Mankind* is something of an exception in that the *Bhagavad Gita* appears as a central text of Hinduism, albeit as one among many others. The "pizza effect," as described by Bharati and Sharpe, becomes less plausible for this reason alone. Moreover, a closer historical analysis reveals a different instigator of Indian enthusiasm for the *Bhagavad Gita*.

4.1. Christianity and the *Bhagavad Gita*

Some European Indologists were receptive to theistic Vaishnavism. In the second half of the nineteenth century, there was discussion within these circles of the possibility of Christian influence on the formation of Krishna bhakti.[64] In 1857, Albrecht Weber advanced the theory that the

Krishna cult might have been influenced by Christianity, or rather that it might constitute a misinterpretation of Christianity.[65] This idea was taken up by Franz Lorinser, a Catholic clergyman from Breslau, in the introduction to his 1869 verse translation of the *Bhagavad Gita*, wherein the *Bhagavad Gita* is described as a text influenced by Christianity. The possibility is discussed sympathetically, if tangentially, in a footnote to the second edition of Albrecht Weber's *Akademische Vorlesungen über indische Literaturgeschichte* (1876).[66] Weber himself, to be sure, did not attach particular importance to the *Bhagavad Gita*. The discussion receded quickly in European Indology, as there was widespread consensus that the *Bhagavad Gita* predated Christianity and even Buddhism, and that any parallels therefore could not be conclusive evidence of any dependence.[67] Both Max Müller[68] and especially Richard Garbe[69] had emphatically rejected the possibility early on.

The same cannot be said of the debates in India. When Lorinser's theories became known there at the start of the 1870s, they unleashed a storm of outrage among nationalist-minded Hindu reformers. In 1874, none other than the aforementioned Kashinath Trimbak Telang held a lecture in front of the Students' Literary and Scientific Society to oppose Lorinser's view that the *Bhagavad Gita* derived from the Bible. In 1873, a condensed version of Lorinser's theories had appeared in English in the *Indian Antiquary*, and so had become easily accessible in India.[70] In 1875, Telang published his lecture as a comprehensive introduction to an English-verse translation of the *Bhagavad Gita* (*Divine Lay*, Bombay 1875).[71] One can assume that Telang's interest in the *Bhagavad Gita* won widespread recognition among the English-speaking Indian elite because, as has been mentioned, he soon went on to produce an academic translation of the *Bhagavad Gita* for Max Müller's *Sacred Books of the East*, published in 1882. Telang was the only Indian academic to work on this project along with leading European Indologists and Orientalists. Telang's work demonstrates the way in which various discourses began to fuse together at the time on a global level, and he was no exception. The 49th volume of the *Sacred Books of the East* on Mahayana Buddhism was translated by the Japanese scholar Takakusu Junijirō. In addition to Telang, other Indian Indologists, such as R. G. Bhandarkar and Manilal Dvivedi, were well-known in Europe too. The influence of these Asian researchers on late nineteenth-century European Indology is still in need of closer investigation.

Telang was not only an internationally recognized Sanskritist and Indologist, but he also advocated for political reform, and in 1885 he was among the founding members of the Indian National Congress.[72] Moreover, he was one of the important early reformers of Maharashtra, a group concerned with revitalizing Hinduism. The latter is evident not only in his translation of the *Bhagavad Gita*, but also in his involvement with the Prarthana Samaj.[73] In Telang's case it is, however, completely clear that, regardless of his involvement with the theistic Prarthana Samaj, he interpreted the *Bhagavad Gita* as a Vedanta text, and specifically as part of Advaita Vedanta. Hence, his explanation in the foreword to his translation in *Sacred Books of the East*: "My aim has been to make that translation as close and literal a rendering as possible of the Gîtâ, as interpreted by the commentators Sankarâkârya, Srîdharasvâmin, and Madhusûdana Sarasvatî."[74]

At the time, such an Advaita Vedantic perspective was anything but a given. A contemporaneous translation of the *Bhagavad Gita* by John Davies sharply criticized any and all Vedantic interpretations;[75] instead, he emphasized Samkhya and Yoga in particular as the leading sources of the text. In doing so, Davies was, in a way, following Thomson's precedent. It is significant, then, that Davies' translation, much like that of Thomson, did not receive much attention in India or Europe.

4.2. *Bhagavad Gita* and "Eastern" Wisdom

Telang maintained close contacts to the Theosophical Society. Even if it was without any apparent particular interest in their esoteric doctrine, this was critical to the Society's further development. In the first volume of *The Theosophist* (1879/80), Telang published a three-part article on the life of Shankara, which reiterated his special interest in Advaita Vedanta. In 1884, he took part in the annual meeting of the Theosophical Society in Adyar (Madras), possibly with the goal of leading preparatory discussions about the founding of the Indian National Congress.[76] Telang's publications on the *Bhagavad Gita* therefore were well-known within the Theosophical Society when, in 1882/83, a disagreement with the English Spiritualist and Swedenborgian William Oxley took place inside the pages of *The Theosophist*. Indian Theosophists refuted "Western" interpretations of Indian sources and took over Telang's argumentation.

4.2.1. "Busiris the Ancient"

In 1881, William Oxley, who had close ties to the Theosophical Society and had even temporarily been a member,[77] published a book in which he developed his Spiritualist-Theosophical theories explicitly relating to the *Bhagavad Gita*, even including verses from Wilkins's translation.[78] The Theosophists thought it necessary to respond to this work for several different reasons. For Blavatsky, it was probably a matter of maintaining an interpretive monopoly in matters of Theosophical doctrine. Oxley's claim to have personally encountered Theosophical Mahatmas posed a threat to her control over these contacts. However, Damodar M. Mavalankar (1857–1885?), the young Indian Theosophist charged with writing the review,[79] took issue with entirely different matters. Oxley claimed that a spirit named "Busiris the Ancient" had revealed himself via a medium as the author of the *Mahabharata*. Here Mavalankar commented that "it requires but a moderate dose of [. . .] national pride [. . .] to view the venerable Busiris as a rival [. . .] to a dignity already honourably occupied in India."[80]

Oxley tried to defend himself in a rebuttal,[81] which immediately prompted a new, extensive review by another Indian Theosophist, T. Subba Row (1856–1890).[82] The arguments and discourses of legitimization put forward would warrant a separate study.[83] In any case, it is clear that the young, Theosophical Brahmans had no wish to see the interpretation of their own traditions usurped by the "Western" side, nor indeed by somebody like Oxley, who had not even mastered Sanskrit, as was emphasized time and again. Mavalankar drives the point home:

> Being but an humble pupil of Brahman-pundits learned in the esoteric interpretation of the Bhagavad-Gita, the "Reviewer" confesses to know little of the Western "School of Thought" [on which Oxley had built his case] which interprets *our* sacred Books it its own way. But, he is pretty sure of his facts when related to Eastern or Aryan esotericism.[84]

As a result of the dispute, Indian Theosophists turned their attention on the *Bhagavad Gita* with renewed vigor and occupied themselves with its interpretation.

4.2.2. Early Theosophy and Bhagavad Gita

To understand the significance of this development, it is important to recall that the Theosophical Society had previously demonstrated no particular interest in the *Bhagavad Gita*. Founded by Helena P. Blavatsky (1831–1891) and Henry Steel Olcott (1832–1907) in 1875, it had relocated its headquarters to India in 1879. The position of the Theosophical Society with regard to the existing religious scriptures was ambiguous. Theosophy was to teach the "Ancient Wisdom" underlying all world religions, but Blavatsky nonetheless emphasized that "the main body of the Doctrines given is found scattered throughout hundreds and thousands of Sanskrit MSS., some already translated—disfigured in their interpretations, as usual—others still awaiting their turn," whose study allowed for the "verification" of Theosophical doctrines.[85]

To prove her case, Blavatsky endeavored to draw evidence as extensively as possible from all sorts of Orientalist works, which, however, also means that her works do not privilege any specific work. This must be kept in mind when Blavatsky engages with the *Bhagavad Gita* in her first major work, *Isis Unveiled* (1877). Therein, she assumes an advanced age for the *Bhagavad Gita* and states, in reference to the foreword of Charles Wilkins's translation, that "the grandest mysteries of the Brahmanical religion are embraced within this magnificent poem."[86] However, neither here nor elsewhere in the early Theosophical Society can one discern a special focus on the *Bhagavad Gita*. This was to change in the 1880s, as Indian members employed the *Bhagavad Gita* against the theory of Busiris and the presumed superiority of "Western" wisdom. This process paralleled debates about the meaning and significance of yoga that were unfolding in the same context, which similarly revolved around questions of authority on ancient wisdom.[87]

4.2.3. Theosophical Orientation toward the Bhagavad Gita

In June of 1882, the first article devoted solely to the *Bhagavad Gita* appeared in *The Theosophist*. Bengali Theosophist and administrative officer Nobin K. Bannerji (d. 1885) was its author, and T. Subba Row provided additional commentary.[88] In a footnote to the article, Blavatsky indicated that the significance of the *Bhagavad Gita* was as "a record of the ancient teachings during the Mysteries of Initiation."[89]

During this time, the *Bhagavad Gita* became the fixed reference within Theosophy for "Hinduism," in contrast to "esoteric Buddhism." The latter played a central role for Blavatsky and Olcott, with both of them having officially converted to Buddhism in 1880 in Sri Lanka. In 1882, in response to the written recommendation of Mavalankar, American Theosophist William Quan Judge (1851–1896) read the *Bhagavad Gita*.[90] The following year, the publisher of *The Theosophist* announced a new series about "the hidden meaning of the Aryan Shastras," which was to commence with a complete commentary on the "esoteric meaning" of the *Bhagavad Gita*.[91] In this context, an "almost perfect identity between the concealed sense of this immortal epic and the Arhat Tibetan Doctrine"[92] is proposed. When William Quan Judge complained in *The Theosophist* in 1884 that Alfred Percy Sinnett's *Esoteric Buddhism* (1883) failed to take into account that "nearly all the leading portions of the doctrine are to be found broadly stated in the Bhagavad-Gita,"[93] Blavatsky emphatically agreed and wrote that "*all* the doctrines given in *Esoteric Buddhism* and far more yet untouched, are to be found in the *Gita*," only to immediately add "and not only there but in a thousand more known or unknown MSS. of Hindu sacred writings."[94]

After Judge returned to the United States at the end of 1884, he ambitiously expanded the American branch of the Theosophical Society. For that purpose, he formed reading groups focusing on the *Bhagavad Gita* and published passages and commentaries to the text in his magazine *The Path*, inaugurated in 1886.[95] From the mid-1880s onward, the *Bhagavad Gita* got a privileged status worldwide within the Theosophical Society that grew even stronger in the subsequent years. At the same time, Indian Theosophists made an effort to bring English translations of the *Bhagavad Gita* to the Indian book market at a reasonable price. In 1885, Tukaram Tatya of Bombay undertook a new edition of the Wilkins translation, equipped with extensive introductory statements by Manilal N. Dvivedi (1858–1898) and Nobin K. Bannerji. All three were Indian members of the Theosophical Society.[96]

4.2.4. Theosophical Appropriation of the Arnold Translation of the Bhagavad Gita

At exactly the same time, a verse translation of the *Bhagavad Gita* by Edwin Arnold (*The Song Celestial*, 1885) was released and immediately taken up with great enthusiasm in Theosophical circles. Edwin Arnold (1832–1904) was a journalist and successful Victorian writer, but had spent a number of years as a young man as the principal of a school in India.[97] The intersections of Victorian religious discourse are reflected in his person in a way that seems almost paradigmatic. While he was strongly anchored in the liberal Anglican Broad Church founded by his father, he also had close contact to Unitarian and liberal religious circles in England and the United States. It is worth mentioning that his second marriage was to the daughter of his friend, the American Transcendentalist William Henry Channing.[98] Channing helped promote Arnold's works in America, and it is certainly conceivable that Arnold was incited or encouraged to complete a translation of the *Bhagavad Gita* by him.

Arnold also had contacts in the Theosophical Society,[99] and his youngest son is said to have later become a Theosophist himself.[100] His success as an author was owed to a poem about the life of the Buddha (*Light of Asia*, 1879), which decisively advanced the burgeoning enthusiasm for Buddhism in Europe and the United States, reaching sixty editions in England and eighty in America.[101] Besides that, however, numerous other translations of religious verse stem from him. By 1875 he had already translated the *Gita Govinda* by Jayadeva, a Vaishnavite bhakti poem of the twelfth century that recounts the love affair of Krishna and Radha, how they separated and then reunited, in twelve songs. In spite of the earlier positive European reception of the *Gita Govinda* (for example, by Goethe),[102] Arnold's translation remained comparatively unknown, as were further translations out of the *Mahabharata* (*Indian Poetry*, 1881; *Indian Idylls*, 1883) and his translation of the *Katha Upanishads* (*The Secret of Death*, 1885), although the latter actually should have fitted in well with the overall positive reception of Advaita Vedanta.[103] He also produced a poetic translation with commentary on the ninety-nine names of God in Islam (*Pearls of Faith*, 1883, seven editions by 1896).

Initially, the *Bhagavad Gita* seems not to have interested Arnold overmuch. He translated other passages of the *Mahabharata*, and beyond that he conceptualized a trilogy of three exemplary works of Hinduism, Buddhism, and Islam, respectively, which were composed of his translations of the *Gita Govinda* (note: not the *Bhagavad Gita*), the life of Buddha, and the ninety-nine names.[104] It follows that the success of his *Bhagavad Gita* translation—though it could not compare with the popularity of his book on Buddha[105]—could not be traced back to a particular preference for the text by Arnold.[106] Rather, it was its enthusiastic reception in Theosophical circles that brought this about. How quickly Arnold's *Bhagavad Gita* gained popularity within Theosophy is illustrated by the will of Blavatsky written in the year of its publication. Blavatsky wrote that she wished that "yearly, on the anniversary of my death some of my friends should assemble at the Headquarters of the Theosophical Society and read a chapter of Edwin Arnold's *Light of Asia* and *Bhagavad Gita* [*Song Celestial*]."[107] Following her wishes, after her death Olcott established White Lotus Day in 1892.[108]

4.2.5. Interpretations of the Bhagavad Gita by Indian Theosophists

Over the course of the 1880s, two Indian Theosophists produced comprehensive interpretations of the *Bhagavad Gita*. At the annual meeting of the Theosophical Society in 1886, T. Subba Row held four lectures on the *Bhagavad Gita*, which were published a year later.[109] The interpretation of the Telugu Smarta Brahman, T. Subba Row, follows Advaita Vedanta. His reading is allegorical and spiritual in its treatment of the poem. The Pandavas are the higher, spiritual side of humanity, and their enemies the Kauravas, the lower side. It is concerned with the victory of the spiritual person and the attainment of immortality. Krishna is the "Logos," who descends to the realm of souls to lend vital support. Popular Hinduism is criticized for contributing to the moral decadence of India.[110] Such commentary demonstrated the allegorical and spiritualized reading that was to become the standard interpretation of the *Bhagavad Gita* in India.

In 1887, the commentary by T. Subba Row was backed by an English translation of Bengali Theosophist Mohini Mohun Chatterji (1858–1936). His translation followed T. Subba Row's allegorical interpretation,[111] and in his case also the alignment with Advaita Vedanta is clear. Prior to his translation of the *Bhagavad Gita*, Chatterji had translated two classic texts credited to Shankara into English (*Atmanatmaviveka*, 1884; *Vivekacudamani*, 1885).

5. Hinduism and the Bhagavad Gita

Over the course of the 1880s, the Indian Theosophical interpretation of the *Bhagavad Gita* gained broader attention. This is particularly evident in the case of Vivekananda (1863–1902) and his followers, who propagated a new Hinduism, the central tenet of which they declared to be Advaita Vedanta. Their reinterpretation of Advaita Vedanta had its origin in the Brahmo Samaj, a major Hindu reform movement in colonial India. Although the *Bhagavad Gita* is one of the three commentaries of Vedanta, the early Brahmo Samaj did not refer much to it. This is apparent in the case of Rammohan Roy (1772–1833), the founder of the Brahmo Samaj. At the beginning of the nineteenth century, Roy advocated for the reconception of Advaita Vedanta as a central philosophy of Hinduism. He was able to do quite well without any particular dependence on the *Bhagavad*

Gita for this purpose.[112] It is only in the context of his argumentation against *sati* (immolation of widows) that he fell back on the *Bhagavad Gita*, among others, as an authoritative scripture ("Shastra") in order to confirm the rejection of "acts based on desire such as concremation," that is, *sati*, in the Hindu tradition.[113] The *Bhagavad Gita* played no part in his philosophical writings. Hence a popularization of the *Bhagavad Gita* did not happen during the reconceptualization of Advaita Vedanta in the Brahmo Samaj.

The *Bhagavad Gita* found its way to Vivekananda through Mohini Mohun Chatterji. Until the mid-1880s, Chatterji was among the most important Indian Theosophists, and he was very close to Blavatsky and Olcott. After a roughly one-year period of disagreement, in 1887, Chatterji left the Theosophical Society.[114] His *Bhagavad Gita* translation of that same year was published by a non-Theosophical publisher in Boston, presumably thanks to his acquaintance with members of the Brahmo Samaj who were in close contact with in Unitarian and liberal religious circles there. It was likely through similar circles in England, where he had undertaken a very successful lecture tour while still a Theosophist in 1884 and 1885, that the London edition of the following year was distributed.

By the second half of the 1890s at the latest, Chatterji had become an official supporter and follower of Vivekananda.[115] Although he quoted from it rather infrequently, Vivekananda referred to the *Bhagavad Gita* on prominent occasions, such as in his opening address to the World Parliament of Religions in 1893.[116] He characterized the *Bhagavad Gita* as a text of Advaita Vedanta, as the "best authority on Vedanta," and as "the only commentary, the authoritative commentary on the Vedas."[117] Evident throughout is an allegorical-spiritual interpretation of the text. Arjuna, to whom Krishan related his teachings in the *Bhagavad Gita*, was "under the control of his emotionalism," but the "goal of man" was to attain eternal consciousness, where there is no space for emotions, only "pure reason." Arjuna "is not what he should be—a great self-controlled, enlightened sage working through the eternal light of reason."[118] For Vivekananda, this demand for deed without desire (Skt. *niṣkāma karman*) is a rejection of "Western" materialism and a materialist view of the world: "Religion is the realisation of spirit as spirit."[119]

In his North American lectures, it was of particular importance to Vivekananda to emphasize that religions were not to be understood as divisive doctrines, but as forms of individual realization that could be arrived at by various routes.[120] He had already made the latter point in his opening speech to the World Parliament of Religions in reference to the *Bhagavad Gita*. Many of his European and American followers also had a particular interest in the text. One can infer a correlation with the popularization of Theosophy in the 1880s. One notable case is that of Sarah Chapman Bull (1850-1911), one of the early and most socially influential followers of Vivekananda in the United States, who bequeathed a large amount of her fortune to the Ramakrishna Mission. She belonged to a circle of Unitarian, liberal religious-minded Bostonians. We know that her interest in Asian religions was piqued by a lecture by Mohini Mohun Chatterji, which was held in 1886 during a tour of the United States.[121]

Another important early supporter of the Ramakrishna Mission was Josephine MacLeod (1858-1949), who was active in the same circles as Chatterji and Bull. We know of her that she had already read the *Bhagavad Gita* in Boston, together with her sister Betty Sturges, before they met Vivekananda in the mid-1890s. The same is true for Laura Glenn (1867-1942), later known as Sister Devamata. She also became interested in Asian religions by reading the *Bhagavad Gita*.[122] Another example is Edward Toronto Sturdy (1860-1957), who likewise encountered Vivekananda in the second half of the 1890s. He previously had been a member of the Theosophical Society, where in the mid-1880s he purportedly had been deeply engaged in study of the *Bhagavad Gita*.[123]

The Theosophical mode of interpretation continued to influence the Hindu reformist appropriation of the *Bhagavad Gita* in the following years. Annie Besant (1847-1933), Blavatsky's successor in the leadership of the Theosophical Society and temporarily president of the Indian National Congress, carried on the tradition. Together with the young Indian Theosophist and later politician Bhagavan Das (1869-1958), Besant published two editions of the *Bhagavad Gita* (1895, 1905) and personally wrote a commentary called *Hints on the Study of the Bhagavad Gita* (1906). Wholly in keeping with the spirit of the allegorical-spiritual interpretation, the central theme of the *Bhagavad Gita* was identified as the internal victory of the spirit (Skt. *manas*) over desire (Skt. *kāma*) in humanity.[124]

Mohandas K. Gandhi (1869-1948) represents a particularly memorable example of the interplay between Theosophical and Hindu interpretations of the *Bhagavad Gita* at the turn of the twentieth century. Gandhi himself reports that his first encounter with the *Bhagavad Gita* took place in a Theosophical context. In 1889, during his stay in London, he got to know two Theosophists, Bertram and Archibald Keightley, who asked him to read the *Bhagavad Gita* together with them. In his autobiography, Gandhi writes:

> They were reading Sir Edwin Arnold's translation—The Song Celestial—and they invited me to read the original with them. I felt ashamed, as I had read the divine poem neither in Samskrit nor in Gujarati. I was constrained to tell them that I had not read the Gita, but that I would gladly read it with them, [. . .] I began reading the Gita with them. [. . .] The book struck me as one of priceless worth. The impression has ever since been growing on me with the result that I regard it today as the book par excellence for the knowledge of Truth.[125]

Theosophy was more formative an influence on Gandhi than he himself admitted afterward.[126] According to his own account, he began to study the *Bhagavad Gita* more intensively with "Theosophist friends" in South Africa around 1903.[127] In 1905, he had Annie Besant's translation of the *Bhagavad Gita* reprinted for the purpose of instructing Indian youths in South Africa, with her portrait on the title page.[128] When Besant protested against the use of her portrait, Gandhi apologized by saying it had happened out of "excessive reverence" for Besant.[129] In terms of content, large sections of Gandhi's version of the *Bhagavad Gita* also run parallel to the allegorical-spiritual interpretation of Theosophy.[130] Just as is in Theosophy, Gandhi formulated the *Bhagavad Gita* as the battle between humanity's higher and lower self, but does not justify the use of violence because the battlefield described is that of human nature.

Starting in the early twentieth century, the *Bhagavad Gita* attained increasing popularity among the educated, mainly English-speaking Hindu elite because of the growing emphasis on the *Bhagavad Gita* in Hindu reform movements. It was only then that it became considered one of the central texts of Hinduism, and the allegorical-spiritual interpretation the norm. Rai Bahadur Lala Baijnath wrote in the year 1908: "For the Hindu it is now the *one* book of books. [. . .] The Gita is as fresh as ever and just as to the Christian is the Bible . . . the Gita is to the Hindu."[131] At the 1910 World Missionary Conference in Edinburgh, the missionary F. J. Western described "the widespread use of the Bhagavad-Gita as a book of theology and devotion" and speaks of it as having been "re-discovered by English educated Hindus."[132] C. F. Andrews, liberal missionary and an eventual colleague of Gandhi's, pointed out in 1912 that "the Bhagavad Gita, which a century ago was scarcely known outside the learned circles of the pandits, [. . .] has been elevated from a position of comparative obscurity to that of a common and well-read scripture for the whole of educated India."[133]

The exclusive status of the *Bhagavad Gita* in India had been widely established by the late 1920s at the latest. So it was that in 1928 Gandhi spoke of how one could attain salvation after death if one carried the message of "Mother Gita" always in one's heart,[134] and that "no Hindu should let a single day pass without the study of [. . .] Bhagavad Gita."[135] Consequently, the popularity of the *Bhagavad Gita* has since been anachronistically written back into history. In 1929, Sarvepalli Radhakrishnan (1888–1975), a leading Hindu thinker of his time and the second president of India, opined that "if the hold which a work has on the mind of man is any clue to its importance, then the Gītā is the most influential work in Indian thought."[136]

6. Political *Bhagavad Gita*

The allegorical-spiritualized reading in accordance with Advaita Vedanta by Theosophists and Hindu reformers enjoys widespread acceptance in present-day Hinduism. In light of this, it is easy to forget that other conventions for interpretation also emerged, which certainly remain relevant even today. They, too, most likely built on the popularization of Theosophy in the 1880s, but aimed for a more political-nationalist reading.

6.1. Krishna as the "Ideal Man"

A number of the Indian Theosophists who championed the *Bhagavad Gita* hailed from Bengal, and they may well have been the conduits through which Theosophical discussions of the *Bhagavad Gita* became well-known. In any case, Bengali reformers discovered the *Bhagavad Gita* for their cause contemporaneously. The Krishna bhakti was deeply anchored in Bengal because of Gaudiya Vaishnavism, and Vaishnavite theism experienced an upswing in the 1880s. At the same time, the reformers saw themselves confronted with Christian missionary criticism of the presumed immorality of young Krishna's love affair with Radha, which was the central motif of the Krishna bhakti in the *Bhagavata Purana*.[137]

This criticism resonated with the Victorian Indian colonial elite of Bengal. By alluding to the *Bhagavad Gita*, the reformers attempted to remodel the figure of Krishna. The Krishna of the *Bhagavad Gita*, a philosophical debater little known to Christian missionaries at that point,[138] was henceforth declared the new standard. The Bengali poet Nabinchandra Sen

(1847–1909) published the first volume of a trilogy to the *Mahabharata* in 1886, in which he recounts how Krishna had created a unified Indian kingdom that lasted for several thousand years before it was destroyed by Brahmans. This kingdom was distinguished by its righteousness, and its foundation was the *Bhagavad Gita*.[139] Just how recent the reorientation toward the *Bhagavad Gita* still was at the time is evident in the fact that Nabinchandra Sen had not yet set eyes on the *Bhagavad Gita* during the drafting of the first volume and only got hold of it afterward, with the result that he released a published and annotated Bengali translation in 1889.[140]

At the same time, over a period of two years (1886–1888), the Bengali poet Bankimchandra Chattopadhyaya (1838–1894) also began publishing a commentary on the *Bhagavad Gita* in his magazine *Pracar*[141] that in a way flanked his major work about the life of Krishna (*Krishnacaritra*, 1886). Just as in Nabinchandra Sen's reading, the *Bhagavad Gita* served to characterize Krishna as a religious national hero, an "ideal man" who could serve as a Hindu equivalent to the figure of Christ.[142] However, even in this Bengali reinterpretation of the figure of Krishna, the *Bhagavad Gita* did not necessarily become a central Hindu text; rather, its reception remains embedded in an extensive rereading of Vaishnavite Puranic literature, including the *Bhagavata Purana*.[143]

6.2. *Bhagavad Gita* as a Call for Armed Resistance

The nationalist interpretation of the *Bhagavad Gita* as first formulated in Bengal took on a radical edge in subsequent years. Starting with Maharashtra, at the end of the nineteenth century, the *Bhagavad Gita* was made into the ideological armor of a militant wing of the anti-British resistance. Krishna's incitement of Arjuna to fight his relatives, with no regard for the consequences, to restore the dharma (Skt. *niṣkāma karman*) was understood as a justification for putting aside established moral values for the sake of the anti-colonial fight for freedom. Consequently, Bal Gangadhar Tilak (1856–1920) wrote in 1897:

> Shrimat Krishna's teaching in the *Bhagavad Gita* is to kill even our teachers and our kinsmen. No blame attaches to any person if he is doing deeds without being motivated by a desire to reap the fruit of his deeds. [. . .] Get out of the Penal Code, enter into the extremely high atmosphere of the *Bhagavad Gita*, and then consider the actions of great men.[144]

Between 1910 and 1911, Tilak wrote a long commentary on the *Bhagavad Gita* in prison. In an explicit critique of one-sided Advaita Vedantic and allegorical-spiritual interpretations, he posited political independence as an indispensable condition for the restoration of religious order (Skt. *dharma*).[145] Following this interpretation, at the turn of the twentieth century, the *Bhagavad Gita* began to provide the legitimization in Maharashtra and, to a lesser extent, in Bengal for an anti-colonial fight for independence that relied on assassination and bombings.[146] This political-militant interpretation, the traces of which can be found even in the Hindu nationalism of today, could not sustain majority support. Instead, it was the allegorical-spiritual interpretation that eventually pushed through in the early decades of the twentieth century. In the person of Aurobindo Ghose (1872–1950), these developments are made visible: while at first he followed Tilak's interpretation, around 1910, his beliefs took a spiritual turn.[147]

6.3. *Bhagavad Gita* and the Ethics of Action

This decidedly political-nationalist interpretation of the *Bhagavad* Gita shows again that it was hardly inevitable for the *Bhagavad Gita* to become one of the scriptural foundations of modern Hinduism. At the same time, political-nationalist and allegorical-spiritual interpretations were not entirely opposed to each other: not only did they share a common theoretical origin, but they also overlapped in practice. Vivekananda advanced not only spiritualistic but also nationalist interpretations.[148] He saw a clear ethic of action laid out in the *Bhagavad Gita*, whereby "a man must be active in order to pass through activity to perfect calmness."[149] He emphasizes this point particularly in regard to his Indian followers, and allows himself this dramatic utterance:

> You will understand the Gita better with your biceps, your muscles, a little stronger. You will understand the mighty genius and the mighty strength of Krishna better with a little of strong blood in you.[150]

Here the *Bhagavad Gita* becomes the basis for the masculine national awakening of India. To the later Indian-Theosophical interpretation, this aspect was not unknown either. Annie Besant and Bhagavan Das established that the *Bhagavad Gita* had historical significance, drawing on the evolution of a "world logos," whereby the unification of humankind and God is made possible through outward effort.[151] Gandhi, too, understood the *Bhagavad Gita* as a call to action: "He who gives up action falls. He who gives up only the reward rises."[152] These interpretations promoting action show how it is possible for nationalist and Spiritualist interpretations to mesh. However, this changes nothing of the result, which was that the Spiritualist reading was to push through in the end.

7. Conclusion: *Bhagavad Gita* and Global Religious History

The present popularity of the *Bhagavad Gita* in India can be traced back to Theosophical debates in the 1880s about the relationship between "Western" and "Eastern" tradition. The context of its popular emergence was the nationalist protest of Indian Theosophists against European Orientalist claims. However, there is no evidence for a "pizza effect," whereby the positive reception in India is the result of the previous high regard held by the text in Europe and the United States. The historical findings as delineated in this chapter seem so self-evident that the question arises of why scholarship has overlooked the Theosophical connection thus far. The answer to this question can help us understand how theoretical presuppositions structure our view of the past. I contend that the Indian Theosophists who played the decisive role twice fell victim to common historiographical ignorance.

First, there exists a conceptual flaw in the academic study of esotericism, because it examines esotericism as a purely "Western" phenomenon.[153] Dissenting voices have not found much of an audience thus far.[154] Consequently, Theosophy is usually examined only as an expression of "Western" esotericism,[155] and its Orientalist notions come under consideration only as a product of European imaginations.[156] There is no conceptual room for questions regarding the possible contributions by Indian Theosophists to the doctrinal progression of the Theosophical Society. However, the Theosophical discussions about the *Bhagavad Gita* retraced in this article make it clear that such a narrow view is insufficient. Second, for a long time, the Orientalism debate neglected questions related to the Indian role in the conceptual formation of modern Hinduism under colonialism.[157] In the case of the *Bhagavad Gita*, this meant that the Indian reception was declared too hastily as nothing more than the adaptation of Orientalist patterns of interpretation from Europe and the United States. Thereby, the active role of the colonized falls from view, and the far-reaching scope of the events in the 1880s outlined in this article is not recognized.

As a result, the reception of the *Bhagavad Gita* raises fundamental questions. Its scholarly investigation necessitates a theoretical foundation that critically reflects and seeks to overcome the structural reasons for current blind spots. Elsewhere I have argued that a global history approach is necessary to adequately study processes of religious transformation of the nineteenth and early twentieth centuries.[158] A global history approach is also helpful for a better understanding of the changing importance of the *Bhagavad Gita*. For one, it deliberately interrogates the role of the colonized within the discourse of colonial power.[159] It investigates the complex forms that assimilation of "Western knowledge" by the colonized takes, and does not simply assume an identical substitution. Colonial discourses are no longer seen as monolithic or invariable; rather, it is their polyphonic and unstable character that comes into view. They exhibit a considerable dynamism and substantial potential for transformation, and in their instability they can simultaneously express resistance.[160] Recent post-colonial studies take particular interest in the entire range of articulations of the colonized. When applied to the reception of the *Bhagavad Gita*, this means that the Indian reaction automatically falls into the specific research focus and no longer runs the risk of being structurally erased.

For another reason, the concept of a global religious history demands to understand colonial history as "entangled histories," because "those entities that stand in relation with one another are themselves in part a product of their entanglements."[161] Entangled histories follow the insight of recent post-colonial theories, whereby all articulations within a discourse refer to each other as "citations." This means that not even Europe experienced history autonomously; rather, because of its "entanglements" with the colonies, the identity formation of Europe was "entangled" with that of the colonies. Even though European knowledge had a hegemonic position, European colonialism was also marked by entanglement. Within such a perspective, it is no longer necessary to conceive of a self-sustained "Western esotericism."[162] Instead, the study of esotericism within religious studies will only benefit from recognizing its subject as a global one.

Finally, global religious history rests on a genealogical approach in the vein of Foucault, who demanded a strict historicizing of research subjects.[163] In this historical sense, "precolonial" can only denote the time directly before the nineteenth century, rather than vaguely indicating thousand-year-old Indian traditions, the continuity of which is simply presupposed.

This chapter provides a concrete example of how fruitful a global perspective is for the writing of religious history. From the perspective of global religious history, however, at least three further central aspects of the reception of the *Bhagavad Gita* that have thus far been insufficiently researched come to light. It demonstrates a need for stricter historicizing of the connection between pre- and post-colonial understandings of the *Bhagavad Gita*. The role of the *Bhagavad Gita* in eighteenth-century India bears particular consideration. If indeed there is an Indian pre-colonial root for the colonial reception of the *Bhagavad Gita*, it must be located in this period. Past research has missed its chance to follow up on this question in depth. A fruitful point of departure would surely be the Brahmanization of Krishna bhakti in Rajasthan in the eighteenth century, mentioned at the outset of this chapter. The related reorientation toward Vaishnavite Vedanta generated renewed interest in the *Bhagavad Gita* within the worship of Krishna. The effect of this development on colonial Hinduism has yet to be examined, even though it seems to have had a direct impact, for example, on Bharatendu Harishchandra (1850–1885).[164] Furthermore, the Indian reception of the *Bhagavad Gita* in colonial India would benefit from a more detailed examination of the various *Bhagavad Gita* commentaries that were published in the nineteenth and early twentieth centuries in regional Indian languages.[165]

Finally, there is a need for future studies of Theosophy in line with a global history approach. If it is true that greater appreciation of the *Bhagavad Gita* within Theosophical circles in England and the United States developed as a result of discussions that took place in the 1880s in India, then this lays bare an entanglement, the implications of which for the ongoing development of Theosophical doctrine at the end of the nineteenth century must be taken into greater consideration. Future research must also strive to examine the Indian influence on Theosophical discussions in Europe and the United States. In the broadest possible terms, it is a matter of recognizing Theosophy as having been a global phenomenon. The same is true of the question of tracing back the present-day popularity of the *Bhagavad Gita* in Europe and the United States. There is much to suggest that the European Romantic and American Transcendentalist preoccupation with the *Bhagavad Gita* did not, as is commonly assumed, play a decisive role. As shown, the influence of European Romanticism and American Transcendentalism has been overestimated. Is, then, the present-day popularity of the *Bhagavad Gita* outside India instead a reaction to its Indian popularization since the 1880s? This would explain why the zenith of Indological research into the *Bhagavad Gita* did not occur until after 1900 and continued for about forty years thereafter.[166] In light of global entangled histories, it is to be assumed that the particular Indological interest in turn reinforced the Indian focus on the *Bhagavad Gita*. In any case, a thorough examination of this web of complex questions would be worthwhile. To conclude, the perspective of global religious history generates unexplored avenues for the further investigation of colonial discourses. It is precisely herein that we find the reason for its relevance.

Notes

1. Eric J. Sharpe, *The Universal Gita: Western Images of the Bhagavad Gita: A Bicentennary Survey* (La Salle, IL: Open Court, 1985); Friedrich Huber, "Religion und Politik in Indien," *Zeitschrift für Mission* 17, no. 2 (1991); Rahul Peter Das, "Die Rolle der Bhagavadgita im indischen Nationalismus der Kolonialzeit," in *Religiöser Text und soziale Struktur*, ed. Walter Beltz and Jürgen Tubach (Halle: Universität Halle, 2001); Catherine A. Robinson, *Interpretations of the Bhagavad-Gita and Images of the Hindu Tradition: The Song of the Lord* (London: Routledge, 2006); Richard H. Davis, *The Bhagavad Gita: A Biography* (Princeton: Princeton University Press, 2015).

2. Agehananda Bharati, "The Hindu Renaissance and its Apologetic Patterns," *Journal of Asian Studies* 29 (1970): 274.

3. Sharpe, *Universal Gita*, 169–70.

4. Richard King, *Orientalism and Religion: Postcolonial Theory, India and "The Mystic East"* (London: Routledge, 1999), 120–21.

5. Robinson, *Interpretations*; Shruti Kapila and Faisal Fatehali Devji, *Political Thought in Action: The Bhagavad Gita and Modern India* (Cambridge: Cambridge University Press, 2013); Davis, *Bhagavad Gita*.

6. Matthew Clark, *The Daśanāmī-Saṃnyāsīs: The Integration of Ascetic Lineages into an Order* (Leiden: Brill, 2006); Christopher Minkowski, "Advaita Vedānta in Early Modern History," *South Asian History and Culture* 2 (2011).

7. Dewan Bahadur K. Rangachari, *The Sri Vaishnava Brahmans* (Madras: Madras Government Museum, 1931); Gérard Colas, "History of the Vaiṣṇava Traditions. An Esquisse," in *The Blackwell Companion to Hinduism*, ed. Gavin Flood (Oxford: Blackwell, 2003).

8. Ursula King, "The Iconography of the Bhagavad Gita," *Journal of Dharma* 7, no. 2 (1982).

9. Catharina Kiehnle, *Jñāndev Studies I and II. Songs on Yoga: Texts and Teachings of the Mahārāṣṭrian Nāths* (Stuttgart: Franz Steiner, 1997); Davis, *Bhagavad Gita*, 65–71.

10. Shankar Gopal Tulpule, *Classical Marāṭhī Literature from the Beginning to A. D. 1818* (Wiesbaden: Harrassowitz, 1979), 359.

11. Hugh van Skyhawk, *Bhakti und Bhakta: Religionsgeschichtliche Untersuchungen zum Heilsbegriff und zur religiösen Umwelt des Śrī Sant Ekanāth* (Wiesbaden: Steiner, 1990), 19.

12. Alan W. Entwistle, *Braj, Centre of Krishna Pilgrimage* (Groningen: Egbert Forsten, 1987).

13. Helmuth von Glasenapp, "Die Lehre Vallabhâcāryas," *Zeitschrift für Indologie und Iranistik* 9 (1933/34); Richard Barz, *The Bhakti Sect of Vallabhācārya* (Faridabad: Thomson Press, 1976).

14. Joseph Thomas O'Connell, "Caitanya's Followers and the Bhagavad-Gita: A Case Study in the Bhakti and the Secular," in *Hinduism: New Essays in the History of Religions*, ed. Bardwell L. Smith (Leiden: Brill, 1976); Tony K. Stewart, *The Final Word: The Caitanya Caritāmṛta and the Grammar of Religious Tradition* (New York: Oxford University Press, 2010).

15. Monika Horstmann, *Der Zusammenhalt der Welt: Religiöse Herrschaftslegitimation und Religionspolitik Mahārājā Savāī Jaisinghs (1700–1743)* (Wiesbaden: Harrassowitz, 2009).

16. Viśvanātha cakravartī: *Sārārtha-varṣiṇī* (Skt., ca. 1704–1709), quoted from Adrian P. Burton, "Temples, Texts, and Taxes: The Bhagavad-gītā and Politico-Religious Identity of the Caitanya Sect" (PhD diss., The Australian National University, 2000).

17. Burton, "Temples," 2–4.

18. Winand M. Callewaert and Shilanand Hemraj, *Bhagavadgītānuvāda. A Study in Transcultural Translation* (Ranchi: Satya Bharati Publications, 1983), 182; Burton, "Temples," 93.

19. Reinhart Hummel, *Indische Mission und neue Frömmigkeit im Westen* (Stuttgart: Kohlhammer, 1980), 52.

20. Mary Lloyd, "Sir Charles Wilkin, 1749–1836," in *Report for the Year 1978*, ed. India Office Library and Records (London: Foreign and Commonwealth Office, 1979).

21. P. J. Marshall, ed., *The British Discovery of Hinduism in the 18th Century* (Cambridge: Cambridge University Press, 1970), 194.

22. Ibid., 193.

23. Alladi Mahaveda Sastry, *The Bhagavad Gita with the Commentary of Sri Sankaracharya. Translated from the original Sanskrit into English* (Madras: Samata Books, 1977 [1897]), 4; P. J. Thomas, *20th Century Interpretations of Bhagavadgita: Tilak, Gandhi and Aurobindo* (Delhi: I. S. P. C. K, 1987), 10. (Skt. "tat idaṃ samastavedārthasārasaṃgrahabhūtaṃ.")

24. Marshall, *British Discovery*, 193.

25. Ibid., 194.

26. Rosane Rocher, *Orientalism, Poetry, and the Millennium: The Checkered Life of Nathaniel Brassey Halhed, 1751–1830* (Delhi: Motilal Barnasidass, 1983), 123–24. See also the "Unitarian" interpretation of Advaita Vedanta by Rammohan Roy (Dermot Killingley, *Rammohun Roy in Hindu and Christian Tradition: The Teape Lectures 1990* [Newcastle upon Tyne: Grevatt and Grevatt, 1993], 135–37).

27. Wilhelm Halbfass, *India and Europe: An Essay of Philosophical Understanding* (Delhi: Motilal Barnarsidass, 1990), 56.

28. Bradley L. Herling, *The German Gita: Hermeneutics and Discipline in the German Reception of Indian Thought, 1778–1831* (London: Routledge, 2006).

29. Günter Kronenbitter, ed., *Friedrich Gentz: Gesammelte Schriften*, vol. VIII, 5 (Hildesheim: Olms-Weidmann, 2002), 300 (letter by Wilhelm von Humboldt to Friedrich Gentz, March 1, 1828).

30. Sharpe, *Universal Gita*, 20.

31. Halbfass, *India and Europe*, 84–99; Andreas Nehring, "Religion und Kultur. Zur Beschreibung einer Differenz," in *Religious Turns—Turning Religions: Veränderte kulturelle Diskurse—Neue religiöse Wissensformen*, ed. Andreas Nehring and Joachim Valentin (Stuttgart: Kohlhammer, 2008).

32. J. Cockburn Thomson, *The Bhagavad-Gita, or a Discourse Between Krishna and Arjuna on Divine Matters: A Sanskrit Philosophical Poem, Translated, with Copious Notes, an Introduction on Sanskrit Philosophy, and Other Matters* (Hertford: Stephen Austin, 1855); John Dowson, *A Classical Dictionary of Hindu Mythology and Religion, Geography, History and Literature* (London: Trübner, 1879), 43–44, 82–83.

33. Thomson, *Discourse*, xvii–cxix.

34. J. Cockburn Thomson, *The Bhagavad-Gita, or The Sacred Lay: A New Edition of the Sanskrit Text, with a Vocabulary* (Hertford: Stephen Austin, 1855).

35. Émile Burnouf, *La Bhagavad-Gîtâ ou le chant du bienheureux: poeme Indien* (Paris: B. Duprat, 1861), VII.

36. Ibid., V–XI.

37. Arthur Anthony Macdonell, *A History of Sanskrit Literature* (London: W. Heinemann, 1900). See Sharpe, *Universal Gita*, 51. On the bibliography of Albrecht Weber, see Asko Parpola, "Publications of the Great Indologist Fr. Albrecht Weber," *Studia Orientalia* 97 (2003).

38. Friedrich Max Müller, *India: What Can It Teach Us?* (New York: Funk & Wagnalls, 1883), 272, see also 109–10.

39. Mishka Sinha, "Corrigibility, Allegory, Universality: A History of Gita's Transnational Reception, 1785–1945," *Modern Intellectual History* 7 (2010): 306–7.

40. Kashinath Trimbak Telang, *The Bhagavadgîtâ with the Sanatsujâtîya and the Anugîtâ*, Sacred Books of the East, vol. 7 (Oxford: Clarendon, 1882).

41. Arthur Christy, *The Orient in American Transcendentalism: A Study of Emerson, Thoreau, and Alcott* (New York: Columbia University Press, 1932), 23.

42. See the list of references in Christy, *Orient*, 278–301.

43. Carl T. Jackson, *The Oriental Religions and American Thought: Nineteenth-Century Explorations* (Westport: Greenwood Press, 1981), 47; Sharpe, *Universal Gita*, 21–22.

44. Ralph L. Rusk, *The Letters of Ralph Waldo Emerson*, 6 vols. (New York: Columbia University Press, 1939), III, 209 (letter by Emerson to Elizabeth Hoar, June 17, 1845). See also Christy, *Orient*, 287; Jackson, *Oriental Religions*, 50; Sharpe, *Universal Gita*, 22. On the problem of Emerson's mixing up Buddhism and Hinduism, see Jackson, *Oriental Religions*, 56.

45. Christy, *Orient*, 23, 167–68; Jackson, *Oriental Religions*, 50, 134.

46. Christy, *Orient*, 287; Jackson, *Oriental Religions*, 52–53. The first U.S. American reprint was probably first published in New York in 1867 (Geo. P. Philes, New York University), while Thomson's 1855 translation seems not to have found many readers in North America.

47. Christy, *Orient*, 26. (The Sanskrit original has *samkhya* for "speculative doctrine" and *yoga* for "practical doctrine.")

48. Ibid., 26.

49. Sharpe, *Universal Gita*, 26–31.

50. Henry D. Thoreau, *Walden*, ed. J. Lyndon Shanley (Princeton: Princeton University Press, 1971), 298.

51. Sharpe, *Universal Gita*, 27.

52. Ibid., 28.

53. Christy, *Orient*, 242; Jackson 1981, *Oriental Religions*, 70–73.

54. Arthur Versluis, *American Transcendentalism and Asian Religions* (New York: Oxford University Press, 1993), 100 (journal entry from May 1846).

55. Christy, *Orient*, 240–48; Versluis, *American Transcendentalism*, 99–104.

56. Jackson 1981, *Oriental Religions*, 59.

57. Samuel Johnson, *Samuel Johnson: Oriental Religions and Their Relation to Universal Religion (India, China, Persia)*, 3 vols. (Boston: J.R. Osgood, 1872); James Freeman Clarke, *Ten Great Religions: An Essay in Comparative Theology* (Boston: J. R. Osgood, 1871); Moncure Conway, *The Sacred Anthology: A Book of Ethnic Scriptures* (New York: H. Holt, 1874). On the background, see Carl T. Jackson, "The Orient in Post-Bellum American Thought: Three Pioneer Popularizers," *American Quarterly* 22 (1970). One should take note that the main interest in the United States at this time increasingly concentrated on Buddhism (See for instance Jackson, *Oriental Religions*, 141–56; Thomas A. Tweed, *The American Encounter with Buddhism, 1844–1912: Victorian Culture and the Limits of Dissent*, 2nd ed. (Chapel Hill: University of North Carolina Press, 2000 [1992]).

58. Frank F. Ellinwood, *Oriental Religions and Christianity: A Course of Lectures Delivered on the Ely Foundation, before the Students of Union Theological Seminary, New York 1891* (London: Nisbet, 1892).

59. Clarke, *Ten Great Religions*, III, 6.

60. Johnson, *Samuel Johnson*, I, 411–40.

61. Jackson, *Oriental Religions*, 111–13.

62. Jackson, "Orient in Post-Bellum American Thought," 78.

63. Conway, *Sacred Anthology*, 479–80.

64. Vasudha Dalmia, *The Nationalisation of Hindu Traditions: Bharatendu Harishchandra and Nineteenth-century Banaras* (Delhi: Oxford University Press, 1997), 401 note 60.

65. Ibid., 392–93.

66. Sharpe, *Universal Gita*, 53; Dalmia, *Nationalisation*, 394.

67. Putative parallels between the *Bhagavad Gita* and the New Testament, especially the Gospel of John, were still brought up by Indologists in later periods, as the examples of Edward Washburn Hopkins (1895 and 1901) and Paul Deussen (1906 and 1911) show (Richard Garbe, *Indien und das Christentum. Eine Untersuchung der religionsgeschichtlichen Zusammenhänge* [Tübingen: Mohr, 1914], 211 note, 246–49).

68. Friedrich Max Müller, *Natural Religion: The Gifford-Lectures Delivered Before the University of Glasgow in 1888* (London: Longmans, Green & Co., 1889), 99–100.

69. Garbe, *Indien*, 228–54. See also Sharpe, *Universal Gita*, 51–58, 110–13.

70. "Traces in the Bhagavad-Gītā of Christian Writings and Ideas: From the Appendix to Dr. Lorinser's Bhagavad-Gītā," *Indian Antiquary* 2 (1873): 283–96.

71. G. A. Natesan, ed., *Kashinath Trimbak Telang: A Sketch of His Life and Career* (Madras: G. A. Natesan, s. a). It is noteworthy that Harichand Chintamani, who was from Bombay as well, had also published an English translation of the *Bhagavad Gita* in the previous year. (See note 86 below.)

72. Charles H. Heimsath, *Indian Nationalism and Hindu Social Reform* (Princeton: Princeton University Press, 1964), 188.

73. Ibid., 108.

74. Telang, *Bhagavadgîtâ*, 35.

75. John Davies, *Hindu Philosophy. The Bhagavad Gita or The Sacred Lay. A Sanskrit Philosophical Poem*, Translated, with Notes, 4th ed. (London: Kegan Paul, Trench, Trübner, 1907 [1882]), 207–8.

76. Matthew Lederle, *Philosophical Trends in Modern Maharashtra* (Bombay: Popular Prakashan, 1976), 223.

77. On William Oxley and his relationship to Theosophy, see Helena Petrowna Blavatsky, *Collected Writings*, 15 vols. (Wheaton, IL: The Theosophical Publishing House, 1950–1991), IV, 99–101, 190–93, 398–99, XI, 302. On the problem of the alleged visits by Mahatmas, see also Alfred Trevor Barker, ed., *The Mahatma Letters To A. P. Sinnett from the Mahatmas M. & K. H.: Transcribed and Compiled by A. T. Barker, in Chronological Sequence Arranged and Edited by Vicente Hao Chin, Jr.* (Chennai: Theosophical Publishing House, 1998), 135–41, 252–53, 267–68.

78. William Oxley, *The Philosophy of Spirit, Illustrated by a New Version of the Bhagavat Gítá, an Episode of the Mahabharat, one of the Epic Poems of Ancient India* (Glasgow: Hay Nisbet, 1881).

79. *The Theosophist*, December 1881, 62–64. This article was published anonymously, but in a different replique (*The Theosophist*, March 1882, 150, footnote), the "reviewer" reveals himself with the initials "D. M."

80. *The Theosophist*, December 1881, 63.

81. *The Theosophist*, March 1882, 150–53.

82. N. C. Ramanujachary, *A Lonely Disciple: Monograph on T. Subba Row, 1856-90* (Madras: Theosophical Publishing House, 1993).

83. *The Theosophist*, May 1882, 192–96 (Subba Row); September 1882, 298–303 (Oxley); October 1882, 18–20, February 1883, 121–23 (Subba Row).

84. *The Theosophist*, March 1882, 150, footnote.

85. Helena Petrovna Blavatsky, *The Secret Doctrine*, Seventh (Adyar) Edition, Collected Writings 1888, 3 vols. (Adyar, Madras: The Theosophical Publishing House, 1979 [1888]), I, xxiii.

86. Helena Petrovna Blavatsky, *Isis Unveiled*, New Edition, Revised and Corrected, and with Additional Material, Collected Writings 1877, 2 vols. (Wheaton, Illinois: The Theosophical Publishing House, 1972), II, 562–63. It should be noted that Hurrychund Chintamon (Harichand Chintamani) from the Arya Samaj in Bombay, the first contact person in India for Blavatsky and Olcott, had already penned a commentary on the *Bhagavad Gita* in 1874 (*A Commentary on the Text of the Bhagavad-Gítá*, London: Trübner; he adopted the English translation by John Cockburn Thomson from 1855). It is not known, however, whether Blavatsky was aware of this edition, which appears not to have been spread widely. To my knowledge, she never refers to this edition. On Harichand Chinatamani, see Marion Meade, *Madame Blavatsky: The Woman behind the Myth* (New York: G. P. Putnam's Sons, 1980), 181, 195–97, 254–55, and J. T. F. Jordens, *Dayānanda Sarasvatī: His Life and Ideas* (Delhi: Oxford University Press, 1978), 203, 209–14.

87. Karl Baier, "Theosophical Orientalism and the Structures of Intercultural Transfer: Annotations on the Appropriation of the Cakras in Early Theosophy," in *Theosophical Appropriations. Esotericism, Kabbalah, and the Transformation of Traditions*, ed. Julie Chajes and Boaz Huss (Beer Sheva: Ben-Gurion University of the Negev Press, 2016).

88. *The Theosophist*, June 1882, 229–31.

89. Blavatsky, *Collected Writings*, IV, 124.

90. Sven Eek, ed., *Dâmodar and the Pioneers of the Theosophical Movement* (Madras: Theosophical Publishing House, 1965), 74.

91. *The Theosophist*, August 1883, 265. This plan could apparently not be implemented right away. The "Notes on the Bhagavad Gita" by T. Subba Row did not appear there before 1887.

92. Blavatsky 1950-1991: V, 68.

93. *The Theosophist*, February 1884, 122.

94. Blavatsky, *Collected Writings*, VI, 147.

95. Meade, *Madame Blavatsky*, 420.

96. *The Theosophist*, August 1885, 278. A second edition was published in 1887. On Dvivedi, see Thaker, *Manilal Dvivedi* (New Delhi: Sahitya Academy, 1983). At the same time, the Tamil translation of the *Bhagavad Gita* by Villavarambal Kuppuswami Iyer was advertised within the Theosophical Society (*The Theosophist*, September 1885, 310). On Tukaram Tatya, see the obituary in *The Theosophist* (Olcott 1898).

97. On Arnold, see Brooks Wright, *Interpreter of Buddhism to the West: Sir Edwin Arnold* (New York: Bookman, 1957).

98. Christy, *Orient*, 248–53.

99. Blavatsky, *Collected Writings*, XII, 718–23. When Arnold embarked on a trip to South Asia in 1885–1886, he was received in grand style by Sumangala, one of the highest Buddhist dignitaries of Sri Lanka, upon mediation by Olcott, who was also present at the reception (Wright, *Interpreter*, 115–16).

100. Wright, *Interpreter*, 56.

101. Jackson, *Oriental Religions*, 143.

102. Translations of *Gitagovinda*: English (William Jones, 1807), German (Friedrich Rückert, 1837), and Latin (Christian Lassen, 1836). Klaus Mylius, *Geschichte der Literatur im alten Indien* (Leipzig: Reclam, 1983), 192–95.

103. Mohini Chatterji briefly reported the publication of the work in *The Theosophist* (March 1885, 146).

104. Edwin Arnold, *The Song Celestial, or Bhagavad-Gîtâ* (Boston: Roberts Brothers, 1885), 188.

105. According to the (not entirely reliable) catalogs of the British Library and the Library of Congress, ten editions were published in England until 1906, while there was no separate new edition in North America, but only a reprint within a collected works edition from 1889.

106. Edwin Arnold praised Davies's translation and probably made heavy use of it (Arnold, *Song Celestial*, 9–10; Wright, *Interpreter*, 125–26).

107. Blavatsky, *Collected Writings*, VI, 322.

108. Blavatsky, *Collected Writings*, VI, 323–24.

109. First in the journal *The Theosophist* in 1887, then as a stand-alone book in 1888, published with Tukaram Tatya in Bombay.

110. T. Subba Row, *Philosophy of the Bhagavad-Gita: Four Lectures Delivered at the Eleventh Annual Convention of the Theosophical Society, Held at Adyar, on December 27, 28, 29 and 30, 1886*, 2nd ed. (Madras: Theosophical Publishing House, 1994 [1912]). See also Ronald W. Neufeldt, "A Lesson in Allegory: Theosophical Interpretations of the Bhagavadgita," in *Modern Indian Interpreters of the Bhagavadgita*, ed. Robert N. Minor (Albany: State University of New York Press, 1986), 13–15.

111. Mohini M. Chatterji, *The Bhagavad Gita or the Lord's Lay, with Commentary and Notes, as well as Reference to the Christian Scriptures*, 2nd ed. (Boston:

Houghton Mifflin Company, 1888 [1887]). See also Sharpe, *Universal Gita*, 93-94; Neufeldt, "Lesson in Allegory," 15-19.

112. Dermot Killingley, "Rammohun Roy's Interpretation of the Vedanta" (PhD diss., University of London), 154, 342; Killingley, *Teape Lectures*, 86-87.

113. Killingley, "Roy's Interpretation of the Vedanta," 154-55 [from the last Bengali treatise on Sati, 1829]. See also Sharpe, *Universal Gita*, 13-14.

114. Eek, *Dâmodar*, 638-39.

115. Vivienne Marie Baumfieldt, "Swami Vivekananda's Practical Vedanta" (PhD diss., University of Newcastle upon Tyne, 1991), 49-50.

116. Swami Vivekananda, *The Complete Works of Swami Vivekananda*, Mayavati Memorial Edition (Reprint), 9 vols. (Calcutta: Advaita Ashrama, 1959-1997), I, 4.

117. Vivekananda, *Complete Works*, VII, 57. (July 18, 1895, Thousand Island Park) ("The Bhagavad Gita is the best authority on Vedanta."); Ibid., III, 244-45 (1897 in Victoria Hall in Madras?) ("As I told you the other day, the only commentary, the authoritative commentary on the Vedas, has been made once and for all by Him who inspired the Vedas—by Krishna in the Gita.")

118. Ibid., I, 460.

119. Ibid., I, 469.

120. Ibid., I, 4, 470, 473-74.

121. Carl T. Jackson, *Vedanta and the West: The Ramakrishna Movement in the United States* (Bloomington: Indiana University Press, 1994), 92.

122. Ibid., 95.

123. Marie Louise Burke, *Swami Vivekananda in the West: New Discoveries*, 6 vols. (Calcutta: Advaita Ashrama, 1984), III, 213.

124. Neufeldt, "Lesson in Allegory."

125. M. K. Gandhi, *The Life and Works of Mahatma Gandhi*, vol. 44, CD-ROM Version, ed. Ministry of Information and Broadcasting, Government of India (New Delhi: Icon Softec, 1999), 142.

126. Michael Bergunder, "Experiments with Theosophical Truth: Gandhi, Esotericism, and Global Religious History," *Journal of the American Academy of Religion* 82 (2014).

127. Gandhi, *Life and Works*, vol. 44, 286-87.

128. Gandhi, *Life and Works*, vol. 4, 271-72, 275. See also I. M. Muthanna, *Mother Besant and Mahatma Gandhi* (Vellore: Thenpulam Publishers, 1986), 82-83.

129. Gandhi, *Life and Works*, vol. 4, 271.

130. Sharpe, *Universal Gita*, 116-19; J. T. F. Jordens, "Gandhi and the Bhagavadgita," in *Modern Indian Interpreters of the Bhagavadgita*, ed. Robert N. Minor (Albany: State University of New York Press, 1986).

131. Rai Bahadur Lala Baijnath: The Bhagavad Gita in Modern Life, Meerut: Vaishya Hitkari, 1908, 50, quoted from Robert N. Minor, ed., *Modern Indian*

Interpreters of the Bhagavadgita (Albany: State University of New York Press, 1986), 4 (emphasis added, M. B.).

132. World Missionary Conference, ed., *Report of Commission IV. The Missionary Message in Relation to Non-Christian Religions. With Supplement: Presentation and Discussion of the Report in the Conference on 18th June 1910* (Edinburgh: Oliphant, 1910), 313–14.

133. C. F. Andrews, *The Renaissance in India: Its Missionary Impact* (London: Baptist Missionary Society, 1912), 146.

134. Gandhi, *Life and Works,* vol. 37, 107 (from "Discourses on the 'Gita' "; the quoted entry is from March 27, 1926). See also Gandhi, *Life and Works,* vol. 64, 255; Friedrich Huber, *Die Bhagavadgita in der neueren indischen Auslegung und in der Begegnung mit dem christlichen Glauben* (Erlangen: Verlag der Ev.-Luth. Mission, 1991), 6.

135. Gandhi, *Life and Works,* vol. 41, 89 (Hindi preface to a Tamil translation of the *Bhagavad Gita* by S. Bharati, 1928).

136. Sarvepalli Radhakrishnan, *Indian Philosophy,* 2nd ed., 2 vols. (London: George Allen, 1929), I, 519.

137. Sharpe, *Universal Gita,* 85–86.

138. For general information, see Sharpe, *Universal Gita,* 32–46. In the conflicts between Christians and Hindus in the first half of the nineteenth century, the *Bhagavad Gita* seems not to have played any role (see Richard Fox Young, *Resistant Hinduism: Sanskrit Sources on Anti-Christian Apologetics in Early Nineteenth-Century India* [Vienna: Institut für Indologie der Universität Wien, 1981]). Even a reception of the Lorinser's thesis that the *Bhagavad Gita* was influenced by Christianity is hardly visible in missionary literature (see Sharpe, *Universal Gita,* 49). However, compare the interesting argument by the Indian theologian Ram Chandra Bose on the *Bhagavad Gita* (see Ram Chandra Bose, *Hindu Philosophy Popularly Explained* [New York: Funk and Wagnalls, 1884], 399–420).

139. Das, "Rolle der Bhagavadgita," 102–3.

140. Ibid.

141. Hans Harder, *Bankimchandra Chattopadhyaya's Srimadbhagavadgita: Translation and Analysis* (New Delhi: Manohar, 2001).

142. Ibid., 173–75.

143. Asit Kumar Bandyopadhyay, "Bankimchandra and Neo-Puranism," in *Bankimchandra Chatterjee: Essays in Perspective,* ed. Bhabatosh Chatterjee (New Delhi: Sahitya Akademi, 1994).

144. From an article of the journal *Kesari* (April 8, 1905), translated from the Marathi original in "Indian Home Proceedings" (London: Indian Office Records), Public Proceeding No. 356 (May 1898). Quoted from John R. McLane, ed., *The Political Awakening in India* (Englewood Cliffs, NJ: Prentice Hall, 1970), 56. See also Sharpe, *Universal Gita,* 71.

145. Lederle, *Philosophical Trends*, 246–78; Robert W. Stevenson, "Tilak and the Bhagavadgita's Doctrine of Karmayoga," in *Modern Indian Interpreters of the Bhagavadgita*, ed. Robert N. Minor (Albany: State University of New York Press, 1986).

146. McLane, *Political Awakening*, 61–69; Sharpe, *Universal Gita*, 72, 81–82; Minor, *Modern Indian Interpreters*, 223; Varuni Bhatia, "Sisir's Tears: Bhakti and Belonging in Colonial Bengal," *International Journal of Hindu Studies* 21 (2017): 5, 13–14.

147. Sharpe, *Universal Gita*, 77–83; Alex Wolfers, "The Making of an Avatar: Reading Sri Aurobindo Ghose (1872–1950)," *Religions of South Asia* 11, no. 2-3 (2017); On the role of Ghose, see also the chapter by Hans Martin Krämer in this volume.

148. On the following, see Harold W. French, "Swami Vivekananda's Use of the Bhagavadgita," in *Modern Indian Interpreters of the Bhagavadgita*, ed. Robert N. Minor (Albany: State University of New York Press, 1986).

149. Vivekananda, *Complete Works*, I, 40 (Karma-Yoga).

150. Vivekananda, *Complete Works*, III, 242 (1897?).

151. Neufeldt, "Lesson in Allegory," 25–28.

152. Gandhi, *Life and Works*, vol. 46, 172.

153. Bergunder, "Experiments"; Michael Bergunder, " 'Religion' and 'Science' within a Global Religious History," *Aries* 16 (2016).

154. Kocku von Stuckrad, "Western Esotericism: Towards an Integrative Model of Interpretation," *Religion* 35 (2005); Kennet Granholm, "Locating the West: Problematizing the Western in Western Esotericism and Occultism," in *Occultism in a Global Perspective*, ed. Henrik Bogdan and Gordan Djurdjevic (London: Acumen, 2013); Egil Asprem, "Beyond the West: Towards a New Comparativism in the Study of Esotericism," *Correspondences* 2, no. 1 (2014); Kocku von Stuckrad, *The Scientification of Religion: An Historical Study of Discursive Change, 1800–2000* (Berlin: De Gruyter, 2014).

155. Nicholas Goodrick-Clarke, *The Western Esoteric Traditions: A Historical Introduction* (New York: Oxford University Press, 2008); Jeffrey D. Lavoie, *The Theosophical Society: The History of a Spiritualist Movement* (Boca Raton, FL: Brown Walker Press, 2013); Wouter J. Hanegraaff, *Western Esotericism: A Guide for the Perplexed* (London: Bloomsbury, 2013); Olav Hammer and Mikael Rothstein, eds., *Handbook of the Theosophical Current* (Leiden: Brill, 2013); see also the chapter by Wouter J. Hanegraaff in this volume.

156. Nicholas Goodrick-Clarke, "The Theosophical Society, Orientalism, and the 'Mystic East': Western Esotericism and Eastern Religion in Theosophy," *Theosophical History* 13, no. 3 (2007); Isaac Lubelsky, *Celestial India: Madame Blavatsky and the Birth of Indian Nationalism* (Sheffield: Equinox, 2012).

157. Michael Bergunder, "What Is Religion? The Unexplained Subject Matter of Religious Studies," *Method and Theory in the Study of Religion* 26 (2014).

158. Ibid., 275–280.

159. Ibid., 277–278.

160. Homi K. Bhabha, *The Location of Culture* (London: Routledge, 1994); Gayatri Chakravorty Spivak, "Can the Subaltern Speak?," in *Colonial Discourse and Post-Colonial Theory: A Reader*, ed. Patrick Williams and Laura Chrisman (New York: Columbia University Press, 1994 [1988]).

161. Sebastian Conrad and Shalini Randeria, "Einleitung: Geteilte Geschichten—Europa in einer postkolonialen Welt," in *Jenseits des Eurozentrismus: Postkoloniale Perspektiven in den Geschichts- und Kulturwissenschaften*, ed. Sebastian Conrad and Shalini Randeria (Frankfurt am Main: Campus, 2002), 17.

162. Goodrick-Clarke, *Western Esoteric Traditions*; Hanegraaff, *Western Esotericism*.

163. Bergunder, "What Is Religion?," 269–273.

164. Dalmia, *Nationalisation*.

165. The Hindi versions by Byas Ji (Lucknow 1880), Umadatta Tripathi (Lucknow 1888), Bhimasena Sharma (Etawah 1897), Ramsvarupa Sharma (Lahore 1897), and Laskhminarayan (Agra 1898) are in particular need of analysis. Important translations into Bengali are those by Hitlal Misra, Kedarnath Datta (= Bhaktivinoda Thakur [1838–1914]), Bhudharcandra Chattopadhyay, Krishnaprasanna Sen, and Gaurisankara Sarman Tarkavisa Bhatta, Kali Prasanna Simha, et al. Translations of the *Bhagavad Gita* into Marathi include those by Moropanta (Bombay 1864), Ramcandra Sastri Modak (Bombay 1851), Vamana (Bombay 1861, Ratnagiri 1862), and Muktesvara (Bombay 1861), and a version in Gujarati is available by Kavi Dhandas (Ahmedabad, Bombay 1850). See Adolf Holtzmann, *Die neunzehn Bücher des Mahabharata* (Kiel: Haeseler, 1893), 129–30; Harder, *Srimadbhagavadgita*, 161; Ulrike Stark, *An Empire of Books: The Naval Kishore Press and the Diffusion of the Printed Word in Colonial India* (Ranikhet: Permanent Black, 2007). (My thanks go to Ulrike Stark [Chicago] for important bibliographical suggestions.) See also Callewaert & Hemraj, *Bhagavadgītānuvāda*, 111–233.

166. Angelika Malinar, *Rajavidya: Das königliche Wissen um Herrschaft und Verzicht: Studien zur Bhagavadgita* (Wiesbaden: Harrassowitz, 1996), 17. In this phase, there is a discussion about whether the *Bhagavad Gita* may originally have been a purely theist text, which was only later reworked into a Brahmanistic-"pantheistic" one (e.g., Adolf Holtzmann, 1891; Richard Garbe 1905), whether it may have been the other way around (Edward Washburn, 1895; Paul Deussen/Otto Strauss, 1906), or whether both may have already been fused originally (Hermann Jacobi 1918).

References

Andrews, C. F. *The Renaissance in India: Its Missionary Impact*. London: Baptist Missionary Society, 1912.

Arnold, Edwin. *The Song Celestial, or Bhagavad-Gîtâ*. Boston: Roberts Brothers, 1885.

Asprem, Egil. "Beyond the West: Towards a New Comparativism in the Study of Esotericism." *Correspondences* 2, no. 1 (2014): 3–33.

Baier, Karl. "Theosophical Orientalism and the Structures of Intercultural Transfer: Annotations on the Appropriation of the Cakras in Early Theosophy." In *Theosophical Appropriations: Esotericism, Kabbalah, and the Transformation of Traditions*, edited by Julie Chajes and Boaz Huss, 309–54. Beer Sheva: Ben-Gurion University of the Negev Press, 2016.

Bandyopadhyay, Asit Kumar. "Bankimchandra and Neo-Puranism." In *Bankimchandra Chatterjee. Essays in Perspective*, edited by Bhabatosh Chatterjee, 246–59. New Delhi: Sahitya Akademi, 1994.

Barker, Alfred Trevor, ed. *The Mahatma Letters To A. P. Sinnett from the Mahatmas M. & K. H.: Transcribed and Compiled by A. T. Barker, in Chronological Sequence Arranged and Edited by Vicente Hao Chin, Jr*. Chennai: Theosophical Publishing House, 1998.

Barz, Richard. *The Bhakti Sect of Vallabhācārya*. Faridabad: Thomson Press, 1976.

Baumfieldt, Vivienne Marie. "Swami Vivekananda's Practical Vedanta." PhD diss., University of Newcastle upon Tyne, 1991.

Bergunder, Michael. "What Is Religion? The Unexplained Subject Matter of Religious Studies." *Method and Theory in the Study of Religion* 26 (2014): 246–86.

———. "Experiments with Theosophical Truth: Gandhi, Esotericism, and Global Religious History." *Journal of the American Academy of Religion* 82 (2014): 398–426.

———. "'Religion' and 'Science' within a Global Religious History." *Aries* 16 (2016): 86–141.

Bhabha, Homi K. *The Location of Culture*. London: Routledge, 1994.

Bharati, Agehananda. "The Hindu Renaissance and Its Apologetic Patterns." *Journal of Asian Studies* 29 (1970): 267–87.

Bhatia, Varuni. "Sisir's Tears: Bhakti and Belonging in Colonial Bengal." *International Journal of Hindu Studies* 21 (2017): 1–24.

Blavatsky, Helena Petrovna. *Collected Writings*. 15 vols. Wheaton, IL: The Theosophical Publishing House, 1950–1991.

———. *Isis Unveiled*. New Edition, Revised and Corrected, and with Additional Material, Collected Writings 1877, 2 vols. Wheaton, IL: The Theosophical Publishing House, 1972.

———. *The Secret Doctrine*. Seventh (Adyar) Edition, Collected Writings 1888, 3 vols. Adyar, Madras: The Theosophical Publishing House, 1979 [1888].

Bose, Ram Chandra. *Hindu Philosophy Popularly Explained*. New York: Funk and Wagnalls, 1884.

Burke, Marie Louise. *Swami Vivekananda in the West: New Discoveries*. 6 vols. Calcutta: Advaita Ashrama, 1984.

Burnouf, Émile. *La Bhagavad-Gîtâ ou le chant du bienheureux: poeme Indien*. Paris: B. Duprat, 1861.

Burton, Adrian P. "Temples, Texts, and Taxes: The Bhagavad-gītā and Politico—Religious Identity of the Caitanya Sect." PhD diss., The Australian National University, 2000.

Callewaert, Winand M., and Shilanand Hemraj. *Bhagavadgītānuvāda: A Study in Transcultural Translation*. Ranchi: Satya Bharati Publications, 1983.

Chatterji, Mohini M. *The Bhagavad Gita or the Lord's Lay, with Commentary and Notes, as Well as Reference to the Christian Scriptures*. 2nd ed. Boston: Houghton Mifflin Company, 1888 [1887].

Christy, Arthur. *The Orient in American Transcendentalism: A Study of Emerson, Thoreau, and Alcott*. New York: Columbia University Press, 1932.

Clark, Matthew. *The Daśanāmī-Saṃnyāsīs: The Integration of Ascetic Lineages into an Order*. Leiden: Brill, 2006.

Clarke, James Freeman. *Ten Great Religions: An Essay in Comparative Theology*. Boston: J. R. Osgood, 1871.

Colas, Gérard. "History of the Vaiṣṇava Traditions: An Esquisse." In *The Blackwell Companion to Hinduism*, edited by Gavin Flood, 229–70. Oxford: Blackwell, 2003.

Conrad, Sebastian, and Shalini Randeria. "Einleitung: Geteilte Geschichten—Europa in einer postkolonialen Welt." In *Jenseits des Eurozentrismus: Postkoloniale Perspektiven in den Geschichts- und Kulturwissenschaften*, edited by Sebastian Conrad and Shalini Randeria, 9–49. Frankfurt am Main: Campus, 2002.

Conway, Moncure. *The Sacred Anthology: A Book of Ethnic Scriptures*. New York: H. Holt, 1874.

Dalmia, Vasudha. *The Nationalisation of Hindu Traditions: Bharatendu Harishchandra and Nineteenth-century Banaras*. Delhi: Oxford University Press, 1997.

Das, Rahul Peter. "Die Rolle der Bhagavadgita im indischen Nationalismus der Kolonialzeit." In *Religiöser Text und soziale Struktur*, edited by Walter Beltz and Jürgen Tubach, 93–109. Halle: Universität Halle, 2001.

Davies, John. *Hindu Philosophy: The Bhagavad Gita or The Sacred Lay. A Sanskrit Philosophical Poem*. Translated, with Notes, 4th ed. London: Kegan Paul, Trench, Trübner, 1907 [1882].

Davis, Richard H. *The Bhagavad Gita: A Biography*. Princeton: Princeton University Press, 2015.

Dowson, John. *A Classical Dictionary of Hindu Mythology and Religion, Geography, History and Literature*. London: Trübner, 1879.

Eek, Sven, ed. *Dâmodar and the Pioneers of the Theosophical Movement*. Madras: Theosophical Publishing House, 1965.

Ellinwood, Frank F. *Oriental Religions and Christianity: A Course of Lectures Delivered on the Ely Foundation, before the Students of Union Theological Seminary, New York 1891*. London: Nisbet, 1892.

Entwistle, Alan W. *Braj, Centre of Krishna Pilgrimage*. Groningen: Egbert Forsten, 1987.
French, Harold W. "Swami Vivekananda's Use of the Bhagavadgita." In *Modern Indian Interpreters of the Bhagavadgita*, edited by Robert N. Minor, 131–46. Albany: State University of New York Press, 1986.
Gandhi, M. K. *The Life and Works of Mahatma Gandhi*. 100 volumes, CD-ROM Version edited by Ministry of Information and Broadcasting, Government of India. New Delhi: Icon Softec, 1999.
Garbe, Richard. *Indien und das Christentum: Eine Untersuchung der religionsgeschichtlichen Zusammenhänge*. Tübingen: Mohr, 1914.
Glasenapp, Helmuth von. "Die Lehre Vallabhâcâryas." *Zeitschrift für Indologie und Iranistik* 9 (1933/34): 268–330.
Goodrick-Clarke, Nicholas. "The Theosophical Society, Orientalism, and the 'Mystic East': Western Esotericism and Eastern Religion in Theosophy." *Theosophical History* 13, no. 3 (2007): 3–28.
———. *The Western Esoteric Traditions: A Historical Introduction*. New York: Oxford University Press, 2008.
Granholm, Kennet. "Locating the West: Problematizing the *Western* in Western Esotericism and Occultism." In *Occultism in a Global Perspective*, edited by Henrik Bogdan and Gordan Djurdjevic, 17–36. London: Acumen, 2013.
Halbfass, Wilhelm. *India and Europe: An Essay of Philosophical Understanding*. Delhi: Motilal Barnarsidass, 1990.
Hammer, Olav, and Mikael Rothstein, eds. *Handbook of the Theosophical Current*. Leiden: Brill, 2013.
Hanegraaff, Wouter J. *Western Esotericism: A Guide for the Perplexed*. London: Bloomsbury, 2013.
Harder, Hans. *Bankimchandra Chattopadhyaya's Srimadbhagavadgita: Translation and Analysis*. New Delhi: Manohar, 2001.
Heimsath, Charles H. *Indian Nationalism and Hindu Social Reform*. Princeton: Princeton University Press, 1964.
Herling, Bradley L. *The German Gita: Hermeneutics and Discipline in the German Reception of Indian Thought, 1778–1831*. London: Routledge, 2006.
Holtzmann, Adolf. *Die neunzehn Bücher des Mahabharata*. Kiel: Haeseler, 1893.
Horstmann, Monika. *Der Zusammenhalt der Welt: Religiöse Herrschaftslegitimation und Religionspolitik Mahārāja Savāī Jaisinghs (1700–1743)*. Wiesbaden: Harrassowitz, 2009.
Huber, Friedrich. *Die Bhagavadgita in der neueren indischen Auslegung und in der Begegnung mit dem christlichen Glauben*. Erlangen: Verlag der Ev.-Luth. Mission, 1991.
———. "Religion und Politik in Indien." *Zeitschrift für Mission* 17, no. 2 (1991): 74–86.
Hummel, Reinhart. *Indische Mission und neue Frömmigkeit im Westen*. Stuttgart: Kohlhammer, 1980.

Jackson, Carl T. "The Orient in Post-Bellum American Thought: Three Pioneer Popularizers." *American Quarterly* 22 (1970): 67–81.

———. *The Oriental Religions and American Thought: Nineteenth-Century Explorations*. Westport: Greenwood Press, 1981.

———. *Vedanta and the West: The Ramakrishna Movement in the United States*. Bloomington: Indiana University Press, 1994.

Johnson, Samuel. *Samuel Johnson: Oriental Religions and Their Relation to Universal Religion (India, China, Persia)*. 3 vols. Boston: J.R. Osgood, 1872.

Jordens, J. T. F. *Dayānanda Sarasvatī: His Life and Ideas*. Delhi: Oxford University Press, 1978.

———. "Gandhi and the Bhagavadgita." In *Modern Indian Interpreters of the Bhagavadgita*, edited by Robert N. Minor, 88–109. Albany: State University of New York Press, 1986.

Kapila, Shruti, and Faisal Fatehali Devji. *Political Thought in Action: The Bhagavad Gita and Modern India*. Cambridge: Cambridge University Press, 2013.

Kiehnle, Catharina. *Jñāndev Studies I and II. Songs on Yoga: Texts and Teachings of the Mahārāṣṭrian Nāths*. Stuttgart: Franz Steiner, 1997.

Killingley, Dermot. "Rammohun Roy's Interpretation of the Vedanta." PhD diss., University of London, 1977.

———. *Rammohun Roy in Hindu and Christian Tradition: The Teape Lectures 1990*. Newcastle upon Tyne: Grevatt and Grevatt, 1993.

King, Richard. *Orientalism and Religion: Postcolonial Theory, India and "The Mystic East."* London: Routledge, 1999.

King, Ursula. "The Iconography of the Bhagavad Gita." *Journal of Dharma* 7, no. 2 (1982): 146–63.

Kronenbitter, Günter, ed. *Friedrich Gentz: Gesammelte Schriften*. Vol. VIII, 5. Hildesheim: Olms-Weidmann, 2002.

Lavoie, Jeffrey D. *The Theosophical Society: The History of a Spiritualist Movement*. Boca Raton, FL: Brown Walker Press, 2013.

Lederle, Matthew. *Philosophical Trends in Modern Maharashtra*. Bombay: Popular Prakashan, 1976.

Lloyd, Mary. "Sir Charles Wilkin, 1749–1836." In *Report for the Year 1978*, edited by India Office Library and Records. London: Foreign and Commonwealth Office, 1979.

Lubelsky, Isaac. *Celestial India: Madame Blavatsky and the Birth of Indian Nationalism*. Sheffield: Equinox, 2012.

Macdonell, Arthur Anthony. *A History of Sanskrit Literature*. London: W. Heinemann, 1900.

Malinar, Angelika. *Rajavidya: Das königliche Wissen um Herrschaft und Verzicht: Studien zur Bhagavadgita*. Wiesbaden: Harrassowitz, 1996.

Marshall, P. J., ed. *The British Discovery of Hinduism in the 18th Century*. Cambridge: Cambridge University Press, 1970.

McLane, John R., ed. *The Political Awakening in India*. Englewood Cliffs, NJ: Prentice Hall, 1970.
Meade, Marion. *Madame Blavatsky: The Woman behind the Myth*. New York: G. P. Putnam's Sons, 1980.
Minkowski, Christopher. "Advaita Vedānta in Early Modern History." *South Asian History and Culture* 2 (2011): 205–31.
Minor, Robert N., ed. *Modern Indian Interpreters of the Bhagavadgita*. Albany: State University of New York Press, 1986.
Müller, Friedrich Max. *India: What Can It Teach Us?* New York: Funk & Wagnalls, 1883.
———. *Natural Religion: The Gifford-Lectures Delivered Before the University of Glasgow in 1888*. London: Longmans, Green & Co., 1889.
Muthanna, I. M. *Mother Besant and Mahatma Gandhi*. Vellore: Thenpulam Publishers, 1986.
Mylius, Klaus. *Geschichte der Literatur im alten Indien*. Leipzig: Reclam, 1983.
Natesan, G. A., ed. *Kashinath Trimbak Telang: A Sketch of His Life and Career*. Madras: G. A. Natesan, s.a.
Nehring, Andreas. "Religion und Kultur: Zur Beschreibung einer Differenz." In *Religious Turns—Turning Religions: Veränderte kulturelle Diskurse—Neue religiöse Wissensformen*, edited by Andreas Nehring and Joachim Valentin, 11–31. Stuttgart: Kohlhammer, 2008.
Neufeldt, Ronald W. "A Lesson in Allegory: Theosophical Interpretations of the Bhagavadgita." In *Modern Indian Interpreters of the Bhagavadgita*, edited by Robert N. Minor, 11–33, 230–32. Albany: State University of New York Press, 1986.
O'Connell, Joseph Thomas. "Caitanya's Followers and the Bhagavad-Gita: A Case Study in the Bhakti and the Secular." In *Hinduism: New Essays in the History of Religions*, edited by Bardwell L. Smith, 33–52. Leiden: Brill, 1976.
Olcott, Henry Steel. "Tookaram Tatya." *The Theosophist* 19 (1898): 627–28.
Oxley, William. *The Philosophy of Spirit, Illustrated by a New Version of the Bhagavat Gítá, an Episode of the Mahabharat, One of the Epic Poems of Ancient India*. Glasgow: Hay Nisbet, 1881.
Parpola, Asko. "Publications of the Great Indologist Fr. Albrecht Weber." *Studia Orientalia* 97 (2003): 189–219.
Radhakrishnan, Sarvepalli. *Indian Philosophy*. 2nd ed., 2 vols. London: George Allen, 1929.
Ramanujachary, N. C. *A Lonely Disciple: Monograph on T. Subba Row, 1856–90*. Madras: Theosophical Publishing House, 1993.
Rangachari, Dewan Bahadur K. *The Sri Vaishnava Brahmans*. Madras: Madras Government Museum, 1931.
Robinson, Catherine A. *Interpretations of the Bhagavad-Gita and Images of the Hindu Tradition: The Song of the Lord*. London: Routledge, 2006.

Rocher, Rosane. *Orientalism, Poetry, and the Millennium: The Checkered Life of Nathaniel Brassey Halhed, 1751–1830*. Delhi: Motilal Barnasidass, 1983.

Rusk, Ralph L. *The Letters of Ralph Waldo Emerson*. 6 vols. New York: Columbia University Press, 1939.

Sastry, Alladi Mahaveda. *The Bhagavad Gita with the Commentary of Sri Sankaracharya: Translated from the Original Sanskrit into English*. Madras: Samata Books, 1977 [1897].

Sharpe, Eric J. *The Universal Gita: Western Images of the Bhagavad Gita: A Bicentennary Survey*. La Salle, IL: Open Court, 1985.

Sinha, Mishka. "Corrigibility, Allegory, Universality: A History of Gita's Transnational Reception, 1785–1945." *Modern Intellectual History* 7 (2010): 297–317.

Skyhawk, Hugh van. *Bhakti und Bhakta: Religionsgeschichtliche Untersuchungen zum Heilsbegriff und zur religiösen Umwelt des Śrī Sant Ekanāth*. Wiesbaden: Steiner, 1990.

Spivak, Gayatri Chakravorty. "Can the Subaltern Speak?" In *Colonial Discourse and Post-Colonial Theory: A Reader*, edited by Patrick Williams and Laura Chrisman, 66–111. New York: Columbia University Press, 1994 [1988].

Stark, Ulrike. *An Empire of Books: The Naval Kishore Press and the Diffusion of the Printed Word in Colonial India*. Ranikhet: Permanent Black, 2007.

Stevenson, Robert W. "Tilak and the Bhagavadgita's Doctrine of Karmayoga." In *Modern Indian Interpreters of the Bhagavadgita*, edited by Robert N. Minor, 44–60. Albany: State University of New York Press, 1986.

Stewart, Tony K. *The Final Word: The Caitanya Caritāmṛta and the Grammar of Religious Tradition*. New York: Oxford University Press, 2010.

Stuckrad, Kocku von. "Western Esotericism: Towards an Integrative Model of Interpretation." *Religion* 35 (2005): 78–97.

———. *The Scientification of Religion: An Historical Study of Discursive Change, 1800–2000*. Berlin: De Gruyter, 2014.

Subba Row, T. *Philosophy of the Bhagavad-Gita: Four Lectures Delivered at the Eleventh Annual Convention of the Theosophical Society, Held at Adyar, on December 27, 28, 29 and 30, 1886*. 2nd ed., Madras: Theosophical Publishing House, 1994 [1912].

Telang, Kashinath Trimbak. *The Bhagavadgîtâ with the Sanatsujâtîya and the Anugîtâ*. Sacred Books of the East, vol. 7. Oxford: Clarendon, 1882.

Thaker, Dhirubhai. *Manilal Dvivedi*. New Delhi: Sahitya Academy, 1983.

Thomas, P. J. *20th Century Interpretations of Bhagavadgita: Tilak, Gandhi and Aurobindo*. Delhi: I. S. P. C. K, 1987.

Thomson, J. Cockburn. *The Bhagavad-Gita, or The Sacred Lay: A New Edition of the Sanskrit Text, with a Vocabulary*. Hertford: Stephen Austin, 1855.

———. *The Bhagavad-Gita, or a Discourse Between Krishna and Arjuna on Divine Matters: A Sanskrit Philosophical Poem, Translated, with Copious Notes, an*

Introduction on Sanskrit Philosophy, and Other Matters. Hertford: Stephen Austin, 1855.

Thoreau, Henry D. *Walden*. Edited by J. Lyndon Shanley. Princeton: Princeton University Press, 1971.

"Traces in the Bhagavad-Gītā of Christian Writings and Ideas: From the Appendix to Dr. Lorinser's Bhagavad-Gītā." *Indian Antiquary* 2 (1873): 283–96.

Tulpule, Shankar Gopal. *Classical Marāṭhī Literature from the Beginning to A. D. 1818*. Wiesbaden: Harrassowitz, 1979.

Tweed, Thomas A. *The American Encounter with Buddhism, 1844–1912: Victorian Culture and the Limits of Dissent*. 2nd ed. Chapel Hill: University of North Carolina Press, 2000 [1992].

Versluis, Arthur. *American Transcendentalism and Asian Religions*. New York: Oxford University Press, 1993.

Vivekananda, Swami. *The Complete Works of Swami Vivekananda*. Mayavati Memorial Edition (Reprint), 9 vols. Calcutta: Advaita Ashrama, 1959–97.

Wolfers, Alex. "The Making of an Avatar: Reading Sri Aurobindo Ghose (1872–1950)." *Religions of South Asia* 11, no. 2–3 (2017): 274–341.

World Missionary Conference, ed. *Report of Commission IV: The Missionary Message in Relation to Non-Christian Religions. With Supplement: Presentation and Discussion of the Report in the Conference on 18th June 1910*. Edinburgh: Oliphant, 1910.

Wright, Brooks. *Interpreter of Buddhism to the West: Sir Edwin Arnold*. New York: Bookman, 1957.

Young, Richard Fox. *Resistant Hinduism: Sanskrit Sources on Anti-Christian Apologetics in Early Nineteenth-Century India*. Vienna: Institut für Indologie der Universität Wien, 1981.

Chapter 3

Theosophying the Vietnamese Religious Landscape

A Circulatory History of a Western Esoteric Movement in Southern Vietnam

Jérémy Jammes

Introduction

In his book *Đạo Giáo, hình nhi thượng học* ("Daoist religion, metaphysics"), subtitled into French as "Daoism: Esoteric teaching," Nguyễn Hữu Đắc (1935) attempted a translation into Vietnamese of the book *La Voie Rationnelle* (1907) by the French occultist Albert de Pouvourville (1861–1940). Nguyễn Hữu Đắc was a follower of a redemptive society in Saigon (Minh Lý Đạo, Ch. Minglidao) and the maternal cousin of Lê Văn Trung, the "interim pope of Caodaism" (following the translation given by Francophone Caodaists)—a newborn religion that appeared in the 1920s in Cochinchina (Southern Vietnam) and the third-most-populous religion of present-day Vietnam. In this book, he proposed a "rationalist" analysis of Daoism, presenting such alchemical practices as the "science of the spirit and the psychology of dharma" (*khoa thần trí tâm lý diệu pháp*) and discussing the "science of esoteric practice" (*khoa pháp môn bí truyền học*). In his argumentation, he directly refers to the Theosophical Society as the "Religious Association of Studies on Communication with Spirits" (Vietnamese *Hội giáo Thông thần học*, or Ch. *huijiao tongshenxue*) and to its authors, notably Charles W. Leadbeater. He presented Caodaism (Cao

Đài religion) and Theosophy as the contemporary catalysts of all of the "religious ways" (*đạo*, Ch. *dao*) in the world, the former from the East, the latter from the West.[1]

Eighty years later, from January 5 to 16, 2015, Mrs. Trần Thị Kim Diệu (b. 1949) conducted a two-week session for some sixty students of the School of the Wisdom in Adyar at the International Headquarters of the Theosophical Society. The theme of her session was "The Science of Theosophy: Foundation and Practice," analyzing Blavatsky's conceptual Diagram of Meditation.[2] In January 2016, after the 140th International Convention, she lectured at the School of Wisdom on "Chinese philosophies" (including Daoism, Confucianism, and Chan Buddhism). Of Vietnamese descent, she spoke as the Chairperson of the European Federation of the Theosophical Society.[3] Moreover, she succeeded Phan Chơn Tôn (1930–2009), also Vietnamese, as General Secretary of the French Section (1992–1997).[4] Both have been prolific authors in the journal *Le Lotus Bleu*: Phan Chơn Tôn published about 160 articles between 1959 and 2014, and Mrs. Trần about 120 articles between 1980 and 2015.

The emergence of the Theosophical Society in the world of Vietnamese beliefs coincided with the colonial period, and "it strikes root mostly among the cultured classes of the natives (the 'Annamites') of that land," according to the General Secretary of the French Section of the Theosophical Society, Charles Blech, who wrote in 1930 regarding the foundation of the Cochinchinese lodge two years earlier.[5] The *Thông thiên học* association naturally plunges us back into this period of interreligious contact: immersed in the movement to reform Buddhism at the beginning of the century, that association claimed membership to the international network of the Theosophical Society and, since being banned in Vietnam in 1975, continues to exist within Vietnamese communities overseas. The prolific products of its Vietnamese actors were rationalist insertions into the dialogues both between representatives of civilizations and between religions, guided as much by a concern for social reform as by a quest for "cultural synthesis," aestheticism, and symbolic comparativism. The conquest of Indochina enabled the expansion of the cultural horizon of the esoteric thinkers and Western occultists of the nineteenth century, further broadening the search for the spiritual treasures of Asia, which at that time focused on the worlds of India and China.[6]

A local religious substrate persisted in the colonial period, nourished by the more or less esoteric codes, values, and symbols that mainly came from the traditions of the three teachings of Confucianism, Buddhism, and Daoism (*Tam Giáo*, Ch. *sanjiao*). But one would be wrong to cling to this notion of a mystical Orient, unchanging throughout the centuries. As Edward Said has noted, a major strand of Western academic discourse has for far too long described "the Orient" as impermeable and unreceptive to change—an immutable Orient, closed in on itself, an essentially religious and wholly self-sufficient Orient.[7] Against such a cloistered depiction, where the Three Doctrines play the role of a single engine, I instead opt for a dynamic, circulatory, and trans-Asian reading of the "Vietnamese Orient" that interacts with philosophies and practices external to Vietnamese culture.

Only a few contemporary authors have mentioned—and those almost anecdotally—that the "works of [the three Spiritists] Flammarion, Allan Kardec, Léon Denis and [the Theosophist] Colonel Olcott have been introduced into Indochina, and have been read, translated, and published."[8] At the same time, Cochinchina was witnessing the appearance of collective impulses in favor of a reform of Buddhism and, largely speaking, of the *Tam Giáo* matrix. These new Sino-Vietnamese or Vietnamese reformed (and reforming) religious movements were the Minh redemptive societies, Caodaism, and Hòa Hảo Buddhism—all of which persist to this day.

The role of the Theosophical Society in the reformist impulse of both Buddhism in Ceylon and politics in India is evident in both historical and ethnographic source material. One of the main sociological characteristics of the Theosophical undertaking is that it was propelled by anti-clerical and sometimes anti-Christian motivations, while fueling a discourse of social and political emancipation.[9] This chapter aims to examine the place and role of the Theosophical Society—the *Thông thiên học* in Vietnamese (Ch. *tongtianxue*, literally "studies of communications with the heavens")[10]—within these reformist religious impulses in Cochinchina.

In general, the implementation of this Western occultist phenomenon in Vietnam has not been studied in depth because of the lack of reliable sources, and also because of the discretion of the members of these circles, as well as their strategies of cultivating secrets about their activity and life. In fact, an academic investigation of the Theosophical circles in Vietnamese contexts and their relational modalities with the colonized populations has so far never been formulated or even mapped out. Even if the researcher is confronted with a lack of rigorous academic sources and simultaneously with a maze of hermetic concepts, secret practices, enigmatic personas, and all kinds of historical or metaphysical intrigues, it is nevertheless possible to find a path through this maze of occultist culture by bringing together different sources of information.[11]

The Theosophical revitalization and rationalization of ancient Buddhist "traditions," which were accepted and considered as representative of ancient pre-colonial values by a large part of the colonized population, led Richard Gombrich and Gananath Obeyesekere[12] to speak of a "transformed Buddhism"—they go so far as to refer to a *Protestant Buddhism*—in which the progressive discourses emanating from the organizational structure of Adyar and of the Theosophical Society in general played a key reforming role. Following these authors, the Theosophical network can be considered a focal point of vitality in Ceylon and in India stimulated by the colonial scientific presence. Becoming a source of hope for the Ceylonese and Indian colonized population, the Theosophical network that was established on colonized lands is a necessary object of study for any researcher interested in political-religious reform movements and disputes.

This study thus naturally turns to the Vietnamese religious situation under colonization, and in particular to its Buddhist institutions—privileged grounds for Theosophical reformist circles—to examine the establishment of the first Theosophical association in Saigon on October 10, 1928.[13] The approximate number of members was fewer than thirty people. In 1952, the first Vietnamese National Section was created, and since then the Vietnamese members have had to report their activities directly to Adyar without the intervention of the French Section (as was previously the case). Once founded, this Vietnamese National Section counted 135 members, and 63 more the year after. Prior to the mass Buddhist protests of the summer of 1963 (against their persecution by the South Vietnamese regime led by Ngô Đình Diệm), the Vietnamese section counted 667 members and 16 lodges. This figure was almost the same between 1961 and 1964, the Theosophical Society esoteric discourse being perhaps too distant from the popular protest and political claims. With the multiplication of philanthropic activities in wartime, the number of Theosophical Society members increased, especially after 1968, and by 1974 it had risen to 1,338 of the 17 million inhabitants of South Vietnam.[14] Of the nineteen Vietnamese lodges, eight were in Saigon, and eleven were in the former southern provinces of Cochinchina and Annam.

I retrace the path and characteristics of the process of the Theosophical Society's spread in Cochinchina, starting from its first official events in the 1920s until it was banned in 1975 on the orders of the new socialist regime. I then point out the different means of dissemination that the Theosophists put in place to establish themselves in Cochinchina. My research reveals how, through the unique circulations of people, goods, and ideas between Vietnam, India, and the West, but also between lay Buddhists, Freemasons, and "reformed Buddhists" (Caodaists, Minh Lý members, etc.), the issue of Theosophical development in South Vietnam and its fertilization under colonial rule may be examined in a new light. This study thus highlights a certain number of people, places, and activities that gradually allowed the Theosophical Society to take part in the reform of Buddhism in twentieth-century Vietnam.

1. The Establishment of the Theosophical Society in Cochinchina (1928–1975)

The Beginning

The years between the 1890s and 1930s saw Confucianism suffer an increasing loss of authority in Indochinese society under French influence. Concurrently, Buddhist pagodas struggled with a considerable loss of interest, which sparked a spirit—and program—of reform among a handful of monks. Catholicism, meanwhile, witnessed a resurgence of followers, facilitated by the goodwill of the colonial authorities. In fact, these decades constituted an exceptional period of transition and recomposition within the religious domain of Vietnamese society.

A first impulse to reform Buddhism began in approximately 1898 with the Cochinchinese Reverend Thiện Quảng's (life: 1862–1911) travels to Tibet, Burma, and India. His trip provided a fertile ground for future affiliation with Theosophical networks in Ceylon and India.[15] A more general movement to reform Buddhism developed in Cochinchina in approximately 1923 on the initiative of the Reverends (*hòa thượng*) Huệ Quang, Khánh Hòa, and Khánh Anh.[16] In particular, this so-called Buddhist Revival movement (*chấn hưng Phật giáo*) aimed to purify dogma, improve the training of monks, restore discipline in monastic circles, translate and edit religious texts into the newly formed romanized writing of the Vietnamese language (the *quốc ngữ*), and print and publish journals.

From a sociological perspective, the movement applied itself to turning the pagoda into a place of worship and assembly, redefining individual practices and community ties by developing a homogenous and unified community that provided an increasing amount of space for the role of women and Buddhist international service organizations in particular.[17] If there is one fact that needs to be emphasized concerning this period, it is Caodaism's self-proclamation as a "reformed Buddhism" in September 1926—a combination of family networks, patron-client ties, political interests, millenarian discourse, and the coordination of spirit-medium messages by a developed sacerdotal hierarchy allowed for rapid and significant waves of Cao Đài conversions among the peasantry and the members of the French- or Chinese-educated indigenous religious, economic, and political elite in Cochinchina and Annam.[18]

The 1920s also marked the beginning of the Theosophical Society's establishment in Cochinchina[19] at the instigation of Phạm Ngọc Đa (his pen name was Bạch Liên), a school principal of a girls' elementary school in the remote town of Châu Đốc on the Cambodian border. Bạch Liên was admitted as a member of the Theosophical Society of France on January 1, 1925.[20] Given the legislative situation in force at the time, French and Vietnamese members of the Theosophical Society in French Indochina were attached to the French Section until 1952, as I have already mentioned above. It was a French citizen, Georges Raimond, who laid the first stone of the Theosophical Society in Cochinchina. An engineer from the École Polytechnique, he was also known as an executive of the Bình Tây distillery (in Chợ Lớn) and as an "employee of the French-Asian Oil Company."[21] A member of the national Theosophical section of France, he created the Theosophical branch called *Cochinchine* ("Cochinchina" or *chi bộ Nam Kỳ*), which operated from 1929 to 1934. The creation of a Theosophical lodge in Saigon on November 1, 1929, was carried out on the associative model of other large national sections that were organized in many countries at the end of the nineteenth century.

Raimond was president of that first lodge, and a Vietnamese trader, Trần Văn Sáo, was named secretary of it. The other leaders were Cochinchinese notables educated at French colonial schools who had positions in the colonial regime of the time: Nguyễn Kim Dinh (provincial councilor), Trần Quang Nghiêm (court bailiff), and two *huyện* or honorary mandarins, Nguyễn Văn Song and a man named Bảo. The secretary of the Bank of Indochina, Nguyễn Kim Muôn, was also said to have been a sympathizer of the movement.[22]

As early as in the first few months, lectures were organized in the provinces on the topic of the links between Buddhism and Theosophy. The public was invited to join the Society. But this Theosophical branch that hoped to constitute itself did not receive the backing of the Cochinchinese authorities. The latter wanted to reduce the scope of the Theosophical Society, undoubtedly fearing both the international ramifications of the

Theosophical Society in Cochinchina and the nationalist dimension of its discourses, which could in turn feed the claims of the nascent Vietnamese independence movement. One year after the founding of this new branch, whose application for formalization was refused by the French government, Raimond returned to France and was never heard of again in Vietnam.

The Leadbeater Branch

Nguyễn Văn Lượng's *Histoire de la Société théosophique du Viêt-nam* ("History of the Theosophical Society of Vietnam") emphasizes the involvement of important international Theosophical bodies in this Cochinchinese project, rejecting the idea of any Masonic initiative. The Cochinchinese Theosophical branch did indeed have the honor of receiving, on November 1, 1929, a visit from a prominent member of the International Theosophical Society, Charles Webster Leadbeater (1854–1934).[23]

Ordained an Anglican priest in 1878, Leadbeater joined the Theosophical Society five years later, the first Christian priest to be converted to Buddhism. The companion of Annie Besant, a "compulsive storyteller with an inexhaustible imagination that allowed him to improvise at will improbable and fantastic stories,"[24] he greatly contributed to the dissemination of the official Theosophical Society doctrine among the less educated social strata, especially with his historical fiction series titled "Rents in the Veil of Time," which was published in the magazine *The Theosophist*.[25] Furthermore, Leadbeater's use of picturesque narrative[26] was, if not revolutionary, at least mechanical and systematic in the hermetic environment of the occultists, and foreshadowed the fantasy literature of the twentieth century. Similarly, his sojourn through the Anglican clergy, and then his abandoning of that clergy, is emblematic of the reformist and protest impulse of Theosophical Society against Christianity's stranglehold on religious thought, that is, on the interpretation and application of texts. All these characteristics could have contributed to Leadbeater's charisma among colonized populations and to a sort of recuperation of the latter's anti-clerical protest discourse, as demonstrated by a series of examples below.

During the years following this visit, the Theosophical Society came to have the wind in its sails in Cochinchina, and went so far as to lend the name of "Leadbeater"—who had just passed away—to a new Theosophical branch (1934–1940).[27] This branch was statutorily attached to the

French Theosophical Section and was said to have obtained, according to the same Theosophical sources (Bạch Liên and Nguyễn Văn Lượng), the local Cochinchinese government's authorization to operate regularly. Its administrative committee was composed of a president, Pierre Alexandre Timmermans, and three vice presidents: Mr. Lê Thành Long (a "retired mandarin"), one Monsieur Soubrier (J. Mus Pharmacy, Saigon),[28] and one Madame Crisas (director of the "Cave Sahel" house). "Advisory members," once again recruited directly from the French colonial milieu or from that of the colonized, add to the list: Mr. Appavou (an official of the Saigon Arsenal), Mr. Thái Du Lực (a commercial clerk in Chợ Lớn), Mr. Huỳnh Bà Nhê (a teacher in Châu Đốc), Mrs. Anna Lê Thị Cang (a Catholic landowner in Gò Công, who saved the journal *Nirvana* from bankruptcy in the 1930s),[29] Mrs. Nguyễn Thị Hai (a teacher in Gò Công), and Ms. Lưu Thị Dậu (assistant principal at the Gia Long high school, Saigon). The mayor of the third arrondissement of Saigon (the Khánh Hội district, Port of Saigon), Nguyễn Văn Lượng (ca. 1906–1990), was also initiated at this point in time.[30]

Based on the Grand Orient archives and other sources, Mr. Timmermans, the new president of the Theosophical Society in Cochinchina, can be identified as a "Three Points" (*Tam điểm*) Masonic brother—to take up the Vietnamese expression that was directly inspired by the French nickname,[31] or perhaps a close relative of his was a Freemason. Indeed, a certain "Albert Timmermans" worked as supervisor of the Indochinese Post Offices in Hanoi and was authenticated as a Freemason.[32] At the same moment, a certain "Pierre Timmermans," also presented as a supervisor of the Indochinese Post Offices in Saigon, became president of the Cochinchinese Theosophical Society.[33]

Born in Marseille on July 28, 1891, Albert Timmermans (according to the same Grand Orient archives) was initiated into the Grand Orient on March 16, 1923, at the Parfaite Sincerité ("Perfect Sincerity") lodge of that same port city before embarking for Indochina, probably a few weeks or months before joining the Fraternité Tonkinoise ("Tonkinese Fraternity") lodge on September 11, 1924, in Hanoi. Other colleagues from the Indochinese Post Office sought to join at the same time.[34]

In the interwar period, three Masonic orders coexisted in Indochina: the Grand Orient, the Grande Loge de France, and the Droit Humain ("Human Right"). Their main disagreement was around the question of initiation and whether women and the colonized populations should be allowed to be initiated. Concerning this thorny issue, the Grand Orient

(GO) was quite hostile to initiating the colonized at this time and called for their inclusion into intermediate Theosophical societies. The Grande Loge de France (GLF), for its part, welcomed the colonized. The Droit Humain (DH) accepted both indigenous people and women in its lodges.[35]

Starting in 1940, the pro-Vichy regime considered the Vietnamese lodges as centers of Masonic protest that had to be eliminated. Following the new anti-sectarian legislation, the meetings of the Leadbeater Branch were explicitly forbidden, and the branch was dissolved in Cochinchina.[36] Its journal, *Niết Bàn* ("Nirvana"), ceased publication.

Postwar Developments

At the end of World War II, the Vichy laws were no longer in force, and the Leadbeater Theosophical Branch reappeared from 1947 to 1950, still in Saigon. In 1949, the year that the French administration created an Associated State of Vietnam with Bảo Đại as head of state, this Theosophical Branch took the name of "Việt Nam." This new name thereby demonstrated the Theosophical path and will to national ambition. In other words, this "Việt Nam" Branch claimed to be the representative of Theosophy for the entire Vietnamese territory once the war would be finished, but to no avail. According to the same process of "Vietnamization," a colonized person assumed the presidency of this association. The right of "primogeniture" was activated, and the honor fell to the oldest Vietnamese Theosophist, Bạch Liên. The vice presidency was given to Phan Vô Ky, a government clerk and director of the Cabinet of the Ministry of Information.[37] He was later replaced by Nguyễn Văn Lượng.

The Theosophical Society surrounded itself with new advisors, such as Mrs. Hồ Thị Cơ, wife of Nguyễn Văn Lượng and a schoolteacher in Phú Lâm; Trần Văn Dinh, a senior secretary at the Court of Saigon; and Pierre Marti, a planter in Đà Lạt.[38] A sign of this Frenchman's prominence in local public life was the naming of a street after the Theosophical Society in Đà Lạt: Thông Thiên Học Street.

This Theosophical branch apparently experienced a major wave of enthusiasm and interest among the Southern Vietnamese in 1951, and in 1952 it was able to form a National Section in Vietnam.[39] The national section acquired headquarters at 466 Võ Di Nguy Street (formerly Louis Berland Street) in Phú Nhuận (a suburb north of Saigon).[40] The plans were drawn up by the architect Nguyễn Mạnh Bảo, who was known less for being a member of the Theosophical Society and more for being a senator in the Parliament and a minister in Ngô Đình Diệm's government in January 1956.[41] The building was modeled after that of Adyar, with an auditorium (with 500 seats), a library (with 700 books provided by Pierre Marti), a meditation room, and a garden with a cutting from a Bồ Đề (*ficus religiosa*) tree—the type of tree under which the Buddha is said to have meditated and attained enlightenment—taken from the Adyar garden by Nguyễn Thị Hai in 1950.[42] From the tree planted in Saigon, several other cuttings were planted in the Theosophical lodges of the Mekong Delta,[43] and then, after 1975, by Vietnamese living overseas in the lodges of Manor (Sydney) and Ojai (California). This practice, present in various pagodas in Vietnam at the time, contributes to the legitimation of a new place of worship by transmitting symbolic power emanating from the reference place of Adyar.

According to Nguyễn Văn Lượng, the plan to create a national section was finally approved by the Caodaist Prime Minister Nguyễn Văn Tâm[44] thanks to the support of a figure from the intellectual and cultural circles of the 1940s and 1950s, René de Berval, a French publicist and director of *France-Asie*.[45] A charter, signed on November 17, 1952, by the international president of the Theosophical Society, C. Jinarajadasa, was sent to Vietnam to consecrate "the statutory birth of the National Section."[46] Mrs. Rukmini Devi Arundale visited Vietnam from Adyar to inaugurate the opening ceremony of the headquarters in the summer of 1952.

The presidency of this new National Section was entrusted to Bạch Liên, who stepped down at the end of his second term (1953-1958). Its secretary general at the time was Nguyễn Văn Lượng. Two women took up the presidency following Bạch Liên. Mrs. Nguyễn Thị Hai (wife of the art professor and publisher Nguyễn Văn Huấn, who was actually the brother of Nguyễn Văn Lượng) was president for fifteen years: from 1959 to 1968, and again from 1972 to November 15, 1973, the date of her death.[47] As for the deputy high school principal Miss Lưu Thị Dậu, she headed the national section between 1969 and 1971, and then from 1973 to 1975.[48]

The Theosophical discourses of these associations never took the marked anti-colonial dimension seen in India, which could have established the Theosophists as competitors to the Communist solution. However, the Theosophical Society could already be identified as an international and philanthropic organization capable of acting as a rallying point for different public—and occasionally political and religious—personalities, French, Vietnamese, but also Indian, British, American, New Zealander and

Australian. The secret Masonic adhesion (Droit Humain) was one of the social and ideological catalysts that made possible the quick and efficient activation of such international connections. It was therefore no surprise that the new socialist regime saw, behind the communicative postures of the Theosophical associations in Vietnam, a potential pole of action and a strategic engine—which inevitably aroused the regime's suspicions.[49] The year 1975 witnessed the banning of Theosophical associations in Vietnam by the new socialist regime. To understand this banishment, it is necessary to reflect on the types of actions taken by the Theosophists in the south of Vietnam and see how the Theosophical Society socially found its roots there, gathering a Vietnamese and potentially subversive "*bourgeoisie* class."

2. "The Path That Leads to the Masters of Wisdom": Translation and Circulation of Models

Buddhist Messianic Dynamics

It is no coincidence that the Theosophical Society was established in the Mekong Delta in Cochinchina. This is attested by the origin of certain members (Bạch Liên and Huỳnh Ba Nhê in Châu Đốc, Anna Lê Thị Cang and Nguyễn Thị Hai in Gò Công, and Ngươn Har[50]), and by the majority of the locations of Theosophical branches. The geographic anchoring of Theosophical Society members in the delta can be understood if we map a regional messianic and millenarian tradition, the *Phật Thầy Tây An*, onto the messianism that animates the Theosophical Society, and in particular the Leadbeater branch.

This regional tradition first appeared in the late nineteenth century in the Seven Mountains site in the western and pioneer land of Cochinchina. The region, renowned for being home to a number of hermits, Buddhist monks, and Daoist masters seeking enlightenment or immortality, took on particular significance in 1849 when Đoàn Minh Huyên (1807–1856), a simple peasant from the Mekong Delta, attained enlightenment and became the *Phật Thầy Tây An*, the "Buddha Master of Western Peace." To his devotees, he became the "living Buddha" (*phật sống*), who announced a new millennium and the coming of the Buddha of the Future (Maitreya), who was to come to save the virtuous, at the precise location of the *Bửu Sơn* Pagoda in the village of Long Kiến, in the province of Long Xuyên. This cult took the name of *Bửu Sơn Kỳ Hương*, the "Strange Fragrance from the Precious Mountain."[51] Through this local myth, we can find in the south of Vietnam the double notions of millenarianism and messianism (via the cult of the Maitreya and the incarnation of the *Phật Thầy Tây An*), which inspired many monk-healers and religious leaders in the nineteenth and twentieth centuries.[52]

An earthly-imminent messianic version of the Maitreya myth eventually came to involve a "catastrophic millenarian scenario" in Blavatskian teachings, in which Maitreya is transcribed as "Maitree-Buddha."[53] Concerning the ensuing messianic belief in Maitreya among Theosophists, Lukas Pokorny writes:

> A most significant task in Besant's theosophical-millenarian project [. . .] was to prepare a bodily vessel for Maitreya to descend into, for his own physical body needed to be kept at his residence in the Himalayas. This shell was discovered in April 1909 by Besant's right-hand man, Leadbeater, [. . .] in the person of the then thirteen-year-old Krishnamurti.[54]

Indeed, this messianic dimension becomes manifest in key aspects of Theosophy, allowing indigenous populations to map their own ideas onto them. Significantly, two senior figures of the Theosophical Society, Annie Besant and C. W. Leadbeater, saw in the person of a young Indian son of a Brahman, Jiddu Krishnamurti (1895–1986), a new Messiah-Legislator of the future cycle. The latter—before he distanced himself from the Theosophical Society and founded his own mystical school in 1927–1929—was presented by other Theosophists of the time as the new Christ-Buddha, of whom he was a reincarnation, as the "vehicle" whom "the Great Teacher" might use when He wished again to speak to the world.[55] Renamed Alcyone, he published, to conclude his initiation, a group of philosophical reflections within a fabulous, and even magical, framework, *At the Feet of the Master*.[56] He was nominated Head of the Order of the Star, an international organization established by the Theosophical Society leadership to prepare for the arrival of a messianic or "World Teacher."

Many Vietnamese translations and exegeses of Theosophical books feed on the messianic dynamics of the Theosophical Society before Krishnamurti formally broke off with it (speech during the annual Star Camp, at Ommen, the Netherlands, on August 3, 1929) by renouncing his avatar status and by dissolving the Theosophical Society's Order of the Star). According to Charles Blech, from 1928 onward, some Vietnamese

Theosophists "quickly take in Krishani's [Krishnaji or Krishnamurti] teachings, so akin to Buddhism."[57] Likewise, Krishnamurti's initiatory book was translated early on by the "first Theosophist" of Cochinchina, Phạm Ngọc Đa.[58] Then it was the turn of a *Commentary on At the Feet of the Master*, translated into Vietnamese by Mrs. Nguyễn Thị Hai and her husband, Nguyễn Văn Huấn (and Huỳnh Hai, a Chinese-Vietnamese Theosophical Society member, provided a Chinese translation). Nguyễn Văn Lượng also penned a commentary on that book in his exegesis *Học Đạo Dưới Chơn Đức Thầy* ("Learning the Way of the Feet of the Master"), which attempts a synthesis and a translation—from English to Vietnamese—of Besant's and Leadbeater's commentaries on Krishnamurti. Nguyễn Văn Lượng chose a pocket format for this book (about twenty pages versus fifty for the original version in English). Finally, a Theosophical branch in the middle of the delta, at Vĩnh Long, took the name of this messianic book, *Dưới Chơn Thầy* ("At the Feet of the Master").[59]

Reading books on this subject thus could offer both an original interpretation and a conceptual reorientation of the local Vietnamese cult of Maitreya. The process thereby revitalized a regional myth by infusing it with syncretic concepts taken from Western and Christian occultist worlds. The link between the *Bửu Sơn Kỳ Hương* and the Theosophical Society would allow the defenders of the regional myth to preserve their orthodox doctrine, on which their temporal millenarian mission depended. In return, the reference to this local myth allowed Theosophists in the provinces, and in particular the western provinces of Cochinchina, to perform a true social and religious function for the population, supporting their propaganda. Such a position wove together a religious vision and a discourse promoting independence that aroused suspicion among the colonial authorities.

Theosophical Literature: Translation and Exegesis

The regional myth of *Bửu Sơn Kỳ Hương* was certainly not the only factor that enabled the Theosophical Society to penetrate into Cochinchina and develop there. A Theosophical literature quickly emerged in the form of translations of books or independent essays about the "classics" of the Theosophical Society, with the aim of popularizing and explaining to the Vietnamese public certain key terms, symbols, and ideas. According to Roland Lardinois's investigation into the global market of "Indianist cultural goods" in the twentieth century, Theosophical publications (in Western and Asian languages) were characterized by their dynamism: "Small Theosophical brochures [. . .] represent 30.2% of the market of books on India after the First World War."[60]

Indeed, Spiritualist, Theosophical, and metapsychological journals and books were circulating in India in the 1920s and 1930s and reached the colonized intelligentsia in India and Ceylon. Theosophical literature was published in Indochina either in French (from the colonial period until 1975) or English (during the American period), and there was also a very large number of publications in Vietnamese.

As a phonetic transcription of the Vietnamese language, the *quốc ngữ* was in fact a script that was easily accessible to all social strata. This system of transcription was chosen both for the translations and the original literary productions of the Vietnamese Theosophical Society, and those of all political and religious movements of the period. The choice to publish in this script and no longer in Chinese characters for exegetic purposes was part of both the Buddhist Revival movement (*chấn hưng Phật giáo*) and the Cao Đài programs.[61] Both aimed to reform Buddhism and the Three Teachings (*Tam Giáo*)'s modes of expression, allowing for a broader and quicker diffusion of Theosophical interpretations of Buddhism beyond the sinological circles of Vietnamese monks, scholars, and intellectuals.

To supply the libraries of the Vietnamese Theosophical lodges, solidarity was established with other sections around the world, and especially with Dutch, English, and Australian lodges. Mrs. Edith Gray, president of the Theosophical Book Gift Institute in the United States, also donated many books to the national section of Vietnam.[62]

The first Cochinchinese Theosophist, Phạm Ngọc Đa (also known as Bạch Liên), wrote the first Theosophical exegeses in romanized Vietnamese script between 1925 and 1930. Right from the start, he applied Theosophical thought to ancient Buddhist concepts (*Luân hồi*, or the wheel of reincarnation; *Quả báo*, or retribution or the law of karma) and popular Vietnamese religious beliefs (*Hồn phách Con Người*, or "man's soul,"[63] and *Thiên Đường Địa Ngục*, or "heaven path and hell") while introducing the messianic ideas and syncretism of the initiatory story of Krishnamurti.[64]

In 1933, *Niết Bàn* ("Nirvana"), the first Theosophical Society bi-monthly in Cochinchina (6,000 copies), was launched under the patronage of Phạm Ngọc Thổ (a *huyện* or an actual functioning district head). Interestingly, he was the father of the pioneer Phạm Ngọc Đa. Nguyễn Văn Lượng was his editor in chief. Lay Buddhist local intelligentsia collaborated for this journal, which provided them with a focal point for reforming Buddhism. That was the case with certain journalists (Bùi Thiên Lượng and Lê Hữu Ty), members of the educational sector (Bạch Liên, Huỳnh Bà Nhê, Nguyễn Thị Hai, Lưu Thị Dậu), publishers (Nguyễn Văn Huấn, Nguyễn Văn Keo), doctors (Nguyễn Văn Dung, Võ Văn Xuôi), and one engineer (Nguyễn Cữu Phú).[65]

Reference works of the Theosophical Society were translated or commented on by Vietnamese teachers or notables (Mrs. Nguyễn Thị Hai, Nguyễn Văn Lượng, etc.) and were made available to the public in the form of books and journals,[66] as well as at conferences. Nguyễn Văn Huấn, for instance, translated (from the French version into Vietnamese) and wrote an exegesis of the central book by Theosophical Society founder Mrs. Blavatsky, *The Voice of Silence* (*Tiếng nói vô thinh*, 1968),[67] making accessible in Vietnamese all the enchanting and colorful sketches of the original English publication. The same Nguyễn Văn Huấn was involved at least as a publisher and copy editor, possibly as a translator, of one of the four canonical scriptures of Caodaism, the *Đại Thừa Chơn Giáo* (literally "the True Teachings of the Mahayana").[68] Dealing with Daoist esoteric practices and moral guidance, this collection of spirit-medium teachings is presented, in the original Vietnamese version, as "a manual of the pill of immortality" (*kinh sách luận về Đơn-Kinh*, Ch. *Jingshu lunyu danjing*).[69] However, it is referred to by its Caodaist and Theosophical French-language translators, editors, and publisher as the "Bible of the Great Caodaist Esoteric Cycle,"[70] which would reveal "the Gospel of the Spirit of Truth" and announce "to the Incarnates the coming Judgement of God."[71] These two designations divulge the two distinct idioms in which the esoteric teachings are presented in this translation: as a Daoist alchemical and meditative manual in the Vietnamese version and as a Theosophical and Spiritist "Bible" in the French version.[72]

New lay methods for learning contemplative meditation (*tham thiền*) were made available through these communication channels, which restructured the master-disciple relationship that had hitherto prevailed. Similarly, Theosophical writings largely adopted a didactic and moralizing tone, sometimes evoking the fear of Hell, to teach "the path that leads to the masters of wisdom" (*Con đường đi đến Chơn Tiên*, literally "The path that leads to the veritable immortals"), "The Construction of the Universe" (*Tạo lập vũ trụ*, literally "The creation of the cosmos"), or "The path of karmic liberation" (*Con đường giải thoát*), to cite only titles of works by Nguyễn Văn Lượng. This Theosophical literature—while overlapping sometimes with Cao Đài literature, as I have already provided an example above[73]—occupies a unique position in published esotericism, as the stories by and of initiates in addition to comparative religious analyses are based on "strange and marvelous adventures, utterly unusual and with amazing characters, [. . .] placed at the heart of events that are supposed to take the place of evidence."[74] In the derivation of Puységur's magnetic somnambulism and the animal magnetism of Mesmer, the genre of "scientific supernatural" or "the science for the marvelous" (*le merveilleux scientifique*, according to Pierssens) is a crucial component of different esoteric and occultist groups in the West—Spiritualism, metapsychology, and of course the Theosophical Society—with which it shares a desire to turn a mystical or religious subject into science. This visual and literary culture of "scientific supernatural" emerged at the beginning of the nineteenth century (with a peak around the middle)[75] and shines through in the works of Jules Verne, Louis Figuier, and Camille Flammarion. Their literary fiction reveals a desire to combine mysticism and positivism, technicism and astronomy, stimulated by "a solemn rhetoric of truthfulness and objectivity mixed with a formidable pathos of terror."[76]

In the West, several authors from the Theosophical Society excelled in this genre.[77] Leadbeater's name and his fantastical style have already garnered our attention. Among the historical figures of the International Theosophical Society who came to Vietnam, I should highlight C. Jinarajadasa, whose literary style mixes the marvelous and the scientific. The "Great White Brotherhood" is a recurring theme in Theosophical writings that designates an esoteric circle that brings together both the mythic keepers of inner Wisdom and "the representatives of this powerful line of Seers and Sages."[78] Concerning this "Great White Brotherhood" (*Quần Tiên Hội* in Vietnamese),[79] Jinarajadasa writes:

> For each of the globes of the Solar System there is a group of ministers of the Logos that execute His Plan in relation to that globe. This group is called the "Hierarchy" of the globe, and on Earth that Hierarchy has been given many names by tradition, the mostly commonly used one now being "the great white Brotherhood." This Brotherhood is not a simple association of Supermen, but a living Body that contains the vital forces of the Logos. It is in truth a "superior Grand Lodge," a model of all the Grand Lodges that have ever existed, and its powerful Officers work from noon to noon without interruption.[80]

In his *Học Đạo Dưới Chơn Đức Thầy* ("Exegesis of *At the Feet of the Master*"), Nguyễn Văn Lượng states that his "study" provided

> mysterious details on the celestial and mystical world that were of great interest to the vast majority of the Vietnamese people, as this was the first time in their lives that laypeople had been informed about celestial things. [. . .] Henceforth for them, the high divinities of Eternal Wisdom were no longer myths, but realities they could attain if they persevered on the path laid out by the Master.[81]

Similar quotations could be multiplied and propagated without changing their sociological meaning, to the effect that these new vocabularies, and the definitions and symbols that go along with them, fed a new mode of occultist rationalization for the Vietnamese. The "translingual practices" at play in the production of Theosophist texts during and after colonial period find another illustration in the famous Theosophical credo—"There is no religion greater than Truth"—which was literally translated into Vietnamese as *"Không tôn giáo nào cao hơn chánh lý."*[82] These publications served as channels for a popularization of scientific concepts, instruments, and methods via integrative stories of mystery, miracles, beliefs, and religious practices. The stories of scientific experiments and discoveries thus share the same register as legends, tales, hagiographies, initiatory stories, and so forth. The genre of scientific supernatural and its mysteriousness thus constitute a crucial component of the Theosophical Society, continuously renegotiating the relationship between science and religion, paving the way in the colonial and later in post-colonial Vietnamese context of a "morally edifying science," or a "savant religiosity."[83]

The Vietnamese Lodges at the Intersection of the International Theosophical Society Network

Subsequent to the beginning of the Theosophical Society in Cochinchina, an international Theosophical network emerged, shaped by an "interactional history," at the points of contact and mutual exchanges between Theosophists in Cochinchina (and later on in South Vietnam) and Western or even Asian societies. For instance, Mrs. Nguyễn Thị Hai was thus delegated by the lodge to attend the International Theosophical Society's jubilee in Madras on December 24, 1935,[84] just as Nguyễn Văn Lượng would be later (figure 3.1).

Beginning in 1952, the new national section was representative of all of Cochinchina and Annam (respectively the south and center of Vietnam), and from that time exchanges and meetings took place at the world headquarters at Adyar. The yearly Adyar Conventions were favorable to such international meetings. The National Section of Vietnam sent representatives to Adyar in 1955 (Phan Văn Hiện, Principal Secretary at the Ministry of Health; with Trương Khương, photographer in Sóc Trăng), in 1956 (Mr. and Mrs. Ngươn Har, and Nguyễn Hữu Kiệt, publisher), and in 1965 (Mrs. Nguyễn Thị Quản and Ms. Lưu Thị Dậu). Moreover, in April and May 1961, General Secretary Nguyễn Thị Hai visited the Theosophical Society lodges in the Philippines, Hong Kong, and Japan.[85] Then she visited Paris and the esoteric center of Huizen (Holland) in August 1971.

Similarly, in 1936, on his way to Java, Singapore, and Sydney, the Sinhalese polyglot C. Jinarajadasa (1875–1953)—head of the Esoteric School and the future international president of the Theosophical Society (from 1946 to 1953)—visited the Leadbeater branch. He gave two talks in French on "Buddha and His Message" and "Theosophy and Brotherhood" (on March 4 and 14, 1936) at the headquarters of the Société Amicale Indochinoise (SAMIPIC [The Indochinese Friendship Society], *Nam Kỳ*

Figure 3.1. A Vietnamese Theosophist in the international networks of the Theosophical Society. *Source:* Nguyễn Văn Lượng, 1981.

Tương Tế Khuyến Học Hội, literally "The Cochinchina Association for Mutual Aid and Education Promotion") on Gallieni Street (later Trần Hưng Đạo) in Saigon.[86] His two-week visit also took him to the provinces of Bà Rịa and Bạc Liêu, where lodges had just been formed.[87] In 1937, Jinarajadasa, on his way to Hong Kong, Shanghai, and Kyoto, was jailed for four days in Saigon for giving a talk at 48 Vassoigne Street.[88] His successor as president of the Theosophical Society, Mrs. Rukmini Devi Arundale (1904–1986),[89] came to Vietnam on two occasions: in 1952 and in 1980. The next president of the Theosophical Society, Sri Ram (1953–1973),[90] visited South Vietnam and the Angkor temple complex in 1955. Several prominent figures of Anglo-Saxon Theosophy also visited Vietnam in this period: Mrs. Helen Zahara (1917–1973) of New Zealand,[91] as well as the Englishman Geoffrey Hodson (1887–1983),[92] who visited regularly and for long periods of time, sometimes with the Perth Theosophist Sandra Chase (as in July 1959).

3. Theosophying the Vietnamese Religious Landscape

Reimagining Buddhist Philanthropy and Preaching

In approximately 1952, the Leadbeater branch was intentionally split into three separate sub-branches in Saigon.[93] Further branches were also created: one in Vĩnh Long (under the name *Dưới chơn thầy*, "At the Feet of the Master"), one in Long Xuyên (with the same name as the city), and one in Châu Đốc (An Giang). The seventh and last branch, located in Tân Châu, adopted a term that was explicit about its goal and its means, *Bác ái* ("Philanthropy"). From this section, new branches could emerge, and by 1975 there were nineteen Theosophical lodges in Vietnam.[94] Eight of these were located in the capital of Saigon after the creation and establishment of two women's branches (*Dung hạnh*, literally "Grace and Good Conduct," and *Saigon*) and three mixed branches (*Minh triết*, "Enlightened Philosophy;" *Từ bi*, "Compassion;" and *Bồ Đề*, "Bodhi"). There was only one branch in the central part of the country in Huế (the *Chơn lý*, or "Truth," branch). The six other branches were located in the Mekong Delta.[95]

Philanthropy was a flagship activity of Vietnamese Theosophists beginning in the 1930s. This typical aspect of the Vietnamese lodges bears the fingerprints of C. Jinarajadasa, who visited Saigon in 1936 and 1937.

Over the course of his several tours in Asia, Europe, and Latin America, he urged "always the necessity for devoted service to or 'Work' for Theosophy."[96] At the same time, "serving the society" was clearly considered a strategic way "to face the incredible propaganda of Christianism which is in vogue in Vietnam."[97]

Indeed, charitable actions clearly reflected the Theosophical Society's concern for its own sociopolitical integration, as they demonstrated the civic responsibility of the Theosophists, who announced themselves as model citizens mindful of their neighbors' welfare. According to the Theosophists, this personal investment of a portion of their financial resources in humanitarian action benefiting the entire Vietnamese population was in response to an aspect of Buddhist ideology that sets great store in compassion. Helping orphans or victims of poverty, setting up nurseries, maternity wards, and so forth, would in this sense be the means for Theosophical Society members to attract good "fortune" in return, through the merits that they acquire and the prophylactic acts they perform in the framework of the liturgical activities of such social foundations. It is doubtlessly within this interweaving of philanthropic activities and lay meditation (to which I will return) that the Theosophical Society's greatest originality lies in terms of social and religious practices.

This was the case, for example, with the women's branch of Saigon, founded by Nguyễn Văn Huấn and his wife, Nguyễn Thị Hai. At the latter's funeral on November 15, 1973, Mrs. Nguyễn Văn Thiệu, the wife of the president of the Republic of Vietnam (1965–1975), came in person to preside over the coffining "to honor her devotion to the social works of women in Vietnam."[98] The home of this Saigon branch[99] served, for example, as a conference center and a place to study Theosophical works, and in particular two primary core texts: Arthur E. Powell's *The Solar System* and Annie Besant's *A Study in Consciousness*. The artist Đinh Văn Bách was responsible for reproducing, in large portfolio format, all the diagrams and charts that elucidate Powell's text. Along with these study seminars, the couple devoted themselves to "training apprentice orators."[100]

The *Kiêm ái* ("Philanthropy") branch of Saigon had the most members and was very active. It was also engaged in the dissemination of Theosophical precepts in the media. Rich in experience gained overseas, especially "in France, Holland, England, and India," Mrs. Lê Hồng Hạnh and Mrs. Trần Kim Thanh established "a large classroom for Theosophical study that brought 50 students together each week," "a spacious lecture hall that 50 to 200 people would come to every Sunday afternoon," and "a monthly 120-page Theosophical journal, *Ánh Đạo* ('Light of the Way') which was widely read and had print runs of up to 1,200 copies," giving access in Vietnamese to articles formerly published in *The Theosophist* (Adyar) and *Le Lotus Bleu* (Paris). Finally, this branch built a center of "Theosophical mysticism or an esoteric center" named *Thanh tâm đạo viện* ("Purity of the Heart") on the side of the hill called Núi Dại (four kilometers from the coastal city town of Vũng Tàu, formerly Cap Saint Jacques). The 50,000 square meters of land was offered by Mrs. Lê Hồng Hạnh, a kindergarten school director in Saigon (after some training in London ca. 1955).[101] This center, which was "under the high patronage of the Huizen Center in Holland," gathered, for a week each summer, "60 to 100 participants from all branches," with a "meditation session each morning and an hour lecture followed by questions and answers."[102]

In the 1960s, the *Thanh Niên Phụng Sự* ("Youth Work") branch in Saigon was directly aided and run by the Frenchman François Mylne. For twenty-three years, he worked together with a group of elders to allow students aged fifteen to twenty-five, most of whom were from Theosophical Society members' families, to acquaint themselves with Theosophical concepts by organizing oral presentations and training them in the art of rhetoric.[103] Evening classes focused on the writings of H. P. Blavatsky. Starting in 1968, F. Mylne led a collective meditation group based on Katherine Beechey's teachings every Sunday morning. This Saigon branch published at its own expense a bi-monthly magazine, *Tìm hiểu Thông thiên học* ("Understanding Theosophy"), which had "print runs of 2,000 copies" and was "distributed free of charge to individuals and people in the administrative service, in the capital and in the provinces."[104]

The 1950s, 1960s, and 1970s witnessed the activities of the *Từ bi* ("Compassion") orphanage, which Nguyễn Văn Lượng's wife led for seven years, and which was first located in the outbuildings of the Nguyễn Văn Lượng's villa.[105] She was assisted by Mr. and Mrs. Ngươn Har. The creation of this institution, with financial assistance from the *Theosophical Order of Service* in Australia and the United States,[106] was authorized on October 10, 1953, by Mai Thọ Truyền,[107] who at the time was government inspector of administrative and financial affairs. From 1960 to 1975, the same Buddhist-oriented term, "compassion," was used to name a free maternity ward with twenty beds (*nhà bảo sanh từ bi miễn phí*) in the village of Bình Đăng (four kilometers from Chợ Lớn). There, Nguyễn Văn

Lượng drew on the patron-client network of his father, who headed the council of village notables. That maternity ward also had a meditation space dedicated to the Bodhisattva Quan Âm (Ch. Guanyin).

The *Chơn Lý* ("Truth") lodge, opened in Huế in May 1955, seemed particularly isolated in the center of the country. Led by Mr. Nguyễn Phước Hòa Giai (member of the Government Delegate Cabinet for Center Vietnam), Lê Văn Mừng, and Nguyễn Hữu Nghị, it followed the model of its sister branches, organizing public lectures, publishing monthly newsletters, and "opening an elementary school for disadvantaged children and providing assistance to war orphans."[108]

Implicit in the above section, the practice and teaching of meditation appear as key activities for understanding Theosophy in Vietnam. The headquarters in Phú Nhuận as well as the provincial representative sections housed meditation rooms from the 1950s onward, which allowed for teaching and study sessions on religious doctrines.

Recasting and Laicizing Meditation

The Theosophical Society's greatest originality doubtlessly lies in this interweaving of philanthropic activities (setting up nurseries, maternity wards, etc.) and lay meditation. From the perspective of religious practices, it effectively pointed the way to a reform of Vietnamese Buddhism. A translation by Nguơn Har and Cao Thị Lan of James Ingall Wedgwood's popularizing book *Meditation for Beginners*[109] is illuminating in this regard. The Theosophical Society was carrying out a form of "laicization of meditation,"[110] that is to say, it was making the practice of meditation accessible to anyone who came in contact with the Theosophical Society. Until then, such ascetic practices were traditionally defined as being a hazardous business, in which only constant supervision by an experienced teacher for more than a year guaranteed the novice real progress and safety. With regard to these meditative practices that were "traditionally" transmitted informally, from one monk to another, the wide dissemination of the practice of meditation through Theosophical translations greatly transformed Buddhism in Vietnam following World War II.[111]

Once they had been given meditation courses (daily, weekly, or in other stages) in these Theosophical centers or at private residences, the meditators returned home and practiced alone, seeking to "enter into contemplation" (*tham thiền*) in order to, according to Wedgwood and his translators, find the "masters of wisdom" (*chơn sư*). Meditative practice was exported from the pagoda, which no longer was the sole place where the Buddhist could seek a form of salvation. Learning meditation was no longer reserved for the Buddhist or Daoist clergy. Meditative practice was now fundamentally different from what could have existed before, because the Theosophical meditator could read esoteric texts on meditation and deepen, and even personalize, his or her own meditative exercises, individually or collectively, without religious intercession.

The encouragement to meditate that these Theosophical publications provided in lay circles had "dramatic" identity effects in the case of the Sinhalese Theravada.[112] Broadening meditation to the mass public did not, contrary to what one might think, lead to the trivialization of the meditative practice, but rather encouraged Buddhists to become involved in the world (in particular by establishing trade relations in social interactions) while still working for their own salvation and the salvation of others (through meditation and philanthropic works). Through privatization and internalization, the practice of meditation was used as part of a progressive project of laicization by the Buddhist clergy, who could thus claim salaries and engage in public activities that were previously forbidden to them. The laicizing of meditation was thus a means for Theosophical members to radically critique the traditional norms of monastic roles in the lives of the faithful, and even the autarkic behavior of the Buddhist clergy and all other clergy (the Catholics were a prime target).

This reformist impulse of Buddhism conveyed the idea that individual responsibility was a necessary component of the personal search for salvation through a sort of "spiritual egalitarianism" in daily life (abstinence, vegetarianism, study, meditation, philanthropy). The charitable actions of the Theosophical lodges in Cochinchina coincided with the Buddhist quest for merits while reflecting the Theosophists' concern to give pledges of their civic sense and to announce themselves as model citizens mindful of their neighbors' welfare.

The Theosophical Society's role in this process of laicizing meditation should be placed alongside the ongoing efforts to translate and distribute publications of canonical Buddhist texts in Theosophical centers. Similarly, Theosophical preachers, who were laypeople, undertook complex exegeses in their public presentations of texts from different religions. The status of these preachings was thus halfway between sermon and presentation. Generally speaking, Theosophy undertook enormous actions through its cohort of orators, who were often scholars, and who maintained all their vitality and rhetorical verve in Vietnam until 1975 (and abroad after that date). These points of contact are important because they define a certain mode of political and religious investment, a new "microphysics of power" based on "dispositions, manoeuvres, tactics, techniques, functionings."[113]

Significantly, the Theosophical Society in Vietnam organized a series of public lectures, inviting various inter-Buddhist sects. The so-called "Congress of Religions" on April 18–19, 1954, for instance, was organized on the premises of the Theosophical Society's headquarters in Phú Nhuận and gathered together representatives of Mahayana, Theravada, Cao Đài religion, Tịnh độ cư sĩ (Pure Land lay Buddhism), and Minh Lý Đạo (a Chinese-Vietnamese redemptive society).[114]

Among the speakers summoned to these Theosophical forums were professor Chung Hữu Thế, the engineer Huỳnh Văn Tuất, and the writer of Khmer origin, Nguơn Har. Mai Thọ Truyền, a well-known lay Buddhist, was often invited to take part in Theosophical forums, as well as to Saigon occultist circles of the time in general. He worked, notably, with René de Berval to set up a committee to organize the arrival of a relic of the Buddha in 1956 (in the Xá Lợi Pagoda), and together the two of them published a history of Buddhism in Vietnam in de Berval's (in many respects) "mystical-literary" journal, *France-Asie*. Mai Thọ Truyền himself embodied the idea and process of the lay reform of Buddhism. Having ascended to the office of Minister of State, he acquired undeniable political authority following the 1950s. From that period onward, his name was closely linked to the ecumenical actions of the Xá Lợi Pagoda and the Society of Buddhist Studies (*Société d'Études Bouddhiques*) in Saigon, which at that time represented both the modern spirit of reform and the politicization of Buddhism.[115]

The case of Mai Thọ Truyền was no exception among the number of oblates who, while accepting religious responsibilities within a pagoda, could perform public activities and claim a corresponding salary. This was also the case with Dr. Cao Văn Trí (director of a hospital), Võ Đinh Dần (president of the Saigon Chamber of Commerce),[116] and the mathematics professor and Caodaist Trần Văn Quế (1902–1980), for example, who was also an orator at the Vietnamese Theosophical Section in the 1950s to 1970s. In 1952, the last of these was appointed Deputy for Research and Reform in the government of Prime Minister Nguyễn Văn Tâm (1952/53). At the same time, he founded, together with Phan Khắc Sửu—a Caodaist and future president of South Vietnam (in 1964/65)—a Caodaist reunification organization (the *Cao Đài Qui Nhứt*). In 1955, he was in Kyoto as a representative of Caodaism at the Congress of National Religions. In

1965, he held the reins of the Saigon-based "Center for the Diffusion of the Great Cao Đài Way in Vietnam" (*Cơ quan Phổ thông Giáo lý Cao Đài giáo Việt Nam*), working together with his friend Đỗ Vạn Lý, the Vietnamese ambassador to India.[117] After 1975, Nguyễn Văn Minh—the government clerk and a Theosophist from the *Kiêm ái* branch of Saigon—became a Cao Đài devotee within that association, participating in its cultural department (*văn hoá vụ*) under the religious name of *Chơn Thiên Minh* (the "Luminous [and] Pure Zen").

Conclusion

From this outline of the history of the Theosophical Society in Cochinchina, some major and specific aspects emerge. First of all, Theosophical thought convinced both Vietnamese and French people, who had a common desire to reform religious institutions, which in the Southeast Asian context also implied a questioning of politics, as religion and politics were intimately linked to one another. Theosophical thought thereby established a system of universal and syncretic meaning that was no longer conveyed by any type of clergy (Buddhist, Christian, etc.), but rather by an associative body that received its orders directly from the spirits (Buddhas, bodhisattvas, saints, etc.).

Its associative members—who were no longer called "adepts"—belonged to the Vietnamese middle-class bourgeoisie and had urbanized lifestyles. The establishment of the Theosophical Society thus corresponds to both a "bourgeoisification of Buddhism" (or rather of its initial followers)[118] and a bourgeoisification of Vietnamese syncretic popular religion, in which Buddhism is an important component in its southern Cochinchina diversity (Mahayana, Theravada, *Phật Thầy Tây An*, *Bửu Sơn Kỳ Hương*), albeit not the only one. Indeed, the Theosophical Society headquarters in Phú Nhuận also attracted, until 1975, various elements of the wider Buddhist reform movements of Cochinchina, such as progressive Buddhist monks, oblates with political offices, but also Caodaists, members of Chinese-Vietnamese redemptive societies, spiritual seekers or laypeople in search of enlightenment and wisdom, and women leaders who were engaged in social and spiritual action. The Theosophical Society, therefore, revealed a sociological group that was perfectly integrated into the intellectual fabric of its time, largely representative of the Vietnamese urban middle class educated at French colonial schools. It allowed for different religious, occultist, and political movements to come together on a path that was lined with the historical events that shook Vietnam in the twentieth century.

The social origin of these Theosophical leaders suggests that membership in the Theosophical circles of Cochinchina took the form of a specific phenomenon of acculturation, or at least that of a response to Western influence. Although assimilation does indeed presuppose acculturation, acculturation does not necessarily result in assimilation. Acculturation can in certain cases reinforce dividing lines and strengthen the integrity of the recipient group, even against those from whom the recipient group borrows certain practices, ideas, or institutions.

Whether in Ceylon or the south of Vietnam, the obvious evolution of meditative activity, for example, is considered by Vietnamese Theosophists an expression of the past in the present, a revitalization of ancestral Buddhist practices and values whose activist tone is a continuation of certain of the Theosophical texts mentioned at the beginning of this chapter. By way of explaining such a phenomenon, Gombrich and Obeyesekere[119] make reference to Eric Hobsbawm's and Terence Ranger's concept of the invented tradition,[120] according to which new movements, such as the Theosophical Society, acquire their legitimacy from previous traditional phenomena. The practice of Theosophical meditation was seen as a re-creation of a lost tradition, or rather as an ancient tradition that should endure. In favor of a traditionalist consciousness, the laicization of meditation made the Theosophical Society accomplice to a project of rereading a historical heritage, notably at a time when the Buddhist clergy were short of breath. Presented as a continuation of the past, this laicization remained an activity that focused individual and collective energy for the purpose of gradual access to a type of salvation that was Buddhist in nature. The Theosophical Society could therefore play an active role in the process of secularization, accelerating the reform and social anchoring of a globalized Buddhism and diversifying local esoteric practices such as meditation. In this sense, colonialism opened the field of religious and philosophical possibilities and referents, expanded exchanges between religions, and allowed movements like the Theosophical Society to try to unify Western and Eastern esoteric traditions into a so-called original unity.

The Theosophical lodges formed a complex meshwork at the crossroads of national and international Buddhist networks, as well as Cao Đài (through editorial and conference collaborations, for instance), Daoist (through their relationship with Minh Lý Đạo, for instance), local Western esoteric (through the journal *France-Asie* and its editorial board) and pro-American networks, to stay with the Vietnamese case. The density of these linkages often took the form of dotted lines, allowing for spatial, conceptual, and social comings and goings. Georges Raimond's fleeting participation in founding the first Theosophical lodge perfectly illustrates the fluidity of the courses taken by members of the Theosophical Society. This figure of French Theosophy played, in Cochinchina, the role of a relay runner, a passer of the torch, providing the local Theosophical Society with international legitimacy. If he seems to have spurred on a movement, his quick disappearance from the Cochinchinese occultist chessboard suggests a number of other actors, this time indigenous ones, who were determined to perpetuate that initial impulse and provide it with a local religious foundation.

The penetration of Theosophical occultist circles and their respective areas of expertise into Cochinchina via the colonizers was of an associative nature. They interfered in colonial society and its political-religious machinery under the guise of Freemasonry, of publications, and of philanthropy and centers to initiate people into Buddhism, meditation, and "Eastern wisdom." The encounters, affinities, and familial complicities (and even nepotism), but also the local reinterpretations, of Theosophical contributions are in line with one of the characteristics of the Theosophical Society: its many descendants can be explained by its doctrinal flexibility and adaptability to local thought—a doctrine that thus appeared to be "often unfaithful, and constantly renewed" in the process of the Theosophical Society's international expansion.[121]

Reflecting its development in India, the Theosophical Society emerged more as an interstitial space than as a small underground and clandestine group. The Theosophical Society in Vietnam took the form of small, innocent, and not particularly coercive or authoritarian associative communities, but which all had a great power of diffusion among both the intelligentsia and the faithful through popular religious movements (Buddhism, Cao Đài, etc.). More than merely a galaxy of disparate elements, this sociological and interactive network seems, from my perspective, to have been unavoidable for Vietnamese occultist networks, and it invites future research in order to examine this complex, multifaceted, and intertwined circulation of people, goods, and ideas. The products of the Vietnamese Theosophical Society themselves—books, brochures, magazines, visuals, translations, and their subsequent translingual practices—need further investigation, not as elements of a linear and definitive process, but as a "circulatory global resource," in which "ideas, practices and texts enter society or locale as one kind of thing and emerge from it considerably transformed to travel elsewhere even as it refers back, often narratively, to the initiating moment."[122] The problematic itself of Theosophical cross-cultural interpretation or syncretism under colonial rule may be questioned in a new light and reconceptualized.

The information this chapter has provided calls for subsequent studies on South Vietnam to take into account the different modes of penetration of Theosophical political and religious principles into several institutions that appeared in Vietnam in the twentieth century: the Buddhist reform movement, the Cao Đài religion, and Indochinese Freemasonry, for example. A comprehensive analysis of the religious tensions and many points of contact created by the colonial situation would be incomplete if the historian, or the anthropologist, were to leave out this type of Theosophical sociability and socialization, which formed a recurring backdrop to the world of Vietnamese belief and to the construction of a Vietnamese category of religion.

Notes

1. Nguyễn Hữu Đắc et al., *Đạo Giáo, hình nhi thượng học (Doctrine du taoïsme—Enseignement ésotérique)* (Saigon: Xuân-Thu At-Hoi nien, 1935), 5, 16. An earlier version of this chapter was published in French in *Péninsule* (2010). This English version has presented me with the opportunity to update my data and approach. I am especially grateful to Huệ Tâm Hồ Tài and Đỗ Thiện for their fruitful comments and insights on this chapter.

2. Krista Umbjärv, "School of the Wisdom in Adyar with Trân-Thi-Kim-Diêu: Report" (2015, www.ts-efts.eu/SoW-Adyar-2015.pdf).

3. A post-graduate in pharmaceutical technology, Mrs. Trân Thị Kim Diệu was born in South Vietnam into a Mahayana Buddhist family. She joined the Theosophical Society in 1972, then more specifically the Joan-of-Arc lodge in Orleans (France), in 1976. She has been working at the French headquarter (Square Rapp) since early 1980s, first as a librarian.

4. Phan Chơn Tôn was a professor in the Department of Biological Sciences at the University of Montreal (1974–1993) who specialized in plant physiology (see the University of Montreal University Assembly, "Minutes of the 514th session, held on December 14, 2009," www.direction.umontreal.ca/secgen/corps_universitaires/documents/AU514_14-12-09_000.pdf). He published in both Vietnamese and French, with the Guérin publishers of Montréal/Toronto (*Le*

Bouddhisme, 1986), and with the Adyar publishers of Paris (*L'Homme . . . Quel Homme?*, 2000); *Le Yoga de Patañjali*, 1998), etc.

5. Charles Blech, *Fifty-fourth Annual General Report of the Theosophical Society for 1929* (Adyar, 1930), 58.

6. Norman Girardot, *The Victorian Translation of China: James Legge's Oriental Pilgrimage* (Berkeley: University of California Press, 2002) and Roland Lardinois, *L'Invention de l'Inde: Entre Ésotérisme et Science* (Paris: CNRS Éditions, 2007).

7. Edward W. Said, *Orientalism* (London: Routledge and Kegan Paul, 1978).

8. Lalaurette and Vilmont, *Le Caodaïsme* (Saigon: Rapport du service des Affaires politiques et administratives de Cochinchine, 1932/33), 1.

9. See Jean-Pierre Laurant, *L'Ésotérisme chrétien en France au XIXe siècle* (Lausanne: l'Âge d'Homme, 1992), 139; Wiktor Stoczkowski, *Des hommes, des dieux et des extraterrestres: Ethnologie d'une croyance moderne* (Paris: Flammarion, 1999), 155. And on the specific role of the Theosophical Society and the Esoteric Christian Union in the formation of Gandhi's notions of Hinduism or Christianity, see Michael Bergunder, "Experiments with Theosophical Truth: Gandhi, Esotericism, and Global Religious History," *Journal of the American Academy of Religion* 82, no. 2 (2014).

10. I have also, though less frequently, encountered the expression *Thiên đạo giáo*, the "religion of the celestial path," to denote the Theosophical Society.

11. I have systematically compared my contemporary interviews (with Vietnamese Minh and Cao Đài devotees) with academic and religious (Theosophical, Buddhist, Minh, Cao Đài, and Theosophist) documents. Concerning the history of the Theosophical Society's spread in Cochinchina in particular, I express my deep gratitude to the Adyar Headquarters members who warmly received me and my research during my visit in May 2015. I would like to especially thank the heads of the administration and of the library, who granted me access to their sources. I have also explored some boxes in the *Grand Orient de France* archives (at 16 Cadet Street, Paris), and I warmly thank the head of the archives, Mr. Pierre Mollier, for his guidance. Finally, there is Nguyễn Văn Lượng's *Histoire de la Société théosophique du Việt-nam* (Montrouge: Presse des Établissements Dalex, 1981), which is actually based on a talk given by his wife, Hồ Thị Cơ, on April 21, 1974, at the Theosophical Society headquarter in Saigon, and translated into French by Ngươn Har.

12. Richard Gombrich and Gananath Obeyesekere, *Buddhism Transformed: Religious Change in Sri Lanka* (Princeton, NJ: Princeton University Press, 1988), 242.

13. Blech, *Fifty-fourth Annual General Report*, 58.

14. According to the *Ninety-Ninth Annual General Report of the Theosophical Society* 1974 (Adyar, 1975).

15. Nguyễn Duy Hình, "Phật Giáo canh tân (thế kỷ XX)," in *Tư tưởng Phật giáo Việt Nam*, edited by a Collective (Hanoi, Ban Khoa Học Xã Hội, 1999).

16. The programmatic nature of this movement has led some Buddhist authors (e.g., Thích Nhất Hạnh, Trần Tri Khách, etc.) to postulate that this meeting was the first concrete initiative to renew Buddhism in Cochinchina.

17. For more on this topic, see the article by Elise DeVido, "'Buddhism for this World': The Buddhist Revival in Vietnam, 1920 to 1951, and Its Legacy," in *Modernity and Re-enchantment: Religion in Post-Revolutionary Vietnam*, ed. Philip Taylor (Singapore: ISEAS, 2007).

18. For more on this topic, see Jérémy Jammes, *Les Oracles du Cao Đài. Étude d'un mouvement religieux vietnamien et de ses réseaux* (Paris: Les Indes savantes, 2014).

19. The spread of the Theosophical Society in Tonkin followed a different strategy and was supervised by the French Freemason Albert Janvier. He founded the Theosophical Society lodge "Dragon" in 1920 in Hanoi (see *The General Report of the Fiftieth Anniversary and Convention of the Theosophical Society, 1925*, Adyar, 1926), when he was still a member of the *Fraternité Tonkinoise* (*Grand Orient Masonic order*). A municipal councilor, treasurer of the Orphanage for Abandoned Métis, and manager of the newspaper *Indochine Républicaine* (Grand Orient de France Archives (GODF), box 1094, Hanoi, Fraternité Tonkinoise 1924/26), he was initiated to Freemasonry on November 30, 1917. He was elevated to the rank of Master on June 6, 1918, and acquired the 18th degree on August 17, 1919, "at the time of his departure to Hanoi and following specific services rendered to the order." He resigned from the Grand Orient Masonic order on January 28, 1927 (ibid., *letter of the Droit Humain from May 5, 1924*, signed by Marius Desbordes, Secretary of the National Council, 3.221; see also Jacques Dalloz, *Francs-maçons d'Indochine (1868–1975)* (Paris: Éditions Maçonniques de France, 2002), 51. The Cao Đài religion in Cochinchina seems to have been the main supporter of the Grand Orient Masonic order (see Jammes, *Les Oracles*, 173–81).

20. Nguyễn Văn Lượng, *Histoire*, 2.

21. Pascal Bourdeaux, "Émergence et constitution de la communauté du bouddhisme Hòa Hảo, contribution à l'histoire sociale du delta du Mékong (1935–1955)" (PhD diss., École pratique des hautes études, 2003), 106.

22. Ibid.

23. According to Gregory Tillet, *The Elder Brother* (London: Routledge & Kegan Paul, 1982).

24. Stoczkowski, *Des Hommes*, 230.

25. Ibid.

26. E.g., Leadbeater's intensive and esoteric-driven use and interpretation of visual materials (symbols, pictures, colorful drawings, explanatory scheme, etc.), especially in his book *The Chakras: The Original Monograph Based on Clairvoyant Investigations* (1927).

27. This point contradicts official and archival data from the period, according to which the Theosophical Society seems, from its very inception, "doomed to

failure," leaving its unofficial members to be diluted "in spiritualist or Caodaist circles" (Bourdeaux, *Émergence et constitution*, 106). This dispersion into local religious movements was by no means that certain, and the Theosophical Society found a certain autonomy with regard to them.

28. The website "Phụng Sự Theosophia" [In the Service of Theosophy] (www.phungsutheosophia.org), created and managed by Huỳnh Công Huấn, states that Mr. Soubrier was president of the Saigon lodge before Mr. Timmermans. The journal *Phụng Sự Theosophia* was founded in the summer of 1978 by overseas Theosophists.

29. According to Hô, *Histoire*, 4.

30. Nguyễn's main books are *Con đường đi đến Chơn Tiên* ("The Path that Leads to the Masters of Wisdom"), *Tạo lập vũ trụ* ("The Construction of the Universe"), and *Con đường giải thoát* ("The Path of Karmic Liberation").

31. Seeking to lend a secretive element to the Masonic lexicon, the Freemasons used three points arranged into a triangle in their correspondence: F∴ for *frères* (brothers), R∴ L∴ for *respectable loge* (respectable lodge), Vén∴ M∴ for *vénérable maître* (venerable master), etc.

32. GODF, box 1094, "Letter to the Droit Humain from August 6, 1924," 50736. Although this letter mentions the name of "Albert Timmermans," one might suppose that it refers to "Pierre Alexandre Timmermans."

33. One of the surnames may have been truncated, or the two names may refer to close relatives. Albert and Pierre Timmermans would certainly know each other very well, as they worked in the same post offices institution, in Hanoi and Saigon, respectively, according to Theosophical Society publications and the Grand Orient archives. To add a piece to the puzzle, the name of Pierre Timmermans as a "receiver at the Post Offices" in the circumscription of Phnom Penh-Kandal is also found in a 1939 administrative report written by the Council of Cambodia's Economic and Financial Interests ("Conseil français des intérêts économiques et financiers du protectorat du Cambodge," www.entreprises-coloniales.fr/inde-indochine/CIEF-Cambodge-1939.pdf).

34. As Jules Grime (initiated in Lyon, lodge of Amis de la Vérité et Fraternité et Progrès) and the chief clerk of Aveyron, Arthur Chevalier (GODF, box 1094, *Membership notices*, 54766). Interestingly, Indochina's Postmaster General Lavallée was a Freemason. See Patrice Morlat, *Indochine Années 1920: Le rendez-vous manqué* (Paris: Les Indes savantes, 2005), 193.

35. For a general definition of the *Droit Humain* and a specific perspective on Vietnam, see Morlat, *Indochine*, 207–9.

36. Interview with the Caodaist dignitary Đinh Văn Đệ, March 2002.

37. Its first secretary was Nguyễn Văn Huấn, a publisher and translator. Its deputy secretary was a retired surveyor, Lâm Vô Võ. Phan Văn Hiền was its treasurer, and Trường Khương assisted him in this task.

38. Nguyễn Văn Lượng, *Histoire*, 8. This information was corroborated by an interview conducted in 2004 with his Vietnamese wife residing in France.

39. It normally takes seven members to form a branch and seven branches to form a national section.

40. The land and the money for construction costs came from a donation by the Nguyễn Văn Lượng couple (according to the website Phụng Sự Theosophia and Hồ, *Histoire*, 11).

41. Nguyễn Văn Lượng, *Histoire*, 10.

42. Ibid.

43. In Gò Công, Cà Mau, Mỹ Tho, Sóc Trăng, and Rạch Giá.

44. Minister from June 25, 1952, to December 19, 1953.

45. See Pascal Bourdeaux, "La revue *France-Asie* (1946–1974), un regard post-colonial sur la 'synthèse culturelle,'" *Péninsule* 56, no. 1 (2010).

46. Nguyễn Văn Lượng, *Histoire*, 23.

47. Ibid., 25.

48. Mrs. Rukmini Devi Arundale and the former Theosophical Society president of France, J.-Émile Marcault, were present on the day when the last national section was inaugurated.

49. The Vietnamese member of the French Section, Huỳnh Ái Chung, was actively involved late in the late 1990s and early 2000s in efforts to obtain permission for the Theosophical Society to be re-formed in Vietnam. But the official legal framework (to be registered as a religion or a research association) does not fit with the ideology and way of implementation of the Theosophical Society (interview with Huỳnh Ái Chung, December 2001, Ho Chi Minh City).

50. Of Khmer origin, Ngươn Har was Inspector of Cambodian Finances; he married a Vietnamese teacher and Theosophical Society member, Trần Thị Kiến (Hồ, *Histoire*, 23).

51. The "precious mountain" is the place of the prophecy's fulfilment; the "strange fragrance" evokes the new millennium and the era of peace and harmony that will follow the apocalypse.

52. A number of them who possessed more charisma managed to develop movements of greater magnitude, revitalizing the *Bửu Sơn Kỳ Hương* cult and lending an important regional political dimension to it. This was the case with Huỳnh Phú Sổ, who in 1939 initiated Hòa Hảo Buddhism. See Huê Tâm Ho Tai, *Millenarianism and Peasant Politics in Vietnam* (Cambridge: Harvard University Press, 1983).

53. Lukas Pokorny, "The Theosophical Maitreya: On Benjamin Creme's Millenarianism," in *The Occult Nineteenth Century: Roots, Developments, and Impact on the Modern World*, ed. Lukas Pokorny and Franz Winter (New York: Palgrave Macmillan), 8, quoting H. P. Blavatsky, *Isis Unveiled: A Master-key to the Mysteries of Ancient and Modern Science and Theology* (Vol. 2—Theology, New York: J. W. Bouton, 1877), 275.

54. Pokorny, "The Theosophical Maitreya," 9–10.

55. See Josephine Ransom, comp., *A Short History of the Theosophical Society (1875–1937)* (Adyar: The Theosophical Publishing House, 2007 [1938]), 474, who quotes Annie Besant. On this topic, see René Guénon's ironic critique: *Le Théosophisme, histoire d'une pseudo-religion* (Paris: Éditions Traditionnelles, 1921), 192, 204.

56. Jiddu Krishnamurti, *At the Feet of the Master: Toward Discipleship* (Adyar: The Theosophical Publishing House, 1910). Also see Laurant, *L'Ésotérisme*, 140: "But the case caused a scandal, and the future teacher of humanity refused the institutional structure of a Church, whatever it was." Convinced at first, Krishnamurti became independent and quickly developed his own influence.

57. Blech, *Fifty-fourth Annual General Report*, 58.

58. Nguyễn Văn Lượng, *Histoire*, 17.

59. The Caodaist spirit-medium Nguyễn Trung Hậu published also in 1927 a poem titled *Dưới chơn Thầy*. Three years later, he became the editor of the first *Revue Caodaïste* (1930–1933), a monthly magazine that published in French the Cao Đài approach of Western esotericism or occultist colonial culture, including of the Theosophical Society. About the genealogy and occultist content of this "Caodaist Journal," see Jérémy Jammes, "Printing Cosmopolitanism, Challenging Orthodoxies: Cao Đài Journals in Twentieth Century Vietnam," *Vienna Journal of East Asian Studies* 10 (2018): 194–202.

60. Lardinois, *L'Invention de l'Inde*, 127. If Theosophical literature seems to collapse "in half in the 1930s, when it represents only 13.9% of the total," the sudden and impressive appearance of neo-Hindu publications suggests that the latter were largely inspired by Theosophical precepts.

61. On the community of Cao Đài exegetes, journalists, and publishers, see Jammes, "Printing Cosmopolitanism."

62. Phụng Sự Theosophia website.

63. Translated by Theosophists as "etheric body and man." According to such beliefs, humans have superior or rational souls (*hồn*, Ch. *hun*) as well as inferior or sensitive souls (*phách*, Ch. *po*). The *hồn* are said to survive death whereas the *phách* would not.

64. Regarding Phạm Ngọc Đa's innovative translation work, see for instance Bạch Liên, *Thông thiên học là gì?* (Canada, 1970, www.thongthienhoc.com/sach%20tthlagi.htm). The two websites www.thongthienhoc.com and www.phungsutheosophia.org contain a profusion of examples of Theosophical translations and exegeses produced in Vietnam, on which my study of Vietnamese Theosophical literature is largely based.

65. Hồ, *Histoire*, 4.

66. The following journals were published in the 1950s–1970s. In Saigon: *Đạo Học* ("Studies on the Dao") and *Bài Giảng* ("Sermons") *by Lương Văn Bối and Nguyễn Văn Lượng*; *Tiến* ("Evolution") by Nguyễn Văn Huấn, *Ánh Đạo* ("Light

of the Dao") by Nguyễn Văn Minh; *Tìm hiểu Thông thiên học* ("Understanding Theosophy") by Nguyễn Thị Hai. In Châu Doc province: *Kỷ yếu Chi-bộ An Giang* ("Bulletin of the An Giang Branch") by Huỳnh Bà Nhê; the monthly journal *Tập sách Phổ Thông Giáo Lý Thông Tin Thiên Học* ("Popularization of the Theosophical Teaching") by Nguyễn Ngọc Lâu. In Long Xuyên province: *Kỷ yếu Long Xuyên* ("Bulletin of Long Xuyên [Branch]") by Huỳnh Từ Hiếu *(*see Hồ, *Histoire*, 5).

67. Published by Ánh Đạo.

68. Phái Chiếu-Minh ("Cao Đài Chiếu-Minh Branch"), *Đại Thừa Chơn Giáo: Le Grand Cycle de l'Ésotérisme* (Saigon: Nguyễn-Văn-Huấn Printing House, 1950).

69. Ibid., 8–9.

70. Ibid., 15.

71. Ibid., 16.

72. On the Kardecian (Spiritist) and Leadbeaterian (Theosophical) style of the translation of this Vietnamese Cao Đài scripture in French, see Jérémy Jammes and David A. Palmer, "Occulting the Dao: Daoist Inner Alchemy, French Spiritism and Vietnamese Colonial Modernity in Caodai Translingual Practice," *Journal of Asian Studies* 77 (2018).

73. Significantly, the Caodaist journalist and exegete Phan Trường Mạnh published in 1954 "The Way of Caodaic Salvation" (*La Voie du Salut Caodaïque, Đường Cứu Rỗi Đạo Cao Đài*), "a bilingual [French and Vietnamese] work that influenced Cao Đài exegetes and especially those who tried to translate Cao Đài thought into French and into Spiritist and theosophical pseudo-scientific concepts" (Jammes, "Printing Cosmopolitanism," 200).

74. Michel Pierssens, "Récits et raisons," in *Des savants face à l'Occulte*, ed. Bernadette Bensaude-Vincent and Christine Blondel (Paris: Éditions La Découverte, 2002), 43.

75. Julian Strube, "Occultist Identity Formations between Theosophy and Socialism in Fin-De-Siècle France," *Numen* 64, no. 5–6 (2017).

76. Pierssens, "Récits et raisons," 61.

77. Examples include *Isis Unveiled* (1877) and *The Secret Doctrine* (1888) by H. P. Blavatsky; *The Masters* (1912) and *The Theosophical Society and the Occult Hierarchy* (1925) by Annie Besant (1912); *The Seven Rays* (1927) by Ernest Wood, etc.

78. Charles Leadbeater, *Les Maîtres et le Sentier* (Paris: Adyar, 1949), 45. He includes his own actions in this derivation of universal "Masters" and "Sages."

79. Literally, the "association of immortals." Cao Đài theology also has a "cave with white clouds" (*Bạch Vân Động*) or "white lodge" in which all the saints reside. Here we can perhaps see the trace of Theosophical influence on Caodaism and the original interpretation of the title of the work by the sixteenth-century Vietnamese poet and soothsayer Nguyễn Bỉnh Khiêm (aka Trạng Trình).

80. Jinarajadasa, *L'Évolution occulte de l'Humanité* (Paris: Publications Théosophiques, 1950), 250–51.

81. Nguyễn Văn Lượng, *Histoire*, 20.

82. Lydia Liu defines translingual practice as "the process by which new words, meanings, discourses, and modes of representation arise, circulate, and acquire legitimacy within the host language due to, or in spite of the latter's contact/collision with the guest language," in which the "host" and "guest" languages represent that of the colonized and the colonizer, respectively. See Lydia H. Liu, *Translingual Practice: Literature, National Culture, and Translated Modernity— China, 1900–1937* (Stanford, CA: Stanford University Press, 1995), 26–27. For a discussion of the concept of "translingual practice" in colonial Vietnam, and especially for its application to Cao Đài texts, see Jammes and Palmer, *Occulting the Dao*. For the Japanese context, see Hans Martin Krämer, *Shimaji Mokurai and the Reconception of Religion and the Secular in Modern Japan* (Honolulu: University of Hawai'i Press, 2015).

83. Pierre Bourdieu, *Choses Dites* (Paris: Éditions de Minuit, 1987), 110.

84. Phụng Sự Theosophia website.

85. *Eighty-Sixth Annual General Report of the Theosophical Society for 1961*, Adyar, 1962.

86. About this Southeast Asia and Australian tour, see Ransom, *Short History*, 535. Both talks were "immediately translated into Vietnamese and printed in full," according to Nguyễn Văn Lượng, *Histoire*, 6.

87. Account related by the Theosophist Nguyễn Thị Quản, delivered on June 18, 1968, at the Theosophical Society headquarters in Saigon and published in the *Ánh Đạo* journal in September 1968 (www.thongthienhoc.com/bai%20 vo%20ts%20jinarajadasa.htm).

88. Phụng Sự Theosophia website.

89. Of Brahman origin, R. Devi married George Arundale (president of the Theosophical Society from 1934 until his death in 1945). A dancer, she contributed to the revival and UNESCO recognition of Bharata Natyam, the oldest classical dance tradition in India. Following the political model of Annie Besant, she joined the Indian Parliament and implemented several educational projects as well as projects for the protection of animals in India.

90. The South Indian Brahmin Sri Ram focused primarily on the practice of meditation, on the transformation brought about in oneself and in the world by individual practice, and finally on the critical spirit necessary to maintain with regard to ancient Theosophical teachings.

91. Phụng Sự Theosophia website. A friend of Geoffrey Hodson, Helen Zahara worked as a secretary in Adyar from 1946 to 1953, and then became assistant editor of the *American Theosophist* magazine. She was Secretary General of the Theosophical Society in Australia from 1957 to 1965 before returning to the United States to work as a program coordinator for the Kern Foundation (https:// questbooks.com/index.php?route=product/author&author_id=1483; Quest Books is the publishing arm of the Theosophical Society in America House).

92. An important figure in the Theosophical Society and the Liberal Catholic Church (founded by Wedgwood), Geoffrey Hodson was the author of more than forty Theosophical books on meditation, health, clairvoyance, etc. His longevity provided a certain legitimacy to his teachings. He was the "director of studies" at the "Wisdom School" of Adyar (https://questbooks.com/index.php?route=product/author&author_id=1210).

93. The *Việt Nam*, *Kiêm ái* ("Philanthropy") and *Thanh niên* ("Youth") branches.

94. Nguyễn Văn Lượng, *Histoire*, 24.

95. The *Huynh Đệ* ("Brotherhood") branch in Gò Công, and five other branches that have the same names as their geographic locations, namely, the *Gò Công*, *Cà Mau*, *Mỹ Tho*, *Sóc Trăng*, and *Rạch Giá* branches.

96. Josephine Ransom, comp., *The Seventy-Fifth Anniversary Book of the Theosophical Society: A Short History of the Society's Growth from 1926-1950* (Adyar: The Theosophical Publishing House, 2005 [1950]), 20.

97. Report of Nguyễn Thị Hai, November 20, 1958, 12 (Adyar Administrative Archives).

98. Nguyễn Văn Lượng, *Histoire*, 25.

99. At 72-74 and 72-76 Nguyễn Đình Chiểu Street (Saigon).

100. Ibid., 24.

101. Interview with the theosophist Huỳnh Ái Chung (December 2001, Ho Chi Minh City).

102. Nguyễn Văn Lượng, *Histoire*, 26.

103. Ibid., 25-26

104. Ibid.

105. C. V. Agarwal, *The Buddhist and Theosophical Movements (1873-2001)* (Varanasi: Maha Bodhi Society of India, 2001 [1993]), 52.

106. Phụng Sư Theosophia website.

107. Nguyễn Văn Lượng, *Histoire*, 31.

108. Phụng Sự Theosophia website.

109. This text *Mới học tham thiền* [Learning contemplative meditation] is available on the Vietnamese Theosophical website www.thongthienhoc.com (www.thongthienhoc.com/sach%20moihocthamthien.htm).

110. Gombrich and Obeyesekere, *Buddhism Transformed*, 239.

111. Ibid., 237.

112. Ibid., 240.

113. Michel Foucault, *Discipline and Punish. The Birth of the Prison* (Harmondsworth: Penguin, 1977), 26.

114. Theosophical Society Annual General Report for 1954. Regarding Minh Lý Đạo, see Jammes, *Les Oracles* and idem, "Divination and Politics and Religious Networks in Southern Vietnam: From the 'Temple of the Three Doctrines' (*Tam Tông Miếu*) to Caodaism," *Social Compass* 57, no. 3 (2010).

115. Mai Thọ Truyền, "Le Bouddhisme au Viêt-nam," in *Présence du Bouddhisme*, ed. René de Berval (Saigon: France-Asie, 1959) and idem, *Le Bouddhisme au Vietnam, Pagode Xá Lợi* (Saigon: Bùi Văn Tạ, 1962). The remains of the famous monk Thích Quang Đức, whose heart was not consumed by the flames during his immolation in 1963, were kept and worshipped in that same pagoda. See Jerrold Schecter, *The New Face of Buddha: Buddhism and Political Power in Southeast Asia* (New York: Coward-McCann, 1967), 179.

116. According to Hồ, *Histoire*, 15, Cao Văn Trí managed the Theosophical Society orphanage.

117. For other biographical details, see Janet Hoskins, "Derrière le voile de l'œil céleste, le rôle des apparitions dans l'expansion du Caodaïsme," *Péninsule* 56, no. 1 (2010).

118. As Gombrich and Obeyesekere, *Buddhism Transformed*, 212, observed in the Sinhalese context. For a comparison with the "bourgeois" Hinduism of the mid-nineteenth-century urban Bengali elite and the key role of this group in the emergence of the modernist Hindu tradition during the age of British empire, see Brian A. Hatcher, *Bourgeois Hinduism, or Faith of the Modern Vedantists: Rare Discourses From Early Colonial Bengal* (Oxford: Oxford University Press, 2008).

119. Gombrich and Obeyesekere, *Buddhism Transformed*, 241.

120. Eric J. Hobsbawm and Terence Ranger, *The Invention of Tradition* (Cambridge: Cambridge University Press, 1983).

121. Also highlighted by Stoczkowski, *Des hommes*, 235.

122. Prasenjit Duara, *The Crisis of Global Modernity: Asian Traditions and a Sustainable Future* (Cambridge: Cambridge University Press, 2015), 73.

References

Agarwal, C.V. *The Buddhist and Theosophical Movements (1873–2001)*. Varanasi: Maha Bodhi Society of India, 2001 [1993].

Bạch, Liên. *Thông thiên học là gì?* [What Is Theosophy?]. Canada, 1970. www.thongthienhoc.com/.

Bergunder, Michael. "Experiments with Theosophical Truth: Gandhi, Esotericism, and Global Religious History." *Journal of the American Academy of Religion* 82, no. 2 (2014): 398–426.

Blavatsky, Helena Petrovna. *Isis Unveiled: A Master-key to the Mysteries of Ancient and Modern Science and Theology*. Vol. 2—Theology. New York: J. W. Bouton, 1877.

Blech, Charles. *Fifty-fourth Annual General Report of the Theosophical Society for 1929*. Adyar: The Theosophical Publishing House, 1930.

Bourdeaux, Pascal. "La revue *France-Asie* (1946–1974), un regard post-colonial sur la 'synthèse culturelle.'" *Péninsule* 56, no. 1 (2010): 163–209.

———. "Émergence et constitution de la communauté du bouddhisme Hòa Hảo, contribution à l'histoire sociale du delta du Mékong (1935–1955)." PhD diss., École pratique des hautes études, 2003.

Bourdieu, Pierre. *Choses Dites*. Paris: Éditions de Minuit, 1987.

Dalloz, Jacques. *Francs-maçons d'Indochine (1868–1975)*. Paris: Éditions Maçonniques de France, 2002.

DeVido, Elise Anne. "'Buddhism for This World': The Buddhist Revival in Vietnam, 1920 to 1951, and Its Legacy." In *Modernity and Re-enchantment. Religion in Post-Revolutionary Vietnam*, edited by Philip Taylor, 250–96. Singapore: ISEAS, 2007.

Duara, Prasenjit. *The Crisis of Global Modernity: Asian Traditions and a Sustainable Future*. Cambridge: Cambridge University Press, 2015.

Foucault, Michel. *Discipline and Punish. The Birth of the Prison*. Harmondsworth: Penguin, 1977.

Girardot, Norman. *The Victorian Translation of China: James Legge's Oriental Pilgrimage*. Berkeley: University of California Press, 2002.

Gombrich, Richard, and Gananath Obeyesekere. *Buddhism Transformed—Religious Change in Sri Lanka*. Princeton, NJ: Princeton University Press, 1988.

Guénon, René. *Le Théosophisme, histoire d'une pseudo-religion*. Paris: Éditions Traditionnelles, 1921.

Hatcher, Brian A. *Bourgeois Hinduism, or Faith of the Modern Vedantists: Rare Discourses From Early Colonial Bengal*. Oxford: Oxford University Press, 2008.

Hồ, Thị Cơ. *Histoire de la Société théosophique du Viêt-nam*. Saigon headquarter conference, unpublished, April 21, 1974.

Ho Tai, Huê Tâm. *Millenarianism and Peasant Politics in Vietnam*. Cambridge: Harvard University Press, 1983.

Hobsbawm, Eric J., and Terence Ranger. *The Invention of Tradition*. Cambridge: Cambridge University Press, 1983.

Hoskins, Janet. "Derrière le voile de l'oeil céleste, le rôle des apparitions dans l'expansion du Caodaïsme." *Péninsule* 56, no. 1 (2010): 211–47.

Jammes, Jérémy. "Printing Cosmopolitanism, Challenging Orthodoxies: Cao Đài Journals in Twentieth Century Vietnam." *Vienna Journal of East Asian Studies* 10 (2018): 175–209.

———. *Les Oracles du Cao Đài. Étude d'un mouvement religieux vietnamien et de ses réseaux*. Paris: Les Indes savantes, 2014.

———. "Divination and Politics and Religious Networks in Southern Vietnam: From the 'Temple of the Three Doctrines' (*Tam Tông Miếu*) to Caodaism." *Social Compass* 57, no. 3 (2010): 357–71.

Jammes, Jérémy, and David A. Palmer. "Occulting the Dao: Daoist Inner Alchemy, French Spiritism and Vietnamese Colonial Modernity in Caodai Translingual Practice." *Journal of Asian Studies* 77 (2018): 405–28.

Jinarajadasa. *L'Évolution occulte de l'Humanité*. Paris: Publications Théosophiques, 1950.
Krämer, Hans Martin. *Shimaji Mokurai and the Reconception of Religion and the Secular in Modern Japan*. Honolulu: University of Hawai'i Press, 2015.
Krishnamurti, Jiddu. *At the Feet of the Master: Toward Discipleship*. Adyar: Theosophical Publishing House, 1910.
Lalaurette and Vilmont. *Le Caodaïsme*. Saigon: Rapport du service des Affaires politiques et administratives de Cochinchine, 1932/33.
Lardinois, Roland. *L'Invention de l'Inde—Entre ésotérisme et science*. Paris: CNRS, 2007.
Laurant, Jean-Pierre. *L'Ésotérisme chrétien en France au XIXe siècle*. Lausanne, Suisse: Éditions l'Âge d'Homme, 1992.
Leadbeater, Charles. *Les Maîtres et le Sentier*. Paris: éd. Adyar, 1949.
Liu, Lydia H. *Translingual Practice: Literature, National Culture, and Translated Modernity—China, 1900–1937*. Stanford, CA: Stanford University Press, 1995.
Mai, Thọ Truyền. *Le Bouddhisme au Vietnam, Pagode Xá Lợi*. Saigon: Bùi Văn Tạ, 1962.
———. "Le Bouddhisme au Việt-nam." In *Présence du Bouddhisme*, edited by René de Berval, 801–10. Saigon: France-Asie, t. XVI, 1959.
Morlat, Patrice. *Indochine Années 1920: Le rendez-vous manqué*. Paris: Les Indes savantes, 2005.
———. "Rivalités entre les missions et les loges maçonniques en Indochine durant les années vingt." In *La Question religieuse dans l'empire colonial français*, 125–73. Paris: Les Indes savantes, 2003.
Nguyễn, Duy Hình, "*Phật Giáo canh tân (thế kỷ XX)*" [Reformed Buddhism in the Twentieth Century]. In *Tư tưởng Phật giáo Việt Nam* [Buddhist Belief in Việt Nam], edited by a Collective, 710–86. Hanoi: Ban Khoa Học Xã Hội, 1999.
Nguyễn, Hữu Đắc et al. *Đạo Giáo, hình nhi thượng học (Doctrine du taoïsme—Enseignement ésotérique)*. Saigon: Xuân-Thu At-Hoi nien, 1935.
Nguyễn, Văn Lượng. *Histoire de la Société théosophique du Việt-nam*. Montrouge: Presse des Établissements Dalex, 1981.
Phái Chiếu-Minh ("Cao Đài Chiếu-Minh Branch"). *Đại Thừa Chơn Giáo—Le Grand Cycle de l'Ésotérisme*. "Cao Đài Đại Đạo" Series ("Great Way of Cao Đài" or "Caodaism" Series). Saigon: Nguyễn-Văn-Huấn Printing House, 1950.
Pierssens, Michel. "Récits et raisons." In *Des savants face à l'Occulte*, edited by Bernadette Bensaude-Vincent and Christine Blondel, 41–62. Paris: Éditions La Découverte, 2002.
Pokorny, Lukas. "The Theosophical Maitreya: On Benjamin Creme's Millenarianism." In *The Occult Nineteenth Century: Roots, Developments, and Impact on the Modern World*, edited by Lukas Pokorny und Franz Winter, 1–25. New York: Palgrave Macmillan, 2020.

Pouvourville, Albert de (alias Matgioi). *La Voie Rationnelle*. Paris: Paul et Louis Chacornac, 1907.
Ransom, Josephine, comp. *A Short History of the Theosophical Society (1875–1937)*. Adyar: The Theosophical Publishing House, 2007 [1938].
———, comp. *The Seventy-Fifth Anniversary Book of the Theosophical Society. A Short History of the Society's Growth from 1926–1950*. Adyar: The Theosophical Publishing House, 2005 [1950].
Said, Edward W. *Orientalism*. London: Routledge and Kegan Paul, 1978.
Schecter, Jerrold. *The New Face of Buddha: Buddhism and Political Power in Southeast Asia*. New York: Coward-McCann, 1967.
Stoczkowski, Wiktor. *Des hommes, des dieux et des extraterrestres: Ethnologie d'une croyance moderne*. Paris: Flammarion, 1999.
Strube, Julian. "Occultist Identity Formations between Theosophy and Socialism in Fin-De-Siècle France." *Numen* 64, no. 5–6 (2017): 568–95.
Tillet, Gregory. *The Elder Brother*. London: Routledge & Kegan Paul, 1982.

Chapter 4

Theosophical Movements in Modern China
The Education Provided by Theosophists at the Shanghai International Settlement

CHUANG Chienhui

Introduction

India and China, two of the four great ancient civilizations of the world, suffered heavily from imperialism in the modern era. In India, the second president of the Theosophical Society, Annie Besant (1847–1933), worked in support of self-rule. The Theosophical Society in India also placed an emphasis on education and established schools for Indians in Varanasi, Kolkata, and other places. The Theosophical movement in South Asia thus influenced politics, modern education, and the Buddhist restoration movement, but it also attempted to promote a similar movement in modern China. Christian missionary schools in China were established in the late nineteenth century. By the 1920s, nationalism had surged among the Chinese. The Chinese became highly concerned with educational rights as a part of the growth of the nationalist movement. Subsequent to the May Thirtieth Movement in 1925, nationalistic Chinese elites pressured the government for the establishment of rights to education; hence, the Chinese government formulated policies for the recovery of educational rights in the same year. During this conflict, the Theosophical Society,

---

The author wishes to acknowledge that this work was supported by JSPS KAKENHI Grant Number 15H06352.

which was promoting alternating communication and interaction between the "East" and the "West" from a pluralistic perspective, established a girls' school for the Chinese in the Shanghai International Settlement. Regardless of whether the timing was appropriate, the Theosophical girls' school was popular with the Chinese. Although the school was instituted by Theosophical missionaries, few Chinese were aware of its difference from other Christian missionary schools. In this chapter, I outline the development of the Theosophical movement in modern China. Furthermore, I discuss the ideals of the Theosophical educational movement, as exemplified by George S. Arundale (1878–1945) and Beatrice Ensor (1885–1974). Subsequently I situate the reception of the Theosophical educational movement in Shanghai against the background of the country's battle against Western hegemony in the early twentieth century.

The Early Theosophical Movement in Modern China

Wu Tingfang (1842–1922) was an important diplomat in modern China and one of the best-known Chinese individuals in the Western world from the late nineteenth century to the early twentieth century. He was famous not only as a diplomat but also as the author of the first Chinese-language Theosophical manual. The first record that Wu acquired membership in the Theosophical Society is from 1916. Wu joined in the United States at Krotona, Hollywood, on August 23, 1916.[1] There were some interesting encounters during his stay in the United States as the Minister of the Qing Dynasty to the United States in 1909. William Walker Atkinson (1862–1932), a pioneer of the New Thought movement, met Wu in the summer of that year. Wu asked Atkinson for his thoughts on the secret of keeping young, though being old.[2] Later in October of the same year, Wu first experienced the work of a trance medium in a Spiritualist demonstration in Washington.[3] This suggests that Wu was curious about Spiritualism at that time.

Wu began his propaganda work for Theosophy in China from the 1910s. During the 1910s, Wu's Theosophical propaganda was related to three Western Baptists: Timothy Richard (1845–1919), Gilbert Reid (1857–1927), and C. Spurgeon Medhurst (1860–1927). Timothy Richard and Gilbert Reid were not Theosophists, but all three figures had similar views regarding the religions of East and West.

If we take Wu as a pioneer of the Theosophical Movement among the Chinese, Medhurst, who originally came to China as a Baptist missionary, should also be considered a pioneer of the Theosophical Movement in China. Spurgeon Medhurst was forced to resign his clerical post in 1904 owing to his involvement with the Theosophical Society.[4] *The International Theosophical Yearbook* first recorded Spurgeon Medhurst's Theosophical Movement in China in 1909.[5] Wu finished his mission as the Qing Dynasty Minister to the United States, Spain, and Peru, and returned to China in 1910. When he returned to Beijing, he immediately resigned because of his dislike for the political corruption prevalent among the Qing. He moved to Shanghai and became engulfed in studying Theosophy.[6] Later, Wu presented a paper about Chinese Civilization at the "First Universal Races Congress" in July 1911, where Annie Besant was on the list of sponsors and accompanied by Gandhi.[7] At this congress, Wu remarked that he preferred Chinese civilization.[8] He explained the concept of Chinese civilization using words from the Confucian classics: "We should treat all who are within the four seas as our brothers and sisters." This point of view may be associated with the first doctrine of the Theosophical Society, namely the doctrine of "universal brotherhood." Wu later stated that he began to study morality and religion after the success of the Xinhai Revolution, which took place from 1911 to 1912.[9]

In Shanghai in 1912, Timothy Richard, Gilbert Reid, and Spurgeon Medhurst founded a research society for discussing "world religions" (*Shijie zongjiao hui*), focusing on the study of comparative religion.[10] In 1913, Spurgeon Medhurst, who had previously published a translation of the Taoist classic *Dao de jing* through the Theosophical Society,[11] gave a speech at Gilbert Reid's International Institute of China (*Shang xiantang*) in Shanghai. He spoke of "the great spontaneity or Natural Law of the universe," "purity," finding "satisfaction in service for others," "worldwide unity," and "life eternal or immortality" as the five "hopes" in Laozi's teaching, which may remind the reader of similar doctrines in Theosophy. The first record of Wu and Medhurst's cooperation for Theosophical propaganda dates from January 1916. Meanwhile, the influential Chinese-language newspaper *Shen Pao* reported that Wu and Spurgeon Medhurst had founded a society for the research of religion in Shanghai.[12] Lectures and speeches held at the International Institute of China were open to people of all nationalities, and local journalists often wrote about them in Chinese and English newspapers.

Starting in January 1916, Wu and Medhurst delivered speeches about Theosophy at the International Institute of China in Shanghai. In March the same year, *The Shanghai Times* posted an announcement about an upcoming lecture by Wu. It said that Wu would talk about "another subject in Theosophy" under the title of "The Human Soul in Its Relation to the Physical Body and Its Consequences." The progress of the lecture was described in one of Chinese magazines for young students as follows:

> Wu Tingfang of the Tongshen Society was invited to the International Institute of China to deliver a lecture on the relation between the soul and the body. There were hundreds of people who came to see his speech. According to Wu's words, the human soul will never die. There is no beginning nor ending in it. [. . .] The human body is like clothes, it's not good to consider it too important. If we don't train ourselves well, we cannot evolve. If we train ourselves well over and over, we will change, becoming perfectly good men, and will arrive at a state of bliss. [. . .] Things which have shapes are *yang*, those without shapes are *yin*. *Yin* comes first, and then *yang* comes afterwards. People know of earthly matters but don't know that there are numerous worlds besides the earth. The *qi* of individuals, the air of emotions, does not occur only within us. It may be felt by others. [. . .] There is a book written by a Westerner, which has collected pictures of *qi* taken with a camera. Many kinds of photos are included, please take a look. (Wu opened the book and showed every page to his audience. There are about 50 pages in the book.) People's goodness and badness are classified according to shapes and colors.[13]

Wu's use of terms such as *ying*, *yang*, and *qi* in his lecture suggests that he combined Theosophy with Daoism when he introduced Theosophy to the Chinese. The "book by a Westerner" that he showed as evidence to the audience is, in all likelihood, Annie Besant's *Thought-Forms*;[14] nevertheless, he did not mention Besant's name, or the Theosophical Society, in the lecture. Furthermore, Wu showed his collections of Western spirit photography to those in attendance to make them believe in the existence of life after death. The only thing he did not mention is what Theosophy was. Gradually, Wu and Medhurst's efforts came to be noticed by the Chinese. In 1916, the education department of Jiangsu Province invited Wu to give a speech about Theosophy as a member of the Tongshen Society (*Tongshen hui*). Tongshen is the Chinese translation of Theosophy, which means "connected with God."[15] This lecture was reported not only in a bulletin of the Jiangsu province's education department, but also in other

Chinese newspapers and magazines. Wu stated that Western science had created doubt about the existence of spiritual matters both in the East and in the West. As for China, in the Confucian classic *The Analects of Confucius*, it is written: "Confucius does not speak about occult violence and spiritual matters," and "How can you know death when you still don't know about life?"[16] Although Confucius did not deny life after death, research into spiritual matters had not been appreciated in the Confucian tradition. A friend of Wu's living in Beijing read Wu's Theosophical lecture in a newspaper and sent him a letter asking what the soul (*linghun*) was. Wu's friend said his view was ridiculous and inappropriate for the modernized world. Wu used his friend's question as an introduction to his talk at the educational department of Jiangsu province.

> I replied to him that this is a profound theory which can't be explained in a letter. If you don't believe in ghosts (*gui*[17]), may I ask you whether you worship your ancestors? Doesn't ancestor worship show a belief in the existence of ghosts? Our Confucius said, "The ghosts' function in morality is huge." Isn't this evidence that the Saint believed in the existence of spirits? As for those who don't believe in it, it is because they know less, so they think it strange. If they study it, then they must suddenly achieve a total understanding. No religion denies the existence of the soul (*linghun*).[18]

Wu's lectures about *soul* were also related with his friends in the International Institute of China. The International Institute of China, the first place where Wu and Medhurst delivered speeches about Theosophy, was established by Gilbert Reid. It was also known as a place for the improvement of cultural exchange and the introduction of different kinds of religions and philosophy. Timothy Richard published a book in 1910 titled *The New Testament of Higher Buddhism*. The *North-China Herald* (*Beihua jiebao*), an influential English-language newspaper in Shanghai, introduced Richard's new book soon after its publication in the following way:

> The general reader and even these students in the West who are now studying Buddhism are left in a confused state of mind as to its real place among the religions of the world, owing to Theosophy, and Edwin Arnold's *Light of Asia*, which was written at a time when the true relation of Higher and Lower Bud-

dhism was not known. This book contains two most important translations—one, the origin of Higher Buddhism called "The Awakening of Faith," and the other, "The Essence of the Lotus Scripture." The first was translated into English before, but by one unacquainted with Buddhist key to the central thought of the True Model Chin Ju. The second has never been translated before, though the Lotus of the Good Law was translated in the Sacred Books of the East. No student of Higher Buddhism should be without this book.[19]

Timothy Richard's missionary work and his relationships with Chinese politicians or intellectuals have been researched in previous studies. He stayed in China for forty-five years and translated many Buddhist classics into English. His views of Eastern religions have also been widely discussed. For example, Son writes:

Richard drew attention to "the Mahayana Buddhism of East Asia" in contrast to the Theravadan tradition that had been the focus of most previous Western scholars and missionaries, and he was immensely interested in the historical relationship between Buddhism and Nestorian Christianity.[20]

Even though Timothy Richard's Buddhist translations were influenced by his Christian cultural background, his views of Eastern religions, unlike those of other Western Baptist missionaries who despised them, were characterized by his seeking communality between Eastern and Western religions. Judith C. Powles points out that even after Medhurst resigned his missionary post, his "nearest friend," Timothy Richard, maintained his connection with him.[21] We may say that Medhurst and Wu's Theosophical movement in the China of the 1910s flourished because of the support of their considerate Christian missionary friends in China. However, their cooperation did not occur simply because of friendship, but as part of a wave of reconsideration of the religious concepts in the 1910s. In addition, Richard, Reid, Medhurst, and Wu were also associated with the Mahayana Association in Japan in 1916.[22] Although the Mahayana Association was not directly connected to the Theosophical Society, many Western members of the association were Theosophists. Theosophy was the impetus that made Christian Baptists such as Timothy Richard translate Buddhist classics through a Christian filter but at the same time seek uniformity.

Medhurst's translation of the *Dao de jing* may be taken as providing a means for illustrating the commonalities between Eastern and Western wisdom. Wu Tingfang tried to encourage the practice of Theosophy as providing a means for the settling of conflicts regarding nations, races, religions, and so on worldwide. Theosophy would play the role of catalyst for the rethinking of religion and also as mediator between Eastern and Western thought systems.

Wu and Medhurst made great efforts in disseminating Theosophical propaganda and forming a Theosophical study group in 1916.[23] However, Wu joined the Constitutional Protection Movement in 1917 and came to be the temporary premier of the Republic of China from May to June, then took on the post as Foreign Minister from September, which meant that he could not stay in Shanghai. Medhurst established the Quest Society in Shanghai, which held lectures on various subjects from religion to alchemy.[24] In 1918, several Theosophists in Shanghai participated in Quest Society events and initiated a "study circle"[25] for Theosophy soon after that. Through these movements in the 1910s, Captain George W. Carter and Hari Prasad Shastri (1882–1956) established the first official Theosophical lodge in China, the Saturn Lodge,[26] on June 26, 1919,[27] in the Shanghai French Concession. It had thirteen members in the beginning and came to have twenty-eight members after one year.[28] Hari Prasad Shastri, a professor, Sanskrit scholar, and Raja Yoga teacher, was its first president.[29] Chinese members held a study circle and gave Chinese-language lectures about Theosophy every Sunday.[30] Though he was extremely busy during the Chinese Civil War, he still provided support to the running of the Saturn Lodge. The Saturn Lodge did not have a regular meeting site in its first year. At first, members' residences, such as that of George Carter, as well as Wu's, were used in the summer.[31] One year later, Wu was elected as honorary president in 1920.

Though Wu was busy at the time, he organized a new lodge in Shanghai in 1922, the Sun Lodge, which was the first lodge run by Chinese natives.[32] Moreover, he pioneered Chinese Theosophical literature with his "Wu Tingfang's theory of soul," the first Chinese-language Theosophical Manual.[33] Wu stayed in South China as part of the Constitutional Government in Canton under Sun Yat-sen (1866–1925), holding the position of Minister of Finance. Cen Chunxuan (1861–1933), the leader of the military government in Canton, forced Wu to hand over the funds for a forthcoming university's establishment in China.[34] Cen wanted to use the funds for his army, so Wu decided to leave Canton with the money in March 1920 and hide in Hong Kong. There he met James H. Cousins (1873–1956), an Irish poet and an active Theosophist. Wu told Cousins that he wanted to help the Theosophical movement and do "all he can in China." Wu offered to send Cousins on a lecture tour of China with his financial support, which would amount to 2,000 rupees.[35] Wu was on his way to Shanghai during this period to escape from threats against him.[36] Wu and Cousins planned to start further propaganda on behalf of the Theosophical Society after political circumstances improved. However, their plan could not be realized because Wu died in June 1922.

In 1921, Spurgeon Medhurst and his wife left Shanghai for Sydney to visit C. W. Leadbeater (1854–1934). He was to live in Australia until his death. Wu and Medhurst's work had significantly facilitated the early Theosophical movement in modern China; however, the progress of the movement declined after Wu's death in 1922.[37]

After Wu's Death

The Theosophical movement in China was reorganized in 1924 by the new president of the Shanghai Lodge, Dorothy M. Arnold (? –1982). Her Theosophical movement in Shanghai was supported by the Hong Kong Lodge's[38] founder and president, Malcolm Manuk (1881–1932), an Armenian born in India. He was a secretary for the Dairy Farm Company and frequently visited Sydney for business purposes. He came to be a member of the Blavatsky Lodge in Sydney in 1926 and remained a member until his death in 1932. It was he who had sent Wu Tingfang's letter to Cousins and arranged their meeting in 1920. Manuk was also active in the Theosophical network between China and Australia. Some former members of the Saturn Lodge, such as H. P. Shastri and Alexander Horne, an American Jewish Theosophist, also played active parts in the re-creation of the Chinese Theosophical movement. Horne endeavored to publish Chinese Theosophical literature, and he was in charge of the "China Publication Fund," which was established by the Shanghai Lodge.[39] Furthermore, Arnold supported the Chinese in reopening the Chinese Lodge under the name of Dawn Lodge in 1924; H. P. Shastri founded the "China Lodge" in 1925 with Chinese Theosophists.[40] Under the guidance of Arnold, Theosophists in China put more emphasis on Theosophical missionary work to the Chinese. Arnold and Chinese members of the Theosophical Society established the first Theosophical school in Shanghai in 1925.

The reason Theosophists in Shanghai decided to resume their lodges and emphasize Chinese publications and education for young Chinese might relate with the situation in modern China. According to the official organ of lodges in the Far East, the *Far Eastern T. S. Notes*, in July 1924, Annie Besant visited London for a Theosophical international meeting. Lodges in China and Japan were not invited; therefore, an article was published criticizing this move in addition to commenting on the isolated position of lodges in the Far East. However, lodges in the Far East continued to follow Besant's leadership and teaching. Subsequent to this issue, members of the Shanghai Lodge were active in propagating Theosophy to young Chinese.[41]

The Besant School in Shanghai

In February 1925, one of the members of the Saturn Lodge who was also a teacher delivered lectures about Theosophy every Wednesday night to his students, aged between sixteen and eighteen years, in the lodge.[42] The movement to cultivate young Chinese Theosophists became more active because of the situation in Shanghai after the May Thirtieth Movement in 1925. As officers of the Shanghai Municipal Police opened fire on Chinese protesting against the international settlement of Shanghai on May 30, 1925, the anger of the Chinese led to a series of anti-imperialist and anti-Christian demonstrations followed by riots. The editorial notes of the *Far Eastern T. S. Notes* commented on this movement in a timely fashion. It said:

> So much has happened since the last issue of these "Notes," both from the standpoint of our Movement and on a national scale, that it is somewhat difficult to visualize events in their real perspective. More than ever would it seem true that China stands at the cross-roads of her destiny, and those who love her most, and dream that she may yet take her place among the great concord of nations who are consciously working for the progress and happiness of humanity, are at times a little fearful lest the pressure of revolutionary forces, now fomenting the consciousness of her people, may unhappily burst asunder the salutary dam of century-old traditions and national customs before these have been supplanted by other standards equally

> beneficial to the national life of people. The hope of China, as of other countries, lies in her Youth, and it is among this section of the community that the disturbing effect of these forces is most apparent. It is our deep conviction that the greatest contribution that Theosophy can make to the welfare of China lies in the educational field. To no other country does this statement apply so forcibly, because we have here a condition prevailing which enables us to offer values which would place the Theosophical Schools in an unchallengeable position in regard to both missionary and government institutions.[43]

From this article, we can learn that the intention behind the establishment of Theosophical schools was not just the propagation of Theosophy, but also to support China in facing the crisis of Western and Japanese imperialism. Another article published in the same issue, written by Dorothy Arnold and Virginia Zee (Xu Renyi), the first president and vice president of Theosophical schools in China, respectively, said:

> A great Leader in the World Youth Movement, such as Dr. G. Arundale, could undoubtedly make a big appeal to that generous element of idealism and altruism which, despite all adverse critics, lies at the heart of the Student Movement in this country, however obscured these qualities may, seemingly, appear in the course of that jarring conflict which always mars the painful transition period through which nations (and individuals) pass as they break with century-old traditions and customs to emerge into a New Era with no familiar landmarks whereby to direct their course.
>
> *We believe in the inherent greatness of China with all our hearts.* We are convinced that she will emerge from the turmoil of conflicting elements, at present struggling for the mastery, purified and united, and it is our belief that by helping her youth to realize the responsibilities and duties of real citizenship we shall be truly serving the cause of Theosophy, which is founded upon the twin rocks of Service and Brotherhood. *A great nation is built up of great individuals.* [. . .] No one has stood more firmly for the highest ideals of citizenship, or contributed more to the spiritual awakening of the race, than our great President, Dr. Annie Besant. [. . .] We cannot hope

that Dr. Besant will personally accomplish a similar miracle for China. [. . .] Her influence, however, can overshadow this country through the great ideals of Spirituality, Truth, Service, Justice, Humanitarian Citizenship, which by example and precept she has ceaselessly taught, and which are the qualities, it is our dream, to be the distinctive feature and stamp of all those who study and teach in the *Besant School in China*.

We hope, in time, that the *Besant Schools* will be widely known to stand for a unique type of education and become a real factor in moulding the young citizens of China. Our plan is that in each important town there shall, eventually, exist a *Besant School for Boys*, a *Besant School for Girls*, and a *Besant Co-educational College*, which would draw its recruits from the two former.[44]

Based on this article about the Theosophical schools that would be founded in China, we may say that they aimed at matching the great achievements of Besant and George S. Arundale in India.

Arundale, the third president of the Theosophical Society, was associated with Besant in the establishment of two Theosophical schools in India in 1913. Subsequently, he worked with Beatrice Ensor, also a Theosophist, on Theosophical education. They established the Theosophical Fraternity in Education in 1915. The Theosophical Fraternity in Education was mainly led by Ensor, and in 1921, to realize the aim of world peace through education, the New Education Fellowship was organized, also by Ensor. The slogans of the New Education Fellowship were child-centered education, social reform through education, international understanding, and the promulgation of world peace.[45]

The Theosophical educational movement in China consulted Arundale in making plans for the establishment of Theosophical schools in China. In 1925, Dorothy M. Arnold, the president of the Shanghai Lodge, wrote to Arundale asking for his assistance in establishing a school in China. On March 19, 1925, Arundale replied to her with a short letter and copies of the pamphlet "Youth," which described the educational work of Theosophists in India and the Western world. In his reply, Arundale pointed out that there were two Theosophical educational movements in India:

In India, we have two movements: (1) The League of Youth, and (2) The Youth Section of the Theosophical Society in India.

Both these movements work very harmoniously side by side, one catering for the general body of young people, and the other for those specially attached to the Theosophical point of view. In the course of our first year's effort, over one thousand young Indians, under 30 years of age, joined the Theosophical Society and the Youth Section.[46]

While its achievements were different, its overall idea was similar to that of the Chinese Theosophical movement undertaken by the Shanghai Lodge. Alexander Horne, ex-editor of the Saturn Lodge's official organ and the secretary of the Shanghai Lodge, obtained capital from American Theosophists to establish the school.[47]

After these preparations, the advertisement column of the well-known Chinese-language newspaper *Shen Pao* on July 1, 1925, announced the imminent opening of a summer school named Peicheng, which later became the Besant School for Girls in Shanghai. It reported that the school would be run by the Truth Proving Society (*Zhengdao xuehui*) and would commence operations in August 1925. The Truth Proving Society was the Chinese name for the Theosophical Society used by the Shanghai Lodge. Peicheng means "educating successful people" in Mandarin Chinese, but it is also a transliteration of Besant's name. According to the advertisement in *Shen Pao*, the Besant School for Girls was founded with the objectives of simply "finding common doctrines in the world, working hard to advance morality, and teaching others to teach themselves." It stated that the aim of the school was to "allow students to be acquainted with knowledge of East and West and to lay emphasis on both moral and physical education in order to cultivate a complete person." The coming of the Besant school was announced not only to the Chinese-speaking population but also to Western residents in Shanghai. An influential English-language newspaper in Shanghai at the time, *The China Press*, introduced the coming Theosophical school as follows:

> Tomorrow will see the opening of a Shanghai school unique in the educational annals of China. It is named The Besant School for Girls, after Dr. Annie Besant, President of the Theosophical Society, whose inspiring service in the cause of Indian education and Indian political unity have received world-wide recognition. The pioneer Theosophical work in China by the late Dr. Wu Ting-fang is also one of the indirect influences

determining the present venture. The school is located in 316 and 317 Bubbling Well Road near Hart Road.

The regular staff consists of four foreign and four Chinese members, Miss Dorothy Arnold being Principal. The curriculum is comprehensive enough for all requirements, including, besides the usual English and mathematical subjects, the principal sciences, ancient and modern history and physical culture with music, stenography and Esperanto as optional studies.

The distinctive feature of the school, however, is the religious teaching offered, which is to be on such broad lines as no Mission or Government would dare to cover. "Every effort," the prospectus reads, "will be made to give students the highest possible teaching in the religions to which they belong. Thus the Buddhists will be given religious instruction by a competent priest of their own faith; the Christians will have the guidance of an enlightened Christian teacher; and the Taoists and followers of the great Confucius will be given every opportunity to study the inspiring teachings of these respective schools of philosophy."

Only free recognition by the founders of the essential unity of the great religions could have suggested and sanctioned such an innovation. In adopting, along with this plan, the motto "Truth, Tolerance and Brotherhood," they aim at a rapprochement between the different faiths and ethical systems and a fusion of different cultures.[48]

This English-language newspaper introduced the forthcoming Besant school as "unique in the educational annals of China." By contrast, *Shen Pao* announced the Besant School for Girls as a school that would cultivate mutual cultural understanding between East and West, a school for building friendship and universal brotherhood, elements that were emphasized by *The China Press*. However, although *The China Press* considered the comparative religion course as a "unique" feature of the Besant school in Shanghai, *Shen Pao* did not mention this at all.

After a session of summer school in August, the Besant School for Girls was opened permanently on September 10, 1925, in the Shanghai International Settlement. Arnold and a former member of the Saturn Lodge taught English lessons; there was also at least one Chinese teacher for Chinese classics. Kiang Kang-hu (1883–1954), a controversial politician and scholar whose thought was said to have influenced Mao Zedong (1893–1976), was its honorary principal.[49] In *Shen Pao*, the Besant School for Girls was announced as accepting boys younger than twelve for the summer school and boys younger than fourteen for the regular Besant School. There also was a dormitory for boarding students,[50] as in Arundale's Theosophical schools in India.[51] An emphasis was placed on Chinese education in the school. Also according to *Shen Pao*, the junior high school (*Yu ke*) at the Besant School for Girls in Shanghai required academic achievement in Chinese for at least four years. It also provided language courses for senior or married women in the afternoon, not only in teaching English but also in Chinese.

Initially, the school shared buildings with Shanghai Lodge at 316 and 317 Bubbling Well Road (currently West Nanjing Road) near Hart Road (currently Hede Road). However, the school went well and expanded, moving to No. 61 Carter Road (currently Shimen'er Road) on May 1, 1926.[52]

In its first year, Shanghai's Besant school followed "the usual course adopted by all schools."[53] The only difference was its operation in accordance with the principles of the Theosophical Society: every effort was made to give the students "the highest possible teaching of religion."[54] In 1926, Arnold reported on the current state of the Besant School for Girls:

> A fine spirit of fellowship is beginning to appear among the students, whose whole attitude has undergone complete transformation since they came under our influence. The sullen suspicion and sense of rebellion which marked their attitude in the early days has entirely given place to feelings of trust and friendship. The formation by the students of a Youth Lodge, "The Besant Lodge," has done much to consolidate the School and testifies to the appreciation of the students themselves of the ideals set before them in their daily spiritual charge, or morning address, based on "At the Feet of the Master."[55]

The Theosophical Youth educational movement moved smoothly in its first year. However, Arnold worried about the school's finances and consulted with Horne. Horne's publicizing of the school to American Theosophists brought about regular contributions.[56] The Besant school's balance between Chinese and Western subjects was different than in the Christian missionary schools in China. Arnold proudly wrote the following:

> The first impression that strikes a visitor to the School is the atmosphere of happiness and freedom from restraint that characterizes the students, who look upon the School as theirs, and have profoundly associated themselves with its development. Many times, parents and students have commended us for the high moral influence permeating the place, and also for the careful attention given to the Chinese side of curriculum. Usually, in the Schools under foreign auspices, the national culture of the students is neglected to their detriment, and we have, therefore, been especially careful to avoid falling into the error of maintaining a high standard in English at the expense of the students' knowledge of their own language.[57]

In the Shanghai of 1926, among private schools run by Westerners, the Besant School for Girls was "unique" in its emphasis on Chinese culture and that it granted its students the freedom to choose their own religious beliefs. The McTyeire School for girls (Zhongxi nüshu) was a well-known girls' school in Shanghai contemporary with Shanghai's Besant school. Heidi A. Ross pointed out that, by the early twentieth century:

> McTyeire's education aims reflected both the accomplishments wealthy families desired in their daughters and the moral character and refined breeding that comprised the mission school's "gospel of gentility": to offer students a firm grounding in Chinese and English through a liberal arts education; to offer a series of elective classes in Western music; to build a wholesome educational environment which would cultivate young Chinese women of high moral character and mental habits; and to provide students with fundamental knowledge of Christianity.[58]

However, after the May Thirtieth Movement in 1925, Chinese elites urged their government to adopt reformist policies promoting educational rights. Education was adopted as an effective method of opposing Western religion and imperialistic thinking. The recovery of the educational rights movement also became more highly regarded by the Chinese after 1925. In September 1926, Shanghai's Besant school announced the coming of a new college in *Shen Pao*'s ad column. They announced their plans to found a new college, with coeducational evening courses in business, science, and the arts, to start on October 1. Thus, the scope of the Theosophical educational program was going to be broadened.

However, the Chinese government also promulgated a series of regulations for educational rights in the same year. Even schools in the international settlement were forced to follow these regulations. Religious curricula, as well as schools having foreign headmasters and principals, became forbidden. Therefore, both the name of the Theosophical Society and its educational goals were omitted from the announcement in the advertisement for the Besant school in *Shen Pao*.

Circumstances soon became even worse. Xu Renyi (Virginia Zee), vice president and one of the founders of the Besant School for Girls, and a keen Chinese Theosophist, left the school suddenly and took many of the Chinese teachers and students with her in January 1928.

Xu Renyi found a new supporter immediately: Luo Jialing. Luo was the wife of Silas Aaron Hardoon. Hardoon's huge Aili yuan residence in Shanghai was named by his wife, and the pair established a Buddhist lodge and university in the gardens there. Xu Renyi borrowed a site in the gardens for a new girls' school, named "Trinity School for Girls,"[59] one week after she left the Besant school. Xu even posted an announcement titled "To the parents of Besant School for Girls' students"[60] in *Shen Pao*, which ran for more than a month. The article criticized the school's character as being incompatible with the Chinese character, stating that the author was no longer able to see any possibility for cooperation. Furthermore, she said that she and her comrades regretted leaving educational work to foreigners and letting them trample on the youth of China. In the end, the Chinese youth had become barbarians and failed to get rid of their servile disposition. Xu said the new school was established owing to student demand; the students wished to benefit from the movement for the recovery of educational rights in China. Xu's father, Xu Xiaonong (?–1932), was a famous scholar and doctor of Chinese medicine in Shanghai; he was the school's principal in name. Xu Renyi's announcement likely affected the reputation of the Besant School for Girls.

The reason for this split is not clear, but it happened soon after Arnold came back to China in the middle of September 1927 from her visit to "leaders of the Theosophical Movement."[61] Also, the Besant school welcomed a new Chinese principal, Kuai Shuping, who had received a master's degree at Oxford University in January 1928.[62] In 1929, the school moved to 1 Ferry Road (currently Xikang Road), a building with an area of 1,973 square meters.[63]

After 1929, private schools established by foreigners were forced to register at the educational bureau of Shanghai. Schools in the International Settlement were not ruled by the Chinese government, but the Chinese government established laws stating that only degrees from registered schools would be recognized. Graduates needed an accepted degree to apply to a university in China. Gradually, the curriculum of the Besant School for Girls came to be similar to that of Christian missionary schools. However, many missionary schools in Shanghai had religious subjects as club activities after the regular classes. When a graduate of McTyeire School for Girls who graduated in 1936 talked about her domestic science lessons, she said, "McTyeire's students were all noble ladies. No one would like to work a sewing machine by foot! Our Home Ec. was taught by [a] Western teacher. She took many flowers and taught us flower arrangement."[64] By contrast, Besant's students knitted sweaters for charity. They considered sports to be important and played basketball, volleyball, and ping-pong in teams at their school. Private girls' missionary schools seldom took sports seriously. Furthermore, many missionary schools run by Westerners had subjects or clubs of Western classical music; Besant had both Western and traditional Chinese music clubs. On the other hand, private schools established by Chinese people often had similar tendencies to Shanghai's Besant school. Although the times made it hard for the Besant school in Shanghai to educate Chinese youth according to the ideal of "universal brotherhood" among religions, philosophies, races, and nations, the Besant school in Shanghai can be seen as a unique pioneer in the history of the Chinese education movement's battle with imperialism and Western civilization.

Cao Jinyuan, the Chinese principal of the Besant school, published an English-language article in the yearbook of the Besant school in 1933. She wrote:

> Present conditions in China reveal this truth in a very remarkable and convincing manner. China does not lack brilliant scientists, clever politicians, able lawyers, and skillful engineers. In fact, in all walks of life, we find many clever and well-trained people. Yet, when the iron-hand of the invader is laid upon China, we feel helpless. Why is this so? China has more schools and educated people than she ever had in all her history, yet

the spirit which made China so great a country in the past seems to be disappeared. [. . .] China is passing through a very critical stage in her history. Whether her ancient civilization will survive this supreme test or not depends mainly upon her sons and daughters.[65]

Principal Cao's family came to be powerful in Shanghai's Besant school in the 1930s. For the educational rights recovery movement, the principal of a registered school could only be Chinese. For this reason, Arnold's official title in the school became "chief English teacher" in the Chinese-language records.[66] Principal Cao's uncle, Cao Yunxian (1881–1937, known as Y. S. Tsao in his lifetime), was principal of Tsinghua University, Beijing, and was a pioneer of Bahá'í Faith propaganda in China. Cao Yunxian's wife was a Theosophist and member of the Besant School Board until 1943.[67] Cao attended Shanghai's Besant school's graduation ceremony and was a member of the school's board in 1935.[68] In 1935, Arnold took one semester's leave because of illness[69] and vanished thereafter. She was called "Founder of Our School" in the yearbook of the Besant School in 1937, although she was not in the group photo of the school faculty. The state of the Theosophical movement in Shanghai after the late 1930s has not yet been fully elucidated; however, as a school where Eastern and Western teachers cooperated, the Besant School for Girls in Shanghai might be viewed as a practical example of the concept of "universal brotherhood."

Conclusion

In the 1910s, Wu emphasized the importance of making the Chinese believe in the existence of life after death. He also emphasized that research on life after death is not superstitious, nor should it be marginalized. He used Confucian and Daoist sayings as a way in, and his collections of Western spiritual photography as evidence. Before introducing the notion of Theosophy, he had to explain the idea of life after death. His Chinese lectures about Theosophy during the 1910s only briefly mentioned what Theosophy and the Theosophical Society were. His first detailed introduction about H. P. Blavatsky and the Theosophical Society was in his first Chinese-language Theosophical manual, published in 1921. The reason might be explained by his conversation with the Indian scholar

Benoy Kumar Sarkar (1887–1949) in 1916, in which Wu asked Sarkar if he knew about Theosophy:

> Wu laughed and said, "Right. These days I'm thinking of visiting Madras when the war is over." When Sarkar enquired if the visit to Madras would be a "pilgrimage," Wu laugh and said, "Right. These days I'm studying (the concepts of) soul, the world beyond death, rebirth, etc. I've given up eating fish and meat. It's my desire to lead a solitary life on a mountain following the ideals of your Buddha." Wu also told Sarkar that he had started a movement among the Chinese youth to reform their eating habits by becoming vegetarians. To promote this movement, he opened a restaurant that served only vegetarian food. "But the customers were limited," the old diplomat told him, "then one night some miscreants set fire to the restaurant . . . and that's why I am very disheartened." Using his personal loss as a metaphor for the political uncertainties in China, Wu remarks, "After all, in every reform movement in the world the pioneers or the pathfinders experience such maladies."[70]

According to this conversation, Wu's concern with Theosophy started from his interest in spirituality, and his Theosophical movement may be defined as a movement for progress and social reform. After Wu returned to China in 1910, he immediately established a society for vegetarianism (*Shenshi weisheng hui*). Then the next year he attended the "First Universal Races Congress" in London and declared his ideal of Chinese Civilization. In his English book *America: Through the Spectacles of an Oriental Diplomat* (1914), Wu mentioned Annie Besant's support as far as two of his ideas were concerned: the citizenship of immigrants and the benefits of vegetarianism. Hu has rightfully pointed out similarities between Wu's political ideas and his Theosophical literature:[71] indeed, Wu's objection to enacting Confucianism as the only Chinese state religion was based on the Theosophical aim of "universal brotherhood."

Around 1918, Chinese intellectuals were working on psychical research in Shanghai to prove the existence of life after death. Many well-known intellectuals were engaged in psychical research to introduce it as a new science in the West. Wu Tingfang's view of the soul was used in support of their theory. Their work was a fusion of psychical research and traditional religious rites. Their research was severely criticized for being based on superstition by members of the New Culture Movement, which criticized traditional values and advocated Western civilization. This made people steer clear of spiritual issues and religions. Those audiences who listened to Wu's Theosophical speeches during the 1910s might have obtained the impression that Theosophy was similar to Spiritualism.

In 1912, the Republic of China was established. Then World War I began in Europe. Chinese intellectuals in the 1910s focused on conflicts between the "old" and "new." They tried to understand what kind of civilization their country needed. In this way, they were enthusiastic about finding solutions for what they regarded as two problems in China: moral bankruptcy and loss of spiritual faith. These attempts to define Chinese culture were intertwined with the aim to renegotiate the meaning of religions and philosophies.[72] Against this historical background, Wu not only added "moral" to the Theosophical Society's Chinese name but also expounded on the existence of life after death. He encouraged the Chinese to conduct research on all kind of religions and philosophies from across the world. Wu's Theosophical propaganda fit the Zeitgeist. Under his leadership, the Theosophical movement conducted research on spirituality, social reform, and anti-colonialist movements. However, since then, the Chinese have considered these activities separately instead of understanding them as parts of the Theosophical movement. Wu Tingfang was one of the pioneers of Spiritualism and vegetarianism in China and was admired for his efforts in gaining equal rights for Chinese immigrants. Because these achievements were based on the aims of the Theosophical Society, the Theosophical impact in modern China should be reassessed.

On the other hand, the unique Theosophical education that the Theosophists aimed to practice failed mainly because of the situation brought about by the rise of Western and Japanese imperialism in China. The Theosophical Society's aim of "universal brotherhood" was a key feature of Theosophical propaganda in China. From the 1910s to the early 1920s, Wu's Theosophical propaganda presented Theosophy, and in particular its internationalist aspects, as an effective theory for Chinese social improvement and as a tool to negotiate cultural conflicts between the East and West in China. Moreover, with the intensification of Western and Japanese imperialism in China, the needs for social improvement changed into a need for national salvation. The educational rights movement and the anti-Christian demonstrations held from the mid-1920s in China were both related to anti-colonialism. The Chinese did not resist Christianity because of anti-religious sentiments; rather, wariness of being culturally colonialized by Christian missionaries was the more important causal factor for those demonstrations. Moreover, the fusion of Eastern and Western thought by foreigners was perceived as dangerous by the Chinese people for the same reason. It was difficult for the Chinese to perceive the difference between "universal brotherhood" and Western cultural colonialism. However, although the Theosophical educational movement and Wu's Theosophical literature have been forgotten by the Chinese, the Chinese Theosophists who participated in its educational movement worked actively in the Chinese educational world. Furthermore, those activities of Wu's Theosophical propaganda, such as human rights and vegetarianism, are remembered by people in Greater China and continue to be practiced as social reform movements even today.

Notes

1. However, when James Henry Cousins, an Irish writer and Theosophist, met Wu in Hong Kong on his way back to Adyar in 1920, he said that Wu "carries a form to apply for fellowship when he is free of official restrictions" (*New India*, May 20, 1920). I am grateful to Kurt Leland for his generous assistance with the membership register. On Cousins, see the contribution by Hashimoto Yorimitsu to this volume.

2. William Walker Atkinson, "The Trail That Is Always New," *The Progress Magazine* 7 (1909). Special thanks to Philip Deslippe for providing the material.

3. "Spirits Converse with Wu Ting Fang: Chinese Minister Attends a Seance and Probes Mysteries of Occult World," *The San Francisco Call*, October 15, 1909.

4. Concerning Spurgeon Medhurst and his "fight" for Theosophy, see Judith C. Powles, "Misguided or Misunderstood? The Case of Charles Spurgeon Medhurst (1860–1927), Baptist Missionary to China," *Baptist Quarterly* 43, no. 6 (2010).

5. Theosophical Society, ed., *International Theosophical Year Book: Giving the History and Organization of the Theosophical Society, a Theosophical Who's Who, the President's Policy etc.* (Adyar: The Theosophical Publishing House, 1937), 225.

6. Ding Xianjun and Yu Zuofeng, "Wu Ting Fang dashi jiyao," in *Wu Tingfang pingzhuan*, ed. Ding Xianjun and Yu Zuofeng (Beijing: Renmin chubanshe, 2005). It says that in 1910, Wu took a break from work owing to his "illness." Also, Wu hoped to "gather Western and Chinese intellectuals who live in Shanghai together for the establishment of a Theosophical Society and carry on research on the essence of religions such as Confucianism, Buddhism, Christianity, and Islam." Unless otherwise indicated, all translations from Chinese or Japanese into English are mine.

7. Besant was together with Gandhi and W. E. B. Du Bois (Michael P. Cowen and R. W. Shenton, *Doctrines of Development* [London: Routledge, 1996], 299). However, although Wu strongly admired Besant, it seems that Wu did not meet her in his lifetime. See Benoy Kumar Sarkar, *Bartaman Yuge Chin Samrajya* (Kolkata: Siddheshwar Press, 1922). The original language is Bengali. I consulted the English digest version from Narayan C. Sen, "China as Viewed by Two Early Bengali Travellers: The Travel Accounts of Indumadhav Mullick and Benoy Kumar Sarka," *China Report* 43, no. 465 (2007).

8. Wu Ting-fang, "China," in *Papers on Inter-racial Problems, Communicated to the First Universal Races Congress, Held at the University of London, July 26–29, 1911*, ed. Gustav Spiller (Miami: HardPress Publishing. Reprinted from London: P. S. King & Son [1911]), 132. Wu's paper was also reported by *The Theosophist* in October 1911 (Adyar: The Theosophical Society, 138).

9. Wu Tingfang, "Zhi Yuan Shikai shu," first appearance in April 20 (1916), in *Wu Tingfang ji*, ed. idem et al. (Beijing: Zhonghua shuju, 1993), 785. Yuan Shi-kai (1859–1916), who desired to establish a Chinese Empire, hoped Wu would come to his camp, but Wu refused many times. In this letter, Wu said that he had given up the idea of searching for fame and fortune for years. He wanted to visit India to study Zen and Brahmanism, etc., but could not anticipate World War I. Wu ironically invited Yuan to visit India together with him someday.

10. "Shijie zongjiao huiquan ying Zhang tianshi," *Shen Pao*, September 14, 1912.

11. Charles Spurgeon Medhurst, *The Tao teh king: A Short Study in Comparative Religion* (Chicago: Theosophical Book Concern, 1905), 134.

12. "Wu Tingfang yanshuo zongjiao," *Shen Pao*, January 14, 1916.

13. *Xuesheng zazhi* 3, no. 4 (1916): 20–21.

14. In Wu's first Theosophical handbook, "Wu Tingfang's theory of soul," he used a similar explanation for *qi*. He said that there were more than ten photographs of *qi* in *Thought Forms*, which had been published by the Theosophical Society's headquarters (Wu Tingfang, *Wu Tingfang linghun xueshuo* [Shanghai: Shanghai lingxun janijiushe, 1921], 7–8).

15. Wu and other Theosophists in China considered Theosophy's Chinese translation and renamed it three times before 1921. In "Wu Tingfang's theory of soul," following the preface, he explained the reasons for these acts of renaming. He stated that he was afraid that the *Tongshen* Society might be misunderstood as a society for connecting with ghosts and gods; hence, he added "moral" (*dao de*) before *tongshen* to illustrate the true aim of the society. However, a Westerner criticized the name, so Wu and his friend came up with a new name, Mingdao, which means "to clarify the natural laws." However, "Wu Tingfang's theory of soul" uses another name to refer to the society: *Linghun xueshuo mingdaohui* (Society for clarifying the theories about the soul).

16. "Zi buyu guili luanshen"; "Wei zhi sheng yan zhi si."

17. *Gui* may refer to both ghost and demon in Chinese.

18. "Wu Zhiyong xiansheng Tingfang yanjiang tongshenxue," *Linshi kanbu yuekan* 14 (1916): 1.

19. Anonymous, "Higher Buddhism," *The North-China Herald*, December 23, 1910, 725–26.

20. Son Ji hye, "East-West Communication and Modern Buddhism: Timothy Richard's Translations of Buddhist Scriptures and His Understanding of Buddhism," *Tōzai gakujutsu kenkyūjo kiyō* 48 (2015): 281.

21. Powles, "Misguided."

22. Mahayana Association membership list, 1916.

23. In August 1916, the Theosophical magazine, *Reincarnation*, wrote about Wu's and Medhurst's Theosophical movement as follows: "It is a pleasure to note that the Legion work has been satisfactorily started in Shanghai, China, where there are now six members and an active Group will probably soon be chartered. Among the members are the well-known names of Wu Tingfang, former Chinese minister to the United States, and Rev. C. Spurgeon." Then, in November of that year, the magazine of the Theosophical Society in Adyar, *The Theosophist*, reported that Wu and Medhurst were forming a Theosophical study circle (*The Theosophist* 38 [1916]: 122).

24. Anonymous, "Obituary: Rev. C. S. Medhurst, Formerly of China," *The North-China Herald*, September 17, 1927.

25. George W. Carter, "From Study Circle to Lodge," *The Saturn Lodge Monthly* 1, no. 1 (1920).

26. Although Wu said that the founder of the first Theosophical lodge in China was "a British man, Carter" (see anon., ed., "Dialogues on Theosophy," *Dr. Wu's Works on Theosophy* [Shanghai: China Publication Fund; this book was published after 1924, but the exact year of publication is unknown], 12), the first president of Saturn Lodge was Hara Prasad Shastri.

27. Ibid.; Carter, "From Study Circle," 20.

28. Anonymous, "The Anniversary Meeting," *The Saturn Lodge Monthly* 1, no. 7 (1921).

29. Hari Prasad Shastri was born in Bareilly, India, and is known as a Sanskrit scholar and Yoga teacher. Shastri graduated from the Hindu College, a school established on the initiative of Annie Besant. According to a report from 1920 in the Adyar Archives (file: Chi-1.22), Shastri should be a member of the U. P. Federation ("Shantidavaka Lodge, Morababad, U. P."); however, no records pertaining to him could be found in records of the U. P. Federation or of the Indian Section of the Theosophical Society. In 1916 he moved to Japan. After teaching at Waseda University and Tokyo Imperial University for two years, he went to China on the offer of his Chinese friend Dr. Sun Yat-Sen and taught at Cangseng mingzhi University, a university established by the famous Jewish businessman Silas Aaron Hardoon (1851–1931). He lived in China for eleven

years and established "Holy Yoga," a study group for Raja Yoga in Shanghai. Wu Tingfang also practiced yoga with him in Wu's own residence. When in Japan, Shastri also had a connection to Paul Richard, the French Indophile esotericist and sometime associate of the Theosophical Society. See the contribution by Hans Martin Krämer to this volume. On the other hand, Shastri was also an agent for the British. See Richard J. Popplewel, *Intelligence and Imperial Defence: British Intelligence and the Defence of Indian Empire 1904–1924* (London: Frank Cass, 1995), 278–79. After moving to Shanghai, Shastri was not only active in the Theosophical movement, but also endeavored in promoting the ideal of Asian Unity. In the 1920s, Shastri established some groups for Asian unity in Shanghai; one of them was the Shanghai Pan-Asian Society [Ch. Yazhou Minzu Xiehui, Jp. Shanghai Dai Ajia Kyōkai]. The Society was led by Shastri and Tongu Hiroshi, a Japanese doctor who was well-known to the local Shanghai people at that time. The society had its official organ, *The Asiatic Review (Daya Zazhi)*, which was a Chinese and English-language magazine. Shastri was the editor of its English pages. We may suggest that Shastri's movements in the Far East during 1916–1929 cooperated with Japanese Pan-Asianism. Special thanks are due to Dr. Craig Smith for the information about the bilingual (Chinese-English) magazine *The Asiatic Review*. The magazine was published in 1920s China by an Asianism group called the Asiatic Association. Shastri was one of its active members and worked as the magazine's English editor.

30. Popplewel, *Intelligence*, 120.

31. Ibid.

32. Kinson Tsiang, "Inauguration of the Dawn Lodge, Shanghai," *Far Eastern T. S. Notes* 2, no. 1 (January–February 1925): 8. Tsiang said the first Chinese lodge was Wu's Sun Lodge, and that Dawn Lodge was the second lodge run by Chinese Theosophists.

33. Wu, *Linghun xueshuo*. As for Wu's Theosophical literature, Chuang (2014) identifies its characteristics as a fusion through his unique view of civilization between East and West. See Chien-hui Chuang, "Chūgoku kara kieta shinchigaku kyōkai," *Studies in Comparative Culture* 111 (2014).

34. Southwest (Xinan) University.

35. Cousins (1920). Two thousand rupees in 1920 would be about 13,200 U.S. dollars today.

36. Though Cousins did not mention the details of Wu's stay in Hong Kong in the article he published in *New India* soon after his return to India, he wrote about it in detail in later years. (See James Henry Cousins and Margaret E. Cousins, *We Two Together* [Madras: Ganesh, 1950], 368–69.)

37. Kinson Tsiang, the president of the Theosophical Society's Dawn Lodge in Shanghai, said: "Although, here in Shanghai, there are two or three branches, yet they have been established by foreigners. It was not until the tenth year of

the Chinese Republic that a new branch, under the name of the 'Sun' Lodge, was organized by Dr. Wu Ting-fang, a learned Chinese, who sympathized very much with the objects; but after his death, as there was no one to hold it together, the Lodge gradually became extinct" (Tsiang, "Inauguration," 8).

38. For a brief history of the Hong Kong Lodge, see Brian Edgar, "Herbert Edward Lanepart (1): Theosophy in Old Hong Kong," https://brianedgar.wordpress.com/2012/11/09/herbert-edward-lanepart-1-theosophy-in-old-hong-kong/. The Theosophical acceptances between Chinese in Shanghai and Hong Kong were different. I introduce these differences in another paper.

39. On Horne, see also the contribution by Boaz Huss to this volume.

40. "Editorial Notes," *Far Eastern T. S. Notes* 2, no. 2 (March–April 1925): 3.

41. "Our President," *Far Eastern T. S. Notes* 1, no. 6 (November–December 1924): 3.

42. "Editorial Notes," *Far Eastern T. S. Notes* 2, no. 1 (January–February 1925): 2.

43. "Editorial Notes," *Far Eastern T. S. Notes* 2, no. 3 (May–June 1925): 1.

44. "The Besant School in China," *Far Eastern T. S. Notes* 2, no. 3 (May–June 1925): 6–7.

45. See Iwama Hiroshi, *Exploring the Sources of UNESCO: New Education Fellowship and Theosophical Society* (Tokyo: Gakuensha, 2008).

46. *Far Eastern T. S. Notes* 2, no. 3 (May–June 1925): 16–17.

47. *Far Eastern T. S. Notes* 2, no. 3 (May–June 1925): 4.

48. "Besant School for Girls to Open Tomorrow," *The China Press*, September 9, 1925.

49. Kiang was one of the founders of the Chinese Socialist Party. He was lowly regarded in previous studies in China after World War I for his cooperation with Wang Jingwei (1883–1944). Kiang left China to Canada to work as a sinologist at McGill University until 1933. His efforts toward introducing Chinese culture to the Western world have been reevaluated in recent studies (See Li Shan, "Jiang Kanghu Beimei chuanbo Zhongguo wenhua shulun," *Shi lin* 2, [2011]). Kiang took Theosophy as an example of the potential of Eastern spirituality to propagate to the West (cf. Wang Zhangcai, "Ouzhan yu Zhongguo wenhua," in *Jiang Kanghu boshi yanjiang lu*, ed. Nanfang University Press (Shanghai: Taipingyang yinshua gongsi, 1923), 176. Kiang also gave a lecture about Confucianism at Shanghai's Theosophical lodge in 1936 ("New Light Shed on Confucius," *The China Press*, January 9, 1936).

50. No. 114-01-00002-0002-002, Shanghai city, Jing'an district official document archives.

51. See Iwama, *Exploring*, chapter 2.

52. The Shanghai Lodge also moved with the school.

53. "School of Theosophists Here Makes Great Strides," *The China Press*, September 12, 1926.

54. Ibid.

55. "The Besant School for Girls," *Far Eastern T. S. Notes* 2, no. 4 (July–October 1926): 9.

56. Anonymous, "A Dollar a Month for China," *The Messenger* 13 (March 1926); Anonymous, "Besant School for Girls—China," *The Messenger* 13 (April 1926).

57. Anonymous, "Besant School for Girls," 8.

58. Heidi A. Ross, "Cradle of Female Talent: The McTyeire Home and School for Girls, 1892–1937," in *Christianity in China: From the Eighteenth Century to the Present*, ed. Daniel H. Bays (Stanford, CA: Stanford University Press, 1996), 214.

59. Its Chinese name is "Zhirenyong nüxue." The school's motto is *Wisdom, Love, and Will*.

60. "Peicheng nüxiao xuesheng jiazhang gongqi."

61. "Sunday Pictorial Section," *The China Press*, September 4, 1927.

62. Anonymous, "Peicheng nüxiao xiaozhang," *Shen Pao*, January 29, 1928.

63. It was reported that this move was due to young men roaming around the school. See Wei Qiang, "Peicheng nüxiao qiaoqian suji," *Zhongguo sheying xuehui huabao* 4, no. 192 (1929).

64. *Mingguo shiqi Shanghai nüzi jiaoyu koushu yanjiu* (Xi'an: Shanxi shifan daxue chuban zongshe, 2014), 16.

65. Cao Jinyuan, "Untitled," *The Besant/Peicheng niankan* (1937 Shanghai Besant Girls' School Yearbook Publication/*1937-nian niankanshe*).

66. She was still identified as "principal" in the 1932 graduation certificate's English version. but her name was omitted in the Chinese version. In 1932, Western teachers of the school were Arnold and Lily Noblston, who had been a member of Theosophical Society ever since Saturn Lodge.

67. No. 114-01-00008-0002-002, Shanghai city, Jing'an district official document archives.

68. *Shen Pao*, July 2, 1935.

69. No. 114-01-00002-0015-051, Shanghai city, Jing'an district official document archives. According to the staff list of Pei-cheng from 1928 to 1954, Arnold worked as chief English teacher until the autumn of 1935 (No. 114-01-00007-0006-012, Shanghai city, Jing'an district official document archives).

70. Sen, "China as Viewed by Two Early Bengali Travellers," 478. His vegetarian restaurant reopened in Shanghai in July 1915.

71. Hu Xuecheng, "Wu Tingfang de tongshenxue yu lingxuesheng ya," *Zheng da shi cui* 22 (2012): 13.

72. About Chinese intellectuals' attempts to define borderlines between science, religion, superstition, and philosophy in modern China, see Max K.

W. Huang, "Zhongguo jindai sixiang zhong de mixin," in *Higashi Ajia ni okeru chiteki kōryū*, ed. Sadami Suzuki and Jian-hui Liu (Kyoto: Kokusai Nihon bunka kenkyū sentā, 2013).

References

"A Dollar a Month for China." *The Messenger* 13, no. 10 (March 1926): 202.
Atkinson, William Walker. "The Trail That Is Always New." *The Progress Magazine* 7 (1909): 25–26.
"Besant School for Girls to Open Tomorrow." *The China Press*, September 9, 1925.
"Besant School for Girls—China." *The Messenger* 13 (April 1926): 240.
Cai, Degui. *Qing hua zhi fu Cao Yunxiang Zhuan ji pian* [Cao Yunxiang, the Father of Tsinghua University: Biography]. Xi'an Shi: Shanxi shi fan da xue chu ban she, 2011.
Cao Jinyuan. "Untitled." *The Besant/Peicheng niankan* (1937 Shanghai Besant Girls' School Yearbook Publication/*1937-nian niankanshe*).
Carter, George W. "From Study Circle to Lodge." *The Saturn Lodge Monthly* 1, no. 1 (1920): 18–19.
Chin, Vicente Hao. "China, Theosophy in." Last modified August 6, 2010. http://theosophy.ph/encyclo/index.php?title=China,_Theosophy_in.
Chin, Vicente Hao. "Theosophy in China." *July 2012 Newsletter*. http://singapore-lodge.org/2012_july_news.htm.
Chuang, Chien-hui. "Chūgoku kara kieta shinchigaku kyōkai [The Theosophical Society that disappeared from China]." *Studies in Comparative Culture* 111 (2014): 245–53.
Cousins, James. "A Visit to Japan." *New India*, May 20, 1920.
Cousins, James Henry, and Margaret E. Cousins. *We Two Together*. Madras: Ganesh, 1950.
Cowen, Michael P., and R. W. Shenton. *Doctrines of Development*. London: Routledge, 1996.
Crow, Carl. *China Takes Her Place*. New York and London: Harper & Bros, 1944.
"Dialogues on Theosophy." In *Dr. Wu's Works on Theosophy*, edited by Anonymous. Shanghai: China Publication Fund, exact year of publication unknown (post-1924).
Ding, Xianjun, and Yu, Zuofeng, ed. *Wu Tingfang pingzhuan* [A critical biography of Wu Tingfang]. Beijing: Renmin chubanshe, 2005.
Edgar, Brian. "Herbert Edward Lanepart (1): Theosophy in Old Hong Kong." https://brianedgar.wordpress.com/2012/11/09/herbert-edward-lanepart-1-theosophy-in-old-hong-kong/.
"Editorial Notes." *Far Eastern T. S. Notes* 2, no. 1 (January–February 1925).

"Editorial Notes." *Far Eastern T. S. Notes* 2, no. 2 (March–April 1925).
"Editorial Notes." *Far Eastern T. S. Notes* 2, no. 3 (May–June 1925).
Feng, Kaiwen, ed. *Zhongguo Minguo jiaoyu shi* [Education History of the Republic of China]. Beijing: Renmin chubanshe, 1994.
Flynt, Wayne, and Gerald W. Berkley. *Taking Christianity to China: Alabama Missionaries in the Middle Kingdom, 1850–1950.* Tuscaloosa: University of Alabama Press, 1997.
"Higher Buddhism." *The North-China Herald*, December 23, 1910.
Hu, Xuecheng. "Wu Tingfang de tongshenxue yu lingxuesheng ya [Wu Ting-fang, Theosophy, and Spiritualism]." *Zheng da shi cui* 22 (2012): 3–20.
Huang, Max K. W. "Zhongguo jindai sixiang zhong de mixin [Superstition in modern Chinese thoughts]." In *Higashi Ajia ni okeru chiteki kōryū* [Exchange of knowledge in East Asia], edited by Sadami Suzuki and Jian-hui Liu, 185–200. Kyoto: Kokusai Nihon bunka kenkyū sentā, 2013.
Iwama, Hiroshi. *Exploring the Sources of UNESCO: New Education Fellowship and Theosophical Society.* Tokyo: Gakuensha, 2008.
Kinouchi, Makoto. *Shanhai rekishi gaido mappu: Zōhō kaiteiban* [Historical guide maps of Shanghai. Revised and supplemented edition]. Tokyo: Taishūkan Shoten, 2011.
Li, Shan. "Jiang Kanghu Beimei chuanbo Zhongguo wenhua shulun [Jiang Kanghu's Dissemination of Chinese Culture in North America]." *Shi lin* 2 (2011). Online version. http://jds.cass.cn/ztyj/shwhs/201605/t20160506_3326282.shtml.
Medhurst, Charles Spurgeon. *The Tao teh king: A Short Study in Comparative Religion.* Chicago: Theosophical Book Concern, 1905.
"New Light Shed on Confucius." *The China Press*, January 9, 1936.
"Obituary: Rev. C. S. Medhurst, Formerly of China." *The North-China Herald*, September 17, 1927.
"Our President." *Far Eastern T. S. Notes* 1, no. 6 (November–December 1924).
"Peicheng nüxiao xiaozhang [Besant Girls' School: Principal]." *Shen Pao*, January 29, 1928.
Pomerantz-Zhang, Linda. *Wu Tingfang (1842–1922): Reform and Modernization in Modern Chinese History.* Hong Kong: Hong Kong University Press, 1992.
Popplewel, Richard J. *Intelligence and Imperial Defence: British Intelligence and the Defence of Indian Empire 1904–1924.* London: Frank Cass, 1995.
Powles, Judith C. "Misguided or Misunderstood? The Case of Charles Spurgeon Medhurst (1860–1927), Baptist Missionary to China." *Baptist Quarterly* 43, no. 6 (2010): 347–64.
Prothero, Stephen R. *The White Buddhist: The Asian Odyssey of Henry Steel Olcott.* Bloomington: Indiana University Press, 1996.
Ross, Heidi A. "Cradle of Female Talent: The McTyeire Home and School for Girls, 1892–1937." In *Christianity in China: From the Eighteenth Century*

to the Present, edited by Daniel H. Bays, 209–27. Stanford, CA: Stanford University Press, 1996.

Sarkar, Benoy Kumar. *Bartaman Yuge Chin Samrajya* [The Chinese Empire in the Present Age]. Kolkata: Siddheshwar Press: 1922.

"School of Theosophists Here Makes Great Strides." *The China Press*, September 12, 1926.

Sen, Narayan C. "China as Viewed by Two Early Bengali Travellers: The Travel Accounts of Indumadhav Mullick and Benoy Kumar Sarka." *China Report* 43, no. 465 (2007): 477–78.

"Shijie zongjiao huiquan ying Zhang tianshi [World Religions Research Society welcomed Master Zhang]," *Shen Pao*, September 14, 1912.

Shu, Xincheng, ed. *Jindai Zhongguo jiaoyu shiliao* [Educational historical materials in modern China], *Jindai Zhongguo shiliao congkan xubian* [Sequel of historical materials in modern China series], Vol. 66. Taipei: Wenhai chubanshe, 1977.

Son, Ji hye. "East-West Communication and Modern Buddhism: Timothy Richard's Translations of Buddhist Scriptures and His Understanding of Buddhism." *Tōzai gakujutsu kenkyūjo kiyō* [Reports of the Kansai University Institute of Oriental and Occidental Studies] 48 (2015): 281–305.

"Spirits Converse with Wu Ting Fang: Chinese Minister Attends a Seance and Probes Mysteries of Occult World." *The San Francisco Call*, October 15, 1909.

"Sunday Pictorial Section." *The China Press*, September 4, 1927.

"The Anniversary Meeting." *The Saturn Lodge Monthly* 1, no. 7 (1921): 119.

"The Besant School in China." *Far Eastern T. S. Notes* 2, no. 3 (May–June 1925).

"The Besant School for Girls." *Far Eastern T. S. Notes* 2, no. 4 (July–October 1926).

The Theosophist (October 1911).

Theosophical Society, ed. *International Theosophical Year Book: Giving the History and Organization of the Theosophical Society, A Theosophical Who's Who, the President's Policy etc.* (Adyar: The Theosophical Publishing House, 1937).

Ting-fang, Wu. "China." In *Papers on Inter-racial Problems, Communicated to the First Universal Races Congress, Held at the University of London, July 26–29, 1911*, edited by Gustav Spiller, 123–32. Miami: HardPress Publishing. Reprinted from London: P. S. King & Son, 1911.

Tsiang, Kinson. "Inauguration of the Dawn Lodge, Shanghai." *Far Eastern T. S. Notes* 2, no. 1 (January–February 1925).

Universal Races Congress, ed. *Papers on Inter-racial Problems Communicated to the First Universal Races Congress, Held at the University of London, July 26–29, 1911*. London: P. S. King & Son, 1911.

Wang, Lunxin. *Qingmo minguo shiqi zhongxue jiaoyu yanjiu* [Studies on middle school education in the Late Qing and Republican periods]. Shanghai Shi: Huadong shifan daxue chubanshe, 2002.

Wang, Zhangcai. "Ouzhan yu Zhongguo wenhua [World War I and Chinese culture]." In *Jiang Kanghu boshi yanjiang lu* [Collection of Dr. Kiang Kanghu's speeches], edited by Nanfang University Press. Shanghai: Taipingyang yin shua gong si, 1923.

Wei, Qiang. "Peicheng nüxiao qiaoqian suji [Shorthand writing of Besant School for Girls' move]." *Zhongguo sheying xuehui huabao* [Pictorial Magazine of Chinese Photography Society] 4, no. 192 (1929): 355.

Wu, Tingfang, *Wu Tingfang linghun xueshuo* [Wu Tingfang's Theory of Soul]. Shanghai: Shanghai lingxue yanjiushe, 1921.

Wu, Tingfang, Ding Xianjun and Yu Zuofeng, eds. *Wu Tingfang ji* [Wu Tingfang Works' Collection]. Beijing: Zhonghua shuju, Xinhua shudian Beijing faxingsuo, 1993.

Wu, Tingfang. *America, Through the Spectacles of an Oriental Diplomat*. Publisher unknown, 1996 [1914]. http://www.gutenberg.org/files/609/609-h/609-h.htm.

"Wu Tingfang yanshuo zongjiao [Wu Ting-fang speeches about religion]," Shen Pao, January 14, 1916.

Wu, Tingguang, ed. *Wu xiansheng (Zhiyong) gongdu* [Mr. Wu (Zhiyong)'s Official Documents]. Taipei: Wenhai chubanshe, 1971.

"Wu Zhiyong xiansheng Tingfang yanjiang tongshenxue [Mr. Wu Tingfang talked about Theosophy]." *Linshi kanbu yuekan* 14 (1916).

Xuesheng zazhi [Student's Magazine] 3, no. 4 (1916): 20–21.

Yang, Jie. *Mingguo shiqi Shanghai nüzi jiaoyu koushu yanjiu* [Oral Studies about Shanghai Women's Education in the Republican period]. Xi'an: Shanxi shifan daxue chuban zongshe, 2014.

Zhang, Liheng, *Cong xifang dao dongfang: Wu Tingfang yu Zhongguo jindai shehui de yanjin* [From the West to the East: Wu Tingfang and the Evolution of Modern Chinese Society]. Beijing: Shang wu yin shu guan, 2002.

Zhang, Liheng, *Wu Tingfang zhuan* [Biography of Wu Tingfang]. Shijia zhuang: Hebei renmin chubanshe, 1999.

Zhang, Liheng, *Wu Tingfang de waijiao shengya* [Wu Tingfang's Diplomatic Career]. Beijing: Tuanjie chubanshe, 2008.

Chapter 5

Absence Unveiled?

The Early Theosophical Society and the Entanglement of History and Historiography

Ulrich Harlass

Introduction

The Theosophical Society became immensely successful on a global scale after its founders Helena Petrovna Blavatsky (1831–1891) and Henry Steel Olcott (1832–1907) moved to India in 1879. Here, crucial concepts of "occult sciences" were revealed to the world through Eastern adepts who allegedly authored the so-called Mahatma letters. Blavatsky claimed them her teachers and spoke in their name; others published with reference to these "masters" who never went public themselves. As the teachings contained in the letters came from a quasi-authoritative source, to question the legitimacy of the adepts meant to jeopardize the legitimacy of the Theosophical project. Written mainly to A. O. Hume (1829–1912) and A. P. Sinnett (1840–1921), the letters attained a central function for early Theosophy: with their public discussion, the "oriental shift" of Theosophy took shape and led to intricate cosmological and anthropological doctrines. Blavatsky's magnum opus, *The Secret Doctrine*, largely elaborated on topics developed in this context. The Mahatma letters themselves were edited and published as late as 1923[1] after they had become a blessing and a curse at the same time. While occult knowledge from hidden masters appeared exclusive and exotic, the existence of these masters had been doubted from the beginning—and the debate continues to this day.[2] The Theosophists spread their exclusive knowledge among readers in India, Europe, the United States, and, to some extent, worldwide, thus making the Theosophical Society both a child of, and an active contributor to, the global history of religion.[3]

The study of esotericism, and the Theosophical Society in particular, has developed into a field of research in its own right over the past two decades. But while abundant fruitful scholarship is taking place, its entrenched adhesion to "Western Esotericism" demands scrutiny.[4] This is of special concern to research on Theosophy, as the Theosophical Society was constituted by—and entangled within—global negotiations of religion, science, and esotericism. Furthermore, Theosophists explicitly referred to non-Western traditions. What is more, Blavatsky is generally treated as the focal point of the historiography of Theosophy, so that the vast majority of introductions and overviews is dominated by "the Old Lady."[5] Most studies identify a pivotal philosophical development between her influential books *Isis Unveiled* (1877) and *The Secret Doctrine* (1888), which is held to be the result of her "oriental shift." The Mahatma letters are assumed to illustrate the developments in Blavatsky's thinking between these works, and in so doing the letters' content is identified with her thought. Blavatsky's ideas, in the form of these letters, so the narrative continues, were then collected and presented by willing collaborators—most notably A. P. Sinnett in his *The Occult World* (1881) and *Esoteric Buddhism*[6] (1883). To maintain this interpretation, a certain narrative is needed, which I am going to discern in this chapter. As we will see further, this narrative comes at a cost. An epistemological barrier emerges on two levels, which I call "absences." The first are sources of Theosophical concepts besides Blavatsky, and the second is the "East" as depicted in scholarly accounts of Theosophy.

As this double absence in the historiography of Theosophy results from the description of early Theosophical teachings and the role of Blavatsky, questions arise, then, regarding the ways in which this problem might be tackled. A focus on the "real" sources of the Mahatma letters seems natural, but this could become the next deflective move. For this would only be part of the problem, because whatever the outcome of such endeavor would be, its historical context—the negotiations of the letters and their meaning—would still remain unanalyzed. Rather than trying to solve the conundrum of the Mahatma letters, I examine contemporary debates about the adept brothers, Sinnett's books, and—as this constitutes a principle thread connecting *Esoteric Buddhism* to *Secret Doctrine*—the septenary constitution of the universe.

First, I consult recent scholarship so as to introduce the topic and substantiate the problem—an absence in the historiography of Theosophy. Consequently, the examination of a particular narrative about early Theosophical teachings, the Mahatmas, and the role of Blavatsky reveals a second absence. Following this is a consideration of interpretations of "East and West." Finally, I investigate nineteenth-century source material commonly identified with the "oriental shift" and the contemporary debate about it. I propose a genealogical approach that provides a better understanding of the early Theosophical Society without reiterating the twofold absence. While the conundrum of the Mahatmas will not be solved here, the suggested perspective on contemporary disputes and claims about them will enable the tracing of how Theosophical teachings emerged, developed, and corresponded. Blavatsky is not omitted in this approach, but she is placed alongside other persons so as to illustrate the procedural and polyphonic character of this context.

Academic Evaluation of the Theosophical Society

Introductions and overviews of the Theosophical Society commonly focus on its early years, which appear as the Society's origin or *Ursprung*. The activities of its founder, Helena Petrovna Blavatsky, occupy a predominant place in the majority of such scholarship. This applies to both her early, or "Western," phase and her "Oriental" phase, when Blavatsky focused on Eastern traditions, from India and Tibet in particular, in her search for the *philosophia perennis*. She not only drew on numerous orientalist sources, but also included the "esoteric" and Spiritualist context of the time. With the Theosophical Society literally moving east, Blavatsky altered her philosophical outlook, the consequences of which she would later express in *The Secret Doctrine*. This interpretation appears historically plausible, for it takes into consideration important developments and crucial topics of modern Theosophy. Still, it raises questions concerning implicit assumptions behind this focus and the main points in this line of argumentation.

Nicholas Goodrick-Clarke, in *The Western Esoteric Tradition*, dedicates his chapter on the Theosophical Society to "Helena Blavatsky and the Theosophical Society."[7] He sees numerous religious movements evolving in reaction to wider scientific developments of the nineteenth century, such as the impact of Darwin's theory of evolution and a crisis of orthodox faith. Goodrick-Clarke discerns two central such movements with an obvious preference: "Whereas Spiritualism simply posited survival after death, Theosophy located human destiny in an emanationist cosmology and anthropology derived from Neoplatonism and oriental religions."[8] Blavatsky appears as Theosophy's driving force, embracing "Eastern" concepts such as karma, reincarnation, and oriental adepts in connection to already established references to "Western" traditions, thus globalizing esotericism: "Blavatsky assimilated Buddhist ideas into her eclectic Theosophy, ultimately equating Buddhism and Advaita Vedanta as the common source of her esoteric doctrine."[9] Joscelyn Godwin also outlines a crucial development in this period, which he terms *The Theosophical Enlightenment*. In a chapter designated "Enter Madame Blavatsky," the author depicts biographical cornerstones to the foundation of the Theosophical Society and focuses on contemporary controversies with a slightly different emphasis in comparison to Goodrick-Clarke: "With the entry of Blavatsky, a rift begins to open between the Western occultists and the proponents of Eastern doctrines, especially Buddhism."[10] This rift is stimulated by disputes over concepts such as a personal god and reincarnation and results in a confrontation between Eastern and Western Theosophists, represented mainly by A. P. Sinnett for the Eastern and Anna Kingsford and Edward Maitland for the Western side.[11] Blavatsky and Olcott, according to Godwin, turned to Buddhism, equating it with the "Aryan" or Brahman doctrine, and combined the two with Western esotericism. This eventually led to Blavatsky's best-known publication: "Much of Blavatsky's later work, in particular *The Secret Doctrine*, is based on information first given out in the 'Mahatma Letters,' supposedly from an esoteric Buddhist source, and on esoteric Hindu teachings,"[12] which come from F.T.S. (Fellow of the Theosophical Society) Subba Row (1856–1890). Godwin follows the quarrels between Spiritualism and Theosophy and identifies Sinnett's publications as focal points. *The Occult World* "challenged the complacency of Western Spiritualists with the claim—if not the proof—that there were living adepts in the East."[13] Whereas Sinnett's book includes a theory contradicting Spiritualist views, explaining Spiritualist phenomena with occultism and not with the agency of the dead, Anna Kingsford's *The Perfect Way*[14] (1881) emphasizes reincarnation and confirms a strong bond with Christianity. After two years of dispute, reincarnation is still an unresolved issue, but with Sinnett's *Esoteric Buddhism*, "the Theosophical system became clearer."[15]

In his conclusion, Godwin stresses the distinctly "Western" character that the heritage of Blavatsky's Theosophy was to attain: "Together with the Western occult tradition, the Theosophists have provided almost all the underpinnings of the 'New Age Movement,' their exoteric reflection, in which there is definitely no parting of the hemispheres. But these efforts are something characteristically Western."[16]

Recently, Jeffrey Lavoie opened the introductory section of *The Theosophical Society* with the chapter "Why study Madame Blavatsky or the Theosophical Society?"[17] He does not answer this programmatic question straightforwardly, but stresses instead the compatibility of Theosophy and Spiritualism and the influence the Theosophical Society had on nineteenth-century intellectual life. According to Lavoie, the impact of Theosophy reaches well into the present.[18] The author's implicit assumption is well represented by the following statement about Blavatsky: "[H]er Theosophy actually affirmed many Spiritualist doctrines and continued to embrace these ideals long after the Society's relocation to India."[19] Despite the observation of their shared history, philosophy, and numerous members belonging to both movements, Lavoie too depicts modern Theosophy as fundamentally Blavatsky's project. This becomes obvious in his claims that he is representing the history of the Theosophical movement with "a fair and balanced sampling of *her* views throughout the years."[20] Furthermore, being *Western* esotericism, modern Theosophy seems to be confined to the Western World, which "could be geographically Europe and North America."[21] Therefore, like his academic peers, Lavoie implicitly inscribes a flaw on Theosophical activities outside these regions, for if an essentially *Western* movement takes place outside the West, what can it be other than dislocated or deviant? It is not the aim of Lavoie to transcend the implicit boundaries, regardless of both the above-mentioned move away from the geographical "West" and the interaction with "Eastern doctrines."[22]

On first balance, we can conclude that there has been a habitual focus on H. P. Blavatsky, who is seen as constituting the center of developments, debates, and activities of the early Theosophical Society in the accounts discussed above. These developments are described as global in scope but Western in substance. Detailed discussions of the origin and development of Theosophy and its doctrines frequently follow this line of argument.[23] This is not surprising because Blavatsky was one of the founders of the Theosophical Society, a dazzling agent and its main public spokesperson. She was met with high veneration on the one hand, and criticism or outright ridicule on the other. This brought her to the fore in countless contemporary sources, corroborating the impression of the Theosophical Society as having been *her* project. What is more, the works mentioned above agree on the importance of the Orient, or the East, in the latter phase of Blavatsky's work, while at the same time they maintain that the Theosophical Society must be understood as "Western Esotericism." Interestingly, James Santucci tentatively expands on this dictum in an article on "The Notion of Race in the Theosophical Society."[24] Santucci, like Goodrick-Clarke, opts for "Global Esotericism" rather than Western. The main reason for this nevertheless pertains to the integration of "Eastern traditions" such as Vedic or Hindu sources rather than the influence of this "East" beyond its ancient scriptures. Nile Green recently pointed to the global scope of nineteenth-century occultism, as "[g]lobal exchange was (and is) a religiously generative process and one that left its stamp in the hybrid character of its occult productions."[25]

What connects these publications is the assumption that the "East" is referred to as a façade, set up by Blavatsky to refurbish the stage on which her *Western* esoteric Theosophical play was carried out. However, if Theosophy is regarded as a Western phenomenon, Theosophy outside the West bears an implicit deficiency. It is the flaw of being either dislocated or basically insignificant, with no need for further investigation.[26] I argue for a global historical perspective considering the strategic character of representations of East and West, or the analysis of "complicated narrative maneuvers."[27] This requires, in my view, taking into account the global history of mutual exchange and the repercussions between positions claiming affiliation to or representation of either East or West. Two aspects of the historiography of the Theosophical Society became apparent: the identification of Blavatsky with the Theosophical Society, and the determination that the Theosophical Society is characteristically "Western." In the next step, I wish to uncover a particular structure in the historical narrative(s) that seems prevalent when establishing Blavatsky as the core of Theosophy—the structure of an absence.

Historical Insignificance or Unexplained Absence?

As we have seen, Blavatsky not only co-founded the Theosophical Society, but she also occupies a central place with her claim that a perennial philosophy underlies all religions in human history in both Theosophical self-conceptions and the historiography of Theosophy. Blavatsky maintains that there is an "esoteric" meaning hidden behind the "exoteric" phenomena that only a few select sages know about—and these specialists have kept it hidden ever since.[28] But while in ancient times the general populace knew of its existence, modern man—the Westerner in particular—has come to forget, and even deny, the true spiritual wisdom of esoteric knowledge and denounce it as magic or superstition, with confessionalism, ritual, bigotry, and real superstition being its substitutes. Theosophical narrative has it that nevertheless mankind is not lost; guardians of the wisdom of old subsist in oriental seclusion, secretly watching over the world and developing the occult sciences. While this can already be found in *Isis Unveiled*, in 1880 a profound step occurred. Reacting to a pressing query, the Mahatma Koot Hoomi took up correspondence with A. P. Sinnett and A. O. Hume via Blavatsky. This correspondence would provide a revelation of occult philosophy to the public, contributing to Theosophy's shift toward its "Oriental period."[29] Occult science did not go public directly through the masters, but indirectly through the publications of the two Englishmen. The former wrote *The Occult World*, which was based on his own experiences with Blavatsky's occult capacities and the first letters he received from Koot Hoomi.[30]

Sinnett became a Theosophist when the Society's founders moved to India in 1879, where he was among their earliest contacts and members[31]— and he would prove their "Godsend."[32] As a distinguished newspaper editor and correspondent from the centers of colonial power, Sinnett introduced Blavatsky and Olcott to Anglo-Indian society both personally and through his journalistic work, for he referred to the Theosophical Society in *The Pioneer* after 1879 and kept India informed about its activities for the next three years.[33] But his role was to become even more crucial with his insights into the occult sciences through the correspondence with the adepts that prompted two publications that initiated a debate on Eastern wisdom that influenced the Society as a whole.

Hume, in turn, wrote several pamphlets and a three-part series titled *Fragments of Occult Truth* (*Fragments*) in the *Theosophist*, later parts of which were written by Sinnett as a consequence of the parting with Hume.[34] After a continuous exchange of letters between the two and the adepts, Sinnett presented a comprehensive account of the philosophical teachings in 1883—*Esoteric Buddhism*. The controversy over the credibility of both the content and the authors of the letters immediately escalated.[35] This debate was connected to earlier disputes,[36] some of which had taken place in the *Pioneer*,[37] but mostly in the two Spiritualist papers *The Spiritualist Newspaper* and *Light*.[38]

Established narratives assume the dependence of modern Theosophy on Blavatsky, with Hume and Sinnett being more or less "editors" of her thought. Thus, the philosophical framework of the Theosophical Society is seen as *her* project, and its eastward turn is represented by the difference between *Isis Unveiled* and *The Secret Doctrine*. Accordingly, Blavatsky appropriated orientalist literature only superficially, so as to "give occultism an eastward orientation."[39] In this process, "[s]he used contemporary scholarship selectively to support her own views, reinterpreting or ignoring aspects of science, orientalism, and the religious traditions of India."[40] If this transformation is but superficial, this will be verifiable in historical sources, for example, the works of Hume and Sinnett. Other influences on Theosophical concepts and Blavatsky can be excluded, then, as they appear insignificant. Hence, when A. P. Sinnett presented *The Occult World* and *Esoteric Buddhism*, the content and impact of these books cannot but affirm this view. My argument points to a different direction by questioning this narrative. Consequently, the next step is to look into both more recent and older scholarly accounts of Sinnett's role.

Theosophical Historiography, A. P. Sinnett, and the Masters

Lavoie correctly states that "[*The Occult World*] brought Theosophy and Helena Blavatsky's Eastern activities to a wider audience in Victorian England"[41] and credits *Esoteric Buddhism* with even stronger approval, for it "was monumental in influencing the future publication of *The Secret Doctrine* and Theosophy as a whole."[42] Brendon French also asserts Sinnett's importance due to his having introduced Blavatsky and Olcott to Anglo-Indian society.[43] Furthermore, "rapturous tones in the *Pioneer* [. . .] caused a flurry of interest in Blavatsky."[44] Three older, in my view essential, works on Theosophical history should also be considered. In an extensive and valuable annotated bibliography on Theosophy, Michael Gomes dedicates a separate chapter to "a shrewd newspaper man, A. P. Sinnett,"[45] and the Mahatma letters. Whereas Gomes depicts earlier letters from the masters to other recipients as "Theosophical legend," Sinnett, with his correspondence and two monographs, is held responsible for presenting the world with the Mahatmas—forcing Blavatsky to react. Joscelyn Godwin argues, tentatively and with a different emphasis, regarding *The Occult World*:

Sinnett's work, which included the first "Mahatma Letters" from Koot Hoomi, challenged the complacency of Western spiritualists with the claim—if not the proof—that there were living adepts in the East whose mastery of psychic powers and knowledge of occultism far exceeded anything yet demonstrated in the West.[46]

Godwin handles Sinnett from a thorough historical perspective with regard to the disputes in which he was involved. K. Paul Johnson, however, takes the discussion to a more speculative level. In *The Masters Revealed*, he holds that there might be historical individuals behind Blavatsky, for whom she covered by "inventing" the masters in order to protect her real interlocutors and herself from colonial persecution.[47] Johnson is interested in the adepts' identity exclusively and mentions Sinnett only *en passant*: he succinctly remarks that Sinnett "wrote two books [*The Occult World* and *Esoteric Buddhism*] based on [the Mahatmas'] letters."[48] Nevertheless, the author frequently refers to Sinnett's writings to corroborate his theses, making Sinnett's publications and correspondence implicitly integral to his argument. The importance of Sinnett popularizing the Theosophical Society in India and providing the public with insights from the Mahatma letters is undoubted. These letters, in turn, contain crucial elements of Theosophical concepts at that time and thus are indispensable. The question arises, then: how are the masters and their letters being assessed?

We find a much more multifarious picture as regards the status of Blavatsky's ominous backers—the Mahatmas—and Sinnett's relationship to them. In his dissertation, Brendan French regrets that, owing to their importance, one would expect "at least a degree of mature critical analysis [. . .] [but that] has not been the case."[49] He does not follow his wish, but treats the masters implicitly as Blavatsky's creation and denies any influence of the Indian context because "Blavatsky *imported* standard motifs of Western esotericism into India [. . .] fashioning an Indicised esotericism."[50] In this view, she brought her Western concept of masters, a concept unknown to the East, to India, which is why she was unsuccessful in Asia. Apart from this Eurocentric perspective, French, against his otherwise thorough treatment of secondary sources and references, and against his own claim to abstain from judgment as to the reality of the adepts, asserts that Blavatsky invented her masters and thus must have conceived of the letters herself. Consequently:

[. . .] the device of the Mahatma letter, with its dynamic of transmission from *guru* (Master) to *chela* (Sinnett and others), conveniently circumvented Blavatsky as the *fons et origo* of Theosophy's claim to meta-empirical insight and oversight.[51]

A focus on claims of meaning and on normative power structures many accounts. But this is mostly confined to Blavatsky's attempts to control Theosophical doctrine, while other participants in the discourse play but minor roles.[52] The question of the adepts remains unclear but is in fact inextricably attached to "the Old Lady." Lavoie argues with minimal substantiation that " 'KH' and 'M' were indeed sub-personalities of Blavatsky."[53] Consequently, *Esoteric Buddhism* "was A. P. Sinnett's compilation of the Mahatma Letters that were covertly written by H. P. Blavatsky as she developed her own cosmological structure of time and spiritual evolution."[54] Therefore, the Mahatmas are neither living adepts who authored the famous correspondence, nor are the letters written by other historical persons—and Sinnett did no more than compile teachings created by Blavatsky.

For Gomes, the case seems clear too: "It has never been explained why Blavatsky should choose to create human Mahatmas, who would eventually require tangible evidence of their existence."[55] Godwin abstains from any judgment in *The Theosophical Enlightenment*. In a more recent article, he keeps the case open and maintains that the early history of Theosophy "is a complex story, involving many nations and characters, but they all revolve around Helena Petrovna Blavatsky (1831–1891)."[56] Godwin remarks that many questions pertaining to the Mahatma letters, the foundation of Sinnett's *Esoteric Buddhism*, remain open, and *The Secret Doctrine* "enlarges on many of the principles outlined in the Mahatmas' letters."[57] K. P. Johnson's particular approach leads him to the opposite assessment: "In truth, her masters constituted not a stable hierarchy but an ever-evolving network."[58] This is to say, Blavatsky actually wrote the letters but with a number of ever-changing teachers behind her. What is more, the wave of criticism and suspicion concerning the adepts' existence caused a crisis that even managed to bring about, according to Johnson, a catharsis: "When HPB was freed from service to hidden Masters, she entered the most productive part of her career [. . .]."[59] This may explain the absence of Sinnett in Johnson's publication—Accordingly, Sinnett only compiled what was genuinely Blavatsky's thought at that time, which only later grew to its full potential.

The above-mentioned authors agree on the correlation of Theosophical thought and the Mahatma letters, and Sinnett's role in their promulgation, as well as on the intimate involvement of Blavatsky. All authors are aware, and sometimes wary of the case, but, except for Godwin, the historical context with regard to the interdependence of Theosophical concepts with the Mahatma letters remains unexplored. Where conflicts are mentioned, they corroborate the origin of Theosophical thought with Blavatsky. As a consequence, other sources connected to the development and negotiation of Theosophical teachings are not taken into consideration. The teachings are reduced to Blavatsky's major publications and their concord with the letters of her reputed masters—which are treated as hers. As none of the authors above examines the letters or their historical context, a consideration of the premises of this position seems advisable. Because references supporting this interpretation are scarce, the justification of the hegemony of Blavatsky appears unclear. I suggest that this position itself must be historicized. It is thus expedient to briefly consult older works to reach for a limited genealogy of the narrative in question.

Bruce Campbell complained in 1980 that accounts on Theosophy predominantly take sides and can be divided between two poles—either "accusatory in tone" or "blanket defenses of Theosophy."[60] Campbell maintains that "[t]he outsider is led to the conclusion that the existence of the Masters and the inspiration of Theosophical writings by them are among the weakest of the Theosophists' claims."[61] Three examples suffice to illustrate the positive handling of the challenging history, but the case could easily be expanded and would be worthy of its own article. The first example is A. T. Barker's full text edition of *The Mahatma Letters* (1923), then the *Readers' Guide to the Mahatma Letters* by George E. Linton and Virginia Hanson (1972), and finally an article in its appendix by Sven Eek, *Alfred Percy Sinnett*.[62] Barker writes from an explicitly "Theosophical" standpoint in a time he conceives of as crisis. He claims to act for "the highest interests of The Theosophical Society,"[63] providing the world with access to its *original* teachings. Merely looking into Sinnett's publications, says Barker, is insufficient, for "it is almost impossible to arrive at the facts [. . .] by studying an edited book of extracts."[64] It is striking in Barker's compilation that, rather than editing the letters according to their appearance, that is, their chronology, he employs thematic chapters that "suggest itself as more or less natural divisions."[65] Barker separates pertinent from impertinent letters with regard to the "original teachings,"[66] and so distorts the chronological sequence and its progressive, often inconclusive or confusing, character. What is more, the compiler does not mention disputes about what to count as Mahatma letter and what not—which is certainly not as clear as he suggests.[67] Barker is obviously dismissive toward Sinnett and his late critique of Blavatsky and defends her and the adepts because "Madame Blavatsky is justified at almost every point in these letters."[68] What is interesting here is not so much the affirmation of the existence of the masters and their lore by a Theosophist, but the corollary of this assumption, namely that the masters' teachings constitute the *original* Theosophical doctrine. Barker indicates that the adepts legitimize Blavatsky against the objections of fraud and fiction, and thus argues that all other possible influences are void. Consequently, the history of contentions can be nothing but a distraction and is eventually of no use for the understanding of Theosophy.

Almost fifty years later, Linton and Hanson attempt to present the original order of the letters, adding annotations for better comprehension. Again, the adepts are declared as delivering original teachings: "[The Masters] evidently foresaw the great revolutionary changes that were to take place in the near future and wished to channel them into more progressive directions and along more spiritual lines."[69] Hence, the adepts are vital to Theosophical thought, being historical persons possessing the key to occult philosophy. The authors recommend Sinnett's books as early classics of Theosophy and praise him for his introducing Blavatsky and Olcott to Anglo-Indian society. The image of Sinnett and his role is ambiguous nevertheless. In the appended article *Alfred Percy Sinnett* from the 1966 *American Theosophist*, Sven Eek gives a less than flattering account of the article's name giver. Sinnett's fame is justified only because he received the letters, but otherwise Eek's reluctance is obvious: "His grasp of Theosophy lacked the depth which comes not merely from intellectual penetration but also from a spiritual identification of one's personal life with the philosophy."[70] In summary, the Mahatma letters and Blavatsky constitute the core of Theosophical thought, while Sinnett "never understood his place in the Theosophical movement."[71]

This example impressively shows that, even while Sinnett is the headliner, he is actually absent from the consideration of the historical events and the meaning given to them at the time. The above extracts reveal a blind spot in the debates regarding the masters, Blavatsky, and her contemporaries. The Anglo-Indian milieu and Indian Theosophists are practically excluded, and the story could have taken place anywhere in the "West," it seems. The assumed "author function"[72] of Blavatsky as *fons et origo* of the doctrines in dispute, which here excludes a considerable part of the context, is not only present in today's academic studies and introductions. It can also be traced to works dating before Barker's edition of the Mahatma letters. What is more, the unexplained absence of a range of speakers—Sinnett, Hume, Row, and others—and the broader historical context already becomes perceptible by exclusively scrutinizing the secondary literature. Therefore, keeping Blavatsky at the core of the historical narrative of Theosophy while dealing with the enigmatic Mahatmas and their letters seems to induce persisting difficulties. For if Blavatsky is held to be the Theosophical Society's fulcrum (often implicitly), and her legitimacy is constitutively bound to the adepts, which was historically the case, it appears to be impossible, then, to dispose of the masters without sacrificing Theosophy as a whole. Discomfort in dealing with this material strikes even the most attentive of scholars who seem to carry on a historical heritage that can be detected in older accounts on the topic. I would argue that it is not necessary to reject Blavatsky's historic importance and the value of countless studies to this end. But, to avoid the problem I have determined, it seems appropriate to take a wider historical scope while still leaving open the question of the Mahatma letters' origin.

In the final section, I wish to conclude this genealogical case study with nineteenth-century sources. The historiographical difficulties revealed above can be grasped, in my view, by employing Foucault's reading of Nietzsche.[73] The attribution of Blavatsky representing variations of the "origin" (*Ursprung*) of Theosophical thought by allocating an author function to her led to a potential disguise of its historical origin (*Herkunft* or descent), which proves to be "the site of a fleeting articulation that discourse has obscured and finally lost."[74] Moreover, the absences detected at this point reveal a *descent* that, as we have seen, also encompasses the scholars ("us")—"the historian's history."[75] As this chapter cannot (and does not want to) claim comprehensiveness, the aim of the following section is to explore whether a genealogical approach proves of further use in dealing with the absences, that is, fruitful for a better understanding of early Theosophical history. This also allows for a connection of the history of the Theosophical Society to academic approaches such as post-colonial studies and global history.

Spiritualism, Occultism, and the Truth?

The publication of *The Occult World* and its reception constitutes an adequate starting point to delve into the discussion about the adepts, their occult teachings, and Blavatsky. "The author seeks to show that the powers of these men, though apparently miraculous, rest on a strictly natural basis,"[76] proclaims Damodar Mavalankar in July 1881. The book sold so well, he later asserts, that it was sold out by October 1881 with a second imprint on its way. In *The Occult World*, Sinnett reports on the incredible powers of the adepts while stressing the natural and scientific character of their occult knowledge. However, the book is not mainly about occult philosophy, but illustrates the phenomena associated with Blavatsky, and in so doing constitutes a firsthand report of "Madame's" abilities. In a programmatic article with the title "Teachings of Occult Philosophy," Sinnett resorts to *Isis Unveiled*, because "Madame Blavatsky is in constant communication, by means of the system of psychological telegraphy that the initiates employ, with her superior 'Brothers' in occultism."[77] The Tibetan brothers share their insight into the *philosophia perennis* with Blavatsky, who is a reliable and authentic speaker of occultism. To understand the unfolding disputes, it is necessary to trace the discussion and its conflicting positions.

Print media were of central significance for the nineteenth-century public debate, with disputes negotiated in a dialogical process in newspapers and magazines. Mark Morrison shows that this applies to the "occult revival" too, which owes much of its success to the periodical culture providing swift and easy access to information.[78] He sees the aim of such periodicals in proselytizing their readers so as "to legitimate occult knowledge in the dominant public sphere in quasi-scientific terms of validation."[79] Furthermore, Alex Owen emphasizes the wide social distribution of newspapers, because they "served both middle-class and plebeian readership [and] point up the major concerns, controversies and issues of the day."[80] Of particular interest here is that "the magazines were also used to air disputes with other occult rivals publicly."[81] For the present discussion, the *Theosophist* (Bombay), and the London-based *Spiritualist Newspaper* and *Light* need to be inspected.

As *The Occult World* proved a hot seller, Stainton Moses saw its benefit in clarifying the otherwise incomprehensible *Isis Unveiled* and shedding light on the knowledge of the mysterious brothers from whom Blavatsky claimed her inspiration. With respect to *Isis Unveiled*, Moses complains that:

> [N]o one has mastered its contents so as to fully grasp the author's plan [. . . thus the reader] sorely needed some more

tangible hold on the history and pretensions of the mysterious brotherhood for which the author made such tremendous claims [. . .] For a long time the answer was of the vaguest. But eventually evidence was gathered, and in this book we have Mr. Sinnett coming forward [. . .] and especially to give us his correspondence with Koot Hoomi, an adept and member of the Brotherhood.[82]

Whereas there is, according to Moses, only a slight difference between Spiritualism and Theosophy—passive mediums and active adepts—*The Occult World* helps followers of both movements in their search for the "whence and whither of humanity."[83]

William Harrison, editor of the *Spiritualist Newspaper*, equally welcomed *The Occult World* by "Mr. A. P. Sinnett, who is known both in London and in India as a good literary man."[84] In a later article, the recent debate shines through when Harrison applauds Sinnett's well-written book again and draws the following two conclusions from it, structurally inverting common accusations against Spiritualism.[85] First, Blavatsky must have been a Spiritualist medium, even if neither she herself nor Sinnett realizes it, but contrive *mistaken theories*. Second, the existence of the adept brothers depends entirely on personal faith rather than evidence. Harrison substantiates his interpretation with a detailed comparison of Blavatsky's alleged abilities with famous Spiritualist mediums like "Mrs. Guppy"[86] and demands for adequate scientific investigations—very much like the Theosophists and other critics regularly expected from the Spiritualists and their mediumistic phenomena.[87]

As the debate continued, the Theosophists predominantly defended two claims in reprints, comments, and articles in the *Theosophist*: First, there is an occult philosophy grounded in centuries of learning that is more rational or scientific than any popular Spiritualist conception of the communication with the dead. Second, the source of that knowledge is a brotherhood of adepts in the Himalayas, to which Koot Hoomi and Morya—the ostensible writers of the Mahatma letters—belong. Obviously, the legitimacy of the Theosophists' claims is connected to the Masters. As we will see below, Sinnett, Hume, Row, and other Indian members supported this notion of adepts and testified as to their existence, lending credibility to the Masters' doctrinal authority. The approval of the brothers also enabled *Esoteric Buddhism* to become another success for Sinnett, as it is based foremost on the adepts' letters and thus constitutes the first direct account of their teachings.

Critics and Defenders of the Mahatmas

The above-mentioned comments on *The Occult World* already foreshadowed criticism of the adepts. In both papers, *Light* and the *Spiritualist*, critical tones are common. A major doubt is expressed, probably by the editor, in the *Spiritualist* in July 1881. The author ascribes the famous "brooch-incident," which prominently features in *The Occult World*,[88] to the agency of spirits rather than adepts. Many authors discuss the phenomena and their origin and thus the existence of the adepts, or refer critically to Theosophy and related topics in the *Spiritualist*. On the other side, Blavatsky, as the *Theosophist*'s editor, annotates anything she finds worthy to comment on or replicate, and numerous other Theosophists contribute a critical mass of "witnesses" for the Mahatmas.[89] Immediately reacting to objections against *The Occult World*, a series of correspondences was published in the *Theosophist* of July 1881. Mirza Moorad Alee—the Indian-born Godolfin Mitford—claimed, "I hereby declare that not only have I within the last few days seen one of the persons so designated at the Headquarters of the Society at Bombay,"[90] but that he and others had known the brothers even before joining the Theosophical Society—which is to say, independently of Blavatsky. Mavalankar joins Alee and reports:

> I have at least seen about half a dozen on various occasions, in broad daylight, in open places, and have talked to them, not only when Madame Blavatsky was in Bombay but even when she was far away and I here. I have also seen them at times when I was travelling. I was taken to the residences of some of them and once when Col. Olcott and Mme. Blavatsky were with me.[91]

S. J. Padshah's declaration reflects the ongoing contentions: "[I] have to thank Madame Blavatsky [. . .] for having given me opportunities to realize what is generally supposed to be the mere creatures of that Lady's imagination—the existence of the 'Brothers.'"[92] Others join in, even with collective confirmations of the masters' existence. M. B. Nagnath and B. G. Mullapoorcar assure: "We have had, on several occasions, the honour to see these 'Brothers' [. . .] they represent a class of living, not 'disembodied' men or ghosts—as the Spiritualists would insist upon."[93]

Sinnett appears at that time rather quiet in the *Theosophist*, but not absent from the debate. In the *Theosophist*'s August 1881 Supplement,

Tookaram Tatya reports on Sinnett's speech at the Bombay meeting of the Theosophical Society, one day after he arrived from England, personally introducing *The Occult World*. Sinnett, then acting vice president of the Society, affirmed new members and answered to requests of his fellows. In Tookaram's words: "He also stated his reasons for affirming most positively that these letters were written by a person quite different from Madame Blavatsky, a foolish suspicion entertained by some sceptics."[94] The quote proves that criticism and doubt concerning the adepts were known and openly discussed among members of the Theosophical Society. Furthermore, Sinnett's reconfirmation of the Himalayan brothers' existence comprised praise of India that obviously appealed to his Indian audience: "It warmed the heart of every native member present to hear an Englishman of literary distinction paying so much respect and reverence to a *Hindu mystic*. National pride was upon every face."[95] A year later, after the first *Fragments* had appeared, which would become part of *Esoteric Buddhism*,[96] Sinnett holds that "the reality of the great occult organization which The Theosophical Society has revealed (though hampered by restrictions that no outsider can understand at first) is plainer to me than ever."[97] He defends Blavatsky and Olcott and the validity and value of the occult sciences in several letters in *Light*.[98]

Blavatsky also speaks up in numerous comments and footnotes, rejecting basically all of Moses's above-mentioned complaints. She highlights, as stated in *The Occult World*, that *Isis Unveiled* was only the entrée to the topic—and ambiguous owing to her poor command of English. She gets habitually polemic, for example, asserting that Spiritualist mediums are but passive and ignorant puppets, while she herself acts fully aware of what would happen and why, with no need for darkened séance rooms. Blavatsky continues confrontationally: "The claims made for a 'Brotherhood' of living men, were never half as pretentious as those which are daily made by the Spiritualists on behalf of the disembodied souls of dead people!"[99] In November 1882, she affirms her own and some other Theosophists' personal visit of the Mahatmas. Her letter comes:

> from an altitude of over 8,000 feet above the sea level, having just enjoyed the privilege of passing 48 hours in the company of those much doubted BROTHERS of ours [. . .] certain of our Theosophists, moreover, who crossed over to Sikhim and made their personal acquaintance, representing additional legal evidence in favour of my claims.[100]

Additional testimony comes from Darjeeling: in *Natives of India*, Mohini Chatterji, Rama Sourindro Gargya, Nobin K. Banerjea, S. Ramiswamier, and Darbhagiri Nath sign as "Chelas who know their Masters."[101]

The adept brothers played a leading role in the quarrels between Spiritualism and Theosophy, for they provided the contested authority and legitimacy for the Theosophists. While with *The Occult World* not much philosophy had yet been provided, Spiritualists such as Harrison or Moses welcomed its publication. But the general tone in the papers remained wary. Although Moses stayed open to the possible existence of adepts and the reconciliation of Spiritualism and Theosophy, many Spiritualists were not convinced, despite correspondence of "natives" as authentic witnesses to the existence of their masters. A more substantial debate goes beyond such abstract affirmations, one that corroborates the thesis of a wider range of positions in Theosophical debates—the discussion of the septenary constitution.

The Septenary Consitution

The septenary or sevenfold constitution is one of the key philosophical concepts in *The Secret Doctrine* and a *novum* in comparison to *Isis Unveiled*. Blavatsky states in *Isis Unveiled* that the reincarnation of an individual is against natural laws and occurs extremely rarely: "If reason has been so far developed as to become active and discriminate, there is no reincarnation on this earth, for the three parts of the triune man have been united together."[102] A decade later, the triune constitution has multiplied to a group of seven comprising the whole cosmos: "The structural framework of the universe, humanity included, is by nature septenary in composition."[103] As we have seen, scholars agree on a significant conceptual difference between *Isis Unveiled* and *The Secret Doctrine*, consisting of a deliberate move from West to East—geographically as well as philosophically—with reference to Oriental (and Orientalist) literature. Nevertheless, the "Orient" is hardly included, "Eastern" scriptures in their Orientalist form put aside, so that the "East" proves to be absent in this current of academic contributions. Philosophical changes between her two publications are depicted to depend almost entirely on Blavatsky's thought, mostly reflecting debates between Spiritualism and Theosophy. Several pivotal sources behind *The Secret Doctrine* seem to have been either disregarded or vaguely treated as authored by Blavatsky herself. Consequently, publications by Sinnett and Hume, as well as the Mahatma letters, have not been analyzed as sources in their own right.

Goodrick-Clarke is an adequate example for the implicit appropriation: while he rightly maintains that the sevenfold constitution was introduced by Hume and developed thenceforth, he concludes by placing an unexplained constriction on Blavatsky: "The first formal statement of the sevenfold principle in humans was actually published in October 1881 by A. O. Hume [. . .] Blavatsky had revised her view in the context of the septenary constitution of humans."[104] These sentences are not accidentally contiguous, but imply that the concept has been derived from Blavatsky. Jeffrey Lavoie holds: "One of Blavatsky's first attempts of dealing with the issues between Spiritualism and *her* Theosophical Society was found in [. . .] 'Fragments of Occult Truth' [. . .] [These] were based on the same idea as *Esoteric Buddhism* only *summarized* by a different recipient."[105] Despite the unknown source(s) of the Mahatma letters, leaving aside other possible actors in this context (Hume indubitably deleted here), both authors declare the teachings from the letters to be Blavatsky's. Hanegraaff, however, follows Godwin's argument from the *Theosophical Enlightenment* and evaluates the development between *Isis Unveiled* and *The Secret Doctrine* as follows: "Blavatsky's shift from a 'Hermetic' to an 'Oriental' perspective is more apparent than real [. . .] [Theosophy] is not only rooted in Western Esotericism, but has remained an essentially western movement."[106]

With the first account of the septenary constitution in the *Theosophist* in October 1881, Hume enters into a three-part dialogue with W. H. Terry, an Australian Theosophist, who declares that the phenomena at séances are real and caused by "disembodied spirits,"[107] that is, dead people's non-physical remains. Based on experience and observation, Terry sees "conclusive evidence that disembodied spirits can and do produce physical and mental phenomena on the surface of this world."[108] Rappings, apparitions, materializations, even communications are caused by "intelligences who consistently maintain that identity of the disembodied spirits of men and women who have lived on this earth."[109] Hume retorts with the septenary constitution of man—a "scientific explanation" exposing Spiritualist ideas as false. Moreover, the interpretation of man as a trinity is not wrong, but inadequate.[110] While after physical death, the three lower principles decompose, there is "a new Ego [. . .] to be reborn in the next higher world of causes,"[111] not on this earth—as Blavatsky asserted in *Isis Unveiled*. Only few Spiritualist phenomena are true and appear to be a dead person's spirit, but are actually unconscious remains of these lower principles.[112]

Other Spiritualists reacted to the harsh criticism and its ostensibly scientific justification, enlarging the debate. In two more *Fragments*, Hume introduces new elements to the theory opposing Terry's arguments, which defended Spiritualism and its phenomena as genuine messages from the dead, so that both men essentially adhere to their stance. In the second *Fragments* in March 1882,[113] Hume emphasizes the adepts' occult abilities to command phenomena Spiritualists ascribed to spirits, hoping they "will accept the aid of that nobler illumination which the elevated genius and untiring exertion of Occult Sages of the East have provided."[114] The final part of the dialogue in September 1882 follows these grooves, and further specifications emerge in Hume's detailed comments. While Terry remains a firm believer in Spiritualism, as "[t]wenty years experience, with the mental and spiritual development it has brought, fail to exhibit any defects in it,"[115] Hume expands on occult science, emphasizing the importance and abilities of the adepts. He also introduces the term *Devachan* (a key concept of *Esoteric Buddhism* and, eventually, *The Secret Doctrine*) as a *gestation state*[116] prior to the next birth, and thus declares mediumship to be dangerous, as it "distinctly disturbs the gestation of the personality, hinders the evolution of its new Egohood."[117] Not only can Spiritualism, according to Hume, be better explained by occult science as cconveyed by the adept brothers, but it even proves to be dangerous and against the law of evolution. The *Fragments*[118] thus reflect a debate illustrating how Spiritualists and Theosophists mark their explanatory authority. With evolution as a key feature and his emphasis on natural laws, Hume connects to state-of-the art (popular) science, still reflecting and including the criticism of Terry in his answers.

Stainton Moses also remarks on the *Fragments* and elaborates on the discussion about "departed human spirits" and its Theosophical criticism. In September 1881, he demands "more clear and positive demonstration"[119] of the Theosophists' claims about occult phenomena and Eastern adepts. Sinnett also contributes several letters to *Light*, defending occult philosophy,[120] and Blavatsky replies repeatedly to Moses. In January 1882, she opposes his charge of contradictions in occult theories, pointing to the *Fragments* for clarification, despite their being a series of answers to Terry's questions.[121] Nevertheless, her own elaboration rests on the principles given by Hume.

It has become obvious that the sevenfold constitution served as the main argument for the legitimacy of Theosophical teachings and the dismissal of Spiritualist conceptions. Formulated in October 1881 by A. O. Hume, several authors joined in, resting their arguments on two claims: the transmittal of the teachings from initiated adepts, and the perennial, yet strictly scientific, character of their lore. While the historical source of the first *Fragments* is unclear, it is Hume who initially presented the seven principles. The sevenfold constitution and its scope developed, then, according to the dispute with Spiritualists, proving that there was a vivid discussion associated with the development of said teachings rather than a finished "doctrine." The case promises to exceed the restriction of Theosophical teachings to Blavatsky and thus proves itself worthy of closer scrutiny. Opening a field of historical debates, influences, and developments hitherto unconsidered, its genealogy is to "[seek] the subtle, singular, and subindividual marks that might possibly intersect [. . .] to form a network that is difficult to unravel."[122] Still, this brief examination seems to be a mostly "Western" discussion. Is there no other crossing of boundaries except beyond the geographical—literally the "export" of Theosophy to India?

Crossing the Boundary—T. Subba Row

T. Subba Row (1856–1890)[123] contributed to the discussion from an explicitly "Brahmanical" point of view, elaborating on manifold topics concerning Theosophy that consequently played an important role in the promulgation of Theosophical legitimacy. What is more, he established an image of India and Hinduism in numerous articles, emphasizing a (neo-)Advaita Vedanta interpretation of Hinduism and its accordance with esoteric Theosophy. Between 1881 and 1883, that is, between *The Occult World* and *Esoteric Buddhism*, Subba Row appeared as an erudite specialist for the esoteric understanding of Advaita Vedanta and Hindu scriptures, which in this form of neo-Vedanta is commonly held as demarcating Neo-Hinduism.[124] In his accounts, Row is eager to defend India and its adepts against intrusions from the "West," corroborating strategic representations of "East" and "West." He furthermore elaborated on the septenary constitution from "a Hindu's" point of view in January 1882.[125] In "The Aryan Arhat Esoteric Tenets on the Sevenfold Principle in Man," Row holds that the old Indian Vedas and Upanishads, if understood correctly, contain the septenary teaching. In so doing, Row not only identifies Theosophy with "Hindu" knowledge, but also equates Brahmanical with Tibetan-Buddhist esoteric lore and establishes the link to the "Hindu" tradition: "[T]he results arrived at (in the Buddhist doctrine) do not seem to differ much from the conclusions of our Aryan philosophy."[126]

Presenting himself as a specialist for this Aryan[127] doctrine and its Sanskrit sources, Row declares that the "Modern psychologists of Europe" are mistaken in assuming the destruction of individuality with the brain's dissolution after death. According to the Aryan philosophers, the mind is constituted by an indestructible "occult power of force,"[128] so that in the evolutionary progress, man's upper principles ascend, and it is impossible for the dead to be invoked at séances.[129] The final aim of this progress is Nirvana, that is, the seventh principle stripped of its individual consciousness. In July 1882, Hume received a letter from Koot Hoomi answering several questions, advising him to read Row's article. The adept concluded that the occult theories are scientific and all the explanations given by Row are in accordance with "Darwin's genealogical tree."[130] Row was even asked to support Hume and Sinnett in their occult progress, but he emphatically refused to teach the two and requested that Blavatsky stop Hume's plan to visit Tibet—not only for training, but for seeking eventual proof of living adepts.[131]

The imbrications of Theosophy with a reinterpreted Vedanta are well researched and its popularity in Theosophical circles is beyond doubt,[132] but Row's part has hardly been investigated—and he contributed to the popularity of the Vedanta with manifold articles on the topic. Blavatsky confirmed his authority by stressing, for example, that he is "a Brahmin, is a VEDANTIN ADWAITEE, of the esoteric Aryan school [. . .] a highly advanced *Chela*."[133] She affirmed: "I know of no better authority in INDIA in any thing, concerning the esotericism of the Adwaita philosophy."[134] Row's (self-)representation as a specialist in Hindu scriptures and their "esoteric Theosophy" makes him a valuable witness of "Eastern" esotericism and its superiority over the decayed Western tradition with its unscientific, if not altogether erroneous, Spiritualism. In 1882, Row, as a Hindu, challenged the claims of the English Spiritualist William Oxley, who maintained contact with—and authorship of—the *Bhagavad Gita* by a European adept, Busiris.[135] Oxley furthermore tried to reconcile Spiritualism and Theosophy because occult philosophy as manifested in the *Fragments* and the Spiritualist belief in reincarnation are "in perfect accord."[136]

Row also argued with other "Hindu" correspondents in the *Theosophist*. Defending Vedanta, he highlighted non-duality against an "Almora Swami," stating that the "esoteric Theosophy" of Hindu writings teaches the unity of matter and spirit (*prakṛti* and *puruṣa*): "It seems to me that the Swamy has entirely misunderstood the Adwaitee doctrine regarding the relation between Prakriti and Purusha."[137] Obviously, there were debates besides Blavatsky's struggle with Spiritualism that connect to the Indian context—here, the identity of India and the interpretation of its religious scriptures. On other occasions, it becomes apparent that Row's contribution to the debates has so far been underestimated: in A. T. Barker's *The Letters of H. P. Blavatsky to A. P. Sinnett*, a separate section is devoted to Row's letters to Blavatsky.[138] His role as a Hindu specialist is apparent here too, and Row was probably one of the reasons behind Blavatsky and Olcott's decision to move to Adyar: "The little of occultism that still remains in India is centred in this Madras presidency."[139]

Row furthermore explained that "there are a good many gentlemen here who sympathise with your aims and objects"[140] and referred to the improvement of his home country's state. He saw a direct link between India's regeneration and the Theosophical Society: "The countenance and support of some men at least of the ruling race seem to be absolutely necessary for initiating any movement or reform. Nevertheless, it is quite clear to my mind, that the real work of reform or regeneration must be commenced by Hindus themselves."[141] Theosophy and national regeneration have not occluded each other, but were connected in this view.[142] Nevertheless, one reason for his refusal to teach Hume and Sinnett was their being English, which illustrates the mutual construction of borders between "East" and "West." In May 1882, Sinnett reports being requested by the adept Morya, who was irritated about Row, to be patient with him because "he is very jealous and regards teaching an Englishman as a sacrilege."[143]

Conclusion

There is a narrative structure in the historiography of the early Theosophical Society common to introductions and more specific accounts. While it is plausible that the Society and its philosophical framework are depicted as a product of H. P. Blavatsky this narrative bears certain limitations. It reveals two lacunae I called absences, both of which seem structurally qualified. The focus on Blavatsky in the reconstruction of the Theosophical Society excludes other influences and sources, so that this narrative brings with it the first absence in Theosophical historiography. This becomes more obvious tracing its main arguments: accordingly, Blavatsky's *Isis Unveiled* and *The Secret Doctrine* demonstrate the literary outcome of Theosophy's "Oriental Shift," while most scholars agree both on the shift itself and on its superficial nature. The "Western esoteric" character of Theosophy is firmly adhered to in this view, and, consequently, the Orient or the East points only to the appropriation of a choice of "Oriental" scriptures taken from Orientalist (i.e., Western) literature. The absence thus proved double-headed, as the Orient is omitted (or at least massively restricted), because according to this perspective, Theosophy is *not* crossing the boundaries of the West. The exclusion of the "East" thus constitutes the second absence.

In both academic as well as Theosophical discussions, the Mahatma letters represent a pivotal source demonstrating said Oriental shift. The letters furthermore constituted the legitimacy of Theosophy after 1881 and Sinnett's *The Occult World*. They are indispensable with regard to their normative power to enforce Theosophical claims, but they bear a historiographical riddle to the present, and with the letters "a conundrum arises."[144] Despite their contested content and unclear origin, the letters are treated as Blavatsky's legacy. In so doing, the narrative plausibility needed to maintain her authority over Theosophical teachings is reiterated and the twofold absence passed on. There is an *author function* that controls and limits the range of possible predicates or "discursive properties" ascribed to Blavatsky. In the words of Foucault: "The different forms of relationships (or non-relationships) that an author can assume are evidently one of these discursive properties."[145] In the case of early Theosophical historiography, it is the relationship(s) between contributors to the debate, including Blavatsky, that comes at the expense of most contributors, who appear secondary or unconsidered when the adepts' teachings are ascribed (in different ways) to Blavatsky.

Although the rationale behind these positions is rarely clear and references are scarce, they have predecessors with a similarly structured narrative stemming from a Theosophical context. These address the case in comparable ways, albeit with a bias toward Theosophy. Such partiality cannot be ascribed to the academic works discussed above, but they partly appropriate the eliminative aspect in similar ways, predominantly treating the letters not as a source *for* but as an expression *of* Blavatsky. Following a genealogical approach, this narrative can be traced even further to historical sources where the adepts are an indispensable means to legitimate the occult sciences as opposed to Spiritualism, and in defense of "oriental Theosophy"—that is, the Theosophical Society. An examination of the debates about Sinnett's *The Occult World* and *Esoteric Buddhism* has proved fruitful for insight into both recent academic and historical debates. While in current scholarship Sinnett's works are depicted as "massively influential" and groundbreaking for the Oriental shift, their historical involvement lacks proportionate attention. Critical examination of the participants and the controversy triggered by *The Occult World* reveals a dialogical process that involves a dispute over the meaning and authority of Theosophy and its doctrines. Here, the adept brothers turn out to have been the fulcrum to legitimate the occult claims.

As a consequence, a network of interacting speakers comes to the fore negotiating manifold topics. The significance ascribed to the adepts proves to be more important in the debates than it appears in scholarly accounts, with Spiritualists such as Moses, Harrison, Massey, the "correspondents" Sinnett and Hume, the Hindu specialists Subba Row, Damodar Mavalankar, and other Indian members struggling over the masters' existence and their teaching. In so doing, they become vital "witnesses" to Theosophical claims as they constantly reaffirm what is at stake: the legitimacy of the Theosophical endeavor as a whole. In this sense, they ascribe the author function of occultism, which here means Theosophy, to the Mahatmas, while simultaneously influencing the topics discussed. Hume, Sinnett, and Row are of particular weight because they published, went into dialogue with their critics, and developed those *adeptic* teachings that were to become a constitutive part of *The Secret Doctrine*—for example, the sevenfold constitution that is held to separate scientific occult Theosophy from erroneous Spiritualism. More than that, subjects hitherto underrated prove essential, most importantly, the distinction between East and West, but also contemporary notions of race and nation. The East/West binary appears strategic in the disputes, serving as a normative marker, for example, when the knowledge of "Western Spiritualists" is outrun by "Eastern adepts"—even if strongly purported by the Anglo-Indian Theosophists themselves, but claimed to be derived from the adepts.[146] Therefore, the recognition of the double absence in Theosophical history opens up new vistas that lay open an actual *Theosophy across boundaries* and that constitute a starting point for further analysis of the (global) history of modern Theosophy.

Notes

1. A. Trevor Barker, *The Mahatma-Letters to A.P. Sinnett from the Mahatmas M. & K.H.*, 1st ed. (London: T. Fisher Unwin, 1923).

2. Cf. René Guénon, *Theosophy: History of a Pseudo-Religion*, ed. James Wetmore (Hillsdale, NY: Sophia Perennis, 2003). In 2003, Guénon's critical account was translated into English for the first time. Cf. Edward Abdill, *Masters of Wisdom. The Mahatmas, Their Letters, and the Path* (New York, New York: Tarcher, 2015), xiii. Abdill leaves no doubt regarding his attitude: "Fortunately we do have some hard evidence that these men existed. We have letters written by them." Equally regarding the authenticity of Blavatsky, e.g.: "according to the Masters and HPB" (xvii). Robert Ellwood, *Theosophy: A Modern Expression of the Wisdom of the Ages* (Wheaton, IL: Quest Books, 1994), vii. Ellwood, in the initial "Note on the Sources," lists Blavatsky's *Isis Unveiled*, *The Secret Doctrine*, *Collected Writings*, and *The Key to Theosophy*, and Barker, *The Mahatma Letters*.

3. Cf. Michael Bergunder, "'Religion' and 'Science' within a Global Religious History," *Aries* 16, no. 1 (2016); Christopher A. Bayly, *The Birth of the Modern World* (Oxford: Blackwell, 2004), 317, 364–65, 479–80; Mark Bevir, "Theosophy and the Origins of the Indian National Congress," *Journal of Hindu Studies* 7, nos. 1–3 (2003); Nile Green, "The Global Occult: An Introduction," *History of Religions* 54, no. 4 (2015); Sebastian Conrad, "A Cultural History of Global Transformation," in *A History of the World*, vol. 4: *An Emerging Modern World, 1750–1870*, ed. idem and Jürgen Osterhammel (Cambridge, MA: Harvard University Press, 2018), 411–625, particularly 559–561.

4. Wouter J. Hanegraaff, "The Globalization of Esotericism," *Correspondences* 3 (2015); Michael Bergunder, "What Is Esotericism? Cultural Studies Approaches and the Problems of Definition in Religious Studies," *Method & Theory in the Study of Religion* 22, no. 1 (2010); Kennet Granholm, "Locating the West," in *Occultism in a Global Perspective*, ed. Henrik Bogdan and Gordan Djurdjevic (London: Acumen Publishing, 2013): Granholm rejects a heuristic category "Western," but struggles in his aim to "use [the West] in a general way," while at the same time "focusing on more specific locations." Egil Asprem, "Beyond the West: Towards a New Comparativism in the Study of Esotericism," *Correspondences* 2, no. 1 (2014); and Marco Pasi, "Kabbalah and Modernity," in *Kabbalah and Modernity*, ed. Marco Pasi, Kocku von Stuckrad, and Boaz Huss (Leiden: Brill, 2010). Pasi attempts to integrate Blavatsky's changing interpretation of Kabbalah, which illustrates the "oriental shift." For a very brief sketch of different approaches, see

Wouter J. Hanegraaff, "Esotericism Theorized: Major Trends and Approaches to the Study of Esotericism," in *Religion: Secret Religion*, ed. April D. DeConick, MacMillan Interdisciplinary Handbooks (London: Macmillan & Co, 2016). For a brief discussion of recent debates in research on "(Western) esotericism," see the introduction to this volume.

    5. Cf. Joscelyn Godwin, *The Theosophical Enlightenment*, SUNY Series in Western Esoteric Traditions (Albany, NY: State University of New York Press, 1994); Michael Gomes, *Theosophy in the Nineteenth Century: An Annotated Bibliography*, Religious Information Systems Series 15 (New York [u.a.]: Garland, 1994); Michael Gomes, *The Dawning of the Theosophical Movement* (Wheaton, IL: Quest Books, 1987); Nicholas Goodrick-Clarke, *The Western Esoteric Traditions* (New York: Oxford University Press, 2008); Wouter J. Hanegraaff, *New Age Religion and Western Culture: Esotericism in the Mirror of Secular Thought*, Studies in the History of Religions 72 (Leiden: Brill, 1996); Jeffrey D. Lavoie, *The Theosophical Society: The History of a Spiritualist Movement* (Boca Raton: BrownWalker Press, 2012); Santucci, James A., "Theosophical Society," in *Dictionary of Gnosis & Western Esotericism*, ed. Wouter J. Hanegraaff (Leiden: Brill, 2006).

    6. Sinnett, Alfred P., *Esoteric Buddhism* (London: Trübner & Co, 1883).

    7. Goodrick-Clarke, *The Western Esoteric Traditions* (New York: Oxford University Press, 2008), 211–28.

    8. Ibid., 211.

    9. Ibid., 219.

    10. Joscelyn Godwin, *The Theosophical Enlightenment* (Albany: State University of New York Press, 1994), xii.

    11. Ibid., 333; cf. Joy Dixon, *Divine Feminine* (Baltimore: The Johns Hopkins University Press, 2001), 25–30.

    12. Ibid., 329.

    13. Ibid., 340.

    14. Anna Kingsford and Edward Maitland, *The Perfect Way or the Finding of Christ* [repr.] ([Whitefish, Mont.]: Kessinger Publ., 1992).

    15. Godwin, *The Theosophical Enlightenment*, 342.

    16. Ibid., 379; cf.: Joscelyn Godwin, "Orientalism," in *Dictionary of Gnosis and Western Esotericism*, ed. Wouter J. Hanegraaff (Leiden: Brill, 2006), 907. More recently, Godwin's evaluation appears persistent. Godwin holds that the Theosophical assessment of the Orient counters "Orientalism," which he understands as a purely negative attitude of representation referring to Edward Said. For a critique of Said, see Robert J. C. Young, *White Mythologies: Writing History and the West*, 2nd ed. (London: Routledge, 2004), 158–80. According to Young, post-colonial theory begins with the critical discussion of Said's concept, resulting in a focus on the global context and the entanglement between "East" and "West."

    17. Lavoie, *The Theosophical Society*.

18. Ibid., 2–9.
19. Ibid., 9.
20. Ibid. My emphasis.
21. Ibid., 6.
22. Cf. Jörg Wichmann, "Das Theosophische Menschenbild und Seine Indischen Wurzeln," *Zeitschrift für Religions- und Geistesgeschichte* 35, no. 1 (1983). In this German article on the "Indian roots of the Theosophical conception of man," the habit of identifying India with its alleged scriptures becomes blatantly obvious. It is a case of the classic Orientalist paradigm of representation.
23. Cf. Olav Hammer and Mikael Rothstein, eds., *Handbook of the Theosophical Current* (Leiden: Brill, 2013); Mark Bevir, "The West Turns Eastward: Madame Blavatsky and the Transformation of the Occult Tradition," *Journal of the American Academy of Religion* 62, no. 3 (1994); Alex Owen, *The Place of Enchantment* (Chicago: University of Chicago Press, 2004); Santucci, "Theosophical Society," 1114–23. Cf. Dixon, *Divine Feminine*, 24–30 in particular. Dixon takes a broader perspective on historical debates and the discursive function of the Mahatma letters. But she is neither concerned with giving an overview over Theosophical teachings, nor clear in her evaluation of the connection between Blavatsky, the letters (or the Mahatmas), and Sinnett.
24. James A. Santucci, "The Notion of Race in Theosopy," *Nova Religio: The Journal of Alternative and Emergent Religions* 11, no. 3 (2008).
25. Green, "The Global Occult," 391.
26. Cf. Dipesh Chakrabarty, *Provincializing Europe: Postcolonial Thought and Historical Difference* (Princeton, NJ: Princeton University Press, 2007). It is this flaw that Chakrabarty analyzes as a characteristic way of writing history—a history modeled after an ideal Europe. Different histories, then, cannot but be inadequate copies of this ideal history.
27. Dixon, *Divine Feminine*, 28.
28. Cf. Helena Petrovna Blavatsky, *Isis Unveiled*. Vol. 1. *Science*, Reprint of the ed. New York 1877 (Pasadena, CA: Theosophical University Press, 1998), v. She introduces her work as "the fruit of a somewhat intimate acquaintance with Eastern Adepts." See also Helena Petrovna Blavatsky, *The Secret Doctrine: The Synthesis of Science, Religion and Philosophy: Occultism*, vol. 3 (Kila, MT: Kessinger Publishing, 1993), xx–xxi: The Eastern Adepts are kept as her teachers, but Blavatsky claims scriptural authority of the "Book of Dzyan," which holds all ancient wisdom and truth.
29. Godwin, *The Theosophical Enlightenment*, 277–81; cf. Bevir, "The West Turns Eastward."
30. Cf. Barker, *The Mahatma-Letters*, Letters I–VIII, 1–37.
31. Cf. Goodrick-Clarke, *The Western Esoteric Traditions*, 219–21.
32. Santucci, "Theosophical Society," 1116.

33. On February 20, 1879, Blavatsky and Olcott are named in the "List of Passengers" in *The Pioneer* 37, no. 2924 (1879), 6; three weeks later, the Society is introduced in a somewhat sceptical manner, with extracts from two of their Indian circulars (no. 2933, 1 and 4). Cf. Alfred P. Sinnett, *Autobiography of Alfred Percy Sinnett*, ed. Leslie Price (London: Theosophical History Centre, 1986).

34. Cf. *The Theosophist* 3 (1882), 17–22, 160–314 and *The Theosophist* 4 (1883), 2–5.

35. Cf. *Light* 2 (1882), 153. The curious yet cautious announcement of *The Occult World* in May 1881 holds: "Mr. Sinnett has had exceptional means of satisfying himself of the existence of those adepts in Occultism of whom we have heard so much from Colonel Olcott, and have read such remarkable accounts in H. P. Blavatsky's 'Isis Unveiled.'"

36. For a brief overview of the discussion even before the foundation of the Theosophical Society, see Stephen R. Prothero, *The White Buddhist: The Asian Odyssey of Henry Steel Olcott* (Bloomington: Indiana University Press, 1996), 44–48.

37. Cf. *The Pioneer* from March 1879 onward, where the Theosophical Society as well as Spiritualism were frequently discussed. From October 1880, one witnesses Sinnett's reports of several "incidents" corroborating Blavatsky's command of occult phenomena, and on October 15, 1881, a series of correspondences illustrated ongoing debates between Indian as Anglo-Indian readers (no. 3436, 7).

38. Cf. *Light* 2 (1882), 78, 98 and *The Spiritualist Newspaper* 19, no. 1 (1881), 1–3, 19–20, 30, 41–42.

39. Bevir, "The West Turns Eastward," 748.

40. Ibid., 759.

41. Lavoie, *The Theosophical Society*, 33.

42. Ibid., 44.

43. Brendan James French, "The Theosophical Masters: An Investigation Into the Conceptual Domains of H.P. Blavatsky and C.W. Leadbeater" (PhD diss., University of Sydney, 2000). French is reserved as to the origin of the letters and does not attempt to solve this riddle. Instead, he holds that their importance is due to their recognition as normative teachings by Theosophists (136–45).

44. Ibid., 134.

45. Gomes, *Theosophy in the Nineteenth Century*, 364.

46. Godwin, *The Theosophical Enlightenment*, 340.

47. Cf. Shery F. Crawford, "The Masters Revealed by K. Paul Johnson (Foreword: Joscelyn Godwin)," *Utopian Studies* 7, no. 2 (1996). In her review, Crawford is highly critical of the speculative and oftentimes forced character of Johnson's reasoning.

48. K. Paul Johnson, *The Masters Revealed*, SUNY Series in Western Esoteric Traditions (Albany, NY: State University of New York Press, 1994), 2.

49. French, *The Theosophical Masters*, 144.

50. Ibid., 129.
51. Ibid., 144.
52. An exception is Dixon, *Divine Feminine*. As noted above, her interest lies elsewhere. Dixon examines the connection between feminism and spirituality, and emphasizes the struggles for authority connected to the Mahatma letters and those claiming to be their mouthpieces—most notably Blavatsky and Sinnett; cf. 24–36, where it is stated that "Sinnett compiled the teachings" (26).
53. Lavoie, *The Theosophical Society*, 193.
54. Ibid., 196.
55. Gomes, *Theosophy in the Nineteenth Century*, 17.
56. Joscelyn Godwin, "Blavatsky and the First Generation of Theosophy," in *Handbook of the Theosophical Current*, ed. Olav Hammer, Brill Handbooks on Contemporary Religion 7 (Leiden: Brill, 2013), 15.
57. Ibid., 26.
58. Johnson, *The Masters Revealed*, 8.
59. Ibid., 12.
60. Bruce F. Campbell, *Ancient Wisdom Revived. A History of the Theosophical Movement* (Berkeley: University of California Press, 1980), vii.
61. Ibid., 61.
62. Sven Eek, "Alfred Percy Sinnett," *The American Theosophist* 7, no. 54 (1966): 164.
63. Barker, *The Mahatma-Letters*, vii.
64. Ibid., xiv.
65. Ibid., v.
66. Ibid., viii.
67. Cf. Curuppumullage Jinarajadasa, *Letters from the Masters of the Wisdom, 1881–1888* (London: Theosophical Publishing House, 1919). Jinarajadasa lists forty letters from the Masters. Among the recipients are H. P. Blavatsky and H. S. Olcott, C. W. Leadbeater, Francesca Arundale, Damodar Mavalankar, the Pandit Pran Nath of Gwalior, and Prince Harisinghji Rupsinghji. For Annie Besant, this is a "priceless booklet of Letters from the Elder Brothers" (v); Cf. Johnson, *The Masters Revealed*, 3–5; Geoffrey A. Barborka, *The Mahatmas and Their Letters* (Adyar [u.a.]: Theosophical Publishing House, 1973). Barborka is convinced of the masters' existence and their teachings. His account comprises a wider spectrum of what counts as "Mahatma Letters" as compared with the works quoted above. He refers to letters to de Fadeyev (11–14), H. S. Olcott (228–30), and Damodar Mavalankar (252–4) and dedicates two chapters to "Testimonials," including further recipients of Mahatma Letters (Chapter XIV–XVI and Appendix I–II); Cf. Sven Eek, *Dâmodar and the Pioneers of the Theosophical Movement* (Madras, India: Theosophical Publishing House, 1965); Cf. Gomes, *Theosophy in the Nineteenth Century*.
68. Barker, *The Mahatma-Letters*, xiii.

69. George Linton and Virginia Hanson, eds., *Readers' Guide to the Mahatma Letters to A. P. Sinnett*, 2nd rev. ed. (Adyar: Theosophical Publishing House, 1988), xv.
70. Ibid., 354.
71. Ibid.
72. Michel Foucault, "What Is an Author?," *Screen* 20, no. 1 (1979).
73. Michel Foucault, "Nietzsche, Genealogy, History," in *Language, Counter-Memory, Practice: Selected Essays and Interviews*, ed. D. F. Bouchard, vol. 20, I (Ithaca, NY: Cornell University Press, 1977).
74. Ibid., 143.
75. Ibid., 157.
76. *The Theosophist* 2, no. 9 (1881), n.p. (supplement).
77. Alfred P. Sinnett, *The Occult World* (London: Trübner & Co., 1881), 158.
78. Mark S. Morrison, "The Periodical Culture of the Occult Revival: Esoteric Wisdom, Modernity and Counter-Public Spheres," *Journal of Modern Literature* 31, no. 2 (2008).
79. Ibid., 5. Interestingly, Morrison emphasizes that Sinnett was an important member for the Theosophical Society not only because of his monographs, but in large part because he was a "professional journalist" (8). Unfortunately, this is the only occasion Morrison refers to Sinnett.
80. Owen, *The Place of Enchantment*, n.p. (Introduction).
81. Morrison, "Periodical Culture of the Occult Revival," 13.
82. *Light* 1, no. 25 (1881), 194; see also *The Theosophist* 2, no. 12 (1881), 258–60. Moses's note was reprinted in *The Theosophist*, following the then-common practice of mutual reception. Manifold cross-references between different popular journals of the time prove the close communicative network.
83. *The Theosophist* 2, no. 12 (1881), 259.
84. *The Spiritualist Newspaper* 19, no. 1 (1881), 1.
85. Ibid., 13.
86. Agnes Guppy (1838–1917); cf. Alex Owen, *The Darkened Room: Women, Power, and Spiritualism in Late Victorian England* (Chicago: University of Chicago Press, 2004), 41–74.
87. *The Spiritualist Newspaper* 19, no. 2 (1881), 13.
88. Cf. Sinnett, *The Occult World*, 56–57. This is one of the major events described in *The Occult World*. Blavatsky allegedly had a lost brooch of Mrs. Hume "precipitated" in the presence of several witnesses. The case went public for the first time in Sinnett's *The Pioneer* in October 1880, nos. 3429, 3 and 3433, 1. There is a series of contributions about "Occult Phenomena," partly about the events ascribed to Blavatsky. Extracts would be reprinted in *The Occult World*.
89. Cf. Eek, *Dâmodar and the Pioneers*. A good deal of his argument is based on these accounts.
90. *The Theosophist* 2, no. 11 (1880), 230.

91. Ibid.
92. Ibid.
93. Ibid.
94. Ibid., no. 11 (August Supplement).
95. Ibid., n.p. Emphasis mine.
96. Sinnett, *Esoteric Buddhism*, mostly 17–20.
97. *The Theosophist* 3, no. 9 (1882), 218.
98. Sinnett was printed with five installments of "Letters on Theosophy" in *Light* 2 (autumn 1882): no. 86389; no. 89, 412; no. 98, 518–19, and no. 99, 534; and *Light* 3 (1883), no. 3, 75.
99. *The Theosophist* 3, no. 12 (1882), 258.
100. *The Theosophist* 4, no. 2 (1883), 50.
101. Ibid., 46.
102. Blavatsky, *Isis Unveiled*. Vol. 1. *Science*, 351.
103. James A. Santucci, "Blavatsky, Helena Betrovna," in *Dictionary of Gnosis & Western Esotericism*, ed. Wouter J. Hanegraaff (Leiden: Brill, 2006), 183.
104. Goodrick-Clarke, *The Western Esoteric Traditions*, 220–21.
105. Lavoie, *The Theosophical Society*, 207. Emphasis mine.
106. Hanegraaff, *New Age Religion and Western Culture*, 455. Cf. Hanegraaff, Globalization.
107. *The Theosophist* 3, no. 1 (1882), 17–22.
108. Ibid., 17.
109. Ibid., 18.
110. Ibid., 17. He occasionally becomes polemic in tone, e.g., concluding that "[Spiritualists] overrate their quality and character."
111. Ibid., 19.
112. Ibid., 20. Hume again wastes no energy on diplomacy, assuring that most phenomena at séances are a "vast mass of trash, frivolous nonsense and falsehood communicated through mediums."
113. *The Theosophist* 3, no. 6 (1882), 159.
114. Ibid., 160.
115. *The Theosophist* 3, no. 12 (1882), 308.
116. Ibid., 309.
117. Ibid., 312.
118. After a long debate between Hume, Blavatsky, and the adepts, they finally parted for good, and in October 1882 the fourth and subsequent parts were due to A. P. Sinnett. *The Theosophist* 4, no. 1 (1883), 2–5.
119. *Light* 1, no. 20 (1881), 156.
120. E.g.: *Light* 2, no. 49 (1882), 389–91; no. 89, 412–14.
121. *The Theosophist* 3, no. 4 (1882), 90.
122. Foucault, "Nietzsche, Genealogy, History," 145.

123. Eek, *Dâmodar and the Pioneers*, 661–73. Eek gives one of the above-mentioned "Theosophical" accounts. Its historical scope is limited, but besides a biographical sketch of Row's, this example shows that there are attempts to approach "Indian" Theosophists and appreciate their role in Theosophical history. Cf. Godwin, *The Theosophical Enlightenment*, 329.

124. Richard King, *Orientalism and Religion: Postcolonial Theory, India and "The Mystic East"* (London: Routledge, 1999). See also Godwin, *The Theosophical Enlightenment*, 307–32.

125. *The Theosophist* 3, no. 4 (1881), 93–98.

126. Ibid., 93.

127. Row's identification of India as "Aryan" (and debates on and depictions of India) is a delicate topic worthy of a separate article. For the ideologically charged implications of "Aryan" as connected not only to race, but also to linguistics, culture, religion, and nation, see Thomas R. Trautmann, *Aryans and British India* (New Delhi: Vistaar Publ., 1997); Susan Bayly, "Race in Britain and India," in *Nation and Religion; Perspectives on Europe and Asia*, ed. Peter van der Veer and Hartmut Lehmann (Princeton, NJ: Princeton University Press, 1999); see also Santucci, James A., "The Notion of Race in Theosophy." While giving a glimpse into the debate on race in the nineteenth century (Orientalist) context, Santucci limits his discussion mainly to the notion of race(s) in "classical" Theosophical publications—*Esoteric Buddhism* and *The Secret Doctrine*. Hence, the focus on said publications leads to philosophical aspects of the evolution of races as constructed therein, but does not analyze the historical context of Theosophical debates and their connection to race. The above-mentioned examples of Row and Mavalankar, and furthermore parts of *The Occult World* and *Esoteric Buddhism*, suggest a different reading of the importance of race in this context. For "race" in Theosophy with a focus on Annie Besant, see Gauri Viswanathan, *Outside the Fold: Conversion, Modernity, and Belief* (Princeton: Princeton University Press, 1998), 187–200,

128. *The Theosophist* 3, no. 4 (1881), 96.

129. Ibid., 97.

130. Barker, *The Mahatma-Letters*, 92.

131. A. Trevor Barker, *The Letters of H. P. Blavatsky to A. P. Sinnett*, Facsimile edition (Pasadena, California: Theosophical University Press, 1973), 323.

132. Cf. Godwin, *The Theosophical Enlightenment*, 307–32; Godwin, "Orientalism"; Nicholas Goodrick-Clarke, "The Theosophical Society, Orientalism, and the 'Mystic East': Western Esotericism and Eastern Religion in Theosophy," Theosophical History 13, no. 1 (2007); Michael Bergunder, Heiko Frese, and Ulrike Schröder, *Ritual, Caste, and Religion in Colonial South India* (Halle [Wiesbaden]: Verlag der Franckeschen Stiftungen, Harrassowitz in Kommission, 2010). Bergunder suggests that this development was not natural but shows further

trajectories in his analysis of Theosophical connections to South Indian Shaiva Siddhanta.

133. *The Theosophist* 3, no. 12 (1882), 297.
134. *The Theosophist* 4, no. 5 (1883), 118.
135. *The Theosophist* 3, no. 3 (1882), 62; See also ibid., no. 6, 152. After Damodar Mavalankar had written the first critical review of the book in the *The Theosophist* 2, no. 3 (1881), 62–64), he later comments in several footnotes on Oxley's letters again, reinforcing his criticism. One reason to reject Busiris, he says, lies in its non-Aryan name—other than, for example Koot-Hoomi. To corroborate his views, he additionally refers to *The Occult World*. For an in-depth discussion of Theosophy and the Bhagavad Gita, see Bergunder's chapter in this volume.
136. *The Theosophist* 3, no. 6 (1882), 151.
137. *The Theosophist* 4, no. 10 (1883), 249.
138. Barker, *The Letters of H. P. Blavatsky to A. P. Sinnett*, 316–23.
139. Ibid., 318.
140. Ibid., 316.
141. Ibid., 319.
142. On a broader scale, Bevir has pointed into that direction. Bevir, "Theosophy and the Origins of the Indian National Congress."
143. Barker, *The Mahatma-Letters*, 70.
144. Santucci, "The Notion of Race in Theosophy," 53.
145. Foucault, "What Is an Author?," 28.
146. The irony of this inversion was described by Viswanathan. Cf. Gauri Viswanathan, "The Ordinary Business of Occultism," *Critical Inquiry* 27, no. 1 (2000).

References

Abdill, Edward. *Masters of Wisdom: The Mahatmas, Their Letters, and the Path*. New York: Tarcher, 2015.

Asprem, Egil. "Beyond the West: Towards a New Comparativism in the Study of Esotericism." *Correspondences* 2, no. I (2014): 3–33.

Barborka, Geoffrey A. *The Mahatmas and Their Letters*. Adyar: Theosophical Publ. House, 1973.

Barker, A. Trevor. *The Letters of H. P. Blavatsky to A. P. Sinnett*. Facsimile edition. Pasadena, CA: Theosophical University Press, 1973.

———. *The Mahatma-Letters to A. P. Sinnett from the Mahatmas M. & K. H.* 1st ed. London: T. Fisher Unwin LTD, 1923.

Bayly, Christopher A. *The Birth of the Modern World*. Oxford: Blackwell, 2004.

Bayly, Susan. "Race in Britain and India." In *Nation and Religion: Perspectives on Europe and Asia*, edited by Peter van der Veer and Hartmut Lehmann, 71–95. Princeton, NJ: Princeton University Press, 1999.

Bergunder, Michael. "'Religion' and 'Science' within a Global Religious History." *Aries* 16, no. 1 (2016): 86–141.

———. "What Is Esotericism? Cultural Studies Approaches and the Problems of Definition in Religious Studies." *Method & Theory in the Study of Religion* 22, no. 1 (2010): 9–36.

Bergunder, Michael, Heiko Frese, and Ulrike Schröder. *Ritual, Caste, and Religion in Colonial South India*. Halle [Wiesbaden]: Verlag der Franckeschen Stiftungen, Harrassowitz in Kommission, 2010.

Bevir, Mark. "The West Turns Eastward: Madame Blavatsky and the Transformation of the Occult Tradition." *Journal of the American Academy of Religion* 62, no. 3 (1994): 747–67.

———. "Theosophy and the Origins of the Indian National Congress." *Journal of Hindu Studies* 8, nos. 1–3 (2003): 99–115.

Blavatsky, Helena Petrovna. *Isis Unveiled*. Vol. 1. *Science*. Reprint of the ed. New York 1877. Pasadena, CA: Theosophical University Press, 1998.

———. *The Secret Doctrine: The Synthesis of Science, Religion and Philosophy. Occultism*. Vol. 3. Kila, MT: Kessinger Publishing, 1993.

Campbell, Bruce F. *Ancient Wisdom Revived: A History of the Theosophical Movement*. Berkeley, CA: University of California Press, 1980.

Chakrabarty, Dipesh. *Provincializing Europe: Postcolonial Thought and Historical Difference*. Edition: New. Princeton, NJ: Princeton University Press, 2007.

Conrad, Sebastian. "A Cultural History of Global Transformation." In *A History of the World*, vol. 4: *An Emerging Modern World, 1750–1870*, edited by Sebastian Conrad and Jürgen Osterhammel, 411–625. Cambridge, MA: Harvard University Press, 2018.

Crawford, Shery F. "The Masters Revealed by K. Paul Johnson (Foreword: Joscelyn Godwin)." *Utopian Studies* 7, no. 2 (1996): 272–74.

Dixon, Joy. *Divine Feminine*. Baltimore: The Johns Hopkins University Press, 2001.

Eek, Sven. "Alfred Percy Sinnett." *The American Theosophist* 7, no. 54 (1966): 164–67.

———. *Dâmodar and the Pioneers of the Theosophical Movement*. Madras, India: Theosophical Publishing House, 1965.

Ellwood, Robert. *Theosophy: A Modern Expression of the Wisdom of the Ages*. Wheaton, IL: Quest Books, 1994.

Foucault, Michel. "Nietzsche, Genealogy, History." In *Language, Counter-Memory, Practice: Selected Essays and Interviews*, edited by D. F. Bouchard, Vol. 20. I. Ithaca, New York: Cornell University Press, 1977.

———. "What Is an Author?" *Screen* 20, no. 1 (1979): 13–34.

French, Brendan James. "The Theosophical Masters: An Investigation Into the Conceptual Domains of H.P. Blavatsky and C.W. Leadbeater." PhD diss., University of Sydney, 2000.

Godwin, Joscelyn. "Blavatsky and the First Generation of Theosophy." In *Handbook of the Theosophical Current*, edited by Olav Hammer, 16–31. Brill Handbooks on Contemporary Religion 7. Leiden: Brill, 2013.

———. "Orientalism." In *Dictionary of Gnosis and Western Esotericism*, edited by Wouter J. Hanegraaff, 906–9. Leiden: Brill, 2006.

———. *The Theosophical Enlightenment*. SUNY Series in Western Esoteric Traditions. Albany, NY: State University of New York Press, 1994.

Gomes, Michael. *The Dawning of the Theosophical Movement*. Wheaton, IL: Quest Books, 1987.

———. *Theosophy in the Nineteenth Century: An Annotated Bibliography*. Religious Information Systems Series 15, New York: Garland, 1994.

Goodrick-Clarke, Nicholas. "The Theosophical Society, Orientalism, and the 'Mystic East'": Western Esotericism and Eastern Religion in Theosophy." *Theosophical History* 13 (2007): 3–28.

———. *The Western Esoteric Traditions*. New York: Oxford University Press, 2008.

Granholm, Kennet. "Locating the West." In *Occultism in a Global Perspective*, edited by Henrik Bogdan and Gordan Djurdjevic, 17–36. London: Acumen Publishing, 2013.

Green, Nile. "The Global Occult: An Introduction." *History of Religions* 54, no. 4 (2015): 383–93.

Guénon, René. *Theosophy: History of a Pseudo-Religion*. Edited by James Wetmore. Hillsdale, NY: Sophia Perennis, 2003.

Hammer, Olav, and Mikael Rothstein, eds. *Handbook of the Theosophical Current*. Leiden: Brill, 2013.

Hanegraaff, Wouter J. "Esotericism Theorized: Major Trends and Approaches to the Study of Esotericism." In *Religion: Secret Religion*, edited by April D. DeConick, 155–70. MacMillan Interdisciplinary Handbooks. London: Macmillan & Co, 2016.

———. *New Age Religion and Western Culture: Esotericism in the Mirror of Secular Thought*. Studies in the History of Religions 72. Leiden: Brill, 1996.

———. "The Globalization of Esotericism." *Correspondences* 3 (2015): 55–91.

Jinarajadasa, Curuppumullage. *Letters from the Masters of the Wisdom, 1881–1888*. London: Theosophical Publishing House, 1919.

Johnson, K. Paul. *The Masters Revealed*. SUNY Series in Western Esoteric Traditions. Albany, NY: State University of New York Press, 1994.

King, Richard. *Orientalism and Religion: Postcolonial Theory, India and "The Mystic East."* London: Routledge, 1999.

Kingsford, Anna, and Edward Maitland. *The Perfect Way or the Finding of Christ*. [Repr.]. [Whitefish, Mont.]: Kessinger Publ., 1992.

Lavoie, Jeffrey D. *The Theosophical Society: The History of a Spiritualist Movement*. Boca Raton: BrownWalker Press, 2012.

Linton, George, and Virginia Hanson, eds. *Readers' Guide to the Mahatma Letters to A. P. Sinnett*. 2nd revised edition. Adyar: Theosophical Publishing House, 1988.

Morrison, Mark S. "The Periodical Culture of the Occult Revival: Esoteric Wisdom, Modernity and Counter-Public Spheres." *Journal of Modern Literature* 31, no. 2 (2008): 1–22.

Owen, Alex. *The Darkened Room: Women, Power, and Spiritualism in Late Victorian England*. Chicago: University of Chicago Press, 2004.

———. *The Place of Enchantment*. Chicago: University of Chicago Press, 2004.

Pasi, Marco. "Kabbalah and Modernity." In *Kabbalah and Modernity*, edited by Marco Pasi, Kocku von Stuckrad, and Boaz Huss, 151–66. Leiden: Brill, 2010.

Prothero, Stephen R. *The White Buddhist: The Asian Odyssey of Henry Steel Olcott*. Bloomington: Indiana University Press, 1996.

Santucci, James A. "Blavatsky, Helena Betrovna." In *Dictionary of Gnosis & Western Esotericism*, edited by Wouter J. Hanegraaff, 177–85. Leiden: Brill, 2006.

———. "The Notion of Race in Theosophy." *Nova Religio: The Journal of Alternative and Emergent Religions* 11, no. 3 (2008): 37–63.

———. "Theosophical Society." In *Dictionary of Gnosis & Western Esotericism*, edited by Wouter J. Hanegraaff, 1114–23. Leiden: Brill, 2006.

Sinnett, Alfred P. *Autobiography of Alfred Percy Sinnett*. Edited by Leslie Price. 1st edition. London: Theosophical History Centre, 1986.

———. *Esoteric Buddhism*. 1st edition. London: Trübner & Co, 1883.

———. *The Occult World*. London: Trübner & Co., 1881.

Trautmann, Thomas R. *Aryans and British India*. New Delhi: Vistaar Publ., 1997.

Viswanathan, Gauri. *Outside the Fold: Conversion, Modernity, and Belief*. Princeton: Princeton University Press, 1998.

———. "The Ordinary Business of Occultism." *Critical Inquiry* 27, no. 1 (2000): 1–20.

Wichmann, Jörg. "Das Theosophische Menschenbild und seine indischen Wurzeln." *Zeitschrift für Religions- und Geistesgeschichte* 35, no. 1 (1983): 12–33.

Young, Robert J. C. *White Mythologies: Writing History and the West*. 2nd ed. London: Routledge, 2004.

Chapter 6

Affinity and Estrangement

Transnational Theosophy in Germany and India during the Colonial Era (1878-1933)

Perry Myers

Introduction

The late Christopher Bayly, in his masterful book *The Birth of the Modern World*, observes that "the tide of nationalism [. . .] drew on indigenous legends, histories, and sentiments about land and people, rather than being a malign imposition of the West."[1] In a notable contrast, Bayly further posits in a later chapter titled "Empires of Religion" that "the Irish, American, Australian, British, and Indian Theosophists of the 1880s were adepts of a self-consciously global and intellectual tradition; they were not representatives of an embattled 'little tradition' of the locality."[2] Bayly's assessment of the "indigenous" nature of nationalism on the one hand and transnational Theosophy on the other reveals a striking paradox in our understanding of the interaction of global and local symbolic capital during the era—a conflicted assessment of the affinities and estrangements, to borrow Bruce Lincoln's nomenclature, generated by the global flow of esoteric religious ideas and how they interacted with, and facilitated,

---

I would like to thank the editors of this volume and the anonymous readers for their helpful and pertinent suggestions and comments, which have greatly improved the quality and accuracy of my work. Errors remain my own.

the emergence of more local, domestic "tides of nationalism." From the late nineteenth century to beyond the First World War, Theosophical ideas and texts traversed the globe, as Bayly rightly suggests, yet these transnational religious affinities also frequently became fused with native sentiments, local traditions, regional histories, and national agendas. As a result, Theosophical subsets developed that recombined or split apart in multivalent ways, posing a challenge to any convenient analytical binaries involving cosmopolitan Theosophical dispositions.[3] Thus, Bayly uncovers—but does not account for—a paradox that points to an incomplete grasp of the relationship between the global and the local and, more specifically, to the nexus between transnational spiritual capital and local or national agendas—the interstices of both the global and local and the sacred and profane.

As Bayly's work demonstrates, and the transnational flow of social, political, and religious sentiments corroborates, recent historiography has exhibited a substantive "transnational turn." Recent decades have seen the appearance of many fruitful conference presentations, monographs, and journal articles on the transnational links between various intellectual movements, scientific influences, cultural networks, histories, and political agendas across the entire globe, from the Far East to India and the Middle East to South and Central America.[4] Transnational approaches thus have provoked a number of important theoretical and historical questions: How, for instance, do the fundamental analyses manifest in transnational approaches account for links between various geopolitical and geocultural spaces; what commonalities do these purportedly cohesive fields exhibit beyond the more obvious spatial and temporal; moreover, in what ways do the actors depicted in these transnational fields negotiate symbolic power or carve out cultural, social, and political capital that renders them more distinct both globally and locally? More generally, how do the answers to these questions contribute to a better understanding of the more comprehensive or systemic questions regarding the practice of transnational history, which, as Pierre-Yves Saunier points out, is not written

> [w]ithout or against the nation, or [restricted] to only analysing long-distance connections and long-range circulations. Rather, a transnational perspective shows how deeply the national fabric and the local or national political debate are intertwined with issues, actors and processes that cut through what we are used to conceiving as local or national.[5]

This chapter cannot answer all of these questions. That remains the goal of a larger project currently in progress.[6] Yet a comparative investigation of German and Indian Theosophy during the late nineteenth and early twentieth centuries offers important insight into how to further challenge still-embedded historiographical silos, national containers, or the neat results of a Hegelian dialectical synthesis. Moreover, this analysis contributes to better fleshing out some kind of order to these seemingly rhizomic transnational flows—their disruptions, departures, and multiple origins—without assuming an "origin filiation and genesis" as their base.[7] To achieve this goal, first I depict some, though not all, pertinent common features of the Theosophical Movement in both Germany and India to illustrate their transnational affinities, and then, second, examine their idiosyncratic Theosophical formulations and local applications—estrangements—in each of these vastly different geopolitical spaces.

Before doing this, however, some historical background is called for. During the decades of the late nineteenth and early twentieth centuries, many spiritually disgruntled Europeans explored new forms of spirituality—frequently Indian traditions—as a means to articulate responses to perceived social, political, and cultural stresses in their nations and empires.[8] In India, Indian intellectuals were similarly disenchanted, though for far different reasons than in Europe, namely because of increased British repression since the 1857 mutiny and the frustrated hopes for liberation from the British Raj. Similar to their Western counterparts, these Indians explored Western religion and philosophy as a means to rearticulate their own sacred heritage and to transform Indian social, political, and cultural paradigms. As a result, a transnational nexus formed between Indian and Western religious innovation—a religious field, in Bourdieu's sense, in which spiritual dispositions formed a common trajectory that traversed traditional geopolitical boundaries and became fused with the unique national political, social, and cultural spheres in each of these geopolitical zones.[9] To put it differently, a circular or transnational flow of unorthodox religious symbolic capital—formulated through Theosophical precepts—merged with domestic agendas and became rearticulated as a heterodox voice in the German and Indian localities.

The Russian émigré Helena Petrovna Blavatsky (1831–1891) and the American Buddhist revivalist Henry Steele Olcott (1832–1907) founded the Theosophical Society in New York in 1875. Its ideas were based on the idea that there is a universal hidden or occult truth in all religions that reconciles scientific, philosophical, and religious epistemes, but can only be accessed by specially trained and adept individuals. Because their Theosophical wisdom was explicitly linked to Indian traditions, these two visionaries moved the Society's headquarters to India in 1879, where it found significant resonance among Indian reformers, subversives, and nationalists. Though often considered marginal by scholars and never large in membership, the Theosophical Society and its ideas nevertheless attracted many important as well as geographically and ideologically diverse intellectuals during the era.[10] The Irish poet W. B. Yeats, for example, was an engaged member of the British Theosophical Society; the painter Wassily Kandinsky (1866–1944) was heavily influenced by Theosophy; Rudolf Steiner (1861–1925), editor at the Goethe archives in Weimar, was president of the German Theosophical Society until 1912, when he founded Anthroposophy, an occult offshoot more explicitly linked with Christian esoteric traditions; and Gandhi studied Theosophy, as did Jawaharlal Nehru. In fact, Gandhi interacted with many Theosophists, including Annie Besant, the Theosophical Society's leader after Blavatsky's death, which ignited his enthusiasm for Hindu traditions.[11] Theosophy generated an appealing scientific spiritual model for these renowned heterodox thinkers in Europe and India that could be molded for diverse national objectives—to forge a distinctive voice that could augment their cultural and social capital, enabling them to engage in ongoing debates on diverse domestic issues. Thus, my work here focuses on how the common transnational features of this newfangled religious field became reappropriated in various local Theosophical subsets, each of which sought to shape domestic agendas, and provides critical insight into the transnational interplay between the sacred and the profane and its impact on the social and political habitus in each geopolitical domain.

Cosmopolitan Theosophical Affinities

One common feature that traversed the global landscape of Theosophical thought and other schools of thought during the era was its explicit criticism of Western material culture and what Theosophists bemoaned as a predominant, yet fragmented, scientific worldview—"the materialistic mind," so-named by the German Theosophist and medical doctor Franz Hartmann (1838–1912).[12] In his view, materialism failed to adequately acknowledge and incorporate human spirituality into the formula for producing human knowledge.[13] Current scientific practice, according to Hartmann, "gives only a partial solution of the problems of the objective world, and leaves us in regard to the subjective world almost entirely in the dark. Modern science classifies phenomena and describes events, but to describe how an event takes place is not sufficient to explain why it takes place."[14] Several decades later, the Austrian-born Rudolf Steiner, by this time the leader of his own esoteric religious movement, Anthroposophy, asserted in the first of six lectures delivered in October 1919 in Zurich that "This natural science [. . .] exceeds its field, if it wants to express something about the innermost essence of the human being. It gives no answer about the innermost essence of the human being [. . .]"[15] Noteworthy in this context, Helmut Zander asserts that Steiner's lifelong theme was the linkage between science and "Geisteswissenschaft."[16] Thus Hartmann and Steiner's criticism of empirical science's predominant role as the exclusive source for determining human knowledge illustrates a consistent ideological thread in the German Theosophical worldview that by no means rejected science in toto, but rather bemoaned its deficient appraisal of the human being—it needed a spiritual corrective.

German Theosophists also expressed disdain for materialism's pervasiveness in the economic sphere. Hartmann, for instance, vehemently criticized the idealized pursuit of pecuniary gain in modern culture: "To employ the intellectual powers for the purpose of 'making money' is the beginning of intellectual prostitution."[17] Decades later, at the end of World War I in 1918 and the Second Reich's demise, Europe, and especially Germany, confronted many perplexing questions about the social, political, and economic constellations of the future, including what many perceived as an urgent need to address socioeconomic inequalities inherent in industrial capitalism and the related ramifications for German culture and society. Steiner explicitly addressed this issue: "One learned to think about capitalism during a time in which this capitalism caused a process of disease in the social organism."[18] These sweeping denunciations of materialism's predominance not only disclose a common Theosophical thread but also condemn what in their view formed the precarious bedrock for both empirical science and industrial capitalism in modern culture and society.

Indian Theosophists during the era likewise criticized the ascendancy of materially derived knowledge and its utilitarian influences on modern culture and society. Bhagavan Das (1869–1958), a Theosophist and activist in the Indian nationalist movement, for instance, wrote in 1909:

> Yet, latterly, men have been hypnotising themselves and have taken to worshipping the machines they have themselves created. The machine has begun to be regarded as more important than the man. Steam-power, electricity-power, powder, ball, gas, metal, and submarine and aeroplane are treated as if they were greater than the mind-power, manas, which discovers and invents and utilises them, and the bread-power, the staff of life, annamapranah, which nourishes and keeps up that mind-power.[19]

Here, aligned with German views of materialist culture, Das also expressed his disdain for the material objectification of human beings, yet the cleavage between this transnational affinity and the emergence of distinctive domestic aims becomes apparent in Das's precise criticism that subtly redounds to Indian religious traditions as materialism's cultural antidote.[20]

More assertive, B. P. Wadia (1881–1958), the Indian labor leader in Madras and nationalist, unconditionally scorned Western materialism in a text composed after the end of World War I, an event that triggered frequent acerbic disdain for the West among Indian esoteric thinkers: "Of course the whole problem is thrown back on the original sin of Materialism, which denies the divinity of men and things, and refuses to see the hand of God in evolution."[21] Thus, like the German Theosophical acolytes, Indian adepts also identified modern Western materialist designs as the culprit behind many of the world's problems.

Yet, despite this criticism of materialism and the predominance of the natural sciences during the era, Theosophists nevertheless embraced Darwinian evolutionary science, a second transnational affinity, but with a Theosophical twist that incorporated spiritual evolution into the Darwinian model. In the Theosophical German-language journal *Sphinx*, for instance, the German philosopher, Theosophist, and writer on mysticism Carl du Prel (1839–1899) posited in an 1886 essay: "The earthly (physical) Darwinism is a truth; but it is only possible, if a transcendental (metaphysical) Darwinism exists."[22] Moreover, du Prel proposed a more extensive application of Darwinian theory: "Yet at the core of Darwin's theory is to be noted: *the genesis of the practical through natural selection*. When raised as this general philosophical concept, the overlap with other areas that Darwin covered becomes self-evidently clear."[23] Based on the broad scope of Darwinian applications implied here, du Prel applied natural selection as a means to reformulate human physical progression and to validate the existence of life after death:

> According to materialistic notions the highest progression of the soul's life would have to coincide with the highest blossoming of the physical being. However, the opposite is the case: the highest transcendental functions come into appearance with the deepest repression of physical being, namely in death. From this emanates that death is not an annihilation, rather the liberation of the transcendental subject from the shackles of the organism with respect to imagination and effect, a disembodiment of the soul, that precisely for that reason can only represent for our senses a de-souling [*Entseelung*] of the body.[24]

In an even grander scheme, the lawyer and colonial acolyte Wilhelm Hübbe-Schleiden (1846–1916), who founded the *Theosophische Vereinigung* in Berlin in 1892, which later became the *Deutsche Theosophische Gesellschaft* in 1894, invoked Darwinian historicism, combined with his reading of Indian religious tenets, and a twist of Hegelian "world historical figures," to substantiate the evolutionary progress of the ethically benevolent individual:

> [T]hus we also see, based on the same reason [biological evolution], in each systematic series of forms, all coexisting individuals, from the cell to the moss and to the tree, from the amoeba to the worm and to the human being, from the savage to Goethe and to Christ, the different levels of the individualistic pre-history of a Christ-Being, spread before us.[25]

Thus, both du Prel and Hübbe-Schleiden embraced the historicism embedded in Darwin's scientific model as an analytical framework for addressing the disconcerting spiritual apprehension that was unsettling for many intellectuals during the Kaiserreich—a co-optation of the past that predicted progress in order to ratify future Theosophical credibility and authority—the perpetuity of the soul and the emergence of "Christlike" beings.

In a slightly different twist, the Indian story begins with the unambiguous equation of science with Theosophy. J. K. Daji (n.d.) redefined scientific evolution to redound to spirituality even more explicitly than these German adaptations in an essay published in the Adyar *Theosophist* (1889):

> In short, evolution is two-sided. A great mystery works from within, and external circumstances guide and control it to a degree inversely proportionate to the progress of evolution in the individual. In the course of evolution the latent power within is awakened, and soon after its awakening it tends to have its own way, unconsciously at first but consciously as soon as self-consciousness is evolved, [. . .] which trains by proper exercise a power within that becomes irresistible when duly developed (will), and that leads eventually, under the guidance of right effort, to the goal, the crown of evolution, the elevation of man to the dignity of man-god.[26]

In Daji's version, evolutionary progression also became a powerful engine for human beings to potentially attain divine-like qualities and thus created an avenue for these Indian Theosophical pundits to enhance their distinction in the public sphere—a convenient nexus of the sacred and the profane.

From a slightly different angle, Curuppumullage Jinarajadasa (1875–1953), polyglot, world traveler, and, postdating the era of our concern, fourth president of the international Theosophical Society in Adyar (1945–53), reiterated this point in 1921: "There is no better preparation for a clear comprehension of Theosophy than a broad, general knowledge of modern science. For science deals with facts, tabulating them and discovering laws; Theosophy deals with the same facts, and though they may be tabulated differently, the conclusions are in the main the same."[27] Here, Jinarajadasa suggests that science and Theosophy differed only in method, rather than results. Moreover, Indian Theosophists employed this logic to sanction their own distinctive status as both sacred and secular agents. A prime example in this respect is the case of B. P. Wadia, who fused spiritual evolution with an Enlightenment-derived emphasis on individual agency to affirm the distinction of the Theosophical pundit:

> Man is striving to become a Perfect Individual—free in mind, morals and activities. The purpose of all evolution is to enable him to attain to that exalted status. The various branches of

the tree of evolution serve the one purpose—to give man the necessary shelter while he is engaged in the Herculean labour of growth unto a Perfect Individuality."[28]

By implication, then, Theosophy provided knowledge of the world equal in stature and import to that of the scientist. In fact, Theosophy and its pundits furnished the rationalized vehicle for unifying evolutionary science and spirituality, which consequently elevated the credibility and authority of the Theosophical adept as a distinctive voice in negotiating knowledge of the world, in both the sacred and profane spheres.

A third affinity of cosmopolitan Theosophical thought stems from its tenet of universality, based on the creed that all religions embody a core occult spiritual truth only accessible to the Theosophical adept. Franz Hartmann expressed this universal prerogative in explicit terms: "All religions are based upon internal truth, all have an outside ornamentation which varies in character in the different systems, but all have the same foundation of truth, and if we compare the various systems with one another, looking below the surface of exterior forms, we find that this truth is in all religious systems one and the same."[29] Thus, by implication, the work and rare insight of the Theosophical pundit penetrate these exterior forms and thereby reveal the universal cohesion of all religions at their core.

In a more concrete formulation, Hartmann fused Christian and Indian traditions to posit a universal path to spiritual rejuvenation: "The way to Christ is yoga."[30] He further asserted that each religion's essence is explicitly embedded in that of the other: "Yet this yoga-doctrine composes not only the essence of the India doctrine of wisdom, but rather it is also the foundation and pinnacle of all true Christianity [. . .]."[31] In Hartmann's view, both Indian and Western religion manifested a unity based on their common link to universal truth, a conveniently constructed axis that both Indian and German Theosophists, as we shall see, transformed into "myth" and used as a form of symbolic political capital to bolster the efficacy of their domestic political and cultural agendas.[32]

Similar to their German counterparts, Indian Theosophists also underscored Theosophy's claim that all religions constitute the manifestation of a universal spiritual web. In reference to what he described as the dualities of all "world-systems"—religious, scientific, or philosophical—Bhagavan Das asserted: "The common fact, running through all these pairs of names, is the fact of the rhythmic swing of the World-process, the diastole and systole of the universal Heart, the inspiration and expiration of the Universal Breath, on all scales, in all departments of Nature, mental as well as material."[33] N. K. Ramaswami Ayyar (n.d.) reiterated Das's view in more mundane terms, yet with tangible political undertones, when he depicted Theosophy as an

> International federation [. . .] the coming type of social evolution in the West. Hinduism had developed this federal type of nationality ages and ages ago. In the West this federal idea is of very recent growth. But this was applied only to one part of the social life, namely the organisation of the state. Hinduism had developed however a much wider and fuller type of federation.[34]

Here, Ayyar extols Hinduism's primary historical position with respect to recent Western historical processes, which had become manifest in the nation state, to reconstitute universal spiritual federalism. Thus, in Ayyar's assessment, Indian religious traditions' vast history and cultural breadth trumped more recent and limited Western social and political development. Here, Das and Ayyar repurposed a shared transnational Theosophical attribute to articulate political capital endowed with local aims—Hindu revitalization as a foundational element for a "wider and fuller" federation in which sacred mandates justify profane objectives.

With far more extensive repercussions, B. P. Wadia linked universal agency with Aryanism and its implicit racial undertones: "As humanity grows into Justice and Liberty, the hand of the Divine Helper will become visible to an increasing extent, till in the culminating civilisation of our Aryan Race, Gods will walk the earth as of old, and the Golden Age will have returned."[35] Wadia defined Theosophical universality in terms of a superior race associated with India—a formulation remarkably similar to, and most frequently associated with, German attempts to yoke their own heritage to an Aryan past long before the ascension of Hitler's fascist ideology.[36] Taking the point further, Jinarajadasa expressed this racially charged universality as a hierarchical superiority: "In the Aryan or Caucasian races we have probably the highest forms, not only in beauty of structure, but also for quick response to external stimuli and high sensitiveness to the finer philosophical and artistic thoughts and emotions."[37] This link, as we shall see, would provide a foundational framework for Indian anti-colonialist aims, and for asserting national identity and political agency for those Indian Theosophists who envisioned a post-colonial future. Yet, remarkably, Aryan universality served equally well to bolster German visions of a colonial empire.

Estrangement: Reformulating Transnational Spiritual Affinities for Secular Agendas

In his 1887 essay "Der Tod," Carl du Prel argued that society's diseases derive from the increasingly powerful emphasis on the individual human being and earthly life. These referenced social diseases (what Tomas Kaiser, in reference to Du Prel, calls "sociale Schäden"[38]—though not stated explicitly, du Prel actually meant Marxist socialism with its proletarian assertions) can only be remedied "if on the one hand resignation is augmented, and equally on the other hand brotherly love, which receives its highest power of motivation only from the doctrine of immortality."[39] Du Prel ever so subtly attributed society's tribulations to materialism, as did most Theosophists, yet he articulated its remedies in Christian idioms that foresaw their postponement to an eternal afterlife—*Unsterblichkeit*. Such readings thinly veil the elite class cohesiveness that pervaded Theosophy during the era and the underlying aim of German Theosophical pundits to reconstitute spirituality while perpetuating the social status quo.

In fact, German Theosophical texts frequently declared the elite stature of those Theosophists who combined intellectual faculties with spiritual prowess. Franz Hartmann, for instance, contended: "Some persons are possessed of great intellectual power, but of little spirituality; some have spiritual power, but a weak intellect; those in which the spiritual energies are well supported by a strong intellect are the elect."[40] Hartmann later reinforced this point in an unambiguous counter to Nietzschean criticisms of Christianity's emphasis on self-renunciation: "A man who attempts to fall in love with himself, or, with other words, to find in himself his own highest ideal, will never succeed in being contented and harmonious."[41] Here, Hartmann's directive appears to focus on individual mandates, yet Hartmann unequivocally defended traditional social class edifices when he implored his readers to respect the practical boundaries of individual class roles:

> The surest sign of the degradation of a people is, if the so-called higher classes look with contempt upon those who perform manual labour; a street-sweeper who gains his right to live

by his work is more respectable in the eyes of Divinity than a bishop who prostitutes his intellect for the sake of gaining £10,000 a year.[42]

While Hartmann somewhat superficially denounces class arrogance—easy to do when one is not the street sweeper—his observation also reinforced rigid class structures by invoking divine approval of their prevailing inequity. Yet Hartmann corroborated the importance of preserving class status quo more explicitly: "Whether an actor plays the part of a king or a servant, the actor is, therefore, not despised, provided he plays his part well."[43] With zealous anti-Nietzschean sentiment, Hartmann further exhorted: "Those who have reached out in their imagination towards a high ideal on earth will find it in heaven; those whose desires have dragged them down will sink to the level of their desires."[44] Though Theosophy claimed to manifest a global spiritual cohesiveness—unity and equality among all religions and their acolytes—and German Theosophists brazenly disdained Christian hierarchies, the Catholic clergy with its entrenched conservation of traditional class rankings in particular, Hartmann indubitably rejected any reconfigurations of the then current socioeconomic paradigm that could be derived from claims to Theosophical universality.

Given the palpable socioeconomic inequalities of the era and the immense social pressures sparked by the growing and insistent proletarian movement, German Theosophists could not just ignore these issues.[45] Rudolf Steiner, as we have seen, painted capitalism as a pernicious causal factor of society's ills. Yet his critique of capitalism espoused no Marxist sympathies; rather Steiner's anti-capitalist narrative reveals perceptible anxieties about Communist influence spawned by the recent October Revolution in Russia and the radical political voices of Rosa Luxemburg and Karl Liebknecht in Germany. In fact, Steiner emphatically rejected Marxist Communism as a viable alternative for resolving Europe's social ills: "At the present time, in which a huge mistrust of private property has developed in wide circles, a radical conversion of private property to common property is being considered. If one would succeed far on this path, then one would see how through this the livability of the social organism is disabled."[46]

Steiner's opposition to Communist ideology is self-evident. Yet in the years following the war, Marxist agendas and the assertion of proletarian agency had become a consequential force in European debates on emerging social and political constellations, a topic Steiner specifically addressed:

> Currently the proletarian supposes to have encountered the basic force of his soul when he talks of his *class consciousness*. But the truth is, that since his ensnarement in the capitalistic economic order, he is searching for a spiritual life that can carry his soul. He searched for *this* consciousness, and replaced what he could not find, with the *class consciousness* that is born out of economic life.[47]

Here, in an attempt to undermine Communist prerogatives, Steiner reformulated Theosophy's disdain for materialism to argue that the proletarian consciousness had been ensnared and misguided by a materialistic worldview in their effort to strengthen the soul (*Grundkraft seiner Seele*), rather than attaining what was really needed: spiritual rejuvenation.

To get to the point, Steiner envisioned social reconstruction largely as a spiritual undertaking that would leave class paradigms unchallenged and intact by relinking the material and spiritual worlds through what he described as a three-pronged social organization composed of economic, legal, and spiritual life. While an in-depth depiction of Steiner's model is not possible here, Steiner furtively sought to counter the societal transformations generated by increasingly pervasive worker demands and union organization that had become linked with an assertive proletarian voting bloc.[48]

To counter one of the cornerstones of Marxist theory—the tendency in industrial capitalism to skewed and inequitable capital accumulation and the relegation of human capital to an interchangeable cog in the machinations of capitalism—Steiner underscored a requisite link between spiritual reconstitution and economic life, which he claimed would generate some sort of utopian generosity among human beings and thus fairly regulate the flow and distribution of capital:

> From the soul worker to the productive manual worker every human being must say whether he wants to serve his own interests without prejudice: I would like that a large enough number of able persons or groups of persons cannot only completely dispose of capital, but rather that they can also through individual initiative attain capital; because only they can judge, by means of the distribution of capital, how their individual capabilities, in a practical fashion, generate goods for the social organism.[49]

For Steiner, then, the postwar social reconstitution of the German nation twisted an Enlightenment-based worldview, in which his three-pronged social model depended on individual initiative and capability, yet which implicitly undermined any challenges to existing class structures. Thus, Steiner's highly nebulous scheme skirted any concrete tactics that might have addressed the pervasive socioeconomic inequalities at hand and as a consequence purposely left traditional class demarcations unscathed as the prevailing framework for the reforging of community consensus and social life after the war:

> Human beings will be divided neither in classes nor in social strata (*Stände*), rather the social organism itself will be structured. Thus through this the human being will be able to be a true human being; because this classification will be such that he will be rooted with his life in each of the three tiers.[50]

Despite his contention that class and rank will no longer exist in his societal model, this new social structure (*Gliederung*) provided no discernible means or avenues to dismantle or even shift prevailing class demarcations.[51] By revising the taxonomy of society's divisions from class to *Gliederung*, Steiner fashioned a narrative that dodged the more contentious nomenclature linked to social change while still assuming the position of iconoclastic authority. In other words, Steiner advocated a hegemony of spiritual life, as Zander confirms, in which "higher insight" is reserved "for an elite class that should guide the sociopolitical debate."[52]

Franz Hartmann redoubled Steiner's more subtle socioeconomic filibuster when he emphatically endorsed class distinctions in his long essay titled "Karma":

> The poverty that comes from God (Sattwa) is easy to bear. A human being who has attained the awareness of his true divine being has no unusual needs; he is glad in his impoverishment, because he then has no riches that burden him with worries and obligations.[53]

Hartmann's callous assessment baldly inferred that any material or pecuniary redistribution would serve only to perpetuate the apprehension and burden of the impoverished—the poverty-stricken in Hartmann's view exult in their abjection. In his calculated and perverted co-optation of Jesus's "Sermon on the Mount," which implicitly rejects Nietzschean cultural criticism, Hartmann conveniently asserted that impoverishment serves as the critical mechanism for achieving spiritual unity with the divine. Both Steiner and Hartmann invoked a spiritual blueprint that purported to right the socioeconomic ship, yet that, calculated or not, preserved class status quo.

Indian Theosophists also weighed in on the debates regarding growing socioeconomic inequality and piggybacked on the internationalization of labor organization, yet, predictably, their convictions were intricately yoked to the colonial nexus between Europe and the Indian subcontinent. B. P. Wadia, in a speech delivered at the first World Congress of the Theosophical Society, held in Paris in 1921, lashed out at the European powers: "The Europe of 1914 is a lost continent. The flood of human passion has drowned it; the fire of human wrath has destroyed it. The humanity of Europe has been soaked and scorched by it."[54] Wadia's vengeful judgment of Europe was understandably filtered through the lens of colonial dominance, India's strengthening independence movement, and its human sacrifices in support of the British war effort.[55] Yet Wadia's anti-European tirade, as we shall see, echoes his vision of India's social reconstruction in a post-colonial world. Unlike Steiner's intangible and esoteric concepts for revamping society after the war, Wadia's aims became concretized in his founding on April 27, 1918, of India's first textile workers' organization, the *Madras Labour Union*.

Wadia documented the Union's founding and early development through a series of speeches delivered to local workers in Madras in the spring of that same year, which he later published in book form in 1921. In the volume's preface, Wadia explicitly linked the Indian workers' movement to the internationalization of labor:[56]

> When [the Labour Union] was started in the early part of 1918, no one dreamed of the effect it would have on its environment generally; it was hoped that besides bettering the lot of the poor drudges and slaves of the economic system it might slowly tend to the creation of class consciousness among the Indian workers.[57]

Here, the universal prerogatives of Theosophy formed the foundational backdrop for the consolidation of international class consciousness. Yet for Wadia, these cosmopolitan ideological flows also portended unequivocal ramifications for addressing class difference and social transformation in India itself. In a speech one month after the Union's establishment, for instance, Wadia implored these workers to acknowledge their agency in the emergence of a new society and Indian independence: "We want you to realize the fundamental spiritual brotherhood of mankind. We want you to recognize that you have something in yourselves which we do not possess, and similarly we have something perhaps which you do not possess."[58] Thus, the transnational field of labor and the expanding agency of an Indian labor movement became grounded in Theosophy's assertion of universal spiritual capital, accessible in Wadia's version across traditional class boundaries.[59] The influence of Gandhi's sociopolitical designs to fortify the marginalized cannot be ignored here, yet despite Wadia's call to worker solidarity and his leadership in their cause, his comments nevertheless discernibly affirm the distinctive differentiation in the talents and social roles of these pundit leaders and laborers, thereby circuitously endorsing the perpetuation of social status quo and division.

Despite Wadia's somewhat paradoxical pronouncement about the division of labor and talents, the political potencies of Theosophy and its support for labor proved highly tangible in India. In contrast to Germany, where elite Theosophists viewed the workers' movement as a threat to the nation-state and the incumbent social class model, in India, Theosophist pundits envisioned impoverished workers as an essential force in the consolidation of national sentiment in support of their aim to thwart British colonial power. Wadia, for instance, linked the emergence and coalescence of a strong labor movement to national political prerogatives, which "will not succeed in the right direction of democracy if Indian working classes are not able to organize their own forces and come into their own."[60] More forcefully, in his very first speech to local textile workers on April 13, 1918, Wadia invoked the powerful Gandhian mantra, *swaraj* (self-rule), as a descriptor for Theosophy's proclaimed universal accessibility, through which any individual could exercise the spiritual and intellectual prowess to uncover the divine within him- or herself: "There is God within each one of you and that God is your only helper, the only person who will bless you, instruct you, inspire you, show the way out of darkness unto light. You are all Gods; you are all divine."[61] Thus Wadia repurposed Theosophy's transnational religious tenet of universal spirituality with the intent of seamlessly unifying India's labor class as a revolutionary corps in India's struggle for independence and national identity. That is,

Wadia co-opted transnational Theosophical spiritual discourse, which he coalesced with domestic social and political aspirations intended to reinvigorate the Indian nation.

Theosophy's spiritual affinities also smoothly coalesced with nationalist sentiments in Germany among Theosophists. To more clearly unpack this fusion of spiritual tenets with secular aims requires a return to the cultural discourses that had emerged from the European Enlightenment. The scientific and cultural revolution provoked by Enlightenment *philosophes* such as Diderot, Rousseau, Newton, and Hume laid the foundation for Britain and France to assert themselves as the cultural inheritors of the revered Greek traditions and the global crucible of cultural superiority—an important element in their unification processes as nation-states.[62] In Germany, despite Immanuel Kant's later importance as an Enlightenment thinker and Johann Gottlieb Fichte's emancipatory call for German unity, the attempt to culturally unify and forge a cohesive national identity floundered until Bismarck's coercive unification in 1871, which established the Second Reich.[63] After the Reich's official declaration in Versailles' Hall of Mirrors, many German thinkers began to eye the global colonial achievements and empires of England and France with envy.[64]

One of these thinkers whom we have already encountered, Wilhelm Hübbe-Schleiden, was an avid traveler and, like numerous European intellectuals and Theosophists of the era, toured India from 1894 to 1896 and published an account of his experiences, *Indien und die Indier*, in 1898.[65] In the report's first pages, Hübbe-Schleiden framed his travel narrative by expounding the similarity and accord between German and Indian culture:

> Because there is no European people so similar to the Hindus as we Germans, and no other people holds so much congruence in its historical development with that of the Hindus, as we. One could really in a certain sense name Germany a "European India" and us Germans the "Western Hindus."[66]

Here, though not specifically named, Hübbe-Schleiden's far-fetched cultural correlation asserts German tradition to be a direct by-product of what many during the era would have called Aryan culture. This historical maneuver subtly revised canonized European historical linkages and consequently subverted the prevalence of Greco-Roman heritage as the ideological engine for European Enlightenment traditions that had forged its route through Rome to the French and British. As a result, Hübbe-Schleiden's co-optation of Indian cultural heritage and its derivative augmentation of German cultural capital in Europe take on palpable political undertones. That is, Hübbe-Schleiden's assessment elevated German tradition as the primal link to an older, more pristine cultural heritage that predated the Greeks: "That not India but rather Hellas saw the first sunrise of our culture, that the beginnings of our spiritual treasures are to be sought among the old Greeks, that is an already long burst dogma of scholarly ignorance."[67] Here, Hübbe-Schleiden's assessment prompted a consequential shift in his view of how the historical claim to cultural superiority within Europe should be traced: "Because, according to the spirit, we, the Germans, are 'the people of thinkers,' not just solely the spiritual inheritors of the old Greeks, but rather our philosophy and our entire spiritual life distinguish us also as the European 'Brahmans' in the sense of these 'spiritual human beings' of the East."[68] Thus, Hübbe-Schleiden rerouted European cultural pathways to circumvent the predominance of Greek heritage as the genesis foundation for European superiority and thereby reconstituted German thinkers as Europe's elite class—European Brahmans.

Yet Hübbe-Schleiden's narrative embodied an even more potent inference. This constructed cultural nexus between German and Aryan roots born in the Indo-Gangetic plain bolstered German claims to cultural superiority in the era's bellicose European discourses of power, yet also reinforced his vision of German nationhood and its projected role on the colonial geoscape: "thus Germany is the territory and thus our people is the root, from which the Anglo-Saxon culture that dominates the world today arose."[69] Here, Hübbe-Schleiden adapts Theosophical spiritual premises to envision Germany as the genesis predecessor and more pristine root of Anglo-Saxon culture and thus brazenly challenged England's entitlement to global colonial dominance. Moreover, he candidly exuded his appetite for a more calculated German colonial vision in his envious praise of British colonial administrative acumen:

> And I returned home as a definitive admirer of the grand mastery and administration of this great empire of 300 million inhabitants through a handful of independent civil servants, whose number does not even reach one thousand. From this administration we Germans could perhaps learn even more than from the Brahmans, at least for the treatment of our colonies, perhaps even for our domestic administration.[70]

Hübbe-Schleiden's German-Indian narrative exposes the conflicted nature of spiritual aims and the practicalities of empire on the one hand, yet equally discloses the intricate and distinctive fusion between spiritual affinities and secular estrangements—a religious taxonomy that legitimizes political ideology.[71]

Among Germany's Theosophical elite, Hübbe-Schleiden was not alone in his jingoistic vision of Germany's position of cultural superiority. Such views were evident in the tirade of Paul Zillmann (1872–1940), who founded and frequently contributed to the Theosophical journal *Metaphysische Rundschau* (1894).[72] In 1914, as Germany's Second Reich began its march to the ghastly trenches of World War I, Zillmann published a brief essay titled "War Edition. To the Sisters and Brothers of the Forrest Lodge! To all that want to become one! To all Theosophists and Occultists of Germany!" Here, Zillmann's entreaty belies the universal mandates of Theosophical harmony, which he recalibrated to accommodate Germany's war agenda. Zillmann's call, notably aimed only at German Theosophists and occultists, exuded the spirited patriotism and cultural perquisites expressed by Hübbe-Schleiden in his German-Aryan historical narrative as he applied them to the colonial landscape, yet which have now been transformed by Zillmann into war fever:

> A victory of Germanhood across the board, a victory of the good without equal, a development of German culture as world culture, a strengthening of the moral substance of humanity through German essence for centuries beyond! A peace that restrains the immature elements of humanity once for all![73]

Here Zillmann boldly linked German victory with the dissemination, preeminence, and the adoption of German culture throughout the world—an application of Theosophical universality with a uniquely German flavor that would purportedly reinvigorate the ethical disposition of humanity: German-based social and cultural engineering for the world. Thus the nationalistic sentiments of these two Theosophical elites, Hübbe-Schleiden and Zillmann, separated by nearly two decades, corroborates how the transnational—universal—objectives of Theosophy became conveniently reconstituted as bellicose assertions intended to buttress the colonial and hawkish aims of the German nation.

As we have seen thus far, German Theosophists frequently tailored Indian-derived Theosophical tenets to mediate domestic concerns and rearticulated those narratives to sanction global German designs—antithetically coalescing Theosophical notions of universal spirituality and brotherhood with colonial aggression, war exuberance, and cultural supremacy. In similar fashion, Indian Theosophists co-opted such homologous Theosophical precepts as a means to reconstitute Indian identity and national unity. That is, like their German counterparts, Indian Theosophists co-opted transnational spiritual currents to reassert their national and anti-colonial aspirations. Just as German Theosophists advocated national objectives based on their reading and application of Theosophical creeds, Indian thinkers also readily tapped into the same Indian-derived reservoir of ideas to congeal nationalist sentiments. Like the Germans we have just reviewed, Indian Theosophists also adapted the Aryan origin myth to reconstitute their religious heritage and cultural identity, which they linked with national objectives.

In the Adyar publication *The Theosophist* (1886), for instance, Mahadev Trimbak Yog inserts his voice into the European debate over Aryan invasion theories that frequently depicted a racially pure ethnic tribe invading the Indus Valley from the Northwest.[74] Yog disputed European thinkers' messy analytical trail that contorted the Aryan origination story as a means to undergird a model of European cultural superiority:

> The existence of a passage in and out of this country in the north-west is as much an evidence of the Aryas having emigrated from, as of their having penetrated into, this country, and probably the former is the stronger, as many signs exist of India having sent colonies into the four quarters of the world. The assertions of Lassen, Weber and other modern Europeans that the sacred Scriptures of the Indians trace their progress from west to east, though that also within India, directly contradicts the Vachans of the Vedas brought in their support, as well as the Vachana of Manu which has an ample testimony in the oldest hymns of the oldest Veda.[75]

Yog's interpretation certainly concurred with European and especially German contentions that an Aryan migratory passageway in India's Northwest had existed and that India was indeed "the original seat of mankind." Yet he inverted common European convictions about the direction of these migratory flows—the metropole and periphery are emphatically reversed in Yog's view—to reclaim for India the cultural capital embodied in being the crucible of the world's pristine Aryan origins and root religion.

Indian Theosophists such as Yog reformulated the Theosophical notion of a single, common spiritual origin, out of which all existent religions emerged to reinforce India's claim to Aryan roots, but there is more to the story. This Theosophical co-optation of historical capital that redounded to India's origin birthright also served as the bedrock for envisioning a resurgence of Hinduism. Whereas European Theosophists were often split on the appeal of tapping into their Christian esoteric heritage, Indian Theosophy and its incumbent national underpinnings became galvanized in the reestablishment of Hinduism's historical distinction and its essential position in formulating Theosophical ideology. In an 1888 essay, N. Chidambaram Iyer proclaimed:

> The Theosophical sun *has risen*, and is progressing steadily, despite the cloudy calumnies and the haze of ignorant misconceptions that at one time ingloriously endeavoured to surround and stifle it. After the bright golden days of Aryan civilization, when Hinduism had smiled and prospered for centuries, it was unfortunately her fate to be overcast by the might of foreign invasion, and for a few centuries to be immersed in cimmerian darkness.[76]

Similar to German Theosophists' emphasis on cultural genealogy, these Indian thinkers also channeled India's respiritualization through the reclamation of India's religious roots. This sentiment proved to be a pervasive thread in Theosophical ideology among Indians for the following decades, which also steadily broadened in scope and energy, and took on new configurations after Gandhi's return to India from South Africa in 1915.[77]

The lawyer and Theosophist S. Subramanya Iyer of Madras, for instance, who founded the Home Rule Movement with Annie Besant, and was also a founding member of the Indian National Congress, corroborated this link between Hinduism and current-day revitalization in his 1910 publication *Some Observations on Hinduism*: "Upon us, therefore, devolves the special responsibility of restoring Hinduism, so far as may lie in our power, to its ancient glory and grandeur."[78] Moreover, Iyer explicitly linked Hinduism's revival with the elevation of national consciousness: "The uplifting of India can only come through the spiritualising of its people and as I have already said it will be far more effective to work upon the growing generation than upon those who are already middle-aged."[79] Another Theosophist, A. S. Rajam, in a short volume tracing the history of the Indian National Congress, linked the rejuvenation of Hinduism explicitly with the emergence of Theosophy in his tribute to Colonel Olcott's first lecture delivered in Bombay in March 1877: "[Theosophy's] contribution in those days lay chiefly on the death-blow it struck to the scepticism towards Hinduism of people influenced by western materialistic thought."[80] Rajam's comparative stance vis-à-vis the materialist West exhibits implicit political undertones. Thus, Theosophy provided a generation of intellectuals with an ideological foundation that inspired Hindu revitalization, but also, to put it more boldly, reveals how spiritual narratives reinforced unique domestic secular ideologies.

In stark contrast, then, to German Theosophists, who frequently denounced their own Christian traditions and pursued innovative esoteric avenues for reconstituting spirituality beyond—or even in direct opposition to—the Christian rubric, Indian Theosophists envisioned a renewed spirituality that emerged hand in hand with the Theosophical reawakening of ancient Hindu wisdom and practice, and with which they ratified paramount political agendas. As a result, bolder assertions among Indian Theosophists quickly ensued during the era and in fact fomented more forceful political directives. In the reprint of a speech from the 1913 Adyar *Theosophist*, for instance, V. P. Madhava Rao (1850–1934), the Diwan of Mysore, asserted: "When young India was in this plight, down descended, as if from the skies, the pioneers of the Theosophic movement to arrest, as it were, the process of denationalisation, and to tell us that we were fools to run after the dazzling objects of sense and lose the inestimable spiritual treasures of which we were heirs."[81] Rao explicitly credited the Indian Theosophical movement with halting India's national demise. Thus, for Rao, Yog, and other Indian Theosophists, Hinduism's revitalization became imbued with palpable political significance. Rajam summarized this sentiment in his call to reverse Indian passivity and to instill India with a more dynamic charge: "[Theosophy] told the Indian people whose general life was yet one protracted passivity, that India was bound to realise and declare her mission to the world."[82] Here, Indian readings of Theosophical doctrine, galvanized through its universal prerogatives, bolstered Hinduism's revival and were then persistently repackaged as political capital and used in support of Indian national assertions.

This process of galvanization was further enhanced by Indian Theosophical responses to Europe's Great War (1914–1918). Though often little known or relegated to footnotes, some 1.5 million Indians served in the Indian Expeditionary Force, and 65,000 Indians died in the war effort in European battles in multiple theaters of war, including the European continent, the Mediterranean, Mesopotamia, and North and East Africa.[83] These victims, and the horrific reports coming from war-torn Europe, provided an important trigger for Indian Theosophists to further assert their political agendas. Bhagavan Das's concept of social reconstruction, as we have seen, was saturated with criticism of the West's materialism, political turmoil, and violence; yet after the war, Das transformed his denunciation of Europe into grander political schemes. In 1921, he invoked Gandhi's term *swaraj* with mutinous overtures in his book *The Meaning of Swaraj or Self-Government*:

> Briefly, there is every reason why India should no longer be a "dependency," a milk-cow of England, to be beaten, starved, and milked at will by torturing processes of forcing. There is also much reason why the friendliest and closest relations between the two should be maintained, to the profit of both, and of other countries as well. The way of reconciliation of these two necessities is embodied in these last two clauses, in the shape of "Swaraj or Self-government, not on Colonial, but on far better lines, and within, not a British Empire, but an Indo-British or British-Indian Commonwealth or Federation."[84]

Like other Indian Theosophical acolytes who focused on Hindu revival, Das's remodeling of India's position and status within the Commonwealth also became linked to national reconstruction. In a more global twist, B. P. Wadia invoked Theosophy's universal prerogatives to frame a historical narrative that strove to elevate India's position in a transnationally constructed concept of nationhood and race:

> In its place to-day we find a more complex State than the family-State, and we are all evolving through nation-State and race-State. The principles of nationality are being utilised to-day as those of the family-State were once used. We are making ourselves one with our respective nations and races, and in

a few centuries we should have completely transcended that
and should be engaged in making ourselves one with a more
complex organism of an international and inter-racial character.
Even to-day there are men and women who are dreaming some
such dreams and aspiring after some such State.[85]

Here, Wadia synthesized Theosophical tenets of universality, which were grounded in the revitalization and application of Hindu traditions, with a political vision that anticipated progress toward a universal brotherhood. Wadia's cultural perspective, and this point is critical, closely approximates under different circumstances and idiosyncratic narrative that of the German Theosophist and cultural chauvinist Paul Zillmann: Indian culture and tradition will eventually endow the world with the formula to engineer a materially and spiritually cohesive global state.

Summary

In German and Indian Theosophy before and after the turn of the century, common formulations for establishing and asserting spiritual capital flowed across geopolitical boundaries, yet these affinities became easily estranged, co-opted and reformulated to address domestic concerns and national agendas—a complex web involving the transnational and the local, the spiritual and the profane. Spiritual affinities forged through the transnational flow of innovative religious narratives became skillfully garnered to assert political capital and agendas in each domestic domain. Moreover, both German and Indian Theosophical subsets reconstituted these common spiritual tenets for contradictory or even opposed secular visions. Given these powerful estrangements, it is perhaps unsurprising that these Theosophical players interact with one another textually only in rare instances in the contact zone of Adyar. Indian Theosophists quote Besant, Olcott, and Blavatsky in their essays, and they frequently reference canonical British thinkers and esteemed literary giants from Herbert Spencer to Wordsworth and Shakespeare, and they also reference Kant, Schopenhauer, and Goethe, all of whose works would have long been available in English. German Theosophists cite the wealth of Sanskrit translations and related scholarly work produced by European intellectuals—German, French, and British—throughout the nineteenth century. Yet engaged interactions between diverse Theosophists about these seemingly incompatible estrangements that I have expounded here are not evident.[86]

This brief excursion into the transnational flows of innovative religious ideas demonstrates, first, the remarkable malleability of a cohesive set of ideas to produce the requisite foundation for diverse and even conflicting secular aims. Second, and this reveals perhaps the most significant feature of this comparison, it illustrates how a spiritual taxonomy can become so seamlessly transformed into political ideology. A common set of Theosophical doctrines served to justify German colonial ambitions, reject Christian influences and traditions, and assert the global predominance of German culture. Yet, similarly, these same spiritual notions proved no less conducive for heterodox Indian Theosophical acolytes to champion Indian anti-colonialism, the revitalization of Hindu tradition and Indian nationhood, and the supersession of the nation-state during the age of empire with an international and interracial state based on Hinduism. That is, this comparison illustrates the degree and depth to which a religious body of knowledge became intricately entangled with the social and political dilemmas and aspirations that concerned each Theosophical subset.

Moreover, I would argue that the analysis of religious narratives incessantly resists inspection as isolated phenomena. The investigation of Theosophy, and in fact religion more generally, requires the consideration of the coercive—social, cultural, and political—aspects of these fields. To put it differently, and in a way more pertinent to my specific topic here, transnational Theosophical spiritual narratives became reified as distinctive political discourses in Germany and India—"eminently strategic discourse[s]."[87] No scholarly examination is perhaps better suited to demand the somewhat bold, nonconforming, and ungrammatical double negative: religion is never not political. Accounting for the political, social, and cultural cleavages in which religious sentiments and religious actors operate and insert their voices yields an indispensable avenue to foster our understanding of religious praxis.

Notes

1. C. A. Bayly, *The Birth of the Modern World, 1780–1914: Global Connections and Comparisons* (Malden, MA: Blackwell Publishing, 2004), 199.
2. Ibid., 365.

3. Bruce Lincoln, *Discourse and the Construction of Society: Comparative Studies of Myth, Ritual, and Classification* (New York: Oxford University Press, 2014), 8–9.

4. See, for example: Mary Louise Pratt, *Imperial Eyes: Travel Writing and Transculturation* (New York: Routledge, 1992); Sugata Bose, *A Hundred Horizons: The Indian Ocean in the Age of Global Empire* (Cambridge: Harvard University Press, 2006); and Kris Manjapra, *The Age of Entanglement: German and Indian Intellectuals across Empire* (Cambridge: Harvard University Press, 2014) just to provide an ever so modest snapshot of this work.

5. Pierre Yves-Saunier, *Transnational History* (New York: Palgrave Macmillan, 2013), 140.

6. Perry Myers, *Spiritual Empires in Europe and India: Cosmopolitan Religious Movements and their National Factions, 1875–1918*; (work in progress, title pending).

7. Yves-Saunier, *Transnational History*, 122.

8. Related, as Michael Bergunder has shown, Europe's documentation, classification and interpretation of the historical record during the era generated a global wave of religious reinterpretation, interaction, and remodeling within the realms of Hinduism, Buddhism and Islam. See Michael Bergunder, "'Religion' and 'Science' within a Global Religious History," *Aries—Journal for the Study of Western Esotericism* 16 (2016).

9. Pierre Bourdieu, *The Rules of Art: Genesis and Structure of the Literary Field*, trans. Susan Emanuel (Stanford, CA: Stanford University Press, 1996), 214.

10. See the work of Wouter Hanegraaff, particularly *Esotericism and the Academy: Rejected Knowledge in Western Culture* (Cambridge UK: Cambridge University Press, 2012), which explores the academic resistance to the inclusion of the occult as a serious object of study. Most work on Indian Theosophy has been constructed through the lens of British Theosophy in India. See Mark Bevir, "Theosophy and the Origins of the Indian National Congress," *International Journal of Hindu Studies* 7, no. 1 (2003); T. Barton Scott, "Miracle Publics: Theosophy, Christianity, and the Coulomb Affair," *History of Religions* 49, no. 2 (2009). In the case of German Theosophy, more abundant scholarly work exists. In German, see Helmut Zander, *Anthroposophie in Deutschland: Theosophische Weltanschauung und gesellschaftliche Praxis, 1884–1945*, 2 vols. (Göttingen: Vandenhoeck & Ruprecht, 2007), which provides an excellent source of the various Theosophical movements and schisms in Germany during its development. In English, see Corinna Treitel, *A Science for the Soul: Occultism and the Genesis of the German Modern* (Baltimore: Johns Hopkins University Press, 2004); and Peter Staudenmaier, *Between Occultism and Nazism: Anthroposophy and the Politics of Race in the Fascist Era* (Leiden: Brill, 2014).

11. See Michael Bergunder, "Experiments with Theosophical Truth: Gandhi, Esotericism and Religious History," *Journal of the American Academy of Religion* 82, no. 2 (2014).

Affinity and Estrangement 243

12. For a detailed overview of Theosophy's claims to scientific validity and its opposition to materialism in Germany, with particular emphasis on Rudolf Steiner, see Zander, *Anthroposophie in Deutschland*, chapter 9.

13. *Lotusblüten* 2 (1894), 507. All translations of German texts are mine. I would like to thank Susanne Myers for assisting me in their accuracy. Errors remain my own.

14. Franz Hartmann, *Magic, White and Black or The Sciences of Finite and Infinite Life* (London: George Redway, 1888), 24. Hartmann lived for an extended period of time in the United States, where he became a U.S. citizen and practiced medicine. Thus, some of his texts, such as *Magic, White and Black*, were written originally in English. For more biographical background on Hartmann, see Walter Einbeck, "Zum Gedächtnis an Dr. Franz Hartmann (1838–1912)," in *Theosophische Kultur, Sonderheft 2* (Leipzig: Theosophischer Kultur-Verlag, 1925); also see my *German Visions of India (1871–1918): Commandeering the Holy Ganges during the Kaiserreich* (New York: Palgrave Macmillan, 2013), especially 104–11.

15. Rudolf Steiner, "Soziale Zukunft. Sechs Vorträge. Zürich, 24. bis 30. Oktober 1919," Rudolf Steiner Online Archiv, 4. Auflage 2010, http://anthroposophie.byu.edu/vortraege/332a.pdf.

16. Zander, *Anthroposophie in Deutschland*, 859.

17. Hartmann, *Magic, White and Black*, 158.

18. Rudolf Steiner, *Der dreigliedrige soziale Organismus: Eine Darlegung der Kernpunkte der sozialen Frage in den Lebensnotwendigkeiten der Gegenwart und Zukunft* (Cleveland, OH: Goetheanum Verlag von Amerika, 1920), 59. For more background on Steiner's social thought, see the first chapters in Peter Staudenmaier, *Between Occultism and Nazism: Anthroposophy and the Politics of Race in the Fascist Era* (Leiden: Brill, 2014).

19. Bhagavan Das, *The Science of Social Organisation or the Laws of Manu in the Light of Atma-Vidya*, vol. 1, *1909* (Adyar: Theosophical Publishing House, 1932).

20. This cleavage is only faintly distinct here, but the predominant penchant for Indian traditions in which Theosophical ideas had been grounded by Blavatsky, Olcott, and Besant became increasingly troublesome for some European Theosophists like Rudolf Steiner and Édouard Schuré in France.

21. B. P. Wadia, *Problems of National and International Politics* (New York: Theosophical Association of New York, 1922), 15.

22. Carl du Prel, "Monistische Seelenlehre," *Sphinx: Monatsschrift für geschichtliche und experimentale Begründung der übersinnlichen Weltanschauung auf monistischer Grundlage* 1 (1886): 9 (in remaining citations the title will be cited only as *Sphinx*). For an intellectually oriented biography of du Prel, see Tomas Kaiser, "Zwischen Philosophie und Spiritismus: (bildwissenschaftliche) Quellen zum Leben und Werk des Carl du Prel" (PhD diss., Universität Lüneburg, 2009).

23. Carl du Prel, *Entwicklungsgeschichte des Weltalls: Entwurf einer Philosophie der Astronomie*, 3rd ed. (Leipzig: Ernst Günthers Verlag, 1882), 15 (emphasis in

original). This text was originally published in 1874 as *Der Kampf ums Dasein am Himmel*.

24. Carl du Prel, "Der Tod," *Sphinx* 2, no. 3 (1887), 306.

25. Wilhelm Hübbe-Schleiden, *Das Dasein als Lust, Leid und Liebe: Die alt-indische Weltanschauung in neuzeitlicher Darstellung. Ein Beitrag zum Darwinismus* (Braunschweig: Schwetschke & Sohn, 1891), 16. For a superb analysis of Hegel's assessment of Indian traditions, see Ranajit Guha, *History at the Limit of World-History* (New York: Columbia University Press, 2003). For a more detailed appraisal of Hübbe-Schleiden's view of India, see my aforementioned book *German Visions of India*, 154–67; and Treitel, *A Science for the Soul*, especially 85–93.

26. J. K. Daji, "Self-knowledge and Self-Culture," in *The Theosophist* 11 (1889), 31–32.

27. Curuppumullage Jinarajadasa, *First Principles of Theosophy*, 2nd ed. (Adyar: Theosophical Publishing House, 1922 [1921]), 5.

28. Wadia, *Problems of National and International Politics*, 11.

29. Hartmann, *Magic, White and Black*, 28

30. "Der Weg zu Christus," in *Lotusblüten* 2 (1894), 559. This represents a chapter in a series of chapters that according to Hartmann was to appear as a book titled *Yoga und Christentum*. This work did appear partially in Vol. 2 of *Hartmanns ausgewählte theosophische Werke*. No author is attributed, but Franz Hartmann was the editor of this Theosophical journal and authored almost every essay or translated those of other Theosophists like Annie Besant.

31. *Lotusblüten* 2 (1894), 500.

32. I am borrowing Bruce Lincoln's use of the term myth, which he defines not as a pejorative term, which indicates falsity, but rather "designate[s] that small class of stories that possess both credibility and *authority*." See Lincoln, *Discourse and the Construction of Society*, 23 (emphasis in original).

33. Das, *Science of Social Organisation*, 34.

34. N. K. Ramaswami Ayyar, *Godward Ho! Or A Synthesis of Religion, Science & Sociology* (Tanjore: published by author, 1914), xxiv (Postscript). Ayyar was a member of the Indian National Congress and received several mentions in Annie Besant's *How India Wrought for Freedom: The Story of the National Congress Told from Official Records* (Adyar: Theosophical Publishing House, 1915).

35. B. P. Wadia, *Problems of National and International Politics*, 10. See Manu Goswami, *Producing India: From Colonial Economy to National Space* (Chicago: The University of Chicago Press, 2013), especially 174–88 on the link between Aryan origins and the emergence of Indian national identity.

36. The link between Indian thinkers and National Socialism is an important one though not critical for my purposes here. See Manjapra, *Age of Entanglement*, especially 102–8.

37. Jinarajadasa, *First Principles of Theosophy*, 28.

38. Kaiser, "Zwischen Philosophie und Spiritismus," 75. Despite Kaiser's reference to du Prel's concerns with the damage to society caused by poverty,

pauperization, and the decay of morals, he does not focus on du Prel's subtle tactic to undermine socialism's potential benefits.

39. Du Prel, "Der Tod," 310. Du Prel wrote a one-page forward titled "Occultismus und Sozialismus" to Franz Unger's *Die Magie des Traumes als Unsterblichkeitsbeweis*, 2nd ed. (Münster: Franz Mickl, 1898). Here du Prel reinforces my point when he embraces socialism and supports the worker movement only as a spiritual undertaking. He posits "that the justified core of the social movement can only develop when Socialism rejects the materialistic falsity and the anarchic outgrowths."

40. Hartmann, *Magic, White and Black*, 40.

41. Ibid., 144.

42. Ibid., 158.

43. Ibid., 164.

44. Ibid., 173.

45. For general background on economic development during the era, see Thomas Nipperdey, *Deutsche Geschichte: 1866–1918*. Vol. 1, *Arbeitswelt und Bürgergeist* (München: C. H. Beck, 1990), especially 268–90; on class society, 414–27. In the German context the link between socialism and occultism has not been adequately studied. In the case of France, Julian Strube has made a strong and perceptive case for the entanglement of French socialism and the occult during the nineteenth century. See Strube, "Socialist Religion and the Emergence of Occultism: A Genealogical Approach to Socialism and Secularization in 19th-century France," *Religion* 46, no. 3 (2016); and his "Occultist Identity Formations Between Theosophy and Socialism in Fin-de-Siècle France," *Numen* 64, nos. 5–6 (2017).

46. Steiner, *Der dreigliedrige soziale Organismus*, 69.

47. Ibid., 19 (emphasis in original).

48. On the political development of the Social Democrats in Germany, see Thomas Nipperdey, *Deutsche Geschichte: 1866–1918*, Vol. 2, *Machtstaat vor der Demokratie* (München: C. H. Beck, 1992), 554–72. A detailed explication of Steiner's model is available in Zander's *Anthroposophie in Deutschland*, chapter 14. Zander contends that Steiner did not focus extensively on the worker, and that he addressed critical questions in this regard only in his addresses that followed the *Kernpunkte* (1306), yet Steiner's sociopolitical preferences are nevertheless tangible and discernible.

49. Steiner, Der *dreigliedrige soziale Organismus*, 64.

50. Ibid., 91.

51. The German word *Gliederung* is a less culturally charged term than class. *Gliederung* can be defined as classification, structure, arrangement, or grouping, none of which contains the political or social ramifications, or the historical content, of the German words *Klasse* or *Stand*.

52. Zander, *Anthroposophie in Deutschland*, 1316.

53. Franz Hartmann, "Karma," *Lotusblüten* 7 (1896), 340.

54. B. P. Wadia, *Will the Soul of Europe Return?* (London: Theosophical Publishing House, 1921), online available at http://www.teosofiskakompaniet.net/BPWadiaWillTheSoulOfEuropReturn_2011.htm.
55. On India's participation in World War I, see footnote 83.
56. B. P. Wadia, *Labour in Madras* (Madras: S. Ganesan, 1921), xix.
57. Ibid., xiii.
58. Ibid., 15.
59. It is critical to reiterate that both German and Indian Theosophists grounded their doctrine in the idea of the existence of an occult spiritual knowledge that all religions purportedly manifest, yet which could only be accessed by a special group of Theosophical pundits—an elite class of spiritual thinkers. This seems to pose few contradictions in German Theosophical concepts of social transformation; in the case of India, and particularly in light of Wadia's labor leadership in Madras, this proves to be more complex, and an issue I have yet to thoroughly work through. A more differentiated scrutiny of the elitism underlying Theosophy and found across various Theosophical subsets forms part of a book-length monograph currently in progress.
60. Ibid., xvi.
61. Ibid., 2. For Gandhi's exposé, see Mahatma Gandhi, *Hind Swaraj or Indian Home Rule* (Ahmedabad: Navajivan Publishing House, 1946 [1909]).
62. On the European Enlightenment, a great place to start remains Peter Gay's classic and in-depth study *The Enlightenment*, 2 vols. (New York: Knopf, 1966; 1969).
63. A wealth of scholarly literature exists on Germany's Second Reich. One might start with David Blackbourn, *History of Germany, 1780–1918*, 2nd ed. (Malden, MA: Blackwell Publishing, 2003); and Sebastian Conrad and Jürgen Osterhammel, eds., *Das Kaiserreich transnational: Deutschland in der Welt, 1871–1914* (Göttingen: Vandenhoeck & Ruprecht, 2004).
64. On German imperialism and colonialism, see Klaus Bade, ed., *Imperialismus und Kolonialmission: Kaiserliches Deutschland und koloniales Imperium* (Wiesbaden: Steiner, 1982); Sebastian Conrad, *Deutsche Kolonialgeschichte* (München: C. H. Beck, 2008), among many other works.
65. Wilhelm Hübbe-Schleiden, *Indien und die Indier, kulturell, wirthschaftlich und politisch betrachtet* (Hamburg: L. Friederichsen & Co., 1898).
66. Ibid., 2. Hübbe-Schleiden drew heavily, of course, on the linguistic links that had been emphasized at the beginning of the nineteenth century by Friedrich Schlegel and Jacob Grimm. For background, see Sheldon Pollock's important essay, "Deep Orientalism? Notes on Sanskrit and Power Beyond the Raj," in *Orientalism and the Postcolonial Predicament: Perspectives on South Asia*, ed. Carol Breckenridge and Peter van der Veer (Philadelphia, PA: University of Pennsylvania Press, 1993); and the older but still useful Raymond Schwab, *The Oriental Renaissance: Europe's Rediscovery of India and the East, 1680–1880*

(Social Foundations of Aesthetic Forms), trans. Gene Patterson-Black (Columbia, NY: Columbia University Press, 1984) (originally published in French in 1950).

67. Hübbe-Schleiden, *Indien und die Indier*, 11. On the importance of Greek tradition in Germany, see Suzanne Marchand, *Down from Olympus: Archaeology and Philhellenism in Germany, 1750–1970* (Princeton: Princeton University Press, 1996); and E. M. Butler, *The Tyranny of Greece over Germany: A Study of the Influence Exercised by Greek Art and Poetry over the Great German Writers of the Eighteenth, Nineteenth and Twentieth Centuries* (Boston: Beacon Press, 1958). On the emergence of the Aryan myth in Europe, see Stefan Arvidsson, *Aryan Idols: Indo-European Mythology as Ideology and Science*, trans. Sonia Wichmann (Chicago: University of Chicago Press, 2006); also important is Thomas Trautmann, *Aryans and British India* (Berkeley: University of California Press, 1997); also see Bruce Lincoln, *Theorizing Myth: Narrative, Ideology, and Scholarship* (Chicago: University of Chicago Press, 1999), especially 64–66.

68. Hübbe-Schleiden, *Indien und die Indier*, 11.

69. Ibid., 2–3.

70. Ibid., 7.

71. This assertion is supported by Bruce Lincoln's work. In *Theorizing Myth*, Lincoln elaborates: "I am inclined to argue that when a taxonomy is encoded in mythic form, the narrative packages a specific, contingent system of discrimination in a particularly attractive and memorable form. What is more, it naturalizes and legitimates it. Myth, then, is not just taxonomy, but *ideology in narrative form*" (147).

72. *Metaphysische Rundschau* was founded in 1894 and was renamed the *Neue Metaphysische Rundschau* in 1897 but continued publication under Zillmann's editorship.

73. Paul Zillmann, "War Edition. To the Sisters and Brothers of the Forrest Lodge! To All That Want to Become One! To all Theosophists and Occultists of Germany!" *Neue Metaphysische Rundschau* 21 (1914): 164 (emphasis in original). Zillmann's entire quote is printed in enlarged font, which frequently served as the equivalent to italics in that era's publications.

74. For background, see Edwin Bryant, *The Quest for the Origins of Vedic Culture: The Indo-Aryan Migration Debate* (Oxford: Oxford University Press, 2001); and Thomas Trautmann, ed., *The Aryan Debate* (Oxford: Oxford University Press, 2005).

75. Mahadev Trimbak Yog, "Are not the Aryas Autochthonous?," *The Theosophist* 8 (1886): 151.

76. N. Chidambaram Iyer, "The Revival of Hinduism," *The Theosophist* 9 (1888): 589–90. I have been unable to find any significant biographical information on Iyer, other than the record of his noteworthy book from 1884, *The Brihat Samhita of Vahara Mihira*.

77. On Gandhi prior to his return, see Ramachandra Guha, *Gandhi Before India* (New York: Vintage, 2013); also see Sugata Bose and Ayesha Jalal, *Modern South Asia: History, Culture, Political Economy*, 3rd ed. (London: Routledge, 2011), especially 104–21.

78. S. Subramanya Iyer, *Some Observations on Hinduism* (Adyar: The Vasanta Press, 1910), 8.

79. Ibid., 22.

80. A. S. Rajam, *The Indian National Congress: Its Evolution* (Madras: Sons of India Limited, 1918), 5.

81. Madhava P. Rao, "A Great Indian on Theosophy," *The Theosophist* 34 (1913): 150.

82. Rajam, *Indian National Congress*, 6.

83. Anne Bostanci, "How was India Involved in the First World War," published October 30, 2014, https://www.britishcouncil.org/voices-magazine/how-was-india-involved-first-world-war. See Santanu Das, *India, Empire, and First World War Culture: Writings, Images, and Songs* (Cambridge: Cambridge University Press, 2018).

84. Bhagavan Das, *The Meaning of Swaraj or Self-Government* (Benares: Gyan Mandal Press, 1921), 21.

85. Wadia, *Problems of National and International Politics*, 28–29.

86. From a textual perspective, this could be, at least in part, due to a linguistic issue. Germans traveling to India certainly spoke English, but still wrote, with the exception of Hartmann, primarily in German. Indian Theosophists were fully competent in English, which was the common language, but most probably could rarely read German. Thus, a written record of dialogues, minutes of meetings, or paraphrased accounts of conversations might be the most conducive source to trace any interaction that took place. Admittedly, I have not adequately researched the voluminous material available that might prove otherwise, nor have I perused the sources in Adyar, where Hübbe-Schleiden and Hartmann spent time. Surely discussions occurred between these Theosophists during their travels, but their documentation, verification and analysis remain open questions at this point.

87. Lincoln, *Theorizing Myth*, 207.

References

Arvidsson, Stefan. *Aryan Idols: Indo-European Mythology as Ideology and Science*, trans. Sonia Wichmann. Chicago: University of Chicago Press, 2006.

Ayyar, N. K Ramaswami. *Godward Ho! Or A Synthesis of Religion, Science & Sociology*. Tanjore: published by author, 1914.

Bade, Klaus, ed. *Imperialismus und Kolonialmission: Kaiserliches Deutschland und koloniales Imperium*. Wiesbaden: Steiner, 1982.

Bayly, C. A. *The Birth of the Modern World, 1780–1914: Global Connections and Comparisons*. Malden, MA: Blackwell Publishing, 2004.

Bergunder, Michael. "Experiments with Theosophical Truth: Gandhi, Esotericism and Religious History." *Journal of the American Academy of Religion* 82, no. 2 (2014): 398–426.

———. " 'Religion' and 'Science' within a Global Religious History." *Aries—Journal for the Study of Western Esotericism* 16 (2016): 86–141.

Bevir, Mark. "Theosophy and the Origins of the Indian National Congress." *International Journal of Hindu Studies* 7, no. 1 (2003): 99–115.

Blackbourn, David. *History of Germany, 1780–1918*. 2nd ed. Malden, MA: Blackwell Publishing, 2003.

Bose, Sugata. *A Hundred Horizons: The Indian Ocean in the Age of Global Empire*. Cambridge: Harvard University Press, 2006.

Bose, Sugata, and Ayesha Jalal. *Modern South Asia: History, Culture, Political Economy*. 3rd ed. London: Routledge, 2011.

Bostanci, Anne. "How was India Involved in the First World War." Published October 30, 2014, https://www.britishcouncil.org/voices-magazine/how-was-india-involved-first-world-war.

Bourdieu, Pierre. *The Rules of Art: Genesis and Structure of the Literary Field*. Translated by Susan Emanuel. Stanford, CA: Stanford University Press, 1996.

Bryant, Edwin. *The Quest for the Origins of Vedic Culture: The Indo-Aryan Migration Debate*. Oxford: Oxford University Press, 2001.

Butler, E. M. *The Tyranny of Greece over Germany: A Study of the Influence Exercised by Greek Art and Poetry over the Great German Writers of the Eighteenth, Nineteenth and Twentieth Centuries*. Boston: Beacon Press, 1958.

Conrad, Sebastian. *Deutsche Kolonialgeschichte*. München: C. H. Beck, 2008.

Conrad, Sebastian, and Jürgen Osterhammel, eds. *Das Kaiserreich transnational: Deutschland in der Welt, 1871–1914*. Göttingen: Vandenhoeck & Ruprecht, 2004.

Daji, J. K. "Self-knowledge and Self-Culture." *The Theosophist* 11 (1889): 30–34; 147–154.

Das, Bhagavan. *The Science of Social Organisation or the Laws of Manu in the Light of Atma-Vidya*. Vol. 1. 1909. Adyar, India: Theosophical Publishing House, 1932.

———. *The Meaning of Swaraj or Self-Government*. Benares: Gyan Mandal Press, 1921.

Das, Santanu. *India, Empire, and First World War Culture: Writings, Images, and Songs*. Cambridge: Cambridge University Press, 2018.

Einbeck, Walter. "Zum Gedächtnis an Dr. Franz Hartmann (1838–1912)." *Theosophische Kultur*, Sonderheft 2 (1925).

Gandhi, Mahatma. *Hind Swaraj or Indian Home Rule*. Ahmedabad: Navajivan Publishing House, 1946 [1909].

Gay, Peter. *The Enlightenment*. 2 vols. New York: Knopf, 1966; 1969.
Goswami, Manu. *Producing India: From Colonial Economy to National Space*. Chicago: The University of Chicago Press, 2013.
Guha, Ramachandra. *Gandhi Before India*. New York: Vintage, 2013.
Guha, Ranajit. *History at the Limit of World-History*. New York: Columbia University Press, 2003.
Hartmann, Franz. *Magic, White and Black or The Sciences of Finite and Infinite Life*. London: George Redway, 1888.
———. "Yoga." *Lotusblüten* 4 (1894): 496–532.
———. "Der Weg zu Christus." *Lotusblüten* 4 (1894): 559–99.
———. "Karma." *Lotusblüten* 7 (1896): 333–52.
Hübbe-Schleiden, Wilhelm. *Das Dasein als Lust, Leid und Liebe: Die alt-indische Weltanschauung in neuzeitlicher Darstellung. Ein Beitrag zum Darwinismus.* Braunschweig: Schwetschke & Sohn, 1891.
———. *Indien und die Indier, kulturell, wirthschaftlich und politisch betrachtet.* Hamburg: L. Friederichsen & Co., 1898.
Iyer, N. Chidambaram. "The Revival of Hinduism." *The Theosophist* 9 (1888): 589–91.
Iyer, S. Subramanya. *Some Observations on Hinduism*. Adyar: The Vasanta Press, 1910.
Jinarajadasa, Curuppumullage. *First Principles of Theosophy*. 2nd ed. Adyar, India: Theosophical Publishing House, 1922 [1921].
Kaiser, Tomas. "Zwischen Philosophie und Spiritismus: (bildwissenschaftliche) Quellen zum Leben und Werk des Carl du Prel." PhD diss., Universität Lüneburg, 2009.
Lincoln, Bruce. *Theorizing Myth: Narrative, Ideology, and Scholarship*. Chicago: University of Chicago Press, 1999.
———. *Discourse and the Construction of Society: Comparative Studies of Myth, Ritual, and Classification*. New York: Oxford University Press, 2014.
Lotusblüten. Vol. 1–16. Leipzig: W. Friedrich, 1893–1900.
Manjapra, Kris. *The Age of Entanglement: German and Indian Intellectuals across Empire*. Cambridge: Harvard University Press, 2014.
Marchand, Suzanne. *Down from Olympus: Archaeology and Philhellenism in Germany, 1750–1970*. Princeton: Princeton University Press, 1996.
Myers, Perry. *German Visions of India (1871–1918): Commandeering the Holy Ganges during the Kaiserreich*. New York: Palgrave Macmillan, 2013.
———. *Cosmopolitan Religious Movements and their Spiritual Empires in Europe and India, 1875–1918*. (Work in progress, title pending.).
Nipperdey, Thomas. *Deutsche Geschichte: 1866–1918*. Vol. 1, *Arbeitswelt und Bürgergeist*. München: C. H. Beck, 1990.
———. *Deutsche Geschichte: 1866–1918*. Vol. 2, *Machtstaat vor der Demokratie*. München: C. H. Beck, 1992.

Pollock, Sheldon. "Deep Orientalism? Notes on Sanskrit and Power Beyond the Raj." In *Orientalism and the Postcolonial Predicament: Perspectives on South Asia*, edited by Carol Breckenridge and Peter van der Veer, 76–133. Philadelphia: University of Pennsylvania Press, 1993.

Pratt, Mary Louise. *Imperial Eyes: Travel Writing and Transculturation*. New York: Routledge, 1992.

Prel, Carl du. *Entwicklungsgeschichte des Weltalls: Entwurf einer Philosophie der Astronomie*. 3rd ed. Leipzig: Ernst Günthers Verlag, 1882.

———. "Monistische Seelenlehre." *Sphinx: Monatsschrift für geschichtliche und experimentale Begründung der übersinnlichen Weltanschauung auf monistischer Grundlage* 1 (1886): 1–10.

———. "Der Tod." In *Sphinx: Monatsschrift für geschichtliche und experimentale Begründung der übersinnlichen Weltanschauung auf monistischer Grundlage* 2, no. 3 (1887): 221–30; 301–11.

Rajam, A. S. *The Indian National Congress: Its Evolution*. Madras: Sons of India Limited, 1918.

Rao, P. Madhava. "A Great Indian on Theosophy." *The Theosophist* 34 (1913): 150–52.

Schwab, Raymond. *The Oriental Renaissance: Europe's Rediscovery of India and the East, 1680–1880 (Social Foundations of Aesthetic Forms)*. Translated by Gene Patterson-Black. Columbia, NY: Columbia University Press, 1984 (originally published in French in 1950).

Scott, T. Barton. "Miracle Publics: Theosophy, Christianity, and the Coulomb Affair." *History of Religions* 49, no. 2 (2009): 172–96.

Staudenmaier, Peter. *Between Occultism and Nazism: Anthroposophy and the Politics of Race in the Fascist Era*. Leiden: Brill, 2014.

Steiner, Rudolf. "Soziale Zukunft: Sechs Vorträge. Zürich, 24. bis 30. Oktober 1919." Rudolf Steiner Online Archiv, 4. Auflage 2010. http://anthroposophie.byu.edu/vortraege/332a.pdf.

———. *Der dreigliedrige soziale Organismus: Eine Darlegung der Kernpunkte der sozialen Frage in den Lebensnotwendigkeiten der Gegenwart und Zukunft*. Cleveland, OH: Goetheanum Verlag von Amerika, 1920.

Strube, Julian. "Occultist Identity Formations Between Theosophy and Socialism in Fin-de-Siècle France." *Numen* 64, nos. 5–6 (2017): 568–95.

———. "Socialist Religion and the Emergence of Occultism: A Genealogical Approach to Socialism and Secularization in 19th-Century France." *Religion* 46, no. 3 (2016): 359–88.

Trautmann, Thomas. *Aryans and British India*. Berkeley: University of California Press, 1997.

———, ed. *The Aryan Debate*. Oxford: Oxford University Press, 2005.

Treitel, Corinna. *A Science for the Soul: Occultism and the Genesis of the German Modern*. Baltimore: Johns Hopkins University Press, 2004.

Unger, Franz. *Die Magie des Traumes als Unsterblichkeitsbeweis*. 2nd ed. Münster: Franz Mickl, 1898.
Wadia, B. P. *Problems of National and International Politics*. New York: Theosophical Association of New York, 1922.
———. *Labour in Madras*. Madras: S. Ganesan, 1921.
———. *Will the Soul of Europe Return?* London: Theosophical Publishing House, 1921. Online available at http://www.teosofiskakompaniet.net/BPWadia WillTheSoulOfEurop Return_2011.htm.
Yog, Mahadev Trimbak. "Are not the Aryas Autochthonous?" *The Theosophist* 8 (1886): 148–59.
Yves-Saunier, Pierre. *Transnational History*. New York: Palgrave Macmillan, 2013.
Zander, Helmut. *Anthroposophie in Deutschland: Theosophische Weltanschaung und gesellschaftliche Praxis, 1884–1945*. 2 Vols. Göttingen: Vandenhoeck & Ruprecht, 2007.
Zillmann, Paul. "War Edition. To the Sisters and Brothers of the Forrest Lodge! To All That Want to Become One! To All Theosophists and Occultists of Germany!" *Neue Metaphysische Rundschau* 21 (1914): 162–66.

Chapter 7

"To Study Judaism in the Light of Theosophy and Theosophy in the Light of Judaism"

The Association of Hebrew Theosophists and Its Missions to the Jews and Gentiles

Boaz Huss

1. Introduction

In December 1925, at the Jubilee congress of the Theosophical Society at Adyar, twelve Jewish delegates founded the Association of Hebrew Theosophists. They had come from different parts of India as well as from Egypt and Europe. The three aims of the nascent Association were:

> To study Judaism in the light of Theosophy and Theosophy in the light of Judaism;
> To spread Theosophical teachings among the Jews;
> To undertake any other activity which could aid in the realization of the objects of the Association.[1]

This article is based on research conducted within the framework of the research project "Kabbalah and the Theosophical Society (1875-1936)," funded by the Israel Science Foundation (grant no. 774/10). I am grateful to Julie Chajes, Hans Martin Krämer, and Julian Strube, who read previous drafts of this paper, for their very helpful comments.

The Jewish association was founded fifty years after the foundation of the Theosophical Society itself. Even before its foundation, many Jews had been active members of the Society, and some of them had similar aims to those held later by the Association. Many Jewish Theosophists believed they had a mission both to the Jews outside the Theosophical fold, as well as to the non-Jewish members of the Theosophical Society. They were interested in initiating a spiritual reform of Judaism through the spreading of Theosophy to the Jews in addition to elevating the standing of Judaism among their fellow Theosophists and enriching Theosophy with Jewish spiritual traditions.

The Jewish Theosophists faced strong opposition within Jewish circles. Several Jewish thinkers denounced Theosophy as incompatible with Judaism and objected to the foundation of the Association of Hebrew Theosophists. They also had to confront the negative image of Judaism held by some of the founders and followers of the Theosophical Society.

This chapter examines the Jewish Theosophists' aspiration to spiritualize Judaism in the light of Theosophy and to elevate the image of Judaism within the Theosophical Society. It discusses the ways in which Jewish Theosophists confronted opposition from Jewish Orthodox circles and responded to the negative image of Judaism within the Theosophical Society. The chapter illustrates that Kabbalah played a central role in the endeavor of the Jewish Theosophists to bring about a spiritual, Theosophical reform of Judaism, as well as in their endeavor to enrich Theosophy with Jewish spirituality. I show that many Jewish Theosophists argued that the Jewish mystical tradition was the source of ancient wisdom and identical with Theosophical doctrines. These claims served to counter the allegations from Jewish opponents that the Jewish Theosophists had distanced themselves from Judaism, as well as to defend Judaism and improve its image in the eyes of non-Jewish Theosophists. Finally, I argue that the Association of Hebrew Theosophists, as well as other Jewish fellows of the Theosophical Society, made a unique attempt, at that time, to create what could be termed a modern, Western, universalistic form of Judaism that embraced Kabbalah and presented Jewish mysticism as the central component of the Jewish tradition. Yet, before turning to discuss the missions of the Association of Hebrew Theosophists to both fellow Jews and the Theosophical Society, and the ways in which they reconciled Judaism and Theosophy, I offer a brief outline of Jewish involvement in the Theosophical Society and of the social and cultural background of the Jewish Theosophists.

2. Jewish Theosophists and the Association of Hebrew Theosophists

Several Jews played an active role in the Theosophical Society from its very beginning. In fact, one of the founding members of the Society was David E. de Lara, an Anglo-Jewish scholar of Sephardic descent.[2] Many other Jews joined Theosophical lodges around the world in the late nineteenth and early twentieth centuries. Some served as officers of sections and lodges, lectured at Theosophical meetings, and published articles and books in Theosophical publications. Among the prominent Jewish fellows of the Theosophical Society in the late nineteenth century were A. D. Ezekiel (d. 1897), who was active in the lodge in Pune, India,[3] and Friedrich Eckstein (1861–1939), who established the Vienna lodge and was its first president.[4] In 1899, Lewis W. Ritch (1868–1952), a Jewish businessman from England, founded the Theosophical lodge in Johannesburg, and several other Jews were active in the South African Theosophical Society in the early twentieth century.[5] Jews were also very active in the German-speaking Theosophical group in Prague, which met at the Salon of Berta Fanta (1866–1918), a central figure in Prague's literary and intellectual circles. Fanta's son-in-law, Hugo Bergman (1883–1975), a philosopher, Zionist activist, and the future rector of the Hebrew University in Jerusalem, took part in the group's meetings. In 1911, Rudolf Steiner gave a series of lectures in Fanta's residence, attended by leading local intellectuals such as Franz Kafka, among others.[6] From the early twentieth century, Jews joined and were also active in other Theosophical centers around the world, including India, China, Iraq, England, Holland, Poland, and the United States.[7]

As mentioned above, in December 1925, twelve Jewish delegates from around the world met at the Jubilee congress of the Theosophical Society at the international headquarters in Adyar and decided to establish a Jewish Theosophical association, the Association of Hebrew Theosophists. Annie Besant, the president of the Theosophical Society, participated in the foundation ceremony and laid the foundation stone for a synagogue at the Adyar compound. In subsequent years, regional sections of the Association were founded in India, England, Holland, and the United States (which became the largest and most active section). There were also individuals who served as national representatives of the Association of Hebrew Theosophists in Italy, Bulgaria, Belgium, Austria, Czechoslovakia, France, Hungary, Poland, and Romania. The activities of the branches included meetings and lectures on Jewish and Theosophical topics, the collection of funds to finance building a synagogue at Adyar, and the publication of two books. The American section of the Association of Hebrew Theosophists published a journal, *The Jewish Theosophist*, which was edited by the president of the section, Henry C. Samuels (1886-1965).[8]

In 1927, a Jewish Theosophical branch affiliated with the Association of Hebrew Theosophists was founded by Kaduri Ani in Basra, Iraq. The rabbinical authorities in Basra, backed by the rabbis of Baghdad and supported by rabbis from England and the United States, opposed the Jewish Theosophists in Basra and ordered Ani and his followers to leave the Theosophical Society. As the Jewish Theosophists refused, the Rabbis excommunicated them. The excommunicated Theosophists, supported by other members of the Basra community, separated from the main Jewish community and created their own, independent community, which they called "Sincere Jews." The excommunication of the group attracted much attention in both the Jewish and Theosophical press and stimulated a fierce debate. Finally, in 1936, the two factions were reconciled and the order of excommunication against the Jewish Theosophists was rescinded.[9]

By the mid-1930s, the branches of the Association of Hebrew Theosophists ceased activity. Nonetheless, Jewish Theosophists continued playing an active role in the Theosophical Society, and some of them continued to be interested in Jewish issues and in the relations between Theosophy and Judaism. As early as the 1930s, a number of Jewish Theosophists had immigrated to Palestine. After the Second World War and the foundation of the state of Israel, more Jewish Theosophists arrived in Israel from Europe, the Middle East, and North Africa. In 1953, the first lodge of the Theosophical Society in Israel was founded in the upper Galilee, followed by other lodges in Haifa, Tel Aviv, and Jerusalem. The Israeli section of the Theosophical Society is still active today.[10]

3. The Jewish Identities of the Hebrew Theosophists

In 1926, Henry C. Samuels, the president of the Association of Hebrew Theosophists' American section, raised a question concerning the Jewish identity of the members of the Association:

> It is of course to be expected that many should wonder just what the A.H.T. is and what kinds of Jews are those who belong

> to it. Correspondence that we receive indicates that some think of us as an association of Jewish mystics, some as reformed Jews and some as Orthodox Jews. There is really much truth in all those expressions, for the fact is that the organization is an association of Hebrew Theosophists, composed of Jews of all phases and elements in Judaism.[11]

Indeed, the members of the Association, as well as those Jews who joined the Theosophical Society prior to the foundation of the Hebrew Association, came from different geographical areas and ethnic backgrounds and had diverse religious affiliations. As mentioned above, the Association of Hebrew Theosophists had sections in India, England, Holland, Iraq, and the United States. Hence, the Jewish Theosophists included Ashkenazy and Sephardic Jews, Iraqi Jews, as well as Indian Jews from the Cochin and Bnei Israel communities. Nonetheless, the Jewish Theosophists did not come from all "phases and elements" of Judaism. Most Jewish Theosophists in Europe and the United States, as well as in India, South Africa, and Iraq, were middle-class, Western-acculturated Jews proficient in European languages. There were several rabbis and scholars who were members of the Theosophical Society and the Association of Hebrew Theosophists, or at least took part in their activities. Most notable among them were Rabbi Arrigo Lates (1879–1918), who headed a Jewish Theosophical group in Livorno, Italy;[12] Joshua Abelson (1873–1940), a liberal orthodox rabbi, who served in Cardiff, Bristol, and Leeds, and was a notable scholar of Jewish studies;[13] Rabbi Edward L. Israel (1896–1941), a Reform rabbi and social activist from Baltimore;[14] and Moses Gaster (1856–1939), a prominent scholar of Jewish studies, a Zionist leader, and the chief rabbi of the English Sephardic community.[15] Yet most Jewish Theosophists did not receive traditional or academic Jewish education. Some of the Jewish Theosophists who came from traditional orthodox homes related that they became estranged from rabbinic Judaism. Thus, for instance, Leonard Bosman (1879–1936), an Anglo-Jewish Theosophist, wrote in his booklet *A Plea for Judaism*: "The writer, brought up in fairly orthodox surroundings from which, he and the whole of a large family, later fell away because the lack of reality behind the too rigid forms and customs, turned almost with contempt from religion to become agnostic and nearly atheistic in his darkness."[16]

Many other Jewish Theosophists shared Bosman's criticism of Jewish orthodoxy and rabbinic Judaism. Already in 1888, A. D. Ezekiel, the

Jewish Theosophist from Pune, dedicated one of the books he printed to "members of our group," who stood by him in his struggle to "overthrow the yoke of the priestcraft" during his controversy with the rabbis of Iraq and Palestine over the publication of a Jewish-Arabic translation of the *Zohar*.[17] Bozena Brydlova/Mrs. W. B. Rubin (b. 1886), the vice president of the American section of the Association of Hebrew Theosophists, wrote in an article published in 1926, that "The Talmud . . . in our modern days seems dreadfully useless and unpractical with its laws that were established to govern conditions which we have long outgrown."[18] Following the excommunication of the Jewish Theosophists in Basra, some Jewish Theosophists attacked the rabbis who issued and supported the ban. S. S. Cohen (1895–1980), one of the founders of the Association of Hebrew Theosophists, who originally came from Basra, described the rabbis of Basra as "primitive, uneducated, half literate, religious autocrats."[19] Henry C. Samuels published an article titled "Fighting the Light (the Story of a Modern Excommunication)," in which he attacked the rabbis who issued the ban: "I affirm with all vehemence of my soul that in this action and attitude those rabbis neither represent Judaism nor the Jew, but a darkness which still besets some of our people."[20]

Although Jewish Theosophists were especially critical of orthodox Judaism, some of them were also critical of liberal Jewish trends. Alex Horne, a Jewish Theosophist active in Shanghai and later in San Francisco,[21] wrote: "Present day Judaism, in both its Orthodox and Liberal branches, has failed to take stock of the spiritual and intellectual needs of the modern Jew."[22] According to Horne, "the Orthodox Jew keeps to the letter of the law and fails to see its mystic meaning. The Liberal Jew disregards the letter but fails likewise to seek its spirit."[23] Horne is sympathetic to the endeavor to re-form Judaism and detach it from the bonds of the past, when they cease to have present-day significance. Yet he is critical of "the liberal Jew" because he "cannot be made to realise that in doing this he throws overboard at the same time much that has a spiritual significance, simply because he had not been trained to perceive spiritual interpretations."[24] Horne's criticism was clearly aimed at the rejection and disparagement of Kabbalah and Hasidism by the Reform and Conservative Jewish movements of his time.

Notwithstanding their varying affiliations within Judaism, many Jewish Theosophists had a strong sense of Jewish national identity. They were sympathetic to Zionism, and some were active in Zionist organizations. *The Jewish Theosophist*, the journal of the American section of the Association, expressed much interest and sympathy with Zionism. In its report on the Fifteenth Zionist Congress held in 1927 in Basel on the tenth anniversary of the Balfour Declaration, the journal stated: "Jews the world over are now celebrating the 10 anniversary of the Balfour Declaration which restored to the Jew his national existence, and it has realized for him a hope that has not waned in the centuries of our 'Goluth.'"[25] The first two issues of the *Jewish Theosophist* each contain a poem by the Jewish national poet and Zionist activist Hayim Nachman Bialik. The title page of the second volume of the *Jewish Theosophist*, published in 1932, carried a pentagram in which the word Zion was inscribed in Hebrew beside the emblem of the Theosophical Society.

4. "To Study Judaism in the Light of Theosophy": The Mission to Jews

The officers of the American section of the Association of Hebrew Theosophists presented themselves and their mission in a letter sent to the Washington Theosophical Lodge in May 1926: "we, Theosophists of the Jewish race feel it is our duty to band ourselves together for the purpose of bringing Theosophy and the Message of the Coming to Jews and to translate the Ancient Wisdom in terms that are familiar in Jewish tradition by linking these truths with the Jewish mystical tradition." According to the letter, the aim of these Jewish Theosophists was "to do publicity work among Jews" and influence them to join the Society: "There is no reason why more of the people who in the past made such valuable contribution to occultism, witness, the Kabalah, the mysticism of the Essenes, and Hassidism should not be influenced to enter the ranks of the Theosophical Society."[26]

Many Jewish Theosophists worked "to spread Theosophical teachings among the Jews," as stated in the second of the three aims of the Association of Hebrew Theosophists. Lila B. Allebach described the Hebrew Theosophists as "The handful of men who at the call of the 'Masters' are assembled to carry forward the work of Universal Brotherhood among those of our ancient faith."[27] Horne stated:

> Too long have we drunk of the well of knowledge without making some attempt to share our inspiration with the rest of our co-religionists. Now that attempt is made and it is the

privilege of every Jewish Theosophist to take a hand in the work of spreading the light, and the spiritual comfort and strength that go with it.[28]

Horne, who criticized both Orthodox and liberal Judaism for lack of a mystical spirit, believed that the Theosophical Society could satisfy the spiritual yearnings of the modern Jew without estranging him from his own religion. Horne argued that Jews had left Judaism to enter the ranks of Christian Scientists, New Thought, and Catholicism because of mystical cravings that could not be fulfilled within contemporary Judaism. According to Horne, these spiritual and mystical yearnings could be satisfied without leaving Judaism in the Theosophical Society:

> The same yearnings, again, have brought some to the T. S, but here, fortunately, instead of estranging them from their race, as the other religious bodies have done, they have been encouraged rather to seek for the beauties in their own faith, and have no doubt been inspired to go back and work among their own people, and share with them the inspiration, the joy, of their newly acquired outlook on life and the universe.[29]

The Jewish Theosophists did not regard their mission as merely recruiting Jews to the Theosophical Society and spreading the light of Theosophy among them. Rather, they believed that they could offer the Jews a better understanding of their own religion through Theosophy. Gaston Polak (1874–1970), the general secretary of the Belgian Theosophical Society and the president of the Association of Hebrew Theosophists, explained that the first declared aim of the Association—to study Judaism in the light of Theosophy—"will help the Jews to understand their own religion."[30] Similarly, Bozena Brydlova/Mrs. Rubin wrote that Theosophy "will assist the Jew in becoming a better Jew, inasmuch as it will aid him in understanding his own religion better."[31]

The Jewish Theosophists regarded the Theosophically inspired reinterpretation of Jewish culture as a means of reforming Judaism spiritually. As we have seen, Jewish Theosophists were critical of rabbinic Judaism and regarded contemporary Judaism as materialistic and unspiritual. They believed that spreading Theosophy to the Jews and interpreting Judaism in the light of Theosophy would provide a way of "spiritualizing unspiritual Judaism." In a book carrying this title, which was published by the American section of the Association, Horne called for:

> a spiritualized Judaism, that will in fact form the foundation of a real, vital, soul inspiring religion—one that will be not merely a compromise between a half-hearted acknowledgment of one's religious inheritance and the attempt to make that acknowledgment as easy and comfortable as possible, but a religion in the true and fullest sense of the word—a channel through which may pour the spiritual aspirations of the people, and instrument that will instruct and elevate.[32]

In another article, Horne explained that, because of the materialism modern Judaism had fallen to, "it needs a reviving breath, a fresh inspiration, a spiritualizing influence. All this we are in a position to give it."[33]

Allebach emphasized the reformative task facing Jewish Theosophists: "Our task should be to re-interpret the faith as to bring it into consonance with the conditions of a new environment and not permit ourselves to look upon the old type of Judaism as ultimate and binding and attempt to incrustate it in a shell of permanence."[34] According to the officers of the Indian section of the Association of Hebrew Theosophists, the task of the Association was "To help our race by bringing them to the light of Theosophy by turning their narrow orthodoxy to a rational broad-mindedness adorned with intelligent spirituality—a spirituality tinged by the high philosophical conceptions of races and cultures other than their own."[35]

As mentioned above, many Jewish Theosophists had a strong sense of Jewish national identity and were supportive of the Zionist movement. Some Jewish Theosophists regarded the Theosophically inspired spiritual reform of Judaism as necessary for a Jewish national revival. Thus, Horne wrote in his *Spiritualizing Unspiritual Judaism*:

> We have too long made the mistake of regarding a nation or a race as nothing more than a political or social unit. We must now realize that a race is a spiritual entity, whose soul is that undefinable yet unmistakable something which vivifies the physical form, keeps it alive and stamps it with the definite characteristic we so easily recognize as we scan the pages of history. To feed that national soul requires spiritual aspiration.[36]

To accelerate the Theosophical spiritual revival of Judaism, Jewish Theosophists actively recruited Jews to the Theosophical Society and spread Theosophical teachings among them. Jewish Theosophists regarded

Kabbalah as the spiritual essence of Judaism, which to them resembled the teachings of the Theosophical Society (or, as some argued, was identical to them). Hence, they were interested in introducing Jewish mystical sources to the modern Jewish public, which did not have much knowledge of Kabbalah in that period.[37] For that purpose, several Jewish Theosophists translated Kabbalistic texts into languages accessible to modern Jews. This began in the late nineteenth century with A. D. Ezekiel, the Iraqi Jewish Theosophist from India, who translated several Kabbalistic texts (including a section from the *Zohar*) into Jewish Arabic for the benefit of members of his community who were not able to read the texts in their original language.[38] Subsequently, Ernst Müller, a Jewish scholar and Zionist from Vienna who was interested in Theosophy and who was to become a dedicated follower of Steiner, translated *Zohar* passages into German together with his friend Hugo Bergman, who was himself affiliated with Theosophical and Anthroposophical circles in Prague. They published these passages in the volume *Vom Judentum* (Leipzig 1913) and in the journal *Der Jude*.[39] Joshua Abelson, a rabbi, scholar, and Theosophist, participated in the translation of the *Zohar* into English, which was published by the Anglo-Jewish Soncino press in the 1930s.[40] In this period, Jewish Theosophists also published many articles and books about Jewish mysticism, which were intended for both Jewish and non-Jewish readers.[41]

Jewish Theosophists were also interested in forming Jewish-Theosophical religious practices. Indeed, the first action of the Association was to lay the foundations for a synagogue in the Adyar compound. Annie Besant laid the foundation stone, and A. B. Salem conducted the ceremony in Hebrew.[42] The plans for the proposed synagogue were published, and efforts were made in subsequent years to secure funds for its building.[43] Nonetheless, the synagogue was never built. Other Jewish Theosophists suggested forming a "Synagogue on Theosophical lines" in cities with large Jewish populations.[44] The founders of the Association of Hebrew Theosophists were interested in creating a Theosophically inspired prayer for the use in the Adyar Synagogue. In a letter published in the first volume of the *Jewish Theosophist*, S. S. Cohen wrote:

> It will also be desirable to prepare, with the help of the rabbis in America, a form of prayer book in Hebrew to be used in our Adyar Synagogue. You know that Jewish prayers nowadays are very dry from the spiritual standpoint, and lack any sense

of high aspiration. If we could give them a Theosophical tone in connection with the Jewish traditional ritual, it would be highly appreciated.[45]

Similarly, S. I. Heiman suggested revising the Jewish prayer book, changing the ritual at the synagogue, and forming a ritual for the Jewish youth similar to that of the Theosophical youth order, "The Round Table."[46]

As mentioned above, the activities of Jewish Theosophists and the foundation of the Association of Hebrew Theosophists and its call for a Theosophical reform of Judaism encountered severe criticism in the Jewish world. For example, the aforementioned Jewish-Arabic translation of a section from the *Zohar*, by A. D. Ezekiel, stimulated much controversy on its publication at the end of the nineteenth century. Leading rabbis from Baghdad, Jerusalem, and Hebron objected to the translation and issued a decree against it. It is not clear whether these rabbis were aware that Ezekiel was a member of the Theosophical Society. His attempt to introduce Kabbalah to wider sectors of the Jewish populations beyond the rabbinic elite—an objective inspired by his Theosophical convictions—was not acceptable to the rabbinic establishment.[47]

Further evidence of the criticism encountered is also attested in the persecution of a group of Jewish Theosophists that operated in Ahmedabad, India, in the first decades of the twentieth century by leaders of the local Jewish community.[48] However, it was particularly the foundation of the Association of Hebrew Theosophists and its various branches at the end of the 1920s that provoked negative reactions in the Jewish world and brought about the excommunication of the Jewish Theosophical group in Basra.

The *Jewish World* in London denounced the foundation of the Association of Hebrew Theosophists, which it described as a "sect" of Jewish Theosophists. The author expressed his fear of the danger inherent in the continuation of Jewish Theosophists, "as if they were loyal and true Jews," and expressed his hope that eventually the Jewish Theosophists would leave Judaism.[49] Like other Jewish opponents of the Jewish Theosophists, the author was especially suspicious of the Christological aspects of the belief in the coming of the world teacher, and denounced a message of Annie Besant to Jewish Theosophists, in which she expressed her hope that the Jews would welcome the world teacher, "whom they ignorantly rejected when he first came to them."[50] Besant's statement was also denounced by the *Jewish Ledger* of New Orleans, which saw in it proof that Jewish

Theosophists, whom it describes as representing an "absurd cult" and an "abnormality," cannot be "strict adherents of the Jewish faith and unquestionable believers in the Unity of God."[51]

Several rabbinic authorities who were asked for their opinion concerning the Jewish Theosophical group in Basra denounced Theosophy as incompatible with Judaism and advised the Jews of Basra to distance themselves from its teachings. The chief rabbi of the British Empire, Rabbi Joseph Hertz, wrote that "Whilst there are certain resemblances between the Jewish Kabala and some aspects of Theosophy, Theosophical teaching is, as a rule, foreign to Judaism, and sometimes against the very fundamentals of our faith. I would strongly urge brothers in Basra to abstain from affiliation with the Theosophy movement."[52] Similarly, Rabbi Dr. Leo Jung of the rabbinical council of the Union of American Orthodox congregations asserted that:

> Jews do not need Theosophy. In the Torah they are taught a philosophical life, not a mystic nothingness. Theosophy leads Jews away from their solid duties with which our lord has crowned us. I would certainly warn my brothers against the surrender of their religious identity, which is inevitable as they lose themselves in the unprofitable mazes of theosophic thought [. . .] Theosophy is a malady of the weak. It is a punishment of ignorance. It is not a religion for men. It robs women of their grace and strength. It deprives youth of its moral stamina.[53]

Following letters received from rabbinic authorities in Baghdad, England, and the United States, Rabbi Ezekiel Sasson, the acting chief rabbi of Basra, sent a message ordering all Jewish Theosophists to resign from the Society on threat of excommunication. Because they refused, the decree of excommunication was issued on May 20, 1931:

> As our final notice to the Theosophical Society has expired on Tuesday, henceforth according to the judgment given by the rabbis of Bagdad, those who are affiliated to the above Society are excluded from the congregation of Israel in circumcision, marriage, and burial, and other matters relating to the community and all the religious affairs of Israel. Furthermore, people who will go to visit them in their lodge will be accused of being affiliated to the Society.[54]

The excommunication stimulated a heated debate in the Jewish press. Some readers supported the ban on the Jewish Theosophists. Thus, Nayim B. Samuel of Bombay applauded the rabbis for "separating the rotten apples from the good ones." Samuel was especially opposed to the liberal stance of the Theosophists: "Theosophy, to my mind aims at establishing a liberal section of the Jews contrary to the teaching of the Torah." Furthermore, Samuel argued that the Jewish Theosophists disturbed the efforts to build a Jewish homeland in Palestine. Hence, "[i]n excommunicating those that are affiliated to the Theosophic society the rabbis of Basra have removed a serious impediment that would have obstructed us Jews, on our way towards the realization of a peaceful homeland in Palestine."[55] The editor of *Israel Messenger*, N. E. B. Ezra, opposed the excommunication of the Jewish Theosophists. Nonetheless, he accused the Jewish Theosophists of detaching themselves from the Jewish congregation: "Mr. Ani and his friends had donned the costumes of beggars in the home of aliens, in the hope of snatching crumbs of bread from other tables when their own table lacks nothing by way of satisfying their hungry souls."[56]

Jewish Theosophists denied that they had distanced themselves from Judaism by joining the Theosophical Society. They emphasized that Jewish Theosophy did not involve the adoption of "external" doctrines, but rather a return to, and a revival of, original Jewish mystical ideas. A person who wrote under the pseudonym "Sofia" acknowledged in an article titled "Jewish Theosophy—a Paradox" that the ideas of the Theosophical Society may indeed be seen at first sight as distant from Jewish ideas. Yet, she wrote:

> Be not too sure that because you do not readily recognize a thought as Jewish it is necessarily un-Jewish; do not insist that all of the truth manifests itself in present day Judaism, and that, because an idea is not today openly advocated from the pulpit it is necessarily untrue. Keep your mind open: study and reflect, and it will gradually be shown to you that fundamental principles of modern Theosophy conform to the spirit of the teachings promulgated by the Jewish mystics and sages of old.[57]

Many other Jewish Theosophists asserted that Theosophical ideas and values were not alien to the Jewish tradition and that Theosophy was compatible with Judaism. In *The Music of the Spheres*, published in 1914, Leonard Bosman took issue with a student of comparative religion who declared "that he cannot reconcile Judaism with the Wisdom religion or

Theosophy" and "a Jewish Theosophist, so-called" who said that "he is also at loss to see their relation."[58] Bosman replied to them by attacking their limited understanding of Judaism and asserted that Judaism and Theosophy can be reconciled through Kabbalah, which stems from the same source as Theosophy and is essentially identical with it:

> [t]hen indeed we can ask "What do they know of Judaism who only know the rites and customs?" Have they heard of the inner doctrine, the *Received* wisdom, the Qabalah or the Doctrine of the Heart, or the Theos Sophia of the Jews? But verily the Secret Doctrine of the Jews is Theos-Sophia and nothing but Theos-Sophia, and hence it is a matter of perfect simplicity to reconcile the two doctrines that emanate from one source.[59]

Similar to "Sofia" and Bosman, other Jewish Theosophists emphasized the identity of Theosophical doctrines and the Kabbalah in order to rebut the accusation that they had turned to alien sources. In his response to his detractors, Kaduri Ani, the leader of the Basra Theosophists, wrote: "Theosophy is not a religion, as you have alleged, but is a philosophical society—the Jewish Kabbalah itself."[60]

Following the assertion of their conviction that the doctrines of the Kabbalah reflected the ancient universal wisdom and was similar to the teaching of Theosophy, the Jewish Theosophists, who aspired to "study Judaism in the light of Theosophy," attempted to revive the knowledge of Kabbalah among the Jews. For that purpose, Jewish Theosophists studied and translated Kabbalistic texts, gave lectures, and published articles and books on Jewish mysticism. As we shall see in the next section, these activities were intended not only to spiritualize Judaism, but also to improve the image of Judaism within Theosophy and enrich Theosophy with Jewish mystical teachings.

5. "To Study Theosophy in the Light of Judaism": The Mission to the Gentiles

In her article "Why Every Jew Should Join the Association of Hebrew Theosophists," Bozena Brydlova praised the Theosophical Society for its tolerance toward the Jews: "Theosophists draw no distinction between race, creed, sex, caste or color. Therefore the Jew enters the organization with no feeling of timidity of misgiving."[61] Brydlova argued that Theosophy would improve the external image of Judaism and the attitude of the Gentiles to the Jews: "Hence Theosophy will tend to make the Gentile see the Jew in his true light and to endow Judaism with its rightful heritage . . . instead of persecuting the Jew because of his religion, the Theosophist hails him with welcome, because he brings into the society a grand old faith that is worth studying and heeding."[62]

The tolerant, universalistic stance of the Theosophical Society, which called for a universal brotherhood of humanity without distinction of race, creed, sex, caste, or color, attracted many Jews, who joined Theosophical branches all around the world. Yet, notwithstanding the tolerant stance of the Society and its declaration of universal brotherhood, a negative image of Judaism and expressions of anti-Semitic sentiment could be found among some of the founders and followers of the Theosophical Society. For example, a negative stance toward Judaism was expressed by the founder of the society, Helena P. Blavatsky.[63] In *The Secret Doctrine*, Blavatsky claimed that, while Jews were acquainted with sorcery and maleficent powers, they knew little of real divine occultism because their national character was "averse to anything which had no direct bearing upon their own ethnical, tribal and individual benefits."[64] According to Blavatsky, gross realism, selfishness, and sensuality were "the idiosyncratic defects that characterize many of the Jews to this day."[65] She emphasized the chasm between Aryan and Semitic religious thought and declared that "There was a day when the Israelite had beliefs as pure as the Aryans have. But now Judaism, built solely on phallic worship, has become one of the latest creeds in Asia, and theologically a religion of hate and malice towards everyone and everything outside of itself."[66] In her *Key to Theosophy*, Blavatsky expressed the idea that universal truth could be found in all religions except Judaism:

> What is also needed is to impress men with the idea that, if the root of mankind is *one*, then there must also be one truth which finds expression in all the various religions—except in the Jewish, as you do not find it *expressed* even in the Kabala.[67]

Similar opinions were voiced by other leading Theosophists. J. D. Buck (1838–1916), the founder of the Theosophical lodge in Cincinnati, claimed in his 1883 article "The Cabbalah" that the key to the secret wisdom of the Kabbalah was lost from Judaism, which had become "a close corporation for commercial speculations and mutual protection."[68] Rudolf Steiner, the general secretary of the German section of the Theosophical Society in the early twentieth century, and later the founder of Anthroposophy, accused the Jews of national egoism, materialism, and abstract thinking and declared that "The Jews have a great aptitude for materialism, but little appreciation of the spiritual world."[69] Although Annie Besant accepted the establishment of the Association of Hebrew Theosophists with enthusiasm, her letter of welcome to the Jewish Theosophists expressed a Christian bias against the Jews:

> I am very glad to welcome the association. It would indeed be splendid if some of the nation which ignorantly rejected the World Teacher when he came to them, using the body of a Jewish disciple as his vehicle, should welcome Him on his return two thousand years later. Who knows what Word He may have for the ancient people to whom He came on His previous visit, Will He lift them back among the nations of the world? St. Paul looked forward to such a revival of his people and likened it to "life from the dead."[70]

Jewish Theosophists responded to the negative portrayal of Judaism by emphasizing the spiritual and mystical resources of Judaism. Although many of them adopted the negative image of Judaism and criticized rabbinic and contemporary Judaism for being materialistic and unspiritual, they claimed that Judaism had spiritual resources and could enrich Theosophy through its mystical heritage. The founders of the Association of Hebrew Theosophists declared that their aim was "to elevate Judaism to its rightful heritage and to enrich Theosophy, the Divine Wisdom that underlies all religion, with the many treasures that are embodied in ancient and modern Judaism, and thus to be of greater service to Humanity, both as Jews and through Judaism, our cherished faith."[71] The Indian section of the Association declared its aim "to serve our Society by enriching it with the Jewish thoughts which have been evolving for many centuries, from the ancient scriptures of our prophets and sages of old."[72] Similarly, Bozena Brydlova asserted that Judaism had much to contribute to the two main interests of Theosophy, investigating the unexplained laws of nature and the powers latent in man: "Ancient Judaism contains a wealth of mysticism concerning these two subjects and constitutes a valuable source of study to the Theosophists."[73]

As mentioned above, Leonard Bosman challenged the declaration of a Theosophist, whom he described as a pagan student of comparative religion, that "he cannot reconcile Judaism with the Wisdom Religion, or Theosophy."[74] Bosman answered that Judaism and Theosophy can easily be reconciled through Kabbalah: "The Secret Doctrine of the Jews is Theos-Sophia and nothing but Theos-Sophia, hence it is a matter of perfect simplicity to reconcile the two teachings, that emanates from One source."[75]

Bosman and many other Jewish Theosophists regarded Kabbalah as the main contribution Judaism could offer to Theosophy. Kabbalah played an important role in "Western esotericism" in general and within Theosophy in particular. The Theosophical Society had been concerned with Kabbalah since its very beginning, and Kabbalistic ideas and concepts had an important place in Blavatsky's doctrines. Yet the attitude of Blavatsky and other Theosophists to Kabbalah was ambivalent, and they denied its Jewish origin.[76]

In contrast to the ambivalent stance of Blavatsky and other occultists toward Jewish Kabbalah, Jewish Theosophists valorized the Kabbalah unequivocally and emphasized its Jewish nature and origins. They underlined the centrality of the Kabbalah in the universal secret doctrine that the Theosophical Society purported to reveal and, as we saw above, claimed there was a similarity, even an identity, between Kabbalah and Theosophy.[77] Thus, for instance, Elias Gewurtz claimed in his article "The Qabbalah," published in *The Theosophist* in 1914: "What was once known to the few as the holy Qabalah is now proclaimed far and wide as Theosophy. It is all the same teaching and emanates from the same source."[78]

Leonard Bosman, Gewurtz's friend and disciple, declared that the members of the Jewish race were the guardians of the universal religious wisdom of the ancients: "We claim here for the Jewish race the honor of being the recipient of such knowledge through their Wise Men but it should be understood that the Qabalah itself is Universal for it is no more Jewish than Pagan, as much Egyptian as Chaldean and Persian."[79] Bosman challenged Blavatsky's ambivalent stance to Judaism and Kabbalah by defining Kabbala as the "Secret Doctrine of the Jews." He asserted the identity of Kabbalah with the teaching of Blavatsky's magnum opus and suggested that the mysterious book of Dzyan, on which Blavatsky's *Secret Doctrine* was allegedly based, was derived from the Zoharic text *Sifra de-Zeniuta*:

> The Inner Teaching of Judaism is the same as that offered in the *Secret Doctrine*, the very name of the *Book of Dzyan* from

which the *Secret Doctrine* was taken, and the Qabalistic work called the *Book of Dzyaniouta* being similar in construction and purpose.[80]

As we have seen in the previous section, Gewurtz, Bosman, as well as many other Jewish Theosophists and members of the Association of Hebrew Theosophists, gave lectures and published articles and books about Jewish mysticism and Kabbalah. The purpose of these lectures and publications was not only to revive Jewish mystical knowledge among the Jews, but also to present Kabbalah (as understood by the Jewish Theosophists) to fellow Theosophists. Thus, for instance, A. D. Ezekiel published an *Introduction to the Kabalah* in 1888 (the only English text published by his printing press).[81] It was addressed to fellow members of the Theosophical Society in India:

> Since the formation of the Theosophical society several enquiries have been made as to the teaching of the Kabalah. With a view therefore to give the general reader some idea of the subject I have thought it fit to reprint without any corrections or additions the "Introduction to the Kabalah."[82]

Many other publications of Jewish Theosophists were also aimed at presenting Kabbalah to non-Jewish Theosophists to demonstrate its compatibility with Theosophy in addition to the contribution made by Judaism to occult and spiritual knowledge. The discussions and presentations of Kabbalah by Jewish Theosophists, which were intended to counter the negative image of Judaism within the Theosophical Society and emphasize the importance of Jewish Kabbalah, were used by Jewish Theosophists to augment their standing within the Society. Several Jewish Theosophists presented themselves as experts in Kabbalah and used their Jewish origins and knowledge of Jewish tradition to enhance their cultural capital within the Society. Non-Jewish Theosophists accepted the claim of Jewish Theosophists that they could contribute their knowledge of Kabbalah to the Society. In a message to the Hebrew Theosophists (very different in its tone than the first message, discussed above), Annie Besant congratulated them for enriching Theosophy with the wisdom of their "occult treatises":

> It is a great happiness to me to see members of the great Hebrew race enriching Theosophy with contributions from

their ancient Faith. Much wisdom is enshrined in their occult treatises, and European philosophy and metaphysics owe much to the subtle genius of the Hebrew Nation. Great have been its sufferings in the past, but the greater still will be its gifts in the future to the human race.[83]

Conclusion

Members of the Association of Hebrew Theosophists, as well as other Jewish Theosophists more generally, attempted to accommodate Judaism and Theosophy. They regarded their mission both as bringing about a spiritual, Theosophical reform of Judaism, and as enriching Theosophy with Jewish spirituality. Kabbalah played a central role in these twin missions to the Jews and Gentiles. The claim that Kabbalah and Theosophy are compatible served to counter allegations from Jewish opponents that Jewish Theosophists had distanced themselves from Judaism and to demonstrate that Theosophical ideas were not alien to Jewish knowledge. The perception of the compatibility of Kabbalah and Theosophy served also as means to defend Judaism, to improve the image of Judaism in the eyes of non-Jewish Theosophists, and to enhance the status of Jews in the Theosophical Society.

The centrality of Kabbalah within a modern Jewish liberal movement was a unique feature of Jewish Theosophy. By the late nineteenth century, knowledge of Kabbalah was restricted in westernized Jewish cultures and was prevalent mostly among traditional Jews in Eastern Europe, the Middle East, and North Africa. Kabbalah was largely rejected and despised among western-acculturated Jewish circles from which most Jewish Theosophists came. Jewish Theosophy offered a unique attempt, at that time, to create a modern, westernized, universalistic form of Judaism that embraced Kabbalah and presented Jewish mysticism as the central component of the Jewish tradition.[84]

The endeavor of Jewish Theosophists to spiritualize Judaism and to create a modern, liberal Jewish mystical movement did not find many followers within Judaism in the first half of the twentieth century. Nor were they able to stimulate much interest in Jewish Kabbalah or elevate the image of Judaism among the non-Jewish public. It was only in a later period, in the last decades of the twentieth century, that Kabbalah became appreciated in wider circles as an essential component of Judaism and valorized as a form of universal mystical knowledge. A spiritual liberal reform of Judaism, quite similar to that suggested by the Jewish Theosophists, was offered with some success by Jewish renewal and neo-Kabbalistic movements.[85] A positive image of Judaism, as a treasure house of universal mystical knowledge, which the Jewish Theosophists attempted to advance in the early twentieth century, is today taken for granted in the Western world, and many non-Jews find much of interest in Jewish Kabbalah. Although they did not have much influence on the current revival of Kabbalah, the members of the Association of Hebrew Theosophists and other early twentieth-century Jewish Theosophists can be seen as the early precursors and heralds of New Age Kabbalah.

Notes

1. The three aims of the Association of Hebrew Theosophists appear in many sources. See, for instance, Gaston Polak, "Appeal to Members of the T.S.," *The Theosophist* 47 (April 1926).

2. John Patrick Deveney, "D. E. de Lara, John Storer Cobb, and The New Era," *Theosophical History* 15, no. 4 (2011).

3. Boaz Huss, "'The Sufi Society from America': Theosophy and Kabbalah in Poona in the Late Nineteenth Century," in *Kabbalah and Modernity*, ed. Boaz Huss, Marco Pasi and Kocku von Stuckrad (Leiden: Brill, 2010).

4. Sibylle Mulot-Déri, "Alte ungenannte Tage," in *Alte unnennbare Tage*, by Friedrich Eckstein (Wien: Edition Ateli, 1992).

5. Shimon Lev, "Gandhi and his Jewish Theosophist Supporters in South Africa," in *Theosophical Appropriations: Esotericism, Kabbalah and the Transformation of Traditions*, ed. Julie Chajes and Boaz Huss (Beer Sheva: Ben-Gurion University of the Negev Press, 2016).

6. Andreas Kilcher, "Kabbalah and Anthroposophy: A Spiritual Alliance According to Ernst Müller," in *Theosophical Appropriations: Esotericism, Kabbalah, and the Transformation of Traditions*, ed. Julie Chajes and Boaz Huss (Beer Sheva: Ben-Gurion University of the Negev Press, 2016), 206; Boaz Huss, "Qabbalah, the Theos-Sophia of the Jews: Jewish Theosophists and Their Perceptions of Kabbalah," in *Theosophical Appropriations: Esotericism, Kabbalah, and the Transformation of Traditions*, ed. Julie Chajes and Boaz Huss (Beer Sheva: Ben-Gurion University of the Negev Press, 2016), 140.

7. Huss, "Qabbalah, the Theos-Sophia of the Jews," 140–42.

8. Ibid., 142–43.

9. Ibid., 143–44.

10. Ibid., 144.

11. Henry C. Samuels, "Basic Information of the Association of Hebrew Theosophists," *The Jewish Theosophist* 1, no. 2 (1926), 8.

12. Marco Pasi, "Teosofia e antroposofia nell'Italia del primo Novecento," in *Storia d'Italia. Annali 25. Esoterismo*, ed. Gian Mario Cazzaniga (Torino: Einaudi, 2010), 586.

13. Benjamin J. Elton, "Conservative Judaism's British Trailblazers," *Conservative Judaism* 63, no. 4 (2012): 64–65; Liz Greene, *Magi and Maggidim: The Kabbalah in British Occultism 1860–1940* (Ceredigion Wales: Sophia Center Press, 2012), 297.

14. "Rabbi Edward L. Israel on Theosophy and the World Teacher," *The Jewish Theosophist* 1, no. 4 (1927).

15. Green, *Magi and Maggidim*, 292–93.

16. Leonard Bosman, *A Plea for Judaism* (Adyar: Association of Hebrew Theosophists, 1926), 16.

17. Huss, "The Sufi Society," 182.

18. Bozena Brydlova, "The Ancient Kabbalah," *The Jewish Theosophist* 1, no. 2 (1926): 28.

19. S. S. Cohen, "Excommunication in a Modern Synagogue," *The Jewish Advocate* (June 1931): 184.

20. Henry C. Samuels, "Fighting the Light (the Story of a Modern Excommunication)," *The Jewish Theosophist* 2, no. 1 (1932).

21. See Huss, "Qabbalah, the Theos-Sophia of the Jews," 139. For more on Horne, see the chapter by Chuang Chienhui in the present volume.

22. Alex Horne, *Spiritualizing Unspiritual Judaism* (Seattle, WA: Association of Hebrew Theosophists, American Section, 1928), 10.

23. Alex Horne, "Theosophy and Modern Judaism," *The Theosophist* 47 (April 1926): 105.

24. Ibid., 105.

25. *The Jewish Theosophist* 1, no. 5 (1927): 4.

26. Typed letter, addressed to the Washington Lodge of the Theosophical Society, with the letterhead "Association of Hebrew Theosophists, American Section," sent from Milwaukee, Wisconsin, on May 20, 1926. I am grateful to Ms. Janet Kerschner, who located this letter and kindly sent it to me. A similar message was printed in an announcement published the same month in *The Messenger*: "We, members of the Theosophical Society and the Order of the Star who are of the Jewish Race, feel that an effort must be made to present the Jewish people our beliefs about the Coming, the existence of the Great White Lodge, Reincarnation, and Karma, from an angel best suited to their historical background and their traditions, and link these truths with the work of the great sages as given in the midrashim, Mishna, Talmud and Kabala." *The Messenger* 13, no. 12 (May 1926): 265. The announcement was reprinted in *The Theosophist* 47 (August 1926): 623–24.

27. Lila B. Allebach, "Our Task As Hebrew Theosophists," *The Jewish Theosophist* 1, no. 3 (1927): 4.

28. Alex Horne, "A Glorious Opportunity," *The Jewish Theosophists* 1, no. 2 (1926): 7.

29. Horne, "Theosophy and Modern Judaism," 14

30. Polak, "Appeal to Members of the T. S.," 103-4.

31. Bozena Brydlova, "Why Every Jew Should Join the Association of Hebrew Theosophists," *The Jewish Theosophist* 1, no. 1 (1926): 7.

32. Horne, *Spiritualizing Unspiritual Judaism*, 10.

33. Horne, "A Glorious Opportunity," 8.

34. Allebach, "Our Task as Hebrew Theosophists," 4.

35. "A Message to Jews in India," *The Jewish Theosophist* 1, no. 4 (1927): 27.

36. Horne, *Spiritualizing Unspiritual Judaism*, 5.

37. Huss, "Qabbalah, the Theos-Sophia of the Jews," 148-56.

38. Huss, "The Sufi Society," 176-83.

39. Boaz Huss, *The Zohar: Reception and Impact* (Oxford: The Littman Library of Jewish Civilization 2016), 305

40. Ibid., 307.

41. Huss, "Qabbalah, the Theos-Sophia of the Jews," 148-56.

42. *The Messenger* 13 (April 1926): 246.

43. *The Jewish Theosophist* 1, no. 1 (1926): 5; *The Jewish Theosophist* 1, no. 4 (1927): 5, 14, 19, 26.

44. S. I. Heiman, "Correspondence," *The Jewish Theosophist* 1, no. 1 (1926).

45. S. S. Cohen, "Correspondence," *The Jewish Theosophist* 1, no. 1 (1926).

46. Heiman, "Correspondence."

47. Huss, "The Sufi Society," 178-91.

48. In an article published in 1931, C. Jinarajadsa cites the testimony of Jacob E. Solomon, a Jewish Theosophist of the Bene Israel Indian community: "In Ahmedabad I was beaten in the Synagogue and excommunicated for protesting the unrighteous actions of the leaders; we formed a separate community and had prayers in my Hall. After seven years we were honorably taken back." *The Theosophist* 52 (June 1931): 363. I have not found any other information concerning the excommunication of Solomon, or of the existence of a separate community of Jewish Theosophist in Ahmedabad.

49. *The Jewish Daily Bulletin* (March 3, 1927): 2.

50. Ibid.

51. Cited in *The Jewish Daily Bulletin* (March 10, 1927): 2.

52. Cited in *The Theosophist* 52 (June 1931): 368; *Israel Messenger* (June 1, 1931): 18.

53. Ibid.

54. The decree is cited by Reuben Ani in a letter published in *The Jewish Advocate* (May 1931): 167.

55. *The Jewish Advocate* (July 1931): 202.

56. *Israel Messenger* (September 4, 1931): 20.

57. Sofia, "The Jewish Theosophist—a Paradox." *The Jewish Theosophists* 1, no. 1 (1926): 21.

58. Leonard Bosman, *The Music of the Spheres* (London: Dharma Press, 1914), 5.

59. Ibid.

60. An English translation of the letter (written originally in Arabic) was published in *The Theosophist* 52 (June 1931): 365–68.

61. Brydlova, "Why Every Jew Should Join the Association of Hebrew Theosophists," 7.

62. Ibid.

63. See Karen Swartz, "Views from the Great White Brotherhood" (PhD diss., Linnaeus University, 2009), 60. Isaac Lubelsky, *Celestial India: Madame Blavatsky and the Birth of Indian Nationalism* (Sheffield: Equinox 2012), 150, 153; Huss, "The Sufi Society," 174; Peter Staudenmaier, "Rudolf Steiner and the Jewish Question," *Leo Baeck Institute Yearbook* 50, no. 1 (2005): 136–37.

64. H. P. Blavatsky, *The Secret Doctrine*. Theosophical Universal Press Online Edition, vol. 1, 230, http://www.theosociety.org/pasadena/sd/sd1-1-11.htm.

65. Blavatsky, *The Secret Doctrine*, vol. 2, 471.

66. Ibid.

67. H. P Blavatsky, *The Key to Theosophy* (London: The Theosophical Publishing Company, 1889), 45.

68. J. D. Buck, "The Cabbalah," *The Theosophist* 5 (1883).

69. Staudenmaier, "Rudolf Steiner and the Jewish Question," 139. On similar expressions in the writing of Steiner's followers see ibid., note 51.

70. *The Jewish Daily Bulletin* (February 17, 1927): 2.

71. "Information of the A.H.T.," *The Jewish Theosophist* 1, no. 2 (1926): 9.

72. "A Message to Jews in India," *The Jewish Theosophist* 1, no. 4 (1927): 27.

73. Brydlova, "Why Every Jew Should Join the Association of Hebrew Theosophists," 7.

74. Bosman, *The Music of the Spheres*, 5.

75. Ibid.

76. Marco Pasi, "Oriental Kabbalah and the Parting of East and West in the Early Theosophical Society," in *Kabbalah and Modernity*, ed. Boaz Huss, Marco Pasi, and Kocku von Stuckrad (Leiden: Brill, 2010); Julie Chajes, "Construction Through Appropriation: Kabbalah in Blavatsky's Early Works," in *Theosophical Appropriations: Esotericism, Kabbalah and the Transformation of Traditions*, ed. Julie Chajes and Boaz Huss (Beer Sheva: Ben-Gurion University of the Negev Press, 2016); Julie Chajes, *Recycled Lives: A History of Rebirth in Blavatsky's Theosophy* (New York: Oxford University Press, 2019), 6–9.

77. Huss, "Qabbalah, the Theos-Sophia of the Jews," 148–56.

78. Elias Gewurtz, "The Qabbalah," *The Theosophist* 36 (November 1914): 172.
79. Bosman, *The Music of the Spheres*, 5–6.
80. Ibid., 6.
81. This book is a reprint of a text entitled "Introduction to the Cabalah," published in London in 1845/46, in the journal *The Voice of Israel*, propagated by "Jews who believe in Jesus of Nazareth as the Messiah," edited by the convert Reverend Ridley Haim Herschell. The "Introduction to the Cabalah" that was published in the *Voice of Israel*, and reprinted by Ezekiel, was an English translation (probably prepared by Herschell) of excerpts from the book on Jewish sects by the Jewish scholar Peter Baer, *Geschichte, Lehren und Meinungen aller bestandenen und noch bestehenden religiösen Sekten der Juden und der Geheimlehre oder Kabbala* (Brünn: Traßler, 1822/23).
82. A.D. Ezekiel, *Introduction to the Kabalah* (Poona: A.D. Ezekiel, 1888), n.p.
83. Annie Besant "A Message from Annie Besant to Hebrew Theosophists," *The Jewish Theosophist* 1, no. 3 (1927).
84. A similar stance was presented by some Western Jewish academic scholars who revalued Kabbalah from a neo-Romantic and Jewish national perspective. See Huss, "Qabbalah, the Theos-Sophia of the Jews," 157–60.
85. Boaz Huss, "The New Age of Kabbalah: Contemporary Kabbalah, the New Age, and Postmodern Spirituality," *Journal of Modern Jewish Studies* 6 (2007).

References

Allebach, Lila B. "Our Task as Hebrew Theosophists." *The Jewish Theosophist* 1, no. 3 (1927): 4–5.
Baer, Peter. *Geschichte, Lehren und Meinungen aller bestandenen und noch bestehenden religiösen Sekten der Juden und der Geheimlehre oder Kabbala*. Brünn: Traßler, 1822/23.
Besant, Annie. "A Message from Annie Besant to Hebrew Theosophists." *The Jewish Theosophist* 1, no. 3 (1927): 2.
Blavatsky, H. P. *The Secret Doctrine*. Theosophical Universal Press Online Edition. http://www.theosociety.org/pasadena/sd/sd1-1-11.htm.
———. *The Key to Theosophy*. London: The Theosophical Publishing Company, 1889.
Bosman, Leonard. *The Music of the Spheres*. London: Dharma Press, 1914.
———. *A Plea for Judaism*. Adyar: Association of Hebrew Theosophists, 1926.
Brydlova, Bozena. "The Ancient Kabbalah." *The Jewish Theosophist* 1, no. 2 (1926): 27–28.
———. "Why Every Jew Should Join the Association of Hebrew Theosophists." *The Jewish Theosophist* 1, no. 1 (1926): 7–8.

Buck, J. D. "The Cabbalah." *The Theosophist* 5 (1883): 44–45.
Chajes, Julie. "Construction through Appropriation: Kabbalah in Blavatsky's Early Works." In *Theosophical Appropriations: Esotericism, Kabbalah and the Transformation of Traditions*, edited by Julie Chajes and Boaz Huss, 33–72. Beer Sheva: Ben-Gurion University of the Negev Press, 2016.
———. *Recycled Lives: A History of Rebirth in Blavatsky's Theosophy*. New York: Oxford University Press, 2019.
Cohen, S. S. "Correspondence." *The Jewish Theosophist* 1, no. 1 (1926): 19.
———. "Excommunication in a Modern Synagogue." *The Jewish Advocate*, June 1931: 184–85.
Deveney, John Patrick. "D. E. de Lara, John Storer Cobb, and the New Era." *Theosophical History* 15, no. 4 (2011): 27–33.
Elton, Benjamin J. "Conservative Judaism's British Trailblazers." *Conservative Judaism* 63, no. 4 (2012): 55–76.
Ezekiel, A. D. *Introduction to the Kabalah*. Poona: A.D Ezekiel Press, 1888.
Gewurtz, Elias. "The Qabbalah." *The Theosophist* 36 (November 1914): 168–72.
Greene, Liz. *Magi and Maggidim: The Kabbalah in British Occultism 1860–1940*. Ceredigion, Wales: Sophia Center Press, 2012.
Heiman, S. I. "Correspondence." *The Jewish Theosophist* 1, no. 1 (1926): 20.
Horne, Alex. "Theosophy and Modern Judaism." *The Theosophist* 47 (April 1926): 105–6.
———. "A Glorious Opportunity." *The Jewish Theosophists* 1, no. 2 (1926): 7–8.
———. *Spiritualizing Unspiritual Judaism*. Seattle, WA: Association of Hebrew Theosophists, American Section, 1928.
Huss, Boaz. " 'The Sufi Society from America': Theosophy and Kabbalah in Poona in the Late Nineteenth Century." In *Kabbalah and Modernity*, edited by Boaz Huss, Marco Pasi, and Kocku von Stuckrad, 167–93. Leiden: Brill, 2010.
———. " 'Qabbalah, the Theos-Sophia of the Jews': Jewish Theosophists and Their Perceptions of Kabbalah." In *Theosophical Appropriations: Esotericism, Kabbalah, and the Transformation of Traditions*, edited by Julie Chajes and Boaz Huss, 137–66. Beer Sheva: Ben-Gurion University of the Negev Press, 2016.
———. "The New Age of Kabbalah: Contemporary Kabbalah, the New Age, and Postmodern Spirituality." *Journal of Modern Jewish Studies* 6 (2007): 107–25.
———. *The Zohar: Reception and Impact*. Oxford: The Littman Library of Jewish Civilization, 2016.
Kilcher, Andreas. "Kabbalah and Anthroposophy: A Spiritual Alliance According to Ernst Müller." In *Theosophical Appropriations: Esotericism, Kabbalah, and the Transformation of Traditions*, edited by Julie Chajes and Boaz Huss, 197–221. Beer Sheva: Ben-Gurion University of the Negev Press, 2016.
Lubelsky, Issac. *Celestial India: Madame Blavatsky and the Birth of Indian Nationalism*. Sheffield: Equinox, 2012.

Lev, Shimon. "Gandhi and His Jewish Theosophist Supporters in South Africa." In *Theosophical Appropriations: Esotericism, Kabbalah and the Transformation of Traditions*, edited by Julie Chajes and Boaz Huss, 245–72. Beer Sheva: Ben-Gurion University of the Negev Press, 2016.

Mulot-Déri, Sibylle. "Alte Ungenannte Tage." In *Alte unnennbare Tage*, by Friedrich Eckstein, 298–300. Wien: Edition Ateli, 1992.

Pasi, Marco. "Teosofia e antroposofia nell'Italia del primo Novecento." In *Storia d'Italia. Annali 25. Esoterismo*, edited by Gian Mario Cazzaniga, 569–98. Torino: Einaudi, 2010.

———. "Oriental Kabbalah and the Parting of East and West in the Early Theosophical Society." In *Kabbalah and Modernity*, edited by Boaz Huss, Marco Pasi, and Kocku von Stuckrad, 150–66. Leiden and Boston: Brill, 2010.

Polak, Gaston. "Appeal to Members of the T.S." *The Theosophist* 47 (April 1926): 103–4.

"Rabbi Edward L. Israel on Theosophy and the World Teacher." *The Jewish Theosophist* 1, no. 4 (1927): 28.

Samuels, Henry C. "Basic Information of the Association of Hebrew Theosophists." *The Jewish Theosophist* 1, no. 2 (1926): 8.

———. "Fighting the Light (The Story of a Modern Excommunication)." *The Jewish Theosophist* 2, no. 1 (1932): 3–4.

Sofia. "The Jewish Theosophist: A Paradox." *The Jewish Theosophists* 1, no. 1 (1926): 21–22.

Staudenmaier, Peter. "Rudolph Steiner and the Jewish Question." *Leo Baeck Institute Yearbook* 50, no. 1 (2005): 127–47.

Swartz, Karen. *Views from the Great White Brotherhood*. PhD diss., Linnaeus University, 2009.

PART II

THEOSOPHY IN LITERATURE, THE ARTS, AND POLITICS

PART II

THEOSOPHY IN LITERATURE, THE ARTS, AND POLITICS

Chapter 8

International Religious Organizations in a Colonial World

The Maha-Bodhi Society in Arakan

Laurence Cox and Alicia Turner

Introduction

Shortly after Mme Blavatsky's death in May 1891, a London correspondent for the New York *Sun* interviewed the Irishman Capt. Charles Pfoundes, who was running the first Buddhist mission in the West on behalf of the Japanese Buddhist Propagation Society (*Kaigai Senkyō Kai*), affiliated with the True Pure Land School (Jōdo Shinshū). Pfoundes was a very public critic of the Theosophical Society and its claim to represent "esoteric Buddhism," but Annie Besant's transition from secularism to Theosophy posed severe, and ultimately successful, competition to Pfoundes's mission.[1] Here is what he had to say about his competitors:

> "I apprehend," he said to the Sun correspondent, "that the theosophists will divide into several branches. First, there will be the Olcott following, and as he is entirely played out with the Hindoo and Parsee factions he must teach Buddhism. Mrs.

Research for this chapter was funded by the Canadian Social Sciences and Humanities Research Council. Our thanks to Wai Phyo Maung, who did substantial research for this piece, and to Douglas Ober and Mitra Barua for their feedback. Any mistakes remain our own.

Besant will have her clientele too. She is now miscredited with the extreme socialistic and anarchistic elements which belong to the secular party, because she is believed by them to have taken up transcendentalism. She will have a small following of spiritualists. Bertram Keightley will probably control the Adyar section, which has recently been vacated by Olcott, and his school will be Hindoo mysticism in Ceylon. The Rev. J. Bowles Daly, a former clergyman of the Established Church and a B.A. of Dublin University, who has been a sort of jackal for Olcott, will have a following whom he will feed upon Cingalese Buddhism and anti-Christian education in America. There will remain the Mark Q. Judge crowd, and opposed to them Professor Cones [Elliott Coues] and his following will represent the agnostic theosophic element.[2]

Our interest here is not with the accuracy of Pfoundes's specific predictions: many of the details were wrong, but something of the general picture did come to pass, if not as quickly as Pfoundes hoped. What this interview points to, however, is that it was entirely possible for a contemporary, moving in much the same world, to analyze the Theosophical Society as a series of emerging factions and leaderships, tied to different ideological positions and local strengths. Although in polemic moments Pfoundes was perfectly capable of inveighing against Theosophy as an essentialized unity, when he thought about it as someone who was himself part of an international religious organization, he had no difficulty in recognizing that it was not a single homogenous thing. As it might have been put in Buddhist terms, like everything else, the Theosophical Society was compounded, devoid of an essence—and hence impermanent.

It is this very compound and impermanent quality that makes the Theosophical Society of such interest today. Like Walt Whitman ("Song of Myself"), it was large, it contained multitudes—but only for a time. We touch on Theosophy whether we are researching the Irish literary revival, the origins of Buddhism in Britain, educational reform in Ceylon, Steiner/ Waldorf schooling, or the contemporary New Age. Often, in fact, it is not those who remained within the changing bounds of organizational membership and ideological orthodoxy who give it significance, but those who left individually, the organizations that split from the Theosophical Society, and those who were influenced by Theosophy without ever being members.

This chapter focuses on one such organization, the Maha-Bodhi Society,[3] which was "theosophical with a small t": founded by onetime Theosophical Society member Anagarika Dharmapala, it used many of the organizing techniques of the Theosophical Society and indeed had Colonel Olcott as its most prominent speaker. Its conception of world Buddhism, too, was at least as closely shaped by the Theosophical Society's perspective of a shared but disparate essence as it was by (for example) Orientalist views of a pristine, original Buddhism to be recovered through archaeology and scholarly work; intra-Theravadin networking processes and Buddhist Councils;[4] or Japanese attempts at exporting particular sects' versions of Buddhism.

However, at least within Buddhist Studies, research too frequently falls back into seeing such bodies as the Theosophical Society or Maha-Bodhi Society as unified wholes. We regularly tell their stories in the top-down terms of founders, texts, orthodoxy, and organizational history. Even when we are critical of the substance of these narratives, we often share this "view from the center," the view most easily found in an organization's own records and often stabilized by later generations of loyalists. It is relatively easy to do so, but to do this falls substantially short of what we should expect of ourselves in terms of the critical ways we have learned to think about religion.

To anticipate, a critical view of international religious organizations[5] is one that asks not only about the founders, but also about the other members, both individually (e.g., plebeian, women, or subaltern participants) and collectively (what networks either adopted or were formed within the organization?). It asks not just about official texts, but about what ordinary members actually said and wrote (and within official publications, which books galvanized them and which left them cold, which sections of the journal they read avidly and which they skipped over). It asks not just what the official line was, how it changed and was refined, but equally how it was challenged, what other perspectives were expressed using the official language, and how people worked with the contradictions of the ideology. Last, it asks not just how the center saw the organization develop, grow, take action, form alliances, and so on, but how this looked from the necessarily multiple perspectives of other groups within such a complex organization, held together by such loose threads.

This critical perspective may be particularly important for the period of "global Buddhism" and the globalization of other religious movements, in which international organizations were sustained across huge differences of class, race, gender, and power, and across vast geographical and cultural distances. This was primarily achieved through the comparatively tenuous medium of books and periodicals; the formal structures of committees and branches; a handful of indefatigable travelers, celebrities, and networkers; and occasional meetings and conferences. This form, perhaps, acquired such significance because it was always a fudge, a more-or-less-conscious glossing over of differences that could (mostly) be contained so long as the branch paid its dues, the center published the next issue, and there were regular visits tying all the disparate strands together. However, this relatively rigid form was filled with the *flows* that Tweed has argued we have to see as primary in a translocative theory of religion,[6] and that take center stage in our own attempts to research the first Western Buddhists in Asia and the first Buddhists in the West.[7]

This chapter introduces the Maha-Bodhi Society and sets it in the wider context of international organizations of the period. It discusses the Maha-Bodhi Society specifically as a "borning organization,"[8] a space that enabled the formation of new religious and political networks, organizations, leaderships, or ideologies in ways that often diverged substantially from their official ideologies and organizational structures. This concept, drawn from social movement studies, can of course be used to characterize Theosophy as a whole: the multiplicity of bodies that were "theosophical with a small t" is a product precisely of this phenomenon. The chapter then moves to the *Arakanese* element within the Society, in terms of its relationship with the Burman sangha, what we characterize as an "independent religious foreign policy" expressed in various parts of India, and its tensions with the parent Maha-Bodhi Society. It concludes with some reflections on how we can understand such organizations more generally.

The Theosophical and Maha-Bodhi Societies as International Religious Organizations

The late nineteenth- and early twentieth-century formation of what is sometimes called "global" Buddhism, with a dual emphasis on pan-Asian or modernist Buddhisms in Asia and the spread of Buddhisms to the West, can hardly be understood without attention to the development of new kinds of international religious organizations, from the Jōdo Shinshū's Buddhist Propagation Society to Ananda Metteyya's Buddhasasana Samagama and his Buddhist Society of Great Britain and Ireland. Such experiences were of course paralleled by other globalizing Asian religions[9] and drew on a wider background of international movements and organizations, ranging from liberal-democratic, socialist, and anarchist networks to free thought, Christian missionary, and temperance bodies.

Founded by Anagarika Dharmapala (David Hewavitarne, 1864–1933) in May 1891, the Maha-Bodhi Society was an international Buddhist organization present in many Asian countries and some Western ones. Its explicit goals included the establishment of Buddhist centers at the four traditional sites of Buddhist pilgrimage in India: the sites of the Buddha's birth, enlightenment, first preaching, and death. Given the near absence of Buddhists in India[10] and the social marginality of the Chittagong tribal Buddhists and Dalit converts of the period, these centers were intended for—and to be funded by—Buddhists outside India.

The Maha-Bodhi Society was thus organized around a new kind of Buddhist internationalism, in which India took the role of a Buddhist holy land that enabled the formation of a pan-Asian and indeed global Buddhist identity. As Dharmapala put it, echoing European nationalist formulations such as that in *Deutschland über alles*, "In all Asia from the banks of the Caspian Sea to the distant islands of Japan, from the snowy regions of Siberia to the Southern limits of the Indian Ocean the blessed influence of the Dharma spread [. . .]."[11]

As is well known, the project of asserting Buddhist presence at and control of the temple at Bodh Gaya, the site of the Buddha's enlightenment, rapidly became extremely contentious in relation to the Mahant (the incumbent priest at what had become a Hindu temple), the British authorities, and ultimately a resurgent Hinduism in which the Theosophical Society, in its Hindu turn under Annie Besant, played a role. As with other such international organizations, however, the blocking of the Maha-Bodhi Society's explicit goal enabled it to fulfill a wide range of "latent" or indirect purposes, most notably as enabling the formation of new kinds of internationally linked, lay Buddhist actors.

This period saw the rise of a new type of international organization: alongside the Theosophical Society, the Maha-Bodhi Society, and organizations such as Pfoundes's Buddhist Propagation Society we find bodies devoted to everything from temperance (the Independent Order of Good Templars) to working-class politics (the International Workingmen's Association). In terms of technological and industrial development, such organizations were made possible by cheaper and faster travel, communications, and the relative deregulation of printing (removal of taxes on printed material, some lifting of censorship). As international organizations, they were also enabled by the imperial relationships that many resisted: the increased flows of people and transport, the spread of European languages and cultural points of reference, and to some extent comparable legal and financial systems. Such organizations also have to be understood as the extension on a new scale of something analogous to what Charles Tilly called a repertoire of contention: a particular combination of modes of formal organization, public meetings and demonstrations, petitions, media statements, and so on, which he understood as having been developed in the West by the 1830s and subsequently spread via imperial relationships.[12]

Such associations shared a number of qualities, such as the capacity to form organizations that spanned continents in more than nominal ways, a focus on periodicals as a primary form of activity, and a tendency to spawn rival organizations or future networks. Perhaps their most important common feature is the fact of organizing itself—in particular, organizing on the basis of formal membership and technical equality between members (in most cases irrespective of class, gender, and race but also cutting across traditional status barriers) and doing so on a public stage, consciously attempting to recruit members. Such societies offered a new way of existing within modernity, based around a common commitment to a goal (however distant—prohibition of alcohol, Buddhist control of Bodh Gaya, socialism, the World Master). This enabled new kinds of sociability in the here and now between people from different social positions who could not have done so without this structure, often with distinctive modes of interaction, such as vegetarianism or temperance, and overlapping commitments to, for example, pacifism or women's rights.[13] This new mode of sociability both overlapped with traditional modes of organizing and enabled new possibilities for members of previously subaltern social strata.[14]

This enabled such organizations to play a powerful role. In the history of global Buddhism, the Theosophical Society and Maha-Bodhi Society were critical catalysts despite their primary purpose lying elsewhere: their journals, branches, and correspondents mapped out, but also constituted, many of the networks that became global Buddhism, so that if we are researching (for example) the formative period of Buddhism in England, we turn not only to the explicitly missionizing focus of the *Kaigai Senkyō Kai* and the Buddhist Society of Great Britain and Ireland but also to the London branch of the Maha-Bodhi Society and the Buddhist Lodge of the Theosophical Society, while Theosophical periodicals and the *Journal of the Maha-Bodhi Society* are key research tools. This point is familiar to researchers in practical terms, but here we want to tease out some implications that are not always taken fully on board.

Local Actors, Movements, and Organizations

For one thing, the process worked very differently in different places. To take one example: in Ireland, unlike many countries, Theosophy was *not* a basis for the development of Buddhism, even though Irish Theosophists abroad at times became Buddhist, and many Dublin Theosophists were as much at home in London. The Irish networks that adopted Theosophy had other fish to fry—culturally and politically—for which Buddhism would not have served them.[15] Ireland had representatives of the Maha-Bodhi Society and the Buddhist Society of Great Britain and Ireland, but other than a brief mention of money being sent for "propaganda," there is no indication that either group engaged in the kind of missionary activity that was going on in London.[16] Instead, when a Buddhist center was finally set up in Dublin for a few years from the later 1920s on, it seems to have been run in association with the Unitarian-derived Order of the Great Companions, and was set up on the initiative of reformist Asian Buddhists.[17]

Local actors, in other words, had different purposes from the main organizations, and we cannot read their politics off from the strategies of the center in any simple way—or, put another way, the unintended and indirect consequences of these organizations were as often the result of the strategies of local actors as they were of the central organizations' "mission creep." More broadly, if the new kind of organization offered unparalleled possibilities for energetic organizers such as Olcott and Besant, Dharmapala and Marx, this was in no small measure because they offered such a range of possibilities to ordinary members for organizing themselves and achieving their own purposes. New networks could be formed, cutting across existing local boundaries; things could be said and done relying on the prestige of what was still in practice mostly a fairly distant center. The interest and enthusiasm available for the wider organization was a powerful resource:

> [T]oo little attention has yet been paid to the ways in which the Maha Bodhi Society and the Theosophical Society functioned

as umbrella organizations within which a variety of local sociopolitical agenda[s] were pursued at various locations linked by these societies, or to how these organizations facilitated the travel of local Asians through port cities, travel that was undertaken for a number of reasons including commerce, intellectual exploration, the cultivation of political/activist ties, and the development of religious institutions. The diaries of Anagarika Dharmapala make very clear how crucial local involvement at each nodal point was to the movement of these societies' leaders, but also that locals associated with the Maha Bodhi Society and the Theosophical Society could pursue their own aims on a wider regional basis through connection to these trans-regional societies and their patronage arrangements that made possible travel as well as liaison with foreign visitors.[18]

As the examples of the Buddhist Theosophical Society in Ceylon[19] or the Arakanese Maha-Bodhi Society show, such aims were often those of a developing national or sub-national elite. Frost writes:

> Entrepôts like Bombay, Madras, Calcutta, Rangoon and Singapore witnessed the emergence of a non-European, western-educated professional class that serviced the requirements of expanding international commercial interests and the simultaneous growth of the imperial state. Learned elites drawn from the ranks of civil servants, company clerks, doctors, teachers, public inspectors, communications workers, merchants, bankers and (above all) the legal profession began to form themselves into intelligentsias by immersing themselves in discursive activity, and quickly developed habits of intellectual sociability that became organized and systematic. The *Bhadralok* of Calcutta, the Theosophists of Madras and the *Peranakan* (local born) Chinese reformers of Singapore, to name but three of these groups, shared similar concerns for reform and oversaw parallel campaigns for religious revival, social and educational improvement and constitutional change. Associational life and journalism flourished in this environment, both in the bureaucratic centres of the British Empire and beyond [. . .] to such an extent that one can fairly speak of a transformation in the public sphere across the Indian Ocean.[20]

Even if this point is not unfamiliar in general, we still know relatively little in most cases about the way this process worked in practice in terms of these international religious organizations and the formation of what was to become global Buddhism. One key issue is the often dramatic contrast between top-down accounts of these organizations, as they were imagined or represented from the center (by their organizational leaderships and in their periodicals, but also in metropolitan perspectives and later reception), and how they appear when viewed through the lens of the individual religious careers and local networks that at times operated through them or were stimulated by them, but can hardly be described as deriving from the core.[21]

In this context, the Theosophical Society and Maha-Bodhi Society can be thought of as "borning organizations." This is not simply a matter of the multiple goals pursued by individual actors who passed through organizations, the emergence of new organizations and networks from the parent organization, or what might be thought of as instrumental, latent, or emergent organizational goals (such as the development of future nationalist elites), but at its deepest represents a tension between "movement" and "organization," of a kind familiar from other religious contexts such as Spiritualism as well as from social movements, and which enabled the formation of new organizations from the same sociocultural milieux.

In other words, while the organization's center typically identified itself with the movement as a whole (and indeed in this period often used this language), we should not fall into the same trap. We can see how multiple movements might feed into a single organization and indeed be central to its emergence (for example, the encounter between Theosophy's international networks and reforming actors within specific Asian Buddhist milieux was often a necessary condition for new "global Buddhist" initiatives). Conversely, as is well known for the Theosophical Society, a single organization could give birth to a multiplicity of other bodies—both competing Theosophical Society organizations but also the Maha-Bodhi Society, other Buddhist organizations, the Anthroposophical Society, the Golden Dawn, and so forth—and contribute to wider movements both literary and political.[22]

We should also remember that whole movements could exist *without* substantial or effective organizations at all. Despite anarchist involvement in the First International, for example, Anderson has shown the much more informal character of the links that connected Asian and European anarchists in this period.[23] Spiritualism, too, was largely a bottom-up movement in this period[24]—arguably part of Blavatsky and Olcott's genius was to marry Spiritualism's existing focus on celebrity and periodicals to models of centralized organizing. Something similar can be said of the freethought movement, which was crisscrossed by periodicals and formal societies, but equally marked by independent discussion halls and alternative school projects.[25] At moments of split—such as the collapse of the First International—the nature of these tensions within the wider movement could reveal themselves, often contradicting the organization's own official perspective. This, of course, is another way of describing the complexities of splits, successor organizations, and networking outcomes.

Social movement theory marks this distinction by speaking of social *movements* (networks of individuals, informal groups, and formal organizations[26]) and social movement *organizations*, which form part of such movements. The extent to which an individual organization dominates a whole movement—and the extent to which movements prioritize organization—is highly variable. In our period, organization building was almost a popular pastime:

> The fashion for organizing spread well beyond Rangoon. In 1899 the western city of Akyab could boast of the presence of the Arakan Jubilee Club, the Hypocris Club, a literary society, and a half dozen others, not to mention the presence of the Young Arakanese Students' Club of Rangoon. [. . .]
> [B]y the late 1890s Buddhist organizations would eclipse all others in the number of associations, membership, and activity.
> Buddhist associations sprang up across colonial Burma in the hundreds at the turn of the twentieth century. [. . .] While some of these were large-scale organizations with branches in multiple towns, like the educational, Pali-examination, and rice-donating associations [. . .] these were well outnumbered by the local and spontaneously formed associations of lay Buddhists that peppered the small towns and villages. Associations became not just the focus of much popular attention, but the driving force behind social movement and innovation.[27]

Even where such bodies did form part of wider organizations, as we shall see, central control could be very weak by today's standards. Thus, in relation both to local branches and to independent bodies, the movement-organization tension becomes an important analytical tool for thinking beyond a single committee.

These issues can be usefully explored through studying how a local organization operated in the broad context of anti-colonial, pan-Theravada Buddhist networking, in this case the Arakanese branches of the Maha-Bodhi Society, particularly in the two decades before and after the turn of the twentieth century.

Arakanese and the Early Days of the Maha-Bodhi Society

Arakan, today's Rakhine province, had been an independent kingdom up to the late eighteenth century, when it was conquered by Burma. It was ceded to Britain less than half a century later following the First Anglo-Burmese War, and included in British Burma following the second Anglo-Burmese War in 1852. Perhaps predictably, Arakanese elites in the late nineteenth and early twentieth centuries did not always see their interests as being identical with those of Burmese Buddhists.

However, Arakan's early inclusion into the British Empire meant that it developed much more quickly in financial terms than elsewhere in Burma. Akyab (now Sittwe) quickly became a cosmopolitan port with a substantial number of Indian, Chinese, and European businessmen who expanded into Arakan in the early nineteenth century to capitalize on the growth of the new province. There was a massive increase in rice production and export from Akyab between 1825 and 1852, the profits from which not only developed the city, but also expanded the connections between Arakan and other port cities under East India Company rule. By the late nineteenth century, Akyab could boast both a multi-ethnic cosmopolitan community and the presence of a number of newspapers and journals. Moreover, there was a growing population of Arakanese businessmen in Calcutta, Arakanese working for the colonial government, and a number of young English-educated Arakanese studying at Calcutta University.

The Maha-Bodhi Society had found its origins in interactions between Olcott and Dharmapala. After Olcott's famous work among Buddhists in Ceylon and an important joint trip to Japan in the spring of 1889, Dharmapala and Olcott met with a group of Buddhist representatives from Japan, Burma, Chittagong, and Ceylon in January 1891 to originate the idea of an organization uniting Asian Buddhists. Dharmapala immediately proceeded to Bodh Gaya, where he embarked on a mission to preserve the site of the Buddha's enlightenment that would become central to the Maha-Bodhi Society,[28] while Olcott traveled through Burma, where he formulated the platform of a united Buddhist alliance.[29] Dharmapala officially formed the Maha-Bodhi Society in Ceylon in May of that year.

Despite the prominent place that Burma, Japan, and Ceylon play in this story of the move from Theosophy to the Maha-Bodhi Society, Arakanese played an important role in those early days. On his fateful first visit to Bodh Gaya, Dharmapala met another pilgrim who had much the same experience and mission. Kiripasaran, a Chittagong-born Buddhist monk who at times identified as Arakanese and Bengali, "cut his finger, making a vow to the Buddha, and a day later sold his sandals and umbrella in order to purchase oil to light the lamps at the shrine."[30] He had dedicated himself to the revival of Buddhism in Arakan and India and was working among the large community of Arakanese, Magh, and Chittagonians in Calcutta at the time. While Kemper highlights the fact that Dharmapala did not pursue the relationship with Arakanese and Chittagonians in Calcutta as much as with Bengalis because of his own elite biases, the Arakan-Chittagong-Calcutta-Bodh Gaya connection would play an important part in the early history of the Maha-Bodhi Society and Buddhist organizing in Arakan.

After founding the Maha-Bodhi Society in late 1891, Dharmapala met Kiripasaran again in Calcutta on his way back to Bodh Gaya, this time taking four Sinhalese monks to the site. It seems likely that Kiripasaran and Dharmapala took inspiration from each other's work and built a bridge between Arakanese and the nascent project of pan-Buddhist organizing.[31] But the connections had started even earlier. Six months prior in February 1891, immediately after Olcott's visit to Burma and en route to Australia, the Buddhist lay elders of Arakan, represented by U Tha Dway, had telegraphed Olcott asking him to visit and provided funds for his trip.[32] The trip had to be delayed until November 1892, but proved a watershed for Buddhist organizing in Arakan and for the Maha-Bodhi Society itself.

Even in the lead-up to this first visit, it is clear that local interests and approaches did not always perfectly ally with the visions of translocal organizing. While the more cosmopolitan elite organizers sought Olcott's presence, they insisted that Dharmapala must accompany him. As Olcott recounts in his diary,

> I have been amused in looking over my papers of that period to see the reason why. The Arakanese people had heard so much

of my work in Ceylon that they wanted me to come and help them in the same way, and wrote to that effect in strong and complimentary language, but—and this is the humorous part of the affair—as they had never had any religious dealings with a white man other than a missionary, and had never seen or heard of a white Buddhist before, their Oriental suspiciousness was excited and their leaders wrote Dharmapala that they wished him to come with me. [. . .]

"The Colonel's presence alone," writes one of our friends to Dharmapala, "would not be enough to popularise the projects of the Maha-Bodhi Society. You have to consider that our priests and laity have had no experience whatever, whether with white or European priests or Buddhists, so you have to come and tell us how faithfully and earnestly the Colonel has worked for the Buddhist movement. Our priests have power over the people in spiritual affairs, so you have to tell Colonel Olcott to embrace every opportunity for making friends with our priests." In another letter the writer thus describes the character of his people: "They are liberal and generous, they usually display their joy in outbursts of enthusiasm, devotion, energy, and generosity to the fullest extent, especially when it is a question of the interests of their country or their religion. On the other hand, they are suspicious and wary about strangers."

Their invitation having been accepted, the local Arakanese editors prepared the way with fervent articles in their English and vernacular journals after this fashion: "He is well worth hearing, and has all the ancient lore of the Buddhist religion at his fingers' ends . . . All the Poongyees (Buddhist monks) and chief priests of the town and district ought to do all they can to welcome and assist this great European High Priest of Buddhism. . . . In fact the Colonel knows more than the Brahmin High Priests about the Laws and Institutes of Manu, and all ancient Scriptures and religions of Hindustan and Burma"—which, if not at all true, is at least enthusiastic enough in all conscience, and carefully hides the "wary and suspicious" side of the national character![33]

The reversal of white privilege, clearly quite amusing to Olcott, is telling about the complexities of local trajectories of translocal projects. Whereas Olcott's white skin had been highly prized as a marker of the importance and validity of the Buddhist revival in Ceylon, here Olcott's white status was a potential threat to Buddhist revival work, marking it as foreign and illegitimate to Arakanese sangha and laity alike. They highly desired his enthusiasm and his expertise, and perhaps the connections and methods he and Dharmapala brought, but the project of Buddhist organizing in Arakan was wary of things too foreign.

The visit was carried out in November of 1892 with Olcott and Dharmapala together. They were enthusiastically received, lecturing across the province to receptive audiences and winning over the local sangha. Arakanese were apparently very receptive to the vision of the Maha-Bodhi Society, especially the project at Bodh Gaya. As Douglas Ober explains, this likely stemmed from the long history of Arakanese and Chittagonian pilgrimage to Bodh Gaya.[34] They formed a branch of the Maha-Bodhi Society, one of the earliest, as well as a ladies' auxiliary. They also donated generously during this trip. Donations of Rs 50,000 were pledged, and Olcott left Arakan with Rs 4,000 in hand.[35] It had been a Burmese donation of Rs 10,000 for missionizing work that had inspired Olcott to host the meeting that would lead to founding the Maha-Bodhi Society; in one short trip, the Arakanese had pledged five times as much. Dharmapala and Olcott were clearly impressed with the financial generosity of the Arakanese and interpreted it as a wholesale endorsement of their plans and their leadership, which as we will see may not have been completely accurate.

Shin Chandra and the Maha-Bodhi Society

While the laypeople were offering their rupees and their gold, the monks made a donation of their own that ultimately would prove equally significant. During their visit to Akyab, Dharmapala and Olcott suggested that the Arakanese should send some young monks to live in Bodh Gaya to help support the revival of Buddhism in India.

> In order to fulfill the request of their two honorable guests, monks and laymen of Sittwe promised that they would explore among monastery complexes in Sittwe and reply within seven days. On the fifth day, Dharmapala, Col. Olcott, and prominent persons in the town came to Sandimar-Rama Monastery, while

Sayadaw was teaching Shin Chandra and Shin Suriya. Laymen of Sittwe introduced their honorable guests to Sayadaw and explained the reason of their visit. Sayadaw instantly agreed to their plan with delight and asked Shin Chandra who was attending next to him if he was willing to go to Mizzima [India]. Shin Chandra had seriously considered the plan and in a brief moment he answered to Sayadaw that it would be better if his friend Shin Suriya came along with him instead of going there alone. When they asked Shin Suriya, he answered that he would go if his friend Shin Chandra went along with him.[36]

Chandra, being the Sanskrit/Pali for moon, was thus joined by Suriya, or sun, on a mission to preserve Buddhism in India and support the Maha-Bodhi Society. The two novices traveled to Calcutta with an Arakanese minor colonial official, Tha Dway, who had originally invited Olcott to Arakan, accompanied by two groups of thirty lay pilgrims. The Moon and Sun novices lived at Bodh Gaya in 1892 and 1893, and helped clean up the site and reestablish a Buddhist presence there. After attacks on Buddhists by locals in February 1893, the Maha-Bodhi Society rented a small place for them to live there, but the space proved unsuitable, and they moved to a building that had been donated by Arakanese merchants in Calcutta.[37] They eventually asked Dharmapala for permission to return to Akyab and set out for home. However, this was not to be the end of Shin Chandra's efforts in India. According to his successor:

> One day a Mandalay based newspaper featured an article entitled "*Sasana* will prosper in India" which said that "the two novices, Shin Sanda and Shin Suriya from the Sandimayama monastery, Akyab, Arakan, were now studying in India by the invitation of Mr. Dharmapala, the head of Mahabodi Society. When they become grown-ups and educated, the Sasana will shine in India as if the "Sun and Moon" appear. That is why Burmese should support Maha Bodhi Society.[38]

After seeing the news, Shin Chandra felt ashamed of his failure and return. After a discussion with the abbot and a search for new donors, he set out again for India. Shin Chandra returned to Calcutta and received an education in Sanskrit, Pali, and "modern sciences" at a monastery run by another Arakanese monk there. This did not end his interaction with the Maha-Bodhi Society; he helped Dharmapala with the 1908 legal battle for Buddhist control of Bodh Gaya, and in particular the Burmese Rest House there, by interviewing King Thibaw, the Burmese king in exile in Ratnagiri, about the history of the rest house. Nor, as we shall see, would this be the end of the Arakanese contribution to Buddhism in India.

Arakanese Networks in the Maha-Bodhi Society

Dharmapala saw Arakan as an important early base of support for the Maha-Bodhi Society, as represented in early issues of the *Journal of the Maha-Bodhi Society*. The *Journal* consistently listed Arakan representatives separately from those for Burma, while the statement of goals included the establishment at Bodh Gaya of a monastery for bhikkhus "representing the Buddhist countries of China, Japan, Siam, Cambodia, Burma, Ceylon, Chittagong, Nepal, Arakan, and Tibet."[39] Mention is made of the Buddhist flag being introduced in "Burma, Siam and Arakan";[40] Dharmapala writes proudly, "To the Buddhists of Burma, Ceylon, Tibet, Sikkim, Chittagong, Arakan and Japan I have personally delivered the great message";[41] while in more mundane mode, the advertising rates section comments, "This Journal has a circulation throughout India, Ceylon, Burma and Arakan [. . .]."[42]

This perspective was one shared by at least some Arakanese Buddhist organizers: Olcott noted on his first visit that those he met were "generous, enthusiastic, patriotic, religious, and—suspicious of foreigners."[43] A snippet in an early issue of the *Journal of the Maha-Bodhi Society* sets the tone:

BUDDHISM IN ARAKAN.

Buddhism appeared in our country during the life-time of our Lord Gautama Buddha: and it is believed that the famous image of the Lord, now in Mandalay [sc. following the Burmese conquest], was molded after His visit to the Arakanese King Srirája. There is no historical evidence to support this, and ought therefore, to be taken for what it is worth. But Buddhism was firmly established as a state religion after the third Convocation [supposedly called by Asoka, i.e. in the third century BCE]. [. . .]

> Tradition says that the Arakanese are descendants of a Colony of Kshattriyas who came to Arakan about thirty centuries ago from India.
> Since its introduction Buddhism has always remained as the national Religion.[44]

The piece was signed Kaung Hla Phru, who was assistant secretary to the Akyab Maha-Bodhi Society.[45] Similarly, we read in 1895 of one of the secretaries of the Akyab society, Tun or Htoon Chan:

> *Arakan History.*—We are informed that Mr. Tun Chan, B.A., B. L., has, in course of preparation, a history of Arakan from the most authentic sources. In order that it may be a thoroughly trustworthy and standard work of reference, Mr. Tun Chan has undertaken an immense amount of literary research.
> To write the history of one's own native land is surely a most commendable undertaking, and Mr. Tun Chan will earn the gratitude and encomiums of his countrymen for so valuable a legacy. We wish him success in his arduous undertaking.—*Arakan News.*[46]

Unsurprisingly perhaps, the Akyab Maha-Bodhi Society organizers were relatively elite figures.[47] Of Kaung Hla Pru, cited above, we subsequently read:

> Kaung Hla Pru, of Akyab, who at the commencement of the Mahá-Bodhi work rendered excellent service to the cause in Arakan, has passed the Burma Myook's [native magistrate] Examination, coming fourth in the list. We wish him all success, and trust that he would again show that energy in the furtherance of the cause.[48]

Individual donors mentioned include Dr. Moung Tha Noo, Asst. Surgeon, Akyab (Rs 50) and Moung Mra Tha Dun, Pensioned Myook, Akyab (Rs 50).[49] The *Journal of the Maha-Bodhi Society* reported that in the funeral procession of Moung Tha Noo's wife, the cortege was "preceded by a body of Police, Phongyis [bhikkhus] and Lugyis [elders]."[50] An apparently more plebeian "Lah Paw Zan, Bailiff" (Rs 10, twice[51]) turns out to be relatively well-heeled himself:

Personal.

Buddhist alms-giving.—This is the ninth year that Maung Hla Phaw Zan Bailiff, of Akyab, Arakan, in accordance with the Buddhistic spirit of liberal alms-giving, has occupied himself during the eight days cold weather vacation in feeding the Buddhist priests.[52]

Along with the historian Htoon [Tun] Chan (BA, BL), figures who appear regularly in the list of committee members/representatives[53] are Chan Htoon Aung, Advocate,[54] and U Mra U, the latter perhaps the Arakan Society's most high-status member:

U Mra U, Akunwoon, Vice-President of the Arakan Maha Bodhi Society, a most energetic, able and devoted Buddhist, has been deservedly honoured by H.E. the Viceroy and Governor-General of India, with the title of A.T.M., the highest known in Arakan.[55]

U Mra U was clearly also a very wealthy individual:

The Vice-President of the Akyab Maha-Bodhi Society, Mr. U. Mra U, A.T.M., has, according to the *Arakan News*, made his son and his grandson to enter the order of Buddhist novices. For over a fortnight Akyab has witnessed a spectacle hitherto unprecedented in the annals of the town. Feeding of Buddhist priests, giving alms to the poor, distributing Buddhist literature, &c., marked this event. The *Arakan News* says that the total expenditure has been about ten thousand rupees.[56]

Other details confirm this sense of a local educated elite. In 1895 U Mra U was an Extra Assistant Commissioner; later, perhaps, a Superintendent in the Excise Service (1922–27). By 1925 Htoon Chan had also become an advocate. He also brought out at least three editions of an "Arakanese Calendar" (by 1918) and was cited by Maurice Collis as an authority on history. Kaung Hla Pru was working in the Assistant Commissioner's Office in Akyab in 1895. Dr. Moung Tha Noo, who served as a civil surgeon combating plague and was introduced to the Prince of Wales, appeared in *Who's Who in Burma*, which gave a rundown of his family:

A.T.M. K.S.M, Civil Surgeon, (retd.) . . . Son of the late U Myat Tha Dun, 1st Grade Myook, and nephew and son-in-law of the late U Shwe Tha, I.S.O, K.S.M., A.T.M., District Superintendent of Police. . . . Prominent relations in Government Service: U Shwe Zan Aung, B.A., K.S.M., A.T.M. Deputy Commissioner and first Burman Commission of Excise, now retired, Cousin and Brother-in-law. Dr. Tha Doe, M.B., Ch.B. (Edin.) Assistant Medical Superintendent General Hospital Rangoon, Eldest son. U Hla Baw Thu, A.T.M., King's Medallist, 1911, District Superintendent of Police, now retired. Brother-in-law. U Saw Hla Pru, B.A., B.L., A.T.M., Additional Deputy Commissioner and District Magistrate, Tavoy. Son-in-law.[57]

Given these connections, it is entirely plausible that "[a]t Akyab the whole European community turned out to meet [Olcott], and the Commissioner of Arakan had a number of European gentlemen to meet him at a private dinner."[58] These well-connected and comfortably well-off Arakanese Buddhist organizers had their own agendas, which—if they coincided with Dharmapala's for a while—were hardly dependent on him in the longer term.

Arakan and Chittagong

Arakan Buddhists had long had a second point of interest in what was then India:[59] the Chittagong Hill Tracts (in present-day Bangladesh) had been a point of refuge for leading Arakanese groups following the Burmese conquest, and in the mid-nineteenth century, reformist Arakanese monks had played a leading role in the revival of Buddhism among the Barua and Chakma groups in Chittagong.[60] A Chittagong branch of the Maha-Bodhi Society had been among the first to be founded,[61] perhaps as a result of Olcott's private lecture, to "a company of Maghs (Boruahs) of Chittagong" in Akyab,[62] while later that same year Dharmapala could write, "The Bhikshus of Burmah, Siam, Japan, Arakan and Chittagong have promised to support the movement [the Maha-Bodhi Society]."[63]

There was a longer backstory: "In 1885 an excellent Buddhist Journal was started in Bengali, in Chittagong."[64] In the same issue, celebrating ten years of the Society, the *Journal of the Maha-Bodhi Society* quoted the *Indian Mirror* thus: "The revival of Buddhism in this country may be said to have commenced with the foundation of the Maha-Bodhi Society in Calcutta, although isolated bodies had been working silently to the same end *at Calcutta, Chittagong and other places*."[65] By this point, Calcutta had its own Buddhist diaspora: "There are about 2,000 Buddhists in Calcutta, natives of Arakan, Burma, Chittagong and Ceylon, and they are the only people who have no place of worship in the metropolis of the British Indian Empire."[66]

The Maha-Bodhi Society began with close connections to this milieu; this community was organized by the Arakanese monk Kiriparasan, whom Dharmapala had met in Bodh Gaya. Kemper observes that the Chittagong Maghs celebrated Wesak together with the Maha-Bodhi Society in the early years and that the Society held events at their vihara, as well as sharing Bengali patrons. However, after this initial honeymoon, Kiriparasan "showed little interest in including this community of Indian Buddhists in his efforts to recover Bodh Gaya,"[67] and he founded a separate organization, the Bauddha Dharmankur Sabha.[68]

Until the mid-1890s, the *Journal of the Maha-Bodhi Society* listed a Chittagong representative; when in 1891 the Society convened an international Buddhist conference at Bodh Gaya, the Chittagong delegates included this representative (Krishna Chandra Chowdry, listed as secretary for a "Buddhist Association") along with Girish Chandra Dewan, given as "Chakma Sub-Chief, Hill Tracts," and Amal Khan Dewan.[69] Dharmapala seems to have consciously cultivated the Chittagong chieftains: when the young Kumar Bhuvanmohan Roy came to study in Calcutta, the *Journal of the Maha-Bodhi Society* made flattering comments on his "very intelligent and amiable appearance."[70] When a couple of years later the same man, now chief, was promoted to Rajah by the British crown, the *Journal* congratulated him and noted that it "shall henceforth feel proud to call our friend a Rajah."[71]

The Arakanese Maha-Bodhi Society: Asserting Independence Through Religion?

In this period, when religious self-assertion had not yet turned fully into national independence movements, Arakanese Buddhists seem to have been pursuing something of an independent foreign policy vis-à-vis Burman Buddhism. They were early supporters of Dharmapala—indeed taking the initiative in contacting Dharmapala to invite Olcott to Akyab and "prepar[ing] the way with fervent articles in their English and vernacular journals."[72] Clearly, however, these journals were not Arakanese Maha-Bodhi Society ones but other, preexisting Arakanese periodicals.

More generally, the Society (or its individual members) already had significant organizational expertise: for example, it was able to organize for Olcott to speak before a crowd of thousands at a pagoda festival.[73] Immediate steps taken following its formation (along with the previously discussed fundraising) included setting up a ladies' auxiliary society[74] "through the perseverance of Mi Thit Sa and Mi Ngway U (the latter had been on a pilgrimage to Buddha Gaya),"[75] and shortly thereafter establishing its own journal:

> *The Arakan Maha Bodhi Society.*—Under the beautiful and appropriate name of *Bodhimandine*, the Arakan Maha Bodhi Society has started a monthly journal, the first number of which was published on the 1st of January [1893]. Started in the interest of the Burmese-speaking people, it should have a large circulation in Arakan and Burma. We wish the journal every success. Subscriptions should be made payable to Kaung Hla Pru, Assistant Secretary, Arakan Maha Bodhi Society, Akyab.[76]

As Dharmapala recognized, then, the Akyab Society had made major contributions in the early years of the Maha-Bodhi Society:

> *Arakan Maha-Bodhi Society.*—Since the beginning of the year 1893 we have received every possible support from our good brother Buddhists of Akyab. If not for the liberality of the Burmese people, I could not have carried on the great work of the Mahá-Bodhi Society with the help of Ceylon Buddhists alone, who, with commendable generosity, have given me all help since the commencement of the movement, and they have shewn the greatest devotion in contributing money to the Mahá-Bodhi Fund. I expect aid from the Burmese and Arakanese, and by the united efforts of the Buddhists of Asia, we shall again resuscitate Buddhism in India.[77]

Indeed, in 1892–1893 Arakan vied with Burma (Rs 1,272 as against Rs 1,297) for donations to the Society, far ahead of any other country.[78] This funding of course represented a connection to Colombo, but the

Akyab branch also followed through as key supporters of the Maha-Bodhi Society's move to a Calcutta base, a politically significant move given the Society's understanding of India as the Buddhist holy land, and therefore the terrain on which pan-Asian Buddhism was to come together:

> [T]he Akyab Maha-Bodhi Society contributed its share and the premises in 2, Creek Row, were engaged in December 1892. It was a meritorious work this establishment of a Buddhist headquarters in the metropolis of India. The Arakan Buddhists deserve thanks for having contributed to the Maha-Bodhi Fund.[79]

Asserting Independence from the International Maha-Bodhi Society

As with the Buddhist Theosophical Society and Theosophical Society, however, the Arakanese eventually parted ways with Dharmapala. The subscription history tells one story: after 1892/1893, no further Arakanese donations appear until 1900/01 (Rs 13), while Burma recorded substantial contributions in 1894/95, 1896/97, 1898/99, and 1899–1900 (Rs 1,101; 1,345; 930, and 773, respectively).[80] This financial silence hints at Arakanese Maha-Bodhi Society interests lying elsewhere than with the central body. It can be set against a certain flow of snippets from the Arakanese press in the *Journal of the Maha-Bodhi Society*, together with congratulatory comments on Tun Chan's Arakanese history and other personal items relating to Akyab Maha-Bodhi Society figures—suggesting perhaps a sense on Dharmapala's part that a closer alliance was still possible.

However, the undercurrent of division between Dharmapala and the Akyab branch remains. Dharmapala's report contains a reference to the Rs 4,000 donated to Olcott in 1892 as being held in trust by Arakanese members.[81] The control of funds seems to have held with it a sense of a control of agenda as well. By 1902, there was still a conflict over the money collected in 1891. Something of this is present in the article quoted above, thanking the Akyab branch for its contribution toward the Calcutta headquarters, because the article continues:

> About Rs 4,000 were deposited in the Bank of Bengal in the name of the officers of the Akyab Maha-Bodhi Society. The

> General Secretary [Dharmapala] made application to Mr. U. Mua [Mra] U., A.T.M., President, and Mr. Moung Chan Htoon Aung, Advocate, the Secretary of the Branch, requesting that this money may be allocated to either of the following: (1) to build a Dharmasala at Isispatna in Benares (2) to build a Resthouse near the railway station in Gaya for the use of Bhikkhus and pilgrims (3) to purchase a printing press for the use of the Maha-Bodhi Journal and Buddhist texts in Devanagri [sic].
>
> Although over a score of times were written to these gentlemen, no response till now of any kind was received in reply thereto. We hope the Fund is quite safe in their hands and trust that they would remit the amount for the Maha-Bodhi work in India for which it was intended.[82]

It may well be that the Akyab Buddhists did not see Benares or Buddhist publishing in Devanagari (a script few in Arakan could read) within their understanding of Buddhist revival. Such projects, like Olcott's white status, may have elicited their suspicion of the foreign. While it is clear that they continued to support the project of expanding Buddhism in India, with their support of Kiripasaran and Chandramani, it is not clear that they supported Dharmapala's leadership or the right of the central organization to decide on the use of funds. But given how Dharmapala and Olcott read the original donations as an endorsement of their efforts, this control of funds was seen by the center as a betrayal. It is not clear whether the real basis for this conflict was financial, organizational, or more politico-religious in character, but (given the status of the Akyab organizers) it is unlikely that it represented either simple embezzlement or an abandonment of interest: most likely they simply turned their interests elsewhere.

By 1904, the conflict between the two had come to a head, and Dharmapala felt justified in publicly condemning and shaming the Akyab members in comparison with other, more centrally compliant branches:

> The Akyab Maha-Bodhi Society has been requested by the President of the Maha-Bodhi Society, to remit the fund which is at present in the Bank of Bengal, Akyab, for the use of the Society's work in India. The Mandalay Maha-Bodhi Society donated Rs. 12,000 to build the Maha-Bodhi Dharmasala at Buddha-Gaya, and the Lanka Maha-Bodhi Society have contributed since 1891 over Rs. 33,000 at different times for

the work of the Society in India. The Trustees of the Akyab Maha-Bodhi Fund are the leading Buddhists of Arakan to whom several communications have been sent urging them to forward the money for paying the bills of the contractor who built the Dharmasala at Isipatana.

The fund was raised for the Maha-Bodhi work in India in October of 1892; and yet the Trustees are making every effort to appropriate the fund for their own use. For 12 years we have made every exertion to get the fund for the work in India; about a hundred letters have been written to different officers of the Society, but without any effect.[83]

While there was never a formal split between the Akyab branch and the parent Maha-Bodhi Society, it is clear that there was a divergent interpretation of purpose and tension over the control of both funds and agenda from the beginning. The center was unable to affect this process substantially. This changing balance was due in turn to the *effectiveness* of transnational organizations like the Maha-Bodhi Society (and Theosophical Society) in mobilizing local actors—who then articulated new purposes for themselves.

In particular, the Arakan Maha-Bodhi Society is an example of the new assertiveness of *lay* Buddhists (often educated and bilingual) and the articulation of new kinds of politics locally in this period. International religious (and other) organizations had disseminated the new mode of organizing very effectively throughout much of the world-system, and theosophical organizations of all kinds played a significant role in this. However, they were more effective at unleashing these new kinds of popular agency than they were at channeling it in the directions intended by the center. As Turner has written elsewhere:

> Burmese, particularly those in Rangoon and Arakan, were initially quite taken with Olcott's rhetoric and Dharmapala's efforts, creating the first branches of the Maha Bodhi Society and providing much of the early funding for the fledgling association. However, by the late 1890s, such international projects no longer held the Burmese imagination. They were overshadowed by more pressing local problems and local efforts. The internationally focused Buddhist efforts that gained longer support came from two of the earliest Europeans to ordain monks; U Dhammaloka, an Irish sailor who became a popular

preacher and reformer, railing against the threats of Christian missionaries and the dangers of drink, and Ananda Metteyya, a Scottish chemist and occult practitioner who sought to create a Buddhist mission to Europe based out of Rangoon.[84]

The Akyab Maha-Bodhi Society's interests shifted toward promoting other white Buddhists, who perhaps were easier to fit into local agendas, at least initially. In 1899 they housed the Bhikkhu Asoka (Gordon Douglas), one of the first Europeans ordained as a Buddhist monk, and after his death formed a library from his book collection. Moreover, at least one stalwart of the Arakan Maha-Bodhi Society appears in the later history of globalized Buddhism. The *Journal of the Maha-Bodhi Society* tells the tale:

A European Buddhist in Arakan

Mr. Allan MacGregor, a European Buddhist, arrived here on the 6th instant. Arrival of this gentleman was eagerly expected by Dr. Maung Tha Noo, with whom Mr. MacGregor had been in communication for some time. [. . .] It is said that this gentleman, for whom a costly silken yellow robe has already been prepared at the cost of Dr. Maung Tha Noo, is going to be ordained here as a Buddhist priest.[85]

This was Ananda Metteyya, who would go on to found the Buddhist Society of Great Britain and Ireland and send his own mission to Britain.[86] We recall that in 1895 Maung Tha Noo "is a member of the Akyab Mahá-Bodhi Society. He takes a great interest in the welfare of the movement, and was foremost in helping the formation of the Mahá-Bodhi Library." Ananda Metteyya had his own agenda in turn, and found other sponsors outside Arakan, but this ordination marks both a continuation of Arakanese commitment to Buddhist globalization and the abandonment of the Maha-Bodhi Society itself as a vehicle for such activities.

Conclusion: From Arakan to Ambedkar

The networks that constituted the Arakan Maha-Bodhi Society already had their own organizational expertise and publications, and it was they who took the lead in inviting Olcott. Through the Maha-Bodhi Society, they were able to establish links independent of the Burman Buddhist centers in Mandalay and Rangoon with the new would-be organization of world Buddhism. Arakanese Maha-Bodhi Society members were involved in establishing the international Maha-Bodhi Society's new center in Calcutta and its early activities at Bodh Gaya; these initiatives overlapped with the development of a long-standing relationship with Chittagong Buddhists and fitted into a broader perception that "Chittagongian, Magh, Arakanese, or Rakhine" constituted a single ethnic group, whether in the Calcutta diaspora's vihara, the reforming temples of Chittagong, or the lay organizations of Akyab.

This chapter has argued that this period saw the birth of a new kind of transnational religious organization. The Maha-Bodhi Society was theosophical with a small t, precisely because the significance of this organizing form went far beyond the Theosophical Society itself. Local organizers could use it to form new kinds of networks and pursue their own agendas in new ways—as the Arakanese in turn were to do with the Maha-Bodhi Society. The traditional "view from the center," focused on founders, texts, and organizational history, misses these local agendas: yet local actors, with their own purposes, were necessary if transnational religious organizations were to spread; and as the Arakanese story shows, the central organization could often exert little real control when agendas diverged. If theosophy, or the Maha-Bodhi Society, became significant, it is precisely because they were able to offer something new and valuable to local networks, for shorter or longer periods. This chapter has sought to explore something of how this interaction appears from the periphery, in a moment when theosophical organizing practices enabled the formation of new kinds of local elite networks in the contested context of Buddhist globalizing within colonial Asia.

Coda

A final twist in the tale comes with the Arakanese novice Shin Chandra, who was sent to develop the Maha-Bodhi Society presence at Bodh Gaya. Sponsored by the Arakanese merchant U Kyi Zayi on his return to India, he stayed first at "the Arakanese Maha Bodhi Society building" and later at a vihara built by U Kyi Zayi for the Arakanese-Indian monk Sayadaw Mahawira, who oversaw Shin Chandra's education. In time, Mahawira would establish a monastery in Kushinagar, one of the four Buddhist holy places in India where Dharmapala sought to establish the Maha-Bodhi Society. Shin Chandra, ordained as Chandramani in 1903, became chief abbot there after Mahawira's death. Eventually becoming the senior Buddhist monk in India, he officiated at the historical mass conversion ceremony of perhaps 500,000 Dalits to Buddhism under B. R. Ambedkar, marking a very different return of Buddhism to India.[87] If in ways no participant of the 1890s could foresee, U Chandramani's eventual career exemplifies the way in which Arakanese Buddhists appropriated the Maha-Bodhi Society's view of India as the Buddhist holy land, but ultimately asserted their own (and Dalit) agendas as the organizational vehicle of the Maha-Bodhi Society was abandoned.

Notes

1. Brian Bocking, Laurence Cox, and Yoshinaga Shin'ichi, "The First Buddhist Mission to the West: Charles Pfoundes and the London Buddhist Mission of 1889–1892," *DISKUS* 16, no. 3 (2014).

2. The report was republished in the *Virginia Chronicle* 5, no. 100 (Anonymous, "Madame Blavatsky's Successor," *Virginia Chronicle*, June 3, 1891, 5, http://virginiachronicle.com/cgi-bin/virginia?a=d&d=T18910603.1.5#).

3. There is no consistency in how "Maha-Bodhi Society" is written (not least because European diacritics were used, giving forms such as *Mahâ-Bodhi and Mahá Bodhi*). If anything, *mahābodhi* would be most in keeping with present-day anglicizations of Pali and Sanskrit. We have opted for Maha-Bodhi Society for simplicity.

4. Tilman Frasch, "Buddhist Councils in a Time of Transition: Globalism, Modernity and the Preservation of Textual Traditions," *Contemporary Buddhism* 14, no. 1 (2013).

5. Today we might say "transnational," by analogy with "transnational social movements" (see e.g. Cristina Flesher Fominaya, *Social Movements and Globalization: How Protests, Occupations and Uprisings Are Changing the World*. London: Palgrave MacMillan, 2014), but in a world that largely consisted of empires, "internationalist" meant something rather more subversive than it does in today's world, where the vast majority of states claim legitimacy as national entities, so that we typically read inter*national* as inter*state* and expect such bodies to be fairly official.

6. Thomas Tweed, "Theory and Method in the Study of Buddhism: Towards 'Translocative' Analysis," *Journal of Global Buddhism* 12 (2011); Thomas Tweed, "Tracing Modernity's Flows: Buddhist Currents in the Pacific World," *The Eastern Buddhist* 43, nos. 1/2 (2012).

7. See our collaboration with Brian Bocking in the broader "Dhammaloka Project." Alicia Turner, Laurence Cox, and Brian Bocking, *The Irish Buddhist: The Forgotten Monk Who Faced Down the British Empire*, New York: Oxford University Press, 2020; and http://dhammalokaproject.wordpress.com.

8. Charles M. Payne, *I've Got the Light of Freedom: The Organizing Tradition and the Mississippi Freedom Struggle* (Berkeley: University of California Press, 2007), 100.

9. E.g. Nile Green (2013), "Forgotten Futures: Indian Muslims in the Trans-Islamic Turn to Japan," *Journal of Asian Studies* 72, no. 3.

10. For exceptions, see Douglas Ober, "'Like Embers Hidden in Ashes, or Jewels Encrusted in Stone': Rāhul Sāṅkṛtyāyan, Dharmānand Kosambī and Buddhist Activity in Colonial India," *Contemporary Buddhism* 14, no. 1 (2013).

11. *Journal of the Maha-Bodhi Society* 7, no. 4 (August 1898): 36–37.

12. Charles Tilly, "Repertoires of Contention in Britain and America, 1750–1830," Center for Research on Social Organization working paper, University of Michigan, 1977. Perera and others have identified both the Maha-Bodhi Society and the Buddhist Theosophical Society in Ceylon as NGOs, pointing to the importance of funding from foreign, particularly Western, sources but also their religious and social service agendas: Sasanka Perera, "Non Governmental Organizations in Sri Lanka: The Dynamics, the Impact, the Rhetoric and the Politics," *Dialogue-Colombo* 25 (1999): 106. Perera, however, emphasizes the impact of Christian organizational models alone; while this is clearly important for understanding, e.g., the development of Buddhist Theosophical Society schools, we want to point to the wider development of new organizing models, transmitted not least via the Theosophical Society: see also Laurence Cox, "The Politics of Buddhist Revival: U Dhammaloka as Social Movement Organiser," *Contemporary Buddhism* 11, no. 2 (2010).

13. Leela Gandhi, *Affective Communities: Anticolonial Thought, Fin-De-Siècle Radicalism, and the Politics of Friendship* (Durham, NC: Duke University Press, 2006).

14. See Alicia Turner, *Saving Buddhism: The Impermanence of Religion in Colonial Burma* (Honolulu: University of Hawai'i Press, 2014), chapter 4 for a detailed discussion.

15. Laurence Cox, *Buddhism and Ireland: From the Celts to the Counter Culture and Beyond* (Sheffield: Equinox, 2013), chapter 4.

16. Cox, *Buddhism and Ireland*, chapter 5.

17. Laurence Cox, "Buddhism in Ireland: The Inner Life of World-Systems," *Etudes irlandaises* 39, no. 2 (2014).

18. Anne Blackburn, *Ceylonese Buddhism in Colonial Singapore: New Ritual Spaces and Specialists, 1895–1935*. Asia Research Institute Working Paper Series, no. 184 (Singapore: Asia Research Institute, National University of Singapore, 2012), 23.

19. Laurence Cox and Mihirini Sirisena, "Early Western Buddhists in Colonial Asia: John Bowles Daly and the Buddhist Theosophical Society of Ceylon," *Journal of the Irish Society for the Academic Study of Religions* 3, no. 1 (2016).

20. Mark Frost, "'Wider Opportunities': Religious Revival, Nationalist Awakening and the Global Dimension in Colombo, 1870–1920," *Modern Asian Studies* 36, no. 4 (2002): 937.

21. Indeed, for some times and places we even get the impression that a local "global Buddhist" milieu may have taken it on itself to invite Olcott or Dharmapala and constitute a Theosophical Society or Maha-Bodhi Society branch as part of its own development and self-assertion on a wider stage. However, it can be hard to identify such situations given that the records of the international organization are that much more likely to be preserved, digitized, etc.

22. There are of course methodological issues here. English- and French-language sources are more likely to have survived, to have been digitized, and to be available to researchers, while turn-of-the-twentieth-century periodicals in Asian languages often require linguistic skills beyond competence in the present-day written language. Similarly, centralized sources—the journal of an international society or a national colonial newspaper, as against the journal of a local branch or a regional newspaper—are also more likely to have survived, to be digitized and available (and, again, to be published in English or French). The fact that even colonial-language and predominantly "centralist" sources can be read against the grain to reveal much greater internal diversity and contention, and the results achieved by research programs such as those of Anne Blackburn or Yoshinaga Shin'ichi, suggests that we probably still underestimate the power of local actors and purposes. The comparison with existing work on such organizations in Britain, the United States, or Ireland (where academic resources are that much greater, and linguistic issues and source availability present fewer problems) is another helpful corrective in this regard—all, of course, tending to highlight that the self-representation of international organizational centers cannot easily be taken as an accurate reflection of reality.

23. Benedict Anderson, *Under Three Flags: Anarchism and the Anti-Colonial Imagination* (London: Verso, 2005).

24. Logie Barrow, *Independent Spirits: Spiritualism and English Plebeians* (London: Routledge and Kegan Paul/History Workshop, 1986).

25. Stan Shipley, *Club Life and Socialism in Mid-Victorian London* (Oxford: History Workshop, 1972); Paul Avrich, *The Modern School Movement: Anarchism and Education in the United States* (Oakland, CA: AK Press, 2005 [1980]).

26. Mario Diani, "The Concept of Social Movement," *Sociological Review* 40, no. 1 (1992).

27. Turner, *Saving Buddhism*, 76.

28. Steven Kemper, *Rescued from the Nation: Anagarika Dharmapala and the Buddhist World* (Chicago: University of Chicago Press, 2015), 186–93.

29. Henry Steel Olcott, *Old Diary Leaves*, vol. IV (1895), 266–82, online at http://www.minhtrietmoi.org/Theosophy/Olcott/OLD%20DIARY%20LEAVES%204.htm; Stephen Prothero, *The White Buddhist: The Asian Odyssey of Henry Steel Olcott* (Bloomington: Indiana University Press, 1996), 127–29.

30. Kemper, *Rescued from the Nation*, 207. Mitra Barua's work on the complex constructions of ethnic and national Buddhist identities in Chittagong and Arakan sheds greater light on the politics of Buddhist identification in this period. D. Mitra Barua, "Thrice Honored Sangharaja Saramedha (1801–82): Arakan-Chittagong Buddhism Across Colonial and Counter-Colonial Power," *Journal of Burma Studies* 23, no. 1 (2019).

31. For a fuller discussion of Kiripasaran's background and contributions, see Douglas Fairchild Ober, "Reinventing Buddhism: Conversations and Encounters in Modern India, 1839–1956" (PhD diss., The University of British Columbia, 2016), chapters 4 and 5.

32. Olcott, *Old Diary Leaves* IV, 287. This may be the same U Tha Dwe as the Extra Assistant Commissioner who helped write Burmese Buddhist law in Akyab (Andrew Huxley, "Three Nineteenth-Century Law Book Lists: Burmese Legal History from the Inside," *Journal of Burma Studies* 13 [2009]); if so, the Burmese and Arakanese stories are much more closely intertwined. However, further research is needed to demonstrate the identity of the two U Tha Dwe/Dways.

33. Olcott, *Old Diary Leaves* IV, 482–84.

34. Ober, "Reinventing Buddhism," 123–25.

35. Olcott, *Old Diary Leaves* IV, 508–9.

36. Aye Thein, *Naingna akyo pyu apo kan yadana myo* (Yangon: Gone tu sape, 2007), 97–98. Translation by Wai Phyo Maung.

37. Hari Bala Kushinayone [Sayadaw Nyanissara], *Mizzima-daytha-tharthana-phyu-a-tayay-akyone* [Missionary Experiences in Majjhimadesa] (Yangon: Pyinnya Alin pya sarpay, 1993), 73–83. Cf. Aye Thein, *Naingna akyo pyu*, 96–102. For more on the status of this building and competitions between different Buddhist groups in Calcutta, see Ober, "Reinventing Buddhism."

38. Kushinayone, *Mizzima-daytha-tharthana-phyu*, 72. Translation by Wai Phyo Maung.

39. E.g., *Journal of the Maha-Bodhi Society* 1, no. 7 (November 1892): 1.

40. *Journal of the Maha-Bodhi Society* 1, no. 9 (January 1893): 3.

41. *Journal of the Maha-Bodhi Society* 2, no. 10 (February 1894): 4.

42. E.g., *Journal of the Maha-Bodhi Society* 3, no. 4 (August 1894).

43. Olcott, *Old Diary Leaves* IV (November 1892), 503.

44. *Journal of the Maha-Bodhi Society* 1, no. 5 (September 1892): 7.

45. *Journal of the Maha-Bodhi Society* 1, no. 10 (February 1893): 1.

46. *Journal of the Maha-Bodhi Society* 4, no. 5 (September 1895): 33.

47. This is true at least so far as they can be traced, which may be circular.

48. *Journal of the Maha-Bodhi Society* 4, no. 12 (April 1896): 100.

49. *Journal of the Maha-Bodhi Society* 2, no. 3 (July 1893): 8.

50. "Dr. Moung Tha Noo is a member of the Akyab Mahá-Bodhi Society. He takes a great interest in the welfare of the movement, and was foremost in helping the formation of the Mahá-Bodhi Library." *Journal of the Maha-Bodhi Society* 4, no. 3 (July 1895): 23.

51. *Journal of the Maha-Bodhi Society* 1, no. 11 (March 1893): 8.

52. *Journal of the Maha-Bodhi Society* 3, nos. 10/11 (February–March 1895): 77.

53. These three also appear as part of the initial welcoming committee for Olcott's founding visit: *Lucifer*, vol. 11, no. 65 (January 1893), reprint from the *Arakan News*: 427.

54. He was still in this position in 1925: Anglo-Burmese Library, "Thacker's Directory 1925—Akyab," transcribed and published 2011, http://abldirectories.weebly.com/1925-akyab.html.

55. *Journal of the Maha-Bodhi Society* 1, no. 10 (February 1893): 3. "(1) Ahmitdan gaung Tazeik-ya Min (meaning 'Recipient of a Medal for Good Service'), indicated by the letters A.T.M. after the name much as the Companionship of the Bath in England is indicated by the letters C.B." Sir Roper Lethbridge, *The Golden Book of India: A Genealogical and Biographical Dictionary of the Ruling Princes, Chiefs, Nobles, and other Personages, Titled or Decorated, of the Indian Empire* (London: Macmillan, 1893), xii.

56. *Journal of the Maha-Bodhi Society* 3, nos. 10/11 (February–March 1895): 75.

57. *Who's Who in Burma, under the Distinguished Patronage of H.E. Sir Harcourt Butler, Governor of Burma: A Biographical Record of Prominent Residents of Burma with Photographs & Illustrations* (Calcutta: Indo-Burma Publishing Agency, 1927), 166.

58. *Lucifer*, vol. 11, no. 65 (January 1893), 428.

59. Swapna Bhattacharya, "A Close View of Encounter between British Burma and British Bengal" (Paper to 18th European Conference on Modern South Asian Studies, Lund, 2004).

60. Barua, "Thrice Honored Sangharaja Saramedha." The Arakan-trained Chittagong native bhikkhu Saramitra/Saramedha Mahasthavir had moved to Chittagong and was beginning to purify monastic practices there by 1864. His students were present in Calcutta at Kiriparasan's *Dharmankur* vihara (Kemper, *Rescued from the Nation*, 274). Paul Williams, *Buddhism: The Early Buddhist Schools and Doctrinal History: Theravada doctrine*, vol. 2 (London: Taylor and Francis, 2005). See also Bhattacharya, "A Close View of Encounter," 13.

61. *Journal of the Maha-Bodhi Society* 1, no. 2 (June 1892): 1.

62. Olcott, *Old Diary Leaves* IV (November 5, 1892), 501.
63. *Journal of the Maha-Bodhi Society* 1, no. 6 (October 1892): 7.
64. *Maha-Bodhi and the United Buddhist World* 10, nos. 8/9 (December 1901–January 1902): 76. (This is the new title of the *Journal of the Maha-Bodhi Society*.)
65. Ibid., 72, our emphasis.
66. *Journal of the Maha-Bodhi Society* 3, nos. 10/11 (February–March 1895): 86. Douglas Ober notes that, in fact, the vast majority of these 2,000 Buddhists listed in the census were Chinese and not of South or Southeast Asian origin.
67. Kemper, *Rescued from the Nation*, 29.
68. Ibid., 208; Ober has written much more extensively on this conflict. Ober, "Reinventing Buddhism," 170–77.
69. *Journal of the Maha-Bodhi Society* 1, no. 12 (April 1893): 4.
70. *Journal of the Maha-Bodhi Society* 3, nos. 10/11 (February–March 1895): 75.
71. *Journal of the Maha-Bodhi Society* 6, nos. 3/4 (July–August 1897): 17.
72. Olcott, *Old Diary Leaves* IV (September 1892), 483.
73. *Lucifer*, vol. 11, no. 65 (January 1893), reprint from the *Arakan News*, 428.
74. This is the first report of a separate women's Buddhist association in Burma for this period. Turner, *Saving Buddhism*, 180n17.
75. *Journal of the Maha-Bodhi Society* 1, no. 9 (January 1893): 1, citing the *Arakan Echo*.
76. *Journal of the Maha-Bodhi Society* 1, no. 10 (February 1893): 1.
77. *Journal of the Maha-Bodhi Society* 3, no. 12 (April 1895): 91.
78. *Maha-Bodhi and United Buddhist World* 10, nos. 8/9 (December 1901–January 1902): 81.
79. Ibid., 78. Arakanese sources mention an early Maha-Bodhi Society building in Calcutta funded entirely by local Arakanese businessmen, perhaps preceding the Creek Row building.
80. *Maha-Bodhi and United Buddhist World* 10, nos. 8/9 (December 1901–January 1902): 81.
81. Anagarika Dharmapala, *Report of the Maha Bodhi Society, From 1891 to 1915* (Calcutta: Maha Bodhi Society, 1915), 12–13.
82. *Maha-Bodhi and United Buddhist World* 10, nos. 8/9 (December 1901–January 1902): 78. This parallels an earlier complaint along similar lines leveled at the Mandalay Maha-Bodhi Society (*Journal of the Maha-Bodhi Society* 7, no. 3 [July 1898]: 20).
83. *Maha-Bodhi and United Buddhist World* 13, nos. 7/8 (November/December 1904): 1.
84. Turner, *Saving Buddhism*, 18.
85. *Maha-Bodhi and United Buddhist World* 10, nos. 8/9 (December 1901–January 1902): 71.

86. John L. Crow, "The White Knight in the Yellow Robe: Allan Bennett's Search for Truth" (MA thesis, University of Amsterdam, 2009); Elizabeth Harris, *Ananda Metteyya: The First British Emissary of Buddhism. The Wheel*, vols. 420–22 (Kandy: Buddhist Publication Society, 1998).

87. Chan Khoon San, *Buddhist Pilgrimage* (Kuala Lumpur: Majujaya Indah, 2009); Himanshu Prabha Ray, "Creating Religious Identities: Buddhist Monuments in Colonial and Post-Colonial India," *Transforming Cultures eJournal* 3, no. 2 (2008).

Journals Consulted

Journal of the Maha-Bodhi Society (1892–1901) continued as *Maha-Bodhi and United Buddhist. World* (1901–) Calcutta.
Lucifer (1887–1897) London.

References

Anderson, Benedict R. *Imagined Communities: Reflections on the Origin and Spread of Nationalism.* Rev. and ext. ed. London: Verso, 1991.

Anglo-Burmese Library. "Thacker's Directory 1925—Akyab." Transcribed and published 2011. http://abldirectories.weebly.com/1925-akyab.html.

———, ed. "Civil List for Burma–1st. Sept. 1942." Published 2014. http://www.ablmembersarea.com/uploads/6/1/8/9/6189761/civil_list_1942.pdf.

Anonymous. "Madame Blavatsky's Successor." *Virginia Chronicle*, June 3, 1891, 5. http://virginiachronicle.com/cgi-bin/virginia?a=d&d=T18910603.1.5#.

Avrich, Paul. *The Modern School Movement: Anarchism and Education in the United States.* Oakland, CA: AK Press, 2005.

Barrow, Logie. *Independent Spirits: Spiritualism and English Plebeians.* London: Routledge and Kegan Paul/History Workshop, 1986.

Barua, D. Mitra. "Thrice Honored Sangharaja Saramedha (1801–82): Arakan-Chittagong Buddhism Across Colonial and Counter-Colonial Power." *Journal of Burma Studies* 23, no. 1 (2019): 37–85.

Bhattacharya, Swapna. "A Close View of Encounter between British Burma and British Bengal." Paper to 18th European Conference on Modern South Asian Studies, Lund, 2004.

Blackburn, Anne. *Locations of Buddhism: Colonialism and Modernity in Sri Lanka.* Chicago: University of Chicago Press, 2010.

———. *Ceylonese Buddhism in Colonial Singapore: New Ritual Spaces and Specialists, 1895–1935.* Asia Research Institute Working Paper Series, no. 184. Singapore: Asia Research Institute, National University of Singapore, 2012.

Bocking, Brian, Laurence Cox and Yoshinaga Shin'ichi. "The First Buddhist Mission to the West: Charles Pfoundes and the London Buddhist Mission of 1889–1892." *DISKUS* 16, no. 3 (2014): 1–33.

Bocking, Brian, Laurence Cox, and Alicia Turner. *A Buddhist Crossroads: Pioneer Western Buddhists and Asian Networks, 1860–1960*. London: Routledge, 2014.

The Budh-Gaya Temple Case. Calcutta: W. Newman & Co., 1895.

Chan Khoon San. *Buddhist Pilgrimage*. Kuala Lumpur: Majujayah Indah Sdn. Bdh, 2009.

Collis, Maurice S. "Arakan's Place in the Civilization of the Bay: A Study of Coinage and Foreign Relations." *Journal of the Burma Research Society* 15 (1925): 34–52.

Corea, J. C. A. "One Hundred Years of Education in Ceylon." *Modern Asian Studies* 3, no. 2 (1969): 151–75.

Cox, Laurence. "The Politics of Buddhist Revival: U Dhammaloka as Social Movement Organiser." *Contemporary Buddhism* 11, no. 2 (2010): 173–227.

———. *Buddhism and Ireland: From the Celts to the Counter Culture and Beyond*. Sheffield: Equinox, 2013.

———. "Inventing Buddhist Modernism: Repertoires in Transition." Paper to Jinbunken Institute for Researches in Humanities, Kyoto University and Research Centre for Buddhist Cultures in Asia, Ryokoku University joint conference "Asian Buddhism: Plural Colonialisms and Plural Modernities," December 12–14, 2014.

———. "Buddhism in Ireland: The Inner Life of World-systems." *Etudes irlandaises* 39, no. 2 (2014): 161–72.

Cox, Laurence, and Mihirini Sirisena. "Early Western Buddhists in Colonial Asia: John Bowles Daly and The Buddhist Theosophical Society of Ceylon." *Journal of the Irish Society for the Academic Study of Religions* 3, no. 1 (2016) 108–39.

Crow, John L. "The White Knight in the Yellow Robe: Allan Bennett's Search for Truth." MA thesis, University of Amsterdam, 2009.

Dharmapala, Anagarika. *Report of the Maha Bodhi Society, From 1891 to 1915*. Calcutta: Maha Bodhi Society, 1915.

Diani, Mario. "The Concept of Social Movement." *Sociological Review* 40, no. 1 (1992): 1–25.

Fahey, David M., ed. *The Collected Writings of Jessie Forsyth, 1847–1937: The Good Templars and Temperance Reform on Three Continents*. NY: Edwin Mellen, 1988.

Flesher Fominaya, Cristina. *Social Movements and Globalization: How Protests, Occupations and Uprisings are Changing the World*. London: Palgrave MacMillan, 2014.

Frasch, Tilman. "Buddhist Councils in a Time of Transition: Globalism, Modernity and the Preservation of Textual Traditions." *Contemporary Buddhism* 14, no. 1 (2013): 38–51.

Frost, Mark. "'Wider Opportunities': Religious Revival, Nationalist Awakening and the Global Dimension in Colombo, 1870–1920." *Modern Asian Studies* 36, no. 4 (2002): 937–67.

Gandhi, Leela. *Affective Communities: Anticolonial Thought, Fin-De-Siècle Radicalism, and the Politics of Friendship*. Durham, NC: Duke University Press, 2006.

Green, Nile. "The Making of Muslim Networks in Japan, c. 1890–1940." Paper to Jinbunken Institute for Researches in Humanities, Kyoto University and Research Centre for Buddhist Cultures in Asia, Ryūkoku University joint conference "Asian Buddhism: Plural Colonialisms and Plural Modernities, December 12–14, 2014."

Harris, Elizabeth. *Ananda Metteyya: The First British Emissary of Buddhism*. The Wheel. Vols. 420–422. Kandy: Buddhist Publication Society, 1998.

———. *Theravada Buddhism and the British Encounter: Religious, Missionary and Colonial Experience in Nineteenth-Century Sri Lanka*. London: Routledge, 2006.

Huxley, Andrew. "Three Nineteenth-Century Law Book Lists: Burmese Legal History from the Inside." *Journal of Burma Studies* 13 (2009): 77–105.

Kemper, Steven. *Rescued from the Nation: Anagarika Dharmapala and the Buddhist World*. Chicago: University of Chicago Press, 2015.

Kushinayone, Hari Bala [Nyanissara, Sayadaw]. *Mizzima-daytha-tharthana-phyu-a-tayay-akyone* [Missionary experiences in Majjhimadesa]. Yangon: Pyinnya Alin pya sarpay, 1993.

Leider, Jacques. "Politics of Integration and Cultures of Resistance: A Study of Burma's Conquest and Administration of Arakan (1785–1825)." In *Asian Expansions: The Historical Experiences of Polity Expansion in Asia*, edited by Geoff Wade, 184–213. London: Routledge, 2014.

Lethbridge, Sir Roper. *The Golden Book of India: A Genealogical and Biographical Dictionary of the Ruling Princes, Chiefs, Nobles, and Other Personages, Titled or Decorated, of The Indian Empire*. London: Macmillan, 1893.

Malalgoda, Kitsiri. *Buddhism in Sinhalese Society, 1750–1900: A Study of Religious Revival and Change*. Berkeley: University of California Press, 1976.

Marx, Karl. *The First International and After: Political Writings vol. 3*. London: Penguin/New Left Books, 1974.

Ober, Douglas. "'Like Embers Hidden in Ashes, or Jewels Encrusted in Stone': Rāhul Sāṅkṛtyāyan, Dharmānand Kosambī and Buddhist Activity in Colonial India." *Contemporary Buddhism* 14, no. 1 (2013): 134–48.

———. "Reinventing Buddhism: Conversations and Encounters in Modern India, 1839–1956." PhD diss., The University of British Columbia, 2016.

Payne, Charles M. *I've Got the Light of Freedom: The Organizing Tradition and the Mississippi Freedom Struggle*. Berkeley: University of California Press, 2007.

Perera, Sasanka. "Non Governmental Organizations in Sri Lanka: The Dynamics, the Impact, the Rhetoric and the Politics." *Dialogue-Colombo* 25 (1999): 104–24.

Prothero, Stephen. *The White Buddhist: The Asian Odyssey of Henry Steel Olcott.* Bloomington: Indiana University Press, 1996.

Ray, Himanshu Prabha. "Creating Religious Identities: Buddhist Monuments in Colonial and Post-Colonial India." *Transforming Cultures eJournal* 3, no. 2 (2008): 145–67.

Shipley, Stan. *Club Life and Socialism in Mid-Victorian London.* Oxford: History Workshop, 1972.

Swearer, Donald K. "Lay Buddhism and the Buddhist Revival in Ceylon." *Journal of the American Academy of Religion* 38, no. 3 (1970): 255–75.

Thein, Aye. *Naingna akyo pyu apo kan yadana myo* [Jeweled city of the nation]. Yangon: Gone tu sape, 2007.

Tilly, Charles. "Repertoires of contention in Britain and America, 1750–1830." Center for Research on Social Organization working paper, University of Michigan, 1977.

Tollenaere, Herman de. "The Politics of Divine Wisdom: Theosophy and Labour, National and Women's Movements in Indonesia and South Asia, 1875–1947." PhD diss., Catholic University Nijmegen, 1996.

Turner, Alicia, Laurence Cox, and Brian Bocking. *The Irish Buddhist: The Forgotten Monk who Faced Down the British Empire.* New York: Oxford University Press, 2020.

———. "Beachcombing, Going Native and Freethinking: Rewriting the History of Early Western Buddhist Monastics." *Contemporary Buddhism* 11, no. 2 (2010): 125–47.

Turner, Alicia. *Saving Buddhism: The Impermanence of Religion in Colonial Burma.* Honolulu: University of Hawai'i Press, 2014.

Tweed, Thomas. "Theory and Method in the Study of Buddhism: Towards 'Translocative' Analysis." *Journal of Global Buddhism* 12 (2011): 17–32.

———. "Tracing Modernity's Flows: Buddhist Currents in The Pacific World." *The Eastern Buddhist* 43, nos. 1/2 (2012): 1–22.

Who's Who in Burma, under the Distinguished Patronage of H.E. Sir Harcourt Butler, Governor of Burma: A Biographical Record of Prominent Residents of Burma with Photographs & Illustrations. Calcutta: Indo-Burma Publishing Agency, 1927.

Williams, Paul. *Buddhism: The Early Buddhist Schools and Doctrinal History: Theravada Doctrine.* Vol. 2. London: Taylor and Francis, 2005.

Yoshinaga, Shin'ichi. "Theosophy and Buddhist Reformers in the Middle of the Meiji Period: An Introduction." *Japanese Religions* 34, no. 2 (2009): 119–31.

Chapter 9

Euro-Asian Political Activist and Spiritual Seeker

Paul Richard and Theosophy

Hans Martin Krämer

Introduction

In its heyday, the Theosophical Society, and the Theosophical movement more broadly, lent expression to a great number of voices far exceeding those of their direct membership. As the most prominent esoteric organization around the turn of the twentieth century, it attracted many people looking for alternative worldviews into its vicinity. Even though many of these individuals may not have shared the core convictions of the Theosophical movement, it still played a crucial role in bringing them together and making them visible to the wider world.

One of these non-Theosophists whose prominence would not have been possible without Theosophy was Paul Richard (1874–1967), a key figure both in the esoteric circles of the early twentieth century and in the contemporary anti-colonial movement. Richard was on intimate terms with several high-profile figures during the 1910s and 1920s. He accompanied Rabindranath Tagore on the latter's first trip through Japan in 1916.[1] Mohandas Gandhi parted from Richard as the "best of friends" when they attended the Indian National Congress in Ahmedabad in 1921.[2] Having an apparent weakness for past and future Nobel Prize winners,[3] Richard also befriended Romain Rolland and Albert Schweitzer during the

1920s.[4] Another prominent close friend of his was the Japanese thinker Ōkawa Shūmei, the only civilian to be placed on the defendants' bench at the International Military Tribunal for the Far East, better known as the Tokyo Trial, after the end of World War II. Richard himself was deemed important—and dangerous—enough for the secret police services of no fewer than three nations—France, Britain, and Japan—to observe and exchange information about him.

And yet today the man has been almost completely forgotten. Academic scholarship on him is virtually nonexistent.[5] Both his prominence during the 1910s and 1920s and his later obscurity may actually have the same explanation: namely, his blend of religion and politics, which was attractive to his contemporaries at the time of World War I but is irritating within the framework of historiographical paradigms regarding modern history. This blending of religion and politics was also a prominent feature of the Theosophical Society at the time, and it is no coincidence that Richard was involved with the Society in the early 1920s, just as he had undoubtedly been inspired by it ever since coming into contact with esoteric circles in Paris in the 1900s.

Both Richard and the Theosophical Society are representative of a configuration of religion and politics that present a challenge to what one might call the methodological secularism inherent in most current humanities and social-science scholarship dealing with the first decades of the twentieth century. The following account of Richard's life and works in his early years (mostly in Europe), the years that saw the peak of his prominence (mostly in Asia), and the period of his involvement with Theosophy therefore focuses on how political activity and spiritual quest were not just two different sides to Richard's personality, but were intimately intertwined and reinforced each other. I conclude by attempting to elucidate how Richard's encounter with Theosophy amplified this particular blend of the political and the religious.

1. Early Life and Political Activism

Paul Antoine Richard was born in southern France in 1874. Although he studied Protestant theology and became a minister of the Reformed Church in Lille in 1900, he seems to have been more interested in social reform than in taking care of the spiritual needs of his congregation, and was thus in constant conflict with the church authorities until he left the ministry three years later, in 1903. He then took up law, receiving his degree in either 1907 or 1908. In the meantime, he had joined the leftist "Ligue française des droits de l'homme et du citoyen" and had undertaken a study trip to a French penal colony in French Guiana, the French possession on the Northern coast of South America, about which he wrote a very critical report. It is also possible that he ran (unsuccessfully) in the French General Elections in 1906.[7] Richard became a barrister (avocat à la cour d'appel) in Paris in 1908 and joined the "Ligue de Défense et de Propagande Républicaine Radicale et Radicale-Socialiste" in 1910.[8] From 1911 to 1914, he also worked for the progressive Paris daily newspaper *L'Aurore*, a representative organ of anti-colonialist, anti-militarist, and internationalist movements in France before the Great War.[9]

Indeed, anti-colonialism was to occupy a position at the heart of Richard's politics. Biographically, this was due to his experiences in French Guiana in 1904/05, but even more so because of his exposure to India. At that time, France had a colony in India consisting of several smaller territories, the most populous of which was in Puducherry (Pondichéry) in Southeast India. This colony had a seat in the French parliament, and Richard went to Puducherry in 1910 to support a candidate in the elections.[10] When he returned to Puducherry in 1914, he would even run for the representative seat himself, although he was soundly defeated. During his first trip, in 1910, Richard met Aurobindo Ghose (1872–1950), the revolutionary activist for Indian independence. Aurobindo had fled to Puducherry to elude the persecution of the British colonial government. He had already spent a year in prison for his involvement in an assassination attempt on a British official and was being sought because he had published an inflammatory article. Ever since this encounter, colonial independence for Asia, and first and foremost India, was very much on Richard's mind.

This did not remain undetected by the authorities. In February 1915, the British Government of India wrote the following in a memorandum on "Seditious Conspiracy in India":

> Paul Richard, to whose association with Arabindo Ghose I have referred in previous reports, has been ordered by the French Government to leave Pondicherry and return to France to serve as a reservist. The real reason of the order is that he has made himself obnoxious to the Governor by his association with political refugees and his anti-British intrigues.

Paul Richard's main object in coming to Pondicherry was to stand for election as Deputy. He enlisted all the extremists on his side and canvassed Pondicherry and Karikal vigorously with their assistance. His election speeches were socialistic and violently anti-British. [. . .] During his stay in Pondicherry he has been in daily association with members of the extremist party, in particular with Arabindo Ghose, with whom he collaborated in the production of the [journal] *Arya*.[11]

Objections by Richard against his forced removal from India were futile, and he was ultimately compelled to leave the country. His political attention now fully focused on Asia, he did not remain in France for long, but took up residence in Japan from 1916 to 1920. Again, the authorities were quick to identify him as a dangerous individual. The Japanese foreign office filed an observation report on him dated December 1916, which described Richard as closely involved with the movement for Indian independence:

He is in regular contact with Indians both in India and abroad, and in order to achieve Indian independence as quickly as possible, he sees the necessity to establish his base in the Far East. With this in mind, he left India and, experiencing a degree of suppression by the British government, arrived in Yokohama in June of this year [1916]. [. . .] Since then, his actions are under strict surveillance, and he has been in contact with the socialists Ōsugi Sakae[12] and Miyajima Nobuyasu[13] as well as Hari Prasad Shastri,[14] the Indian we already reported about earlier.[15]

While Richard's personal association with Japanese socialists could not be corroborated by evidence from any other sources,[16] there are other hints that radical politics were high on his agenda. James Cousins, an Irish poet who taught English Literature at Keiō University in Tokyo in 1919 and 1920 and frequently met with Richard,[17] reminisced in 1950:

I recall a conversation, partly in Japanese, partly in English, that tried to be highly anglicised but only succeeded in being Japanised pidgin, a conversation in the drawing-room of Paul and Mi[r]ra Richard, at whose home in the suburbs of Tokyo

I was a frequent visitor. Politics were then at the top of the conversational bill among people who trusted one another to keep confidences intact. I was regarded as one such, I don't know why. On that occasion I heard more socialism talked than I had done since my early twenties, when I was a devotee of Robert Blatchford with his spicy weekly paper, "The Clarion."[18]

Richard and Cousins also cooperated in the production of the English-language *Asian Review* in 1919 and 1920, a sister journal to *Ajia jiron*, the organ of the radical pan-Asianist society, Kokuryūkai.[19] While the articles he wrote for the English-language journal were comparatively tame, several openly pan-Asianist articles of his were published in *Ajia jiron*, such as one on Japan's role in fighting against racism in international relations,[20] and another on the need to establish a federation of Asian nations.[21] The Japanese police observation report from December 1916 continued:

Recently, the suspect said to someone as follows: "In India, revolutionary thoughts are spreading everywhere. There is no way Britain will be able to suppress them, no matter what means they will resort to. It is thus a matter of humaneness to release these Indians from the British yoke. And there is absolutely no other way but to rely on Japanese help in order to realize this. [. . .] There are 200 million people in India, but due to British oppression they are not allowed to carry weapons, not even the smallest knife. This kind of control really overshoots the mark. The first question to resolve before a revolutionary movement can take off is thus that of importing weapons and ammunition. Currently, this can only be achieved by Japan. Right now, in the middle of the Great War in Europe, is the best opportunity for this. This is why I came to Japan to persuade the Japanese people and office-holders and to ask for their help."[22]

While we have no other evidence that Richard really came to Japan to canvass for arms for India, he certainly made no secret of his ideas regarding Japan taking a leading role in the task of liberating Asia from the yoke of Western colonialism and imperialism. He attempted to drum up support for this aim during numerous talks he gave while in Japan and in a series of books, articles, and pamphlets he authored. The best-known of these was *To Japan*, published in a quadrilingual edition in 1917, with his original French, English, and Chinese translations as well as a Japanese rendition by Ōkawa Shūmei.[23] In this work, Richard addressed Japan as "a liberator of nations" and stated:[24] "Debtor of Asia, take pride in returning to her nations, a hundredfold increased, all that they gave to thee. In exchange for the old lessons of these masters now slaves, return to them their freedom, the mastery of themselves."[25]

Richard certainly was not just speaking figuratively, as he made abundantly clear: "Liberate and unify Asia; for Asia is thy domain. Asia is thy field of action and, if needed, thy field of war; thou knowest it well."[26] In the end, Richard saw Japan "at the head of a free federation of Asia,"[27] as he explained more explicitly in a work published in 1920 during the last year of his stay in Japan:

> Awaken Asia! [. . .] Awaken Asia by organising her, by uniting her. And to that end, be not masters, but allies of her peoples. Cease you also to cherish against them prejudices of race. Treat them as brothers, not as slaves. Those who are slaves liberate that they may become your brothers. Form with them a single family. Organise the League of Nations of Asia—the United States of Asia.[28]

Richard certainly struck a chord with an important section of the Japanese elite. Although at that time "virtually unknown in the West, Richard became a celebrity in Japan. In 1919–1920 it would probably have been difficult to find well-educated Japanese who did not recognize his name."[29] After leaving Japan in 1920, Richard's main focus returned to India, and he did not stop at empty theorizing. Richard stayed with Mohandas Gandhi for a few days in December 1921, while also attending a session of the Indian National Congress and giving a lecture in Ahmedabad containing his "Message of India."[30] He also had a brief dispute with Gandhi over the future course of the non-violence movement, publicized in the newspaper *Young India* in early 1922.[31]

In the evidence presented so far, Richard appears as a politically minded individual who was active in various movements, especially the anti-colonial movement in India. He also had a clear idea of the role Japan should play in international politics, an idea that he tirelessly put forth during his four-year stay in that country. This picture of Richard is not exactly wrong, but it is certainly incomplete. One hint at the missing dimension can be seen in the biographical synopsis of Aurobindo Ghose given above. The year 1910, when Richard met Aurobindo, also marked the latter's increasing turn away from politics and toward spirituality. When in prison in 1908 and 1909, Aurobindo had had a spiritual experience, and when Richard met Aurobindo in Puducherry in 1910, the latter was not just hiding there from the British, but also beginning to become known as a yogi. Indeed, he was later (in 1926) to open an ashram in Puducherry. The reason Richard sought him out in the first place was not because of Aurobindo's politics, but because he had come to India "to meet some Yogis there if possible and wanted some one [sic!] to direct him."[32]

Richard, however, had not begun his spiritual quest in 1910, but rather much earlier. Neither was he to give it up during his period of political activity. Instead, the two dimensions were intertwined, and each can only fully be explained by reference to the other.

2. Paul Richard as a Spiritual Seeker in Asia

As already mentioned above, Richard had studied Protestant theology and worked as a parson for three years. Although he quit the ministry in 1903, he never stopped searching for the spiritual fulfillment the Reformed Church of France apparently could not give him. The first alternative route Richard sought out that we know of was that of a Masonic Order. We have conflicting evidence concerning the date he joined, but it may have been in 1905.[33] Richard himself later reminisced that he became a member "in the mistaken belief that some worthwhile secret knowledge would be vouchsafed to me," but "withdrew just before reaching the final thirty-second degree."[34]

Around 1907 or 1908, Richard, perhaps already disillusioned by Freemasonry, joined a branch of the Mouvement Cosmique in Paris. This movement had been founded around 1900 by Max Théon, an occultist teacher residing in Tlemcen, Algeria. Boaz Huss has characterized the goals of the Cosmic Movement as follows:

> The Cosmic Movement claimed to restore the lost perennial wisdom, the "cosmic tradition," which antedated all religions, and united and harmonized science and theology. The declared

objectives of the Movement were to improve the state of humanity and to demonstrate to the "psycho-intellectual" human being the true object and aim of life and the extent to which human capacities could be developed. The Cosmic Movement aspired to spiritualize humanity, and raise it to a higher level, teaching that through evolution, human beings could achieve a state of complete immortality. Spiritual practices played an important role in the Movement.[35]

Richard's "growing interest in esoteric, mystical and occult subjects"[36] drew him to this group. Another member of the group from 1905 onward was Mirra Morriset, née Alfassa. Mirra visited Tlemcen for the first time in 1906,[37] but when she went there for the second time in 1907, Richard was also there.[38] Richard soon left the circle of Max Théon, but he moved in with Mirra, who was later (in 1911) to become his second wife. More than anything else, it was Mirra's "untiring encouragement"[39] that propelled Richard's interest in spirituality, and it was also she who prompted him to write his first two books in this area. In 1911, the 300-page *L'Éther vivant et le Réalisme supra-nerveux* was published as part of the series *Bibliothèque de synthèse philosophique* in Paris. Three years later, Richard published another 300-page book simply titled *Les Dieux*.

In *Les Dieux*, written between his two trips to India in 1910 and 1914, Richard aims at overcoming the dualism between rational knowledge of nature and intuitive knowledge of self, in other words, between science on the one hand, and religion and philosophy on the other, which had already been the central goal of his first book, *L'Éther vivant*.[40] The attempt to "combine the findings of both experimental science and the occult sciences" had been strategically central to all occultist endeavors since the second half of the nineteenth century, in that it served to "demonstrate the emptiness of materialism,"[41] which was indeed one of Richard's foremost goals.

In their estrangement from each other, writes Richard in *Les Dieux*, both sides suffer. Religious "belief is merely the laziness of the intellect, which does not want to follow the heart into its profound experience," while the scientific negation of the metaphysical is "nothing but the laziness of the heart refusing to elevate its inner faculties, to exercise its proper organs of perception."[42] By contrast, the "complete human" (l'homme intégral) thinks rationally and transcendentally at the same time.[43] This new thought, however, cannot reveal itself wholly in just one of our verbal syntheses, in just one of our theoretical definitions. One needs all religions, all dogmas, all morals, all philosophies, and all teachings by all masters in order to furnish the idea [of the new thought] with the multiple elements of its complete manifestation.[44]

Richard was quite serious when he was speaking of "all religions," "all philosophies, and all teachings by all masters." Around the same time he was writing *Les Dieux*, he was also compiling "a selection of some two thousand passages from the sacred texts of the major religions."[45] This selection was later published in several installments in *Arya*, the journal that Richard and Aurobindo began to coedit in Puducherry from 1914 onward (see below) and that was published in book form in 1922, under the title *The Eternal Wisdom*.[46] Examples attesting to the eclecticism of this work are contained in the chapter "Contemplation," which includes quotations from *Buddhacarita*, Laozi, *The Imitation of Christ*, *Bhagavad-gita*, *Laws of Manu*, Dharmapada, Confucius, Ramakrishna, Baha-Ullah, *The Book of Golden Precepts*, *Kathna-Upanishad*, and Giordano Bruno.[47] In other chapters, Richard also included excerpts from modern Western authors such as Voltaire, Kant, or Schopenhauer, as well as Egyptian, Mexican, and Druidic authors.

Yet the study of the available wisdom of mankind was only one pillar on which the "new thought" Richard developed in his 1914 *Les Dieux* was to rest. The other was meditation, through which one "opens the secret doors of knowledge" and "develops ignored faculties." In other words, Richard sought to combine the external knowledge of things that science could achieve with the internal knowledge open through Spiritualist means:

> Accordingly, he [the complete human] will unify the knowledge of inner causes and the disciplines of methodical introspection, of intuitive investigation, with the exterior knowledge of things and the means of superficial experimentation.[48]

Les Dieux was published shortly before Richard set out for India for the second time, now accompanied by his wife, Mirra. In Puducherry, Richard not only engaged in political action, but also tried to work productively with Aurobindo's yogic teachings by fusing them with insights based on his Western philosophical training. The result was the publication of the journal *Arya*. As Aurobindo somewhat self-ironically commented later (in a letter to Dilip Kumar Roy in 1934), he had merely seen himself as a poet and politician until 1914, and it was only Richard's idea for *Arya* that had made him into a philosopher.[49] The journal had the following program:

> The Review will publish:
> - Synthetic studies in speculative Philosophy.
> - Translations and commentaries of ancient texts.
> - Studies in Comparative Religion.
> - Practical methods of inner culture and self development.[50]

Although Richard was cut off from his Indian sources of wisdom while in Japan from 1916 onward, he certainly did not cease to publish spiritual texts. More precisely, none of the books and articles he authored during this period has a purely spiritual focus, such as *Les Dieux* or some of his later works such as his 1921 *The Scourge of Christ*. Instead, he typically combined the calls for spiritual and political liberation in his works of this period. This can best be shown by going back to the two works already quoted above.

One of those works quoted from was *The Dawn over Asia*, in which Richard writes: "Awaken Asia! [. . .] Awaken Asia by organising her, by uniting her." This passage, without the ellipsis, in fact reads as follows: "Awaken Asia! Awaken her in two ways. For your work must be double: at once material and spiritual. Awaken Asia by organising her, by uniting her."[51] This is Richard's *basso continuo* in his works from the late 1910s. Echoing what he wrote in *Les Dieux* on the relationship between science and religion, any political action, according to Richard, is meaningless without the accompanying appropriate spiritual attitude. Because of India's superior spirituality, for instance, the country must become a nation independent from the morally degenerate Europe. Japan's leading role in Asia, too, had a religious grounding, writes Richard:

> Land loved by the Gods, they too are reconciled in thee. While everywhere their religions interchange malediction, thy benevolent cults, instead of excluding complete each other: one being that of the divine immanence, of the One in all, in space where move the living forces of nature, in time where dwell the ancestors, living too; and the other that of the transcendence, of all in one, beyond time and space, in the eternal repose of the supreme benediction. [. . .] And around them,

in the shelter of their benevolence, other religions may come to raise their altars, to be pacified, perhaps purified at this contact. And as thou hast received in the past the religion of the Orient, thou receivest to-day that of the Occident [. . .] But was it not necessary that all, meeting thus, should learn to form together, in unity, the more perfect religion of the future. [. . .] As it is in thee that they assemble, so it is from thee that they await their possible synthesis of harmony, their festival of light, O child of the Sun![52]

Richard here picks up on the Orientalist trope of Japanese religious syncretism,[53] but, unusual for his time, he reverses its negative evaluation and rather sees in it the positive reconciliation of religions. Richard's conflation of politics and religion is perhaps most curious where militant political rhetoric blends with religious hyperbole drawing on biblical language, such as toward the end of *To Japan*:

This voice is the voice of the Lord of thy work. He will accomplish this work with thee, but he can also accomplish it without thee, against thee. To the Lord of the Nations who to-day tills this earth to found there the Kingdom of his Justice, what nation could long offer resistance? He advances amidst the peoples, and his Judgement precedes him. Vanquished already are those who resist him; victors from now are those who fight with him. [. . .] Hail to thee [i.e., Japan], warrior, in whom salute each other the archangel of Force and the archangel of Peace.[54]

While these words already had a somewhat exhortative tone to them, they were still infused more with hope for than with anxiety about Japan's foreign policy. The balance tipped somewhat during his stay in Japan, when worries regarding Japanese imperialism came to outweigh his hopes for Japan as the liberator of Asia from Western colonialism. In this, Richard's development paralleled that of Tagore, whose stance toward Japan also changed markedly between his first and second visits to that country in 1916 and 1924, respectively.[55]

After Paul and Mirra Richard departed from Japan and returned to India in 1920, Paul's contacts with Japan never broke off, but his attention was, again, increasingly absorbed by Indian affairs. His personal life took an abrupt turn when he separated from Mirra, who was to stay on at the

Aurobindo ashram, eventually becoming the center of veneration there as "The Mother." Paul Richard cut all contacts with her, and indeed the ashram has later mostly disavowed Richard's spiritual or formative role for Mirra before 1920. Yet this was not the end of Richard's spiritual quest.

One further facet of this was indirectly visible in his stopping at Haifa, Palestine, on his way back to Europe from India in 1922. Although we do not know for sure, it is likely that he stopped there to visit the center of Bahaism, if not to pay a visit directly to Abdul Baha ('Abdu'l-Bahá, born 'Abbás Effendí, 1844–1921). Baha had only died in November 1921, and Richard may not have been aware of his death. The two had met twice, in 1911 and 1913, and Baha was impressed enough to issue one of his tablets, with which he attempted to spread his faith, to Richard in 1914. Also, the two Richards were in very close contact with a follower of the Bahá'í Faith in the 1910s. This was the Irishwoman Dorothy Mary Hodgson, who accompanied the Richards to Japan in 1916, remained in Tokyo with the Richards all throughout their sojourn in Japan, and returned with them to India. She then chose to stay on with Mirra in Aurobindo's ashram, where she is today known as Datta.[56]

3. Paul Richard and Theosophy

Paul Richard was not a member of the Theosophical Society, nor did he subscribe to Theosophy openly at any time of his life. In fact, Sri Aurobindo argued that this was an advantage of the Richards in a letter from 1914:

> Richard is not only a personal friend of mine and a brother in Yoga, but he wishes like myself, and in his own way works for a general renovation of the world by which the present European civilisation shall be replaced by a spiritual civilisation. In that change the resurrection of the Asiatic races and especially of India is an essential point. He and Madame Richard are rare examples of European Yogins who have not been led away by Theosophical and other aberrations. I have been in material and spiritual correspondence with them for the last four years.[57]

Yet, Theosophy being the strongest presence in the occultist-esoteric field of the early twentieth century, Richard was certainly exposed to and influenced by it rather heavily, a fact that is documented by both his life and his writings, even though rarely acknowledged by himself explicitly.

This is particularly evident if one considers how Richard did not privilege one religion over another, even though Christianity remained preeminent in Richard's mind, and presented a strong universalist framework, in which truth was sought within a multitude of teachings. This is obvious in the eclectic makeup of *The Eternal Wisdom*, with its quotes from traditions all over the world, as well as in *Les Dieux*. The various religious traditions of the Orient had always been a center of gravity in occultist writings. When Helena Blavatsky's *Isis Unveiled* (1877) moved "the idea of a 'primordial wisdom,' with Egypt and India as the primary centers, [. . .] into the center of attention,"[58] she thus made an eclectic choice that was not unprecedented. It was Blavatsky's synthesis, however, and the later physical move of the Theosophical Society to India, that proved to have a tremendous impact in the late nineteenth and early twentieth centuries on anyone interested in the occult, including Richard.[59] Or, as Yoshinaga Shin'ichi has put it, with reference to Richard:

> The process of compiling a work by extracting from old and new, Western and Eastern religion, philosophy, and thought is a method that may be called a staple of modern esotericism such as Theosophy, as can be seen in the works of Blavatsky.[60]

Richard himself acknowledged his awareness of Theosophy as early as 1910. When he wrote his first book, he was certainly aware of Theosophy as one spiritual way *en vogue* in the circles he frequented around that time: "So, I began my first book, entitled *The Living Ether*. It was highly colored by the Theosophical and spiritualist ideas which were popular at the time."[61] It seems that Richard had already seen a connection between his first spiritual teacher, Max Théon, and Helena Blavatsky, a connection that was probably fictitious, but that was alleged by Mirra Richard.[62]

When Richard first came to India in 1910, he paid a visit to the headquarters of the Theosophical Society in Adyar, where he "was introduced to Annie Besant and her protegé [Jiddu] Krishnamurti."[63] Although in hindsight (that is, after having met Aurobindo), Richard downplayed the significance of this visit, it is entirely possible that, given the relative proximity of Adyar to Puducherry (around 140 km) and the prominence of the Theosophical Society in Europe, Richard had Adyar in mind when he originally agreed to leave for Puducherry from Paris. Another indirect connection is through James Cousins, his close collaborator in Tokyo in 1919/20. Cousins had been called to Adyar by Annie Besant to edit the journal *New India* in 1915 and even cofounded a Tokyo chapter of the Theosophical Society in February 1920.[64] Indeed, the Richards were identified as Theosophists only a few weeks after their arrival in Japan. On May 31, 1916, they met the playwright Akita Ujaku, who was at that time busy spreading the Bahá'í Faith in Japan. Akita described Richard as a "Theosophist, having just come through India, who talked about Swedenborg and Anna [sic!] Besant,"[65] although we find no other clear evidence of Richard referring to the Theosophical Society during his four-year sojourn in Japan.

It is more difficult to find direct evidence of Theosophical tenets or even influences in Richard's thought, as manifested in his writings. Certainly, one could see in the program of *Arya*, quoted above, parallels to the three official objectives of the Theosophical Society, as formulated in their final version in 1896:

1. To form a nucleus of the Universal Brotherhood of Humanity, without distinction of race, creed, sex, caste or colour.

2. To encourage the study of comparative religion, philosophy and science.

3. To investigate unexplained laws of Nature and the powers latent in man.[66]

The latter two items closely parallel the program of *Arya* and Richard's more general interests, that is, the study of both comparative religion, broadly conceived (i.e., including philosophy), and of "practical methods of inner culture and self development," in the words of the *Arya* program.

Richard certainly had at least a limited knowledge of Theosophy by the early 1910s, after first meeting Aurobindo, but before becoming involved more deeply with him in 1914. He had read the works of Blavatsky, as evidenced by his quoting from the *Book of Golden Precepts* in his *The Eternal Wisdom*, which he put together during this period. Richard categorized the work as belonging to the tradition of Buddhism, although it was actually made up by Blavatsky, who wrote "that it is a work given to mystical students in the East."[67] Richard quoted the work as saying: "Silence thy thoughts and fix all thy attention on the Master within whom thou seest not yet, but of whom thou hast a presentiment." This is a slightly altered quote from Fragment I ("The Voice of the Silence") of Blavatsky's *The Voice of the Silence, Being Chosen Fragments from the "Book of the Golden Precepts,"* where she writes: "Silence thy thoughts and fix thy whole attention on thy Master whom yet thou dost not see, but whom thou feelest."[68] The differences in wording, especially between "to feel" and "to have a presentiment" as well as "thy Master" and "the Master," can most likely be explained through the possibility that Richard drew upon the French translation of *The Voice of the Silence*, published in 1899 (*The Eternal Wisdom* was originally written in French and then translated into English by Aurobindo).[69]

The Eternal Wisdom was conceived as several books (only the first of which was published), each consisting of different sections. The titles of Book I and II read "The God of All: The God Who Is in All" and "The Discovery and the Conquest of the Divine in Oneself," respectively, while one of the sections read "The Conquest of Self." In other words, not only is the inner divinity of humans, a staple of the modern esoteric tradition,[70] a central premise of this work, but techniques for accessing this divine within, stressed in the Theosophical Society since the ascent of Annie Besant,[71] were also crucial for Richard's program.

Somewhat surprisingly, inner divinity plays no role in *Les Dieux*, the monograph that Richard wrote around the same time he collected the aphorisms for *The Eternal Wisdom*, even though the monograph was obviously devoted to the very question of divinity. Instead, in *Les Dieux*, the divine is to be found not within, but among humans, especially the weak and small.[72] Only a few chosen among humans are divine (Richard calls them "the great servants"), and in the end, only one chosen among them ("the servant of servants") becomes the focus of Richard's argument. One can see here, on the one hand, that the social question was still very much on Richard's mind, and indeed the question of theodicy overshadows the whole book. On the other hand, his interest is still very much with Christianity, as can be seen by his focus on the idea of one savior. Indeed, his struggle with Christianity would not leave him throughout his spiritual quest.[73]

Yoshinaga Shin'ichi has argued that an indirect, but strong, connection between Richard's thought and that of the Theosophical Society may be detected in the writings he authored during his stay in Japan. When Richard spoke of the "Lord of the Nations" in his 1917 *To Japan* (see above), Yoshinaga suggests that he was not just thinking in abstract terms of the sort of messianic figure common in esoteric thought, but rather that he was thinking in concrete terms of the "world teacher" Krishnamurti, whom he had, after all, met personally in 1910.[74] Given the vague character of Richard's description of the "Lord of the Nations," his generally universalistic approach eschewing association with a particular faith or school, and lack of further references to Krishnamurti during his entire stay in Japan, however, it seems somewhat unlikely that Richard specifically had Besant's protégé in mind when writing his exhortatory address to the Japanese nation in 1917.

Richard was perhaps most strongly drawn toward Theosophy in the period between his separation from Mirra in 1920 and his return to Europe in 1922. In fact, we know that he headed to Adyar after he left Mirra in Puducherry in November 1920, before secluding himself in a village at the foot of the Himalayas.[75] Over the course of these months, he published several pieces in bona fide Theosophical journals. In the 1921 volume of *The Herald of the Star*, published by Jiddu Krishnamurti between 1912 and 1927, Richard published a poem, which painted an apocalyptic scene of a world inhabited by humans, Gods, *asuras*, demons, and titans.[76] A month later, a longer letter by Richard, ostensibly written to the Order of the Star in the East, was published in the same journal. In the letter, Richard described his own quest as "[h]aving been, for these last fifteen years, all over the world, in search of divine men for the Divine Work."[77] He saw that it would be necessary to downplay religious differences in this work: Richard regarded different gurus—such as Abdul Baha, Aurobindo, or Krishnamurti—as avatars of the divine, as reincarnations of "Christs, Buddhas, and Krishnas," his goal being to "associate them in a collective divine body" and to achieve "synthesis, harmony, unity—in religion first."[78] While this was intended as a point of admonition to the adherents of Krishnamurti not to isolate themselves from other movements with similar goals, Richard saw the Order of the Star in the East as sharing his goal of a unity of religion and politics:

> This Association of Avataras—this manifestation of the Supreme in a collective body—in a spiritual family of human gods—that is the new thing which has been until now impossible, but which should now become possible and will be tried. And this new thing is but the beginning of greater ones. For this Union of Divine Men, this unity of divine thoughts is the first step towards the unity of man—a step more decisive and efficient than covenants of presidents and kings of this earth. [. . .] A League of Asia—a new civilisation of Asia, as the cradle of this superman—an international *ashram*, for the chosen ones of all races and religions, as the centre of this New Asia—these are but the minor points of this Grand Realisation.[79]

At around the same time, Richard composed a longer poem for *The Theosophist*, the flagship journal of the Theosophical Society, founded in 1879 by Blavatsky and published in Bombay and Adyar. The poem contained the vision of a new god that will transcend all currently worshipped gods and will come with a new virtue; also important, however, is the social revolution the new age of this new god will bring about:

> Every time you see, in this world, the great ones becoming little ones surpassing the great, the Prince becoming vagabond and the vagabond king of souls and prince of peoples, recognise there the new Spirit of the ancient Buddha. [. . .] But now, when, in this world, you will see rising from the most tormented the purest song of joy, from the most despised and downtrodden raying out the greatest love, and from the most accursed the greatest benediction [. . .] Recognise there the Spirit of the new God—His new Virtue![80]

Richard's contributions to these two openly Theosophical journals did not contain anything that one would characterize as specifically part of the Theosophical worldview. Yet he still consciously sought Theosophical circles as an audience for airing his own thoughts, apparently seeing at least a basic compatibility.

Indeed, instead of speaking about a specific influence of Theosophy on Richard's thought and action, we might rather think of a broad convergence of historical processes. Richard's writings and deeds fall within a general trend of the times exemplified, pioneered, and popularized by Theosophy, the success of which after 1880 had "changed the fragmented esoteric landscape into a more or less coherent discourse."[81] The focus on comparative religion with a practical, universalist aim, not quite leaving behind spiritism and the goal of developing some inner dormant faculties of individuals, while at the same time not neglecting the dimension of social reform[82] or even outright politics, was certainly a trademark of the Theosophical movement. The Theosophical movement did intense preparatory work along these lines; that is, it made the concern with science that had always been characteristic of Spiritualists a foremost priority, also turning the study of religion itself into a science. At the same time, this scientific study of religion entailed a new and serious orientation toward the East. Both trends were popularized in Europe by the Theosophical movement around the turn of the twentieth century, and this popularization in turn made possible the encounter of someone like Paul Richard with occultist circles in Paris in the first decade of the twentieth century. Furthermore, the connection established in Theosophy between esotericism, science, and the need to experience and study the East was also crucial for Richard, who lived this connection in a particularly meaningful way, adding to it the anti-colonial impetus he also shared with Theosophy. Having come all this way, it may have seemed natural to him to briefly cooperate with the Theosophical Society in the early 1920s, even though he was soon to abandon that cooperation.

Conclusion

Anti-colonial movements have been among the most studied topics in the historiography of modern Asia. Their treatment has, however, usually been limited to political history, and if their ideological underpinnings have been scrutinized, the focus has frequently been on left-wing political thought.[83] Religion has more or less naturally vanished from the field of vision of such a historiography. This is perhaps more true of Japan or China than of India, where the connection between nationalism and religious ideologies has been more marked.

Nonetheless, the tendency to isolate the two factors intellectually can also be seen in South Asia. The Indian historian S. Srinivasachari, who acted as interpreter during the first encounter between Richard and Aurobindo, later reminisced:

> [Paul Richard] told me that he took interest in occult matters much more than in politics which in the present instance had offered him a chance to visit India and he would consider his purpose achieved if he could come into contact with persons who are engaged in Mystic practices seriously and would not regret much his failure in this election.[84]

While it may have been the case that Richard was not overly interested in the election of 1910, this should not be construed to imply a general indifference to politics. Yet, just as political history tends to ignore religious factors, religious studies approaches tend to downplay the political factor. Politics is somehow seen as not genuine when dealing with someone or some group that is supposed to be a religious actor, just as religion is seen as illegitimate in the conduct of politics.

In the case of Richard, and indeed most of his network, however, the relationship between politics and religion was constitutive of their thought and actions. Richard thought that political independence for India was only possible if India could also assert its spiritual independence. The latter, in turn, was India's (and by extension Asia's) most important asset. By contrast, European civilization was thoroughly discredited in Richard's mind, especially since the watershed moment of World War I. In fact, Europe had vanquished any legitimate right for spiritual leadership long ago, as Richard's frustration with Christianity as it existed in European church institutions showed. A civilization that had lost its spiritual foundation, however, also could claim no right to lead politically. The only possible counterweight to a Europe on the downswing was Japan, idealized by Richard as spiritually superior and a potentially benevolent leader of Asia. As one of the handful of scholars working on Richard today has written: "Richard's despair over the decline of Western civilization was linked to his Theosophical [!] convictions that only the East could save mankind."[85]

While this fusion of spiritual and political arguments may seem obscure in the political landscape of today, it was actually very attractive in the early twentieth century, as becomes most obvious if one considers the success of one of Richard's interlocutors, namely the Nobel prize winner Rabindranath Tagore, whose political arguments and views on Asia closely resembled those of Richard.[86]

Occidental criticism of the occident based on a rejection of materialism was, of course, not entirely new by Richard's time. Historian Suzanne Marchand has stressed the "emergence [around 1900] of an avantgarde cultural pessimism [in Germany] that called into question the West's cultural superiority";[87] events in East Asia, and specifically Japan's victory in the Russo-Japanese War of 1905, "offered opportunities for engagements with new kinds of 'otherness' for those weary of other forms of alterity, and sick of bourgeois culture at home."[88] Tracing the genealogy of such modes of criticism back even further, the literary historian Rita Felski has described how such movements had already formed toward the end of the nineteenth century and turned toward Spiritualism and the orient as the supposed authentic source of spirituality. The political associations of earlier esoteric movements, however, had been purely domestic, and the fusion between political activities focused on the liberation of Asia from colonialism and spirituality of the esoteric type is more typical of the 1910s and 1920s.

The Theosophical Society under Annie Besant is a good example of this trend. Indeed, Theosophy is mentioned by Felski as an example of the turn toward the orient, although she does not explore its political dimension in the twentieth century.[89] Both the Theosophical Society and Paul Richard (as well as other prominent figures such as Tagore) were part of a powerful global movement of the 1910s and 1920s, namely, anticolonialism, and they both imbued it with a spiritual twist. Theosophy is relevant when researching Paul Richard not because he was a card-carrying member, but because of the structural similarities based in global trends that both shared. Theosophy was one trend that crucially informed the thinking of people like Richard, Aurobindo, Tagore, or Ōkawa Shūmei, whom Yoshinaga Shin'ichi has called "religious intellectuals."[90] Put differently, ideas put forward within the institutional frameworks of Theosophy were attractive to a broad base of people, not only its followers in the narrow sense. Richard shared many of these ideas, and he in turn proved to be attractive for a vast network of people without ever becoming a truly central figure of that network.

Notes

1. Stephen N. Hay, *Asian Ideas of East and West: Tagore and His Critics in Japan, China, and India* (Cambridge, MA: Harvard University Press, 1970), 126.

2. Mohandas Gandhi, *The Collected Works of Mahatma Gandhi, Volume 22: December 1921–March 1922* (New Delhi: Ministry of Information and Broadcasting, Government of India, The Publications Division, 1966), 461.

3. Gandhi was supposed to receive the Nobel Prize in Peace in 1948 but was assassinated before that decision could be formally reached and announced.

4. He corresponded with Rolland in 1921 and visited him several times in 1924 and 1925. See Romain Rolland, *Inde: Journal 1915–1943* (Paris: Albin Michel, 1960), 27–28, 54–58, 78–79, 99. Richard's connection to Albert Schweitzer could not be verified beyond Richard's claims that he had a conversation with him in 1928. See Michel Paul Richard, *Without Passport: The Life and Work of Paul Richard* (New York: Peter Lang, 1987), 103.

5. There is one article in Japanese (Yoshinaga Shin'ichi, "Ōkawa Shūmei, Pōru Rishāru, Mira Rishāru: aru kaikō," *Maizuru kōgyō kōtō senmon gakkō kiyō* 43 [2008]), a very brief introduction to Richard's life and work in English (Christopher W. A. Szpilman, "Paul Richard: To Japan, 1917, and *The Dawn over Asia*, 1920," in *Pan-Asianism: A Documentary History, Volume 1: 1850–1920*, ed. Sven Saaler and Christopher W. A. Szpilman [Lanham: Rowman & Littlefield, 2011]), and a brief appearance in the Indologist Stephen N. Hay's book on Rabindranath Tagore (*Asian Ideas*). To my knowledge, no other academic publication exists that

would even mention Richard. The *Dictionary of Gnosis & Western Esotericism* does not include Richard in its "Index of Persons," despite encompassing more than 4,000 entries. Richard's wife is taken up under her maiden name, Mirra Alfassa.

6. Unless noted otherwise, all biographical information is taken from the memoirs that Richard left behind unpublished, which were expanded and edited by his son Michel Paul Richard. See Richard, *Without Passport*. Further details of his biography have been elucidated by Yoshinaga Shin'ichi (see "Ōkawa Shūmei," 95–98).

7. Peter Heehs, "Archival Notes: In Pondicherry—1910 and After," *Sri Aurobindo: Archives and Research* 12, no. 2 (1988): 199. This is uncertain. A list of all candidates for the general elections of 1906 does not give a "Richard" as a candidate in any of the nine electoral districts of the city of Lille. See Géo Behaime and Edouard Tonnier, *Tableau des élections générales législatives des 6 et 20 mai 1906* (Paris: Georges Roustan, 1906), 53–54. Two Richards (no first names given) are listed as defeated candidates for the districts Chalon-sur-Saône (ibid., 65) and Epinal in the Vosges (ibid., 86).

8. Heehs, "In Pondicherry," 200. The latter probably refers to the "Parti républicain, radical et radical-socialiste," founded as the first political party in France in 1901.

9. Heehs, "In Pondicherry," 113. *L'Aurore* ceased publication in 1914.

10. Richard himself in his memoir claims that he traveled to India to stand for election himself, but that the elections were then canceled: "all plans for the election had changed" (Richard, *Without Passport*, 55). This is certainly not true, but in 1910 Richard campaigned for the candidate Paul Bluysen, who was to prove victorious. See Heehs, "In Pondicherry," 200–1.

11. Quoted in: "Documents in the Life of Sri Aurobindo: Sri Aurobindo, the Mother and Paul Richard 1911–1915," *Sri Aurobindo: Archives and Research* 13, no. 1 (1989): 111.

12. (1885–1923), head of the Japanese anarchist movement, killed by military police in 1923.

13. Also known under the name Miyajima Sukeo (1886–1951), well-known Japanese anarchist.

14. Hari Prasad Shastri (1882–1956), in Japan from 1916 to 1918, was a teacher of yoga and Buddhism. See Anthony Dunne and Richard Bowen, "Trevor Pryce Leggett, 1914–2000," in *Britain & Japan: Biographical Portraits*, vol. 4, ed. Hugh Cortazzi (London: Japan Library, 2002), 325–27. Ōkawa Shūmei claims to have met Richard first at a lecture by Sāstrī in Tokyo in October 1916. See Yoshinaga, "Ōkawa Shūmei," 97.

15. Document from the Diplomatic Archives of the Ministry of Foreign Affairs of Japan. Gaikō shiryōkan, Gaimushō kiroku, Taishō-ki, 1-mon seiji, 6-rui sho-gaikoku naisei, 3-kō Yōroppa, sono ta, 2-gō Kakkoku naisei kankei zassan, folder 2-21-1: "Eiryō Indo no bu kakumeitō kankei (bōmeisha o fukumu)," 749–50.

16. There appears to be no mention at all of Richard in publications by Ōsugi or Miyajima.

17. On Cousins, see the contribution by Hashimoto Yorimitsu to this volume.

18. James Henry Cousins and Margaret E. Cousins, *We Two Together* (Madras: Ganesh, 1950), 352.

19. For more details on the cooperation between Cousins and Richard on this journal, see Hashimoto Yorimitsu, "Airurando shinchigakuto no Ajiashugi? Jeimuzu Kazunzu no Nihon taizai (1919–1920) to sono yoha," in *Ajia o meguru hikaku geijutsu/dezain-gaku kenkyū: Nichiei-kan ni hirogaru 21-seiki no chihei*, ed. Fujita Haruhiko (Ōsaka University, 2013), 31–34.

20. Paul Richard, "Jinshu-teki sabetsu teppai mondai to Nihon kokumin no tenshoku," *Ajia jiron* 3, no. 4 (1919).

21. Paul Richard, "Mazu Ajia renmei o jitsugen seyo," *Ajia jiron* 3, no. 5 (1919). Cousins later had second thoughts about whether he and Richard were truly helping the cause of the anti-colonial liberation of Asia or rather "subtly paving the way for the subsequent attempt to civilize Asia, in Japan's own way, which ended in tragedy" (Cousins and Cousins, *We Two*, 351).

22. *Gaikō shiryōkan*, 750–51.

23. The Japanese translation was reprinted in 1924, 1925, 1941, and 1958; shorter excerpts can be found in numerous other Japanese works of the prewar period.

24. Paul Richard, *Au Japon*. Quadrilingual edition (no publisher given, 1917), 20.

25. Ibid., 26.

26. Ibid., 30.

27. Ibid., 32. In contrast to the legacy to Japanese pan-Asianism I have stressed here, Stephen Hay rather attributes the "concept of the unity of Asian civilization" in Richard's thinking to the influence of Rabindranath Tagore. See Hay, *Asian Ideas*, 127.

28. Paul Richard, *The Dawn over Asia* (Madras: Ganesh, 1920), 6. Strangely, a Japanese translation of this work has been published in 1959. This translation is available in only one library in Japan today.

29. Szpilman, "Paul Richard," 289.

30. Gandhi, *Collected Works*, 119, 122.

31. Ibid., 460–63.

32. This is according to the later recollections of the interpreter present at the first meeting between Richard and Aurobindo. See S. Srinivasachari, "Freedom Movement in India: Some Jottings from Old Memories (unpublished manuscript)," *Sri Aurobindo: Archives and Research* 12, no. 2 (1988): 189.

33. Heehs, "In Pondicherry," 199.

34. Richard, *Without Passport*, 33. Apparently, Richard was member of a lodge of the Ancient and Accepted Scottish Rite, which has thirty-three degrees, although the final one is reserved for members of a central steering council.

35. Boaz Huss, "Madame Théon, Alta Una, Mother Superior: The Life and Personas of Mary Ware (1839–1908)," *Aries—Journal for the Study of Western Esotericism* 15 (2015): 214.
36. Richard, *Without Passport*, 49.
37. Huss, "Madame Théon," 218–19.
38. Richard, *Without Passport*, 50–51
39. Richard, *Without Passport*, 54.
40. Paul Richard, *L'Éther vivant et le Réalisme supra-nerveux* (Paris: H. Daragon, 1911).
41. Antoine Faivre, "Christian Theosophy," in *Dictionary of Gnosis & Western Esotericism*, ed. Wouter J. Hanegraaff (Leiden: Brill, 2006), 266. For the specific French context, see Julian Strube, "Occultist Identity Formations Between Theosophy and Socialism in Fin-de-Siècle France," *Numen* 64, nos. 5–6 (2017).
42. Paul Richard, *Les Dieux* (Paris: Librairie Fischbacher, 1914), 12.
43. Richard, *Les Dieux*, 13.
44. Richard, *Les Dieux*, 19.
45. Richard, *Without Passport*, 58–59.
46. This book was translated into Japanese by Ōkawa Shūmei and published in installments in the journal *Dō*. This translation was also published in book form in 1924 and again in a second edition in 1942. See Tejaswini Ramesh Barve, *Ōkawa Shūmei (1886–1957) to Aurobindo Ghose (1872–1950): Ōkawa no kōdō o sasaeta shisōteki haikei no kenkyū* (PhD diss., Ōsaka University, 2013), 65–68, available online at http://hdl.handle.net/11094/26227.
47. Paul Richard, *The Eternal Wisdom* (Madras: Ganesh, 1922), 131.
48. Richard, *Les Dieux*, 23–24.
49. "Documents in the Life of Sri Aurobindo: Sri Aurobindo, the Mother and Paul Richard 1911–1915," *Sri Aurobindo: Archives and Research* 13, no. 1 (1989): 103.
50. "Arya," *Sri Aurobindo: Archives and Research* 13, no. 1 (1989): 78.
51. Richard, *Dawn*, 6.
52. Richard, *Au Japon*, 21–22.
53. In a departure from earlier observers of Japan, who had tended to stress how Shinto, Buddhism, and Confucianism compete with each other, this view became pronounced by the end of the nineteenth century, prominently exemplified by Okakura Tenshin in his *Ideals of the East*, written in English in the 1903 original. See Kakuzo Okakura, *The Ideals of the East with Special Reference to the Art of Japan* (New York: Dutton, 1920), 7–8.
54. Richard, *Au Japon*, 35.
55. See Krishna Dutta and Andrew Robinson, *Rabindranath Tagore: The Myriad-Minded Man* (London: Bloomsbury, 1995), 203. Dutta and Robinson, however, prefer to see the change less in Tagore, but in his Japanese audience, whose "response was cooler and cooler still."
56. Richard, *Without Passport*, 79.

57. "Documents," 97.

58. Wouter J. Hanegraaff, *New Age Religion and Western Culture: Esotericism in the Mirror of Secular Thought* (Leiden: Brill, 1996), 450–51.

59. On the complicated question of the sources and precursors of the Theosophical Society, see Karl Baier, *Meditation und Moderne: Zur Genese eines Kernbereichs moderner Spiritualität in der Wechselwirkung zwischen Westeuropa, Nordamerika und Asien* (Würzburg: Königshausen & Neumann, 2009), vol. 1, 179–428.

60. Yoshinaga, "Ōkawa Shūmei," 99.

61. Richard, *Without Passport*, 54.

62. This is found in her *The Agenda*. Paul Richard also claims Théon "had at one time been associated with Madame Blavatsky" (Richard, *Without Passport*, 50).

63. Richard, *Without Passport*, 57.

64. See Hashimoto, "Airurando," 29–30, 36–38.

65. Yoshinaga, "Ōkawa Shūmei," 97.

66. Quoted in Hanegraaff, *New Age*, 448.

67. Theosopedia, the Theosophical Encyclopedia. "Book of Golden Precepts," http://theosophy.ph/encyclo/index.php?title=Book_of_Golden_Precepts. On Blavatsky's writing of this book, which she claimed she translated from a "metaphysical manuscript [that] was engraved on thin oblong squares that appeared within the astral light," see Jeffrey D. Lavoie, *The Theosophical Society: The History of a Spiritualist Movement* (Boca Raton: BrownWalker, 2012), 228–29.

68. Helena P. Blavatsky, *The Voice of the Silence, Being Chosen Fragments from the "Book of the Golden Precepts"* (London: The Theosophical Publishing Company, 1889), 16.

69. Barve, "Ōkawa Shūmei," 66. In the French edition that Richard probably used, this sentence reads "Fais taire tes pensées, et concentre toute ton attention sur le Maître, que tu ne vois pas encore mais que tu pressens." See Helena P. Blavatsky, *La Voix du silence: Fragments choisis du "Livre des préceptes d'or"* (Paris: Publications Théosophiques, 1907), 30.

70. Olav Hammer, *Claiming Knowledge: Strategies of Epistemology from Theosophy to New Age* (Leiden: Brill, 2004), 55.

71. See James A. Santucci, "Theosophical Society," in *Dictionary of Gnosis & Western Esotericism*, ed. Wouter J. Hanegraaff (Leiden: Brill, 2006), 1121.

72. Richard, *Les Dieux*, 253.

73. This is most prominently visible in his 1921 *The Scourge of Christ*, a diatribe against Christianity, which shows how Christianity remained Richard's main referent, even if *ex negativo*.

74. Yoshinaga, "Ōkawa Shūmei," 98.

75. Ibid., 100.

76. Paul Richard, "Celui qui vient," *The Herald of the Star* 11 (June 1922).

77. Paul Richard, "The Avatars," *The Herald of the Star* 11 (July 1922): 251.
78. Ibid., 251–52.
79. Ibid., 252–53.
80. Paul Richard, "Sept chants," *The Theosphist* 43, no. 4 (January 1922): 368.
81. Hammer, *Claiming Knowledge*, 81.
82. Although the first generation of Theosophical leaders was less openly political, even Olcott founded dozens of reform schools in Sri Lanka in the 1880s. See Helmut Zander, *Anthroposophie in Deutschland*, vol. 1 (Göttingen: Vandenhoeck & Ruprecht, 2007), 93–94.
83. It is frequently overlooked that spiritism and occultism emerged within the context of socialism in nineteenth-century France, a tradition that goes a long way toward explaining how the two elements fused in Richard's thought. See Julian Strube, "Socialist Religion and the Emergence of Occultism: A Genealogical Approach to Socialism and Secularization in 19th-Century France," *Religion* 46, no. 3 (2016), and idem, "Socialism and Esotericism in July Monarchy France," *History of Religions* 57, no. 2 (2017).
84. Srinivasachari, "Freedom," 191.
85. Szpilman, "Paul Richard," 288.
86. Stephen Hay argues that "Richard influenced Tagore's thought [. . .] they were certainly thinking along converging lines, and each probably exerted some influence on the other." See Hay, *Asian Ideas*, 126.
87. Marchand, Suzanne L. *German Orientalism in the Age of Empire: Religion, Race, and Scholarship* (Cambridge: Cambridge University Press, 2009), 373.
88. Ibid.
89. Rita Felski, *The Gender of Modernity* (Cambridge, MA: Harvard University Press, 1995), 132–37.
90. Yoshinaga, "Ōkawa Shūmei," 100.

References

"Arya." *Sri Aurobindo: Archives and Research* 13, no. 1 (1989): 78–79.
Baier, Karl. *Meditation und Moderne: Zur Genese eines Kernbereichs moderner Spiritualität in der Wechselwirkung zwischen Westeuropa, Nordamerika und Asien*. 2 vols. Würzburg: Königshausen & Neumann, 2009.
Barve, Tejaswini Ramesh. "Ōkawa Shūmei (1886–1957) to Aurobindo Ghose (1872–1950): Ōkawa no kōdō o sasaeta shisōteki haikei no kenkyū [Ōkawa Shūmei and Aurobindo Ghose: Research on the ideological background that supported Ōkawa's activities]." PhD diss., Ōsaka University, 2013. http://hdl.handle.net/11094/26227.

Behaime, Géo, and Edouard Tonnier. *Tableau des élections générales législatives des 6 et 20 mai 1906.* Paris: Georges Roustan, 1906.

Blavatsky, Helena P. [H. P. B.]. *The Voice of the Silence, Being Chosen Fragments from the "Book of the Golden Precepts."* London: The Theosophical Publishing Company, 1889.

———. *La Voix du silence: Fragments choisis du "Livre des préceptes d'or."* Paris: Publications Théosophiques, 1907.

Cousins, James Henry, and Margaret E. Cousins. *We Two Together.* Madras: Ganesh, 1950.

"Documents in the Life of Sri Aurobindo: Sri Aurobindo, the Mother and Paul Richard 1911–1915." *Sri Aurobindo: Archives and Research* 13, no. 1 (1989): 94–111.

Dunne, Anthony, and Richard Bowen. "Trevor Pryce Leggett, 1914–2000." In *Britain & Japan: Biographical Portraits.* Vol. 4, edited by Hugh Cortazzi, 323–33. London: Japan Library, 2002.

Dutta, Krishna, and Andrew Robinson. *Rabindranath Tagore: The Myriad-Minded Man.* London: Bloomsbury, 1995.

Faivre, Antoine. "Christian Theosophy." In *Dictionary of Gnosis & Western Esotericism*, edited by Wouter J. Hanegraaff, 258–67. Leiden: Brill, 2006.

Felski, Rita. *The Gender of Modernity.* Cambridge, MA: Harvard University Press, 1995.

Gaikō shiryōkan, Gaimushō kiroku, Taishō-ki, 1-mon seiji, 6-rui sho-gaikoku naisei, 3-kō Yōroppa, sono ta, 2-gō Kakkoku naisei kankei zassan, folder 2-21-1: "Eiryō indo no bu kakumeitō kankei (bōmeisha o fukumu) [British India: involving revolutionaries (including those in exile)]," 749–53. Observation report on Paul Richard.

Gandhi, Mohandas. *The Collected Works of Mahatma Gandhi*, vol. 22: *December 1921–March 1922.* New Delhi: Ministry of Information and Broadcasting, Government of India, The Publications Division, 1966.

Hammer, Olav. *Claiming Knowledge: Strategies of Epistemology from Theosophy to New Age.* Leiden: Brill, 2004.

Hanegraaff, Wouter J. *New Age Religion and Western Culture: Esotericism in the Mirror of Secular Thought.* Leiden: Brill, 1996.

Hashimoto Yorimitsu. "Airurando shinchigakuto no Ajiashugi? Jeimuzu Kazunzu no Nihon taizai (1919–1920) to sono yoha [Irish Theosophists' Asianism? James Cousins's stay in Japan and its aftermath]." In *Ajia o meguru hikaku geijutsu/dezain-gaku kenkyū: Nichiei-kan ni hirogaru 21-seiki no chihei* [Comparative art and design studies of Asia: The horizon between Japan and Britain in the 21st century], edited by Fujita Haruhiko, 27–43. Funding report written at Ōsaka University for the Japan Society for the Promotion of Sciences, 2013.

Hay, Stephen N. *Asian Ideas of East and West: Tagore and His Critics in Japan, China, and India.* Cambridge, MA: Harvard University Press, 1970.

Heehs, Peter [P. H.]. "Archival Notes: In Pondicherry—1910 and After." *Sri Aurobindo: Archives and Research* 12, no. 2 (1988): 198–206.

———. "Archival Notes: Sri Aurobindo, the Mother and Paul Richard 1911–1915." *Sri Aurobindo: Archives and Research* 13, no. 1 (1989): 112–21.

Huss, Boaz. "Madame Théon, Alta Una, Mother Superior: The Life and Personas of Mary Ware (1839–1908)." *Aries* 15 (2015): 210–46.

Lavoie, Jeffrey D. *The Theosophical Society: The History of a Spiritualist Movement.* Boca Raton: BrownWalker, 2012.

Marchand, Suzanne L. *German Orientalism in the Age of Empire: Religion, Race, and Scholarship.* Cambridge: Cambridge University Press, 2009.

Okakura, Kakuzo. *The Ideals of the East with Special Reference to the Art of Japan.* New York: Dutton, 1920.

Richard, Michel Paul. *Without Passport: The Life and Work of Paul Richard.* New York: Peter Lang, 1987.

Richard, Paul. *L'Éther vivant et le Réalisme supra-nerveux.* Paris: H. Daragon, 1911.

———. *Les Dieux.* Paris: Librairie Fischbacher, 1914.

———. *Au Japon.* Quadrilingual edition including translations into English (*To Japan*; trans. Mirra Richard), Chinese (*Gao Ribenguo*; trans. Matsudaira Yasukuni), and Japanese (*Koku Nihonkoku*; trans. Ōkawa Shūmei). Tōkyō: No publisher given, 1917.

———. "Jinshu-teki sabetsu teppai mondai to Nihon kokumin no tenshoku [The Problem of the elimination of racial discrimination and the mission of the Japanese people]." *Ajia jiron* 3, no. 4 (1919): 23–27. Reprinted in *Kokuryūkai kankei shiryō*, vol. 7, 155–56.

———. "Mazu ajia renmei o jitsugen seyo [First of all, let's actualize an Asian Union]." *Ajia jiron* 3, 5 (1919): 27–32. Reprinted in *Kokuryūkai kankei shiryō*, vol. 7, 187–89.

———. *The Dawn over Asia.* Madras: Ganesh, 1920.

———. *The Eternal Wisdom.* Madras: Ganesh, 1922.

———. "Celui qui vient." *The Herald of the Star* 11 (June 1922): 223.

———. "The Avatars." *The Herald of the Star* 11 (July 1922): 250–53.

———. "Sept chants." *The Theosophist* 43, no. 2 (November 1921): 148–50; 43, no. 3 (December 1921): 251–53; 43, no. 4 (January 1922): 365–68.

Rolland, Romain. *Inde: Journal 1915–1943.* Paris: Albin Michel, 1960.

Santucci, James A. "Theosophical Society." In *Dictionary of Gnosis & Western Esotericism*, edited by Wouter J. Hanegraaff, 1114–23. Leiden: Brill, 2006.

Srinivasachari, S. "Freedom Movement in India: Some Jottings from Old Memories." *Sri Aurobindo: Archives and Research* 12, no. 2 (1988): 186–91.

Strube, Julian. "Occultist Identity Formations Between Theosophy and Socialism in Fin-de-Siècle France." *Numen* 64, nos. 5–6 (2017): 568–95.

———. "Socialist Religion and the Emergence of Occultism: A Genealogical Approach to Socialism and Secularization in 19th-Century France." *Religion* 46, no. 3 (2016): 359–88.

———. "Socialism and Esotericism in July Monarchy France." *History of Religions* 57, no. 2 (2017): 197–221.

Szpilman, Christopher W. A. "Paul Richard: *To Japan*, 1917, and *The Dawn over Asia*, 1920." In *Pan-Asianism: A Documentary History, Volume 1: 1850–1920*, edited by Sven Saaler and Christopher W. A. Szpilman, 287–95. Lanham: Rowman & Littlefield, 2011.

Theosopedia, the Theosophical Encyclopedia. "Book of Golden Precepts." http://theosophy.ph/encyclo/index.php?title=Book_of_Golden_Precepts.

Yoshinaga Shin'ichi. "Ōkawa Shūmei, Pōru Rishāru, Mira Rishāru: aru kaikō [Ōkawa Shūmei, Paul Richard, Mirra Richard: An unexpected encounter]." *Maizuru kōgyō kōtō senmon gakkō kiyō* 43 (2008): 93–102.

Zander, Helmut. *Anthroposophie in Deutschland*, 2 vols. Göttingen: Vandenhoeck & Ruprecht, 2007.

Chapter 10

An Irish Theosophist's Pan-Asianism or Fant-asia?

James Cousins and Gurcharan Singh

HASHIMOTO Yorimitsu

1. Synaesthesia Echoed by *Fantasia* (1940)

Walt Disney's *Fantasia* (1940) is one of the most popular works echoing synaesthesia. It begins with Bach's *Toccata and Fugue in D minor*, and the word *fugue* had been a common metaphor signifying synaesthesia since as early as 1912, when František Kupka (1871–1957) named his seminal artwork based on Theosophical visions *Disks of Newton (Study for "Fugue in Two Colors")*.[1] Disney had seen a color organ performance in 1928, and Leopold Stokowski (1882–1977), the conductor of the animation, was fascinated by Alexander Scriabin's *Prometheus* (1912), the Clavilux color organ, and synaesthesia. In 1937, Disney began to make *The Sorcerer's Apprentice* starring Mickey Mouse and underlining it with music played by the Philadelphia Orchestra conducted by Stokowski. The episode was expanded into a bigger project of "The Concert Feature," and then the well-known visual musical artist Oskar Fischinger (1900–1967) was invited

---

This chapter is loosely based on Hashimoto Yorimitsu, "Airurando shinchigakuto no Ajiashugi? Jeimuzu Kazunzu no Nihon taizai (1919–1920) to sono yoha," in *Ajia o meguru hikaku geijutsu dezain-gaku kenkyū: Nichiei kan ni hirogaru 21 seiki no chihei*, ed. Fujita Haruhiko (Graduate School of Letters, Osaka University, 2013).

to work at the Disney Studio in 1938 as a "motion picture cartoon effects animator."[2] Fischinger's experimental abstract works in visual music were highly appreciated by, for instance, Baroness Hilla Rebay (1890–1967). Influenced by Theosophy and Kandinsky's theories of spirituality and abstraction, Rebay collected non-objective paintings and films, including Fischinger's, and made them available to the public in the Solomon R. Guggenheim Museum from 1939 onward.[3] On the other hand, Disney wanted the product to be "sort of near-abstract, as they call it—not pure."[4] After his agonizing days at Disney, Fischinger left the studio convinced that Stokowski had stolen his idea. According to him, the film *Toccata and Fugue in D minor* "is really not my work, though my work may be present at some points; rather it is the most inartistic product of a factory."[5]

How and where then did Stokowski get his idea? This is somewhat obscure in the biographies, but according to James H. Cousins (1873–1956), Stokowski experienced illumination from Adyar in 1927.[6] Cousins, an Irish writer and Theosophist, received a letter from Stokowski and his wife announcing that this renowned conductor had come across some pamphlets about the Brahmavidya Ashrama and found there exactly what he was in search of. This school of universal study was founded by the Theosophical Society in 1922, based on Cousins's plan and concept. Seeing the letter, Theosophical Society President Annie Besant (1847–1933) said that they could stay at Leadbeater Chambers even though they were not members.[7] However, according to Stokowski, things were slightly different.

> She [Besant] was head of the Theosophical Society. She had come to Philadelphia and stayed with us, so she invited us to the World Conference of Theosophists even though we weren't theosophists [sic] at all. That's where we met Krishnamurti and there was also Bishop Leadbeater, who was the head of the liberal Catholic Church in Australia.[8]

No matter who invited whom, Stokowski was heavily impressed by Jiddu Krishnamurti (1895–1986). Two years later in Eerde Castle in the Netherlands, whose noble owner adored Krishnamurti as the World Teacher and donated the estate to his Order of the Star in the East, Stokowski talked excitedly about spiritual art to him.

> I was very impressed by a light-color organ called the "Clavilus" invented by Thomas Wilfred of New York. He has developed

what seems to me a new art of color in form and motion, and it occurred to me that there are aspects of music that are extremely immaterial, that are almost pure spirit—and that some day an art might develop that would be immaterial, pure spirit [. . .][9]

This idea may be the basis for *Fantasia*. Cousins, for instance, firmly believed that Stokowski showed "special enthusiasm over an attempt to equate the vibrations of certain musical tones with certain spectral colors, an aspect of artistic collaboration that he was to develop later, with Walt Disney, in the color-sound film 'Fantasia.'"[10] If not as Theosophists or abstract artists, it is very certain that Stokowski and Disney tried to express synaesthesia in a more tangible way. Once Disney claimed that he "saw" orange in some passage of Bach's music, to which allegedly Stokowski replied: "Oh, no, I see it as purple."[11]

This episode might indicate what Cousins unintentionally contributed to the appropriation, albeit not the propagation, of Theosophy. Fortunate or unfortunate, Cousins was not a creative poet or thinker. In admiration of Annie Besant especially, he stuck to Theosophy's orthodoxy. Not afraid to be plagiarized, he simply and passionately preached its "universal brotherhood" based on common artistic expression in the form of something like synaesthesia or aura rather than esoteric initiation and evolution. As recent studies have emphasized, Cousins started as an Irish nationalist poet before reaching out to a transnational network bridging Europe and India.[12] He devoted himself to the propagation of Theosophy, but his global network went far beyond his scope and intention. Few studies, however, have dealt with his days in Japan, although he happened to connect with or expand several local networks there. As he coincidentally connected Stokowski with the Theosophical Society, his activity brought about unknown by-products across India and Japan. For instance, Cousins boldly used Besant's polemical political pamphlet *India: A Nation. A Plea for Indian Self-Government* (1915) as a university textbook in Tokyo,[13] where Indian expats and their sympathizers had been suspected of their commitment to subversive political activities by the Anglo-Japanese authorities, who were keen on protecting the alliance between the two nations. Sharp criticism of British imperialism in India and the ideal of universal brotherhood were, however, later appropriated by the Japanese government, which began to consider Pan-Asianism to be convenient for Japan's imperialism. Synaesthesia, on the other hand, was less appreciated as a means of meditation, but rather as a useful style to enrich or inspire avant-garde painting.

2. Cousins, Belated or Unintentional Benefactor

When Cousins was invited to Japan from India in 1919, he came there as a self-appointed prophet, expected to teach or preach Theosophy and Oriental spirituality to an overly westernized Japan. He openly identified himself as the second Lafcadio Hearn (1850–1904), known as the best interpreter of Japanese culture, possibly owing to their common origin in Ireland. Hearn, as one can see in the title of his masterpiece, *Kokoro* (heart/mind), had emphasized the unchanging character of the Japanese mentality, going back before superficial westernization. "[T]he wonderful pertinacity of the Japanese spirit and its power of continuity" had reminded Cousins of "a big oyster," which would suddenly open and swallow the attacker.[14] After paying a courtesy call to Hearn's Japanese widow, Setsuko, Cousins proudly recorded that he was the first man in the fifteen years since her husband's death who had "recalled him vividly" to her.[15] Following the same position, Cousins was also attracted by Eastern spirituality, which, in his case, was Indian Aryanism based on Theosophy that bridged East and West. In May 1919, at Noguchi Yone's (1875–1947) invitation, Cousins came to Tokyo to teach modern English poetry at Keiō University (figure 10.1). Both the organizer and the intention of such a visit remain obscure, but Cousins's arrival was significantly important for Theosophy in Japan, as had been the visit of the co-founder of the Society, Colonel Henry Steel Olcott (1832–1907), in 1889. Cousins planned to stay in Japan for at least two years and asked his wife Margaret, a famous suffragist and Theosophist in India, to join him after the first year. However, Cousins was suddenly asked by Annie Besant to return to India and to end his contract. His stay thus was cut short. Even so, during the ten months from May 1919 to March 1920, he worked for and contributed several articles to *The Asian Review*, the English journal of the well-known Pan-Asian association Kokuryūkai (Black Dragon Society). The masthead of the journal listed Cousins as "Literary Adviser" alongside the Frenchman Paul Richard, who had also come to Japan from India and who was "General Adviser" to the magazine.[16] In February 1920, Cousins established the Tokyo Lodge of the Theosophical Society. These complex and contradictory activities were recorded in his diary-like travelogue, *New Japan* (1923).

An Irish Theosophist's Pan-Asianism or Fant-asia?

A JAPANESE POET'S SMILE (RIGHT)—PAGE 36

Figure 10.1. James H. Cousins and Noguchi Yone. From Cousins, *New Japan*.

Cousins's *New Japan* begins with his disappointment with westernized Japan. Noguchi Yone, who came to fetch him, wore an old-fashioned English suit; the buildings in Yokohama and Tokyo were much too modernized. In several articles contributed to *The Asian Review*, he repeated similar criticism of the thin veneer of Japanese westernization, stating that it lacked spirituality. For instance, he saw that Russian futurism had been introduced and imitated in the areas of music and paintings, the results of which were, for him, spiritless. Cousins was surprised to hear Scriabin-like music in *Blue Flames* (1919), composed by Yamada Kōsaku (Kôsçak Yamada; 1886–1965); to Cousins, this only indicated the power of the Japanese assimilation of Western modernism, although he did not mention Scriabin's devotion to Theosophy.[17] Cousins might have unconsciously followed in the footsteps of Olcott, who had asked the Japanese to preserve Buddhism against the tidal wave of westernization.[18] However, unlike Olcott, who had referred to India as a negative example for Buddhists, Cousins praised the spirit of India; the same spirit had been ignored and lost in Japan, though it would lead the way to "the One Divine Being." For instance, Cousins referred to Abanindranath Tagore (1871–1951) or Nandalal Bose (1882–1966), whose paintings were products of "the instinct and tradition of the Indian race." According to him, their arts revealed "a shifting scene in the drama of the soul,"[19] echoing the sentiments of AE, that is, the Irish Theosophist poet George William Russell (1867–1935).

Not surprisingly, Cousins did not appreciate the art of the well-known contemporary traditional Japanese painter Yokoyama Taikan (1868–1958), for instance, *Sansō Mugetsu* ("The Waterfall," according to *New Japan*) (1919), although Abanindranath Tagore and Nandalal Bose respected Yokoyama and were even inspired by his paintings.[20] Cousins's adored friend and Abanindranath's uncle, Rabindranath Tagore, highly welcomed and appreciated Yokoyama during his stay in India in 1903. Yokoyama sought to integrate Western concepts into his traditional Japanese paintings by combination, contrast, and juxtaposition. His attempt was succinctly illustrated in the earlier masterpiece, *Mayoi Go* [Stray Child] (1902), which shows Japan disoriented among the sages, namely, Buddha, Confucius, Laozi, and Jesus. In traditional depictions, the three men representing Buddhism, Daoism, and Confucianism are expected to be in happy harmony. Yokoyama, however, added the newcomer Jesus as a representation of westernization. As such, his work features a bewildered young Japan in a Western-style painting that adopted such art techniques as shading and shadowing. This problematic stance was shared by Rabindranath Tagore. Tagore invited Yokoyama to Calcutta and possibly wrote an introductory note for Cousins to Yokoyama. However, Cousins met Yokoyama, "the foremost progressive painter in Japan," as he had been told, only to find his paintings interesting but not inspiring, technically polished crafts lacking spirituality. Yokoyama also adapted himself to Cousins's India-centered spirituality, stating that "we Japanese have no originality. We do not invent or think. We take pleasure in going over and over the same subjects. Our art is all in its technique. We look to India for ideas."[21]

Cousins began to deny or ignore these Japanese elements in or influences on Indian painting. Modern Indian painting, of which Cousins appreciated its traditional Indian spirituality derived from antiquity, was actually nearly hybrid, combining inspirations from British and Japanese academic paintings, such as those by Yokoyama. Repeating an anachronism, Cousins declared that eighteenth-century Japanese woodblock print artist Kitagawa Utamaro's ladies were "lineal descendants of the Shakti of India."[22] Possibly because of this patronizing attitude, Cousins, who had once been marked by the Japanese and British authorities as dangerous when he had been adviser to the pro-Indian-revolution magazine *The Asian Review*, rarely referred to Japanese artists.[23]

3. Cousins's Appreciation of Koumé and Gurcharan Singh's Appropriation of Cousins?

The exception is Tami Koumé or Kume Tamijūrō (1893–1923), a modern Japanese painter. Cousins appreciated Koumé's spiritual abstract expression exclusively.[24] Intentionally or not, Cousins did not point out that Koumé, while studying at St. John's Wood Art School in London, came to know Ezra Pound and collaborated with Pound on a Nō dance.[25] In 1918, Koumé returned to Japan, and his painting *Off England* (1918) became known as one of the few examples of Vorticism in Japan. In 1919, Koumé painted *Ine no shōzō* (A Portrait of Ine), which can be attributed to Ine Brinkley, daughter of Irish journalist Francis Brinkley (1841–1912) and his Japanese wife, Yasu.[26] In the same year, Koumé depicted a similar portrait, *Fusha no hi* (Grief of the Wealthy), also known as *Madame Karina* (1919), in a more academic style. Ine's brother, Jack Ronald Brinkley (1887–1964), was a member of the Tokyo Lodge;[27] Cousins must have met Koumé via Jack Brinkley's introduction. In February 1920, according to *New Japan*, Cousins was shocked to see the "synthesis" in Koumé's paintings at his studio:

> It was an oil painting in which heads, arms, hands, legs, a flaming brand, and splashes of fire and blood were thrown together in what appeared to be confusion. Closer scrutiny, however, revealed clear design [. . .]. The picture seemed to cut across the process of the universe just at the point at which (one might imagine) the concrete might fly off in fragments towards the absolute.[28]

Cousins devoted a chapter to Koumé in another book, *Work and Worship* (1922), in which he quoted Koumé's words "When I stood on the summit of pure spiritual vision, I was an artist, not a painter, a poet without song."[29] Using similar rhetoric, Cousins praised what he saw as Koumé's vision that sprung from a deeper spiritual soul, comparing his struggle with that of Indian Bengali school painters and the Irish poet

AE. Strangely, however, Cousins did not quote any of Koumé's spiritual art, except for *Grief of the Wealthy*.

Koumé may or may not have become a member of the Theosophical Society, but Cousins's influence is obvious. Soon after Cousins left for India, Koumé, with a reference to Annie Besant (obviously her 1905 *Thought-Forms*, showing abstract art–like painting in explaining aura reading), described his paintings as adhering to the "Etherism School" because he depicted an aura or ether using his chosen medium (figure 10.2).[30] Allegedly, during a stay in New York in 1921, Georgette Leblanc, Maurice Maeterlinck's former mistress, praised Koumé as truly a medium painter. Possibly based on his Theosophical network, Koumé's private exhibition was held at Pound's house with the help of Jack Brinkley in Paris in 1922. Unfortunately, after coming back to Japan, Koumé was crushed to death in Tokyo during the Great Earthquake of 1923. Although most of his works were lost, forgotten, or disregarded, Koumé might have been one of the few Japanese painters who tried to follow or to see the vision of contemporary abstract art firsthand.

Another artist Cousins observed during his stay in Japan was Gurcharan Singh. Singh arrived in Japan in 1919 to study industrial ceramics. Soon he came to know two famous potters, Bernard Leach (1887–1979) and Antonin Raymond (1888–1976), who was also a well-known Czech architect and Theosophist.[31] Possibly through Raymond's introduction, Singh met Cousins and then joined the Tokyo Lodge as one of its first

Figure 10.2. Koumé and his "Etherist" painting, Snow Covered Road at Dusk (1920). From *Asahi Shinbun*, May 1, 1920.

members. Singh supported Cousins, and Cousins also found in Singh's "Indo-Japo-Chinese" pottery (Fig. 10.3) a symbol of the cultural unity of Asia, because his work was "Chinese in model, Japanese in substance, Indian in craftsmanship."³² Ironically and interestingly, Cousins realized this "cultural unity of Asia" on his way back to India. Calling at Kōbe, he traveled around Nara, the old Japanese capital, guided by Singh. After seeing the mural painting in the old temple of Hōryūji, he recognized that it was from Ajanta, India, via China and Korea, as suggested by Okakura Kakuzō (1862–1913) in his *Ideals of the East* (1903), the well-known book on Pan-Asianism. According to Cousins, Japanese art "blended, as Okakura points out, the abstract beauty of the Indian model with the strength of the Tang era in China, and to these added a delicacy and completeness that was later to establish itself as the special mark of Japan."³³

Having been asked to do so by Annie Besant, Cousins had to quit his work in Japan after only ten months. His mission, however, seemed to have been successful. During his stay in Japan, he found that Indian spirituality was nearly ignored and at best mimicked superficially in Japan's superficial westernization. Ironically, it was only on his way back to India

Figure 10.3. Cultural unity of Asia? "An Indo-Japo-Chinese Vase by Gurcharn [sic] Singh." From Cousins, *New Japan*.

that he became aware of the ideal of the unity of Asia or the Asian brotherhood. In his open letter to Besant, "A Visit to Japan" in *New India*, he proudly reported that he successfully founded the Tokyo Lodge after his lecture. According to Cousins, Keiō University asked him to "lecture on 'Religion in Education' with special reference to how we had solved the difficulty of different creeds in India at the same colleges." Although any official document or private mention of Theosophy has not been found, it is easy to guess that Cousins emphasized the Theosophical Society as the key to synthesize the different religions and to solve the racial or religious conflicts.[34]

The message seemed to have been received very well. Among the audience were the above-mentioned Jack Brinkley and Gurcharan Singh. Accidentally, a British legal adviser to the Japanese Foreign Office asked Brinkley to meet Kon Buhei, well-known as "Nut Captain" because of his vegetarian diet of taking nuts as his staple food, and who worked for the Japan-Europe line at Nippon Yusen Kaisha.[35] Kon had visited the Theosophical Society headquarters in India on each occasion when "he had taken his ship seventeen times to London." As he bought and read books, he had been attracted to Theosophy in general. After he retired from the ocean-liner company, he devoted himself to the translation and dissemination of works on Theosophy as a core member of the Tokyo lodge. Another important member of the lodge was D. T. Suzuki; Cousins found that he was "a great scholar, author of several books." He expected that Suzuki's wife, Beatrice, was "very capable and quietly earnest," noting that her mother was a member of the Theosophical Society in New York. As for the English media, he boasted that the principal English papers would "print anything I send[t] them on Theosophical matters." He might have meant Hugh Byas, editor of the *Japan Advertiser*, who printed his poem and several articles on his lecture and appeared often in *New Japan*.[36]

Calling at a port in India, Cousins tried to connect and expand the networks across Asia. He had received a letter of invitation from Wu Tingfang, former First Chinese Ambassador to the United States.[37] During his stay in America, particularly after the so-called Boxer Rebellion, Wu devoted himself to defending the right and cause of his country. In his hard days in the United States, he seemed to be moved by Besant's address concerning the equality of human beings and to have experienced a séance to perceive the afterworld as its ideal embodiment of the equality of human beings. At that time, Wu worked as Chancellor of Exchequer to the Canton Government and had "fled from Canton (a move in the political game) and was practically hiding in Hong Kong." Cousins successfully met Wu and, according to the report of a British agent who had sensed his suspicious movements, confirmed the ongoing Theosophical network between India and China, which he wished to expand and strengthen in the future.[38] At the same time, Cousins met Manuk, a member of the Theosophical Society, in Hong Kong, as well as Mensen Fones in Singapore, who wanted to build a connection with Theosophists in China. Cousins introduced Wu to Fones and emphasized that his stay and trip had encompassed the respective lodges and Theosophists. His report ends with the following optimistic remark: "I feel that a very considerable Theosophical advance is soon to be made in China as well as in Japan; and Korea will shortly show a desire for Theosophical work when the two Koreans are present in the Tokyo lodge for their country to prepare the way."

His 1929 open letter to Besant indicated that each of the lodges, and the Theosophists themselves, had developed beyond his originally intended scope and object.[39] After attending the World Congress of the Theosophical Society in Chicago in 1929, Cousins and his wife, Margaret, crossed the Pacific and called at Yokohama, Shanghai, Hong Kong, and Singapore, where he met the same Theosophists nearly ten years later. Manuk and Fones were still representative members, although the network had not spread out; rather, it had developed independently. For instance, he was surprised to see Dorothy Arnold's "Besant School for Girls" in Shanghai, and he frankly reported to Besant: "I feel sure your modesty will stand the shock when I tell you" about the namesake of the school placed above the entrance.[40] In Yokohama, Cousins met Captain Kon on September 27, 1929, but the Tokyo Lodge had been nearly shut down. Kon was a core member of the lodge, but he identified himself as a member of the Order of the Star in the East. Kon translated *At the Feet of the Master* (1910) as *Arakan-dō* in 1925, and therefore the dissolution of the Order in 1927 shocked him deeply. Cousins spent October 6–9, 1929, in Kyoto in the home of D. T. and Beatrice Suzuki. He met the Canadian fantasy writer Lily Adams Beck (actual name: Elizabeth Louisa Moresby; 1862–1931) and Nisoji Tetsugai, a "keen member of the Theosophical Society" in Kyoto. Possibly because of her ambition to form a Pan Asian Women's Association, Margaret Cousins "addressed the Buddhist Women's College" or Kyoto Women's College to be exact, the predecessor of Kyoto Women's University, arranged by Professor Nisoji.[41] Meanwhile, Cousins did, or could, not touch upon the details of the lodge, because their activities were not closely related to Theosophy itself.

Through Captain B. Kon, the wave of the Theosophical enlightenment rippled. Separately from Cousins, he and his books had become a beacon for potential Theosophists or artists interested in synaesthesia. For instance, Moroi Saburō (1903–1977), a young and brilliant composer, was attracted to Theosophical matters via Kon. In 1927, Moroi founded a group of seven composers called Surya. According to the "manifesto" in the program distributed at the first concert, "We are a group of seven musicians. Surya means the sun god in Sanskrit, and we Surya always express our work by the seven."[42] Moroi asked Kon to name the group, and Kon chose this Sanskrit term probably referring to the Theosophical idea of the Order of the Star in the East. Coincidentally, the group was founded in the same year the Order of the Star in the East dissolved, but Surya, in spite of its short activity, left a significant footprint on art history. Inspired by Kon and synaesthesia, Moroi composed and played a series called *Lyricism in the Music* in 1930. This work and idea connected Moroi with Onchi Kōshirō (1891–1955), a leading artist in the Sōsaku Hanga [Creative Print] movement. Onchi borrowed Moroi's books concerning Theosophy, possibly told by Kon to do so. Furthermore, Onchi came across Besant and Leadbeater's *Thought-Forms*, which drastically changed his art. Onchi was impressed by the works of Kandinsky, which Yamada Kósçak had brought from Europe. For Cousins, as we have seen, Yamada's music seemed to be a superficial imitation of synaesthesia art without Theosophy. Ironically, Yamada's appropriation might be similar to Onchi's works of art, in which woodblock print signified rhythm via color and composition.[43]

Onchi seemed to be detached from both academic as well as esoteric circles. Through the 1930s and 1940s, he developed his way of synaesthesia inspired by *Thought-Forms* into woodblock prints, which were not appreciated or valued in Japan at that time. Meanwhile, Disney's *Fantasia* was not shown in Japan because of World War II. When film director Seo Mitsuyo, sponsored by the Navy Ministry of Japan, made a propaganda animation movie, *Momotarō umi no shinpei* (Momotarō's divine sea warriors), he personally saw a confiscated copy of *Fantasia*, possibly in 1944, with the help of the Japanese navy. Shocked deeply, Seo realized that Japan would be defeated by a United States that was wealthy enough to make such a splendid and luxurious masterpiece.[44] Ironically, it was Onchi's abstract expression in his woodblock prints that some American occupation army officers after the war, such as Ernst Hacker, William Hartnett, and Oliver Statler, were startled to find and estimate its rhythmical style developed independently based on the echoes of Western avant-garde. In 1954, Onchi's works were exhibited at the 18th Annual Exhibit of American Abstract Artists in New York, whereas *Fantasia* was publicly screened for the first time in Japan in the following year.

4. Gurcharan Singh's Appropriation of Cousins?

As Cousins's activities were used or developed unexpectedly in Japan, Gurcharan Singh, Cousins's hope for representing the cultural unity of Asia, continued to connect networks of India and Japan across Asia. In his *Ideals of the East* (1903), Okakura starts with the oft-quoted passage "Asia is one"[45] and emphasizes the spiritual element commonly found in Asia. His words are based on experiences and exchanges in India in 1901, particularly appropriating the non-dualism of Swami Vivekananda's Advaita.[46] Furthermore, Okakura proposes that Japan is an example of unity, declaring that Japan is "a museum of Asiatic civilisation."[47] Therefore, according to Okakura, the Japanese mission was "not only to return to our own past ideals, but also to feel and vivify the dormant life of the old Asiatic unity."[48] Meanwhile, just as Vivekananda's disciple Nivedita (1867–1911), originally an Irish woman named Margaret Noble, unconsciously stretches Okakura's idea of Asia to including "the extreme west of Ireland,"[49] in her introduction to the *Ideals of the East*, Cousins also changed the heartland of Asia from Japan to India. After returning to India in 1921, Cousins contributed the article "The Cultural Unity of Asia" to *The Asian Review*; in this work, he begins with Okakura's "Asia Is One" and emphasizes that "In Asia[,] all roads lead to India,"[50] and that, therefore, India would serve "as a healing of the nation."[51]

In spite of Cousins's estimation, Cousins and Singh seemed to have no contact anymore with each other; there is no mention of Singh in Cousins's writings after *New Japan*. A British Foreign Office Secret Report in July 1920 quoted Cousins's open letter to Annie Besant in 1920. Cousins reported that the Tokyo Lodge had expanded its circle of membership into Korea, China, and India, and he noted that "a scion of the princely families of the Punjab" named Gurcharan Singh would assist in the exchange of Theosophical students between India and Japan.[52] Certainly Singh descended from a noble family in Punjab, but the family in Delhi was not as wealthy as Cousins had expected. On the other hand, Singh got into close contact with the circle of Yanagi Sōetsu (also known as Yanagi Muneyoshi,

1889–1961) and studio potters such as Bernard Leach, Hamada Shōji (1894–1978), and Tomimoto Kenkichi (1886–1963). After seeing Cousins off at the pier in March 1920, Singh was encouraged by Yanagi to go and see pottery in Korea in summer. This experience moved and impressed Singh significantly. In his letter to Leach, dated August 25, 1920, he says, "I came here [Korea] to stay for a week. Three weeks have already passed, and yet I don't want to leave this place." According to the same letter, he met "Mr. Asagawa [i.e., Asakawa]" and would like to extend his stay because he loved Korea "next to my motherland."[53] Yanagi also reported in a letter to Leach about his friendship with Singh, who "had a good journey to Korea in this summer." According to Yanagi, Singh had "loved Korea & was loved by the Koreans very deeply" and he "saw most of the Koreans whom I saw in this Spring, so" they "had much talk about them & also of 'the Korean Questions.'"[54] Furthermore in his article "His Journey to Korea," Yanagi explained about an Indian friend named "S" who had seen a white vase with lotus design and had taken a picture together with Mr. "A."[55] This must be the picture showing Asakawa Takumi (1891–1931) with Singh, who has not been identified except for the "Indian potter Singu."[56]

Meanwhile, Asakawa and his older brother Asakawa Noritaka (1884–1964) played a significant role in the reevaluation of Korean art. During

Fig. 10.4. Gurcharan Singh, Asakawa Takumi, and his brother Asakawa Noritaka's white vase. This is Gurcharan Singh's own picture; the caption says "Dear Singu [sic], 31 August 1920, Takumi." From Anuradha Ravindranath's archive concerning Gurcharan Singh, New Delhi, India.

their stay in Korea from 1914 onward, the Asakawa brothers were deeply impressed by Korean art and particularly taken with white porcelain, which had been forgotten and neglected in traditional ceramic art history and even among the Korean people. They devoted themselves, as Yanagi also would do later, to appreciating and collecting Korean ceramic and folk art; thanks to the donation of the readers and supporters, including Gurcharan Singh's 100 yen,[57] an unusually high amount of money donated by one person. Their efforts in this direction culminated in the Korean Folk Art Museum, which opened in 1924. Their devotion to Korean art for the benefit of the colonized Koreans, going against the forced assimilation of the same by the Japanese, could be linked to the so-called Orientalists' patronizing sympathy. As Kikuchi Yuko and Kim Brandt criticize, this is simply a Japanized Orientalism.[58]

5. Gurcharan Singh's Lotus Pattern: from Aryan to Asian?

Yanagi, exactly and consciously following in the footsteps of George Birdwood, William Morris, and Okakura, lamented and warned about the deteriorated chimera of Korean pottery and Japanese designs and techniques.[59] Interestingly, Yanagi's advice to Gurcharan Singh from British India inspired Singh to make another hybrid pottery appreciating and appropriating Korean forms. Returning to Japan in 1920, he decided to become a studio potter himself, using his own kiln like Yanagi's friends Leach, Hamada, and Tomimoto. Originally a graduate in geology of the Prince of Wales College in India, Singh studied ceramics at the Higher Technical School in Tokyo. Leach and his experience in Korea might have changed the course of his plan from an industrial potter to a more artistic one. The white vase, his representative work during his stay in Japan, possibly made in 1921, indicates how profoundly he was influenced by the vases he had seen in Korea; apart from the color and the shape, the engraved lotus and its bud pattern follows the same design.[60] Through this vase, Singh might have represented the unity or harmony of Asia in this flower native to India, whose pattern once had been considered as descended from the Greek or Egyptian palmette motif.[61]

Back in India, he devotedly revived "Delhi Blue Potteries," which—much like Korean white porcelain—had been nearly forgotten, and became one of the founders of modern Indian pottery, with the aim of raising the lower status accorded to a handcraft potter to the higher one commanded by an artist.[62] Although his activity might be considered an appropriation of the Arts and Crafts movement or a ceramic version of the Swadeshi or Buy Indian campaign, the fact that he discovered the value of craftsmanship through the fused European-Asian movement in Japan and Korea should not be overlooked. Although, while in India, he did not come into contact with Japanese and Korean circles except for Bernard Leach, he developed and perfected the design of the lotus pattern, which he had seen in Korea, in later works such as Delhi blue pot and plate in the 1970s.[63] Moreover, he distanced himself from the murkiness of politics exactly through things such as his favorite design of the lotus, symbolizing a soul untainted by its surrounding mud. If William Morris or George Birdwood had seen the combination of the shape and the pattern, they might have detested them as "a violation of everything like artistic and historical consistency in art."[64] The lotus pattern, however, was not an imitation or appropriation according to demand in the Western market, such as the blue and white willow pattern, which circulated mainly in the nineteenth century. This lotus, transferred and rediscovered through the aforementioned complex set of interrelationships, seems to be a representation of an Asian design by Asians for Asians. He thus became one of the founders of modern Indian pottery. This activity might explain why Singh kept his distance from Cousins or Theosophy.

However, in the 1970s, as a master studio potter, Gurcharan Singh made the *Three Symbol Vase* (Fig. 10.5). It has three faces with sacred words from Islam, Hinduism, and Sikhism, suggesting that the "three creeds are one." Essentially, Sikhism bridges Hinduism and Islam, as Trimurti and Advaita are also popular concepts in Indian society, but such a three-faced vase is not common in Indian pottery. This idea might have been inspired by the shamrock, the symbol of Ireland, in which the three leaves denote trinity, or three in one. A more plausible inspiration would be the *sansan-zu*, a painting of the three sages tasting sour wine from a vase; the *sansan-zu*, as Okakura explained, Cousins repeated, and Yokoyama appropriated in the aforementioned *Mayoi Go*, represents that Confucianism, Taoism, and Buddhism are one, although each expresses the same truth differently. According to Okakura's *Book of Tea*,

> The Sung allegory of the Three Vinegar Tasters explains admirably the trend of the three doctrines. Sakyamuni, Confucius, and Laotse once stood before a jar of vinegar—the emblem of life—and each dipped in his finger to taste the brew. The

matter-of-fact Confucius found it sour, the Buddha called it bitter, and Laotse pronounced it sweet.[65]

The three different expressions might correspond to the three faces of the vase. Furthermore, Singh was also among the group of Japanese folk art dilettantes Garakutasyu, which included Antonin Raymond. The topic of the three sages is common in folk painting. Alternatively, it might have been Singh's own revision of Theosophy or "Asia is one."

Whatever may be the case, Cousins successfully propagated Theosophy in Japan, and he was also influenced by Koumé and Singh. As their interpretation or appropriation of Theosophy suggests, the Tokyo Lodge ceased its activities soon after Cousins left. Even if Cousins offered simplified perspectives on the history, culture, and people of Asia, his activities indicated cultural diversity, not unity, in the interrelationship between Theosophy and art in Asia.

Figure 10.5. Gurcharan Singh, *Three Symbol Vase* (1970s). From Ravindranath, *Pottery and the Legacy of Sardar Gurcharan Singh* (1998).

Notes

1. Tessel M. Bauduin, "Abstract Art as 'By-Product of Astral Manifestation,'" in *Handbook of the Theosophical Current*, ed. Olav Hammer and Mikael Rothstein (Leiden: Brill, 2013), 437.

2. William Moritz, *Optical Poetry: The Life and Work of Oskar Fischinger* (Bloomington: Indiana University Press, 2004), 83.

3. Kerry Brougher et al., eds., *Visual Music: Synaesthesia in Art and Music since 1900* (New York: Thames & Hudson, 2005), 240.

4. Moritz, *Optical Poetry*, 84.

5. Ibid., 85.

6. The most detailed bibliography, Oliver Daniel's *Stokowski: A Counterpoint of View* (New York: Dodd, Mead, 1982), and the more recent study by William Ander Smith, *The Mystery of Leopold Stokowski* (Rutherford: Fairleigh Dickinson University Press, 1990), have no reference to his connection and sympathy with Theosophy, guided by Cousins. According to Manly P. Hall's dubious recollection, however, Stokowski, who had been requested by Disney to organize the images for *Fantasia*, visited his home one day asking for advice on how various scenes should be filmed. Hall recalled that "there are vague incidents in the film as I suggested them to Stokowski." See Louis Sahagun, *Master of the Mysteries: The Life of Manly Palmer Hall* (Port Townsend: Process, 2008), 84.

7. James H. Cousins and Margaret E. Cousins, *We Two Together* (Madras: Ganesh, 1950), 464.

8. Oliver Daniel, *Stokowski: A Counterpoint of View* (New York: Dodd, Mead & Company, 1982), 206.

9. "Stokowski and Krishnamuriti: A Conversation," *International Star Bulletin* (May 1929): 5.

10. Cousins, *We Two Together* (Madras: Ganesh, 1950), 465.

11. Bob Thomas, *The Walt Disney Biography* (London: New English Library/Times Mirror, 1977), 118.

12. See Gauri Viswanathan, "Spirituality, Internationalism, and Decolonization: James Cousins, the 'Irish Poet from India,'" in *Ireland and Postcolonial Theory*, ed. Clare Carroll and Patricia King (Cork: Cork University Press, 2003); and idem, "Ireland, India, and the Poetics of Internationalism," *Journal of World History* 15 (March 2004).

13. James H. Cousins, *New Japan* (Madras: Ganesh, 1923), 47.

14. James H. Cousins, "Some Elements in Modern Japanese Culture," *Asian Review* (July 1920): 492.

15. Cousins, *We Two Together* (Madras: Ganesh, 1950), 365.

16. On Richard, see the chapter by Hans Martin Krämer in this volume.

17. Cousins, "Some Elements in Modern Japanese Culture," 493.

18. For an overview of the reception of Theosophy in modern Japan, see Yoshinaga Shin'ichi, "Meijiki Nihon no chishikijin to shinchigaku," in *Hyōi no kindai to poritikkusu*, ed. Kawamura Kunimitsu (Tokyo: Seikyūsha, 2007).

19. James H. Cousins, "Indian Painting," *Asian Review* (March 1920): 175.

20. Partha Mitter, *Art and Nationalism Colonial India, 1850–1922* (Cambridge: Cambridge University Press, 1997), 292–94.

21. Cousins, *New Japan*, 224.

22. James H. Cousins, "Introduction," in *Muraqqa-i-Chughtai: Paintings of M. A. Rahman Chughtai* (Jahangir Book Club, c. 1930), 1.

23. Paul Richard, Cousins's colleague at the *Asian Review*, had been marked by the British government. According to "Further Report by Agent P." (FO371/3065, December 20, 1916) (R. K.), "Sabarwal [Indian revolutionist and Theosophist] and M. Richard are becoming intimate friends. Both are extreme haters of the British and this dangerous union is very inauspicious." Another "Report by Agent P" (FO371/3068, August 28, 1917) expanded the details of Richard, who posed "to know all about the Hindu Scriptures, religion and philosophy" although his knowledge was "very shallow." Warning that his wife Mirra Richard prepared anti-British propaganda, the reports gossiped about the potential scandal of a love affair between her and Hirasawa Tetsuo, a student of Waseda University. This Agent P is Hari Prasad Shastri, Indian lecturer of the Gita Society at Waseda University, Tokyo. After leaving for Shanghai from Tokyo in April 1918, he became one of the core members of the Theosophical Society in China. Interestingly, however, there seems to be no record or report about the relationship between Shastri and Cousins.

24. For more details, see Omuka Toshiharu, *Nihon no avangyarudo geijutsu 'Mabo' to sono jidai* (Tokyo: Seidosha, 2001). This is the most extensive treatment of Tami Koumé and his life, although it does not touch upon his relations with James H. Cousins and Ine Brinkley.

25. For further details, see Sung Hae-kyung, *Seiyō no mugen nō: Ieitsu to Paundo* (Tokyo: Kawade Shobōshinsha, 1999). Koumé's in-depth knowledge and experience of Phantasmal Nō seems to be closely related to his painting style and spiritual interests. Lily Adams Beck, mentioned below, who was closely associated with the Theosophical Society, considered Nō to be like a séance. Not only that, she also emphasized that "in the Noh, thought is a creative thing, and therefore the dragon soul animates a dragon body." It is obvious that this idea of emotions being externalized and materialized was informed by Besant's *Thought-Forms*. See Lily Adams Beck, "The Ghost-Plays of Japan," in idem, *The Perfume of the Rainbow* (New York: Dodd, Mead, 1923), 129.

26. Ine Brinkley has been known solely as a model of Kinu Wheeler in novelist Shiga Naoya's "Ōtsu Junkichi" (1912). See, for instance, Namai Tomoko, "Ine Burinkuri no koto nado," *Shiga Naoya zenshū geppō* 21 (2001).

27. Adele S. Algeo, "Beatrice Lane Suzuki and Theosophy in Japan," *Theosophical History* 11, no. 3 (July 2005): 4–5.

28. Cousins, *New Japan*, 238–9.

29. Cousins, *Work and Worship: Essays on Culture and Creative Art* (Madras: Ganesh, 1922), 149.

30. Koumé Tamijūrō, "Etherism III," *Asahi Shinbun*, September 13, 1920. Using this material, Omuka has already suggested that Koumé was inspired by Besant's *Thought-Forms*. See Omuka Toshiharu, " 'Tami no yume' to modanizumu: Kume Tamijūrō to Ezura Paundo," in *Nihon no avangyarudo geijutsu 'Mabo' to sono jidai* (Tokyo: Seidosha, 2001), 207. See also "Materurinku fujinga tataeta tamashii no gaka," *Tōkyō Nichi Nichi Shinbun* (May 8, 1923). In his obituary, Cousins admired Koumé's realistic painting, such as that of Madame Karina, "a celebrated dancer in London with the deliberation and particularity of the classicists, and with a chastity only possible to an Oriental." Cousins, however, stressed Koumé's interest in the vision and the mystery of the universe, quoting his words: "One day I shall express the pure negotiation of spirit with spirit." See James H. Cousins, "A Serious Loss to Japanese Art," *Japan Advertiser* (May 4, 1924). Koumé seems to have been appreciated by Yamada Kōsaku, who was severely criticized by Cousins, and provided two illustrations based on Etherism for his song "Shimangedō" [Angulimala] (1920). It is worth noting that not only Theosophists but also several members of Taireidō [the way of the Great Spirit] were drawn to Koumé's Etherism. Taireidō was a kind of religion based on psychotherapy, which became popular between 1916 and 1929. At Koumé's exhibition at the Imperial Hotel on April 30–31, 1920, several members of Tairedō approached him and suggested that he join the society. See Takahashi Gorō, "Kōreiteki kaiga," *Taireidō* (September 1920). Not surprisingly Koumé's Etherism and his paintings were introduced as a methodology similar to the Great Spirit. See Itō Nobuji, "Kōreiteki geijutsu II," *Taireidō* (November 1920). Using the same context, the journal briefly expounded on Kandinsky's *The Art of Spiritual Harmony* (1914), which would suggest the affinity with Koumé's Etherism. Anonymous, "Bi no reiteki kaichō," *Taireidō* (January 1922). I am very grateful to Yoshinaga Shin'ichi for sharing these rare sources related to Taireidō.

31. On Raymond, see the chapter by Helena Čapková in this volume.

32. Cousins, *New Japan*, 322.

33. Ibid., 320.

34. James H. Cousins, "A Visit to Japan," *New India* (May 20, 1920). The *Japan Advertiser* on January 16, 1920, announced that Cousins was to deliver a second series of lectures, "Religion and Education," on January 28 and "the Survival of Death" on February 11 at Keiō University in Tokyo. See also "Lack of Religion in Japan's Education," *Japan Advertiser* (January 31, 1920). *Japan Times & Mail* and *Japan Adveriser*, dated February 18, 1920, reported that the Tokyo Lodge of the Theosophical Society was formed on February 15, 1920. Not surprisingly, a

member of the Theosophical Society Point Loma criticized that the Tokyo lodge had "no connection with the Universal Brotherhood" in a letter to the editor of the *Japan Advertiser* dated February 20, 1920. The writer E. S. Stephenson, lecturer at the Imperial Naval College, Yokosuka, was the most aggressive and persistent of all those who wrote such letters questioning the authenticity of Theosophy. After Cousins had left and the activities of the Tokyo Lodge were declining, the Mahayana Theosophical Society of Kyoto was inaugurated according to the article "Kyoto Theosophists" in *Japan Times & Mail* from May 31, 1924. The article "Theosophists Meet" in *Japan Times* (June 17, 1924), for instance, reported that D. T. Suzuki, Beatrice Suzuki (mentioned below), and Yamabe Shūgaku (Buddhist scholar who co-translated *Buddhist Psalms* with Lily Adams Beck in 1921 in the series *Wisdom of the East*) arranged a meeting to welcome and hear Rabindranath Tagore at Kyoto City Hall.

35. This British adviser must have been the British lawyer Thomas Baty (1869–1954), who was as pro-Japanese as Hugh Byas (1875–1945). Although Byas changed his attitude and criticized Japan's invasion of China, Baty became a passionate defender of the Japanese position and ambition in China. See "Seamen and Vegetarianism: N.Y.K.'s 'Nut Captain,'" *Japan Weekly Chronicle* (June 1, 1916): 892. This is a news report about the recent arrival of the N.Y.K. ship Katori-maru from Europe and its captain Kon's nut diet of "over ten years," which might suggest the point of time when he joined the member of the Theosophical Society. Then the news reported about another vegetarian on the same ocean-liner, "Dr. Thomas Baty, the new Adviser to the Foreign Office, who came out to Japan." Captain Kon and Baty "used to eat at the same table as the distinguished Englishman" and Baty took "eggs and cheese besides vegetables, whereas the Japanese officer eats [ate] nothing but nuts save an occasional dish of vegetables and a little bread." This long-term companionship would last after the ship landed.

36. Hugh Byas was also sub-editor of the *New East* (1917–18), sponsored by the British ambassador to Japan. Robertson-Scott edited this pro-British, anti-German, and anti–Pan-Asianist propaganda organ and criticized Annie Besant's sympathetic attitude toward both India and Theosophy. Possibly because of a desire to promote a mutual understanding in a broad sense, a number of Japanese intellectuals, in spite of their detachment from political affairs, contributed informative and interesting articles to this monthly magazine. D. T. Suzuki's essays on Zen, for instance, became a prototype of his later *Zen and Japanese Culture*. To name a few, Yanagi Muneyoshi and Bernard Leach were mentioned in *New Japan*. Cousins might have referred to or contacted the contributors to *New East* and reversed the network for the Theosophical mission. Not long after Cousins met Leach, Cousins contributed "Lines (To an Artist in Clay)" to *Japan Advertiser* (July 6, 1919). Comparing the process of pottery "from dust to dust" with reincarnation, he praised potter as lord, probably expecting Leach to join the Theosophical Society. Around the same time, Leach was interested in Theosophy

and Zen, as well as in the works of Jinarajadasa, P. D. Ouspensky, and so forth, but he eventually came to devote himself to Bahá'í. As for his spiritual wanderings, see Lowell Johnson, *Reginald Turvey: Life and Art* (Oxford: G. Ronald, 1986), 44.

37. On Wu, see also the chapter by Chuang Chienhui in this volume.

38. FO262/1459, Appendix to Secret Abstract for October 1920, 359. According to the report, Cousins "[h]as written to Dr. Wu Ting Fang, saying that he wishes to come to China and asking if Dr. Wu can find him employment."

39. James H. Cousins, "The End of a Fruitful American Tour," *Theosophist* (December 1929).

40. On the Shanghai school, see the chapter by Chuang Chienhui in this volume. In Shanghai, H. P. Shastri, British Agent P, played a pivotal role in the branch of the Theosophical Society and the Asiatic Association. Although no official British documents have yet been found, Japanese Ministry of Foreign Affairs documents suggest that he reported on the core members of a "Universal Brotherhood of Humanity," including Sun Yat-sen, Rabindranath Tagore, Vasili Eroshenko (a Russian anarchist), and communists possibly including Agnes Smedley. The Besant School for Girls in Shanghai, therefore, would have been very convenient to distract from the President of Theosophical Society's advocacy of Indian autonomy and emphasize solely female education. For further details, see my forthcoming paper "H. P. Shastri as Intelligence Broker in Tokyo, Shanghai and London."

41. Cousins, "The End of a Fruitful American Tour," 365.

42. Nakajima Kenzō, *Ongaku to watakushi: Shōgen, gendai ongaku no ayumi* (Tokyo: Kōdansha, 1974), 77.

43. For further details, see Kuwahara Noriko, *Onchi Kōshirō kenkyū* (Tokyo: Serika Shobō, 2012), 309–11.

44. Tezuka Osamu, "Moetsukiru/Momotarō umi no shinpei," in *Tezuka Osamu Essay Shū*, vol. 8 (Tokyo: Kōdansha, 1997), 191.

45. Okakura Kakuzō, *The Ideals of the East: With Special Reference to the Art of Japan* (London: John Murray, 1903), 1.

46. On the modern reinterpretation of Advaita Vedanta and its modern appropriation outside of India, see also the chapter by Michael Bergunder in this volume.

47. Okakura, *The Ideals of the East*, 7.

48. Ibid., 223.

49. Ibid., xiv.

50. James H. Cousins, "The Cultural Unity of Asia," *Asian Review* (March–April 1921): 225.

51. Cousins, *Asian Review* (March–April 1921): 228. A similar appropriation can be found in the following passage from his wife's writings: "Asia is one by links of religion, fundamental custom, temperament, attitude to life, and, above all, by its ideal of women." See Margaret E. Cousins, *The Awakening of Asian*

Womanhood (Madras: Ganesh, 1922), 16. During his stay in India (1901–1902), Okakura was planning to invite Vivekananda to a conference similar to the 1893 World's Parliament of Religions in Chicago, but the project was cancelled. Meanwhile, Margaret, possibly inspired by this idea, organized an All Asian Women's Conference at Lahore in 1931 after she had "scattered the seed-thought" for the conference during the tour from Chicago to India via Japan and China in 1929. See Cousins, *We Two Together* (Madras: Ganesh, 1950), 504.

52. James H. Cousins, "A Visit to Japan," *New India* (May 20, 1920): 8–9 and Public Record Office, FO 371 5350, F 2119/6/23.

53. G. C. Singh to Bernard Leach, 25 August 1920, 2340. Bernard Leach Archive, Crafts Study Centre, Bath.

54. Yanagi Muneyoshi, "Letter to Leach, 31 October 1920" [the original text is in English], in *Yanagi Muneyoshi zenshū*, vol. 21-1 (Tokyo: Chikuma, 1989), 639.

55. Yanagi Muneyoshi, "Kare no Chōsenkō," in *Yanagi Muneyoshi zenshū*, vol. 6 (Tokyo: Chikuma, 1981), 73.

56. For instance, see frontispiece, *Yanagi Muneyoshi zenshū*, vol. 6.

57. Yanagi's magazine *Shirakaba* (silver birch), March 1921, reported the list. See Yanagi Muneyoshi, "Chōsen Minzoku Bijutsukan kifukin hōkoku," in *Yanagi Muneyoshi zenshū*, vol. 6 (Tokyo: Chikuma, 1981), 642.

58. Kikuchi Yuko, *Japanese Modernisation and Mingei Theory: Cultural Nationalism and Oriental Orientalism* (London: Routledge Curzon, 2004). Meanwhile, according to Brandt, Yanagi is Okakura's successor because of their shared "Orientalism for Orientals," and his idea of the Korean Folk Museum "seems an almost uncanny expression of Okakura's notion of Japan's special curatorial role in the preservation of Asiatic civilization." See Kim Brandt, *Kingdom of Beauty: Mingei and the Politics of Folk Art in Imperial Japan* (Durham: Duke University Press, 2007), 27 and 30.

59. Yanagi Muneyoshi, "Richōyō manroku," in *Yanagi Muneyoshi zenshū*, vol. 6 (Tokyo: Chikuma, 1981), 206.

60. As for the research on Gurcharan Singh, including his white vase and photographs, I would like to thank the courtesy and generosity of the Delhi Blue Pottery Trust, especially Mansimran Singh, Managing Trustee, and Trustee Anuradha Ravindranath.

61. George C. M. Birdwood, *The Industrial Arts of India*, vol. 2 (London: Chapman and Hall, 1884), 415. Asian indebtedness to "Aryan culture" had been emphasized in British imperialistic discourse. In the aforementioned British propaganda magazine *New East*, the similarity between Buddhist art in the Ajanta Caves in Maharashtra and Hōryūji Temple in Japan was explained as an example of "a distant Greek influence from Gandara." See "Our Fresco Illustration," *New East* (July 1917): 18.

62. This is noteworthy because of his noble origin. As for the reference, see *Revised Pedigree-Tables of the Families Mentioned in the Revised Edition of Chiefs*

and Families of Note in the Punjab (Lahore: Government Printing, 1940), 136–7 and 145. I would like to thank Mansimran and Mary Singh, J. P. Singh, and Gauri Sharma, who let me know about this and gave me the copy of this document.

63. In his *Pottery in India* (1979), Singh highly estimated Korean pottery, supplying the photographs of his own collection. Singh's other collection of Japanese, Chinese, and Korean porcelain was kept in the Government Museum and Art Gallery, Chandigarh. According to Mansimran and Mary Singh, the assassination of Indira Gandhi by her Sikh bodyguards and the subsequent hate crimes against Sikhs made him decide to donate his collection. This nearly forgotten but important collection includes studio pottery by Barnard Leach, Tomimoto Kenkichi, and others. As for the research at the Government Museum and Art Gallery, Chandigarh, on December 13, 2012, I would like to acknowledge and appreciate the kindness of Mansimran and Mary Singh, Anuradha Ravindranath, K. I. Singh Bhullar, Kanika Ashish Butail, and, last, but not least, the curatorial assistant Seema Gera.

64. Birdwood, *The Industrial Arts of India*, vol. 2, 417.

65. Okakura Kakuzō, *The Book of Tea* (New York: Duffield & Company), 58–59.

References

Algeo, Adele S. "Beatrice Lane Suzuki and Theosophy in Japan." *Theosophical History* 11, no. 3 (2005): 3–16.

Anonymous. "Bi no reiteki kaichō" [Spiritual harmony of beauty]. *Taireidō* (January 1922): 36–40.

Bauduin, Tessel M. "Abstract Art as 'By-Product of Astral Manifestation.'" In *Handbook of the Theosophical Current*, edited by Olav Hammer and Mikael Rothstein, 429–51. Leiden: Brill, 2013.

Beck, Lily Adams. *The Perfume of the Rainbow*. New York: Dodd, Mead, 1923.

Birdwood, George C. M. *The Industrial Arts of India*. Vol. 2. London: Chapman and Hall, 1884.

Brandt, Kim. *Kingdom of Beauty: Mingei and the Politics of Folk Art in Imperial Japan*. Durham: Duke University Press, 2007.

British Government, Public Record Office. "Further Report by Agent P." FO371/3065. December 20, 1916.

———. "Report by Agent P." FO371/3068. August 28, 1917.

———. FO371/5350, F 2119/6/23.

———. "Appendix to Secret Abstract for October 1920." FO262/1459.

Brougher, Kerry et al., eds. *Visual Music: Synaesthesia in Art and Music since 1900*. New York: Thames & Hudson, 2005.

Cousins, James H. "Indian Painting." *Asian Review* (March 1920): 175.

———. "A Visit to Japan." *New India* (May 20, 1920): 8-9.
———. "Some Elements in Modern Japanese Culture." *Asian Review* (July 1920): 492.
———. "The Cultural Unity of Asia." *Asian Review* (March-April 1921): 225.
———. *Work and Worship: Essays on Culture and Creative Art*. Madras: Ganesh: 1922.
———. *New Japan*. Madras: Ganesh, 1923.
———. "A Serious Loss to Japanese Art." *Japan Advertiser* (May 4, 1924).
———. "The End of a Fruitful American Tour." *Theosophist* (December 1929): 361-66.
———. *Muraqqa-i-Chughtai: Paintings of M.A. Rahman Chughtai*. Lahore: Jahangir Book Club, c. 1930.
Cousins, James H., and Margaret E. Cousins, *We Two Together*. Madras: Ganesh, 1950.
Cousins, Margaret E. *The Awakening of Asian Womanhood*. Madras: Ganesh, 1922.
Daniel, Oliver. *Stokowski: A Counterpoint of View*. New York: Dodd, Mead, 1982.
Hashimoto Yorimitsu. "Airurando shinchigakuto no Ajiashugi? Jeimuzu Kazunzu no Nihon taizai (1919-1920) to sono yoha. [An Irish Theosophist's Asianism? James Cousins's stay in Japan and its aftermath]." In *Ajia o meguru hikaku geijutsu/dezain-gaku kenkyū: Nichiei-kan ni hirogaru 21-seiki no chihei* [Comparative Art and Design Studies of Asia: The horizon between Japan and Britain in the 21st century], edited by Fujita Haruhiko, 27-43. Funding report written at Ōsaka University for the Japan Society for the Promotion of Sciences, 2013.
Itō Nobuji. "Kōreiteki geijutsu II" [Spiritual art II]. *Taireidō* (November 1920): 38-41.
Johnson, Lowell. *Reginald Turvey: Life and Art*. Oxford: G. Ronald, 1986.
Kikuchi, Yuko. *Japanese Modernisation and Mingei Theory: Cultural Nationalism and Oriental Orientalism*. London: Routledge Curzon, 2004.
Koumé, Tamijūrō. "Etherism III." *Asahi Shinbun*, September 13, 1920.
Kuwahara Noriko. *Onchi Kōshirō kenkyū* [Research on Onchi Kōshirō]. Tokyo: Serika Shobō, 2012.
"Materurinku fujinga tataeta tamashii no gaka" [Spiritual painter praised by Mrs. Maeterlinck]. *Tōkyō Nichi Nichi Shinbun* (May 8, 1923).
Mitter, Partha. *Art and Nationalism Colonial India, 1850-1922*. Cambridge: Cambridge University Press, 1997.
Moritz, William. *Optical Poetry: The Life and Work of Oskar Fischinger*. Bloomington: Indiana University Press, 2004.
Nakajima Kenzō, *Ongaku to watakushi: Shōgen, gendai ongaku no ayumi* [Music and me: A testimony on the history of contemporary music in Japan]. Tokyo: Kōdansha, 1974.

Namai Tomoko. "Ine Burinkuri no koto nado" [On Ine Brinkley]. *Shiga Naoya zenshū geppō* [Newsletter to complete works of Shiga Naoya] 21 (2001): 6–8.

Okakura Kakuzō, *The Ideals of the East: With Special Reference to the Art of Japan*. London: John Murray, 1903.

———. *The Book of Tea*. New York: Duffield & Company, 1923. First published in 1906.

Omuka Toshiharu. *Nihon no avangyarudo geijutsu 'Mabo' to sono jidai* [Japanese Avant-Garde Art 'Mavo' and its Time]. Tokyo: Seidosha, 2001.

"Our Fresco Illustration." *New East* (July 1917): 18.

Revised Pedigree-Tables of the Families Mentioned in the Revised Edition of Chiefs and Families of Note in the Punjab. Lahore: Government Printing, 1940.

Sahagun, Louis. *Master of the Mysteries: the Life of Manly Palmer Hall*. Port Townsend: Process, 2008.

"Seamen and Vegetarianism: N.Y.K.'s 'Nut Captain.'" *Japan Weekly Chronicle*, June 1, 1916: 892.

Singh, Gurcharan. *Pottery in India*. New Delhi: Vikas, 1979.

———. "Letter to Bernard Leach, 25 August 1920, 2340." Bernard Leach Archive, Crafts Study Centre, Bath.

Smith, William Ander. *The Mystery of Leopold Stokowski*. Rutherford: Fairleigh Dickinson University Press, 1990.

"Stokowski and Krishnamuriti: A Conversation." *International Star Bulletin*, May 1929.

Sung, Hae-kyung. *Seiyō no mugen nō: Ieitsu to Paundo* [Phantasmal Noh in the West: Yeats and Pound]. Tokyo: Kawade Shobō Shinsha, 1999.

Takahashi Gorō. "Kōreiteki kaiga" [Spiritual painting]. *Taireidō* (September 1920): 40–42.

Tezuka Osamu. "Moetsukiru/Momotarō umi no shinpei" [Burnout/Momotarō's divine sea warriors]. In *Tezuka Osamu essei shū* [Essays by Tezuka Osamu]. Vol. 8. Tokyo: Kōdansha, 1997 (originally published in 1984).

Thomas, Bob. *The Walt Disney Biography*. London: New English Library/Times Mirror, 1977.

Viswanathan, Gauri. "Spirituality, Internationalism, and Decolonization: James Cousins, the 'Irish poet from India.'" In *Ireland and Postcolonial Theory*, edited by Clare Carroll and Patricia King, 158–76. Cork: Cork University Press, 2003.

———. "Ireland, India, and the Poetics of Internationalism." *Journal of World History* 15 (2004): 7–30.

Yanagi Muneyoshi. "Chōsen Minzoku Bijutsukan kifukin hōkoku" [Report of donation to the Korean Folk Art Museum]. In *Yanagi Muneyoshi zenshū* [Complete works of Yanagi Muneyoshi]. Vol. 6. Tokyo: Chikuma, 1981.

———. "Kare no Chōsenkō [His journey to Korea]." In *Yanagi Muneyoshi zenshū*. Vol. 6. Tokyo: Chikuma, 1981.

———. "Letter to Leach, 31 October 1920" [the original text is in English]. In *Yanagi Muneyoshi zenshū*. Vol. 21-1. Tokyo: Chikuma, 1989.

———. "Richōyō manroku [Essay on Korean ceramics during the Joseon Dynasty]." In *Yanagi Muneyoshi zenshū*. Vol. 6. Tokyo: Chikuma, 1981.

Yoshinaga, Shin'ichi. "Meijiki Nihon no chishikijin to shinchigaku [Japan's intellectuals and Theosophy during the Meiji era]." In *Hyōi no kindai to poritikusu* [The Modernity of Spirit Possession and Politics], edited by Kawamura Kunimitsu, 115–46. Tokyo: Seikyūsha, 2007.

Chapter 11

Theosophy as a Transnational Network

The Commission of the Golconde Dormitory in Puducherry (1935–ca. 1948)

Helena Čapková

Introduction

> Our eight months at the Ashram (in 1938) were extremely fruitful and instructive. Not only was the life in this Indian monastery the revelation of another way of life, but the conditions under which the work of the building was done were so remarkable when compared to those we had known in this materially bewildered world, that we lived in a dream. No time, no money, were stipulated in the contract. There was no contract. Here indeed was an ideal state of existence in which the purpose of all activity was clearly a spiritual one.[1]

This quote reflects upon the experiences of Antonín Raymond (1888–1976) when he worked as the key architect on the Golconde dormitory, the newly commissioned house for yoga practice in the Sri Aurobindo ashram in Puducherry (figure 11.1). Raymond and his wife and co-designer, Noémi Pernessin Raymond (1889–1980), were active participants in architectural, spiritual, and Theosophical networks in Japan in the interwar period. The Raymonds' complex net of connections, membership in the Theosophical

Society, combined with their admiration for the Orient and its arts, were instrumental in the process of commissioning the Golconde, which resulted in an extraordinary architectural achievement. The transnational approach taken in this study offers an unexpected insight into the concept and design process of this building, which is considered by architectural historians as the prime example of Indian modernism.[2] Hence, instead of focusing on the architectural and construction elements and processes of this project, the core of this text deals with the networks of contacts and personal stories of some key agents—the Raymonds and Zina and Stefan Łubienski (1893–1976)—involved in the early stages of this creative encounter.

One more membership proved to be crucial for uncovering the transnational and Theosophical history of the Golconde. Both couples were members of the "Garakutashū" (1919–1940), which can be translated as "Circle for Studying Curios," that is, all the ordinary, everyday things that were becoming a part of modern Japanese culture. The eccentric artist and leader Mita Rinzō (1876–1960) created in his Tokyo home a temple—Heibonji or "temple of the ordinary"—devoted to the worship of collecting. He used this temple as a meeting place for intellectuals with a passion for things, religion, folklore, history, spirituality, and new ideas coming from abroad.

Figure 11.1. A long view of Golconde, 1948, Puducherry, photographer unknown, photographs copyright Sri Aurobindo Ashram Pondicherry, India.

The group was composed of both male and female members from diverse occupations and interests. It included people such as the American anthropologist Frederick Starr (1858–1933); Indian studio potter Sardar Gurcharan Singh (1898–1995); journalist and Indian revolutionary Keshoram Sabarwal; Polish artist and diplomat Stefan Łubienski and his partner, dancer and medium Zina Łubienski; journalist and political activist Miyatake Gaikotsu (1867–1955); Matsudaira Yasutaka (1867–1930), who had studied at the Royal Agricultural College in London in the 1880s and was a promoter of modern agricultural science in Japan; as well as the Czech/French/American architects and couple the Raymonds. Their friends, chemical engineer and occultist Philippe Barbier Saint Hilaire (later known as Pavitra; 1894–1969) and architect Bedřich Feuerstein (1892–1936), also took part in the circle's activities and parties. It is significant that Singh, Sabarwal, Łubienskis, Noémi Raymond, and Saint Hilaire were all members of the Theosophical Society (figure 11.2).

Figure 11.2. Group photo, from left: Stefan Łubienski, Antonín and Noémi Raymond, Philip St. Hilaire, Zina Łubienski, Keshoram Sabarwal, and two men, Tokyo, early 1920s, photographer unknown, photographs copyright private collection.

Using the methodology developed in the work of Ikegami Eiko, in which she presented her "search for horizontal and voluntary social associations intersecting at several points with cultivation of beauty," I argue that Garakutashū and the Theosophical Society in Tokyo were such associations from which, "when intersected, a set of unforeseen complex social dynamics emerged." Ikegami further introduces the phenomenon of the conglomeration of networks, which also applies here and happens when networks start to overlap spontaneously and become more tightly knit.[3]

The Theosophical Society in 1920s Tokyo

The history of Theosophy in Japan commenced with the visit of one of the Society's founders, Col. Henry Steel Olcott (1835–1907), to Japan in 1889. From then on, the local history of the Society in Japan became intertwined with the concurrent revival of Buddhism, growing nationalistic sentiments, and the developing ideology of Pan-Asianism.[4] The crucial figure for Theosophy in Japan in the interwar era was James H. Cousins, who worked as a professor of Keiō University in Tokyo for ten months in 1919/20.[5] As recent studies have emphasized, Cousins started out as Irish national poet and then reached out for transnational networks bridging Europe and India.[6] He devoted himself to the propagation of Theosophy, but his global network went far beyond his scope and intention. Few studies, however, have dealt with his days in Japan, although he happened to connect with or expand several local networks. During this time, he managed to fulfil his mission and found the Theosophical Society lodge called Tokyo International Lodge. In a letter to the headquarters of the Theosophical Society in Adyar from February 15, 1920, Cousins referred to the lodge as a mother lodge for foreigners and local members, who could then form a new lodge (figures 11.3 and 11.4 on pages 378 and 379). In fact, an exclusively Japanese lodge, where discussions would be led in Japanese, and the translation of literature into Japanese was being prepared. Cousins marveled that "some current members were in Japan only temporarily and that they would bring the message of Theosophy to their respective countries, such as two American educationalists, a Korean, a Greek, a Kashimiri, a Bengali and five permanent Japanese members." The variety of nationalities and equally male and female representation seemed very important to the Theosophical Society. Further, Cousins wrote about his contact with Shanghai Theosophical Society leader Wu Tingfang[7] and his wish to be back to India very soon.

The number-one member and an ongoing liaison with the Adyar headquarters was Buhei Kon, more commonly known as Captain Kon. He was probably the only Japanese member who met the president of the Theosophical Society, Annie Besant (1847–1933), and senior members of the Theosophical Society in Adyar while his ship was anchoring at Madras port a few years before. Per Kon's letter from February 15, 1928, the great issue that the Theosophical Society faced in Japan was twofold: lack of good leaders-teachers and the language problem. In the same year, he established Miroku Lodge with Miss Casey, which became primarily aimed at the Japanese members.

Other members counted Jack Brinkley, an Irish/Japanese who joined Theosophy in London during the war. Coincidently, his sister Ine was a model to another member and accomplished modern abstract painter, Koumé Tami (or Kume Tamijūrō; 1893–1923).[8] In his book *New Japan*, James Cousins mentioned the two Theosophists-artists: Kume in the chapter on Japanese painting and painters, and the above-mentioned potter Gurcharan Singh, whom he had met on the way back to India in Kyoto. He describes the latter as an impersonator of the ideal Asian man of the future:

> The tall Indian put his farewell into the palm-to-palm salutation of his race. When the crowd on the quay had become a human blur, and my little group was lost among it, I could still see, above the dark turban, the hand of blessing, hands that were destined to mould a thing of beauty, symbolizing the cultural unity of Asia, in the shape of a vase, Chinese in mode, Japanese in substance, Indian in craftsmanship.[9]

Another important member was Mme Ina Metaxa, a Greek-Russian who, according to Cousins, was to soon return to Greece. However, Metaxa stayed in Japan for another few years and continued to be an important member. Mme Ina Metaxa (1864–?), a Russian of Greek antecedents and a refugee from the Ukraine, was born Countess Kapnist in Greece, but marriage to her Russian husband, a lawyer, brought her to his estate in Russia. Aristocrats and Czar supporters were driven out of the country after the revolution and sought refuge in the United States and subsequently

Keio University
Mita
TOKYO, Japan
15 February, 1920

My dear Jal,

You will have already, I hope, heard by cable the good news that the first lodge of the T. S. in Japan has been formed. On putting their signatures to the application for a Charter for the Tokyo International Lodge, the new Fellows authorised me to cable their greetings to the President. I have so many indications of the activity of Powers beyond my own mind that I am sure the work will go on well, and that it will have the President's blessing. If I had been acting according to my own desire I should now be packing up to return to India; but this sudden realisation of a dream seems to indicate work here for Gretta and myself for the coming year. You will see from the papers enclosed that we have eleven Fellows. They are full of eagerness for study and work, and we are organising activities beginning next week. One good feature is that several of the new Fellows are here only temporarily and will take the message of Theosophy to their countries -two American educationists, a Korean, a Greek, a Kashmiri, a Bengali. There are five permanent Japanese in the Lodge, and they guarantee several more at once, so that the continuity of the Lodge is assured. The Tokyo International Lodge is intended to link up outlying students and foreigners, and be a mother Lodge for Fellows until local lodges can be formed. Shortly there will be exclusively Japanese lodges, at least one in a couple of months, in which study can be carried on more efficiently in the language of the country. For this purpose textbooks are being put into Japanese, and a magazine in the language (or perhaps in English and Japanese) will be published in the next autumn. Japanese young women can be found, but it will take Gretta to get at them first. Her presence here for some months will be invaluable to the work.

Now for the enclosed papers. I sent you previously the application of Captain Kon for Fellowship, and request for his registration as a Centre. He acts as Secretary of the Lodge for the present. He is member No 1.

Mr J. Brinkley is son of an Irishman and a Japanese mother. He speaks and writes Japanese expertly as well as English. He found Theosophy during the war when the President when he joined in London. I have posted his letter to the British section asking for his transfer here, and enclose a copy of the letter. Please take the transfer as an accomplished fact, and count him as number 2.

I enclose applications from (3) Madame Metaxa, a Greek-Russian lady who some time will return to Greece and work up the T.S. there; Mr J. N. Bhowmick, a Bengali Brahman, who is studying here, and will return to India via America to work enthusiastically for Theosophy; (5) Mr G. Singh, a Kashmiri Sikh of high family who later will have much property at his command, and means, after completing his work in America and Europe, to devote himself to the betterment of the conditions of his people and the running of industries and educational establishments on Theosophical lines; (6) Mr Sang Soong Oh, a

Figures 11.3 (*above*) and 11.4. (*opposite*) James H. Cousins's letter to the Theosophical Society HQ in Adyar refers in detail to the foundation of the first Theosophical Society lodge in Japan, the Tokyo International Lodge. Letter of February 15, 1920. Theosophical Society Archives, Theosophical Society HQ Adyar, India.

Korean Christian who believes that the message of Theosophy will be a great boon to his country. His voluntary coming into the Society opens up happy anticipations of work in Korea in a year's time; (7) Miss Olive Bayles, an American educationist travelling in the East, likely to visit India this year; (8) Miss Anna Wiebalk, same as Miss Bayles, both very happy at having come upon the application of true principles (that is Theosophical principles) to education. When they return to America they will be of much service to the work there; (9) Mr T. Koumé, a Japanese artist seeking deeper inspiration for his work; (10) Mr Park, a Japanese Christian senior student in Imperial University; (11) Mr B. Gokan, a student. The students are of age, and no parental authority is needed.

On the assumption that these names will be accepted as FTS, I also enclose the application for the Charter of the Tokyo International Lodge. Note that the signatories are, (1) a pure Japanese elder, (2) an Anglo-Japanese, (3) a Korean, (4) an Indian, (5) an American, (6) a Greek, (7) a Japanese -and the individual acting as go-between is an Irishman. So it is a fairly representative list.

As regards finance I am not at the moment clear, but I am going according to the paragraph no 2 at foot of the fellowship application form, and taking Kon as transferred from your unattached list to this lodge. Brinkley is paid through London, but if there is any irregularity in any way let me know and I shall set it right. Do not delay the enrolments and charter on a money point which will be settled on hearing from you. So meantime I send, on the basis of one yen equalling two shillings, the equivalent turned into rupees at bank exchange rate. If there is any difference we can adjust it.

```
          Fellowship fees
              Kon, Metaxa,Bhowmick, Singh,
              Sang Soon, Bayles,Wiebalk,
              Koume, Park,Gokan, - (10)
              Certificate of Fellowship  5s
              Annual Subscription        5s
                                       10 @ 10s      100s
          Charter fee                                 20s
                                                     120s
                                        Equivalent 60 yen
```

If there was plenty of money lying about headquarters, or some monied person would donate the price of a cable, it would help us, to get word of our authorisation quickly. "Cousins, Keiogijuku, Tokyo, Charter issued" would do.

I have word from Dr Wu-ting-Fang that he will pay expenses of a tour in China. So it is not improbable that Gretta and I may make our way through Korea and China back to India, leaving lodges formed on the way. I hope so.

Have a look at G's staria-map. No more at present.

With namaskarams to the President,

Ever yours,

James H Cousins

in Japan.[10] Metaxa was an avid writer and political commentator; she published extensively about feminism and on art subjects. She accommodated the Łubienskis, the Raymonds, and Saint Hilaire at her home after the earthquake of 1923, and their spirits seem very much aligned, as confirmed by both Stefan Łubienski and Saint Hilaire[11] (figure 11.5). She published a book on Japan, *Le Japon mystique*, in 1927 and dedicated her second book, *Evening Glow*, published in 1931, to Rabindranath Tagore. Her trail then disappeared, probably in Europe, after she published the article "Cultural Traits of East and West" in *Contemporary Japan: A Review of Far Eastern Affairs*, a propaganda vehicle of the Foreign Affairs Association of Japan in November 1942.

The future leading force of the Theosophical Society in Japan, Suzuki Daisetsu (1870–1966) and his wife, Beatrice Lane Suzuki, joined with her mother, Mrs. Erskine Hahn, MD. The first membership group included three Indians:

Figure 11.5. Mme. Metaxa and Stefan and Zina Łubienski at her Tokyo home, early 1920s, photographer unknown, photographs copyright private collection.

J. N. Bhowmick a Bengali Brahman who is studying in Japan, who will return to India via America, Mr Gurcharan Singh of high family who later will have means and property, after completing his work in America and Europe to devote himself to betterment of conditions, industries and educational activities.[12]

The last Indian was Keshoram Sabarwal, who, like Singh, later became associated with Garakutashū. Sabarwal was then a journalist, correspondent of the *Bombay Chronicle* and the *Japan Times*. In a confidential memorandum from 1919, Sabharwal is presented as complicit in the Indo-German conspiracy. In the report, Sabarwal is said to have acted as secretary to a well-known Indian revolutionary against British Raj, Rash Behari Bose. Keshoram Sabarwal had worked as a secretary of Lala Lajpat Rai and escaped to Japan to continue to live there to work with Bose.[13] Bose settled in Japan in 1915 and found support by Japanese Pan-Asianists, the same network that was familiar to James Cousins and had also supported Mirra and Paul Richard during their stay in Japan from 1916 to 1919.[14] The Richards and the ideas of Sri Aurobindo (1872–1950) were very influential in spiritual/nationalistic circles in Japan and through Keshoram Sabarwal it reached Singh and Philippe Saint Hilaire, who devoted most of his later life to Sri Aurobindo and his ashram.

In a letter dated October 30, 1924, to the Theosophical Society headquarters from the secretary of Mahayana Lodge in Kyoto, Beatrice Suzuki suggested that Tokyo International Lodge be abrogated and should return the charter. Two lodges existed in parallel, Mahayana in Kyoto and Orpheus in Tokyo (figures 11.6 and 11.7 on pages 382 and 383). The two lodges were linked and, for example, on October 11, 1924, K. R. Sarbarwal, an Indian member of the Orpheus, held a lecture on the Arya Samaj for the members of Mahayana lodge. Orpheus Lodge was formed and led by Saint Hilaire from May 1924. The secretary, and later the leader was Dirk van Hinloopen Labberton (1874–1961), a Dutch Indologist who became the first General Secretary of the Theosophical Society in Indonesia, when the treasurer was Sabarwal. Labberton lead the lodge until his departure in 1926, when the lodge was suspended. Among other members were Stefan Łubienski and Mme Metaxa. Saint Hilaire left Japan in the summer of the same year and became only loosely involved with the Theosophical Society until he immersed himself into the teachings of integral yoga of Sri Aurobindo. Unexpectedly, in summer 1925 he briefly returned to

Rec'd. July 1924

Give your aid to the few strong hands that hold back the powers of darkness from obtaining complete victory. Then do you enter into a partnership of joy, which brings indeed terrible toil and profound sadness, but also a great and ever increasing delight.

("Light on the Path")

THEOSOPHICAL SOCIETY.

-o-o-o-o-o-o-

ORPHEUS LODGE.

INNER REGULATIONS.

1. The ORPHEUS Lodge is formed to study the eternal teachings of the Divine Wisdom, most specially in the form given at this time to the world through the channels of the Theosophical Society.

2. The Members of the Lodge claim to adhere to the three aims of the T.S..

3. They propose particularly to acquire the profound understanding of :
    a) The progressive evolution of the soul by successive incarnations and under the rule of KARMA.
    b) The existence of the GREAT WHITE LODGE, the Hierarchy of Adepts, and the spiritual direction of Cosmic Evolution.

4. They shall endeavour to make their Lodge a radiating center of love and of study, keeping always in mind that a theosophical lodge can and must be a transmittor of spiritual forces within the region where it is placed.

5. The Committee of the Lodge consists of :
    a) President
    b) Secretary
    c) Treasurer.
   The members of the Committee are elected for a period of SIX months.
   A Chairman is selected among the members of the Committee or among the other members of the Lodge.

6. All important matters will be settled by the majority of the votes. However, the admission into the Lodge of a new member must be decided unanimously, absent members duly consulted.

Figures 11.6 (*above*) and 11.7 (*opposite*). The foundational document of the Orpheus Lodge, Tokyo, established on May 22, 1924. Theosophical Society Archives, Theosophical Society HQ Adyar, India.

7. When a question is to be settled by voting, if requested by one member, the votes are given secretly.

8. The Meetings of the Lodge are of two kinds : Private and Semi-public.
   The members of the Lodge only attend Private Meetings. Guests, whether F.T.S. or not, may be invited to attend Semi-public Meetings.

9. The Lodge is a non-political organisation and keeps itself aloof from political activities.

Tokyo, May 22nd 1924.

The Members of the ORPHEUS LODGE :

Tokyo, staying with Łubienski and planning to go to the convention in Adyar in December.[15]

Noémi Pernessin Raymond and Theosophy

Upon clarifying the membership of Singh, Sabarwal, the Łubienskis, and Saint Hilaire in the Theosophical Society, we have one important Garakutashū ally left—Noémi Raymond. Outstanding painter and graphic designer Noémi Pernessin Raymond (1889–1980) was French, educated as graphic designer in the avant-garde Teachers College in New York City where she joined the New York circle of the Theosophical Society in 1919 and commenced her lifelong study of esoteric thoughts and religions. She befriended some members, particularly St. Clair Breckons and her husband Stanley whose network became crucial to the Raymonds' future careers. The Breckons also introduced the Raymonds to the partner of Frank Lloyd Wright, Miriam Noel. Wright then became Antonín Raymond's teacher in his laboratory in Taliesin and later his employer. With Wright, the Raymonds travelled to Japan to work on his major project, the Imperial Hotel, which began their journey to creating a famous architectural firm in Japan.

An important source of information about her and Antonín's spiritual and creative dialogue is their correspondence during the 1920s and 1930s. Noémi always reported about her visits to the Theosophical meetings during her stay in New York. In a letter from December 1923, she noted the split and struggle that was happening in the Society and that only the explanation from Dr. Archibald Keightley convinced her that joining Besant's Society would be wrong. From this letter, we know that Noémi was a member of the Theosophical Society in America formed by Ernest Temple Hargrove, J. D. Buck, and others, which had its headquarters in New York City until 1942, when it was evidently disbanded. The Theosophical Society published the periodical *Theosophical Quarterly*. Dr. Keightley, who was mentioned frequently in the correspondence, was very active in this branch of the Society. The reference to the Besant Society indicates the split within the organization, which took place in the Theosophical Society in 1895. The correspondence also contains doubts Noémi had about the different treatment of women in the various Theosophical circles. Even more relevant correspondence in relation to Noémi's search for spiritual fulfilment may be found in letters exchanged with Philippe Saint Hilaire, who had been given the name Pavitra by Sri Aurobindo in 1925. Correspondence with Pavitra starts in 1927 and lasts many decades. In letters from New York, Noémi refers to visits to the Theosophical Society and conversations with Dr. Keightley. Pavitra's Japanese friends seemed very pleased that he was in the salon of Dr. Gose (Sri Aurobindo) and spoke, on the other hand, with suspicion of actions by the Besant society in Adyar. Unlike Pavitra, Noémi continued exploring Theosophy, but not exclusively, and asked questions to Sri Aurobindo which Pavitra communicated and posted the answers back to her in Japan. The bond between them and other Japanese friends from the Garakutashū was profound and they mention Heibonji, Łubienski, and others frequently.

It was Singh who introduced the Raymonds to Heibonji and his circle of 33 members of all sorts of classes and professions, mostly art/craft related (figure 11.8). Noémi became Heibonji's student of ink painting and calligraphy.[16] One female member was a geisha, a biwa player. They held monthly meetings at a member's house, a tea house, or a temple.

Figure 11.8. Group photo, from the left: Philip St. Hilaire, Gurcharan Singh, Stefan and Zina Łubienski and Noémi Raymond, Tokyo, early 1920s, photographer unknown, photographs copyright Sri Aurobindo Ashram Pondicherry, India.

Friends, spouses, children were invited, and a typical day was enjoyed by producing art, holding discussions, and making food. Raymond confessed that he learnt the significance of ink as a medium of self-expression in the Asian art context during the Garakutashū meetings. When one of the members died, Raymond was offered a membership and inherited the area of horse collecting, to which he gladly obliged. Research into Garakutashū documents, introduced only in a very limited degree in this chapter, provides the leads for research of other networks related to the circle; such as diplomatic alliances, the network of revolutionaries and political activists on the run, who used the circle as a conveniently obscure location for meetings, professional liaisons among scientists and university professors, and the network of the Theosophical Society in Japan.

Stefan Łubienski

The impressions of Garakutashū captured in the letters and memoirs of its Theosophical/foreign members are very similar. The common line is that they experienced a profound bond and intensive learning about Japanese tradition and art in a way that was deeply inspirational. Stefan Łubienski, composer, fine artist, and educator was a Polish nobleman who learned about Anthroposophy from his mother and as a youth became attracted to Theosophy. This set of esoteric teachings became a lifelong inspiration to him and led him Eastward. It was the search for superior culture and arts that brought him to Japan where he and his partner Zina stayed from 1921–1926. He focused mainly on learning about Nō theater, and taught music and composition to support his stay (figure 11.9). Upon his arrival, he published the book *Między Wschodem a Zachodem: Japonja na straży Azji. Dusza mistyczna Nipponu, etc.* ("Between the East and the West: Japan as a Guardian of Asia. Mystical Spirit of Japan, etc.") back in Poland in 1927.[17] The Łubienskis became good, intimate friends with the Raymonds and with the French ambassador in Japan, poet and playwright Paul Claudel (1868–1955). From diplomatic circles, there was only a small step to the network of successful industrialists who were inspired and profited from their experiences abroad. One of them was Raymond's client, Hoshi Hajime (1873–1952), who founded a pharmaceutical school in 1922 to expand his pharmaceutical empire and commissioned the young Antonín Raymond with building the campus. The monumental concrete building of the auditorium gained great acclaim for the young architect.

Figure 11.9. Zina and Stefan Łubienski performing at a children's Christmas party at Atami (?), early 1920s, photographer unknown, photographs copyright private collection.

Hoshi also supported several exhibitions highlighting foreign artists' work in Japan in one of the floors of his trendy pharmaceutical shop, and to make the connection even tighter, he employed Saint Hilaire, who had been trained as chemical engineer. By then, however, as noted by Łubienski, Saint Hilaire's view of life and career was changing and soon he went to Tibet in 1924 and then through Theosophical circles to Puducherry, to begin to work with Sri Aurobindo Ghose.

In April 1923, the Shiseidō Gallery in Tokyo opened the exhibition *Pōrando Bijutsu Seisakuten* ("Polish Artistic Production"), displaying the spiritually charged artwork of Zina and Stefan Łubienski. Among the works were the woodblock prints *Power That Created the World*, *Resurrection*, and *Female Ghost*.[18] The Łubienskis lectured at Jiyū Gakuen ("Free College"), a progressive school for girls founded by Christian activist Hani Motoko in Ikebukuro, Tokyo, which can be viewed as a busy transnational artistic intersection used by all of the above-mentioned artists; the school building itself was designed by Frank Lloyd Wright in 1921. Stefan also taught Polish language and Polish literature at Waseda University, opened a small music school, and gathered a group of young fine artists around him; again, he understood this activity as a background for the spiritual foundations of musical expression.

Łubienski returned to Poland via Siberia, and in 1927 he published the aforementioned book *Between the East and the West*, through which he intended to provide a contemporary perspective on Japan, its history, and its culture. In the conclusion to the book, he states that East and West need to exist in equilibrium. Indeed, the story of Stefan Łubienski confirms that Theosophy can be interpreted, in Sixten Ringbom's words, as the connecting link.[19]

Theosophy and Artists

The concept of *Theosophy* itself was loose enough to incorporate the strands of various "world religions" and appealed to a global audience sympathetic to the idea of a "universal brotherhood" at once at odds with, yet inherently part of, the imperial hierarchical system. Scores of anthropological texts and translations of sacred texts published during the heyday of the Theosophical Society movement emphasized the importance of unseen and supernatural powers in Eastern belief systems and supplied Western countries with exciting new material (in their own languages) and nourished a never-sated appetite for the "Orient" and the "exotic." The "evidence," gathered by an assortment of academics, imperial civil servants, religious missionaries, and cosmopolitan travelers, was then assimilated into Theosophical texts such as Blavatsky's *Isis Unveiled* (1877), which was characteristic in its fusion of Western and Eastern spiritual traditions.[20]

Theosophists believe in the existence of no fewer than six occult "planes of existence," including the physical world, each characterized by finer rates of vibrational energy and by closer unity with God. In their influential book *Thought-Forms*, Annie Besant and Charles Leadbeater argue that thoughts and feelings create vibrations, invisible to the untrained eye, which manifest as various shapes and colors depending on their clarity and spiritual content. From undefined feelings of affection to the complex vibrations created by meditation, these mental vibrations surround each one of us and are felt by others. Good mental vibrations, materialized in by the fantastic blue shapes created by spiritual devotion, create harmonious and progressively more spiritually advanced societies.[21] This insight in particular inspired artists internationally. Besant made a direct appeal to artists in the preface to *Thought-Forms*, recognizing the difficulties inherent in the artist's task of trying to represent spiritual forces using the standard methods of art and craft. This was both an acknowledgement of those who were trying to connect the immaterial/material divide in their work and an invitation to others to join the movement. Besant recognized the artistic contributions in her book as follows:

> To paint in earth's dull colours the forms clothed in the living light of other worlds is a hard and thankless task; so much the more gratitude is due to those who have attempted it. They needed coloured fire, and had only ground earths.[22]

While these ideas might, to borrow the words of Gauri Viswanathan, "pose the sorts of challenges to critical thinking that secular intellectuals would prefer not to contemplate," they should be carefully considered. They represented challenges for the artists involved, and they had an impact on their creativity.[23] Examining the relationship between Theosophical thought and the arts opens up different potential interpretations of modern culture, suggesting that disenchantment was not the only option available.[24]

As Viswanathan reminds us, the Theosophical Society was a "cosmopolitan movement that acquired worldwide adherents." In today's language, it was a society that quickly went global.[25] This emphasis on the "worldwide" and the "international" is of particular interest if we consider it not only in relation to the ambitions of the Theosophical Society, but also within the wider context of the connections between the Theosophical Society, the visual arts, and, for example, the world of empires in this period. Theosophical ideas often were not transferred between artists institutionally but rather were absorbed by artists through reading and conversation and, as time passed, gradually mixed with other influences, becoming constituent ingredients in the composition of what would be called the "New Age" movement. The critical significance of the relationships between art, visual culture, and mysticism in the twentieth century has—with the exception of a few well-known cases, such as those of Wassily Kandinsky and Piet Mondrian—been left untapped. This is possibly because, as the historian Alex Owen has suggested, "the very notion of mysticism and the occult seems to run counter to our conception of modern culture and the modern mind set."[26] Recently, a research network called "Enchanted Modernities" examined the extent to which Theosophy had a critical impact on the arts and produced a body of evidence documenting the potency of its impact across national and disciplinary boundaries.[27] For architecture, the terrain has been explored predominantly while the Theosophical Society membership of the individual designers became clear. This applies to the work of Claude F. Bragdon (1866–1946), including his own writing, *The Beautiful Necessity, Seven Essays on Theosophy, and Architecture*; Johannes L. M. Lauweriks (1864–1932); Karel de Bazel (1869–1923); and Rudolf Steiner (1861–1925).[28] In this chapter, the relationship between Theosophy and the architects may not be necessarily formalized but is significant nonetheless.

A potent example of the less formal connection between Theosophy and the arts is the architectural project of the Golconde dormitory. The Raymonds were approached with the unlikely commission of the Golconde because of the Theosophical connections they had built in Japan. Moreover, it was Theosophy and, generally, their commitment to new spirituality that created an avenue for mutual understanding between the ashram members and spiritually tuned designers.

The Golconde Dormitory Project

Although announced in the letters that were frequently exchanged between the Raymonds and Saint Hilaire or, as he was known by then, Pavitra, Raymond's office formally received a commission to design a dormitory for the Sri Aurobindo Ashram in Puducherry in southeast India in 1935 (figure 11.10). Plans were made in Japan and sent to a local team in Puducherry in 1937, before Raymond visited India with his family for a few months. The plans were finalized within six months, and Raymond believed that the dormitory would be erected within a similar time frame. However, when the contractors and building material began entering the ashram, Sri Aurobindo, on addressing the project's potential for seriously disrupting the life of the community, decided that the construction activity itself would become a part of the life of the community, which instead would build the dormitory slowly by itself.[29] This decision had a crucial impact not only on the length of the construction activity itself, but also on the building methods and processes, which had to be transferred by the team to a largely inexperienced team of builders, as well as on the way in which the building would be executed (figure 11.11).

As noted above, it was Philippe Barbier Saint Hilaire, or Pavitra, who successfully convinced the ashram that the Raymonds were spiritually the best-equipped designers to conceive the dormitory. The building was

Figure 11.10. Pavitra in Sri Aurobindo Ashram, Puducherry, undated, photographer unknown, photographs copyright Sri Aurobindo Ashram Pondicherry, India.

conceived upon the request of the Mirra Richard (née Alfassa; also known as the Mother; 1878–1973), the spiritual leader of the Sri Aurobindo Ashram, a female complement to Sri Aurobindo.[30] Mirra was especially impressed by the cooperation between the Raymonds, which was to her an epitome of cooperation of the male and female principles. This indeed was a strength of the couple: their interdisciplinary collaboration, their passion for experimentation, and their commitment to the syncretic spiritual expression they were developing in 1930s. Noémi became more active in the architectural office in the 1930s, and her talent materialized in Golconde in the interior design, furnishings, woven design of sliding doors, and wall design of the dormitory.[31] Raymond called two young architects to help him on-site: George Nakashima (later Sundarananda) (1905–1990)

Figure 11.11. Golconde under construction, 1942, Puducherry, photographer unknown, photographs copyright Sri Aurobindo Ashram Pondicherry, India.

(figure 11.12) and František Sammer (1907–1973), who came to him upon completion of an internship and assistantship at Le Corbusier's studio in Paris and the Soviet Union. Golconde and the experience of the ashram had a formative effect on Nakashima, who became a lifetime member of the community and produced a number of works for the ashram as well as for the new town project of Auroville nearby. Although he often returned to India, his life was to be primarily spent in the United States, where his wooden furniture design became extremely popular and synonymous with a new, postwar modern living interior.[32]

Raymond was seeking the best solution for the hot and humid local climate and oriented the building to face the sea breeze that permeates the dormitory and cools the interiors. The north and south facades are constructed from moveable louvers that let the cool in or provide a pleasant shade. The woven wooden sliding doors do not obstruct the circulation of air and provide privacy required for solitary yoga practice. Like the building, the garden also is a hybrid of modernist, local, and Japanese

Figure 11.12. George Katsutoshi Nakashima (Sundarananda) at Sri Aurobindo Ashram Golconde Guest House, undated, photographer unknown, photographs copyright Sri Aurobindo Ashram Pondicherry, India.

garden design, with the last of these evinced by the inclusion of the characteristic stone lanterns.

Golconde is not only a unique collective living space, but it was also planned for the purposes of spiritual awakening and the stimulation of the spiritual advancement of the *sādhaks*, the members of the ashram. According to the Mother, all of Divine nature was manifested as beautiful on the physical plane. Therefore, she insisted on the beauty of Golconde architecture.[33] The perfection that the designers and the Mother aimed for was also present in a number of little discrepancies, or imperfections. For example, the concrete walls were left bare, and the sides of the building were whitened only with the local, seashell-based stucco finish, which was also used in the interior. Sammer insisted on a quite rough polishing of the concrete building components, so that the numberings, marks, and scratches created over the course of the construction process would remain visible. This approach, which considers the natural imperfect state of materials as possessing the ultimate aesthetic perfection, shows the deep impact of the Japanese aesthetic admired by all those creatively involved in the construction process.

The Mother reportedly insisted on the beauty and perfect execution of the building, which was supposed to motivate the harmony between meditation and physical work conducted by the *sadhaks*. The model for the dormitory was provided by the mountain cave communities in Golconde, not far from Puducherry, where disciples lived in separated caves in close proximity to their guru. Analogically, the Raymonds' Golconde building is such a composition of caves, detached from the everyday world and within which one could realize *sādhana*, that is, spiritual practice in order to overcome the ego.[34]

Conclusion

In 1938, the *Theosophical Quarterly* printed Noémi Raymond's letter of greeting to the Annual Convention. She sent it from Puducherry in French India, where she was staying and working on the project of Sri Aurobindo Ashram dormitory. She wrote:

> Away from strife, rush, greed and noise, away from all mechanization and artificialities, sheltered from any anxiety, the disciples of the Ashram also seek the Divine Life. As I see them daily going about their labours, looking much like angels that have never known incarnation, I think of you all, the fighters, the warriors, who must reach the Divine through sweat and blood. I know then what Theosophy gives of confidence and power, and know too that nowhere else we find a guidance so true and so complete, ranging from the field of pure Spirit to world politics, from problems of personal conduct to problems of the Soul.[35]

This commentary that Noémi Raymond shared with her international readership highlights the difference between the world of the late 1930s, gearing toward the great conflict of World War II, and the place where spirituality is at the core of daily conduct. The Raymonds found in the Ashram an alternative and a partner in their Theosophical study and in their ambition to design a new modernist structure that would by rooted in Eastern tradition, or rather that could overcome the duality between East and West and bridge them in a new, universal style. Golconde dormitory is an alien and hybrid structure that was built harmoniously into the colonial landscape of Puducherry harbor. The architectural success has received praise from an international specialist audience, yet its unconventional design cannot be attributed exclusively to the geniuses of designers. As described above, this design also was the product of the contemporary intrinsic connections among transnational artistic and spiritual networks.

The Theosophical Society meetings and Garakutashū events offered a modern environment that resonated with foreigners who were artistically inclined and who were searching for new spiritual experiences and progress in Japan. Perhaps they even used the events for underground political activities and the exchange of information. Certainly the encounter had a profound impact on their experience of Japan and on their work in theater, design, and architecture. For the Raymonds, the meeting with Heibonji formed their insight into Japanese art and prompted their attention to folk objects, found ordinary things, and Japanese traditional craft. It was these inspirations that later, and in retrospect, became central to their design work. Moreover, these are the clues to their original aesthetic that fused Japanese, Asian, and European views on design (figure 11.13). From the

Figure 11.13. One of the rooms in Golconde Puducherry, undated, photographer unknown, photographs copyright Sri Aurobindo Ashram Pondicherry, India.

point of view of architectural history, the intersection of leisurely horizontal networks in the sense of Ikegami Eiko, as explained above, of the Theosophical Society in Japan and the Garakuta Circle indeed provided an unexpected impulse or a spark for creating one of the best architectural creations in twentieth-century India.

Notes

1. Shraddhavan, ed., "Golconde: A Look Behind, Part 1: The Building," *Mother India* (January 1989): 26–27.

2. Ashok Dilwali, Robi Ganguli, and Vir. Mueller Architects, *Golconde: The Introduction of Modernism in India* (New Delhi: Urban Crayon Press, 2010).

3. Eiko Ikegami, *Bonds of Civility: Aesthetic Networks and the Political Origins of Japanese Culture* (Cambridge: Cambridge University Press, 2005), 4, 368, 376.

4. The history of nineteenth-century Theosophy in Japan has been researched by Yoshinaga Shin'ichi and his team, with the attendant publications appearing in both English and Japanese. Cf. Yoshinaga, Shin'ichi, et al., *Hirai Kinza ni okeru Meiji bukkyō no kokusaika ni kansuru shūkyōshi/bunkashi-teki kenkyū*, Research Report for Grants-in-Aid for Scientific Research for the Japanese Society for the Promotion of Science, Research no. 16520060, https://kaken.nii.ac.jp/report/KAKENHI-PROJECT-16520060/165200602006kenkyu_seika_hokoku_gaiyo/.

5. More on Cousins in Japan: James H. Cousins, *New Japan: Impressions and Reflections* (Madras: Ganesh, 1923); James H. Cousins and Margaret E. Cousins, *We Two Together* (Madras: Ganesh, 1950); Hashimoto Yorimitsu, "Airurando shinchigakuto no Ajiashugi? Jeimuzu Kazunzu no Nihon taizai (1919–1920) to sono yoha," in *Ajia o meguru hikaku geijutsu/dezain-gaku kenkyū: Nichiei-kan ni hirogaru 21-seiki no chihei*, ed. Fujita Haruhiko (Osaka: Graduate School of Letters, Osaka University, 2013), 27–43. See also the contribution by Hashimoto Yorimitsu to this volume.

6. See Gauri Viswanathan, "Spirituality, Internationalism, and Decolonization: James Cousins, the 'Irish poet from India,'" in *Ireland and Postcolonial Theory*, ed. Clare Carroll and Patricia King (Cork: Cork University Press, 2003); and idem, "Ireland, India, and the Poetics of Internationalism," *Journal of World History* 15 (March 2004).

7. On Wu Tingfang, see the contribution by Chuang Chienhui to this volume.

8. For more details, see Toshiharu Omuka, "'Tami no yume' to modanizumu: Kume Tamijūrō to Ezura Paundo," in *Nihon no avangyarudo geijutsu 'Mavo' to sono jidai* (Tokyo: Seidosha, 2001). This is the most extensive paper concerning

Tami Koumé and his life, although it does not touch upon his relations with James H. Cousins and Ine Brinkley.

9. Cousins, *New Japan*, 322.

10. "What Can Be Done to Save Russia Quickly?," *The Sun*, June 30, 1918, Section 5 Magazine Section, Page 7, Image 47, http://chroniclingamerica.loc.gov/lccn/sn83030431/1918-06-30/ed-1/seq-47/.

11. Stefan Łubienski, *Vor der Schwelle: Lebenserzählung eines polnischen Künstlers und Suchers* (Driebergen, Holland: Selbstverlag, 1974), 161; Antonin Raymond, *An Autobiography* (Rutland: C.E. Tuttle, 1973), 95.

12. Quote from Cousins's letter to the headquarters of the Theosophical Society in Adyar from February 15, 1920.

13. Radhanath Rath et al., *Rashbehari Basu—His Struggle for India's Independence* (Calcutta: R. Basu Smark Samity, 1963), 551. Some later correspondence shows Sabharwal move to China.

14. Yukiko Sumi Barnett, "*India in Asia*: Okawa Shūmei's Pan-Asian Thought and His Idea of India in Early Twentieth-Century Japan," *Journal of the Oxford University History Society* 1 (2004). On the Richards, see the contribution by Hans Martin Krämer to this volume.

15. Philippe Barbier Saint Hilaire, *Itinéraire d'un enfant du siècle: de l'école polytechnique à l'Ashram de Sri Aurobindo* (Paris: Buchet Chastel. 2001), 117–26.

16. Raymond, *Autobiography*, 78.

17. Stefan Łubienski, *Między Wschodem a Zachodem: Japonja na straży Azji. Dusza mistyczna Nipponu, etc.* (Warszawa: Gebethner and Wolff, 1927). Stefan Łubiensky's autobiography *Vor der Schwelle: Lebenserzählung* was illustrated by the painting by S. Wyspianski (1869–1907).

18. "Porando Bijutsu Seisakuten [Exhibition of Polish Art]," in *Shiseidō Gyararī shichijūgonenshi: 1919–1994*, ed. Tomiyama Hideo (Tōkyō: Shiseidō: Hatsubai Kyūryūdō, 1995), 253–54.

19. Sixten Ringbom, *The Sounding Cosmos: A Study in the Spiritualism of Kandinsky and the Genesis of Abstract Painting* (Åbo [Finland]: Åbo Akademi, 1970).

20. Helena Petrovna Blavatsky, *Isis Unveiled: A Master-Key to the Mysteries of Ancient and Modern Science and Theology*, Vol. 1, *Science*, Vol. 2, *Theology* (Pasadena: Theosophical University Press, 1972).

21. Annie Besant and Charles Leadbeater, *Thought-Forms: A Record of Clairvoyant Investigation* (London: Theosophical Publishing Society, 1901)

22. Ibid., 5.

23. Gauri Viswanathan, "The Ordinary Business of Occultism," *Critical Inquiry* 27, no. 1 (2000): 4.

24. For further reading: Maurice Tuchman et al., *The Spiritual in Art: Abstract Painting 1890–1985* (New York: Los Angeles County Museum of Art and Abbeville Press, 1986); Alexandra Monroe, *The Third Mind: American Artists Contemplate Asia, 1860–1989* (New York: Solomon R. Guggenheim Museum, 2009).

25. Viswanathan, "Ordinary Business," 4.

26. Alex Owen, *The Place of Enchantment: British Occultism and the Culture of the Modern* (Chicago: University of Chicago Press, 2004), 6.

27. *Enchanted Modernities: Theosophy, Modernism and the Arts, c. 1875–1960* was a three-year network project exploring "what the visual, material and performing arts can tell us about the relationships between Theosophy, modernity and mysticism c. 1875–1960." See "Enchanted Modernities. Theosophy, Modernism and the arts, c. 1865–1960," University of York, Department of History of Art, http://hoaportal.york.ac.uk/hoaportal/enchanted-modernities-index-project.jsp. The network published a book: Sarah V. Turner, Christopher M. Scheer, and James G. Mansell, eds., *Enchanted Modernities: Theosophy, the Arts and the American West* (Somerset: Fulgur Press, 2019).

28. For further reading: Jonathan *Massey, Crystal and Arabesque: Claude Bragdon, Ornament, and Modern Architecture* (Pittsburgh: University of Pittsburgh Press, 2009); Susan R. Henderson, "J.L.M. Lauweriks and K.P.C. de Bazel: Architecture and Theosophy," in *The Religion Imagination and Modern Architecture*, ed. Renate Hejduk and Jim Williamson (New York: Routledge, 2011); Marty Bax, *Organic Architecture. Rudolf Steiner's Building Impulse* (Amsterdam: Iona Stichting, 1993).

29. Shraddhavan, ed., "Golconde. A Look Behind, Part 3: The Buildings (1)," *Mother India* (March 1989): 176.

30. More on Mirra Alfassa in Boaz Huss, "Madame Théon, Alta Una, Mother Superior: The Life and Personas of Mary Ware (1839–1908)," *Aries* 15 (2015): 218–22. See also the contribution by Hans Martin Krämer to this volume.

31. Shraddhavan, ed., "Golconde. A Look Behind, Part 4: The Buildings (1)," *Mother India* (April 1989): 241.

32. George Nakashima, *The Soul of a Tree: A Woodworker's Reflections* (New York: Kodansha USA, 2012).

33. Shraddhavan, ed., "Golconde. A Look Behind, Part 1: The Building," *Mother India* (January 1989): 25.

34. Idem, "Golconde. A Look Behind, Part 13: Conclusion," *Mother India* (February 1990): 91.

35. In *Theosophical Quarterly* 35, no. 3 (1938): 245.

References

Bax, Marty. *Organic Architecture: Rudolf Steiner's Building Impulse*. Amsterdam: Iona Stichting, 1993.

Besant, Annie, and Charles Leadbeater. *Thought-Forms: A Record of Clairvoyant Investigation*. London and Benares: Theosophical Publishing Society, 1901.

Blavatsky, Helena Petrovna. *Isis Unveiled: A Master-Key to the Mysteries of Ancient and Modern Science and Theology.* Vol. 1, *Science.* Vol. 2, *Theology.* Pasadena: Theosophical University Press, 1972.
Cousins, James H. *The New Japan: Impressions and Reflections.* Madras: Ganesh & Co., 1923.
Cousins, James H., and Margaret E. Cousins. *We Two Together.* Madras: Ganesh, 1950.
Dilwali, Ashok, Robi Ganguli, and Vir Mueller Architects. *Golconde: The Introduction of Modernism in India.* New Delhi: Urban Crayon Press, 2010.
Hashimoto Yorimitsu. "Airurando shinchigakuto no Ajiashugi? Jeimuzu Kazunzu no Nihon taizai (1919–1920) to sono yoha [An Irish Theosophist's Pan-Asianism? James Cousins's stay in Japan (1919–1920) and its aftermath]." In *Ajia o meguru hikaku geijutsu dezain-gaku kenkyū: Nichiei-kan ni hirogaru 21-seiki no chihei* [Comparative Art and Design Studies of Asia: The horizon between Japan and Britain in the 21st century], edited by Fujita Haruhiko, 27–43. Osaka: Graduate School of Letters, Osaka University, 2013.
Helfrich, Kurt G. F., and William Whitaker, eds. *Crafting a Modern World: the Architecture and Design of Antonin and Noémi Raymond.* New York: Princeton Architectural Press, 2006.
Henderson, Susan R. "J.L.M. Lauweriks and K.P.C. de Bazel: Architecture and Theosophy." In *The Religion Imagination and Modern Architecture,* edited by Renate Hejduk and Jim Williamson, 164–75. New York: Routledge, 2011.
Huss, Boaz. "Madame Théon, Alta Una, Mother Superior: The Life and Personas of Mary Ware (1839–1908)." *Aries* 15 (2015): 210–46.
Kirita Kiyohide, ed. *Suzuki Daisetsu kenkyū kiso shiryō* [Fundamental Sources for Research on Suzuki Daisetsu]. Kamakura: Matsugaoka Bunko, 2005.
Łubienski, Stefan. *Między Wschodem a Zachodem: Japonja na straży Azji. Dusza mistyczna Nipponu, etc.* [Between East and West: Japan as a Guard of Asia, Mystical Spirit of Japan, etc.]. Warszawa: Gebethner and Wolff, 1927.
———. *Vor der Schwelle: Lebenserzählung eines polnischen Künstlers und Suchers.* Driebergen, Holland: Selbstverlag, 1974.
Massey, Jonathan. *Crystal and Arabesque: Claude Bragdon, Ornament, and Modern Architecture.* Pittsburgh: University of Pittsburgh Press, 2009.
Monroe, Alexandra. *The Third Mind: American Artists Contemplate Asia, 1860–1989.* New York: Solomon R. Guggenheim Museum, 2009.
Nakashima, George. *The Soul of a Tree: A Woodworker's Reflections.* New York: Kodansha USA, 2012.
Omuka Toshiharu. *Nihon no avangyarudo geijutsu "Mavo" to sono jidai* [Japanese Avant-Garde Art "Mavo" and Its Time]. Tokyo: Seidosha, 2001.
Owen, Alex. *The Place of Enchantment: British Occultism and the Culture of the Modern.* Chicago: University of Chicago Press, 2004.
Rath, Radhanath et al. *Rashbehari Basu—His Struggle for India's Independence.* Calcutta: R. Basu Smark Samity, 1963.

Raymond, Antonin. *An Autobiography.* Rutland: C.E. Tuttle, 1973.
Ringbom, Sixten. *The Sounding Cosmos: A Study in the Spiritualism of Kandinsky and the Genesis of Abstract Painting.* Åbo [Finland]: Åbo Akademi, 1970.
Saint Hilaire, Philippe Barbier. *Itinéraire d'un enfant du siècle: de l'école polytechnique à l'Ashram de Sri Aurobindo.* Paris: Buchet Chastel. 2001.
Shraddhavan, ed. "Golconde: A Look Behind." Part 1–13. *Mother India.* January 1989–February 1990.
Sumi Barnett, Yukiko. "India in Asia: Okawa Shūmei's Pan-Asian Thought and His Idea of India in Early Twentieth-Century Japan." *Journal of the Oxford University History Society* 1 (2004): 1–23.
Tomiyama Hideo, ed., *Shiseidō Gyararī shichijūgonenshi: 1919–1994* [75 Years Shiseidō Gallery: 1919–1994]. Tōkyō: Shiseidō: Hatsubai Kyūryūdō, 1995.
Tuchman, Maurice et al. *The Spiritual in Art: Abstract Painting 1890–1985.* New York: Los Angeles County Museum of Art and Abbeville Press, 1986.
Turner, Sarah V., Christopher M. Scheer, and James G. Mansell, eds. *Enchanted Modernities: Theosophy, the Arts and the American West.* Somerset: Fulgur Press, 2019.
University of York, Department of History of Art. "Enchanted Modernities. Theosophy, Modernism and the arts, c. 1865–1960." http://hoaportal.york.ac.uk/hoaportal/enchanted-modernities-index-project.jsp.
Viswanathan, Gauri. "The Ordinary Business of Occultism." *Critical Inquiry* 27, no. 1 (2000): 1–20.
———. "Spirituality, Internationalism, and Decolonization: James Cousins, the 'Irish Poet from India.'" In *Ireland and Postcolonial Theory*, edited by Clare Carroll and Patricia King, 158–76. Cork: Cork University Press, 2003.
———. "Ireland, India, and the Poetics of Internationalism." *Journal of World History* 15 (March 2004): 7–30.
"What Can Be Done to Save Russia Quickly?" *The Sun*, June 30, 1918. http://chroniclingamerica.loc.gov/lccn/sn83030431/1918-06-30/ed-1/seq-47/.
Yoshinaga, Shin'ichi, et al. *Hirai Kinza ni okeru Meiji bukkyō no kokusaika ni kansuru shūkyōshi/bunkashi-teki kenkyū* [Hirai Kinza and the globalization of Japanese Buddhism of the Meiji era: A study in religious and cultural history]. Research Report for Grants-in-Aid for Scientific Research for the Japanese Society for the Promotion of Science, Research no. 16520060. https://kaken.nii.ac.jp/report/KAKENHI-PROJECT-16520060/165200602006kenkyu_seika_hokoku_gaiyo/.

Chapter 12

From Healer to Shaman
Theosophy and the Making of Esoteric Bali

Yan Suarsana

1. Introduction: The Hidden Influence of Theosophy on Balinese Tradition

When Friedrich Demolsky landed on Bali in October 1995, he was on a journey to his inner self. Stricken by illness and personal crisis, he had retired from his position as a judge in Austria, setting out for a one-year trip to "bring his life back into balance," as he told me. Having abandoned his original plan to travel through India's *Little Tibet*, the old Buddhist kingdom of Ladakh, he finally made his way to the tropical island of Bali after an invitation from a boyhood friend who was running a business there.

Six weeks later, Dr. Demolsky had met his future wife, whose brothers worked as healers (*balian*) within the traditional medical sector. Three of them operated as *balians* (*apun* or *uat*), a type of healer combining "the physical actions of massage with the [. . .] manipulation of mystical forces, through mantras and offerings,"[1] with *uat/urat*, meaning "channels [of] various fluids that transmit the life force and that remove waste products."[2] Cured from severe depression by his brothers-in-law, Dr. Demolsky was deeply impressed by their powers and skills, and soon felt the desire to help his "brothers and sisters out there" as well as the *balians* themselves who had healed him. Together with his wife, Ketut, he set up an organization in 1999 to provide the healing powers of his brothers-in-law (and later of other *balians* as well) to a broader customer base, not only in Bali, but also further afield via the internet. The website is still online today.

However, Friedrich Demolsky was not an ordinary tourist. Not only had he devoted himself to magic and shamanism for several decades before his arrival in Bali, but in his younger years, he had served as a member of the Rosicrucian Order (AMORC) together with his former wife, who held a temple degree from that organization. Fascinated by the teachings of Helena Blavatsky and Annie Besant, Dr. Demolsky tracked the installation and proclamation of Jiddu Krishnamurti as the new World Teacher, which finally led him to the headquarters of the Theosophical Society in Adyar, where he spent some time studying (today, a copy of Blavatsky's *Secret Doctrine* is still among the books in his personal library in Bali).

His vast interest in magic, shamanism, and esoteric systems of knowledge such as Rosicrucianism and Theosophy has prompted him to develop a complex theory on the work of his brothers-in-law. As the name of his wife's organization, *Balishaman*, suggests, Dr. Demolsky sees the *balians'* healing skills not just as a form of traditional medicine, as it is usually perceived.[3] In engaging critically with the work of Mircea Eliade,[4] he has published extensively[5] on his concept of shamanism as the "second cultural achievement of mankind," which he sees as having developed from earlier animistic cultures.[6] When the oldest of the "world religions," Hinduism, came to the Malayan archipelago, it was faced with a local culture that was still animistic in character. This clash resulted in an amalgamation of the two, which Dr. Demolsky calls a "magic culture." The spread of Islam in the wider region from the eleventh century onward finally brought an end to this, leaving only the tiny island of Bali to form a "Hindu enclave" within the Muslim environment of the archipelago. Thus magic culture—and with it, shamanism—could survive in Bali up to this very day. Therefore, magic shamanism is an element deeply rooted in Balinese culture and cannot be adopted by outsiders through imitation or education, as Dr. Demolsky told me. Today, Friedrich Demolsky lives in Bali to support his wife with her work and labels himself the "spiritus rector" of her organization.

At first glance, the seamless collaboration of representatives of the traditional Balinese context with an esoteric theorist from Europe hardly seems surprising, because the global image of Bali as the "island of the Gods" or "of a thousand temples" has become firmly ingrained in the popular mindset in recent decades—because of the Indonesian government's master plan for modern mass tourism with Bali as its main target. However, the picture of Bali as a place of esoteric wisdom on which Demolsky relies is much older and has contributed not only to recent images of Bali as a spiritual paradise, but also to the idea of Balinese tradition as being representative of Indian culture and the "world religion" of Hinduism, as I argue. This esoteric conception of Bali dates back to colonial times, when the island was forcefully opened to foreign travelers and, at least as important, global discourses of religion and culture. Among the first to arrive in colonial Bali were members of the Theosophical Society in the Dutch East Indies, who set the scene for what was to become "Esoteric Bali" in the 1970s.

Indeed, Theosophical ideas of Balinese culture and religion are not as marginal as one might think. While research has largely focused on the conceptualization of Balinese religion as part of worldwide Hinduism in the twentieth century,[7] the entanglement of the discourse on Indian religion with Theosophy in India and the Dutch East Indies has been widely overlooked. While esotericism in Bali is at present (in great part, but not exclusively) a touristic phenomenon, the situation is different if one looks at the negotiation processes that helped to establish the "traditional" sphere of Balinese culture during the first half of the twentieth century. In India, Theosophists were instrumental in establishing Hinduism as a "world religion" in the late nineteenth century. Thus, it can be argued that this discourse was somewhat "copied" over to Bali in the early twentieth century, when the Dutch colonial administration started to (re-)construct Balinese society as an essentially *Indian* culture, with Balinese religion as part of worldwide Hinduism. And yet, while recent activities of the Theosophical Society in Bali are rather rare and Theosophical influences have become invisible in traditional contexts, the entanglement of the discourse on Balinese tradition with the conceptualization of "Esoteric Bali" becomes evident when we look at today's scene of New Age esotericism in Bali, as the example of Fritz Demolsky suggests. Therefore, to investigate the role of the Theosophical Society in shaping the various images of the tiny island of Bali, let us begin with the end of the story—today.

2. The Esotericization of Balinese Medicine

When it comes to the idea of esoteric wisdom in Bali, one might immediately think of Elizabeth Gilbert's bestselling book[8] *Eat Pray Love* (2006) and the attendant motion picture featuring Julia Roberts (2010). Here we find Liz, a middle-aged American woman, traveling to Ubud, Bali's cultural capital, consulting a local "medicine man,"[9] that is, the high-caste *balian* Ketut Liyer, who "reveals a new path to peace, leaving her ready to love again."[10] And indeed, if we look a bit more closely at Bali's traditional medical sector, we can find that several of its adherents professionally are organizing themselves to provide services specifically for non-Balinese people—by combining their medical knowledge with concepts of New Age esotericism.

Now, the fact that they are doing so is not astounding, as one could simply speak of fulfilling the needs of those who come to Bali. Yet two other issues need to be looked at more closely. First, why they are coming, and second, why it is that the combination of traditional Balinese concepts of healing and soundness with New Age culture seems so plausible and appealing to both international and local adherents of esotericism in Bali?

To address the first issue, it is necessary to start by approaching the second one. The combination of foreign concepts with a sector that used to be relatively closed to outsiders is in need of explanation. What is now called "traditional medicine" was established as an alternative to academic medicine in colonial times when it was characterized as "Volksheilkunde" (folk medicine) in the extensive study by Wolfgang Weck (1937), who worked as the chief government doctor in the Dutch East Indies.[11] Since then, scholars have sketched the influence of Tantric traditions on Balinese theories of healing that reached Bali through its Indo-Javanese heritage.[12] As Balinese history suggests, it was the Javanese Brahman Mpu Kuturun who brought the first medical manuscripts from East Java to Bali in the eleventh century. These manuscripts are named *usada* in old Balinese, derived from the Sanskrit word *ausada* ("curative"), which is also used in Ayurvedic texts.[13] While in the pre-colonial period, knowledge of *usada* was exclusively held by Brahmin scholars who served as doctors, counselors, or chroniclers at the various royal courts of Bali, the forceful integration of the island into the colonial state of *Nederlands-Indië* at the beginning of the twentieth century brought a decisive change to that situation. As the Dutch saw Brahmin court officials as representatives of the religious sphere, they were widely excluded from the political system of the new state.[14] However, those former high-caste court physicians, now somewhat unemployed, soon managed to reestablish themselves within the diffuse sphere of "traditional" medicine that emerged in parallel to the introduction of health centers and hospitals led by European doctors.[15] Still today, Brahmin scholars (such as the above-mentioned Ketut Liyer from Gilbert's book) function as the backbone of the informal health-care sector of Bali, where health is understood not only in a strictly medical sense, but also with respect to more general concerns, such as crop failure or domestic and political frictions.[16] Known as *balian usada* (for their knowledge of ancient medical manuscripts), high-caste doctors are now supported by a vast array of folk healers, mediums, and magicians, often combining their therapeutic knowledge with various traditions and techniques, such as yoga, even martial arts, or elements from academic medicine.[17]

In the case of the *Balishamans*, we find the practices of some of these low-caste (*commoner*) healers (especially *balian apun* and *tetakson*[18]) conceptualized through ideas obviously derived from New Age esotericism. While Demolsky's concept of shamanism as "the 'primal religion' of mankind"[19] was initially shaped by Mircea Eliade,[20] the idea of shamanistic spirituality as an archaic form of religion has been popularized in New Age circles through the works of Carlos Castaneda,[21] where it not only aroused interest in the "primordial" wisdom of indigenous peoples, but also boosted enthusiasm for "Eastern" spirituality.[22]

However, much more popular than the *Balishamans* is the Balinese guru Ratu Bagus, who began to work as a healer after "a vision from the Divine"[23] during "one of his meditations on the slopes of Mount Agung."[24] In 1988, Ratu founded a little ashram on his farmland in Karangasem (Eastern Bali), where he was surrounded by a community of local followers after some spectacular curative treatments.[25] In 1993, Italian yoga teacher Gino di Simone "discovered" the group and invited its head, Ratu Bagus, to Italy.[26] When a group of Italian travelers visited the ashram two years later, they found a gathering of young men practicing some kind of *Osho*-style shaking meditation combined with martial arts techniques and the defense of rocks and coconuts thrown at them by their guru.[27] Ten years later, the group appears to have completely changed: the ahsram has turned into a modern studio with European and several dressed-up Balinese people practicing *Shaking Yoga*, a kind of "Bio Energy Meditation [that] works on freeing and strengthening our natural life energy."[28] Among them, the kindly, smiling guru is wearing a shiny white robe instead of his sweatpants and T-shirt from a previous decade.[29]

Actually, the Ratu Bagus movement has developed from a local phenomenon of some poor villagers to a global transcultural movement within only ten years, attracting people especially from Europe, North America, and Australia. According to his own statement, Ratu Bagus is represented so far in several Western countries through coordinators and countless "Shaking Groups."[30] His ashram is still located in Karangasem on the side of the holy mountain *Gunung Agung* and is run by Balinese followers of the guru, providing accommodations for spiritual tourists and rooms for workshops. Ratu himself has undertaken several journeys to Europe to spread his teachings; there, he combines New Age concepts with Balinese ideas of healing and sickness, declaring Bali as a center of spiritual energy.[31] While most of the ashram's visitors obviously are of Western origin, Ratu Bagus is far from being a purely touristic movement. In 2009, the guru was awarded with the Hindu Muda Award by the organization of a prominent representative of traditional Bali, Dr. Arya Wedakarna, for his achievements in "strengthening Hindu affiliation among the young generation."[32]

The rapid transformation of the Ratu Bagus movement raises two principal issues: First, how was it possible that this small, village-based group could develop into a global esoteric movement attracting mostly people from Western countries? And second, why is it that this globalized esoteric guru is simultaneously perceived as an important actor of Balinese Hinduism by his compatriots? (This issue is similar in the case of the *Balishamans*, as it seems here that local practitioners of the traditional medical sector do not have the slightest problem with the terminology and concepts of magic and New Age shamanism).[33] To answer these questions, one should look not so much at the teachings of the particular groups, but at esoteric concepts of Bali in general, concepts that are plausible both in an international and a local, "traditional," context. Now, if we want to understand why those ideas of Esoteric Bali seem so self-evident today, we have to trace their origins back in history to a time when such ideas were initially introduced to the cultural context of Bali—by proponents of the Theosophical Society.

3. Esoteric Bali as Part of the Spiritual Trail

One of the backbones of today's esoteric scene in Bali is spiritual tourism. Spiritual travelers have been widespread in Bali since the 1970s, when hosts of hippies and other seekers followed the so-called Spiritual Trail to Bali.[34] The starting point was a newly emerged fascination for Bali in the United States and Europe that was grounded by the influence of Asian religion on pop culture and the New Age wave of the late 1960s[35]—a development that led to a veritable boom in spiritual tourism to Asian countries.[36] In hippie contexts, the works of former Bali-ethnographers Gregory Bateson (1904–1980) and Margaret Mead (1901–1978) certainly had an influence:

> Bateson was at that time living in the hippy mecca of Southern California as one of its Western gurus, while Mead's writings and public appearances had been important in developing ideas of liberation from the boringly puritanical mainstream of middle America. Both were active proponents of alternative lifestyles, of which Bali's culture was perhaps the most perfect example.[37]

Western Bali enthusiasm was paralleled by the plans of Indonesia's central government in Jakarta to establish the island as the country's most prominent target of international mass tourism after years of economic stagnation and political chaos.[38] When concepts of luxury and package tourism in the form of the giant Bali Beach hotel had failed, the provision of a "more personalized experience of Bali"[39] was fostered from the mid-1960s onward. This included the idea of an individualized cultural tourism (*pariwisata budaya*), where visitors were accommodated in bungalow hotels and small hostels often run by local families. "Not being able to afford the plush Bali Beach, the hippies of the late 1960s and early 1970s preferred [. . .] the informal arrangements of staying in people's houses"[40] that had developed "into a semi-formal system of 'home-stays,' in which families were permanently geared to a flow of foreign guests."[41] This way, travelers "who wanted to know more about Bali could also come into close contact with one group of Balinese on a day-to-day basis."[42] These "young people, who fostered an interest in Indian gurus and the use of drugs to achieve enlightenment," combined the "pre-war image of Bali as a rich religious culture" (as propagated by *pariwisata budaya*) with their "hippy ideas about the mystical East," while "in many cases the lack of a common language led them to romanticize the Balinese lifestyle."[43] Therefore, the hippie and New Age tourists of the 1970s can be seen as the founders of today's Esoteric Bali, as they put the island on the global map of spirituality as a paradise of Eastern knowledge and wisdom.

However, these developments cover only one part of the two questions raised above. While New Age tourism explains the mere existence of the global image of Bali as a spiritual or esoteric paradise, the question of the plausibility of this image to both the tourists themselves and the Balinese who represent it is still unanswered. Therefore, we must take one more step back in time, to the invention of Bali as an Indian and spiritual paradise at the beginning of the twentieth century through representatives of colonialism, Neo-Hinduism, and Theosophy.

4. "Indian Bali" as a Product of Colonial History

New Age and "hippie ideas" of Balinese culture and religion would not have gained international popularity if Western tourists (and the Balinese themselves) had not been able to engage in concepts that had been part of the global image of Bali for several decades already. Such concepts date back to colonial times, when Bali was initially integrated into the international infrastructure (and therefore awareness) through the island's rough and final conquest by Dutch army forces in 1908. What matters in our case is that the new rulers introduced the idea of Bali as an essentially Indian culture and of Balinese religion as a derivate of worldwide Hinduism—concepts that would later set Bali on the New Age map of Indian/Eastern spirituality. While Indian influences on Balinese culture (as, for example, in the case of traditional medicine) are doubtlessly traceable via the Indo-Javanese kingdoms of old, the idea of Bali as part of the Indian hemisphere was rather new in a local context, as it had not been part of political or religious discourses on the island in the pre-colonial period. The "Indianization" of Bali rather can be described as the result of complex historical processes of negotiation that began in the middle of the nineteenth century and were connected to global discourses on religion, culture, and civilization.

With the initiation of the gradual colonization of the island by the Dutch from 1846, Bali became an arena for the negotiation of certain European Orientalist conceptions of religion and society. It was, however, as early as 1817 that the British Orientalist and colonial politician Thomas Raffles (1781–1826) shaped the assumption of Bali as being some kind of museum of the great Indo-Javanese *Majapahit* empire, which had dominated the archipelago from the fourteenth to the sixteenth centuries.[44] Raffles's theory of Bali as "little India" went on to become a core concept of Dutch colonial politics: having almost completely wiped out the higher Balinese aristocracy during their final campaign of conquest in 1908, the Dutch sought to reestablish Bali's social structures based on the model of an (idealized) Indian society, with certain inconsistencies caused by Balinese customs perceived as local distortions of the "original" system.[45] "They were especially keen to make a clear distinction between the three highest status categories (collectively Triwangsa, i.e. Brahmana, Satria and Wésia [. . .]) and the large residual population, who were now all to be classed as Sudra, despite the many differences amongst them."[46]

For our purposes, the religious policy is of special interest. Here, the image of Bali as a "little India" fostered a conviction of Balinese religion as being a "legitimate part of the world religion of Hinduism,"[47] which had to be protected against the influence of Islam and Christianity in order to secure peace on the island. This perception of the nature of Balinese religion was adopted by Balinese intellectuals working as civil servants or schoolteachers for the Dutch administration who had been educated in Dutch colleges. In such a way, the first "Hindu" organization, called *Stiti Bali*, was founded in 1917 by the district head of Sukasada, I Goesti Bagoes Tjakra Tanaja, and Ketoet Nasa alongside several religious magazines propagating the subject of "Balinese Hinduism."[48] While supporters of the traditional nobility favored a more localized interpretation of their newfound religion, it was the group of young and upcoming commoners (*jaba*) in Dutch services who sought to unite Balinese religion with what was conceptualized as the world religion of Hinduism (as propagated by Indian Neo-Hinduists).[49] Tjakra Tanaja "wanted to call the religion *agama Hindu Bali*, with the emphasis on the Hindu element, a form of defense of the hierarchy and particularly of the position of the *tri-wangsa*."[50] However, what both groups had in common was the perception of the Balinese as a single people and a stronghold of Hinduism—ideas completely new to the Balinese context at the time.[51]

The second aspect of the formation of a specific Balinese identity is also crucial. The image of Bali as an exotic paradise originally propagated by the second generation of Dutch colonialists and Orientalists (often born in the Dutch East Indies) attracted an increasing number of European artists, cultural travelers and tourists from the 1930s onward. While nineteenth-century European Orientalists such as Rudolph Friederich and Robert van Hoëvell (1812–1879) were more interested in Indian influences on Balinese high culture,[52] scholars including Frederick Albert Liefrinck (1853–1927) were drawn to the simple life of the ordinary people of Bali, focused on constructing detailed accounts on local arts and cuisine, and drew the picture of old *Bali Aga* villages as "the true, republican, if not democratic, nature of Balinese society."[53] It is hardly surprising that the Dutch colonial administration drew on images such as the latter to give Bali a more positive reputation after the devastating conquest of 1908 that had caused international debate. Six years after the Balinese high court had been massacred by colonial forces, the Dutch steamboat company KPM advertised Bali as the "Garden of Eden"[54] and in this way established the image of Bali as an exotic and paradisiacal tourist destination. This strategy proved to be highly successful: in the decades to follow, countless articles in magazines like *National Geographic*, books (such as Vicki Baum's best-selling novel *A Tale from Bali*[55]), and films would attract not only tourists from the upper middle class, but also many artists, dropouts, or spiritual seekers (such as, for example, German painter Walter Spies [1895–1942]), followed by a new generation of scholars (such as the above-mentioned Gregory Bateson and Margaret Mead), who "were at the forefront of modern anthropology, developing it as a profession and making the study of the cultures of the world truly scientific."[56]

5. The Coming of Theosophy

With these two points in mind—the colonial conception of Bali as an outpost of Indian culture, and the provision of a basic traveling infrastructure—it is of course hardly astonishing that the Theosophical Society would soon direct its attention to this "Indian island." While its founders, the New York lawyer Henry Steel Olcott (1832–1907) and German-Russian aristocrat Helena Petrovna Blavatsky (1831–1891), had originally been "committed to the moral and philosophical 'uplift' of spiritualism,"[57] Olcott's interest in Asian religion soon led to a certain "shift" in the orientation of his organization in 1877, when he claimed in a letter to an Indian acquaintance "that the mission of the Theosophical Society was not to reform Spiritualism but to import Asian wisdom to the United States."[58] For that purpose, the Theosophical Society merged with an important Indian reform society in May 1878, "renaming their ecumenical organization 'The Theosophical Society of the Arya Samaj,'"[59] while Swami Dayanand Saraswati (1824–1883), who had founded the Arya Samaj in 1875, was anointed the "'supreme religious Teacher, Guide and Ruler' of this new amalgamation."[60] In December 1878, Olcott and Blavatsky eventually settled in Bombay, where a branch of the Theosophical Society had already been founded by some of Olcott's Indian correspondents,[61] to intensify their collaboration with Hindu reformers. Yet, while "Olcott's mission in India, he announced, was not to reform Hindus but 'to get you Eastern people to help us reform Europe and America' [. . .], the Theosophical Society was destined to wield its primary influence not in the West but in the East."[62] By struggling "for a modern revitalization of 'Aryavarta' or ancient India," Theosophy had a large share in establishing the idea of Indian Hinduism as the universal, prototypical religion of the mystical East.[63] Furthermore, "its creative interpretation of Brāhmanism as including the scientific and moral doctrines of Western rationalism"[64] attracted a large number of Indians from the Western-educated elite who not only "were ready to welcome a reformulation of their religious heritage,"[65] but also were prepared to reform Indian society as a whole. Thus, it is not surprising that Theosophists were heavily involved in the formation of the Indian National Congress (INC), including not only prominent Indian Theosophists such as Narendranath Sen, the editor of the *Indian Daily Mirror*, but also Scotsman Allan O. Hume (1829–1912), one of the INC's founders,[66] and Annie Besant (1847–1933), "who became the only Western woman ever to be elected as president of the Indian National Congress."[67]

Despite its conceptual focus on India, the Theosophical discourse on Indian religion can be characterized as a global phenomenon from its beginnings. This assumption is not merely indicated by the fact that Indian lodges were organized by both Westerners and Indian "members of the new English-orientated, educated classes,"[68] but by Theosophy's global popularity at the end of the nineteenth century, when branches of the Theosophical Society were founded in numerous countries around the world. This way, Theosophy shared a big part in shaping the global discourse on religion by heavily relying on colonial negotiation processes about the "West" and the "East." "Theosophy, thus, provides an outstanding example of the complex entanglements of the global religious history of the nineteenth and early twentieth centuries."[69]

One of the main fields of Theosophical activity at that time was in the Dutch East Indies.[70] After the first lodge in Java had been founded in 1881, the Dutch East Indies were recognized by the Theosophical Society headquarters in Adyar as an autonomous section in 1912, "with Annie Besant announcing that '[i]t is pleasant to chronicle the formation of the National Society in Java, which now feels strong enough to stand on its own feet [. . .].' "[71] In 1930, nearly half a percent of the Dutch population in Java were members of the Theosophical Society—the highest amount of adherents in a ruling colonial population worldwide;[72] 50 percent of them were of local origin, who were often part of the nobility or bureaucratic elite of the colonial administration: as in India, the Theosophical Society supported "the participation of educated members of the native nobility in the political affairs of the Indies," so "it is not surprising to find that quite a considerable number of members of the Volksraad [the colonial parliament] were Theosophists. [. . .] Their number was proportionally much higher than the percentage of Theosophists among the total population."[73] In 1921, "five out of the Volksraad's thirty-nine members were Theosophists," and just as in India's INC, "Theosophists continued to be well presented among Volksraad delegates."[74] When the high prevalence of Dutch Theosophical Society members in the colonial bureaucracy is considered, the implication is close at hand that Theosophical ideas about Indian religion played a role in the conceptualization of Balinese religion as a form of worldwide Hinduism at the beginning of the twentieth century, as I have elaborated above. Though most of the Javanese and European members of the Theosophical Society in Dutch East India were nominally Muslim or Christian, "it was predominantly through their agency that images of India, Hinduism, and Buddhism were disseminated among the wider population of the Indies."[75]

The integration of Bali into Dutch East India (and therefore into the global discourse on Indian religion) at the beginning of the twentieth century resulted almost immediately in the visit of Theosophists from Java. In 1915, only seven years after the Dutch had forcefully opened the way to the island, Mas Djono came to Bali, followed by Javanese prince Mangkoe Negoro VII the same year. From 1918 to 1921, Javanese Theosophist Raden Mas Soetatmo Soeriokoesoemo (1888–1924) traveled the island: "He viewed Bali as being religiously purer than Java and supported 'Balinese religion' as a counterweight to orthodox Javanese Islam."[76] Soetatmo was not only a member of the Paku Alam ruling dynasty of Yogyakarta, but also a Volksraad delegate and a political theorist.[77] His nationalist ideas were "based on Theosophical interpretations of Indian concepts such as the caste system, interpretations that had been advanced mainly by Europeans,"[78] and which he could find manifested in similar form in Bali through the "reorganization" of Balinese society by the colonial administration. In this context, the newly introduced "Sudra" caste attracted his attention:

> Like Theosophists in other countries, who were defending social hierarchies perceived as being under threat by socio-cultural change, Soetatmo associated the new political ideas promoting egalitarianism [which he rejected] with what the Theosophical Society called *sudra*, the lowest "caste" of a given society, incapable of the wise esoteric insights of their social superiors.[79]

During the 1930s, the *Nederlandsch-Indische Theosofische Vereeniging* opened several lodges in Bali.[80] In 1934, its General Secretary, Van Leeuwen, spent his holidays in Bali, and met with some of his fellow Theosophists in Denpasar.[81] Three years later, another member of the Theosophical Society central committee in Bandung, Raden Mas Koesoemodihardjo, came to Bali for a "propaganda trip"[82] and gave an account of the *Adnjana Nirmala* lodge with sixteen members, headed by the north-Balinese noble I Gusti Ketoet Djelantik.[83] It was at about the same time that an Indonesian translation of a lecture on bhakti by Annie Besant, which had been published by the lodge in Batavia, circulated in Bali.[84]

Koesoemodihardjo was not only interested in Theosophical activities in Bali. During his journey, he also addressed several branches of a reformist Hindu organization called *Bali Darma Laksana*, a religious association that had been founded in 1937 (the same year as Koesoemodihardjo's trip) by local intellectuals after the model of the above-mentioned *Stiti Bali*. There, he detected a "great deal of interest"[85] in Theosophy and recorded the notion that "the tenets of theosophy have much in common with the doctrine of the *lontars*"[86] (palm leaf manuscripts) held by influential families and priests.

The enthusiasm of Balinese Hindu reformists for Theosophical ideas can be understood when considering that these organizations were in intense contact with representatives of Indian Neo-Hinduism who shared the idea of Balinese religion as part of worldwide Hinduism and were themselves often deeply entangled with Theosophy, as I have shown above. In 1927, Indian poet and reformist Rabindranath Tagore (1861–1941) visited Java and Bali and was "warmly received by Dutch and Javanese Theosophists as well as Balinese 'Hindu' intellectuals."[87] He declared "that the Balinese were real Hindus,"[88] proposing the invitation of Indian Brahmins to foster a "Hindu Renaissance"[89] in Bali. The year 1933 saw the publication of the first Indonesian translation of the Bhagavad Gita, which had previously been rather unknown in the Balinese context,[90] but had been established by Indian Neo-Hinduists as the central scripture of Indian religion during the nineteenth century.[91]

The connection of Balinese Hindu reformers with both Javanese Theosophists and Indian Neo-Hinduism must not be underestimated. While Theosophy in Bali (unlike in Java) never was a movement of wider political influence, this entanglement could support the wider dissemination of Theosophical ideas through concepts of Indian religion and culture propagated by the exponents of worldwide (Neo-)Hinduism. In Java, Theosophy certainly had a direct effect on the image of Indian religion.[92] By contrast, similar effects in Bali seem rather indirect, although the *Adnjana Nirmala* lodge was still active in the 1950s. Today, Theosophical activities on the island are rather marginal.[93] However, not only did the Neo-Hindu conceptualization of Balinese religion as part of the world religion of Hinduism represent the leading guideline for the colonial administration, but it also continued to be an important element of religious politics of the Republic of Indonesia from 1945 on. The new government, presided over by long-serving nationalist and half-Balinese Soekarno (1901–1970), established a constitutional system in which the legal acknowledgment of a "religion" (*agama*) was linked to certain criteria to secure peace and stability in this vast multiethnic state—criteria that were drawn from the global discourse on "world religions." While the principles of the Indonesian constitution (*Pancasila*) only speak of "the belief in the one and only God" (*ketuhanan yang maha esa*) as the "center of the philosophy of the state,"[94] it was the Ministry of Religion (*Departemen Agama*) that extended the requirements for the legal acceptance of a religious group as *agama* to conditions such as the possession of a holy book and international recognition, while simultaneously not limiting it to a single ethnic group (such as in Bali):[95]

> According to these conditions, the Balinese did not profess a proper "religion" (*agama*) but possessed only "beliefs" (*kepercayaan*) [. . .]. Consequently, if the Balinese did not want to become the target of Muslim or Christian proselytizing, they had no other recourse than to reform their religion in order to make it eligible for the status of *agama*.[96]

In this sense, Balinese intellectuals and politicians lobbied massively for their religion to be considered part of worldwide Hinduism, once again stressing the *Indian* roots of Balinese culture and spirituality.[97] It is not surprising that the *Parisada Hindu Dharma Indonesia* (PHDI), which was founded in 1964 to represent all Indonesian (mostly Balinese) adherents of the newly accepted *agama Hindu*, was in intense contact with reformist groups in India[98]—just like the various religious societies of the colonial period. Based on their model of (Neo-)Hinduism, Balinese religion was propagated as being substantially monotheistic, with the Vedas as holy scripture, "despite the fact that they had not been known in Bali before the twentieth century."[99]

In this context, the popularization of Esoteric Bali by hippies and other spiritual tourists in the 1970s becomes even more plausible. While there seems to be no direct link between Balinese Theosophists and postwar esotericists on the island, the line can be drawn rather indirectly, namely by considering the continuity of religious politics with the image of Balinese religion as part of universal Hinduism from the colonial to the republican era—a concept that was propagated by representatives of Neo-Hinduism and Theosophy alike.

6. Conclusion: Across all Boundaries— Theosophy and Esotericism in Bali

The debate on the character and the ontological status of contemporary esotericism is still ongoing and has not been solved in the current state of research. Contradicting "purely heuristic"[100] approaches (such as Kocku von Stuckrad's concept of "the esoteric as an element of discourse"[101]), Michael Bergunder has suggested an understanding of the subject from a perspective grounded in cultural studies. In his eyes, esotericism, as a "mere construct of the esotericism researchers," has "strictly speaking no historical existence"; this "gives rise to the [. . .] question as to why such a subject should be at all constructed."[102] Instead, Bergunder sees esotericism as an "identity marker"[103] within a specific historical discourse that can be traced in historical sources. As a mere identificational positioning, it is, however, substantially empty, and its content therefore determined by the concepts of the various historical contexts in which it is negotiated.

As current research suggests, an esoteric identity marker can be found for the first time in the second half of the nineteenth century, namely in the form of "a close synchronous esoteric network between the Theosophical Society and related organizations as guiding authorities."[104] It is clear that Theosophy massively relied on concepts that had been widespread in much earlier times. However, at this point, the identificational self-positioning as "esoteric" cannot be traced further back than to the second half of the nineteenth century. From the current state of research,

> it is to be expected that the self-understanding of the predecessors [such as Spiritualism or French Occultism] differ[s] in many points from those of the successors [Theosophy] [. . .], so that the reconstruction of an esoteric tradition need not to be synonymous with the reconstruction of common key elements

of content, but rather go together with the demonstration of conceptual transformation processes and fractures.[105]

In this sense, esotericism is understood as a historical subject that can be reconstructed by tracing "an unbroken line of reception and tradition"[106] that, in the case of Esoteric Bali, leads us back to Theosophy in the nineteenth century.

There is no evidence (yet) for an unbroken line conceptually connecting Theosophical activities on the island in the colonial period and the popularity of Esoteric Bali in the 1970s. However, what I have tried to show is that recent exponents of the global esoteric discourse on the island (such as the *Balishamans* or Ratu Bagus) are nevertheless *indirectly* connected to Theosophy in Bali: both through the entanglement of the Theosophical Society with Indian and Balinese (Neo-)Hinduism, in addition to its entanglement with the political structures of the colonial administration that led to the dissemination of Theosophical concepts of (Balinese) Hinduism and Eastern spirituality into the whole archipelago—ideas that the founders of today's esoteric scene in Bali (the spiritual tourists of the seventies) could rely on. Moreover, the genealogical complexity of this entanglement indicates that the esoteric discourse in the form of Theosophy and its later New Age derivatives was global *from its very beginnings*. In the case of esotericism in Bali, Orientalist ideas of the "Mystical East" coincided with the administrative perception of the island's political structure as a form of Indian caste society that initiated a constant process of negotiation of Balinese religion and tradition in the light of Indian Neo-Hinduism—a cross-boundary discourse that would eventually establish Bali as a major location of esoteric spirituality. In combining theories of New Age shamanism and Balinese Neo-Hinduism, Fritz Demolsky, together with his Rosicrucian and Theosophical background, gives a perfect example for this global amalgamation.

Notes

1. Fred B. Eiseman, Jr., *Bali: Sekala & Niskala, Volume 1: Essays on Religion, Ritual, and Art* (Hong Kong: Periplus Editions, 1990), 140.
2. Ibid.
3. See for example Angela Hobart, *Healing Performances of Bali: Between Darkness and Light* (New York: Berghahn Books, 2003); Eiseman, Bali, 135–45;

Wolfgang Weck, *Heilkunde und Volkstum auf Bali* (Jakarta: P.T. Intermasa, 1986 [1937]).

4. See Mircea Eliade, *Shamanism: Archaic Techniques of Ecstasy* (Princeton, NJ: Princeton University Press, 1964).

5. Balishaman, "Artikelübersicht," http://balishaman.com/artikel_uebersicht.htm (all internet references as seen in May 2015).

6. See Friedrich Demolsky, "Das Alter des Schamanismus," http://balishaman.com/Das_Alter_des_Schamanismus-Teil1.htm.

7. See for example Michel Picard, "From *Agama Hindu Bali* to Agama Hindu and Back: Towards a Relocalization of the Balinese Religion?," in *The Politics of Religion in Indonesia: Syncretism, Orthodoxy, and Religious Contention in Java and Bali*, ed. Michel Picard and Rémy Madinier (London: Routledge, 2011); Leo Howe, *Hinduism and Hierarchy in Bali* (Oxford: James Currey, 2001); Adrian Vickers, *Bali: A Paradise Created* (Tokyo: Tuttle, 2012).

8. Elizabeth Gilbert, *Eat Pray Love: One Woman's Search for Everything Across Italy, India and Indonesia* (London: Bloomsbury, 2006).

9. E.g., ibid., 242.

10. Ibid., back cover.

11. See Weck, *Heilkunde*.

12. See Hobart, *Healing Performance*, 13.

13. See ibid., 15.

14. See Michel Picard, "Cultural Tourism, Nation-Building, and Regional Culture. The Making of a Balinese Identity," in *Tourism, Ethnicity, and the State in Asian and Pacific Societies*, ed. Michel Picard and Robert E. Wood (Honolulu: University of Hawai'i Press, 1997), 186. This split of Balinese society, however, was of much broader consequences than intended here, as I outline in a later section of this chapter.

15. See ibid., 15–21.

16. See ibid., 53–54.

17. See ibid., 22–23; Angela Hobart, Urs Ramseyer, and Albert Leeman, *The Peoples of Bali* (Cambridge, MA: Blackwell, 1996), 174–200.

18. The *balian tetakson* functions as a medium between men and ancestors/gods and is usually female. See ibid.

19. "[. . .] die 'Urreligion' der Menschheit." Balishaman, "Phänomen Schamanismus. Urreligion der Menschheit oder vorreligiöse Disziplin?," http://www.balishaman.com/phaenomen.htm.

20. See Eliade, *Shamanism*.

21. See for example Carlos Castaneda, *The Teachings of Don Juan: A Yaqui Way of Knowledge* (Oakland: University of California Press, 1968).

22. See Hartmut Zinser, *Esoterik: Eine Einführung* (München: Wilhelm Fink, 2009), 62; Kocku von Stuckrad, *Schamanismus und Esoterik: Kultur- und wissenschaftsgeschichtliche Betrachtungen* (Leuven: Peeters, 2003), 153–54.

23. Ratu Bagus Energy Meditation, "Ratu Bagus—His Life and His Work," https://www.ratubagus.com/en-ratu-life-work.

24. Ibid. Visionary experience is often seen as a vocation to work as *balian* (see Hobart, *Healing Performance*, 23).

25. Lucy Williams, *"Shaking the Foundations": A Portrait of Ratu Bagus* (San Francisco: Blurb, 2008), 18.

26. See Thierry Renard, *Ratu Bagus* (Gourdinne: F. Bercy, 2006), 16–17.

27. See An Brone and Leopoldo Antinozzi, eds., "Visiting the Ashram," filmed 1995, https://www.youtube.com/watch?v=rsqG_gDVCVE (video no longer available).

28. Ratu Bagus Energy Meditation, "The key to happiness," https://www.ratubagus.com/english.

29. See Ratu Bagus Energy Meditation, "Ratu Bagus way to happiness PART 1," published September 27, 2009, https://www.youtube.com/watch?v=0m-3mwARgVho (video no longer available).

30. See Ratu Bagus Energy Meditation, "Around the World," https://www.ratubagus.com/around-the-world.

31. See Renard, Ratu Bagus, 7–10; Williams, "Shaking the Foundations," 8–12; see also Yan Suarsana, "Die Insel der Weisheit: Balinesische Esoterik und globale Religionsgeschichte," *Zeitschrift für Religionswissenschaft* 23, no. 2 (2015): 324–26.

32. "[. . .] yang mampu membawa kebangaaan akan Hindu dikalangan generasi muda [. . .]." As seen in May 2015 on http://vedakarna.net/ida-panditampu-nabe-parama-daksa-natha-ratu-bagus-raih-hindu-muda-award-2009-tokohhindu-internasional [website no longer available].

33. This might also be the case for the many *balians* we do not know who do the same with other esoteric traditions.

34. See Vickers, *Bali*, 256.

35. See Hubert Knoblauch, *Populäre Religion: Auf dem Weg in eine spirituelle Gesellschaft* (Frankfurt a. M./New York: Campus, 2009), 110.

36. See Dallen J. Timothy and Paul J. Conover, "Nature Religion, Self-Spirituality and New Age Tourism," in *Tourism, Religion and Spiritual Journeys*, ed. Dallen J. Timothy and Daniel H. Olsen (London: Routledge, 2006).

37. Vickers, *Bali*, 256.

38. See Michel Picard, *Bali: Cultural Tourism and Touristic Culture* (Singapore: Archipelago Press, 1996), 45–49.

39. Vickers, *Bali*, 254.

40. Ibid., 255.

41. Ibid., 256.

42. Ibid.

43. Ibid.

44. See Thomas S. Raffles, *The History of Java*, vol. II (London: Black, Parbury & Allen, 1817), 61.

45. See Howe, *Hinduism*, 21–22.

46. Ibid., 22.

47. Michel Picard, "What's in a Name? Agama Hindu Bali in the Making," in *Hinduism in Modern Indonesia: A Minority Religion Between Local, National, and Global Interests*, ed. Martin Ramstedt (London: Routledge/Curzon, 2004), 59.

48. See ibid., 59–60.

49. Balinese reformers were in contact with Indian Neo-Hindus, as I outline below.

50. Frederik Lambertus Bakker, *The Struggle of the Balinese Intellectuals: Developments in Modern Hindu Thinking in Independent Indonesia* (Amsterdam: VU University Press, 1993), 41.

51. See ibid., 59–64.

52. See Margaret Wiener, *Visible and Invisible Realms: Power, Magic, and Colonial Conquest in Bali* (Chicago: University of Chicago Press, 1993), 93.

53. Vickers, *Bali*, 129. See also ibid., 116–30; Wiener, *Visible and Invisible Realms*, 93.

54. Vickers, *Bali*, 131.

55. See Vicki Baum, *Liebe und Tod auf Bali* (Amsterdam: Querido, 1937).

56. Ibid., 167. See ibid., 130–75.

57. Stephen Prothero, *The White Buddhist: The Asian Odyssey of Henry Steel Olcott* (Bloomington: Indiana University Press, 1996), 51.

58. Ibid., 63.

59. Ibid., 68.

60. Ibid.

61. See ibid., 67.

62. Ibid., 78.

63. See Michael Bergunder, "Experiments with Theosophical Truth: Gandhi, Esotericism, and Global Religious History," *Journal of the American Academy of Religion* 82, no. 2 (2014): 403–4.

64. Mark Bevir, "Theosophy and the Origins of the Indian National Congress," *International Journal of Hindu Studies* 7, nos. 1–3 (2003): 105.

65. Ibid., 104.

66. See ibid., 109–11.

67. Ibid., 112.

68. Bergunder, "Experiments," 404.

69. Ibid.

70. Madame Blavatsky is said to have visited Java three times. See Herman de Tollenaere, "The Theosophical Society in the Dutch East Indies, 1880–1942," in *Hinduism in Modern Indonesia: A Minority Religion Between Local, National, and Global Interests*, ed. Martin Ramstedt (London: Routledge/Curzon, 2004), 36.

71. Ibid.

72. Herman de Tollenaere, *The Politics of Divine Wisdom: Theosophy and Labour, National, and Women's Movements in Indonesia and South Asia, 1875–1947* (Nijmegen: Katholieke Universiteit, 1996), 107.
73. Tollenaere, "The Theosophical Society," 39.
74. Ibid.
75. Ibid., 38.
76. Ibid., 41.
77. See ibid., 38.
78. Ibid.
79. Ibid.
80. See Bakker, *The Struggle*, 43.
81. See Tollenaere, "The Theosophical Society," 41–42.
82. Bakker, *The Struggle*, 43.
83. See Tollenaere, "The Theosophical Society," 42.
84. See Bakker, *The Struggle*, 43.
85. Ibid.
86. Ibid.
87. Tollenaere, "The Theosophical Society," 40.
88. Bakker, *The Struggle*, 36.
89. Martin Ramstedt, "Hindu Bonds at Work: Spiritual and Commercial Ties Between India and Bali," *The Journal of Asian Studies* 67, no. 4 (2008): 1239.
90. See Bakker, *The Struggle*, 42–43.
91. See Michael Bergunder, "Die Bhagavadgita im 19. Jahrhundert: Hinduismus, Eosterik und Kolonialismus," in *Westliche Formen des Hinduismus in Deutschland*, ed. idem (Halle: Verlag der Franckeschen Stiftungen, 2006). See also the contribution by Michael Bergunder to this volume.
92. Tollenaere, "The Theosophical Society," 38.
93. However, in 2013, the conference of the *Indo-Pacific Federation of the Theosophical Society* was held in Bali (see Olga Gostin, "The 12th Triennial Indo-Pacific Conference, 1–6 Nov 2013 from Dr. Olga Gostin Adelaide," http://ipf-ts.org/blog/12th-triennial-indo-pacific-conference-1-6-nov-2013-dr-olga-gostin-adelaide).
94. Edith Franke and Katrin Gotterbarm, "Kritik durch Anpassung? *Aluk to dolo* und Christentum im *Pancasila*-Staat Indonesien," in *Religionsinterne Kritik und religiöser Pluralismus im gegenwärtigen Südostasian*, ed. Manfred Hutter (Frankfurt a. M.: Peter Lang, 2008), 219–20.
95. See Manfred Hutter, "Innerhinduistischer Pluralismus in Indonesien als Ursache für Kritik," in *Religionsinterne Kritik und religiöser Pluralismus im gegenwärtigen Südostasian*, ed. Manfred Hutter (Frankfurt a. M.: Peter Lang, 2008), 130; Picard, "From *Agama Hindu Bali*," 124.
96. Ibid.
97. See ibid., 123–30.

98. See Ramstedt, "Hindu Bonds at Work"; Yadav Somvir, "Cultural and Religious Interrelations Between Modern India and Indonesia," in *Hinduism in Modern Indonesia: A Minority Religion Between Local, National, and Global Interests*, ed. Martin Ramstedt (London/New York: RoutledgeCurzon, 2004).
99. Picard, "From *Agama Hindu Bali*," 125.
100. Michael Bergunder, "What Is Esotericism? Cultural Studies Approaches and the Problems of Definition in Religious Studies," *Method and Theory in the Study of Religion* 22 (2010): 9.
101. Kocku von Stuckrad, *Was ist Esoterik? Kleine Geschichte des geheimen Wissens* (München: C. H. Beck, 2004), 20.
102. Bergunder, "What Is Esotericism?," 28.
103. Ibid., 20.
104. Ibid., 28.
105. Ibid., 30.
106. Ibid., 28.

References

Bakker, Frederik Lambertus. *The Struggle of the Balinese Intellectuals: Developments in Modern Hindu Thinking in Independent Indonesia*. Amsterdam: VU University Press, 1993.
Balishaman. "Artikelübersicht." http://balishaman.com/artikel_uebersicht.htm.
———. "Phänomen Schamanismus. Urreligion der Menschheit oder vorreligiöse Disziplin?" http://www.balishaman.com/phaenomen.htm.
Baum, Vicki. *Liebe und Tod auf Bali*. Amsterdam: Querido, 1937.
Bergunder, Michael. "Die Bhagavadgita im 19. Jahrhundert: Hinduismus, Eosterik und Kolonialismus." In *Westliche Formen des Hinduismus in Deutschland*, edited by idem, 187–216. Halle: Verlag der Franckeschen Stiftungen, 2006.
———. "Experiments with Theosophical Truth: Gandhi, Esotericism, and Global Religious History." *Journal of the American Academy of Religion* 82, no. 2 (2014): 398–426.
———. "What Is Esotericism? Cultural Studies Approaches and the Problems of Definition in Religious Studies." *Method and Theory in the Study of Religion* 22 (2010): 9–36.
Bevir, Mark. "Theosophy and the Origins of the Indian National Congress." *International Journal of Hindu Studies* 7, nos. 1–3 (2003): 99–115.
Brone, An, and Leopoldo Antinozzi, eds. "Visiting the Ashram." Filmed 1995. https://www.youtube.com/watch?v=rsqG_gDVCVE.
Castaneda, Carlos. *The Teachings of Don Juan: A Yaqui Way of Knowledge*. Oakland, CA: University of California Press, 1968.

Demolsky, Friedrich. "Das Alter des Schamanismus." http://balishaman.com/Das_Alter_des_Schamanismus-Teil1.htm.

Eiseman, Fred B., Jr. *Bali: Sekala & Niskala, Volume 1: Essays on Religion, Ritual, and Art*. Hong Kong: Periplus Editions, 1990.

Eliade, Mircea. *Shamanism: Archaic Techniques of Ecstasy*. Princeton, NJ: Princeton University Press, 1964.

Franke, Edith, and Katrin Gotterbarm. "Kritik durch Anpassung? *Aluk to dolo* und Christentum im *Pancasila*-Staat Indonesien." In *Religionsinterne Kritik und religiöser Pluralismus im gegenwärtigen Südostasian*, edited by Manfred Hutter, 215–30. Frankfurt a. M.: Peter Lang, 2008.

Gilbert, Elizabeth. *Eat Pray Love: One Woman's Search for Everything Across Italy, India and Indonesia*. London: Bloomsbury, 2006.

Gostin, Olga. "The 12th Triennial Indo-Pacific Conference, 1–6 Nov 2013 from Dr. Olga Gostin Adelaide." http://ipf-ts.org/blog/12th-triennial-indo-pacific-conference-1-6-nov-2013-dr-olga-gostin-adelaide.

Hobart, Angela. *Healing Performances of Bali: Between Darkness and Light*. Oxford: Berghahn Books, 2003.

Hobart, Angela, Urs Ramseyer, and Albert Leeman. *The Peoples of Bali*. Cambridge, MA: Blackwell, 1996.

Howe, Leo. *Hinduism and Hierarchy in Bali*. Oxford: James Currey, 2001.

Hutter, Manfred. "Innerhinduistischer Pluralismus in Indonesien als Ursache für Kritik." In *Religionsinterne Kritik und religiöser Pluralismus im gegenwärtigen Südostasian*, edited by Manfred Hutter, 129–39. Frankfurt a. M.: Peter Lang, 2008.

Knoblauch, Hubert. *Populäre Religion: Auf dem Weg in eine spirituelle Gesellschaft*. Frankfurt a. M.: Campus, 2009.

Picard, Michel. *Bali: Cultural Tourism and Touristic Culture*. Singapore: Archipelago Press, 1996.

———. "Cultural Tourism, Nation-Building, and Regional Culture. The Making of a Balinese Identity." In *Tourism, Ethnicity, and the State in Asian and Pacific Societies*, edited by Michel Picard and Robert E. Wood, 181–214. Honolulu: University of Hawai'i Press, 1997.

———. "From *Agama Hindu Bali* to *Agama Hindu* and Back: Towards a Relocalization of the Balinese Religion?" In *The Politics of Religion in Indonesia: Syncretism, Orthodoxy, and Religious Contention in Java and Bali*, edited by Michel Picard and Rémy Madinier, 117–41. London/New York: Routledge, 2011.

———. "What's in a Name? Agama Hindu Bali in the Making." In *Hinduism in Modern Indonesia: A Minority Religion Between Local, National, and Global Interests*, edited by Martin Ramstedt, 56–75. London: RoutledgeCurzon, 2004.

Prothero, Stephen. *The White Buddhist: The Asian Odyssey of Henry Steel Olcott*. Bloomington: Indiana University Press, 1996.

Raffles, Thomas S. *The History of Java. Volume II*. London: Black, Parbury & Allen, 1817.
Ramstedt, Martin. "Hindu Bonds at Work: Spiritual and Commercial Ties Between India and Bali." *The Journal of Asian Studies* 67, no. 4 (2008): 1228–50.
Ratu Bagus Energy Meditation. "Around the World." https://www.ratubagus.com/around-the-world.
———. "Ratu Bagus—His Life and His Work." https://www.ratubagus.com/en-ratu-life-work.
———. "Ratu Bagus Way to Happiness PART 1." Published September 27, 2009. https://www.youtube.com/watch?v=0m3mwARgVho.
———. "The Key to Happiness." https://www.ratubagus.com/english.
Renard, Thierry. *Ratu Bagus*. Gourdinne: F. Bercy, 2006.
Somvir, Yadav. "Cultural and Religious Interrelations Between Modern India and Indonesia." In *Hinduism in Modern Indonesia: A Minority Religion Between Local, National, and Global Interests*, edited by Martin Ramstedt, 255–63. London: RoutledgeCurzon, 2004.
Stuckrad, Kocku von. *Schamanismus und Esoterik: Kultur- und wissenschaftsgeschichtliche Betrachtungen*. Leuven: Peeters, 2003.
———. *Was ist Esoterik? Kleine Geschichte des geheimen Wissens*. München: C.H. Beck, 2004.
Suarsana, Yan. "Die Insel der Weisheit: Balinesische Esoterik und globale Religionsgeschichte." *Zeitschrift für Religionswissenschaft* 23 no. 2 (2015): 320–42.
Timothy, Dallen J., and Paul J. Conover. "Nature Religion, Self-Spirituality and New Age Tourism." In *Tourism, Religion and Spiritual Journeys*, edited by Dallen J. Timothy and Daniel H. Olsen, 139–55. London: Routledge, 2006.
Tollenaere, Herman de. *The Politics of Divine Wisdom: Theosophy and Labour, National, and Women's Movements in Indonesia and South Asia, 1875–1947*. Nijmegen: Katholieke Universiteit, 1996.
———. "The Theosophical Society in the Dutch East Indies, 1880–1942." In *Hinduism in Modern Indonesia: A Minority Religion Between Local, National, and Global Interests*, edited by Martin Ramstedt, 35–44. London: RoutledgeCurzon, 2004.
Vickers, Adrian. *Bali: A Paradise Created*. Tokyo: Tuttle, 2012.
Weck, Wolfgang. *Heilkunde und Volkstum auf Bali*. Jakarta: P.T. Intermasa, 1986.
Wiener, Margaret. *Visible and Invisible Realms: Power, Magic, and Colonial Conquest in Bali*. Chicago: University of Chicago Press, 1993.
Williams, Lucy. *"Shaking the Foundations": A Portrait of Ratu Bagus*. San Francisco: Blurb, 2008.
Zinser, Hartmut, *Esoterik: Eine Einführung*. München: Wilhelm Fink, 2009.

Chapter 13

Effects of Theosophy on Russian Cultural History

Björn Seidel-Dreffke

General Introduction

The cultural history of Russia, particularly since the nineteenth century, is characterized by the interplay between three contending contemporary modes of thought, which, although occasionally joining forces, were more commonly locked in fierce competition for control over Russian spiritual and intellectual life. These are the material(ist) worldview, the idealistic worldview, and what might be best described as the mystical occult worldview. Theosophy played an important role in the third of these.[1] Quite a few Russian intellectuals gravitated toward all three poles throughout the course of their lives. For the most part, such intellectuals declared the attainment of the mystical-occult view to be the zenith of this manner of spiritualistic searching for genuine insight into the true nature of things.

The search for "true spirituality" became a constitutive element in the lives of many intellectuals. The result was a cultural boom affecting, among other things, literature, art, music, theater, and philosophy, eventually peaking in the so-called "Silver Age" of Russian culture. Movements that professed an interest in "the occult" naturally existed in Russia before the nineteenth century. In this regard, Russian Freemasonry ("masonstvo"), which in recent years has garnered considerable interest, played an important role.[2]

Russian Freemasons as Trailblazers for Theosophy in Russia

Masonic lodges were already extant by the late eighteenth century, not only in the central metropoles of Moscow and St. Petersburg, but also in more rural areas, and they had a lasting influence on contemporary and subsequent Russian spiritual life. Among the leading representatives of Freemasonry were, for example, Nikolay Ivanovich Novikov, Alexej Mikhailovich Kutuzov, Alexandr Alekseyevich Petrov, Ivan Sergeyevich Turgenev, Ivan Vasiljevich Lopuchin, and for a while Nikolay Mikhailovich Karamzin. For a long time, Russian Freemasons were considered by their contemporaries to be keepers of secret, elite knowledge. Recent research suggests, however, that on the contrary, the transmission of their specialized knowledge and of their society was a matter of utmost importance to them:

> In the circle of Muscovite freemasons and Enlightenment philosophers, the culturally optimistic concepts of Voltaire and the *Encyclopédistes* combined with pietistic, hermetic-theosophical, and mystic tendencies. The majority of such masonry were self-professed followers of "enlightened absolutism."[3]

There is a discernable overlap between Freemasonic ideas and the Theosophy of Helena Petrovna Blavatsky. For one, Freemasonry was among the spiritual informants of Theosophy; for another, the spread of Freemasonic concepts in Russia paved the way for the reception of occult worldviews there. As such, a number of noteworthy parallels between Freemasonic thought and Blavatsky's Theosophy are contextualized below.

Among the Freemasons, there is a certain religious-moral demand on personality that is likewise a central point of the doctrine outlined in Blavatsky's Theosophy. In either case, importance was placed on the reining in of passion, the favoring of spiritual and moral values, and the advocacy of such values as opposed to aspirations focused solely on material well-being. In the case of the Freemasons, as would subsequently be the case with other movements, including Theosophy, components of the practical actualization of this goal were asceticism, self-observation, and a constant striving for self-fulfillment. Already within Freemasonry, the stated goal was to kill off the "old me" and thereby make way for spiritual rebirth.

Another common thread between Blavatsky's Theosophy and Freemasonry emerges from the endeavor to separate from official, institutionalized state religion. Value was placed above all on the spiritual aspects of religiosity. Like the Freemasons, Blavatsky's Theosophy later developed a mystical philosophy of nature. God was experienced primarily via knowledge of nature. A "unio mystica" was sought. One read Jakob Böhme. Fervent acceptance of pietistic and quietistic concepts was arrived at over the course of discussions of Freemasonic concepts in Russia. Rosicrucian understandings were adopted as well.

This spiritual background offered fertile ground for the growing interest in Theosophy in the late nineteenth and especially the beginning of the twentieth century. Russian poet and philosopher Maximilian Alexandrovich Voloshin, for example, was a member of a French masonic lodge before developing an interest in Theosophy. Later he turned more toward Anthroposophy. Unlike others, he retained close ties to Theosophy and sought to find a middle ground between Theosophy and Anthroposophy so that both directions would harmonize in his work.

It would surely be of considerable academic interest to expand "Russian culture and Freemasonry" as a field of intellectual inquiry. This question was previously pursued in the context of a research field "Enlightenment and Esotericism" at the University of Halle in Germany. At the time, research centered on, for example, the relationship of Alexander Sergeyevich Pushkin (1799–1837) to Freemasonry, which can be established from several of his works.[4] Until shortly before the ban on Russian Freemasonry in 1822, Pushkin was a member of the lodge "Ovid," which had its headquarters in Chișinău (in Bessarabia). A succinct example of Freemasonic influence on the poet is Pushkin's drama "Mocart i Sal'ieri" (Mozart and Salieri, 1830/31). One can assume that the symbolism in Mozart's work, which stems from Freemasonic interests, was at any rate known to Pushkin. Mozart and Salieri embody different standpoints in relation to the nature of art. Mozart embodies God-given genius, whereas Salieri exemplifies the "craftsman" who knows what is needed to create good art besides talent. This "craftsman symbolism" relies on symbols that were typical of the Freemasons (ceremonial goings-on behind locked doors, a dagger, a man dressed in black and referred to as "brother," a ritually symbolic act of murder, typical dualism such as "light and dark," "life and death," "paradise and hell"). At the same time, one recognizes a certain reversal of Freemasonic ideas, which Pushkin regarded with increasing cynicism, given after all that Salieri plans to actually murder Mozart.

On August 6, 1822, after the convention of the Holy Alliance in Verona, Alexander I passed a ban on Freemasonry in Russia. Although the tsar had himself sympathized with Freemasonry for some time, political machinations now moved him to take measures against the supposed conspiracies among the Freemasons directed at him. Alexander's successor, Nicholas I, reinforced the ban in 1826, primarily because of the prominent participation of Freemasons in the Decembrist revolt.[5] Thereafter, the heyday of Freemasonry in Russia came to a close.

The First Wave of Theosophical Aspirations in Russia in the Nineteenth and Early Twentieth Centuries (a Historical Overview)

Although Freemasonry had by that point infiltrated broad swathes of the cultural elite, occult thinking nevertheless attained a new level of quality and quantity in the nineteenth century. Both in terms of self-estimation and in their assessment by outsiders, occult systems had advanced. In Russia, occultism came to be of interest in certain circles of society in the late nineteenth and early twentieth centuries, particularly among the *intelligentsia*.[6] The reception of occult theories progressed on any number of levels. For some, it was an adventure that went no further than the levitating of tables and calling upon the ghosts of the dead; for others, it became a philosophy or even a science; whereas yet others found it laughable nonsense. In any case, the overall effect was that, at the turn of the century, the occult became a topic discussed with fervor both in the media and in private conversations. Certain components of occult systems were popularized and "researched," such as tarot, somnambulism, mesmerism, astrology, and so forth. Furthermore, individual occult movements became active or reformed. However, according to Maria Carlson, "the two most important movements in fin de siècle Russia were Theosophy [i.e., the Theosophy of Blavatsky] and Spiritualism. They had the largest number of adherents and dominated the journals and publications."[7] At the start of the twentieth century, several smaller societies in Moscow and St. Petersburg formed with the goal of studying the fundamental tenets of Theosophy. It was also an opportunity for people who held an interest in spirituality, but had turned their backs on official religion.

There is regretfully little scholarship on the history of Theosophy in Russia. The first founder of a Theosophical circle in Moscow was a certain Anna Nikolajewna Goncharova, who was sadly known to few, but who traveled often and was likely personally acquainted with Blavatsky. Thanks to the initiative of the German actress Marie von Strauch-Spettini, a good friend of Marie von Sivers, a leading figure in the German Theosophical Society and later wife of Rudolf Steiner, a German circle was founded in St. Petersburg at the end of 1902 that aimed to spark a Theosophical movement in Russia. However, the founder of this circle passed away soon after, and it was some time before regular Theosophical meetings took place in Russia.

The Russian Theosophical circle in St. Petersburg was brought into existence by Anna Alexejewna Kamenskaya in 1904. Her society, which was independent from the Theosophical Society, succeeded in unifying the German and the Russian circles in the city. Kamenskaya also attempted to spread the doctrine of Theosophy in writing. In St. Petersburg in 1906, she published under the pseudonym "Alba," a name she retained throughout her whole life. One of her early titles was "Tasks of Theosophy." In this work, the author is concerned with detailing first the theoretical and then the practical tenets of Theosophy that were, in her opinion, particularly meaningful for Russia. On the practical side, she called for spreading religious-ethical norms in order to reshape society, above all a reorientation toward a code of conduct that had been rejected by the Orthodox Church. This code of conduct gave individuals the freedom to choose the religious system they felt most drawn to, and it valued female spirituality (despite a rather conservative understanding of family life), marital fidelity, diligence, and the view that communal work was important for societal development.

In theory, her conclusions can be interpreted as containing a hidden polemic against the religious philosopher Vladimir Sergeyevich Solovyov, who submitted the teachings of Blavatsky to harsh criticism in his "A Story of the Antichrist" (1899–1900). Kamenskaya insisted that Theosophy was not a form of Neo-Buddhism, nor was it material pantheism, nor an artificially created religio-philosophical system. She claimed that Theosophical teachings were so important for Russia because only they could resolve the conflict between "god-seekers" and "god-builders," two early twentieth-century Christian branches independent of the Russian Orthodox Church. Furthermore, the author described Theosophy as being compatible with Christianity, if only to appeal to Russian Christians. Subsequently, Kamenskaya expanded on the premises detailed in her book through her lectures, for example, at a meeting of the "Russian Philosophical Society" in St. Petersburg dedicated explicitly to Theosophy.

From the very start, it was primarily women who stood at the pinnacle of the movement in the Russian chapters of the Theosophical

Society. Another important personality who pushed Theosophy forward in Russia in the early years was Anna Pavlovna Filosofova, who was also an active member of the emancipation movement in England.

Aside from in the two major cities of the country (Moscow and St. Petersburg), Theosophy did not at first spread far. Nonetheless, several Theosophical societies that considered themselves independent from any umbrella organization were sprinkled throughout the Russian countryside. One of the best-known was led by F. F. Pisareva, who owned a small estate near Kaluga. Over the course of the next few years, the Kaluga chapter grew to be one of the most active in Russia. The majority of the Theosophical texts that had appeared in Russia beginning in early 1905 were translations from English that Pisareva herself produced. Nikolai Pawlowitsch Pisarev (her husband) founded a publishing house, Lotos, in 1908. By the time of the Revolution, the publishing house had produced twenty-one books, an impressive number for the time.

At the beginning of 1908, there were up to 1,000 members across the various Russian Theosophical societies. This allowed Kamenskaya to legally found the "Russian Theosophical Society" on November 17, 1908, in St. Petersburg. Concurrently, the first Theosophical periodical, *Vestnik teosofii* ("The Theosophy Herald") was created with the aim of introducing Theosophy into Russian life. The appearance of the "Herald" was, in a manner of speaking, the launchpad for further periodicals, among them *Ottuda* ("From There") and *Teosofskoe obozrenie* ("Theosophical Review"). Consequently, additional active groups were founded in other cities.

One might describe this as the peak of the Theosophical movement in Russia. The reason that Russians were drawn specifically to Theosophy is described by author and cultural anthropologist Viktor Borisowitsch Fedyushin:

> The basic concept of Theosophy is close to the Russians' heart, since it describes a scientific-religious synthesis with a tendency for the fraternization of all people, and with the idea of the birth of a new, spiritual human. In the eyes of the Russians, it is impossible to separate God from the incarnation of His truth. Truth without beauty and goodness is unthinkable, no more the good without the beautiful than the beautiful without the good. And so many Russians saw in Theosophy a general fusion of differences, which appealed very much to their mentality.[8]

This statement by Fedyushin coincided with Russian religious philosophical views of the "Russian mission," although in this context it was also a matter of distancing oneself from the "decadent" West. The aspirations for the historical mission of Russia, held by Russian Theosophists and religious philosophers alike, were similar. It was believed that the new "master race" much touted by Theosophy would appear in Russia. Because of characteristics developed through centuries of incessant suffering, such as empathy, sense of community, altruism, innate spirituality, and the ability for co-creation with God (not submission to godly reign, as advanced in the West, but creation on an equal footing with God), Russians felt themselves destined to lead the imminent new age.

The divide of the aggregated worldwide Theosophical Society greatly shocked Russian Theosophists, and the split replicated itself in Russia. On the one hand, numerous members of the Society, including leading intellectuals such as Andrei Bely (real name: Boris Nikolaevich Bugaev) and Voloshin became followers of Rudolf Steiner's Anthroposophy, which went on to gain a firm footing in Russia. On the other hand, several leading Russian Theosophists followed the example of Kamenskaya and Pisareva by remaining in the English-Indian Society under the chairwomanship of Annie Besant.

This final rupture was, however, foreshadowed in certain tendencies toward cleavage within Russian Theosophy by one important point of contention among Russian Theosophical groups at the time, which was that of alignment with either England or Germany. These two directions were spearheaded by Kamenskaya on the one side and Anna Rudol'fovna Mintslova on the other. Kamenskaya pledged herself repeatedly and adamantly to Besant, whereas Mintslova aligned herself more with Steiner. While Mintslova may have been relatively autonomous with regard to doctrine, she oriented herself with Steiner by handing the authority over her Moscow activities to him (Kamenskaya operated from St. Petersburg) and emphasizing that these activities were accountable entirely to his discretion. Consequently, she wanted to found her own society in Moscow, one that would be clearly separate from that in St. Petersburg.

Steiner's response was placatory.[9] On March 23, 1908, in a letter to Mintslova from Berlin, he wrote that he considered Kamenskaya's statements as, above all, a Western-inspired theoretical inflection, and that Russian folk spirit and depth were brought to light particularly by Lev Nikolayevich Tolstoy.

The constantly simmering conflict that resulted from the opposition of English and German Theosophy in Russia had, years before the secession of Steinerians from Theosophy in 1912/13, already induced a cleft that was recognized by the leadership in Adyar. Because of this, the group of Russians who in 1913 had to make a choice between the Anthroposophical Society and the Theosophical Society was not very sizable. Even before the definitive secession, many Russian Theosophists had taken a rather conciliatory stance toward Steiner, whom many still considered an important part of the movement. Translations of Steiner continued to appear in the Theosophical press, and Theosophists remained informed of his activities. In 1910, Kamenskaya still sent a book order for the library's German section to von Sivers, but relations between the leadership in St. Petersburg and Berlin became increasingly strained.

In 1912, Kamanskaya, Steiner, and von Sivers met in Helsinki for what likely would be the last time. The meeting turned into a dispute that eventually resulted in an ultimate split, in part because of personal differences. The formalization of the international divisions of the Theosophical Society that took place in 1913 barely made a splash in Russian Theosophical papers, because the separation had long since occurred in Russia. Neither was Russian membership greatly affected by events in Berlin. While in Germany the Theosophical Society lost a large number of its members to Anthroposophy, in Russia the numbers for the most part remained stable.

Theosophy in Russia after the Revolutions of 1917

Beginning in 1917, Theosophical activities in Russia increasingly became a target for persecution by both the political authorities and from conservative circles. In 1918, all chapters of the Theosophical Society in Russia were shut down by the Bolsheviks. Blavatsky's *Secret Doctrine* was added to the index of forbidden books, and, if found, confiscated. Kamenskaya herself barely escaped arrest. Many staunch Theosophists who could not—and did not want to—renounce the doctrine emigrated, especially to Europe and the United States. Kamenskaya herself went to Geneva. But Russian Theosophists abroad lacked cohesion. The tendency toward division, which had been apparent from the very beginning of the Theosophical movement in general, proved to be a stumbling block for emigrant Theosophists as well.

The circumstances for Russian Anthroposophists were no better. The Communist ideology that won the upper hand in Russia, or rather the Soviet Union, in subsequent years rejected any and all religious activity, in some cases even by punishing it. The Russian Orthodox Church alone could protect itself from this ban, because a large percentage of Russians held ties to the Church, and an across-the-board ban would have led to the Bolsheviks losing their ideological hold on the population. It is common knowledge that in his youth, before joining the Bolshevik movement, Joseph Vissarionovich Stalin had received training as a priest. Stalin again called upon the services of the Russian Orthodox Church in World War II, when he gave it more freedom in order to kindle nationalist sentiment in Russians and thereby spur them on to fight. Other religious groups, communities, and sects were, however, rigorously outlawed and persecuted. Russian Anthroposophists had the advantage that, because of the worldwide network of Anthroposophy, they had many opportunities and a wide range of potential destinations for emigration. In 1920, however, there were also a few well-organized Theosophical circles abroad: in Finland, Tallinn and Riga, in Bulgaria, Czechoslovakia, Germany, Switzerland, the United States, and even China.

In 1924, Kamenskaya's efforts were met with success, and Besant granted official recognition to the "Russian Theosophical Society Outside Russia," which in 1925 was confirmed by Russian statutes as well. At least a few Russian Theosophical conventions could be carried out abroad in 1933 and 1937. Hardly any material from the convention of 1937 has been preserved; conversely, the minutes from the 1933 convention in Paris were documented in great detail in the periodical *Vestnik* ("The Herald"). At this convention, Kamenskaya was chosen once more as General Secretary for the next three years.

At the start of the convention, much was made of the reading of the preliminary greetings by Besant and Dr. George Arundel, among others. The convention was devoted above all to anniversary dates: ten years of contact between individual groups to form the entire organization of the Russian Theosophical Society, fifteen years of community in Russia, twenty-five years since its actual foundation, and finally eleven more years of activity of the journal *Vestnik* abroad. The main purpose was to strengthen unity and to build upon the feeling of community. Another focal point for discussion was the development of strategies for the rebuilding of ties with the French Theosophical Society. The highlight of the convention was Kamenskaya's public reading, in Russian, of "The

Fate of Russia in the Past and the Future." However, the effectiveness of Russian Theosophy abroad waned after the demise of its leaders, especially following World War II.

Thanks to the actions of Nicholas Konstantinovich Roerich and Helena Ivanovna Roerich, however, the doctrine, if in a certain personalized, changed form, returned to the awareness of Western European culture, not as a typically Russian phenomenon, however, but in the universal appropriation that Blavatsky had always advocated. It was not until 1991 that an official refounding of the Russian Theosophical Society took place. There was a Theosophical underground in the Soviet era, but next to no scholarship on this topic exists, bar the trailblazing work of Birgit Menzel.[10]

Theosophy and Its Effects on Russian Intellectual Art and Literature

Blavatsky's Theosophical model of the universe increasingly gained traction with various circles of the Russian *intelligentsia* in the late nineteenth and early twentieth centuries.[11] Many intellectuals were concerned with questions of realizing the "self" and the redefinition of one's relationship to God. Blavatsky's Theosophical model of the universe was used as a basis for the development of personal views that were no longer bound to fixed tradition, and that saw the individual as his or her own creator. What is more, the individual was believed to be capable of transporting him- or herself into the world of the invisible with his or her own power. In doing so, Blavatsky's Theosophy demonstrated aspects of the search for the "new human," which was to define the turn of the century in Russia.

To those who wished to turn their backs on the Church without having to fall into atheism, Theosophy suggested a means to continue believing in a godly principle without having to commit to a certain religion. Many Russian intellectuals were of the opinion that the institution of the Church no longer placed sufficient emphasis on inner piety. This condition was pan-denominational. In the situation of uncertainty and crisis at that time, people could turn to Theosophy in order to imagine themselves as part of a system structured according to stable principles. In Theosophy, the apocalyptic mood of the period was mitigated by a cosmology that did not predict the end of the world and that saw every paradigm shift as a legitimate step toward a better future. Those who might, in the new situation, find themselves feeling alone now saw themselves surrounded by a crowd of apparently helpful beings who surely (if invisibly) stood by their side in every situation.[12]

Consequently, Theosophy contributed to the strengthening of the "anti-millenarian camp" in Russia. Many Russian intellectuals, although not exclusively intellectuals, read an approaching apocalypse into the self-anticipating and ultimately self-fulfilling ongoing processes of societal change. One need hardly be surprised, then, that the "Antichrist" as literary figure made an appearance in the work of numerous authors. Among followers of Theosophy, this was not the case. Theosophists saw all upheavals simply as being symptomatic of the transition into a new age, and Theosophy as a means through which one might best master this transition (for example, through the mental reappraisal of earlier reincarnations, etc.). To followers of a strictly scientific worldview, Theosophy suggested the possibility of entering into the world of the "inexplicable" and the "supernatural" with the aid of academic methods.

Finally, Theosophical cosmology also delivered a foundation for the reinforcing of belief in the Russian mission and was incorporated by several intellectuals into theories of the Russian soul. The concept of a Russian mission had already been voiced in the Middle Ages and was later reiterated by, for example, nineteenth-century Slavophiles. Such concepts often came to be incorporated into occult models of the universe.[13] Russian intellectual expectations of a new golden age were also supported by these.

To the action-oriented Russian intelligentsia, Theosophy was particularly interesting on the basis of its practical dimensions. It was also an impetus to the women's emancipation movement. As has been described, women were frequently in positions of leadership within the Theosophical Society. Because Theosophical ideology supported equality between the sexes, there existed no prescribed limitations to female creativity. Blavatsky often took issue with the role of women in society and demanded a higher valuation of women.[14] In her stories and travelogues, she addresses this and other topics, such as the defense of peoples oppressed by white colonial powers, some of which are still relevant today.[15] Reception of and discussions about Blavatsky's Theosophy took place in Russia at the turn of the twentieth century, at different levels and in different ways.

The public activities of Russian Theosophical circles described earlier soon bore fruit, so that turn-of-the-century Russia confronts us with a series of Russian artists, philosophers, and writers who intensively engaged with the phenomenon of Theosophy, were influenced by it, were intrigued initially before developing a strong aversion, or became followers and apostles of Blavatsky's doctrine. The early reception of Theosophical texts by representatives of Russian spiritual life dates back to the nineteenth century.

For example, the "grandfather of realism" in Russia, Tolstoy, subscribed to various Theosophical journals for some time. Moreover, he read Buddhist texts, whose publication in Russian owed to the significant participation of the Theosophical Society, and he was also interested in the works of Blavatsky. He borrowed several aphorisms for his anthology *Na kazhdyj den'* ("For Every Day") from her book *The Voice of the Silence* (1899). Although he was acquainted with leading Russian Theosophists, his stance regarding Theosophical doctrine remained critical to the last.

A similarly critical position toward Blavatsky's Theosophy found clear expression in the work of the philosopher Solovyov. The philosopher first expressed himself in relation to her teachings in a review of her *Key to Theosophy* (1889) and later in in an essay for Sergei Alexeyevich Vengerov's lexicon of authors.[16] Here Solovyov criticized both the theoretical basis of the concept of Theosophy and specific passages in concrete works, in which he took pains to analyze the concept of God in Theosophy, which was in his opinion unclear. Blavatsky herself had read Solovyov's review of *The Key to Theosophy* and had written an extensive riposte, which was not, however, printed by the Russian press, and was only published at all after her death.[17] The unfolding of the disagreement therefore remained largely hidden from the public. In Solovyov's philosophical system, engagement with the "East" played an important role, which accounts for the cryptic criticism of Blavatsky in his *Povest' ob Antichriste* ("Stories of the Antichrist," 1899).[18]

The philosopher Nikolai Alexandrovich Berdyaev also came into contact with Blavatsky's Theosophy. He described the encounter, which was to have a profound impact on his life, in his philosophical autobiography *Samopoznanie* ("Self-knowledge," published in 1949). In 1916, he devoted an extensive essay on the topic titled "Teosofija i Antroposofija v Rossii" ("Theosophy and Anthroposophy in Russia," reprinted in 1991). Berdyaev sought to classify the phenomenon "Theosophy" in a philosophical context and stated characteristics for the differentiation between Theosophy and Anthroposophy.

At the outset of his career, the Russian philosopher and mystic Peter Demianovich Ouspensky (1878–1947) adhered to a mode of thought more in keeping with Theosophy. Though he later favored the ideas of George Ivanovich Gurdjieff (1866–1949),[19] in his early works Ouspensky's efforts centered on the unification of philosophy and science so often proclaimed by Theosophy, frequently citing Blavatsky's work throughout.[20] Gurdjieff himself had at one point tackled the Theosophy of Blavatsky after first coming into contact with Theosophical texts in 1907. He was a Greek-Armenian esotericist, writer, and composer, and worked first in Russia, then later in France. There are visible parallels with Theosophical interpretations of Buddhist and Hindu ideas present in his works.[21]

Theosophy experienced a new dimension of engagement via Russian Symbolism. How widespread the effects were surely ties into the fact that in Russian Symbolism, more so than in any other literary direction, one's worldview was made a factor of relevance to literary history, ". . . as in this particular case, the worldview generates the diversity of artistic Symbolic imagery."[22]

A new understanding of the world that covered all sides of human interest (from the cosmic to human evolution) was precisely what Theosophical doctrine strove for. Symbolism had first to generate its own imagery, and, in the search for usable patterns, encountered Theosophy.

> Today many scholars are unaware of the degree to which Theosophical vocabulary and imagery left their subtle mark on the art and literature of the Silver Age: the frequent use—indeed, overuse—of adjectives such as "light," "silent," "bright," "spiritual" . . . , the concept of harmony; the notion of theurgy; the images of Eternity and the Call; the idea of correspondences; the central figure of the Triangle; the images of the spider and the web (Maya, the world illusion); the circle, the wheel, and the spiral (of reincarnation); the Initiate and the initiation; the idea of the Path; the Abyss; the struggle of Light and Darkness; the notion of the Master and the Brotherhood; the secret society; the color white and the metal silver, exotic Eastern vocabulary; and the like—these are the commonplaces of Theosophy that entered artistic discourse almost unnoticed. An awareness of this occult subtext on the figurative and semantic level opens fresh perspectives that can lead to new interpretive possibilities.[23]

Of course, Theosophy was not the only influential theoretical current during Russia's "Silver Age." Consequently, there were a number of writers who briefly "flirted" with Theosophy but gave it up soon after and moved on to other theoretical systems, such as Vyacheslav Ivanovich Ivanov, Aleksei

Mikhailovich Remizov, and Valery Yakovlevich Bryusov. Recently, Ivanov's relationship to Theosophy and to the other schools of thought that characterized the "Silver Age" has become an object of historical research. In particular, his relationship with the Theosophist Mintslova is of interest in this regard.[24] Because Ivanov attempted to design his own religious cosmos, the Theosophical traces in his works are marginal, but sufficient enough to identify him as an author who operated in the context of the "occult Renaissance" of the "Silver Age."

With authors who stood in the shadow of a certain kind of scandalous infamy, such as Kuzmin, the parallels to occult texts such as Blavatsky's *Secret Doctrine* are openly acknowledged.[25]

Another author who was attracted to Theosophical ideas was Daniil Leonidovich Andreev. This writer, who was rediscovered after the Perestroika of the 1980s, devised an image of pan-unity in *Roza mira* ("Rose of the World," 1958; first published in 1991), which corresponded with Theosophical considerations in many aspects.[26] Of course, even in the context of Russian Symbolism there were also authors who were familiar with the principles of Theosophy and rejected them out of hand from the very start, such as Dmitry Sergeyevich Merezhkovsky and Zinaida Nikolayevna Gippius. Yet others sided with Steiner's Anthroposophy without first detouring to Blavatsky's Theosophy, such as the poet and translator Lev Lvovich Kobylinsky (pen name Ellis). There were also Theosophists who themselves tried their hand at literary forms to spread the doctrine, like the translator Pavel Ivanovich Batyushkov.

Among the Symbolists, there were also "committed Theosophists, such as Konstantin Balmont, Nikolai Minsky, Max Voloshin, and Andrei Bely."[27] In Bely's case in particular, his engagement with Theosophy was persistent. He later became a dedicated Anthroposophist and polemicized against the Theosophists from an Anthroposophical standpoint. Voloshin was interested in both systems of thought and only attained a removed, critical distance toward them in the second half of his creative career. In addition to Russian Symbolism, there was another group that put forward Theosophical ideas on its own terms, namely the authors of so-called "light fiction." Because of their popularity, they were effective inspirations for engagement with Theosophy. Among these was the writer Vera Ivanova Kryzhanovskaya, who was so fascinated by the exotic and mysterious elements of Blavatsky's ideas that she wrote several novels based in such a context.[28] Another name worth mentioning is that of Blavatsky's sister, the children's book author Vera Petrovna Zhelikhovskaya, whose oeuvre also includes works about her sister.[29]

The novelist Vsevolod Sergeyevich Solovyov (brother of philosopher Vladimir Sergeyevich Solovyov), who was personally acquainted with Blavatsky, played a particularly important role. He was a member of the Theosophical Society from 1884 to 1886, and in 1893 he published a series of articles titled *Sovremennaja zhrica Izidy* ("A Modern Priestess of Isis").[30]

Aside from philosophers and poets, Blavatsky's Theosophy also inspired the art world. At the beginning of the twentieth century in particular, the trend in art circles was to convey through drawing those phenomena that elude the perceptive ability of the human eye. For this reason, theories dealing with the so-called fourth dimension of space were followed with interest, and there was considerable effort to allow the viewer to experience these, or to at least make them accessible via art.

Theosophical imaginings of ether, astral light, or human auras stimulated the search for the possibility of their reproduction. In response to Theosophical attempts to visualize the invisible energies and powers hidden within a person, artists experimented with the depiction of thought forms, or attempted to contribute to the study of spiritual powers by creating artworks that were meant to generate a certain tone or pleasant reverberation in the soul of the viewer.

Certain Theosophical concepts are reinterpreted in the works of Russian avant-garde artists such as Wassily Wassilyevich Kandinsky, Kazimir Severinovich Malevich, Pavel Nikolayevich Filonov, and Mikhail Fyodorovich Larionov. Building up from foundational Theosophical ideas, they attempted to develop their own systems and, by extension, new concepts regarding the function of art, the creative process, and the reception of art. It is worth noting, however, that several of them straddled the fine line between Theosophy and Anthroposophy, because Rudolf Steiner, unlike Blavatsky, had developed his own theory of art. Kandinsky, for example, is known to have consulted Theosophical texts at the beginning of his artistic career as part of the development of his theory of objectless art. In his work "About the Spiritual in Art," he explicitly mentions *The Key to Theosophy* as a work that gave him deep insight into the connection between art and existence.

The Russian Symbolic poet Andrei Bely counts among those who built their art theory model in the contested in-between of Theosophy and Anthroposophy. According to Bely, artistic creation was equivalent to a certain form of world perception, so that this preoccupation with both models, Theosophy and Anthroposophy, led to him further develop his theory of perception in such a context. However, the fact that Theosophical models played a role in the creation of Bely's theoretical conceptions even before those of Steiner is evidenced, for example, by his 1909 essay "Ėmblematika smysla" ("Emblems of the Senses"), as well as the accompanying author's notes. He even cites passages from the *Book of Dzyan*, the stanzas of which formed a central component of her *Secret Doctrine*. The *Book* was purportedly translated by Blavatsky, although some scholars claim she wrote it herself.

> [W]e go from us, as tiny sand grains of existence, to us, as Adam Kadmon, as universe, where I, you, he—are one, where father, mother, and son are one, according to the message of the holy book of "Dzyan." "For father, mother, and son became one once more" (1st verse). And this Oneness—is a symbol of the revealed secret knowledge.[31]

In this essay, Bely investigates the possibility of creating an epistemological model capable of grasping all aspects of existence. In this vein, he studies the potential of various such models that deal with philosophy and the history of science. According to the models he designed and sketched, he assigns Blavatsky's Theosophy to the same tier as, for example, epistemology, religion, metaphysics, theurgy, theology, and ethics. He also clearly expresses his expectations for Theosophy, to which he assigns a high rank, although he deems the current "Eastern" variety not equal to the task:

> Theosophy is a system of systems; it is equally an otherworldly view of the world and the nature of humanity; it is not transformative; it is not overbearing, its purpose is that of completion; it brings an end to Chaos; it systematizes the sum of senselessly emerging images, forms, and norms. Theosophy as we know it today appears at times in the form of gnostic syntheses, other times as the progeny of earlier magicks, theurgies, and religious systems; its effectiveness rests upon the fact that it has yet to soar to the level of functionality possible of true Theosophy, in the present epoch Theosophy is no more than the beginning of a series of growing flows, both old and new, that are now not yet fixed; for this reason its significance, so terrible it freezes the soul to ice, is hidden from us: to bring the drama of our perceptions into a system without demanding a price or suffering, senseless; it strides forth towards its tsardom—there, where one closes one's eyes, where one lets one's arms sink, where the heart ceases to beat [. . . .][32]

In Bely's opinion, only Steiner's Anthroposophy offered the adequate, anticipated solution and expanded Theosophy to that for which it was intended—a comprehensive epistemological model.

His critical engagement with Theosophical theories trails off thereafter with a short summary of those elements that he found dissatisfactory. Scattered through his diaries, letters, and article commentaries are enough pointers to catch the drift of his actual critique of Theosophy—namely, its Eastern component.

At this point, it is appropriate to mention Nicholas Konstantinovich Roerich, who considered himself a true student and follower of Blavatsky. Not only did he follow her spiritually, but he also retraced her steps in actuality by traveling through the East, particularly in Tibet, in search of legendary Shambhala and accompanying rumored Mahatma. He visualized the Theosophical doctrine not just through his paintings, but also in poems, in reviews of literature and art, and in philosophical essays. He was supported in this by his wife, Helena Ivanovna Roerich, who herself also modeled her writings on Blavatsky's teachings.

To complete the picture, it bears noting that both the actor Mikhail Aleksandrovich Chekhov and the composer Alexander Nikolayevich Scriabin went through Theosophical phases. What is more, my investigations into literary history at the turn of the century in Russia reveal that occult, and particularly Theosophical, traces are to be found in the works of authors that until now have hardly been analyzed in this respect.[33] The following examples are provided to compensate for this oversight in previous research.

The works of the writer Nikolay Stepanovich Gumilyov provide ample opportunity for Theosophical analysis. As already proven by the research of Nikolay Alekseevich Bogomolov,[34] Gumilyov was more receptive to the works of Blavatsky than has previously been assumed. Furthermore, archival evidence suggests that he attempted to found a "geosoficheskoe" ("geosophical") society that was to connect Theosophical theories specifically to phenomena of geological interest. Not for nothing did he choose the word "geosophy" (*geosofiya*), similar to "Theosophy" (*teosofija*). He also likely drew upon Theosophical literature for notions regarding the future mission of the Slavic people, which primarily found expression in his works *Romanticheskie cvety* ("Romantic Flowers") and *Ognennyj stolp* ("The Burning Pillar"). Another leading motif in Gumilyov's works is that of androgyny, which borrows from Blavatsky's concept of human development.

Another author little known in relation to his receptiveness of the occult is Mikhail Alekseevich Kuzmin. Although in his case it would be an exaggeration to call him a consistent, undeviating follower of occult theories, one can nevertheless identify temporary occult-influenced phases, in which the theories of Blavatsky's *Secret Doctrine* played an important role. Definitive in this regard is his volume of verse *Seti* ("Nets"), his poem "Adam" from the collection *Nezdeshnie Vechera* ("Not These Evenings"), and his poem "Iskusstvo" ("Art") from the book *Paraboly* ("Parables"). Kuzmin's diaries, having now been released to the national archive, offer extensive new material for researchers.

The case of Vjacheslav Ivanov, a leading representative of Russian Symbolism, provides further fertile ground for investigation. By reputation alone, he represented a central figure of Symbolism, to whom flocked numerous persons, both Theosophically and Anthroposophically inclined. Among the visitors to his literary salon, the "Tower," were Bely and Voloshin, as well as the latter's first wife, Margarita Wassiljewna Sabashnikova, who first expressed an interest in Theosophy before later becoming an adherent of Steiner and who spent many years as a member of his inner circle. For some time, Ivanov also maintained close ties with Mintslova, who sought to unite herself, him, and Bely in a "misticheskij kruzhok" ("mystical triangle"). His work *Lira Novalisa* ("The Lyra Novalis") offers a starting point for textual analyses tracing the occult in his work. References to Theosophy are also discernable in the work of Alexander Alexandrovich Blok, Sergej Mitrofaniovich Gorodecky, Konstantin Dmitriyevich Balmont, and Aleksei Mikhailovich Remizov.

In addition to questions associated with purely literary research, investigations for the sake of expanding knowledge of the cultural history of the "Silver Age" in Russia would also be of use. Particularly at the start of the twentieth century, there was a relatively active print culture among Theosophical publishers, from which *Vestnik teosofii* ("The Theosophy Herald") and *Voprosy teosofii* ("Questions of Theosophy") were read with enthusiasm. There is a wealth of material regarding Theosophical authors, Theosophical takes on philosophical problems, existential questions, social ideas, and so forth of interest to the researcher.

After the October Revolution, all activities promoting the reception and distribution of occult theoretical models were increasingly inhibited by the Soviet Union. Nevertheless, there were "underground" attempts to maintain them. The dedicated researcher can infer important information about occult subcultures from KGB archives now increasingly open to the public.[35] Whether it would be worthwhile at this juncture to take Theosophy alone under the microscope, or whether it would be prudent at first to focus more broadly on the whole phenomenon of occultism, must be determined accordingly over the course of these investigations.

A few names that could become interesting points of reference for the topic of the occult in Russia are listed as follows: Sofya Gitmanovna Kaplun-Spasskaya (1901–1962), who had personal relationships with several literary representatives of the "Silver Age" (for example, with Kuzmin). Moreover, she was much inspired by Bely and left behind letters that bear witness to how Bely's occult interest found lasting resonance with her. Another important name is Lidiya Dmitriyevna Ryndina (1882–1964), who participated in the organization of various secret lodges. The occult interests of Boris Mikhailovich Zubakins, who was not so much interested in the organization or institutionalization of occult circles, but instead attempted to use his personal experiences to convince others of the occult worldview he had distilled from various sources, have recently become well-known. Gregory Ottonovich Mebes and Nikolai Nikolaievich Aseev also bear mentioning. In 1955, the latter published an article titled "Posvjatitel'nye ordena v SSSR" ("Initiatory Orders of the USSR") in a journal called *Vestnik Instituta po izucheniyu istorii i kul'tury SSSR* ("Herald of the Institute for the Study of History and Culture in the USSR"). Tellingly, this particular volume, which, as a publication officially acknowledged and supported by state authorities, ought to be in the central libraries of Moscow and St. Petersburg, is missing.

Official publications on the subject of occultism from the Soviet era are few and far between. It is to be presumed that there are various manuscripts and typescripts of the subculture scene housed in private archives that are still awaiting assessment and could thereby serve to make a certain page of Soviet subculture more transparent.

In 1991, after Perestroika, the Theosophical Society in Russia was refounded. Ever since, Theosophical publications of all ilk are flooding the Russian market, and, as book trade statistics reveal, they sell well. It would be useful to determine audience response patterns, as well as expectations of and dealings with occult literature by contemporary readers. The multifaceted, modern, sprawling Russian literary scene ought also be investigated for traces of occult systems for interpreting the world.

Besides literature, Theosophy, as well as occultism more broadly, was productive in other cultural spheres, such as philosophy and art. In this context, one can think of Solovyov, Berdyaev, Pavel Alexandrovich Florensky, Kandinsky, Malevich, Filonov, and Larionov, to start with. Also noteworthy is the intense scholarly interest of Dr. Helen Westgeest (University of Leiden, Netherlands) into the effects of Theosophy and Anthroposophy in art history, within which context Russian artists have recently come into play.

Modern Russian society since Perestroika has been showered with countless Western theories and models that intersect and generate yet more models. The role of Theosophy in this incomprehensible multitude of frameworks for interpreting the world is nowhere near as slight or as outdated as the ambition toward ever new innovations in this current age would have one assume.

Today, there are several Theosophical Societies in Russia. The circle around Tatyana Nickolaevna Mickushina and her society, which seeks an ethical basis for the new world within Theosophical doctrine, has proven itself particularly productive. A number of their works have now been translated into English, including "Words of Wisdom" (2009), "Good and Evil" (2010), "The Masters about Karma" (2007), "The Sutras of the Ancient Teaching" (2014), "Morya" (2015), "Sanat Kumara" (2013), and "Saint Germain" (2012).

The Russian philosopher and faith healer Arkady Naumovich Petrov provides another example of the incorporation of Theosophical ideas into one's own cosmology and anthropogony.[36] Most of his works have been translated into German, but a translation of his works into English is still pending. Some Theosophical concepts that he has adapted are those of the various cycles and "humanities" (Hyperboreans, Lemurians, Atlanteans, etc.), which he assumes to have once determined the fate of the Earth. He also supports his theories with the Theosophical notion of the sevenfold "bodies" from which humans are composed. Likewise, within his cosmology, which encompasses various planets, one can find numerous leanings toward the world model of Theosophy, for example, the use of the descriptor "sphere moon."

The relationships between the German Theosophical Society and the various Russian Theosophical societies are diverse. Members of the society "Temple of the People," which is headquartered in Halcyon, California, associate actively with their colleagues in St. Petersburg. A large number of the publications of the German Society are also translated into Russian, and there are regular exchange trips.

Prospective Research Directions

The study of the traces of Theosophy within Russian cultural history remains a blind spot in Slavic Studies in Germany. Those few researchers who turned their attentions toward the topic for their dissertations soon changed course at the start of their academic careers. Lasting milestones are the investigations of Henrieke Stahl-Schwaetzer and Renata von Maydell.[37] On an international scale, new standards for the study of the traces of Theosophy in Russia are being set by scholars in the United States. Of note is the work of the aforementioned Maria Carlson, but there are also American scholars of Theosophy as a general phenomenon who relate their work to the Russian case. As the literature about Theosophy is extensive, and the references to Russian thinly dispersed throughout, I forgo individual bibliographical references.

Meanwhile, the academic landscape in Russia remains as skeptical as ever toward all that is spiritual or occult; however, there has been a flood of literature from apologists that must first be examined in terms of their substance. The search for traces of Theosophical thinking plays a role in unearthing the connection between national identity and Russian culture.[38] In art history also, there are several artists whom one can hardly bypass in the investigation of Theosophical influences.[39]

Theosophy is among the most formative phenomena in the cultural history of Russia, and this despite Theosophical ideology having introduced "Western" concepts such as the special place of the individual in the world, religious freedom, and unorthodox understandings of the progress of humanity and the cosmos. Russian intellectuals later gave these ideas their own color, and Theosophical ideas, thus transformed, had a certain reflexive influence on European processes of cultural and artistic production. In particular, before the Russian Revolution of 1917 and after Perestroika, Theosophy became a means to cross national borders and to bring oneself closer spiritually to the representatives of different nationalities. Nowadays, this approach is implemented especially through the newly founded Russian Theosophical Societies, personal contacts, and the exchange of Theosophical texts, and less so through scholarly discourse.

Furthermore, it is worth noting that Blavatsky herself is a largely untapped literary source. Aside from her Theosophical works, she also wrote numerous fantastical stories and travelogues, the analysis of which would be of scholarly benefit.

Another important field for research would be an investigation into questions of differences and similarities between Theosophy and Anthroposophy, as well as other occult models, which so far are no more than fragmentarily available and can therefore only be rudimentarily discussed in the existing literature. Questions of terminology (e.g., occult vs esoteric) are equally important for future research, as there is no academic consensus of yet.

Another desideratum is the expansion of methodology for the study of the effects of occult worldview models visible in literary texts. As there are relatively few works concerned with this problem, there is much potential for development of a methodological process. Such scholarship would yield material for research into theories of transcendence (as opposed to immanence); research into reception, intertextuality, semiotics, and the expansion of theories of literary studies, by which the respective methodological approach would always hinge on the concrete research questions of the moment.

Finally, for the sake of broader international academic discourse, it is essential to determine the extent to which actors in other countries have made note of Russian Theosophists and their effect on culture. Transgressing the historical relevance of Theosophy within the sphere of Russian culture, such a perspective would highlight the global connections that have characterized a highly diverse movement whose manifold influences can be felt up to the present day.

Notes

1. For the history of Theosophy in Russia, see Björn Seidel-Dreffke, *Die russische Literatur Ende des 19. und zu Beginn des 20. Jahrhunderts und die Theosophie E. P. Blavatskajas: Exemplarische Untersuchungen* (Frankfurt: Haag + Herchen, 2004).

2. Readers who wish to know more about this trend are recommended to consult the works of Gabriela Lehmann-Carli, particularly Gabriela Lehmann-Carli, "Aufklärungsrezeption, 'Prosveščenie' und Europäisierung: Die Spezifik der Aufklärung in Rußland," *Zeitschrift für Slawistik* 39, no. 3 (1994); idem, "Der russisch-westliche Streit um das 'alte' und das 'neue' Rußland: Historiographie, Geschichtsverständnis, Kulturkonzepte und Aufklärung (1700–1825)," in *Tätigkeitsbericht* (Potsdam: Forschungszentrum Europäische Aufklärung, 1997), 30–33; idem, "Freimaurerei in russischer Rezeption und Adaption als kulturelle Übersetzung," in *Kultur als Übersetzung: Klaus Städtke zum 65. Geburtstag*, ed. Wolfgang Stephan Kissel (Würzburg: Königshausen & Neumann, 1999); Gabriela Lehmann-Carli, Michael Schippan, and Birgit Scholz, eds., *Russische Aufklärungs-Rezeption im Kontext offizieller Bildungskonzepte (1700–1825)* (Berlin: Spitz, 2000).

3. Lehmann-Carli, "Freimaurerei," 50.

4. See e.g. Nathan Rosen, "The Magic Cards in the 'Queen of Spades,'" *The Slavic and East European Journal* 19 (1975); Lauren G. Leighton, *The Esoteric Tradition in Russian Romantic Literature: Decembrism and Freemasonry* (University

Park, PA: Pennsylvania State University Press, 1994); Markus Wolf, *Freimaurertum bei Pushkin: Einführung in die russische Freimaurerei und ihre Bedeutung für Pushkins literarisches Werk* (Munich: Otto Sagner, 1998); Boris Bashilov, *Pushkin i masonstvo* [Pushkin and Freemasonry] (Moscow: M.I. Novikov, 2011).

5. Decembrists were aristocratic officials who on December 14, 1825, refused to pledge their fealty to the new tsar, Nicholas I. The Decembrist revolt was the first revolutionary movement opposing tsarist autocracy in Russia.

6. The term "intelligentsia" was first brought into discussion by the Russian writer Pyotr Dmitryevich Boborykin (1836–1921) in the 1860s. Soon it became associated not only with the marker of a certain social class, but also with a kind of "moral consciousness" of society. It was later used in Russia, especially in the Soviet era, for those who did spiritual work (as opposed to physical work). Later the term was incorporated into other languages (East German: *Intelligenz*). Here I retain the Russian designation. Compare, e.g., Jutta Scherrer, *Die Petersburger religiös-philosophischen Vereinigungen* (Wiesbaden: Harrassowitz, 1973); idem, *Russkaja emigratsija do 1917 goda: Laboratorija liberal'noj revolyutsionnoj mysli* [Russian Emigration before 1917: A Laboratory of Liberal Revolutionary Thoughts] (St. Petersburg: Russian Academy Press, 1997); idem, *Requiem für den Roten Oktober: Rußlands Intelligencija im Umbruch 1986–1996* (Leipzig: Leipziger Univ. Verlag, 1996); Dmitry Sergeyevich Likhachov, *Rußland: Seele, Kultur, Geschichte* (Augsburg: Pattloch-Verlag, 1994); idem, *The National Nature of Russian History* (New York: Columbia University Press, 1990).

7. Maria Carlson, *"No Religion Higher Than Truth": A History of the Theosophical Movement in Russia, 1875–1922* (Princeton: Princeton University Press, 1993), 5.

8. Viktor Borisowitsch Fedyushin, *Russlands Sehnsucht nach Spiritualität: Theosophie, Anthroposophie und die Russen* (Schaffhausen: Novalis Verlag, 1988), 74.

9. See Rudolf Steiner, "Zur Geschichte und aus den Inhalten der ersten Abteilung der Esoterischen Schule 1904–1914: Briefe, Rundbriefe, Dokumente und Vorträge," in *Rudolf Steiner Gesamtausgabe*, vol. 264, ed. Rudolf Steiner-Nachlaßverwaltung (Dornach: Rudolf Steiner Verlag, 1996).

10. Birgit Menzel et al., eds., *The New Age of Russia: Occult and Esoteric Dimensions* (Munich et al.: Sagner, 2012), 11–28 (introduction, foreword and afterword); ibid., 448; Birgit Menzel, "The Occult Revival in Russia Today and Its Impact on Literature," *The Harriman Review* 16, no. 1 (2007).

11. In Russia, Larisa Petrovna Dmitrieva has published a great number of biographical works about Blavatsky.

12. More on this topic available in the research of Michael Hagemeister, including Michael Hagemeister, ed., *Visionen der Zukunft um 1900: Deutschland, Österreich, Russland* (Paderborn: Fink, 2014); idem, ed., *Mythen Europas*, vol. 7: *Moderne* (Regensburg: Pustet, 2009); see also Boris Groys, *Die neue Menschheit: Biopolitische Utopien in Russland zu Beginn des 20. Jahrhunderts* (Frankfurt:

Suhrkamp, 2005); Karl Pinggera, *Russische Religionsphilosophie und Theologie um 1900* (Marburg: Elwert, 2005).

13. Karl Löwith, *Weltgeschichte und Heilsgeschehen* (Stuttgart: Metzler, 1983).

14. See Helena Petrovna Blavatsky, "Brevno i suchok" [The Stem and the Branch], in idem, *Skrizhali karmy* [The Tablets of Karma], trans. Konstantin Jurjewich Burminstrov (Moscow: Lotos Press, 1995); idem, "Progress i kul'tura [Progress and Culture]," in *Skrizhali karmy* [The Tablets of Karma] (Moscow: Lotos Press, 1995).

15. See idem, *Erzählungen und Reiseberichte*, ed. Björn Seidel-Dreffke (Fichtenwalde: Frank Göpfert, 1999).

16. See Vladimir Sergeyevich Solovyov, "Blavatskaja, E. P. [Helena Petrovna Blavatsky]," in *Kritiko-biograficheskij slovar* [Critical Biographical Dictionary], vol. 3, ed. Sergei A. Vengerov (St. Petersburg: Lan', 1892); idem, "Retsentsia na knigu E. P. Blavatskoj 'The Key to Theosophy' [Review of H. P. Blavatsky's 'The Key to Theosophy']," *Russkoe Obozrenie* 3 (1890).

17. To be found under the title "Neo-Buddhism," in Helena Petrovna Blavatsky, ed. *Collected Writings*, vol. 12: *1889–1890* (Wheaton: The Theosophical Publishing House, 1980).

18. See Björn Seidel-Dreffke, "Blick nach Osten—Wohl oder Wehe? V. S. Solovyovs Auseinandersetzung mit E. P. Blavatskaja," in *Russkie pisatel'nicy i literaturnyj process v konce XVIII—pervoj treti XX v.* [Russian Female Writers and the Literary Process from the End of the 18th Until the First Third of the 20th Centuries], ed. Mikhail Shmil'evich Fajnshtejn and Frank Göpfert (Wilhelmshorst: Frank Göpfert, 1995). Compare Ludolf Müller and Vladimir Sergeyevich Solovyov, "Gedenken zur hundertsten Wiederkehr seines Todestages," in *Südwestfunk: Manuscript for the radio show broadcast on 24 July 2000*, broadcast manuscript from July 24, 2000; Vladimir Sergeyevich Solovyov, *Eine kurze Erzählung vom Antichrist*, trans. and annot. Ludolf Müller (Munich: Köhler, 1990).

19. George Ivanovich Gurdjieff (1873–1949) created his own mystic-occult model of thought for which Indian philosophy, Egyptian lore, and Persian thought functioned as sources. He had a relatively large number of followers in Russia.

20. See Peter Demianovich Ouspensky, *Tertium Organum: Kluchi k zagadkam mira* [Tertium Organum: The Key to Puzzles of the Universe] (St. Petersburg: Trud', 1911); idem, *Tsetvertoe izmerenie* [The Fourth Dimension] (St. Petersburg, 1910).

21. Compare John G. Bennett, *Gurdjieff: Ursprung und Hintergrund seiner Lehre* (München: Heyne, 1989).

22. Gudrun Langer, *Kunst—Wissenschaft—Utopie: Die "Überwindung der Kulturkrise" bei V. Ivanov, A. Blok, A. Bely und V. Chlebnikov* (Frankfurt: Klostermann, 1990), 25.

23. Carlson, *History of the Theosophical Movement in Russia*, 9–10.

24. Nikolay Alekseevich Bogomolov, "Iz predistorii 'Liry Novalisa' [On the Prehistory of Novalis's Lyra]," in *Russkaja literatura nachala XX veka i okkul'tizm*:

Issledovanija i materialy [Russian Literature at the Beginning of the Twentieth Century and Occultism: Research and Documents], ed. idem (Moscow: Novoe Literaturnoe Obozrenie, 1999); idem, "Vyacheslav Ivanov i Kuzmin: K istorii otnoshenij" [Vjatscheslav Ivanov and Kuzmin: On the History of Their Relationship], in ibid.

25. Compare Nikolay Alekseevich Bogomolov, "Tetushka iskusstv: Okkul'tnye kody v poėzii Kuzmina" [The Aunt of the Arts: The Occult Codes in Kuzmin's Poetry], in *Russkaja literatura nachala XX veka i okkul'tizm: Issledovanija i materialy* [Early Twentieth-Century Russian Literature and Occultism: Research and Documents], ed. idem (Moscow: Novoe Literaturnoe Obozrenie, 1999).

26. More recently, in Germany an Andreev-group under the name of "Blume der Welt" ("Flower of the World") has formed, the goals of which closely overlap with those of the Theosophical Society. The leadership is held by composer Alexander Sojnikov. The first Andreev-meeting in Germany took place in March 2000. There is increasing interest in the roots of his works. A dissertation written by Lena Müller at the University of Potsdam in 2002 (unpublished) illustrates Andreev's relationship to Blavatsky's Theosophy.

27. Carlson, *History of the Theosophical Movement in Russia*, 159.

28. For a detailed analysis of the reception and effect of the works of Vera Ivanova Kryzhanovskaya, see Seidel-Dreffke, *Russische Literatur*, chapter 4.

29. See e.g. the following reprints of Zhelikhovskaya's works: Vera Petrovna Zhelikhovskaya, *Radda-Baj, Pravda o Blavatskoj* [Radda-Baj, The Truth About Blavatsky] (Moscow: Lotos Press, 1992); Zhelikhovskaya, "Videnie v kristalle: Rasskaz" [Visions in the Crystal], in *Chudo rozhdestvenskoj nochi* [The Miracle of the Night Before Christmas] (St. Petersburg: Lotos Press, 1994).

30. For more details about Solovyov's relationship to Theosophy, see Seidel-Dreffke, *Russische Literatur*, chapter 5.

31. Andrei Bely, "Ėmblematika smysla" [The Emblematics of Meaning], in *Simvolizm kak miroponimanie* [Symbolism as Understanding of the World], ed. L.A. Sugaj (Moscow: Respublika, 1994), 39.

32. Ibid., 44–45.

33. See Björn Seidel-Dreffke, "Literarische Verhexung: Das Blavatskaja-Bild in Vs. S. Solovyovs 'Sovremennaja žrica Izidy' (1893)," in *Tagungsband zur 11. Fachtagung der Fachgruppe Slavistik in der DGO "Russische Kultur und Gender Studies: Interkulturelle Annäherungen" 11/16–11/18/2000*, ed. Elisabeth Cheauré and Carolin Heyder (Berlin: Deutsche Gesellschaft für Osteuropakunde, 2002); idem, "'Science-fiction' oder 'okkulter Roman': Die Werke V. I. Kryzhanovskayas," *Anzeiger für Slavische Philologie* 28/29 (2000/1); idem, "Die Polemik mit der Theosophie Blavatskajas als Vehikel der Auseinandersetzung mit dem Osten im Rußland der Jahrhundertwende," in *Osteuropäische Lektüren: Beiträge zur 2. Tagung des Jungen Forums Slavistische Literaturwissenschaft*, ed. Mirjam Goller (Frankfurt: Lang, 2000); idem, "Von der Heiligen zur Hexe: Frauengestalten

in den Werken von Vsevolod S. Solovyov," *Anzeiger für Slavische Philologie* 25 (1998).

34. Bogomolov, *Russkaja literatura*.

35. Compare Bernice Glatzer Rosenthal, ed., *The Occult in Russian and Soviet Culture* (Ithaca: Cornell University Press, 1997); Linda Dalrymple Henderson, "The Merging of Time and Space: The Fourth Dimension in Russia from Ouspensky to Malevich," *Structurist* 15 (1975–76); Edward Kasinec and Boris Kerdiman, "Occult Literature in Russia," in *The Spiritual in Art: Abstract Painting 1890–1985*, ed. Edward Weisberger (Paris: Persee, 1986); Lauren G. Leighton, *The Esoteric Tradition in Russian Romantic Literature: Decembrism and Freemasonry* (Philadelphia: Pennsylvania University Press, 1994); Bronislav Malinovskij, *Magija, Nauka, Religija* [Magic, Science, Religion] (Moscow: Nauka Press, 1998); Veit Loers and Ingrid Erhardt, ed., *Okkultismus und Avantgarde 1900–1915* (Frankfurt: Ostfildern, 1995); Rolf Fieguth, ed., *Orthodoxien und Häresien in den slavischen Literaturen* (Vienna: Gesellschaft zur Förderung Slawistischer Studien, 1996); James Webb, *The Occult Underground* (La Salle: LLC, 1974).

36. Works in German translation: Alexandr Petrov, *Neue Erde: Baum des Lebens, Teil II* (Neuss: Kanda Zentrum Verlag, 2013); idem, *Sphäre Mond: Baum des Lebens, Teil III* (Neuss: Kanda Zentrum Verlag, 2014); idem, *Sphäre Merkur: Baum des Lebens, Teil V* (Neuss: Kanda Zentrum Verlag, 2015); idem, *Sphäre Venus: Baum des Lebens, Teil VI* (Neuss: Kanda Zentrum Verlag, 2016) (all works translated by Björn Seidel-Dreffke).

37. See Henrieke Stahl-Schwaetzer, *Renaissance des Rosenkreuzertums: Initiation in Andrej Belys Romanen* Srerebrjanyj golub' *und* Peterburg (Frankfurt et al.: Peter Lang, 2002); Renata von Maydell, *Vor dem Thore: Ein Vierteljahrhundert Anthroposophie in Russland* (Bochum: Projekt-Verlag, 2005) (with interesting commentary on the history of Theosophy in Russia).

38. See Isabel Wünsche, *Harmonie und Synthese: Die russische Moderne zwischen universellem Anspruch und nationaler kultureller Identität* (Munich: Fink, 2008).

39. See Alexander Graeff, *Kandinsky als Pädagoge* (Aachen: Shaker, 2013); Hans-Peter Riese, *Kunst/konstruktiv konkret: Gesellschaftliche Utopien der Moderne* (Munich: Deutscher Kunstverlag, 2008).

References

Bashilov, Boris. *Pushkin i masonstvo* [Pushkin and freemasonry]. Moscow: M.I. Novikov, 2011.

Bely, Andrei. "Ėmblematika smysla [The Emblematics of Meaning]." In *Simvolizm kak miroponimanie* [Symbolism as Understanding of the World], edited by L. A. Sugaj, 25–90. Moscow: Respublika, 1994.

Bennett, John G. *Gurdjieff: Ursprung und Hintergrund seiner Lehre*. München: Heyne, 1989.
Blavatsky, Helena Petrovna, ed. *Collected Writings*. Vol. 12, *1889-1890*. Wheaton: The Theosophical Publishing House, 1980.
———. "Brevno i suchok" [The plank and the twig]. In *Skrizhali karmy* [The Tablets of Karma], translated by Konstantin Jurjewich Burminstrov, 256-70. Moscow: Lotos Press, 1995.
———. "Progress i kul'tura [Progress and Culture]." In *Skrizhali karmy*, [The Tablets of Karma], translated by Konstantin Jurjewich Burminstrov, 271-86. Moscow: ZMF, 1995.
———. *Erzählungen und Reiseberichte*, edited by Björn Seidel-Dreffke. Fichtenwalde: Frank Göpfert, 1999.
Bogomolov, Nikolay Alekseevich. "Tetushka iskusstv: Okkul'tnye kody v poėzii Kuzmina" [The Aunt of the Arts: The Occult Codes in Kuzmin's Poetry]. In *Russkaja literatura nachala XX veka i okkul'tizm: Issledovanija i materialy* [Russian Literature at the Beginning of the Twentieth Century and Occultism: Research and Documents], edited by idem, 145-86. Moscow: Novoe Literaturnoe Obozrenie, 1999.
———. "Iz predistorii 'Liry Novalisa' Vjach. Ivanova [On the Prehistory of Novalis's Lyra]." In *Russkaja literatura nachala XX veka i okkul'tizm: Issledovanija i materialy* [Russian Literature at the Beginning of the Twentieth Century and Occultism: Research and Documents], edited by idem, 203-10. Moscow: Novoe Literaturnoe Obozrenie, 1999.
———. "Vyacheslav Ivanov i Kuzmin: K istorii otnoshenij" [Vjatscheslav Ivanov and Kuzmin: On the History of Their Relationship]. In *Russkaja literatura nachala XX veka i okkul'tizm: Issledovanija i materialy* [Russian Literature at the Beginning of the Twentieth Century and Occultism: Research and Documents], edited by idem, 211-24. Moscow: Novoe Literaturnoe Obozrenie, 1999.
Carlson, Maria. *"No Religion Higher than Truth": A History of the Theosophical Movement in Russia, 1875-1922*. Princeton: Princeton University Press, 1993.
Fedyushin, Viktor B. *Russlands Sehnsucht nach Spiritualität: Theosophie, Anthroposophie und die Russen*. Schaffhausen: Novalis Verlag, 1988.
Fieguth, Rolf, ed. *Orthodoxien und Häresien in den slavischen Literaturen*. Vienna: Gesellschaft zur Förderung Slavischer Studien, 1996.
Graeff, Alexander. *Kandinsky als Pädagoge*. Aachen: Shaker, 2013.
Groys, Boris. *Die neue Menschheit: Biopolitische Utopien in Russland zu Beginn des 20. Jahrhunderts*. Frankfurt: Suhrkamp, 2005.
Hagemeister, Michael, ed. *Mythen Europas*, vol. 7: *Moderne*. Regensburg: Pustet, 2009.
———, ed. *Visionen der Zukunft um 1900: Deutschland, Österreich, Russland*. Paderborn: Fink, 2014.

Henderson, Linda Dalrymple. "The Merging of Time and Space: The Fourth Dimension in Russia from Ouspensky to Malevich." *Structurist* 15 (1975–76): 97–108.

Kasinec, Edward, and Boris Kerdiman, "Occult Literature in Russia." In *The Spiritual in Art: Abstract Painting 1890–1985*, edited by Edward Weisberger, 361–66. Paris: Persee, 1986.

Langer, Gudrun. *Kunst—Wissenschaft—Utopie: Die "Überwindung der Kulturkrise" bei V. Ivanov, A. Blok, A. Bely und V. Chlebnikov*. Frankfurt: Klostermann, 1990.

Lehmann-Carli, Gabriela. "Aufklärungsrezeption, 'Prosveščenie' und Europäisierung: Die Spezifik der Aufklärung in Rußland." *Zeitschrift für Slawistik* 39, no. 3 (1994): 358–82.

———. "Der russisch-westliche Streit um das 'alte' und das 'neue' Rußland: Historiographie, Geschichtsverständnis, Kulturkonzepte und Aufklärung (1700–1825). In *Tätigkeitsbericht*, 30–33. Potsdam: Forschungszentrum Europäische Aufklärung, 1997.

———. "Freimaurerei in russischer Rezeption und Adaption als kulturelle Übersetzung." In *Kultur als Übersetzung: Klaus Städtke zum 65. Geburtstag*, edited by Wolfgang Stephan Kissel, 47–58. Würzburg: Königshausen & Neumann, 1999.

Lehmann-Carli, Gabriela, Michael Schippan, and Birgit Scholz, eds. *Russische Aufklärungs-Rezeption im Kontext offizieller Bildungskonzepte (1700–1825)*. Berlin: Spitz, 2000.

Leighton, Lauren G. *The Esoteric Tradition in Russian Romantic Literature: Decembrism and Freemasonry*. Philadelphia: Pennsylvania State University Press, 1994.

Likhachov, Dmitry Sergeyevich. *The National Nature of Russian History*. New York: Columbia University Press, 1990.

———. *Rußland: Seele, Kultur, Geschichte*. Augsburg: Pattloch-Verlag, 1994.

Loers, Veit, and Ingrid Ehrhardt, eds. *Okkultismus und Avantgarde. Von Munch bis Mondrian. 1900–1915*. Frankfurt: Ostfildern, 1995.

Löwith, Karl. *Weltgeschichte und Heilsgeschehen*. Stuttgart: Metzler, 1983.

Malinovskij, Bronislav. *Magija, Nauka, Religija* [Magic, Science, Religion]. Moscow: Nauka Press, 1998.

Maydell, Renata von. *Vor dem Thore: Ein Vierteljahrhundert Anthroposophie in Russland*. Bochum: Projekt-Verlag, 2005.

Menzel, Birgit et al., eds. *The New Age of Russia: occult and esoteric dimensions*. Munich: Sagner, 2012.

Menzel, Birgit. "The Occult Revival in Russia Today and Its Impact on Literature." *The Harriman Review* 16, no. 1 (2007): 1–14.

Müller, Ludolf, and Vladimir Sergeyevich Solovyov. "Gedenken zur hundertsten Wiederkehr seines Todestages." In *Südwestfunk: Manuskript zur Sendung vom 24.07.2000*. Broadcast manuscript from July 24, 2000.

Ouspensky, Peter Demianovich. *Tsetvertoe izmerenie* [The Fourth Dimension]. St. Petersburg, 1910.

———. *Tertium Organum: Kluchi k zagadkam mira* [Tertium Organum: The Key to Puzzles of the Universe]. St. Petersburg: Trud', 1911.

Petrov, Alexandr. *Neue Erde: Baum des Lebens, Teil II*, translated by Björn Seidel-Dreffke. Neuss: Kanda Zentrum Verlag, 2013.

———. *Sphäre Mond: Baum des Lebens, Teil III*, translated by Björn Seidel-Dreffke. Neuss: Kanda Zentrum Verlag, 2014.

———. *Sphäre Merkur: Baum des Lebens, Teil V*, translated by Björn Seidel-Dreffke. Neuss: Kanda Zentrum Verlag, 2015.

———. *Sphäre Venus: Baum des Lebens, Teil VI*, translated by Björn Seidel-Dreffke. Neuss: Kanda Zentrum Verlag, 2016.

Pinggera, Karl. *Russische Religionsphilosophie und Theologie um 1900*. Marburg: Elwert, 2005.

Riese, Hans-Peter. *Kunst/konstruktiv konkret: Gesellschaftliche Utopien der Moderne*. Munich: Deutscher Kunstverlag, 2008.

Rosen, Nathan. "The Magic Cards in the 'Queen of Spades.'" *The Slavic and East European Journal* 19 (1975): 255–75.

Rosenthal, Bernice Glatzer, ed. *The Occult in Russian and Soviet Culture*. Ithaca: Cornell University Press, 1997.

Scherrer, Jutta. *Die Petersburger religiös-philosophischen Vereinigungen. Die Entwicklung des religiösen Selbstverständnisses ihrer Intelligencija-Mitglieder 1901–1917*. Wiesbaden: Harrassowitz, 1973.

———. *Requiem für den Roten Oktober: Rußlands Intelligencija im Umbruch 1986–1996*. Leipzig: Leipziger Univ.-Verl., 1996.

———. *Russkaja emigratsija do 1917 goda: Laboratorija liberal'noj revolyutsionnoj mysli* [Russian emigration before 1917: A laboratory of liberal revolutionary thought]. St. Petersburg: Russian Academy Press, 1997.

Seidel-Dreffke, Björn. "Blick nach Osten—Wohl oder Wehe? V. S. Solovyovs Auseinandersetzung mit E. P. Blavatskaja." In *Russkie pisatel'nicy i literaturnyj process v konce XVIII–pervoj treti XX v.* [Russian Female Writers and the Literary Process from the End of the 18th Until the First Third of the 20th Centuries], edited by Mikhail Shmil'evich Fajnshtejn and Frank Göpfert, 127–42. Wilhelmshorst: Frank Göpfert, 1995.

———. "Von der Heiligen zur Hexe: Frauengestalten in den Werken von Vsevolod S. Solovyov." *Anzeiger für Slavische Philologie* 25 (1998): 129–46.

———. "'Science-fiction' oder 'okkulter Roman': Die Werke V. I. Kryzhanovskayas." *Anzeiger für Slavische Philologie* 28/29 (2000/1): 129–37.

———. "Die Polemik mit der Theosophie Blavatskajas als Vehikel der Auseinandersetzung mit dem Osten im Rußland der Jahrhundertwende." In *Osteuropäische Lektüren: Beiträge zur 2. Tagung des Jungen Forums Slavistische Literaturwissenschaft, Berlin 1998*, edited by Mirjam Goller, et al., 225–34. Frankfurt: Peter Lang, 2000.

———. "Literarische Verhexung: Das Blavatskaja-Bild in Vs. S. Solovyovs 'Sovremennaja žrica Izidy' (1893)." In *Tagungsband zur 11. Fachtagung der Fachgruppe Slavistik in der DGO "Russische Kultur und Gender Studies: Interkulturelle Annäherungen" 11/16–11/18/2000*, edited by Elisabeth Cheauré and Carolin Heyder, 423–40. Berlin: Deutsche Gesellschaft für Osteuropakunde, 2002.

———. *Die russische Literatur Ende des 19. und zu Beginn des 20. Jahrhunderts und die Theosophie E. P. Blavatskajas: Exemplarische Untersuchungen (A. Bely, M. A. Voloshin, V. I. Kryzhanovskaya, Vs. S. Solovyov)*. Frankfurt: Haag + Herchen, 2004.

Solovyov, Vladimir Sergeyevich. "Retsentsia na knigu E. P. Blavatskoj 'The Key to Theosophy' [Review of H. P. Blavatsky's 'The Key to Theosophy']." *Russkoe Obozrenie* 3 (1890): 15–21.

———. "Blavatskaja, Elena Petrovna [Helena Petrovna Blavatsky]." In *Kritiko-biograficheskij slovar'* [Critical Biographical Dictionary], vol. 3, edited by Sergei A. Vengerov, 315–19. St. Petersburg: Lan', 1892.

———. *Eine kurze Erzählung vom Antichrist*. Translated and annotated by Ludolf Müller. Munich: Köhler, 1990.

Stahl-Schwaetzer, Henrieke. *Renaissance des Rosenkreuzertums: Initiation in Andrej Belys Romanen 'Srerebrjanyj golub' und 'Peterburg.'* Frankfurt: Peter Lang, 2002.

Steiner, Rudolf. "Zur Geschichte und aus den Inhalten der ersten Abteilung der Esoterischen Schule 1904–1914: Briefe, Rundbriefe, Dokumente und Vorträge." In *Rudolf Steiner Gesamtausgabe*, vol. 264, edited by Rudolf Steiner-Nachlaßverwaltung, 117–21. Dornach: Rudolf Steiner Verlag, 1996.

Webb, James. *The Occult Underground*. La Salle: LLC, 1974.

Wolf, Markus. *Freimaurertum bei Pushkin: Einführung in die russische Freimaurerei und ihre Bedeutung für Pushkins literarisches Werk*. Munich: Sagner, 1998.

Wünsche, Isabel. *Harmonie und Synthese: Die russische Moderne zwischen universellem Anspruch und nationaler kultureller Identität*. Munich: Fink, 2008.

Zhelikhovskaya, Vera Petrovna. *Radda-Baj. Pravda o Blavatskoj* [Radda-Baj. The Truth About Blavatsky]. Moscow: Lotos Press, 1992.

———. "Videnie v kristalle: Rasskaz" [The Vision in the Crystal: A Tale]. In *Chudo rozhdestvenskoj nochi* [The Miracle of the Night Before Christmas], edited by E. V. Dushechkina, 168–70. St. Petersburg: Lotos Press, 1993.

Contributors

Michael Bergunder is Professor of Religious Studies and Intercultural Theology at Heidelberg University. His areas of interest include theories and methods in religious studies, Tamil religious history since the eighteenth century, the history of esotericism, and the study of global Pentecostalism. Among his publications are *Ritual, Caste, and Religion in Colonial South India* (as co-editor) and *The South Indian Pentecostal Movement in the Twentieth Century*.

Helena Čapková (Tokyo/Kyoto, Japan) is a researcher, exhibition curator, and art history professor at Ritsumeikan University, Kyoto. She has written extensively on transnational visual culture in Japan and Europe. Her publications include "The Hawk Princess at the Hawk's Well: Neo-Noh and the Idea of a Universal Japan" (2019); "'From Decorative Arts to Impressive Local Constructions and Materials'—On the New Japonisme for the Czechoslovak Republic (1918–1938)" (2018); "Bauhaus and Tea Ceremony: A Study of Mutual Impact in Design Education Between Germany and Japan in the Interwar Period" (2017); "'Believe in Socialism . . .': Architect Bedřich Feuerstein and His Perspective on Modern Japan and Architecture" (2016); and "'Careless Shell'—Transnational Exploration of Czechoslovak and Japanese Surrealisme" (2015).

CHUANG Chienhui is a lecturer at Kobe Women's University in Japan. She obtained her PhD in Japanese Literature from Osaka University in 2013. Her research covers the Theosophical movement in modern China and Japan, as well as post-colonial literature in the modern Far East, with a particular focus on the movements led by Wu Ting-fang and H. P. Shastri. Her paper *The Theosophical Movements in China before W. W. II* was published by the Japanese Association of Comparative Culture in 2014.

Laurence Cox is Associate Professor in Sociology at the National University of Ireland Maynooth. He is author of *Buddhism and Ireland* (Equinox, 2013) and co-editor of *A Buddhist Crossroads: Pioneer Western Buddhists and Asian Networks 1860–1960* (Routledge, 2014) as well as several books in social movement studies. With Alicia Turner and Brian Bocking, he is co-author of *The Irish Buddhist: The Forgotten Monk Who Faced Down the British Empire*, a biography of U Dhammaloka (Oxford: Oxford University Press, 2020).

Wouter J. Hanegraaff is Professor of History of Hermetic Philosophy and Related Currents at the University of Amsterdam, The Netherlands. Alongside numerous articles and seven edited volumes, he is the author of *New Age Religion and Western Culture: Esotericism in the Mirror of Secular Thought* (Leiden: Brill, 1996/Albany: State University of New York Press, 1998); *Lodovico Lazzarelli (1447–1500): The Hermetic Writings and Related Documents* (Tempe: ACMRS Press, 2005; with Ruud M. Bouthoorn); *Swedenborg, Oetinger, Kant: Three Perspectives on the Secrets of Heaven* (West Chester: Swedenborg Foundation Press, 2007); *Esotericism and the Academy: Rejected Knowledge in Western Culture* (Cambridge: Cambridge University Press, 2012); and *Western Esotericism: A Guide for the Perplexed* (London: Bloomsbury Academic, 2013).

Ulrich Harlass is a post-doctoral researcher at the Institute of Religious Studies of the University of Bremen, where he teaches on the global history of religion. His research interests include the Theosophical Society and its so-called "oriental shift," postcolonial perspectives on nineteenth-century global discourses on religion, and the global entanglement of the academic discovery of Buddhism as a world religion. He is the author of *Die orientalische Wende der Theosophischen Gesellschaft* (Berlin: De Gruyter, 2020).

Hashimoto Yorimitsu is Professor for Comparative Literature at Osaka University, Japan. His specialty are narrative and visual exchanges between Britain and Asia around the twentieth century. Recently he has been working on British intelligence activities concerning (counter) Indian revolution movements, especially Agnes Smedley, H. P. Shastri, and Hideo Nakao. Major publications include *Yellow Peril, a Collection of Historical Sources*, 4 vols. (Edition Synapse, 2012); "A Modern Symposium? Goldsworthy Lowes Dickinson and Letters from and to a Chinese Official," in Anne Tomiche, ed., *Comparative Literature as a Critical Approach*, vol.

5 (Classiques Garnier, 2017); "Indo no tōgeika Gurucharan Sin" [Indian Potter Gurcharan Singh], *Mingei*, 2015, March–June.

Boaz Huss is Professor of Jewish Thought at Ben-Gurion University. His research interests include the history of Kabbalah, Western Esotericism, New Age Culture, and New Religious Movements. His recent works include *Mystifying Kabbalah: Academic Scholarship, National Theology, and New Age Spirituality* (Oxford: Oxford University Press, 2020), *Zohar: Reception and Impact* (Liverpool: The Littman Library of Jewish Civilization, 2016); and the co-edited volume (with Julie Chajes) *Theosophical Appropriations: Esotericism, Kabbalah and the Transformation of Traditions* (Jerusalem: Bialik Institute, 2016).

Jérémy Jammes is Professor in Asian Languages and Civilization at the Institut d'Études Politiques de Lyon (Lyon Institute of Political Studies). He has published widely on Southeast Asian geopolitics and religions, including a monograph on Vietnamese Cao Đài religion, and co-edited volumes on evangelical networks, Muslim piety, and contemporary geopolitical issues in Southeast Asia. From 2016 to 2018 he was director of the Research Institute of Asian Studies, Universiti Brunei Darussalam, and from 2017 to 2019 editor-in-chief of the Springer Book Series *Asia in Transition*. Between 2010 and 2014, he served in Bangkok as Deputy Director, Head of Publications, and Strategic Adviser of the Research Institute on Contemporary Southeast Asia (IRASEC).

Hans Martin Krämer is Professor for Japanese Studies at Heidelberg University (since 2012). After obtaining his PhD degree, he spent a year each as guest researcher at Harvard University and the International Research Center for Japanese Studies in Kyoto. His specialization is in modern Japanese History, and his publications have mainly dealt with the history of education, religion, and human-animal relations. His recent work has been devoted to processes of the exchange of knowledge about religion, especially Buddhism, between Japan and abroad, and his most recent publication in this area is the volume *Buddhism and Modernity: Sources from Nineteenth-Century Japan* (Honolulu: University of Hawai'i Press, 2020), co-edited with Orion Klautau.

Perry Myers is Professor of German Studies at Albion College, United States. His most recent book is *German Visions of India, 1871–1918:*

Commandeering the Holy Ganges during the Kaiserreich (Palgrave, 2013). He is currently nearing completion of a comparative research project that explores cosmopolitan religious movements in England, France, Germany, and India (1875–1932) and their sociopolitical idiosyncrasies with the tentative title *Spiritual Empires in Europe and India: Cosmopolitan Religious Movements and their National Factions (1875–1932)*. He was recently awarded a research fellowship at the *Institut d'Études Avancées de Paris* for 2020–21.

PD Dr. Phil. Björn Seidel-Dreffke: Born in 1963, he is a Slavist author, translator, and lecturer. He studied Russian Language and Literature in the former Soviet Union (1982–1987) with a concentration in scientific research and publications in the field of Russian spirituality and their influence on Russian literature and Culture. In 2004, he published his "Habilitation," titled "Russian Literature at the End of the 19th and the Beginning of the 20th century and the Theosophy of H.P. Blavatsky." He is a translator of Russian spiritual writings from 2004 to 2017.

Julian Strube is working on a post-doctoral project about "Religious Social Reform in the Context of Unitarianism and the Brahmo Samaj" at the Cluster of Excellence "Religion and Politics," University of Münster. He is currently preparing the publication of his third book about "Tantra in the Context of a Global Religious History," which focuses on exchanges between Bengali and Western intellectuals in colonial Bengal. The leading themes of his research are the relationship between religion and politics, as well as the debates about the meaning of religion, science, and philosophy since the nineteenth century. In 2015, he received his PhD in Religious Studies for his dissertation about the relationship between *Socialism, Catholicism, and Occultism in Nineteenth-Century France* (published by De Gruyter in 2016).

Yan Suarsana is Professor for Religious Studies at the University of Bremen, Germany. He has published on the global history of Christianity, including two books about Pentecostalism in the context of colonialism and globalization. Another focus of his work lies in the post-colonial approach to religious history of the nineteenth and twentieth centuries, especially in India and South East Asia.

Alicia Turner is an Associate Professor of Humanities and Religious Studies at York University in Toronto. Her work focuses on the intersections of religion, colonialism, secularism, and nationalism with a focus on Buddhism in Burma. She is the author of *Saving Buddhism: The Impermanence of Religion in Colonial Burma* (Honolulu: University of Hawai'i Press, 2014). Along with Laurence Cox and Brian Bocking, she is the co-author of *The Irish Buddhist: The Forgotten Monk Who Faced Down the British Empire* (New York: Oxford University Press, 2020).

Index

Abelson, Joshua, 257, 262
Advaita Vedanta, 66, 75, 79, 80–81, 84, 182, 199
agency, 4–5, 10, 20n21, 182, 194, 224–29, 232, 304–305, 412
Agrippa, Cornelius, 32, 37
Akyab (Sittwe), 290–91, 294–95, 297–306, 310n32, 311n50
Alcott, Bronson, 72
Allebach, Lila B., 259, 261
Ananda Metteyya (Allan MacGregor), 284, 304–305
anarchism, 245n39, 282, 285, 289, 337n12, 366n40
Ani, Kaduri, 256, 265–66
Anthroposophy, 8, 262, 268, 289, 386, 427, 431–33, 436, 438–39, 441, 442–43. *See also* Steiner, Rudolf
anti-colonialism, 4–5, 10, 13–15, 17, 20n24, 29–30, 65–66, 80, 84–90, 110–18, 121–22, 125, 133–36, 141n59, 143n82, 168–69, 185, 187, 217, 223, 226–27, 231–36, 241, 281, 290–91, 295, 306, 309n22, 317, 319, 321–22, 327, 334–36, 359, 338n21, 395, 403–404, 407–16, 435
Arakan, 14–15, 281, 284, 288, 290–307, 310. *See also* Burma

architecture, 16, 117, 352, 373–75, 384, 386, 390–96
Arnold, Dorothy, 156, 158–59, 161, 162–63, 164, 166, 355
Arnold, Edwin, 78–79, 83, 96, 153
art, 9, 14–18, 118, 128–29, 226, 345–47, 350–53, 356–61, 364n30, 367n61, 368n63, 374–75, 377, 380, 385–89, 409–10, 425, 427, 434–45
  folk, 16, 359, 361, 395
Arundale, George S., 143, 150, 158–59, 162
Arundale, Rukmini Devi, 118, 127, 140n48, 143n89
Arya (journal), 320, 325, 326, 330
Aryans, 11, 76, 78, 182, 199–200, 211n127, 212n135, 226–27, 233–37, 244n35, 247n67, 267, 348, 359, 367n61
Arya Samaj, 6, 22n37, 50–51n10, 95n86, 381, 410
Asakawa Noritaka, 358–59
Asakawa Takumi, 358–59
Asia, 1–2, 4–9, 11–16, 30, 43, 71–72, 74, 79, 82, 96n99, 110–11, 114, 121–22, 125, 128, 133, 143n86, 149, 153–54, 172n29, 187, 267, 284–85, 287–89, 291, 301–302,

461

Asia *(continued)*
    306, 309n22, 312n66, 317–23,
    326–28, 332, 334–35, 338n21,
    349–51, 353–54, 357, 359–61,
    367n61, 377, 386, 395, 406, 410.
    See also Arakan, Burma, China,
    Hong Kong, India, Indonesia,
    Japan, Korea, Singapore, Sri
    Lanka, Vietnam
Association of Hebrew Theosophists,
    11, 253–72, 273n26
Atkinson, William Walker, 150
Australia, 119, 122, 129, 143n86, 156,
    197, 217, 346, 405
Ayurveda, 404

Bạch Liên, 114, 116, 117, 118, 119,
    122, 123, 141
Baha, Abdul. *See* Bahaism
Bahaism, 166, 328, 330, 332, 366n36
Balfour declaration, 259
Bali. *See* Indonesia
Balishaman, 402, 405–406, 416
Bateson, Gregory, 406–407, 410
Bely, Andrei, 431, 438–43
Bengal. *See* India
Bergman, Hugo, 255, 262
Besant, Annie, 5, 7–8, 16, 18, 82–83,
    86–87, 115, 120–21, 128, 149,
    151, 152, 157–60, 167, 170n7,
    171n29, 208n67, 220, 237, 240,
    243n20, 255, 262–64, 268, 270–
    71, 281–82, 285, 287, 329–32,
    335, 346–48, 352–57, 363n25,
    364n30, 365n36, 377, 388–89,
    402, 411, 413, 431, 433. See also
    Thought-Forms (book)
Besant School, 160–66, 355, 366n40
Bhagavad Gita, 10, 65–90, 94n67,
    94n71, 95n86, 96n96, 98n138,
    100n165–66, 200, 413
bhakti, 67, 73, 79, 84, 89, 413

Bhaktivedanta, Abhay Charanaravinda, 67–68
Bharati, Agehananda, 65, 68, 73
Bialik, Hayim Nachman, 259
Bible, 74, 83, 327
Blavatsky, Helena Petrovna, 4–7,
    10–12, 17–18, 20n22, 29–39,
    47–49, 50–51n10, 51n16, 52n22,
    58n49, 76–79, 81–82, 95n86, 110,
    123, 129, 166, 179–203, 204n2,
    204n4, 206n23, 206n28, 207n33,
    207n37, 208n52, 209n88, 219–20,
    240, 243n20, 267, 269–70, 281,
    290, 329–33, 388, 402, 410,
    419n70, 426–29, 432, 434–45
Bodh Gaya (Buddha Gaya, BuddhaGaya). *See* Maha-Bodhi Society
Bose, Nandalal, 350
Bosman, Leonard, 257, 265–66,
    269–70
Brahmanism, 66–70, 77, 89, 100n166,
    170n9, 199–200, 411
Brahmo Samaj, 51n10, 80–81
Brinkley, Jack, 351–52, 354, 377
Britain. *See* United Kingdom
Britten, Emma Hardinge, 36–43,
    46–49, 58n86
Brotherhood of Humanity, 267, 330,
    366n40
Brydlova, Bozena, 258, 260, 266–68
Buck, J. D., 267–68, 384
Buddhism, 2, 5, 7, 14, 29–30, 32,
    37–38, 49n2, 55n45, 71, 77–79,
    149, 153–54, 169n6, 182, 200,
    242n8, 281–307, 309n21, 330,
    349–50, 401, 412, 429, 436–37
    in the West, 79, 93n44, 93n57, 219,
        282, 284, 286, 287, 305
    Mahayana, 74, 110, 111–15, 119–
        23, 127–36, 138n16, 154, 161,
        164, 281, 283, 284, 291, 312n66,
        339n53, 350, 360, 376

reform, 5, 11, 110–14, 122–23, 130–34, 140n52, 287, 289, 294, 299
Theravada, 15, 96, 111–12, 282, 288, 291–94, 296–307, 310n30
Zen (Chan), 110, 133, 170n9, 365, 366n36
Bulwer-Lytton, Edward, 37, 41
Burma, 9, 14–15, 113, 284, 290–302, 304–306, 312n74. See also Arakan
Burnouf, Émile-Louis, 69–70
Burton, Richard, 41

Calcutta. See India
Cambodia, 114, 139n33, 140n50, 296
Caodaism, 109–14, 118, 123, 132–33, 138n19, 141n59, 142n72–73, 142n79
Cao Jinyuan, 165–66
Cao Yunxian, 166
Castaneda, Carlos, 405
Ceylon. See Sri Lanka
Chaldea, 6, 10, 33, 38, 43–45, 48, 269
Chan Buddhism. See Buddhism, Zen (Chan)
Chandra, Shin (U Chandramani), 294–96, 303, 306–307
Channing, William Henry, 73, 78–79
Chatterji, Mohini Mohun, 80–82, 96n103, 196
Chattopadhyay, Bankimchandra, 85
China, 6, 8, 12–13, 43, 47, 110, 121–22, 132–33, 149–69, 170n15, 171–72n29, 173n49, 174–75n72, 255, 288–89, 291, 296, 312n66, 321–22, 334, 353–55, 357, 363n23, 365n35, 366n38, 367n51, 368n63, 377, 397n13, 433. See also Hong Kong
Chinese redemptive societies, 109, 111, 132–33

Chittagong, 285, 291–92, 294, 296, 299–300, 306, 310n30, 311n60
Christianity. See also Bible
  Anglican, 78, 115
  Catholic, 74, 113, 116, 131, 144n92, 228, 260, 346
  liberal, 72, 78, 81–82, 144, 346
  missionaries, 2, 5, 7, 47, 72, 83–84, 98n138, 149–51, 154–58, 162, 165, 169, 285, 287, 293, 304–305
  Orthodox, 181–82, 429, 433
  Protestant, 15, 30, 318, 323
  Unitarian (see Unitarianism)
Clarke, James Freeman, 72
Cohen, S. S., 258, 262–63
colonialism. See anti-colonialism
Communism. See Socialism
Confucianism, 73, 110–11, 113, 151, 153, 160–61, 166–67, 169–70n6, 173n49, 325, 339n53, 350, 360–61
Conway, Moncure, 71, 72–73
Cousin, Victor, 71
Cousins, James H., 15–16, 156, 169n1, 172n36, 320–21, 329–30, 338n19, 338n21, 345–61, 362n6, 363n23–24, 364n30, 364–65n34, 365–66n36, 366n38, 376–79, 381, 396n5, 396–97n8, 397n12

Daoism, 109–11, 119, 123, 131, 134–35, 152, 166, 350
Darwin, Darwinism, 181–82, 200, 222–23
Das, Bhagavan, 82, 86–87, 221–22, 225–26, 239
Dee, John, 32, 37
Demolsky, Fritz, 401–403, 405, 416
dharma, 85–86, 109, 285, 414
Dharmapala, Anagarika, 14, 283, 285, 287–88, 291–96, 299–305, 307, 309n21

Disney, Walt, 345–47, 356, 362n6
Dutch East India. *See* Indonesia
Dvivedi, Manilal N., 74, 78
Dzyan, book of, 206n28, 269–70, 440

Eckstein, Friedrich, 255
education, 7–8, 12, 114, 123, 126–27, 130, 133–34, 143n89, 149–53, 157–60, 166–69, 257, 282, 288, 290, 341n82, 354, 376, 381, 402
    for girls, 160–66, 366n40, 387
Egypt, 6, 10, 34, 36–38, 43–45, 48, 50n8, 56n61, 253, 269, 325, 329, 359, 448n19
Eliade, Mircea, 402, 405
Emerson, Ralph Waldo, 71, 72, 73. *See also* Transcendentalism
England. *See* United Kingdom
Ensor, Beatrice, 150, 159
entanglement / entangled histories, 1, 3–4, 8–9, 12, 17, 29, 49–50n3, 51n16, 88–90, 179–80, 205n16, 241, 245n45, 403, 411, 413–14, 416
Eknath, 66–67
Esoteric Buddhism (book), 180–82, 185–88, 193, 195, 197–99, 203, 211n127
Essenes, 259
evolution, 42, 86–87, 181–82, 188, 198, 200, 211n127, 222–25, 323–24, 347, 437
Excommunication, 256, 258, 263–65, 274n48
Ezekiel, A. D., 255, 257–58, 262–63, 270, 276n81
Ezra N. E. B., 265

Fanta, Berta, 255
Felt, George Henry, 33–38, 54–55n33–44
Feuerstein, Bedřich, 375

Fischinger, Oskar, 345–46
Fludd, Robert, 32, 37
Folk medicine, 120, 164, 401–406, 444
France, 15–16, 32–33, 46–48, 67–71, 109–18, 122–23, 126, 128–29, 132–35, 136n1, 136n3, 136n4, 137n11, 138n19, 140n49, 141n59, 155, 171n29, 233–34, 240, 245n45, 255, 309n22, 318–20, 321–23, 331, 337n8, 384, 386, 340n69, 341n83, 348, 375, 384, 386, 394, 415–16, 427, 433, 437
Franck, Adolphe, 33, 53n29
Freemasonry, 135–36, 138n19, 323, 425–28

Gandhi, Mohandas Karamchand, 5, 82–84, 87, 137n9, 151, 170n7, 220, 232, 237, 239, 248n77, 317, 322, 336n3
Gaster, Moses, 257
gender, 283–84, 286. *See also* education for girls
Germany, 9, 13, 48, 69, 71, 206n22, 217, 219–22, 224–28, 230, 232–38, 240–41, 242n10, 245n45, 245n48, 245n51, 246n59, 248n86, 255, 262, 268, 335, 365n36, 410, 427–29, 431–33, 444, 449n26
Gewurtz, Elias, 269–70
Ghose, Aurobindo, 15, 86, 319–20, 323, 325–26, 328–32, 334, 336, 338n32, 373, 381, 384–85, 387, 390–95
global history, 1–3, 18, 22n37, 29, 31, 88–90, 180, 184, 191, 204, 217–18
globalization, 2–3, 283–84, 305
Goethe, Johann Wolfgang, 79, 220, 223, 240
Greece, Ancient, 13, 34, 50n8, 233–34, 247n67, 359, 367

Index

Harrison, William, 193, 196, 203
Hartmann, Franz, 220–21, 225, 227–28, 230–31, 243n14, 244n30, 248
Hasidism, 258
healing. *See* medicine
Hegel, Georg Wilhelm Friedrich, 69, 219, 223, 244n25
Heiman, S. I., 263
Hermetism, 37, 53n30, 111, 115, 197, 426
Hertz, Joseph, 264
Hinduism, 2, 5, 7, 10, 13, 17, 32, 37, 46, 49n2, 65–90, 93n44, 98n138, 137n9, 145n118, 182, 184, 195, 199–203, 220, 226, 233, 237–41, 242, 285, 293, 360, 402–403, 406–16, 437
  Neo-Hinduism, 17, 141n60, 199, 407–409, 413–16, 419n49
Hippie culture, 16, 406–408, 415
Holland. *See* Netherlands
Hong Kong, 126–27, 155–56, 169n1, 172–73, 354–55
Horne, Alexander, 156, 160, 162, 258–61
Hübbe-Schleiden, Wilhelm, 223, 233–35, 246n66, 248n86
Humboldt, Wilhelm, 69
Hume, Allan Octavian, 179, 185–86, 191, 193, 197–203, 209n88, 210n112, 210n118, 233, 411

India, 1, 4–10, 12–13, 15–17, 29, 34, 42, 44–45, 49, 49n2, 50n8, 56n61, 65–70, 73–90, 95n86, 98n138, 100n165, 111–13, 118–22, 133, 135, 143n89, 143n90, 149, 156, 159–62, 166–67, 170n7, 170n9, 171n29, 179–80, 183, 185, 190, 193–94, 203, 207n33, 211n123, 211n127, 217–18, 221–22, 242n10, 244n35, 248n86, 253, 255, 257, 261–63, 268, 270, 274n48, 284–85, 291–92, 294–307, 319–24, 327–28, 334, 337n10, 347, 351–52, 354–55, 357–60, 366n51, 373–77, 380–81, 390–92, 396, 401, 431, 448n19
  in the Orientalist imagination, 4, 6, 10, 13, 17, 29–31, 33, 36–38, 43, 46–48, 51n16, 69, 87–88, 110, 181, 186–87, 195, 199–201, 206n22, 219–20, 223–26, 231–41, 243n20, 244n25, 246n59, 326–27, 329, 335, 348–53, 365n36, 403, 407–16
Indian National Congress (INC), 5, 8, 74–75, 82, 238, 244n34, 317, 322, 411–12
Indology, 65, 69–74, 90, 94n67, 381
Indonesia, 16–17, 126, 381, 401–16
International Society for Krishna Consciousness (ISKCON), 67
Ireland, 9, 15, 156, 169n1, 217, 220, 281–82, 284, 286–87, 304–305, 309n22, 320, 328, 345–48, 350, 351–52, 357, 360, 376–77
Isis Unveiled (book), 47, 56n54, 77, 180, 185–86, 192, 195–97, 202, 204n2, 206n28, 207n35, 329, 388
Islam, 2, 79, 242, 360, 402, 409, 412
Israel, 8, 11, 256, 264, 267. *See also* Palestine
Israel, Edward L., 257
Israel Messenger (journal), 265, 273n26
Iyer, S. Subramanya, 237–38

Japan, 5, 8–9, 12, 15–16, 74, 126, 154, 157–58, 168, 171n29, 281, 283, 285, 291–92, 296, 299, 317–18, 320–22, 326–28, 330–32, 334–35, 336n5, 337n12, 337n13, 337n14,

Japan *(continued)*
　337n15, 338n21, 338n23, 338n27,
　338n28, 339n46, 339n53, 339n55,
　347–61, 364n34, 365n35, 365n36,
　366n51, 367n58, 367n61, 373–77,
　380–81, 384–88, 390, 392,
　394–96, 396n4
Java. *See* Indonesia
Jewish Theosophist, The (journal), 256,
　259
Jinarajadasa, Curuppumullage, 118,
　124–27, 208n67, 224–26, 274n48,
　365–66n36
Jnandev, 66–67
Johnson, Samuel, 47, 72
journals. *See* print media
Judaism, 11, 43, 253–72. *See also*
　Association of Hebrew Theosophists; *Jewish Theosophist, The*;
　Kabbalah
　Liberal / Reform, 11, 254, 257–58,
　260–61, 263, 265, 271–72
Judge, William Quan, 7–8, 38, 77–78
Jung, Leo, 264

Kabbalah, 6, 10–11, 21n31, 33–34,
　37–38, 48, 53n29–31, 55–56n49,
　204–205n4, 254, 258, 261–63,
　266–72. *See* also Judaism
Kafka, Franz, 255
Kamenskaya, Anna Alexejewna,
　429–34
Kandinsky, Wassily, 220, 346, 356,
　364n30, 389, 439, 443
Keightley, Archibald and Bertram,
　82–83, 282, 384–85
Keiō University (Tokyo), 320, 348,
　354, 364n34, 376
Kingsford, Anna, 7, 182
Kiripasaran, 292, 303
Koesoemodihardjo, Raden Mas, 413
Kon Buhei, 354–56, 365n35, 377

Koot Hoomi und Morya, 185–87,
　192–93, 200, 212n135
Korea, 353, 355, 357–60, 367n58,
　368n63, 376
Koumé, Tami (i.e. Kume Tamijūrō),
　351–52, 361, 363n24–25, 364n30,
　377, 396–97n8
Krishnamurti, Jiddu, 8, 21n33,
　120–22, 141n56, 329, 331–32,
　346, 356, 402
Kuzmin, Mikhail Alekseevich, 438,
　441–43

language. *See* translation
Laozi, 73, 151, 325, 350
Lara, David de, 255
Leach, Bernard, 352, 358–60, 365n36,
　368n63
Leadbeater, Charles Webster, 7–8, 109,
　115–17, 119–21, 124, 126–27,
　138n26, 142n72, 156, 208n67,
　346, 356, 388
Lévi, Éliphas, 33, 53n29
Liberal Judaism. *See* Judaism,
　Liberal / Reform
Light (journal), 192, 194, 198
Llull, Ramon, 37
literature, 9–10, 14–18, 29, 47, 70,
　85, 115, 121–25, 155–56, 167,
　169, 186, 191, 196, 202, 320, 376,
　387–88, 425, 434–45
Lorinser, Franz, 74, 98n138
Lotus Bleu, Le (journal), 110, 128–29
Łubienski, Zina and Stefan, 16,
　374–75, 380–81, 384–88

magic, 33–34, 37–48, 120, 185, 402,
　405–406, 440
magnetism, 35, 39, 43, 45–48, 124
Maha-Bodhi Society, 14–15, 281–307,
　285–86, 291–309
Mahabharata (book), 70, 76, 79, 84–85

Index

Mahatmas, Mahatma Letters, 7, 76, 94n77, 181, 186–88, 191, 194–95, 203, 206n23
Maitland, Edward, 7, 182
Maitreya, 119–21
Manuk, Malcolm, 156, 355
Marxism. *See* Socialism
Massey, Charles Carleton, 203
Materialism, 11, 13, 15, 17, 43–44, 81, 220–23, 227, 229, 238–39, 245n39, 260–61, 268, 324
Mavalankar, Damodar M., 76–77, 192, 194, 203, 208n67, 211n127, 212n135
Mead, Margaret, 406–407, 410
Medhurst, Spurgeon, 150–56, 171n23
medicine, 34, 164, 220, 243n14, 401–406, 408
media, 128, 286, 354, 428. *See also* print media
meditation, 5, 69, 110, 118, 123, 128–31, 134–35, 143n90, 144n92, 325, 347–48, 388, 394, 405
Mesmerism. *See* magnetism
messianism, 119–22, 331
Metaxa, Ina, 377, 380, 381
millenarianism, 120
Mintslova, Anna Rudol'fovna, 431, 438, 442
Mirandola, Pico della, 32, 37
missionaries. *See* Christianity, missionaries
modernity, 11, 145n118, 284, 286, 349, 374, 389–90, 392–95, 398n27
monism, 69
Moses, Stainton, 192–93, 195–96, 198, 203, 209n82
Mother, The. *See* Richard, Mirra
Müller, Ernst, 262
Müller, Friedrich Max, 70–71, 73–74
music, 17, 39, 160–61, 163, 165, 345–47, 349, 356, 386–88, 425

Myanmar. *See* Burma
mysticism, 11, 124, 129, 222, 254, 259, 262, 266, 268, 270–71, 281–82, 389, 398n27

Nakashima, George Katsutoshi, 391–92, 393
Nederlandsch-Indische Theosofische Vereeniging, 413
Neo-Hinduism. *See* Hinduism, Neo-
Neoplatonism, 36–37, 182
Netherlands, 17, 120, 122, 126, 128–29, 255, 257, 346, 381, 403–404, 408–13, 443
New Age, 5, 183, 272, 282, 389, 403–408, 416
newspapers. *See* print media
Nguyễn Văn Lượng, 115–18, 121–23, 125–26, 129–30, 137n11, 139n38, 140n40, 141n66, 143n86
Nirvana, 200

occultism, 6, 13, 17, 31–34, 36–39, 41–48, 51n16, 55n47, 56n54, 56n60, 58n78, 58n86, 109–11, 115, 121, 124–25, 132, 134–35, 141n59, 179, 182–87, 190–203, 207n35, 207n37, 209n88, 219–20, 225, 235, 242n10, 245n45, 246n59, 259, 267, 269, 270–71, 304–305, 323–24, 328–29, 333–34, 341n83, 375, 388–89, 415–16, 425–26, 428, 435, 437–38, 441–43, 445–46, 448n19
occult science, 179, 185, 195, 198, 203, 324
October Revolution, 228, 442
Okakura Kakuzō (a.k.a. Tenshin), 339n53, 353, 357, 359–61, 367n51
Ōkawa Shūmei, 318, 322, 336, 337n14, 339n46

Olcott, Henry Steel, 5–7, 21n33–34, 29–31, 34–36, 48–49, 52n22, 54n39, 54–55n43, 58n82, 76–77, 79, 81, 95n86, 96n99, 111, 179, 182, 186, 190, 194–95, 201, 207n33, 207n35, 208n67, 219–20, 238, 240, 243n20, 281–83, 287, 290–96, 299–305, 309n31, 311n53, 341n82, 348–50, 376, 410–11

Onchi Kōshirō, 356–57

Order of the Star in the East. See Krishnamurti, Jiddu

Orientalism / orientalist scholarship, 4–6, 10, 29–31, 33, 38, 42, 44, 48, 50n8, 53n30, 65–66, 68–69, 74, 77, 87–88, 181, 186, 196, 202, 205n16, 206n22, 211n127, 246n66, 283, 327, 359, 367n58, 408–10, 416

oriental shift, 5, 50n4, 179–81, 185, 197, 202, 203, 204n4

Orphic Circle, 39–41, 44

Orthodox Judaism, 11, 254, 256–58, 260, 264

Osho, 405

Ōsugi Sakae, 320

Oxley, William, 75–76, 200, 212n135

Palestine, 8, 256, 258, 265, 328. See also Israel

Pan-Asianism, 15–16, 172, 284–85, 302, 321, 338n27, 345, 347–48, 353, 355, 365n36, 376, 381

Pavitra. See Saint Hilaire, Philippe Barbier

Perestroika, 18, 443–45

Pfoundes, Capt Charles, 281–82, 285

philanthropy, 112, 118, 127–28, 130–31, 135

philosophy, 1, 11, 17, 33, 37, 42–43, 48, 66, 68–72, 80–81, 111, 120, 134, 153, 160–61, 165, 168, 174n72, 180–81, 183–86, 190, 192–93, 196, 198, 200–201, 211n127, 219–20, 222, 225–26, 234, 255, 261, 264, 266, 270–71, 324–26, 329–30, 410, 414, 425, 427–29, 431, 435–37, 439–44, 448n19

Pioneer, The (journal), 7, 185–86, 207n33, 207n37, 209n88

Pisareva, F. F., 430–31

Polak, Gaston, 260, 272n1

post-colonialism, 4, 49n3, 65, 88–89, 125, 191, 205n16, 226–27, 231

pottery. See art

Pound, Ezra, 351

Pouvourville, Albert de,'109

Prel, Carl du, 222–23, 227, 243n22, 244–45n38–39

print media, 7, 31, 39–40, 110, 113, 116–17, 122–23, 128–29, 132, 134–35, 139n28, 141n59, 141–42n66, 142n73, 209n82, 218, 222, 235, 244n30, 256, 258–59, 262, 276n81, 283, 286–87, 291, 293, 296–97, 299–305, 309n22, 319–22, 325–26, 329–30, 332–33, 348, 428, 433, 436, 443

Pushkin, Alexander Sergeyevich, 427

Raimond, Georges, 114–15, 135

Ramakrishna Mission, 82

Ratu Bagus, 405–406, 416

Raymond, Antonin, and Noémi Pernessin, 16, 352–53, 361, 373–75, 380, 384–86, 390–96

reform, social, 6, 11, 12, 15, 70, 159, 163, 167–69, 201, 220, 282, 288, 305, 318, 333, 341n82, 411

Reform Judaism. See Judaism, Liberal / Reform

Reid, Gilbert, 150–51, 153, 154

Index

reincarnation, 42, 46, 55n45, 58n82, 120, 122, 182, 196, 200, 273n26, 332, 365n36, 437
Richard, Mirra, 15, 324–25, 327–29, 332, 363n23, 381, 390–94
Richard, Paul, 15, 317–44, 348, 363n23, 381
Richard, Timothy, 150–51, 153–54
Ritch, Lewis W., 255
Romanticism, 48, 69–70, 73, 89, 276n84
Rosicrucianism, 41, 55n45, 402, 416, 427
Roy, Rammohan, 50–51, 80–81, 92n26
Rubin, Mrs. *See* Brydlova, Bozena
Russia, 17–18, 228, 349, 377, 425–54
Russian Revolution. *See* October Revolution

Sabarwal, Keshoram, 375, 381, 384
Saint Hilaire, Philippe Barbier (a.k.a. Pavitra), 375, 380–85, 387, 390–91
Salem, A. B., 262
Samuel, Nayim B., 265
Samuels, Henry C., 256, 258
Sanskrit, 44, 46, 68–70, 74, 76, 77, 155, 171n29, 200, 240, 295, 307n3, 356, 404
Saraswati, Dayananda, 6, 51n10, 410
Sarkar, Benjoy Kumar, 166–67
Sasson, Ezekiel, 264
Schlegel, August Wilhelm, 69
Scholem, Gershom, 33, 53n31
schools. *See* education
science, 1, 4, 13, 18, 31, 34, 43, 109, 110, 124–25, 153, 167, 174n72, 180, 186, 221–25, 323–26, 330, 333–34, 428, 437
  occult, 179, 185, 195, 198, 203, 324
Scriabin, Alexander Nikolayevich, 345, 349, 441

Secret Doctrine, The (book), 179–82, 186, 196–98, 202–203, 204n2, 206n28, 211n127, 267, 270, 402, 432, 438, 440, 442
secularism, 281, 318
Semitic, 11, 267
Sen, Nabinchandra, 84–85
septenary constitution, 12, 181, 196–99, 200, 203
sevenfold constitution. *See* septenary constitution
Shamanism, 402, 405, 406, 416
Shankara, 66, 68, 75, 80
Shastri, Hari Prasad, 155–56, 171n26, 171–72n29, 172, 320, 337n14, 363n23, 366n40
Sifra de-Zeniuta (book), 269–70
Singapore, 126, 288, 355
Singh, Gurcharan, 345–61, 368n63, 375, 377, 381, 384–85
Sinnett, Arthur Percy, 7, 12, 78, 179–82, 185–98, 200–203, 207n35, 207n37m, 208n52, 209n79
Socialism, 119, 173n49, 227, 245n39, 282, 285, 286, 319–21, 341n83
Soeriokoesoemo, Raden Mas Soetatmo, 412
Solovyov, Vladimir Sergeyevich, 429, 436
Solovyov, Vsevolod Sergeyevich, 439, 443
South Africa, 83, 237, 255, 257
Spiritism, 42, 71, 141n59, 333, 341n83
Spiritualism, 6, 32–40, 43–46, 53n25, 75, 87, 122, 124, 150, 168, 181–83, 185, 191–99, 200–203, 207n37, 289, 290, 325, 333, 335, 415, 428
Spiritualist Newspaper, The, 192–93
Sri Aurobindo. *See* Ghose, Aurobindo
Sri Lanka, 5, 7, 9, 55n45, 77, 96n99, 303, 308n12, 341n82

Steiner, Rudolf, 8, 17–18, 220–21, 228–31, 243n12, 243n18, 243n20, 245n48, 255, 262, 268, 275n69, 390, 429, 431–32, 438–42
Stokowski, Leopold, 345–47, 362n6
Subba Row, Tallapragada, 7, 12, 76–77, 80, 182, 191, 193, 199–201, 203, 211n127
Sundarananda, *see* Nakashima, George Katsutoshi
Suzuki, Daisetsu Teitarō, 354, 355, 365, 380, 381

Tagore, Abanindranath, 350
Tagore, Rabindranath, 15, 317, 327, 335–36, 338n27, 339n55, 341n86, 350, 365n34, 366n40 365–66, 380, 413
Talmud, 258, 273n26
Tatya, Tukaram, 79, 195–95
Telang, Kashinath Trimbak, 70, 74–75
theism, 69, 73, 75, 84, 100n166
Theosophist, The (journal), 75, 77, 78, 96n103, 129, 170n8, 171n23, 185, 192–94, 236, 269, 333
Theravada. *See* Buddhism, Theravada
Thomson, John Cockburn, 69
Thoreau, Henry David, 71–72. *See also* Transcendentalism
Thought Forms (book), 152, 170n14, 352, 356, 363n25, 364n30, 388–89
Tibet, 78, 113, 161, 192, 200, 296, 387, 441
Tilak, Bal Gangadhar, 85–86
Tingley, Katherine, 8
Tolstoy, Lev Nikolayevich, 431, 436
Transcendentalism, 70–73, 79, 89, 282
translation, 66–85, 95n86, 96n96, 96n106, 100n165, 109, 119–25, 130, 135, 141n64, 151, 152, 154, 155, 240, 258, 262–63, 330–31, 354, 388, 430, 432
of the term "Theosophy," 12–13, 109, 170n15
translingual practices, 125, 135, 143n82
Tsinghua University (Beijing), 166

Unitarianism, 68, 72, 78, 81, 82, 287
United Kingdom, 39, 48, 78, 81, 89, 96n105, 128, 186, 200, 201, 217, 219, 232, 233, 234, 239, 240, 242n10, 256, 257, 264, 282, 285, 286–88, 291, 305, 319–21, 363n23, 365n35, 366n40, 367n61, 411, 430, 431
United States, 2, 31, 32, 39, 46, 68, 70–73, 78, 79, 82, 87, 89, 93n57, 129, 150, 151, 180, 243n14, 255, 256, 257, 264, 354, 392, 406, 410, 432–33
Universal Brotherhood, 16, 126, 151, 158, 161, 165–69, 232, 236, 240, 259, 267, 330, 347, 365n34, 366n40, 388
Upanishads, 66, 70, 79, 200, 325

Vaishnavism, 66–67, 73, 79, 84, 85, 89
Vedanta (*and* neo-Vedanta), 66–70, 72, 73, 75, 79, 80–81, 84, 86, 89, 92n26, 97n117, 182, 199–201
Vedas, 43, 68, 81, 97n117, 200, 414
vegetarianism, 131, 167–69, 286, 354, 365n35
Vietnam, 10–11, 109–48
Vivekananda, Swami, 80–82, 86, 97n117, 357, 367n51
Voice of Silence, The (book), 123, 330–31, 436
Volksheilkunde. *See* folk medicine

Voloshin, Maximilian Alexandrovich, 427, 431, 438

Wadia, B. P., 222, 224–26, 231–33, 239–40
Waseda University (Tokyo), 171n29, 363n23, 387
Weber, Albrecht, 70, 73–74, 236
Western Buddhism. *See* Buddhism, in the West
Western Esotericism, 12, 51n16, 184, 202
Wilkins, Charles, 68–69, 71, 72, 75–76, 77, 78
women. *See* gender
world religions, 17, 403, 409, 414
World Teacher. *See* Krishnamurti, Jiddu
World War I, 168, 222, 235, 335
World War II, 117, 256, 318, 356, 394, 433
Wu Tingfang, 12, 150–56, 160–61, 166–68, 169n1, 169n6, 170n7, 170n9, 170n14–15, 171n23, 172–72n37, 354–55, 366m38, 376–77

Xu Renyi (a.k.a. Virginia Zee), 158, 164

Yamada Kōsaku (a.k.a. Kôsçak Yamada), 349, 356, 364n30
Yanagi Muneyoshi (a.k.a. Yanagi Sōetsu), 357–59, 365, 367n58
Yog, Mahadev Trimbak, 236–38
Yoga, 5, 69, 75, 77, 155, 171–72n29, 225, 328, 373, 381, 392, 405
Yokoyama Taikan, 350, 360
Yone Noguchi, 348, 349

Zee, Virigina. *See* Xu Renyi
Zen Buddhism. *See* Buddhism, Zen (Chan)
Zillmann, Paul, 235, 240
Zionism, 255, 257–59, 261, 262
Zohar (book), 258, 262, 263, 269
Zoroastrianism, 33, 48, 53n30